About the Cover

The design shown on the cover is from the computer-generated motion picture Permutations *made by the film maker John Whitney using a computer graphic program developed by Dr. Jack Citron, a physicist and computer scientist. Dr. Citron devised the algorithm which generates the abstract geometric designs seen in the film. This algorithm, based on transformations of the sine function, contains 60 parameters which can be varied to produce a nearly endless variety of geometric shapes.*

From the algorithm, a program for a digital computer connected to a display unit was written. The program directs the computer to list the available parameters on the screen of the display unit. Mr. Whitney then creates a motion-design by selecting numerical values with a light pen for the parameters he wants changed. The computer calculates these values and displays the resulting design on the screen. Mr. Whitney records the parameters of the designs he wants to use and decides how much time should elapse in the film between various designs. This information is entered into the computer, which then produces the desired sequence of designs on the display-unit screen and controls the shutter and film-advance mechanisms of the motion-picture camera which photographs them.

The resulting film is then edited and colored. The coloring and final sequencing of images are done with an optical printer which employs a special motion-picture projector in optical alignment with a motion-picture camera. Colored filters are placed between the projector's film gate and light source, and then the black-and-white film is run through the projector and photographed in color.

ANALYSIS OF ELEMENTARY FUNCTIONS

ROBERT H. SORGENFREY · EDWIN F. BECKENBACH

Editorial Advisers · ANDREW M. GLEASON · ALBERT E. MEDER, JR.

HOUGHTON MIFFLIN COMPANY · BOSTON

Atlanta • Dallas • Geneva, Ill. • Hopewell, N.J. • Palo Alto • Toronto

ABOUT THE AUTHORS

ROBERT H. SORGENFREY, Professor of Mathematics, University of California, Los Angeles. Dr. Sorgenfrey, a topologist, has been Chairman of the Committee on Teaching and has won the Distinguished Teaching Award at U.C.L.A. He has been a team member of the National Council of Teachers of Mathematics (NCTM) summer writing projects.

EDWIN F. BECKENBACH, Professor of Mathematics, Emeritus, University of California, Los Angeles. Dr. Beckenbach is currently Chairman of the Committee on Publications of the Mathematical Association of America. He has also been a participant in Educational Services Inc. projects abroad, and has been a team member and coordinator of the NCTM summer writing projects.

Editorial Advisers

ANDREW M. GLEASON, Hollis Professor of Mathematics and Natural Philosophy, Harvard University, is prominently associated with curriculum changes in mathematics. Professor Gleason was Co-chairman of the Cambridge Conference which wrote the influential report *Goals for School Mathematics.*

ALBERT E. MEDER, JR., Professor of Mathematics and Dean of the University, Emeritus, Rutgers University, The State University. Dr. Meder was Executive Director of the Commission on Mathematics, College Entrance Examination Board.

PRINTED IN THE U.S.A.

ISBN: 0-395-27932-1

CONTENTS

1. The Algebra of Functions

2. Polynomial Functions

6. General Logarithmic and Exponential Functions; Applications

7. The Circular Functions Sine and Cosine

SYMBOLS

(The first few symbols listed should be familiar from earlier work and are not defined in the text.)

		PAGE
$=$	equals *or* is equal to	
$\neq$	does not equal	
$<$	is less than	
$>$	is greater than	
$\leq$	is less than *or* equal to	
$\geq$	is greater than *or* equal to	
$\in$	is an element (*or* member) of	
$\cap$	intersection	
$\cup$	union	
$\{\ \}$	set	2
$\{\ :\ \}$	set builder	3
$\mathcal{R}$	the set of real numbers	4
$f(x)$	the value of the function f at x (read f of x)	6
$f\colon x \to f(x)$	the function f which associates $f(x)$ with x	7
$\mathcal{R} \times \mathcal{R}$	the Cartesian product of $\mathcal{R}$ with itself	12
$\overline{P_1P_2}$	the line segment with endpoints P_1 and P_2	13
dist (P_1, P_2)	the distance between the points P_1 and P_2	13
I	identity function	20
$\lvert x \rvert$	the absolute value of x	20
$[x]$	the largest integer $\leq x$	20
sgn	signum or sign function	21
D_f	the domain of the function f	26
$f + g$	the sum of the functions f and g	26
fg	the product of the functions f and g	26
$f - g$	the difference of the functions f and g	27
$\dfrac{f}{g}$	the quotient of the functions f and g	28
f^n	the nth power of the function f (n a positive integer)	28
$g \circ f$	the composition of g with f	33

CREDITS

PAGE	
Cover, ii	Courtesy of John Whitney, and Dr. Jack Citron of the Los Angeles IBM Scientific Center
xiv	California Computer Products, Inc.
51	Courtesy of Mrs. George D. Birkhoff
52	The Metropolitan Museum of Art
53	Alinari
54	Richard Davis, Design Photographers International
108	Dick Smith, North Conway, N.H.
146	Courtesy of Columbia University Library, D. E. Smith Collection
147	*left* — National Portrait Gallery, London
	right — The Bettmann Archive
150	National Aeronautics and Space Administration
192	The Bettmann Archive
193, 194	Brookhaven National Laboratory
195	Southern California Edison Company
196	National Park Service, U.S. Department of the Interior
228	Ralph Crane, LIFE Magazine © Time Inc.
	diagram — Courtesy of Prof. Thomas R. Kane
261	State of Israel Government Press Office
262	*left* — State of Israel Government Press Office
	right — Israel Information Service
263	Geological Survey, U.S. Department of the Interior
264	*left* — Robert Young, Design Photographers International
	right — George Martin, Design Photographers International
304	Nova Scotia Information Service
337	Wide World Photos
341	Tennessee Valley Authority

1

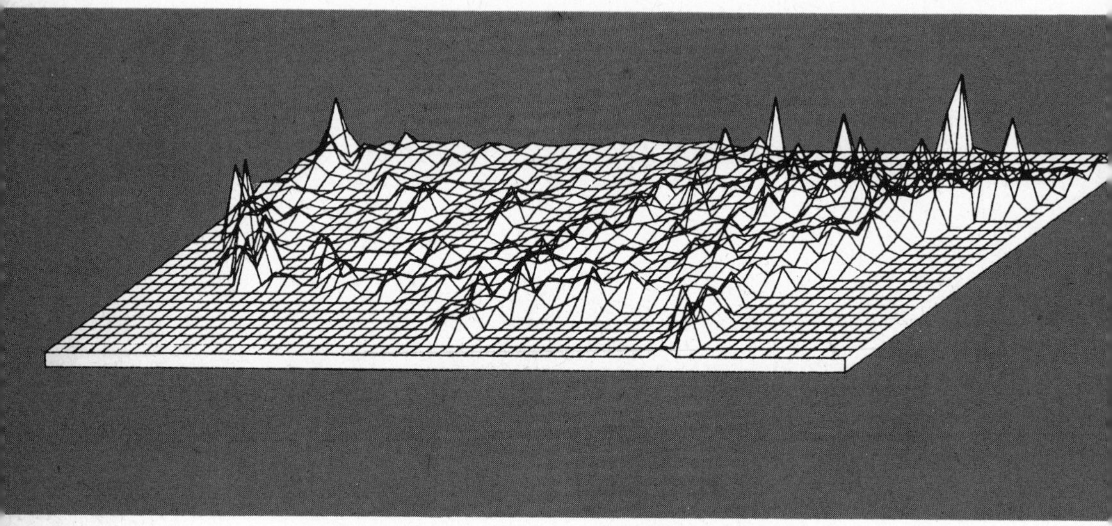

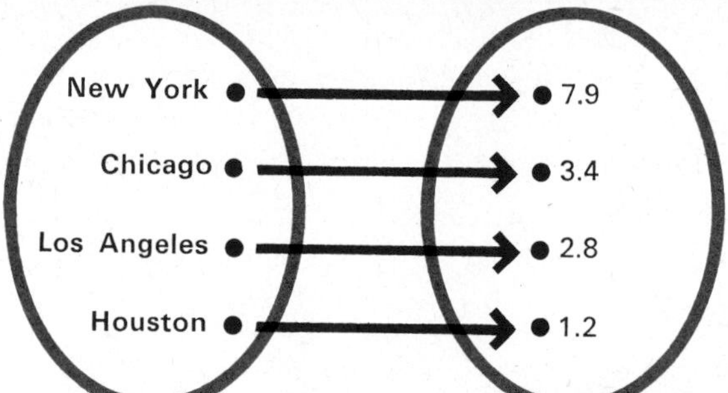

The map appearing above shows the population distribution in the United States. It was drawn by a computer connected to a digital plotter. A function may be interpreted as a mapping from its domain to its range. If the function contains a small number of ordered pairs, it can be conveniently illustrated by a mapping diagram such as the one above, which gives the 1970 population in millions for four United States cities.

The Algebra of Functions

You have probably been told many times that the notion of a function is of basic importance in mathematics and in its applications to other fields, such as physical and life sciences, engineering, and economics. In fact, by now you may have worked with functions enough to have some appreciation for the truth of this statement.

In most of this book, we shall study polynomial, logarithmic, exponential, and circular functions — functions which, because of their basic nature, are called "elementary functions."

In this first chapter, we shall reintroduce the idea of a function in general and shall establish some terminology and notation.

■ Ordered Pairs, Mappings, and Graphs

1–1 Functions as Sets of Ordered Pairs

In mathematics, the word *function* is not used in quite the same way as in ordinary conversation. Before we give a mathematical definition, however, let us look at one of the ways the word is used in ordinary conversation. Consider the following sentence:

> The cost of mailing a letter is a function of the weight of the letter.

What is the meaning of the word *function* when used in this sense? Let us agree to measure cost in cents and weight in ounces and assume that the postage rate is 15¢ per ounce or fraction thereof. Thus if the weight of a letter in ounces is 1.3, the cost in cents is 30; if the weight is 3.0, the cost is 45; and if the weight is 2.7, the cost is 45. Indeed, with each positive real number (the weight), there is associated a definite natural number (the cost). We can think of the *postage function* as associating with each member of the set of positive real numbers a unique (one and only one) member of the set of natural numbers.

Using this example as a guide, we can now state an intuitive definition of *function* as used in mathematics.

> A *function* associates with each member x of one set a unique member y of a second set. (This second set may or may not be the same as the first.)

A symbol which is used to represent any member of a specified set is called a **variable.** Thus the symbols x and y above are variables.

The statement displayed above is a description of what a function *does*, rather than what it *is*, but it can nevertheless be taken as a working definition. In this book, the members of the two sets mentioned in the definition will usually be numbers, but this need not be the case. In the following example, the first set is a set of words and the second set is a set of nonnegative rational numbers. Notice that the association described is indeed a function according to the working definition, because it associates with each word a unique number.

EXAMPLE 1. A function which might be of use in linguistics is the one which associates with each word the rational number expressing the ratio of the number of occurrences of consonants to the number of occurrences of vowels in the spelling of the word. Thus, associated with the word "sleep" is the rational number $\frac{3}{2}$; we may indicate this association by means of an ordered pair: (sleep, $\frac{3}{2}$).

a. Complete these ordered pairs:

(eat, ?), (drink, ?), (little, ?).

b. Find three ordered pairs of the form (? , 1) belonging to this same function.

Solution: **a.** (eat, $\frac{1}{2}$), (drink, 4), (little, $\frac{4}{2}$) = (little, 2).
b. For example, (at, 1), (read, 1), (California, 1).

The idea of *ordered pair* is used in giving a precise definition of function. As you no doubt remember from your earlier work, the ordered pair (x, y) is not just the set having x and y as members. The latter would be written $\{x, y\}$ or, equally well, $\{y, x\}$. As the name implies, in an *ordered* pair, the order in which the members are considered is important. Thus if $x \neq y$, there are two different ordered pairs having x and y as members: one in which x is considered to be first [we write this one (x, y)], and the other in which y is considered to be first [written (y, x)]. We see that

$$(x, y) = (u, v) \text{ if and only if } x = u \text{ and } y = v.$$

We also admit (x, x), $(3, 3)$, and so forth, as ordered pairs. In the ordered pair (x, y), x is called the **first component** and y the **second component.**

In our working definition of function, we required that with each member x of a first set of objects the function associate a unique member y of a second set. As in Example 1, we may represent this association by means of the ordered pair (x, y). The function itself, the totality of all such associations, may therefore be represented as a *set of ordered pairs*. This set cannot contain two different ordered pairs (x, y) and (x, z), $y \neq z$, having the same first component because then both y and z would be associated with x, violating the uniqueness part of the working definition. This discussion leads us to a precise mathematical definition of function:

> A **function** is a set of ordered pairs such that no two different ordered pairs in the set have the same first component.

If for any ordered pair (x, y) in a function as just defined, we consider y to be the member associated with x, then we have a function in the sense of the working definition.

In mathematics, a **relation** is defined to be *any* set of ordered pairs. Thus a function is a special kind of relation. Notice that the definition of function (as well as that of relation) is given in terms of two very basic concepts, *set* and *ordered pair.*

Let us see how our definition of a function can be applied. According to it, the relation

$$f = \{(0, 3), (1, 2), (2, 4), (3, 3)\}$$

is a function, but the relation

$$r = \{(0, 1), (1, 2), (1, 3)\}$$

is not a function. We can check that f associates with each member of the set $\{0, 1, 2, 3\}$ a unique member of the set $\{2, 3, 4\}$: with 0 is 3, with 1 is 2, with 2 is 4, and with 3 is 3. In the case of r, however, both 2 and 3 are associated with 1; therefore r is not a function.

Notice that two ordered pairs in a function may have the same *second* component. In Example 1, both of the ordered pairs (at, 1) and (read, 1) are in the function; that is, 1 is associated with both of the words "at" and "read" (and, of course, many others).

Because functions are *sets* (of ordered pairs), they can often be described conveniently by using *set-builder* notation. For example, the function

$$\{(0, 0), (1, 3), (2, 6), (3, 9), (4, 12), (5, 15)\}$$

can be designated by

$$\{(x, y): x \in \{0, 1, 2, 3, 4, 5\} \text{ and } y = 3x\}.$$

This is read "the set of all ordered pairs of the form (x, y), where x is a member of the set $\{0, 1, 2, 3, 4, 5\}$ and $y = 3x$." The same function can be specified as

$$\{(x, 3x): x \in \{0, 1, 2, 3, 4, 5\}\}.$$

Set-builder notation is particularly useful in describing functions which are *infinite* sets of ordered pairs; most important functions are of this kind (see Examples 2(b) and 2(c) below).

Almost all of the functions we shall study are sets of ordered pairs of *real numbers.*

It will be useful to agree that $\mathcal{R}$ *designates the set of real numbers.*

We shall use this notation throughout this book.

EXAMPLE 2. Which of the following are functions?

a. $K = \{(x, y): x \in \mathcal{R}, y \in \mathcal{R}, \text{ and } y^2 = x - 1\}$
b. $F = \{(x, y): x \in \mathcal{R}, y \in \mathcal{R}, \text{ and } y = x^2 - 1\}$
c. $G = \{(x, y): x \in \mathcal{R}, y \in \mathcal{R}, \text{ and } y = (x + 1)(x - 1)\}$
d. $S = \{x + y: x \in \{1, 2\} \text{ and } y = 3x\}$

Solution: **a.** Some of the ordered pairs in K are $(1, 0)$, $(2, 1)$, and $(2, -1)$. Because K contains different ordered pairs with the same first component, K is *not* a function.

b. If the ordered pairs (x, y_1) and (x, y_2) belong to F, then $y_1 = x^2 - 1$ and $y_2 = x^2 - 1$, and therefore $y_1 = y_2$. Thus $(x, y_1) = (x, y_2)$, and F does *not* contain *different* ordered pairs with the same first component. F is a function.

c. Because for every x in $\mathcal{R}$, $(x + 1)(x - 1) = x^2 - 1$, the sets G and F are the same. Thus G is a function.

d. Since $S = \{4, 8\}$, S is not a set of ordered pairs. Therefore S is not even a relation, much less a function.

We find it convenient to have names for functions. Almost any symbol may be used to name a function, but f, F, g, and ϕ (Greek letter phi, pronounced fē or fī) are often employed for this purpose.

Two functions are **equal** if and only if they are the *same* set of ordered pairs.

We have an instance of this in Example 2 above, where we found that $F = G$.

ORAL EXERCISES

1. In your own words, tell what a relation is.
2. How can you tell whether or not a given relation is a function?
3. In (4, 7), what is the first component? In this ordered pair, what is 7 called?
4. Tell whether or not each of the following is a function, giving a reason for your answer: (4, 7), {4, 7}, {(4, 7)}.

Tell whether or not the following sets are functions.

5. $\{(1, 2), (2, 3), (3, 4)\}$
6. $\{(2, 1), (3, 2), (4, 3)\}$
7. $\{(1, 3), (2, 3), (3, 3)\}$
8. $\{(3, 1), (3, 2), (3, 3)\}$
9. $\{(a, b), (b, a)\}$
10. $\{(a, x), (a, y), (a, z)\}$
11. $\{(6, 6)\}$
12. $\{((1, 2), 3), ((2, 3), 5), ((1, 3), 4)\}$

WRITTEN EXERCISES

In Exercises 1–12, find at least four members of the given set and tell whether or not each set is a function.

A

1. $\{(x, y): x \in \mathcal{R} \text{ and } y = x + 1\}$
2. $\{(x, x + 1): x \in \mathcal{R}\}$
3. $\{(x, 2): x \in \mathcal{R}\}$
4. $\{(2, y): y \in \mathcal{R}\}$
5. $\{(x, y): x \in \mathcal{R} \text{ and } y \in \mathcal{R}\}$
6. $\{(z, z): z \in \mathcal{R}\}$
7. $\{(x, x^2 - 1): x \in \mathcal{R}\}$
8. $\{(x, y): x \in \mathcal{R} \text{ and } y = \sqrt[3]{x}\}$

EXAMPLE. $\{(x^2, 2x + 1): x \in \mathcal{R}\}$

Solution: Taking x to be, in turn, 0, 1, -1, 2, and -2, we find that the following ordered pairs are in the set: $(0, 1)$, $(1, 3)$, $(1, -1)$, $(4, 5)$, and $(4, -3)$. Since the set contains different ordered pairs with the same first component, the set is not a function.

B

9. $\{(x, y): x \in \mathcal{R}, y \in \mathcal{R}, \text{ and } y^3 = x\}$
10. $\{(x^2, x - 1): x \in \mathcal{R}\}$
11. $\{(x^2, x^2 + 1): x \in \mathcal{R}\}$
12. $\{((x, y), x + y): x \in \mathcal{R} \text{ and } y \in \mathcal{R}\}$

Which of the following pairs of functions are equal?

13. $\{(0, 1), (1, 2), (2, 3)\}$, $\{(x, x + 1): x \in \{0, 1, 2\}\}$
14. $\{(x, x + 1): x \in \{0, 1, 2\}\}$, $\{(x - 1, x): x \in \{1, 2, 3\}\}$
15. $\{(x, y): x \in \mathcal{R} \text{ and } y = 2x\}$, $\{(2z, z): z \in \mathcal{R}\}$
16. $\{(x, 2x): x \in \mathcal{R}\}$, $\{(x^2, 2x^2): x \in \mathcal{R}\}$

C

Since functions are sets (of ordered pairs), we may form the union of two functions and also their intersection.

17. Show that there are functions F and G whose union, $F \cup G$, is not a function. (*Hint:* Consider the functions $F = \{(1, 1), (2, 2)\}$ and $G = \{(1, 2), (3, 4)\}$, and write out the set $F \cup G$. Can you give a simpler example?)
18. Show that if F and G are functions, then their intersection, $F \cap G$, is a function.

1–2 Functions as Mappings

The function $F = \{(-1, 2), (0, 1), (1, 2), (2, 5)\}$ associates with each member of the set $\{-1, 0, 1, 2\}$ a unique member of the set $\{1, 2, 5\}$, and each member of this second set is associated with at least one member of the first set. We call $\{-1, 0, 1, 2\}$ the *domain* of F and $\{1, 2, 5\}$ the *range* of F. In general, we have the following definition:

> The **domain** of a function f is the set of all first components of ordered pairs in f. The **range** of f is the set of all second components of ordered pairs in f.

EXAMPLE 1. Find the domain and range of each of the functions.

a. $g = \{(x, x^2 + 1): x \in \mathcal{R}\}$
b. $h = \{(x^2, x^2 - 1): x \in \mathcal{R}\}$

Solution: **a.** Since every real number occurs as the first component of some ordered pair in g, the domain of g is $\mathcal{R}$. For every x in $\mathcal{R}$, $x^2 \geq 0$ and therefore $x^2 + 1 \geq 1$. Moreover, for every number $y \geq 1$, there is at least one x in $\mathcal{R}$ such that $x^2 + 1 = y$. Consequently the range of g is $\{y: y \geq 1\}$. (When we write an inequality like $y \geq 1$, we understand that $y \in \mathcal{R}$.)

b. For every $x \in \mathcal{R}$, $x^2 \geq 0$; and for every $z \geq 0$, there is an $x \in \mathcal{R}$ such that $x^2 = z$. Therefore the domain of h is $\{z: z \geq 0\}$. The function h can now be rewritten as $h = \{(z, z - 1): z \geq 0\}$. From this we see that the range of h is $\{z - 1: z \geq 0\}$, or, with $y = z - 1$, $\{y: y \geq -1\}$.

Let f be any function, and let x be any member of its domain. We know that there is exactly one ordered pair in f which has x as its first component. We denote the second component of this ordered pair by $f(x)$. In other words, $f(x)$ is the unique member associated with x by the function f. We call $f(x)$ the **value** of f at x; $f(x)$ is usually read "f of x." For instance, if $\phi = \{(1, a), (2, b), (3, c)\}$, then the value of ϕ at 2 is b; that is, $\phi(2) = b$. Notice that it would make no sense to ask for $\phi(-1)$, the value of ϕ at -1, because -1 is not in the domain of ϕ.

EXAMPLE 2. If $F = \{(x, y): x \in \mathcal{R} \text{ and } y = 4 - x^2\}$, find

$$F(1), F(0), F(2), F(-2), F(a), F(2 - a),$$

where $a \in \mathcal{R}$.

Solution: The domain of F is $\mathcal{R}$, so each of the numbers $1, 0, 2, -2, a$, and $2 - a$ is in the domain of F. If $x = 1$, then

$$y = 4 - 1^2 = 4 - 1 = 3,$$

and therefore $(1, 3) \in F$. Thus $F(1) = 3$. Similarly,

$$F(0) = 4 - 0^2 = 4,$$
$$F(2) = 4 - 2^2 = 0,$$
$$F(-2) = 4 - (-2)^2 = 0,$$
$$F(a) = 4 - a^2,$$
$$F(2 - a) = 4 - (2 - a)^2 = 4a - a^2.$$

In this example the problem of finding $F(x)$, given x, is merely a matter of substituting in the formula $F(x) = 4 - x^2$.

We can now give another widely used "working definition" of *function:*

> A function f is a rule which assigns to each member x of one set a unique member $f(x)$ of a second set.

Some care must be used in interpreting the word "rule." In many cases the rule used to find $f(x)$ is a mathematical formula. Thus in Example 2, we have the rule $F(x) = 4 - x^2$. But in Example 1 of Section 1–1, no such mathematical formula is available.

Instead of using set-builder notation to describe the function F in Example 2, we might write more briefly

$$F\colon x \rightarrow 4 - x^2.$$

This can be read "F is the function which associates with each number x the number $4 - x^2$." If the function F had not had a letter name, we would have written simply

$$x \rightarrow 4 - x^2,$$

which can be read "the function which associates with each number x the number $4 - x^2$."

Let us look at another example of the notation introduced in the preceding paragraph:

$$g\colon x \rightarrow \frac{x}{x^2 - 1}.$$

We observe that this notation gives no information about the domain of g. Let us, however, make the following agreement:

> Except when the contrary is stated, all functions which occur in this book have domains which are subsets of $\mathcal{R}$.

Could the domain of g be all of $\mathcal{R}$? Not if the values of g are to be real numbers. Notice that if $x = 1$ or -1, the expression $\dfrac{x}{x^2 - 1}$ becomes meaningless. We therefore adopt the following convention:

When notation of the form $F\colon x \to F(x)$ is used, the domain of F is taken to be the most inclusive subset of $\mathcal{R}$ for which the formula or rule for $F(x)$ produces a real number.

Thus the domain of $g\colon x \to \dfrac{x}{x^2 - 1}$ is the set $\{x\colon x \in \mathcal{R} \text{ and } x \neq 1 \text{ or } -1\}$.

EXAMPLE 3. What is the domain of the function $\phi\colon x \to \sqrt{4 - x^2}$ according to the agreements made in the preceding paragraph?

Solution: The quantity $4 - x^2$ is nonnegative if and only if $-2 \leq x \leq 2$. Hence $\sqrt{4 - x^2}$ is a real number if and only if $-2 \leq x \leq 2$. Therefore, the domain of ϕ is the set $\{x\colon -2 \leq x \leq 2\}$.

There are various ways of picturing functions. One of these is to regard a function as a *mapping* from its domain to its range. This nomenclature is inspired by cartography: With each point of land in Ohio, say, there is associated a unique point on a given map of Ohio. To picture a function as a mapping, we draw figures to represent its domain and range and then use arrows to indicate the association given by the function. Such a representation for the function $f = \{(a, x), (b, y), (c, x), (d, z)\}$ is shown in Figure 1–1.

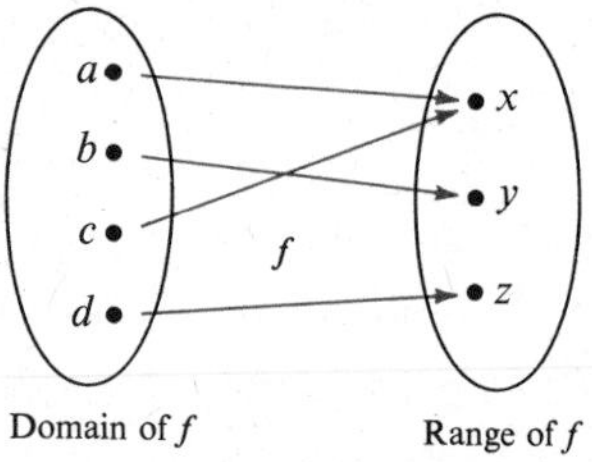

Figure 1–1

EXAMPLE 4. For the function f pictured in Figure 1–1, find $f(a)$, $f(b)$, $f(c)$, and $f(d)$.

Solution: Since in Figure 1–1 there is an arrow from a to x, $f(a) = x$. Similarly, $f(b) = y$, $f(c) = x$, and $f(d) = z$. (We would, of course, get the same results by using the set-of-ordered-pairs description of f.)

Notice that Figure 1–2 is not the pictorial representation of a function, because more than one arrow starts at b. Both of the ordered pairs (b, x) and (b, y) are in the relation pictured, and therefore this relation is not a function.

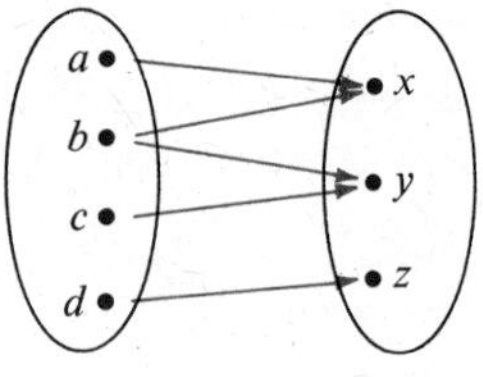

Figure 1–2

The interpretation of a function as a mapping suggests some terminology which is, in fact, in common use. If $f(a) = b$, we say that f **maps** a onto b and that the **image** of a under f is b. Both of these statements are equivalent to saying that the value of f at a is b. If $f(a) = b$, we also say that a is a **pre-image** of b under f. A member of the range of a function may have more than one pre-image. Thus for the function pictured in Figure 1–1, x has pre-images a and c.

The idea of a *function machine* may help us understand what a function does. If f is a function, we may envision the f-machine as a box with "input" and "output" openings. The input opening will accept only members of the domain of f. If a member x of the domain of f is fed into the input opening, a mechanism inside the box (whose nature need not concern us) operates on x and, having done so, ejects $f(x)$ from the output opening. A schematic version of the "square-root-machine," that is, the f-machine for $f\colon x \to \sqrt{x}$, is shown in Figure 1–3. "Function machines" actually do exist: Modern high-speed digital and analog computers are examples.

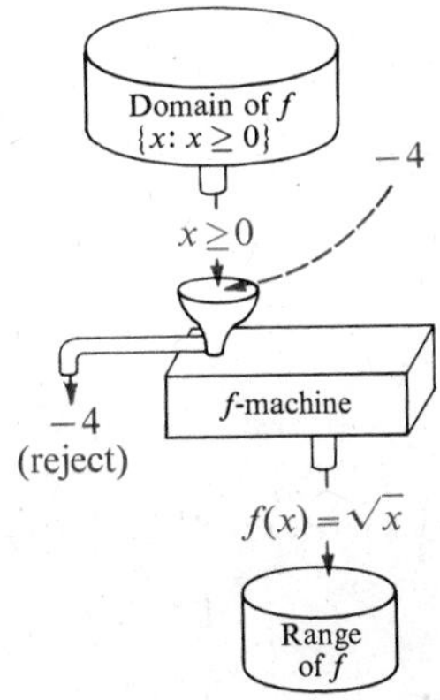

Figure 1–3

ORAL EXERCISES

For the function $f = \{(0, 0), (1, 3), (2, 4), (3, 3), (4, 0)\}$, find

1. the domain of f.
2. the range of f.
3. the value of f at 2.
4. the image of 1.
5. the number into which 4 is mapped.
6. the pre-images of 3.
7. a member of the range having only one pre-image.

Consider the following diagrams:

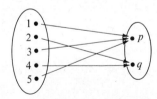

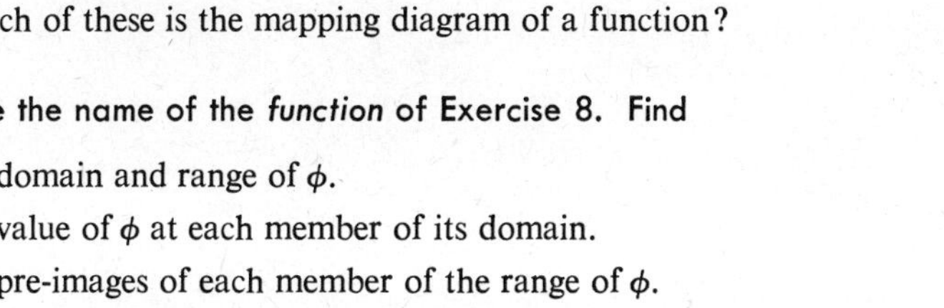

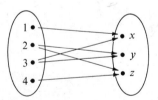

8. Which of these is the mapping diagram of a function?

Let ϕ be the name of the *function* of Exercise 8. Find

9. the domain and range of ϕ.
10. the value of ϕ at each member of its domain.
11. the pre-images of each member of the range of ϕ.

Exercises 12–19 concern the function $g\colon x \to 3 - x$.

12. The function g maps 2 onto __?__.

13. The function g maps __?__ onto 2.
14. What is the image of 0? of -1? of 3?
15. What is the pre-image of 3? of -1? of 4?
16. Find $g(6)$, $g(2)$, and $g(5)$.
17. If $g(y) = 2$, find y.
18. For each real number r, $g(r + 1) =$ __?__.
19. Find a number s such that $g(s) = s$.

In Exercises 20–25, find the domain of h under the convention stated on page 8.

20. $h: x \rightarrow \frac{x}{2}$
21. $h: x \rightarrow \frac{2}{x}$
22. $h: x \rightarrow \frac{1}{x^2 - 4}$
23. $h: x \rightarrow \frac{1}{x^2 + 4}$
24. $h: x \rightarrow \sqrt{x}$
25. $h: x \rightarrow \sqrt[3]{x}$

WRITTEN EXERCISES

A

1. Write out as sets of ordered pairs the two relations pictured on page 9 in Oral Exercise 8.

Find the domain and range of each of these functions:

2. $\{(-2, 4), (-1, 1), (0, 0), (1, 1), (2, 4)\}$
3. $\{(x, 3): x \in \{1, 2, 3\}\}$
4. $\{(x, -x): x \text{ is a positive integer}\}$
5. $\{(z, z^2 + 1): z \in \mathcal{R}\}$
6. $I: x \rightarrow x$
7. $F: x \rightarrow -x^2$
8. $G: x \rightarrow -x^3$
9. $\{(x^2, x): x \in \{0, 1, 2\}\}$
10. $\{(x^3, x^2): x \in \{0, 1, 2\}\}$
11. $\{(x - 1, x + 1): x \in \mathcal{R}\}$

For the function $f: x \rightarrow x^2 - 1$, find these values:

12. $f(0)$
13. $f(2)$
14. $f(-2)$
15. $f(\frac{3}{2})$

For the function $g: x \rightarrow 2x - 1$, find a pre-image of these values:

16. 3
17. 0
18. $\frac{1}{2}$
19. -7

Using the convention stated on page 8, find the domain of each of these functions:

20. $F: x \rightarrow \frac{1}{2}(2x - 1)$
21. $\phi: x \rightarrow \frac{x}{x + 1}$
22. $h: x \rightarrow \frac{x}{x^2 + x}$
23. $G: x \rightarrow \sqrt{x - 1}$
24. $H: x \rightarrow \sqrt[3]{x - 1}$
25. $k: x \rightarrow \sqrt{\frac{x}{(x - 1)^2}}$

In Exercises 26–40, express the requested value of the given function in simple form. In each case, also indicate any necessary restrictions which must be placed on the literal symbols in order that the answer be meaningful.

EXAMPLE. $f\left(\frac{1}{r}\right)$, given the function $f\colon x \to \frac{x^2}{x+1}$

Solution: Since the symbol $\frac{1}{r}$ must name a number, we must have $r \neq 0$. Moreover, since the domain of f does not contain -1, we must have $\frac{1}{r} \neq -1$, or $r \neq -1$. If $r \neq 0, -1$, then

$$f\left(\frac{1}{r}\right) = \frac{\left(\frac{1}{r}\right)^2}{\left(\frac{1}{r}\right) + 1} = \frac{\frac{1}{r^2}}{\frac{1+r}{r}} = \frac{1}{r(1+r)}.$$

B

26. $f(a-1)$, given $f\colon x \to (x+1)(x+2)$

27. $f(2c)$, given $f\colon x \to x^2 + x + 1$

28. $f(-z)$, given $f\colon x \to x^4 + 2x^3 + 3x^2 + 4x + 5$

29. $f\left(\frac{1}{y}\right)$, given $f\colon x \to x^2 + 1$

30. $f\left(\frac{1}{z}\right)$, given $f\colon x \to x + \frac{1}{x}$

31. $f\left(\frac{1}{z}\right)$, given $f\colon x \to \frac{x}{x+1}$

32. $f\left(\frac{1}{a+1}\right)$, given $f\colon x \to \frac{1}{x-1}$

33. $f\left(\frac{1}{a}+1\right)$, given $f\colon x \to \frac{1}{x-1}$

34. $f(x-a)$, given $f\colon x \to x^2 - a^2$

35. $f\left(\frac{x+a}{a}\right)$, given $f\colon x \to \frac{x+1}{x-1}$

C

36. $f(2+h) - f(2)$, given $f\colon x \to x^2 + 1$

37. $f(z+h) - f(z)$, given $f\colon x \to x^2 + x + 2$

38. $\frac{f(x+h) - f(x)}{h}$, given $f\colon x \to x^2$

39. $\frac{f(y+h) - f(y)}{h}$, given $f\colon x \to x^2 - x + 2$

40. $\frac{f(x+h) - f(x)}{h}$, given $f\colon x \to \frac{1}{x}$

1–3 Cartesian Coordinates

The mapping diagrams introduced in Section 1–2 are not particularly useful in depicting functions which contain infinitely many ordered pairs. Fortunately, we have another way of picturing any function whose domain and range are subsets of $\mathcal{R}$. Such a function is a set of ordered pairs of real numbers and is therefore a subset of the set of *all* such pairs. The latter set is called the **Cartesian product** of $\mathcal{R}$ with itself and is denoted by $\mathcal{R} \times \mathcal{R}$.

We can represent ordered pairs of real numbers as points in a plane by setting up a one-to-one correspondence between $\mathcal{R} \times \mathcal{R}$ and the set of points in the plane. To establish such a correspondence, choose two mutually perpendicular lines in the plane which intersect at a point O, the **origin,** as shown in Figure 1–4(a) and also in Figure 1–4(b). Designate one of these lines as the *first axis* and the other as the *second axis.* Next, using convenient units of length (ordinarily, but not necessarily, the same), make each axis into a number line having O as its zero point.

To associate a point with an ordered pair (r, s) of real numbers, we draw (perhaps mentally) two lines: one parallel to the second axis through the graph of r on the first axis, and the other parallel to the first axis through the graph of s on the second axis. The point of intersection of these lines is the **graph** of (r, s).

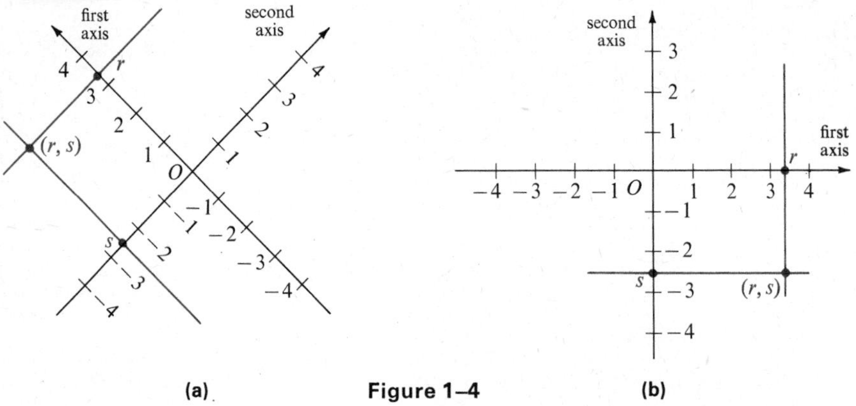

Figure 1–4

By reversing the procedure just described, we can start with any point in the plane and find an ordered pair of numbers corresponding to it. The components of this ordered pair are the **coordinates** of the point. The first coordinate is the **abscissa** of the point, and the second is the **ordinate** of the point.

This one-to-one correspondence between points and ordered pairs is called a **rectangular Cartesian,** or **Cartesian, coordinate system** in the plane. A plane equipped with a Cartesian coordinate system is called a **Cartesian plane.** Once a coordinate system has been chosen, it is customary to refer to the point P having coordinates (r, s) as "the point $P(r, s)$" or "the point (r, s)."

In drawing a coordinate plane on a sheet of paper or a chalkboard, we usually arrange that the first axis extend horizontally to the right and the second axis extend vertically upward, as in Figure 1–4(b). Moreover, because the symbol (x, y) is so frequently used to denote an arbitrary ordered pair, we usually call the first axis the ***x*-axis** and the second axis the ***y*-axis,** and we label them as shown in Figure 1–5. The coordinate axes separate the plane into four **quadrants,** which are customarily given roman numerals as in Figure 1–5.

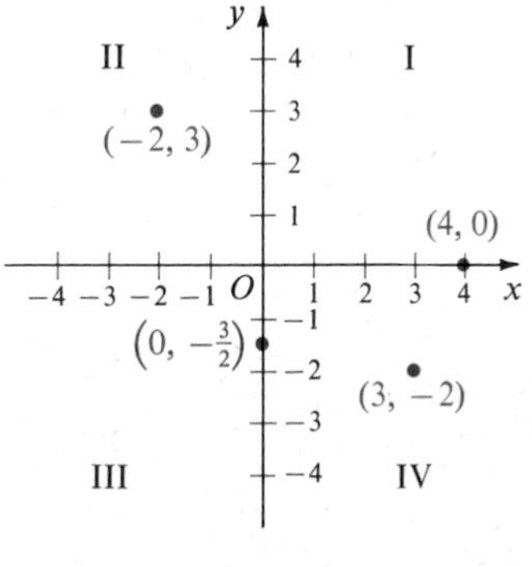

Figure 1–5

Two points $P_1(x_1, y_1)$ and $P_2(x_2, y_2)$ determine a line segment $\overline{P_1P_2}$. The length of $\overline{P_1P_2}$, that is, the distance between P_1 and P_2, is given by the **distance formula**

$$\text{length } \overline{P_1P_2} = \text{dist}(P_1, P_2) = \sqrt{(x_2 - x_1)^2 + (y_2 - y_1)^2}.$$

Figure 1–6 suggests a proof of this formula based on the Pythagorean Theorem. Notice that either or both of the differences $x_2 - x_1$ and $y_2 - y_1$ might be negative, but that this does not affect the validity of the distance formula because the differences are squared. Since

$$\sqrt{(x_2 - x_1)^2 + (y_2 - y_1)^2} = \sqrt{(x_1 - x_2)^2 + (y_1 - y_2)^2},$$

either expression may be used in calculating distances.

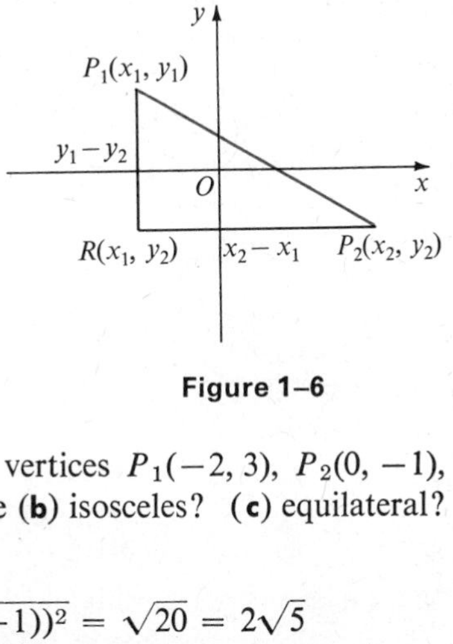

Figure 1–6

EXAMPLE 1. a. Draw the triangle having vertices $P_1(-2, 3)$, $P_2(0, -1)$, and $P_3(2, \frac{5}{2})$. Is the triangle **(b)** isosceles? **(c)** equilateral?

Solution:

a. $\text{length } \overline{P_1P_2} = \sqrt{(-2 - 0)^2 + (3 - (-1))^2} = \sqrt{20} = 2\sqrt{5}$

$\text{length } \overline{P_2P_3} = \sqrt{(0 - 2)^2 + (-1 - \frac{5}{2})^2}$

$= \sqrt{\frac{65}{4}} = \frac{\sqrt{65}}{2}$

$\text{length } \overline{P_1P_3} = \sqrt{(-2 - 2)^2 + (3 - \frac{5}{2})^2}$

$= \sqrt{\frac{65}{4}} = \frac{\sqrt{65}}{2}$

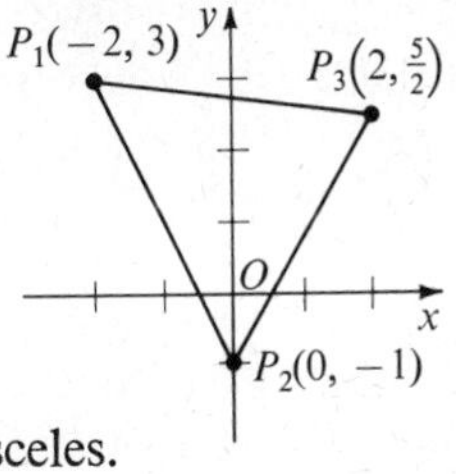

b. Since length $\overline{P_2P_3}$ = length $\overline{P_1P_3}$, the triangle is isosceles.

c. Since length $\overline{P_1P_2} \neq$ length $\overline{P_1P_3}$, the triangle is not equilateral.

We next introduce a method of describing the *direction* of a line segment $\overline{P_1P_2}$, one which is useful in differential calculus, a subject we shall study beginning in Chapter 3.

While driving in mountainous terrain, you may have seen a warning sign saying "20% grade ahead." This means that the portion of the road ahead rises 20 feet for every 100 feet of horizontal distance traversed. [See Figure 1–7 (not drawn to scale).] The 20% is the "rise" divided by the "run," $\frac{20}{100} = \frac{1}{5}$, expressed as a percent. We can use this simple idea to describe the direction of a line segment in a Cartesian plane.

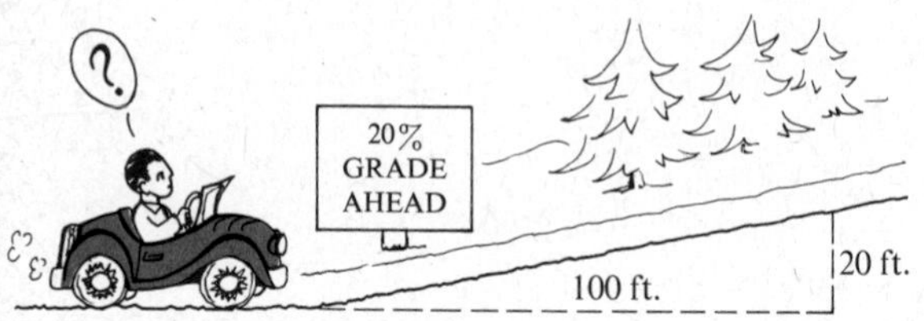

Figure 1–7

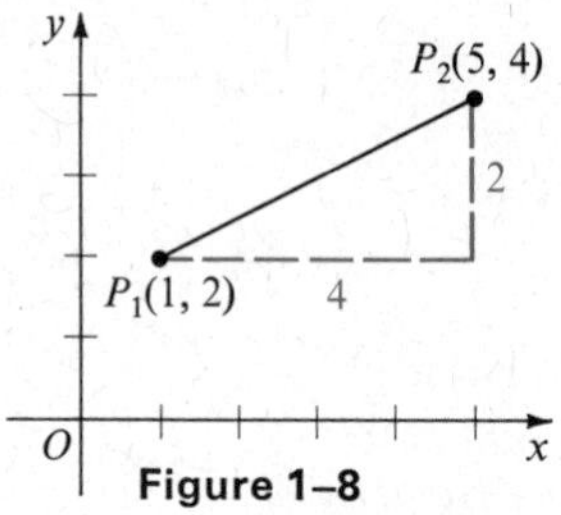

Figure 1–8

Consider, for example, the points $P_1(1, 2)$ and $P_2(5, 4)$ shown in Figure 1–8. As we traverse the segment $\overline{P_1P_2}$ from P_1 to P_2, the vertical change (rise) is $4 - 2 = 2$, and the horizontal change (run) is $5 - 1 = 4$. We call the quotient

$$\frac{\text{rise}}{\text{run}} = \frac{\text{vertical change}}{\text{horizontal change}} = \frac{2}{4} = \frac{1}{2}$$

the *slope* of the segment $\overline{P_1P_2}$.

> For any points $P_1(x_1, y_1)$ and $P_2(x_2, y_2)$, with $x_1 \neq x_2$, the **slope of the segment** $\overline{P_1P_2}$ is $\dfrac{y_2 - y_1}{x_2 - x_1}$.

The condition $x_1 \neq x_2$ in this definition rules out vertical segments. *Vertical segments have no slope.* If the segment $\overline{P_1P_2}$ is *horizontal*, then $y_1 = y_2$, and the slope of the segment $\overline{P_1P_2}$ is 0. Notice that saying a segment has *no* slope is different from saying a segment has slope *zero.*

Since $\dfrac{y_2 - y_1}{x_2 - x_1} = \dfrac{-(y_1 - y_2)}{-(x_1 - x_2)} = \dfrac{y_1 - y_2}{x_1 - x_2}$, we see that in calculating the slope of $\overline{P_1P_2}$ it does not matter whether the coordinates of P_2 or of P_1 occur first in the differences appearing in the numerator and denominator; the choice must be the same, however, for both numerator and denominator.

EXAMPLE 2. Draw the line segments from the point $(-1, 2)$ to each of the points $(1, 8)$, $(2, 5)$, $(3, 4)$, $(5, 2)$, $(7, 0)$, $(3, -3)$, $(-2, -1)$, and $(-2, 6)$. Then find the slope of each of these segments and label each segment with its slope.

Solution: After some practice, slopes can be calculated mentally. Be careful, however, when some coordinates are negative. For example, the slope of the segment joining $(-1, 2)$ and $(-2, -1)$ is

$$\frac{(-1) - 2}{(-2) - (-1)} = \frac{-3}{-1} = 3.$$

The required slopes are shown in red.

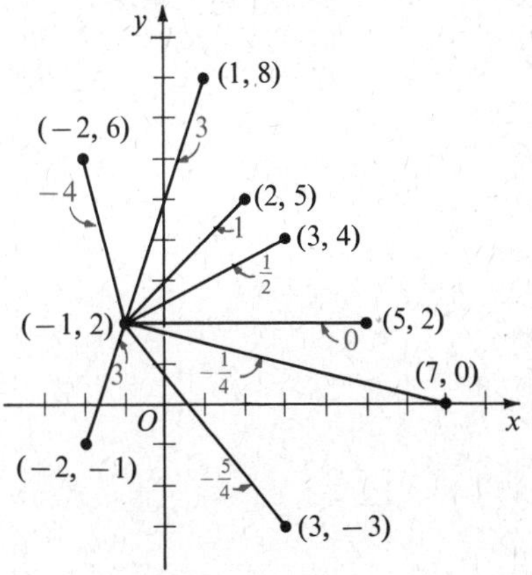

As we look at the diagram above, we see that segments which are inclined upward as we go to the right have positive slope, while those which are inclined downward as we go to the right have negative slope. We see also that the more steeply inclined a segment is, the greater the absolute value of its slope.

Two line segments are **parallel** or **perpendicular** if and only if the lines on which they lie are respectively parallel or perpendicular. In Section 2–2, we shall show that if two nonvertical segments have slopes m_1 and m_2, respectively, then the segments are

parallel if and only if $m_1 = m_2$,
perpendicular if and only if $m_1 m_2 = -1$.

Since the condition $m_1 m_2 = -1$ is equivalent to $m_2 = -\frac{1}{m_1}$ and to $m_1 = -\frac{1}{m_2}$, we say that two nonvertical segments are perpendicular if and only if their slopes are *negative reciprocals* of each other.

EXAMPLE 3. Show that the triangle having vertices $P_1(8, 5)$, $P_2(1, -4)$, and $P_3(-1, 2)$ is a right triangle.

Solution: If we draw the triangle, we see that the right angle, if there is one, must be at the vertex P_3. The slope of $\overline{P_3P_1}$ is $\frac{5 - 2}{8 - (-1)} = \frac{1}{3}$, and the slope of $\overline{P_3P_2}$ is $\frac{2 - (-4)}{-1 - 1} = -3$. Since $\frac{1}{3} \cdot (-3) = -1$, $\overline{P_3P_1}$ and $\overline{P_3P_2}$ are perpendicular, and the angle at P_3 is a right angle.

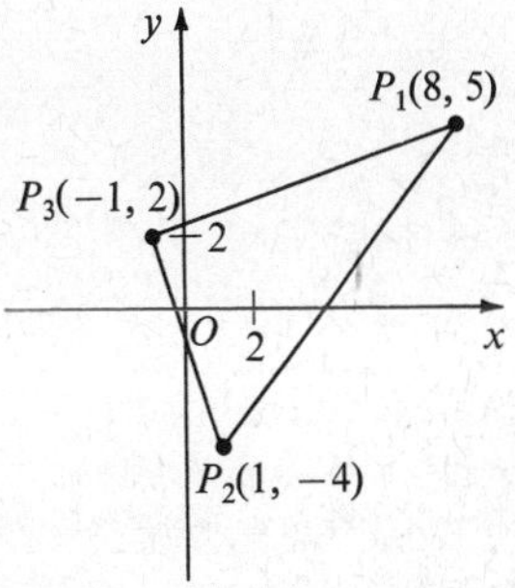

ORAL EXERCISES

State whether each of the following points lies on the x-axis, the y-axis, both, or neither.

1. $(0, 3)$
2. $(-2, 0)$
3. $(0, -10)$
4. $(0, 0)$
5. $(1, 1)$
6. $(-2, -3)$

Complete the statements in Exercises 7 and 8.

7. A point lies on the x-axis if and only if. . . .
8. A point lies on the y-axis if and only if. . . .

In Exercises 9–16, state the distance between the given pair of points.

9. $(0, 0), (0, 3)$
10. $(2, 0), (2, 3)$
11. $(0, 1), (0, 5)$
12. $(2, 1), (2, 5)$
13. $(0, 0), (-2, 0)$
14. $(0, 1), (-2, 1)$
15. $(-1, 0), (2, 0)$
16. $(-1, 3), (2, 3)$

In Exercises 17–20, find the slope of the segment joining the given pair of points.

17. $(0, 0), (2, 3)$
18. $(0, 1), (3, 4)$
19. $(2, 2), (5, 4)$
20. $(0, 0), (2, -3)$

WRITTEN EXERCISES

In Exercises 1–6, (a) draw the segment $\overline{P_1P_2}$ and find (b) its length and (c) its slope.

A

1. $P_1(0, 0), P_2(3, 4)$
2. $P_1(0, 0), P_2(-4, 3)$
3. $P_1(-1, -1), P_2(2, 3)$
4. $P_1(-1, 6), P_2(6, -6)$
5. $P_1(2, -3), P_2(-1, 0)$
6. $P_1(-1, -2), P_2(-4, -3)$

In Exercises 7–12, determine whether or not the triangle ABC is (a) equilateral, (b) isosceles (but not equilateral), (c) right.

7. $A(5, -3), B(-1, -1), C(3, 1)$
8. $A(0, 7), B(-4, -2), C(5, 2)$
9. $A(2, -2), B(2\sqrt{3}, 2\sqrt{3}), C(-2, 2)$
10. $A(0, 2), B(7, -2), C(6, 1)$
11. $A(7, 0), B(-2, -4), C(2, 5)$
12. $A(0, 1), B(3, 2), C(5, -4)$

In Exercises 13–16, determine whether or not the quadrilateral *ABCD* is a square, a rectangle (but not a square), a parallelogram (but not a rectangle), or a trapezoid.

13. $A(0, 2)$, $B(5, 4)$, $C(2, -1)$, $D(-3, -3)$

14. $A(-2, 0)$, $B(1, 1)$, $C(0, 4)$, $D(-3, 3)$

15. $A(1, 0)$, $B(3, 0)$, $C(0, 6)$, $D(0, 3)$

16. $A(-3, 2)$, $B(0, 4)$, $C(4, -2)$, $D(1, -4)$

In Exercises 17–20, a point *A* and numbers *m* and *d* are given. Find the coordinates of a point *P* such that the slope of $\overline{AP}$ is *m* and the length of $\overline{AP}$ is *d*. (There are two correct answers in each case.)

B

17. $A(0, 0)$, $m = \frac{3}{4}$, $d = 5$

18. $A(0, 0)$, $m = -1$, $d = 2$

19. $A(1, 2)$, $m = -\frac{4}{3}$, $d = 10$

20. $A(2, 2)$, $m = 2$, $d = 2$

In Exercises 21–26, find the number *t* so that the segment joining the given points will be (a) parallel and (b) perpendicular to the segment joining the points $(-3, 0)$ and $(1, 2)$.

21. $(0, 0)$, $(1, t)$

22. $(0, 2)$, $(2, t)$

23. $(3, -2)$, $(4, t)$

24. $(0, 2)$, (t, t)

25. $(1, 1)$, $(t + 1, t - 1)$

26. (t, t), $(t + 1, 2t)$

1–4 Graphs of Equations and Functions

Any *set* of ordered pairs of real numbers corresponds to a *set* of points in a Cartesian plane.

EXAMPLE 1. Graph the ordered pairs which belong to the function

$$g = \{(x, x^2): x \in \{-2, -1, 0, 1, 2\}\}.$$

Solution: The function may be rewritten as follows:

$$g = \{(-2, 4), (-1, 1), (0, 0), (1, 1), (2, 4)\}$$

The set of points graphed at the right is the *graph* of the function *g*.

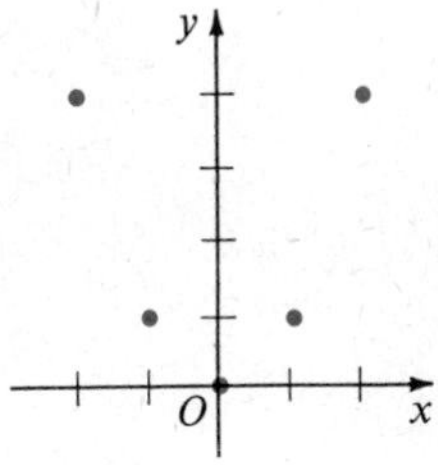

If *f* is *any* function whose domain and range are subsets of $\mathbb{R}$, then

$$\begin{aligned}\text{the } \textbf{graph} \text{ of } f &= \{\text{point } (x, y): (x, y) \in f\} \\ &= \{\text{point } (x, f(x)): x \in \text{domain of } f\}.\end{aligned}$$

The solution set of an *equation* in two (real) variables is a set of ordered pairs of real numbers, and the **graph of the equation** is the set of all points (x, y) such that (x, y) is in the solution set. We see that the graph of a *function* f is the same as the graph of the *equation* $y = f(x)$.

EXAMPLE 2. Replace the question marks so that each ordered pair is in the solution set of the equation $2x - 3y - 6 = 0$.

$(0, ?)$, $(?, 0)$, $(1, ?)$, $(?, 1)$,
$(-3, ?)$, $(?, -1)$

Then graph these ordered pairs.

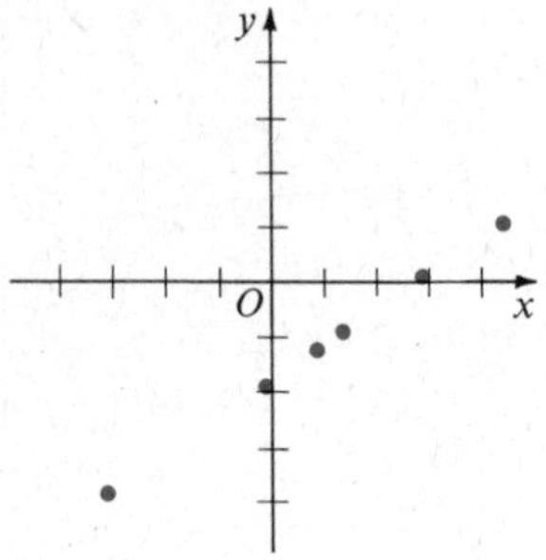

Solution: The completed ordered pairs are $(0, -2)$, $(3, 0)$, $(1, -\frac{4}{3})$, $(\frac{9}{2}, 1)$, $(-3, -4)$, $(\frac{3}{2}, -1)$. The graph is shown at the right.

We notice that the graphs of the six ordered pairs of Example 2 appear to lie on a line, and we might guess that the *complete* graph of the equation $2x - 3y - 6 = 0$ *is* this line. This guess is correct:

The graph of any equation of the form

$$Ax + By + C = 0, \qquad (*)$$

where A, B, and C are real numbers and not both A and B are zero, is a line. Conversely, every line is the graph of an equation of this form.

For proofs of these statements, see Exercises 33 and 34, pages 25 and 26. It is natural to call equations of the form (*) **linear equations.**

EXAMPLE 3. Find an equation of the form (*) in the three cases

a. $A = 2, B = -3, C = -6$;
b. $A = 2, B = 2, C = -6$;
c. $A = 2, B = 0, C = -6$.

Graph these equations in the same coordinate plane.

Solution: The three equations are

a. $2x - 3y - 6 = 0$;
b. $2x + 2y - 6 = 0$;
c. $2x - 6 = 0$.

Since each of these equations is of the form (*), in each case we need only find two points whose coordinates satisfy the equation and then draw the line which they determine, as shown on page 19. It is often a good idea, however, to graph one or two additional points to guard against mistakes.

In the diagram at the right we have used arrowheads to indicate that the lines continue indefinitely. For simplicity, however, we shall omit such arrowheads from graphs in the future.

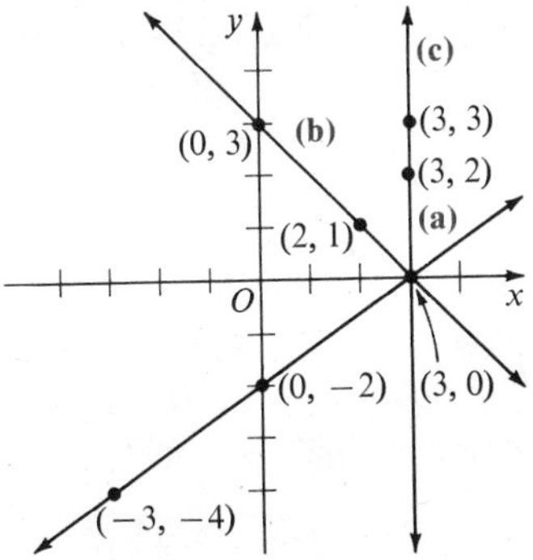

The abscissa of a point where a graph intersects the x-axis is called an **x-intercept** of the graph; **y-intercept** is defined similarly. Thus the x- and y-intercepts of the line in Example 3(a) are 3 and -2, respectively.

In Example 3(c), we notice that $B = 0$ and that the graph is a *vertical* line. It can be shown that the graph of $Ax + By + C = 0$ is a vertical line if and only if $B = 0$.

If $B \neq 0$, the equation $Ax + By + C = 0$ can be written equivalently in the form

$$y = -\frac{A}{B}x - \frac{C}{B},$$

or, with $m = -\dfrac{A}{B}$ and $b = -\dfrac{C}{B}$, in the form

$$y = mx + b. \tag{†}$$

On the other hand, (†) can be written equivalently as

$$mx + (-1)y + b = 0,$$

which is in the form $Ax + By + C = 0$, with $B \neq 0$. The graph of *equation* (†) is the same as the graph of the *function*

$$f\colon x \to mx + b.$$

Functions of this form are called *linear*.

> A function f is **linear** if there are numbers m and b such that $f\colon x \to mx + b$.

We can conclude from the discussion above that:

> The graph of every linear function is a nonvertical line and every nonvertical line is the graph of some linear function.

In the diagram for Example 3, the lines labeled **(a)** and **(b)** are the graphs of the linear functions $x \to \frac{2}{3}x - 2$ and $x \to -x + 3$, respectively. The line labeled **(c)** is not the graph of *any* function.

Note: The word "linear" means slightly different things in different mathematical contexts. For example, the function $f\colon x \to mx + b$ is "linear" even if $m = 0$, but the polynomial $mx + b$ is "linear" (see Chapter 2) only if $m \neq 0$, and the "linear" term in the polynomial $mx + b$ is mx. We shall discuss linear functions at greater length in Sections 2–1 and 2–2.

Now we shall introduce some special functions and draw their graphs. Notice that the first two of these special functions are linear functions.

Constant functions. A constant function is one all of whose values are the same number. If this number is c, then the function can be expressed as

$$\{(x, y)\colon y = c\}, \quad \text{or} \quad \{(x, c)\}, \quad \text{or} \quad x \to c.$$

The domain of the function is $\mathcal{R}$. Its graph is a horizontal line which intersects the vertical axis at the point $(0, c)$, as shown in Figure 1–9.

The symbol c is often made to do double duty and serve not only as the name of a *number*, but also as the name of the constant *function* all of whose values are the number c. There is some danger in doing this. We must, for example, make a clear distinction between the statements

$$f = 0 \qquad \text{and} \qquad f(x) = 0.$$

The first of these equates two *functions* and means that f is the constant function all of whose values are zero. The second statement equates two *numbers* and means that f is a function whose value is zero at the particular member x of its domain.

The identity function. This function, which will be denoted by I, is the one which maps each number onto itself. Thus $I = \{(x, y)\colon y = x\}$, or $I = \{(x, x)\}$, or $I\colon x \to x$. The graph of I is a straight line through the origin which is equally inclined to the axes, as shown in Figure 1–10.

The absolute-value function. The absolute value $|x|$ of a real number x is defined to be x if $x \geq 0$ and $-x$ if $x < 0$. Thus if $x \neq 0$, $|x|$ is the *positive* number of the pair x and $-x$. The absolute value $|x|$ may be interpreted as the distance from the origin to the graph of x on the number line. The absolute-value function is $\{(x, y)\colon y = |x|\}$, or $x \to |x|$. Its graph is shown in Figure 1–11.

The "greatest-integer" function. The symbol $[x]$ is often used in number theory to denote the greatest integer which does not exceed x. For example,

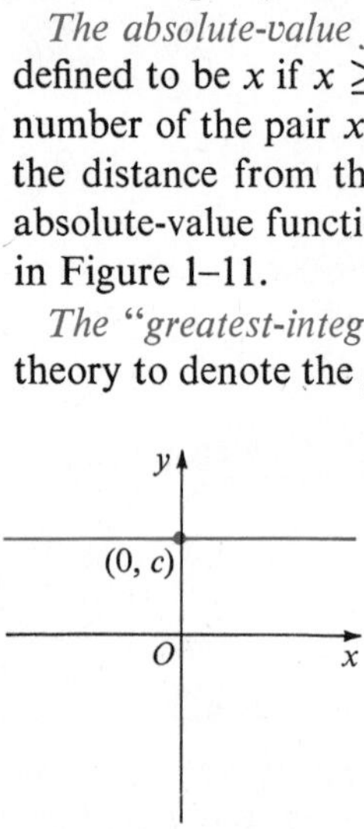

Figure 1–9

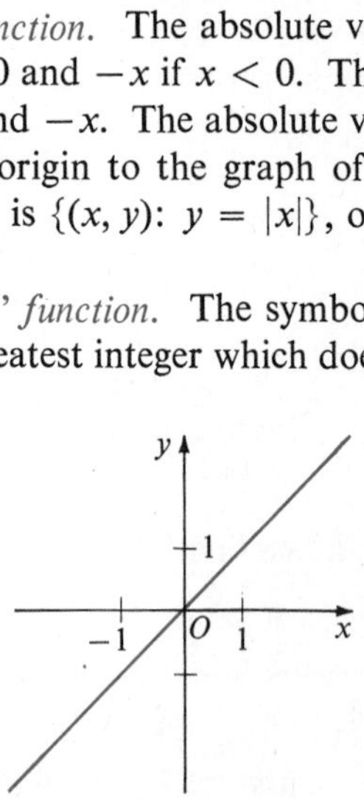

Figure 1–10

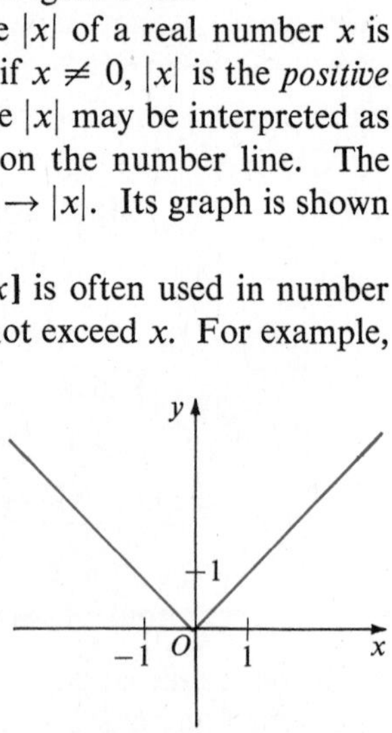

Figure 1–11

$[\frac{7}{3}] = 2$, $[2] = 2$, $[-\frac{7}{3}] = -3$, and $[-\frac{1}{2}] = -1$. (Do not confuse [ ] with the grouping symbols [ ].) The function $\{(x, y): y = [x]\}$, or $x \to [x]$, is the greatest-integer function. Notice the device used in Figure 1–12 to make clear which of certain questionable points are in the graph. Since $[2] = 2$, the point (2, 2) is in the graph, and it is shown as a solid dot. The point (2, 1) is shown as a hollow dot to indicate that it is not in the graph although points near it are.

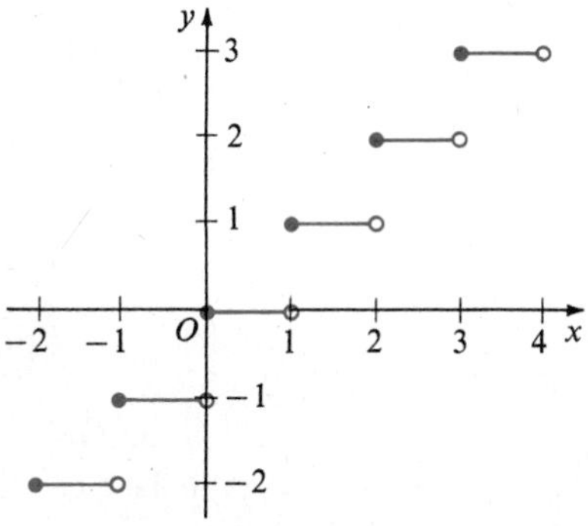

Figure 1–12

The signum function. This function, which is sometimes called the *sign* function, is usually named *sgn*. It is defined by the formula

$$\text{sgn}: x \to \begin{cases} 1 & \text{if } x > 0 \\ 0 & \text{if } x = 0 \\ -1 & \text{if } x < 0 \end{cases}$$

This is an example of a *piecewise definition* of a function. The graph of sgn is shown in Figure 1–13.

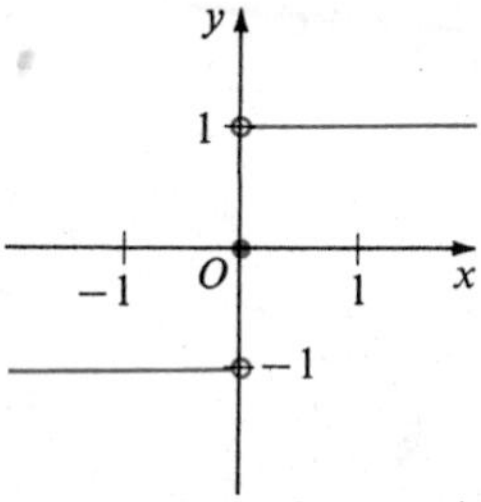

Figure 1–13

When the name of a function contains more than one letter, as is the case with sgn, we often omit the parentheses in the functional-value symbol. Thus we write sgn x instead of sgn (x). We must, however, use parentheses in some cases. The value of sgn at the number $x + 2$ is written sgn $(x + 2)$.

The fact (page 3) that different ordered pairs in a function cannot have the same first component has a simple graphical interpretation:

> No vertical line intersects the graph of a function in more than one point.

(See Figure 1–14.) You should check that each of the graphs of the special functions we have discussed passes this "vertical-line test."

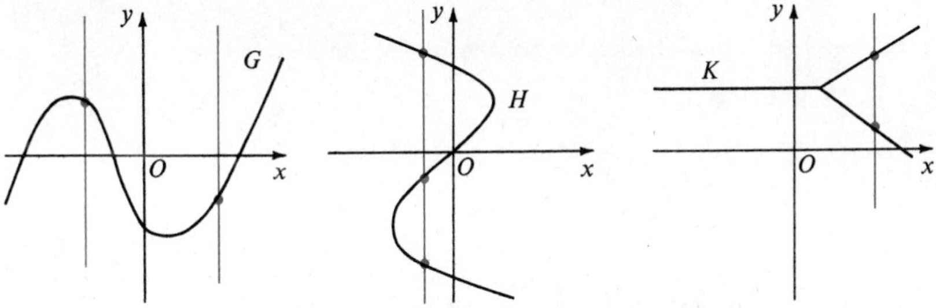

G passes the vertical-line test. *H* and *K* do not.

Figure 1–14

The domain of each of the special functions we have discussed is all of $\mathcal{R}$. Let us consider the graph of a function whose domain is not all of $\mathcal{R}$.

EXAMPLE 4. Draw the graph of $f: x \to \sqrt{25 - x^2}$.

Solution: By agreement (page 8), the domain of f is $\{x: -5 \le x \le 5\}$. Since $f = \{(x, y): y = \sqrt{25 - x^2}\}$, we observe that the graph of f consists of all points whose coordinates satisfy the equation $y = \sqrt{25 - x^2}$. If (x, y) *does* satisfy this equation, then $y^2 = 25 - x^2$, or $x^2 + y^2 = 25$. Since the left-hand member of the last equation is the square of the distance from $(0, 0)$ to (x, y), we see that the point (x, y) lies on the circle

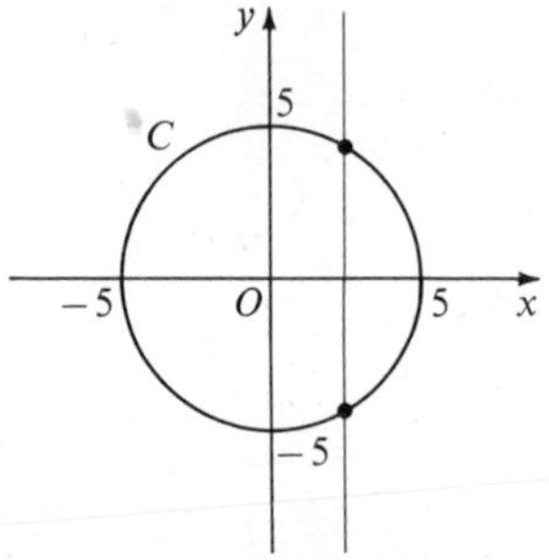

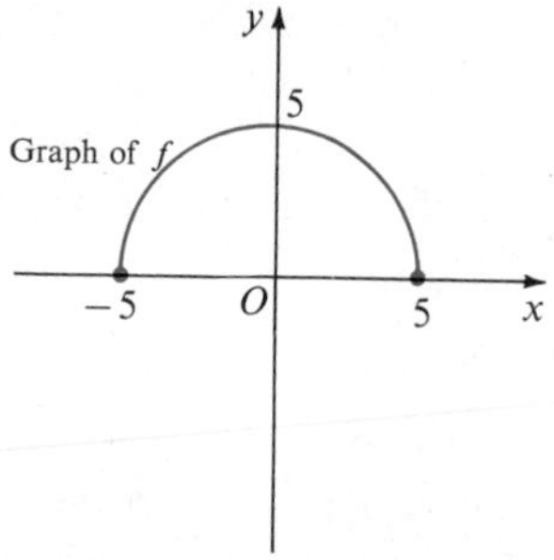

C of radius 5 with center at the origin. But C is not the graph of f; indeed, C is not the graph of *any* function because it fails to pass the vertical-line test. All we have shown is that the graph of f is a *subset* of C. When we recall, however, that the symbol $\sqrt{}$ means the *nonnegative* square root, we see that the graph of f is the part of C which lies on or above the x-axis. Notice that the circle C is the graph of the *equation* $x^2 + y^2 = 25$.

ORAL EXERCISES

In Exercises 1–8, state whether or not the given equation is linear.

1. $x + 2y + 3 = 0$
2. $x^2 + 2y + 3 = 0$
3. $2x + 1 = 0$
4. $(x + 2y)(x - 2y) = 0$
5. $2x + 3y = \frac{1}{2}(x + 1)$
6. $|x| + |y| = 1$
7. $-\frac{4}{3}[x] + y = 2$
8. $[-\frac{4}{3}]x + y = 2$

In Exercises 9–14, state whether or not the function f is linear.

9. $f: x \to -x$
10. $f: x \to 2|x| + 3$
11. $f: x \to \dfrac{2 - x}{3}$

12. $f: x \to \dfrac{2 - x}{x}$ **13.** $f: x \to 5$ **14.** $f: x \to \dfrac{x - 1}{x - 1}$

Give the *x*- and *y*-intercepts of the lines pictured below. (Integer points are marked on the axes.)

15.

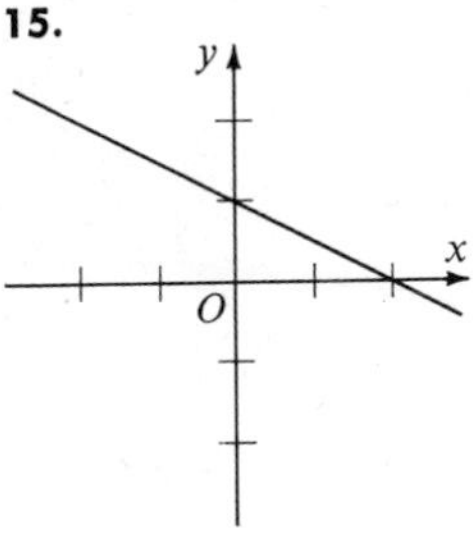

16.

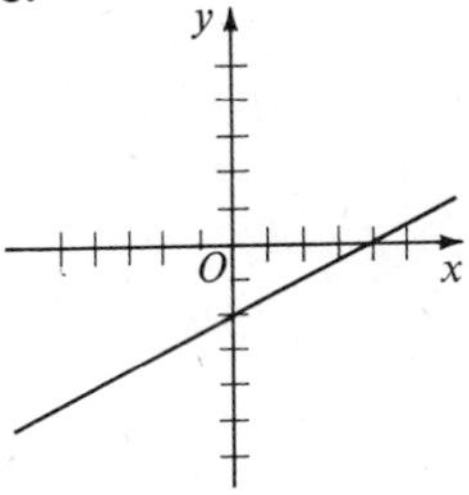

17.

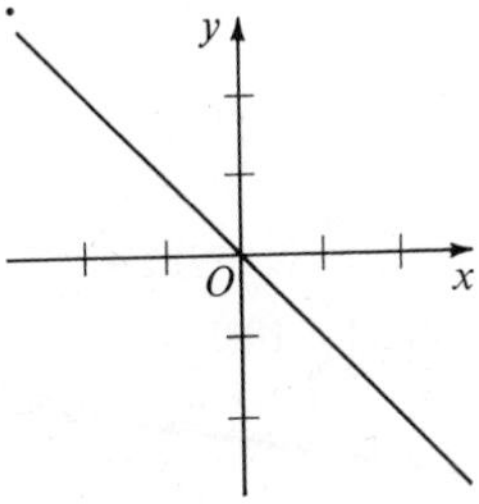

Give the following numbers:

18. $I(-2)$

19. $|-2|$

20. $[-2]$

21. $\text{sgn}\,(-2)$

22. $\text{sgn}\,(2\frac{1}{2})$

23. $[2\frac{1}{2}]$

24. $|2\frac{1}{2}|$

25. $[-2\frac{1}{2}]$

Give the range of each of these functions:

26. I

27. sgn

28. $x \to |x|$

29. $x \to [x]$

30. $x \to \sqrt{25 - x^2}$

31. $x \to -\sqrt{25 - x^2}$

State whether or not the set of points pictured is the graph of a function.

32.

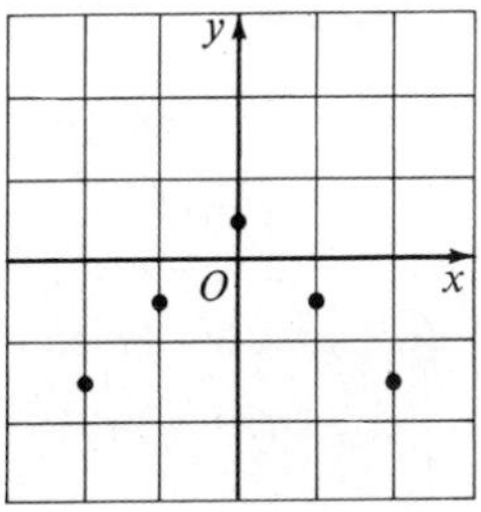

34.

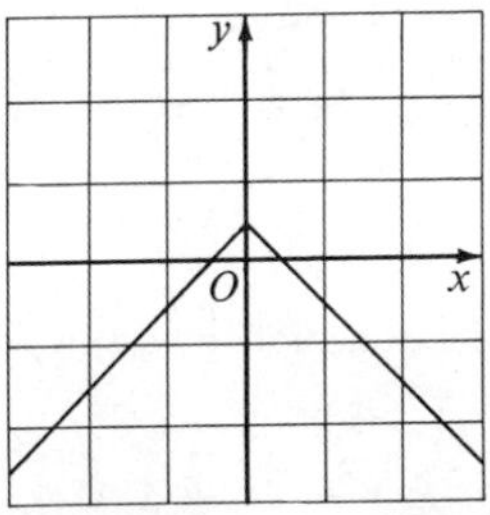

36.

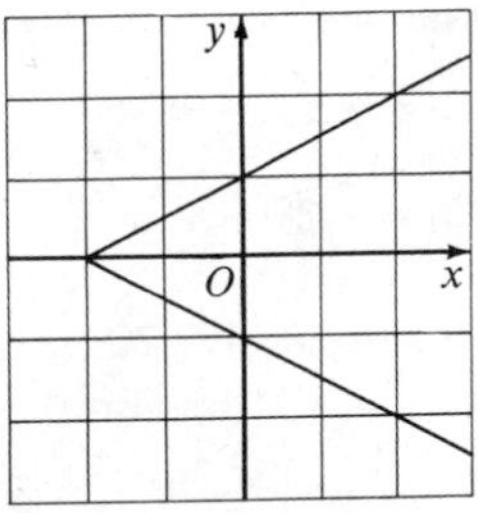

33.

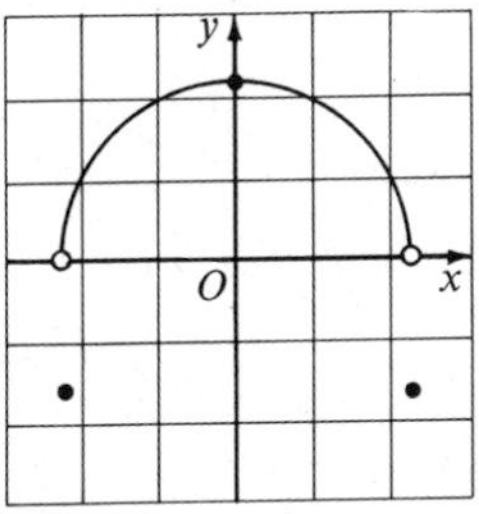

35.

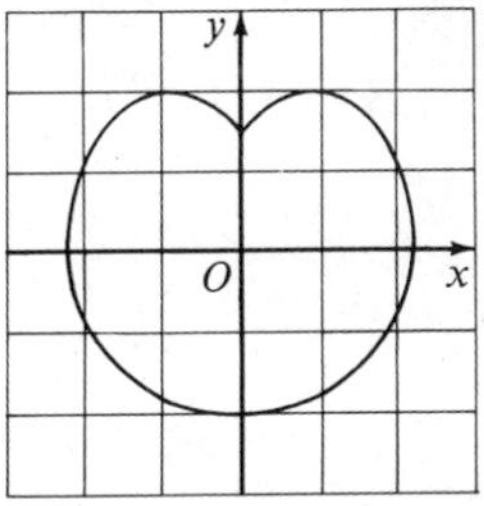

37.

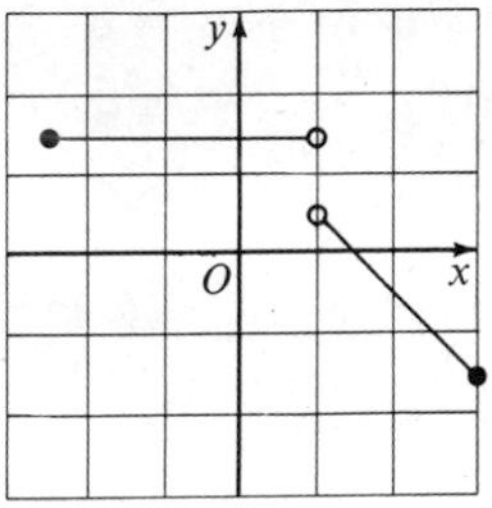

WRITTEN EXERCISES

Draw the graph of each of these functions.

A

1. $\{(-1, 2), (0, 1), (1, 0), (2, -1)\}$
2. $\{(x, x+2): x \in \{-2, -1, 0, 1, 2\}\}$
3. $\{(x+2, x): x \in \{-2, -1, 0, 1, 2\}\}$
4. $\{(x, x^2): x \in \{-2, -1, 0, 1, 2\}\}$
5. $\{(x, 4-x^2): x \in \{-2, -1, 0, 1, 2\}\}$
6. $\{(x, [x]): x \in \{-1\frac{1}{2}, -\frac{1}{2}, \frac{1}{2}, 1\frac{1}{2}, 2\frac{1}{2}\}\}$

7.

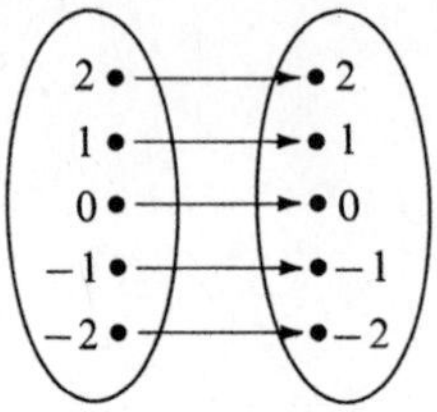

9.

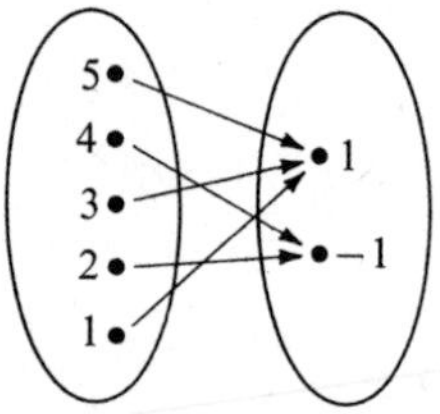

8.

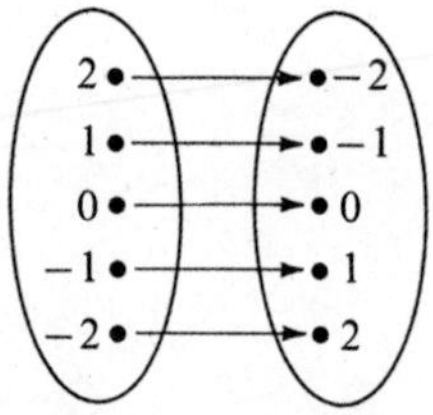

10.

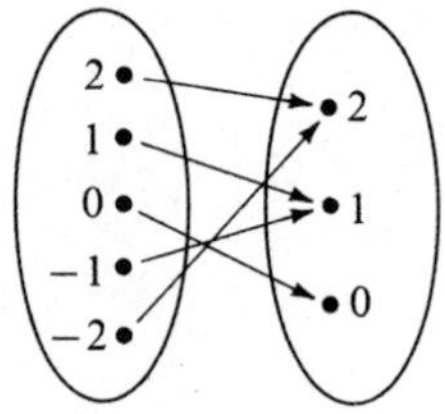

Draw the graphs of the lines whose equations are given in Exercises 11–16.

11. $x + 2y - 4 = 0$
12. $x - 2y - 4 = 0$
13. $2x - 3 = 0$
14. $y = 2x - 1$
15. $y - 1 = 2(x + 1)$
16. $\frac{x}{3} - y = 1$

In Exercises 17–22, graph the equation given in the (a) part and the function given in the (b) part.

17. a. $y = 2x + 1$ b. $f: x \to 2x + 1$
18. a. $y = -x + 2$ b. $f: x \to -x + 2$
19. a. $x - 2y + 4 = 0$ b. $f: x \to \frac{1}{2}x + 2$
20. a. $2x + 3y = 6$ b. $f: x \to -\frac{2}{3}x + 2$
21. a. $x^2 + y^2 = 4$ b. $f: x \to \sqrt{4 - x^2}$
22. a. $x^2 + y^2 = 4$ b. $f: x \to -\sqrt{4 - x^2}$

In Exercises 23–26, graph the given function.

B

23. $f: x \to \begin{cases} 1 & \text{if } x \geq 0 \\ -2 & \text{if } x < 0 \end{cases}$

24. $g: x \to \begin{cases} x & \text{if } x \geq 0 \\ -2 & \text{if } x < 0 \end{cases}$

25. $h: x \rightarrow \begin{cases} x & \text{if } x \geq 0 \\ -x & \text{if } x < 0 \end{cases}$

26. $F: x \rightarrow \begin{cases} -1 & \text{if } x < -1 \\ x & \text{if } -1 < x < 1 \\ 1 & \text{if } x > 1 \end{cases}$

In Exercises 27–30, graph the two functions described.

EXAMPLE. **a.** $x \rightarrow \text{sgn } x - 2$ **b.** $x \rightarrow \text{sgn } (x - 2)$

Solution: **a.** We notice that the ordinate y of any point (x, y) which satisfies $y = \text{sgn } x - 2$ is 2 less than the ordinate of the point with the same abscissa satisfying $y = \text{sgn } x$. Therefore the graph of the function in (**a**) can be obtained by lowering the graph of sgn 2 units.

b. If $x > 2$, then $x - 2 > 0$ and thus $\text{sgn } (x - 2) = 1$.
If $x = 2$, then $x - 2 = 0$ and thus $\text{sgn } (x - 2) = 0$.
If $x < 2$, then $x - 2 < 0$ and thus $\text{sgn } (x - 2) = -1$.

We can use these results to obtain the graph in (**b**) below.

a.

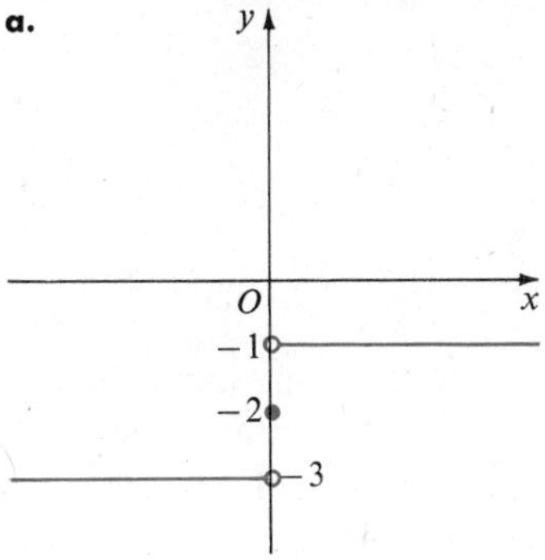

b.

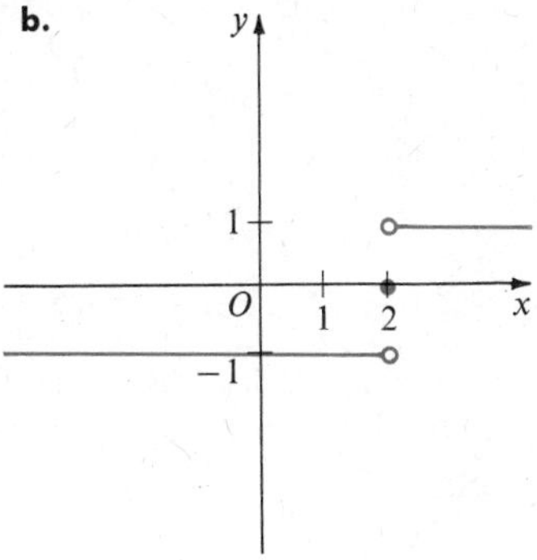

27. a. $x \rightarrow |x|$ **b.** $x \rightarrow -|x|$

28. a. $x \rightarrow \text{sgn } x + 1$ **b.** $x \rightarrow \text{sgn } (x + 1)$

29. a. $x \rightarrow |x| - 1$ **b.** $x \rightarrow |x - 1|$

30. a. $x \rightarrow -\text{sgn } x$ **b.** $x \rightarrow \text{sgn } (-x)$

C **31.** Draw the graph of the function $x \rightarrow x \cdot \text{sgn } x$. What is the standard name for this function?

32. Draw the graph of the function $s: x \rightarrow \dfrac{x}{|x|}$. What is the domain of s? Compare the graphs of s and sgn. Are these functions equal?

In Exercises 33 and 34, use the following fact from plane geometry: The line which is the perpendicular bisector of a segment $\overline{HK}$ is the set of all points equidistant from the points H and K.

33. Show that every line is the graph of some linear equation. [*Hint:* Let L be a line and choose points $H(r, s)$ and $K(u, v)$ so that L is the perpendicular bisector of $\overline{HK}$. Show that the following statements are equivalent:

$$P(x, y) \text{ is on } L$$
$$\text{dist}(P, H) = \text{dist}(P, K) \qquad (1)$$
$$\sqrt{(x-r)^2 + (y-s)^2} = \sqrt{(x-u)^2 + (y-v)^2}$$
$$2(u-r)x + 2(v-s)y + (r^2 + s^2 - u^2 - v^2) = 0 \qquad (2)$$

Is the last equation linear?]

34. Show that the graph of every linear equation is a line. [*Hint:* Let $Ax + By + C = 0$ be a linear equation. Equation (2) of Exercise 33 suggests that we choose numbers r, s, u, and v such that

$$2(u-r) = A,\ 2(v-s) = B,\ r^2 + s^2 - u^2 - v^2 = C. \qquad (3)$$

(Show that this choice can be made by solving the first two of equations (3) for u and v, and then eliminating u and v from the third equation.) The given equation is now the *same* as (2). Let H be the point (r, s) and K be (u, v). Use the fact that equations (2) and (1) are equivalent to show that the graph of $Ax + By + C = 0$ is $\{P\colon \text{dist}(P, H) = \text{dist}(P, K)\}$.]

Operations on Functions

1–5 The Operations of Arithmetic

If we have two **real-valued functions,** that is, functions whose ranges are subsets of $\mathcal{R}$, we can add and multiply them in a natural way. Thus for the functions $F\colon x \to 2x$ and $G\colon x \to 1 - x$, we call the function $F + G\colon x \to (2x) + (1 - x)$ the *sum* of F and G and the function $FG\colon x \to (2x)(1 - x)$ the *product* of F and G.

Similarly, the sum and product of $f\colon x \to \frac{1}{x}$ and $g\colon x \to \sqrt{x}$ are, respectively, the functions

$$f + g\colon x \to \frac{1}{x} + \sqrt{x} \quad \text{and} \quad fg\colon x \to \frac{1}{x}\sqrt{x}.$$

But since we may add and multiply $\frac{1}{x}$ and $\sqrt{x}$ only when both expressions are defined, we must take the domains of $f + g$ and fg to be the set of numbers common to the domains of f and g, that is, the set

$$D_f \cap D_g = \{x\colon x \neq 0\} \cap \{x\colon x \geq 0\} = \{x\colon x > 0\}.$$

In general:

The **sum** and **product** of the functions f and g are, respectively, the functions

$$f + g\colon x \to f(x) + g(x), \text{ and}$$
$$fg\colon x \to f(x) \cdot g(x).$$

The domain of each of $f + g$ and fg is $D_f \cap D_g$, where D_f and D_g are the respective domains of f and g.

EXAMPLE 1. Given $f\colon x \to \dfrac{x}{x-1}$ and $g\colon x \to \dfrac{2}{1-x^2}$, find **(a)** the domain and **(b)** formulas for the values of $f + g$ and fg.

Solution: **a.** $D_f = \{x\colon x \neq 1\}$, $D_g = \{x\colon x \neq 1 \text{ or } -1\}$. Therefore,

$$D_{f+g} = D_{fg} = D_f \cap D_g = \{x\colon x \neq 1 \text{ or } -1\}.$$

b.
$$\begin{aligned}(f+g)(x) &= \frac{x}{x-1} + \frac{2}{1-x^2}\\ &= \frac{x}{x-1} - \frac{2}{x^2-1}\\ &= \frac{x(x+1)}{x^2-1} - \frac{2}{x^2-1}\\ &= \frac{x^2+x-2}{x^2-1}\\ &= \frac{(x+2)(x-1)}{(x+1)(x-1)}\\ &= \frac{x+2}{x+1}\end{aligned}$$

$$\begin{aligned}(fg)(x) &= \frac{x}{x-1} \cdot \frac{2}{1-x^2}\\ &= \frac{-2x}{(x-1)(x^2-1)}\\ &= \frac{-2x}{(x-1)^2(x+1)}\end{aligned}$$

The formulas in **(b)** are valid only for those numbers in the domains of the functions, that is, $\{x\colon x \neq 1 \text{ or } -1\}$. Although the simplified formula for $(f + g)(x)$ is meaningful when $x = 1$, this number is *not* in the domain of $f + g$.

If c is a number and f is a function, we define cf to be the function, whose domain is that of f, such that $cf\colon x \to cf(x)$. Notice that if we regard c to be a constant *function* (page 20), then by the definition of the product of two functions, $cf\colon x \to c(x)f(x) = cf(x)$. Thus the definitions of cf are consistent whether we regard c as a number or as a constant function.

The function $(-1)f$ is written $-f$ and is called the **negative** of f. The function $f + (-g)$ is written $f - g$ and is called the **difference** of f and g.

The **reciprocal,** $\dfrac{1}{g}$, of a function g is defined to be the function

$$\frac{1}{g}\colon x \to \frac{1}{g(x)}.$$

Since zero denominators are not allowed, the domain of $\frac{1}{g}$ is $\{x: x \in D_g$ and $g(x) \neq 0\}$. The function $f \cdot \frac{1}{g}$ is written $\frac{f}{g}$ and is called the **quotient** of f and g. The domain of $\frac{f}{g}$ is the set $\{x: x \in D_f \cap D_g$ and $g(x) \neq 0\}$.

If n is a positive integer, we define the ***n*th power,** f^n, of a function f to be the function having the same domain as f such that $f^n: x \to [f(x)]^n$. Thus if $f: x \to \sqrt{x}$, then $f^4: x \to [f(x)]^4$, or (since $[f(x)]^4 = [\sqrt{x}]^4 = x^2$) $f^4: x \to x^2$. The domain of f^4 is $\{x: x \geq 0\}$ because this set is the domain of f. Notice that $f^2 = f \cdot f$, $f^3 = f \cdot f^2$, and so on.

EXAMPLE 2. Let $f: x \to |x|$ and $g = \text{sgn}$. Find a formula for determining the values of each of the functions $f + g$, $f - g$, fg, $\frac{f}{g}$, and g^2. Draw graphs of these functions.

Solution: The domain of both f and g is $\mathcal{R}$, so $D_f \cap D_g = \mathcal{R}$.

$$(f+g)(x) = f(x) + g(x) = |x| + \text{sgn } x = \begin{cases} x+1 & \text{if } x > 0 \\ 0 & \text{if } x = 0 \\ -x-1 & \text{if } x < 0 \end{cases}$$

$$(f-g)(x) = f(x) - g(x) = |x| - \text{sgn } x = \begin{cases} x-1 & \text{if } x > 0 \\ 0 & \text{if } x = 0 \\ -x+1 & \text{if } x < 0 \end{cases}$$

$$(fg)(x) = f(x)g(x) = |x| \text{ sgn } x = \left.\begin{cases} x \cdot 1 = x & \text{if } x > 0 \\ 0 \cdot 0 = 0 & \text{if } x = 0 \\ (-x)(-1) = x & \text{if } x < 0 \end{cases}\right\} = I(x)$$ (See page 20.)

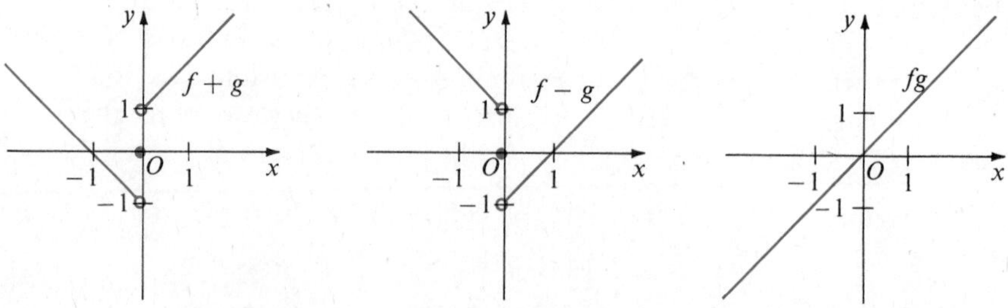

$$\left(\frac{f}{g}\right)(x) = \frac{f(x)}{g(x)} = \frac{|x|}{\operatorname{sgn} x} = \begin{cases} \dfrac{x}{1} = x & \text{if } x > 0 \\ \text{undefined} & \text{if } x = 0 \\ \dfrac{-x}{-1} = x & \text{if } x < 0 \end{cases}$$

$$g^2(x) = [g(x)]^2 = [\operatorname{sgn} x]^2 = \begin{cases} 1 & \text{if } x \neq 0 \\ 0 & \text{if } x = 0 \end{cases}$$

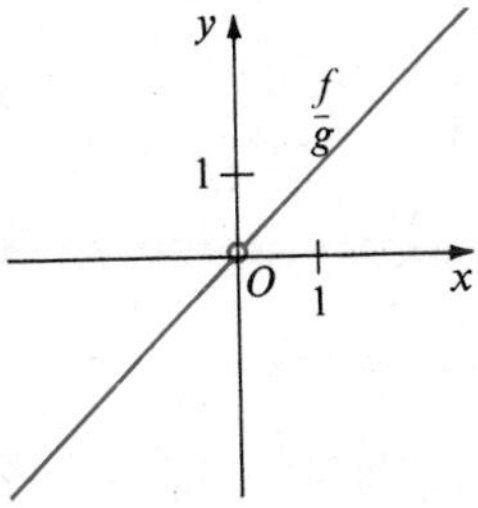

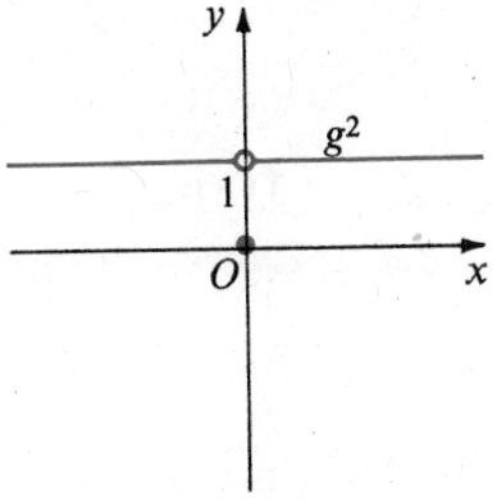

The arithmetic (arith-MET-ic) operations we have defined above for functions obey certain basic rules of the kinds which hold in the system of real numbers. For example, the theorem below asserts that *multiplication is distributive over addition.*

Theorem 1.

Let f, g, and h be real-valued functions. Then

$$f(g + h) = fg + fh.$$

Note: On the right-hand side of the equation, we follow the usual practice of carrying out the multiplications before the addition, and thus we write simply $fg + fh$ instead of $(fg) + (fh)$. On the left-hand side of the equation, $f(g + h)$ is the *product* of the function f and the function $g + h$. It is *not* the value of f at $g + h$. (We shall consider the "function of a function" idea in the next section.)

Proof

To show that the two functions are equal (see the definition on page 4), we shall show that they have the same domain and that each x in their common domain has the same image under each function.

(Proof continued)

The domain of $g + h$ is $D_g \cap D_h$; therefore, the domain of $f(g + h)$ is $D_f \cap (D_g \cap D_h)$, or $D_f \cap D_g \cap D_h$. The domains of fg and fh are $D_f \cap D_g$ and $D_f \cap D_h$, respectively; therefore, the domain of $fg + fh$ is $(D_f \cap D_g) \cap (D_f \cap D_h)$, which is equal to $(D_f \cap D_f) \cap (D_g \cap D_h)$, or $D_f \cap D_g \cap D_h$. Hence the domains of $f(g + h)$ and $fg + fh$ are the same set,

$$D = D_f \cap D_g \cap D_h.$$

For any x in D,

$$\begin{aligned}[f(g + h)](x) &= [f(x)][(g + h)(x)] && \text{(Definition of product of functions)}\\ &= f(x)[g(x) + h(x)] && \text{(Definition of sum of functions)}\\ &= f(x)g(x) + f(x)h(x) && \text{(Distributive law for real numbers)}\end{aligned}$$

$$\begin{aligned}\text{and } [fg + fh](x) &= (fg)(x) + (fh)(x) && \text{(Definition of sum of functions)}\\ &= f(x)g(x) + f(x)h(x). && \text{(Definition of product of functions)}\end{aligned}$$

Therefore

$$[f(g + h)](x) = [fg + fh](x).$$

We have shown that the functions $f(g + h)$ and $fg + fh$ have the same domain, and that on that domain they have the same formula. Therefore they are the same function.

ORAL EXERCISES

1. Explain why the domain of $f + g$ and fg is taken to be $D_f \cap D_g$. Could it just as well be taken to be $D_f \cup D_g$?
2. What are the function values of $f - f$ and of $\frac{f}{f}$? What are the domains of these functions?

For each of the pairs of functions f and g given below, describe the domain of $f + g$, $f - g$, fg, $\frac{f}{g}$, and g^2. Then state a formula for the value of each of these functions at a member x of its domain.

3. $f\colon x \to x + 1,\ g\colon x \to x - 1$
4. $f\colon x \to 6,\ g\colon x \to 2$
5. $f\colon x \to x,\ g\colon x \to \frac{1}{x}$
6. $f = 1,\ g = I\ (I\colon x \to x)$
7. $f = I,\ g\colon x \to |x|$

WRITTEN EXERCISES

For each of the pairs of functions f and g described below, write as sets of ordered pairs the functions $f + g$, $f - g$, fg, $\frac{f}{g}$, and g^2.

EXAMPLE. $f = \{(0, 1), (1, 6), (2, 3), (3, 3)\}$, $g = \{(1, 2), (2, 0), (3, 6), (4, 1)\}$

Solution: The domain of each of $f + g$, $f - g$, and fg is the set $D_f \cap D_g = \{0, 1, 2, 3\} \cap \{1, 2, 3, 4\} = \{1, 2, 3\}$, and therefore

$$f + g = \{(1, 6 + 2), (2, 3 + 0), (3, 3 + 6)\} = \{(1, 8), (2, 3), (3, 9)\},$$

$$f - g = \{(1, 4), (2, 3), (3, -3)\}, \text{ and}$$

$$fg = \{(1, 12), (2, 0), (3, 18)\}.$$

Since $g(2) = 0$, the domain of $\frac{f}{g} = \{1, 3\}$, and

$$\frac{f}{g} = \left\{\left(1, \frac{6}{2}\right), \left(3, \frac{3}{6}\right)\right\} = \left\{(1, 3), \left(3, \frac{1}{2}\right)\right\}.$$

Finally, $g^2 = \{(1, 4), (2, 0), (3, 36), (4, 1)\}$.

A

1. $f = \{(1, 2), (2, 4), (3, 6)\}$, $g = \{(1, 1), (2, 2), (3, 2)\}$
2. $f = \{(1, 6), (2, 4)\}$, $g = \{(0, 0), (1, 3), (2, 2)\}$
3. $f = \{(2, 4), (3, 1), (4, 6)\}$, $g = \{(2, 2), (3, 0), (4, 3)\}$
4. $f = \{(1, 0), (2, -4), (3, 5), (4, 1)\}$, $g = \{(1, 0), (2, 2), (3, 0), (4, 2), (5, 3)\}$

5.

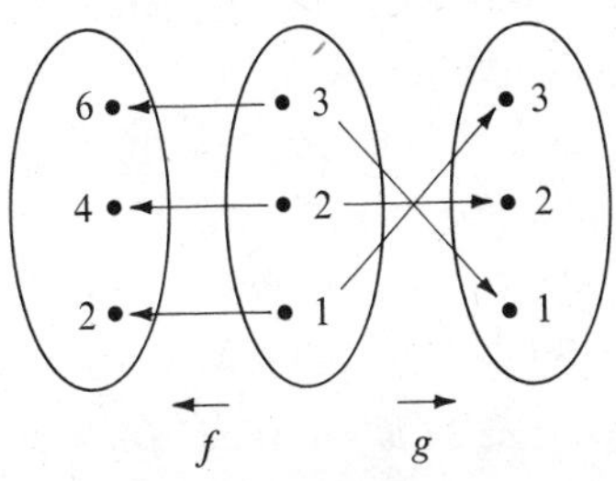

6.

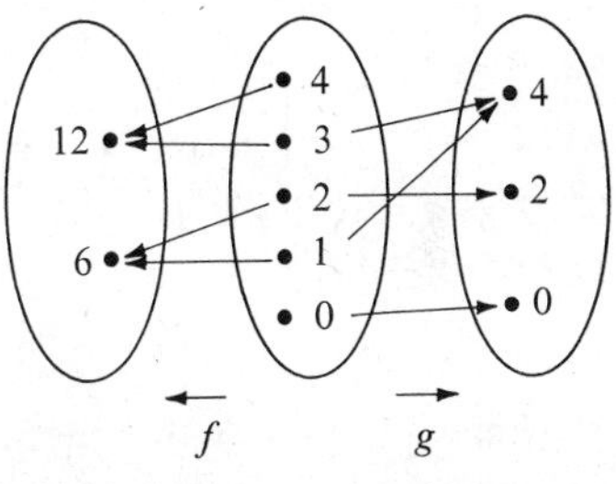

7. $f = \{(x, 2x): x \in \{0, 1, 2\}\}$, $g = \{(x, x - 1): x \in \{0, 1, 2\}\}$
8. $f = \{(x, x + 1): x \in \{0, 1, 2, 3\}\}$, $g = \{(x, x^2): x \in \{1, 2, 3\}\}$

For each of the pairs of functions f and g in Exercises 9–16, find the domain and a formula for the values of $f + g$, fg, and $\frac{f}{g}$.

9. $f: x \to 6x,\ g: x \to 2$
10. $f: x \to 2,\ g: x \to x$
11. $f: x \to x,\ g: x \to x^2 + 1$
12. $f: x \to x^2,\ g = I$

13. $f: x \to x^2,\ g: x \to \frac{1}{x}$

14. $f: x \to x - 1,\ g: x \to x^2 - 1$

15. $f: x \to x^2,\ g = \text{sgn}$

16. $f: x \to |x|,\ g = I$

In Exercises 17–20, find a formula for the value of the given function at x, and evaluate the function at 0 and at 2.

17. $I^2 + I$

18. $I^2 - 4I + 4$

19. $I^3 - 2I^2 + 4$

20. $I^4 + 2I^2 + 1$

In Exercises 21–30, draw the graph of the given function. In these exercises, A: x $\to$ |x|, S: x $\to$ sgn x, and G: x $\to$ [x].

B

21. $S - A$

22. $I + S$

23. $I - S$

24. $A - I$

25. $\frac{A}{I}$

26. $2(I \cdot S)$

27. $\frac{1}{2}(I + A)$

28. $G + S$

29. $G \cdot S$

30. $I - G$

In the exercises below, you are asked to prove some algebraic properties of addition and multiplication of functions. Before starting these exercises, you should reread the proof of Theorem 1 on page 29. Notice that the symbols 0 and 1 name constant *functions,* not numbers. If *f, g,* and *h* are real-valued functions, prove the statements in Exercises 31–37.

C

31. $(f + g) + h = f + (g + h)$ (Associative property of addition)

32. $(fg)h = f(gh)$ (Associative property of multiplication)

33. $0 + f = f$ (Existence of additive identity)

34. $1f = f$ (Existence of multiplicative identity)

35. $f + g = g + f$ (Commutative property of addition)

36. $fg = gf$ (Commutative property of multiplication)

37. If $D_f = \mathcal{R}$, $f + (-f) = 0$ (Existence of additive inverses)

38. Show by example that the statement in Exercise 37 is *not* true if $D_f \neq \mathcal{R}$.

39. Show by example that the following statement is *not* true in general: If $D_f = \mathcal{R}$ and $f \neq 0$, then $f\left(\frac{1}{f}\right) = 1$.

Discussion: Suppose we have a system in which addition and multiplication are defined, and suppose that the elements of the system are closed under these operations. If the operations have the properties stated in Exercises 31, 32, 33, 35, and 37, and in Theorem 1, page 29, the system is called a **ring.** If, in addition, it contains a member 1 which satisfies the property of Exercise 34, the system is a **ring with unit element.** A ring in which multiplication is commutative (the property of Exercise 36) is a **commutative ring.** We see, therefore, that the system F of all real-valued functions whose domains are $\mathcal{R}$ is a *commutative ring with unit element.*

A **field** can be described as a commutative ring with unit element in which each member except the additive identity has a multiplicative inverse (that is, if $m \neq 0$, then there is a member $\frac{1}{m}$ such that $m\left(\frac{1}{m}\right) = 1$). The system $\mathcal{R}$ of real numbers, for example, is a field, as is the system of rational numbers. In view of Exercise 39, however, we see that the system F of the preceding paragraph is *not* a field.

1–6 Composition of Functions

In addition to the arithmetic ways of combining two functions discussed in Section 1–5, there is another way, called *composition*, which has no counterpart in the algebra of numbers. The idea behind the composition of two functions is a kind of "chain reaction" in which the functions are "applied" one after the other. For example, the amount of money a man earns is ordinarily a "function" (in the conversational sense used on page 1) of the length of time he works, and the amount of income tax he pays is a "function" of the amount of money he earns. Thus the amount of tax is ultimately a "function" of the length of time he works.

To illustrate this more specifically, consider the case of an unmarried man who earns \$5 an hour. Let f be the function $t \to 5t$ (this might be earnings as a function of time), and let g be the function $x \to \frac{1}{4}(x - 600)$ (this might be the tax as a function of earnings). Let us see what happens if we "apply" f to a specific number, say 140, and then g to the result: We have $f(140) = 700$, and then $g(f(140)) = g(700) = \frac{1}{4}(700 - 600) = 25$ (tax corresponding to 140 hours worked).

EXAMPLE 1. Using the functions f and g of the preceding paragraph, find a formula for $g(f(t))$.

Solution: Since $f(t) = 5t$ and $g(x) = \frac{1}{4}(x - 600)$, we have $g(f(t)) = \frac{1}{4}(f(t) - 600) = \frac{1}{4}(5t - 600) = \frac{5}{4}t - 150$.

To take another example, let $f\colon x \to 4x$ and $g\colon x \to \sqrt{x}$. If $x \geq 0$, $f(x) = 4x$ is nonnegative and is thus in the domain of g. Therefore we have $g(f(x)) = g(4x) = \sqrt{4x} = 2\sqrt{x}$. The association $x \to g(f(x))$ gives us a new function, which we denote by $g \circ f$ and call the *composition* of g with f. Notice that the domain of f, D_f, is $\mathcal{R}$, but that some members of this set must be excluded from the domain of $g \circ f$: If x is negative, then $f(x) = 4x$ is negative and is therefore not in the domain of g. In order to be in the domain of $g \circ f$, a number x must not only be in the domain of f, but must also be such that $f(x)$ is in the domain of g. In this example, $D_{g \circ f} = \{x\colon x \geq 0\}$.

In general:

> The **composition** of the function g with the function f is the function
> $$g \circ f: x \rightarrow g(f(x)).$$
> The domain of $g \circ f$ is the set
> $$\{x: x \in D_f \text{ and } f(x) \in D_g\}.$$

EXAMPLE 2. Given $f: x \rightarrow \dfrac{x^2 - 1}{x - 2}$ and $g: x \rightarrow \dfrac{1}{x^2}$. Find

a. the domain of $g \circ f$;
b. a formula for the values of $g \circ f$.

Solution: **a.** Since $D_f = \{x: x \neq 2\}$ and $D_g = \{x: x \neq 0\}$, the domain of $g \circ f$ is the set

$$D_{g \circ f} = \left\{x: x \neq 2 \text{ and } f(x) = \frac{x^2 - 1}{x - 2} \neq 0\right\}$$
$$= \{x: x \neq 2, 1, \text{ or } -1\}.$$

b. If $x \neq 2, 1,$ or -1, then $(g \circ f)(x) = g(f(x)) =$
$$g\left(\frac{x^2 - 1}{x - 2}\right) = \frac{1}{\left(\dfrac{x^2 - 1}{x - 2}\right)^2} = \frac{(x - 2)^2}{(x^2 - 1)^2}.$$

If the range of f is contained in the domain of g, then the domain of $g \circ f$ is the domain of f. This is true in many important cases, and some authors *require* that this condition be fulfilled in order for $g \circ f$ to have any meaning. A mapping diagram illustrating this case, in which R_f, the range of f, is contained in D_g, is shown in Figure 1–15.

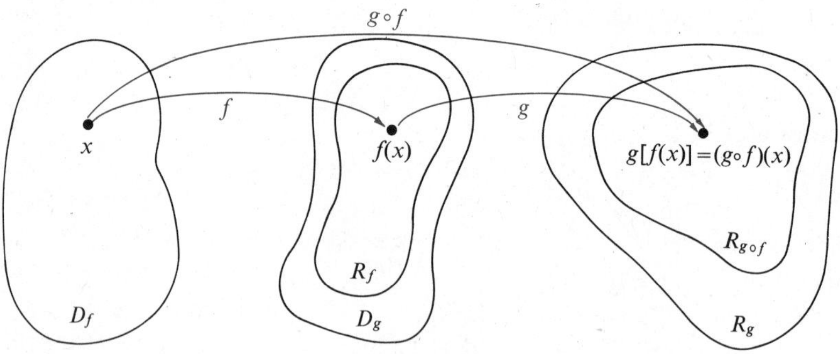

Figure 1–15

Warnings: (1) Do not confuse the composition $g \circ f$ with the product gf. (2) Notice the "backwards" nature of the notation $g \circ f$; f is applied *first*, and g is applied *second*.

EXAMPLE 3. If $F: x \to x - 2$ and $A: x \to |x|$, find formulas for the values of

a. $A \circ F$;
b. $F \circ A$.

Then graph the functions in (**a**) and (**b**).

Solution: Since the domains of F and A are both $\mathcal{R}$, the range of each is contained in the domain of the other. Therefore the domain of each of the composite functions is $\mathcal{R}$.

a. $(A \circ F)(x) = A(F(x)) = A(x - 2) = |x - 2|$.
b. $(F \circ A)(x) = F(A(x)) = F(|x|) = |x| - 2$.

a.

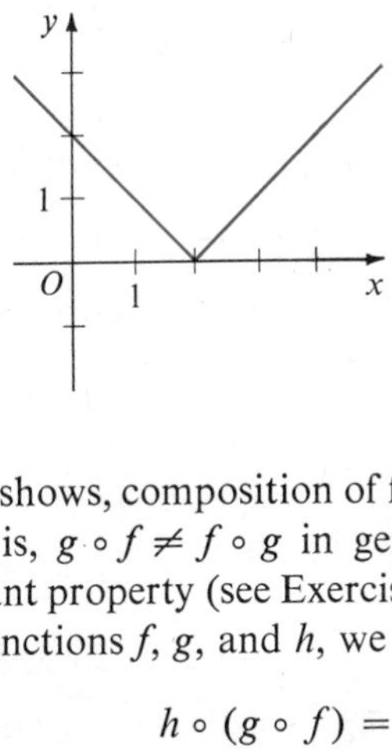

b.

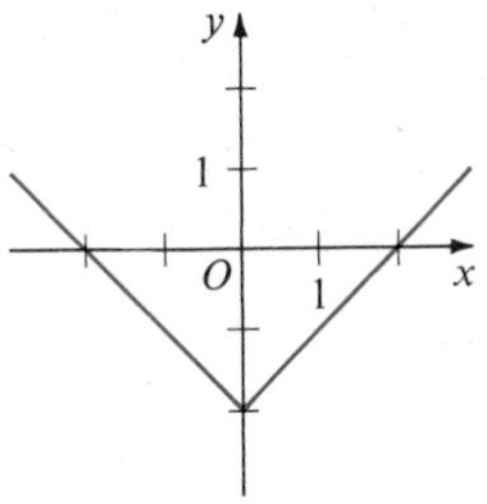

As Example 3 shows, composition of functions is *not* always a commutative operation; that is, $g \circ f \neq f \circ g$ in general. Composition does, however, have the important property (see Exercise 29 on page 38) of being associative: For any three functions f, g, and h, we have

$$h \circ (g \circ f) = (h \circ g) \circ f.$$

The identity function, $I: x \to x$, serves as an "identity element" for the operation of composition; we can show (Exercise 28, page 38) that for any function f, $f \circ I = I \circ f = f$.

It is often useful to be able to express a given function as the composition of two simpler functions. Part (a) of Example 3, for instance, shows that for $\phi: x \to |x - 2|$, we have $\phi = A \circ F$, and both

$$A: x \to |x| \qquad \text{and} \qquad F: x \to x - 2$$

are simpler than ϕ.

EXAMPLE 4. Express $\phi: x \to \sqrt{x^2 + 1}$ as the composition of two simpler functions.

Solution: We seek functions f and g such that $\phi = g \circ f$, that is, such that $\phi(x) = g(f(x))$. Since in this example $\phi(x) = \sqrt{x^2 + 1}$, we want

$$\sqrt{x^2 + 1} = g(f(x)). \tag{1}$$

This equation suggests that we let

$$f(x) = x^2 + 1. \tag{2}$$

Then (1) becomes

$$\sqrt{x^2 + 1} = g(x^2 + 1). \tag{3}$$

To simplify matters, let us set $x^2 + 1 = y$. Then (3) becomes

$$\sqrt{y} = g(y). \tag{4}$$

Equations (2) and (4) define the required functions f and g; $f: x \to x^2 + 1$ and $g: y \to \sqrt{y}$, or, because it does not matter what letter we use for the variable, $g: x \to \sqrt{x}$.

We can check our results by observing that

$$(g \circ f)(x) = g(f(x)) = g(x^2 + 1)$$
$$= \sqrt{x^2 + 1} = \phi(x)$$

for all $x \in \mathcal{R}$, and therefore $g \circ f = \phi$.

For the functions $F: x \to x^2$ and $G: x \to \sqrt{x + 1}$, we find that

$$(G \circ F)(x) = G(F(x)) = G(x^2)$$
$$= \sqrt{x^2 + 1} = \phi(x),$$

where ϕ is the function of Example 4. We see from this that a function can sometimes be expressed as the composition of two functions in more than one way.

We can illustrate the idea of composition of functions using function machines (page 9). Given functions f and g, we can construct a $(g \circ f)$-machine by hooking up a g-machine in series (or tandem) with an f-machine, as shown schematically in Figure 1–16.

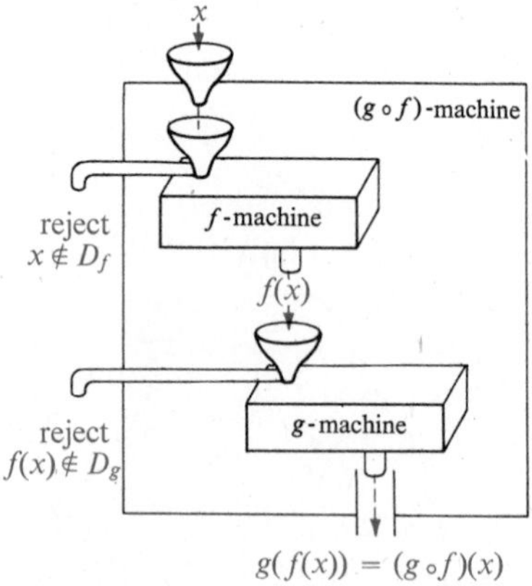

Figure 1–16

ORAL EXERCISES

In Exercises 1–10, find the domain of $g \circ f$ and find $(g \circ f)(x)$ for each x in this domain.

1.

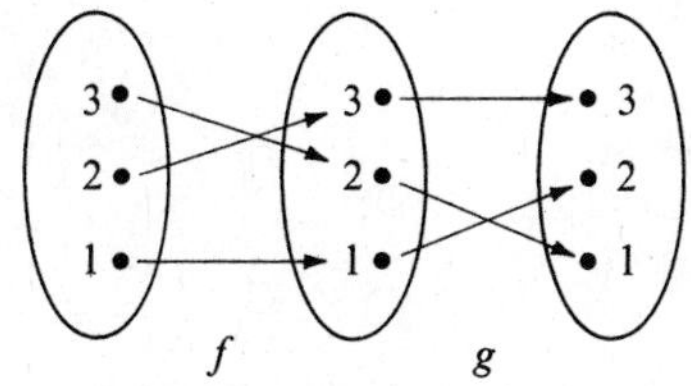

2.

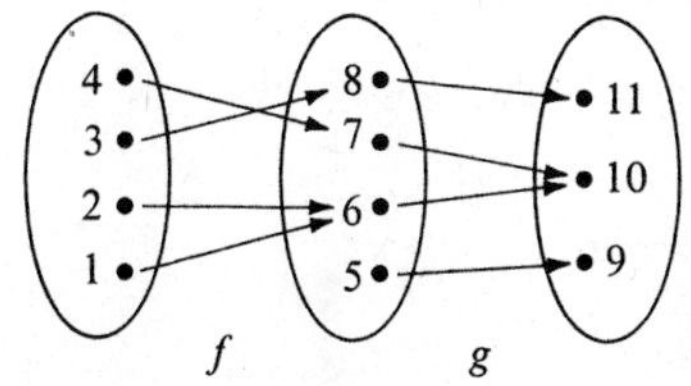

3.

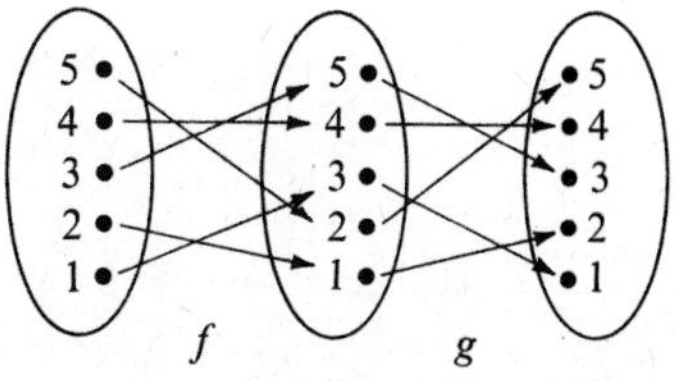

4.

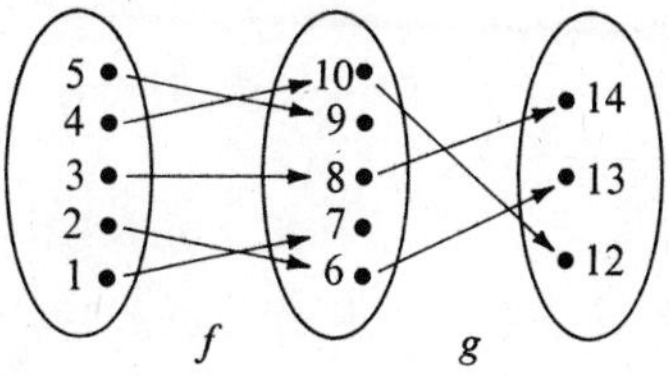

5. $f = \{(1, 2), (2, 1), (3, 3)\}$, $g = \{(1, 5), (2, 6), (3, 4)\}$

6. $f = \{(1, 1), (2, 2), (3, 3)\}$, $g = \{(1, 4), (2, 5), (3, 6)\}$

7. $f = \{(1, 2), (2, 2), (3, 2)\}$, $g = \{(1, 4), (2, 5), (3, 6)\}$

8. $f = \{(1, 2), (2, 3), (3, 4)\}$, $g = \{(1, 5), (2, 6), (3, 7)\}$

9. $f = \{(1, 3), (2, 1), (3, 2)\}$, $g = \{(1, 2), (2, 3), (3, 1)\}$

10. $f = \{(1, 3), (2, 1), (3, 2)\}$, $g = \{(1, 3), (2, 1), (3, 2)\}$

In Exercises 11–16, find the domain of $g \circ f$ and give a formula for $(g \circ f)(x)$.

11. $f\colon x \to x^2,\ g\colon x \to x + 1$

12. $f\colon x \to x + 1,\ g\colon x \to x^2$

13. $f\colon x \to x - 1,\ g\colon x \to \frac{1}{x}$

14. $f\colon x \to \frac{1}{x},\ g\colon x \to x - 1$

15. $f\colon x \to \sqrt{x},\ g\colon x \to x^2$

16. $f\colon x \to x + 1,\ g\colon x \to x - 1$

WRITTEN EXERCISES

In Exercises 1–20, find the domain of $g \circ f$ and give a formula for $(g \circ f)(x)$.

A

1. $f\colon x \to 2x,\ g\colon x \to x^2 + 4$

2. $f\colon x \to x^2 + 4,\ g\colon x \to 2x$

3. $f\colon x \to x - 1,\ g\colon x \to \sqrt{x}$

4. $f\colon x \to \sqrt{x},\ g\colon x \to x - 1$

5. $f\colon x \to x^2,\ g\colon x \to \sqrt{x}$

6. $f\colon x \to 2x,\ g\colon x \to \sqrt{4 - x^2}$

7. $f: x \to -x^2$, $g: x \to \sqrt{x}$

8. $f: x \to \frac{1}{x}$, $g: x \to x^2 - 1$

9. $f: x \to x^2 - 1$, $g: x \to \frac{1}{x}$

10. $f: x \to x$, $g: x \to x^2 + 2$

11. $f: x \to x^2 + 2$, $g: x \to x$

12. $f: x \to |x|$, $g: x \to x + 2$

13. $f: x \to x + 2$, $g: x \to |x|$

14. $f: x \to |x|$, $g: x \to \text{sgn}\ x$

15. $f: x \to \text{sgn}\ x$, $g: x \to |x|$

16. $f: x \to x^3$, $g: x \to \sqrt[3]{x}$

17. $f: x \to \frac{1}{x}$, $g: x \to \frac{1}{x}$

18. $f: x \to \frac{1}{x - 1}$, $g: x \to \frac{x + 1}{x}$

19. $f: x \to \frac{x + 1}{x}$, $g: x \to \frac{1}{x - 1}$

20. $f: x \to 1$, $g: x \to x^2 - 1$

In Exercises 21–26, find functions f and g, both simpler than ϕ, such that $\phi = g \circ f$.

B 21. $\phi: x \to (x + 1)^5$ (*Hint:* Let $f(x) = x + 1$.)

22. $\phi: x \to (x^2 + 1)^5$ (*Hint:* Let $f(x) = x^2 + 1$.)

23. $\phi: x \to \sqrt{x^2 + 4}$

24. $\phi: x \to \frac{1}{x^2 + 1}$

25. $\phi: x \to \frac{1}{x^2 - 1}$

26. $\phi: x \to \sqrt{1 - x^2}$

27. Verify that $h \circ (g \circ f) = (h \circ g) \circ f$ for $f: x \to x^2$, $g: x \to x + 1$, $h: x \to \frac{1}{x}$.

C 28. Prove that for every function f, $f \circ I = f$ and $I \circ f = f$ ($I: x \to x$).

29. Prove that if f, g, and h are functions, then $h \circ (g \circ f) = (h \circ g) \circ f$.

30. Draw a mapping diagram, similar to the one in Figure 1–15, illustrating the case in which the range of f is not contained in the domain of g.

1–7 Inversion of Functions

We know that a function may map *different* members of its domain onto the *same* member of its range. If this does *not* happen, we say that the function is *one-to-one*.

> A function f is **one-to-one** if and only if for any two different members x_1 and x_2 of its domain, $f(x_1) \neq f(x_2)$.

The equivalent "contrapositive" way of saying this is, "f is one-to-one if and only if $f(x_1) = f(x_2)$ implies $x_1 = x_2$."

EXAMPLE 1. Determine whether or not each of the following functions is one-to-one.

a. $A: x \to |x|$ **b.** $F: x \to x - a$

Solution: **a.** A is not one-to-one because $-2 \neq 2$, for instance, but $A(-2) = |-2| = 2$ and $A(2) = |2| = 2$.

b. F is one-to-one because if $x_1 \neq x_2$, then $x_1 - a \neq x_2 - a$ and therefore $F(x_1) \neq F(x_2)$.

The definition given on page 38 is equivalent to the statement that a function f is one-to-one if and only if no two different ordered pairs in f have the same *second* component. Therefore (see Figure 1–17):

A real-valued function is one-to-one if and only if no horizontal line intersects its graph in more than one point.

This horizontal-line test might be combined with the vertical-line test on page 21 as follows:

A relation is a one-to-one function if and only if no vertical or horizontal line intersects its graph in more than one point.

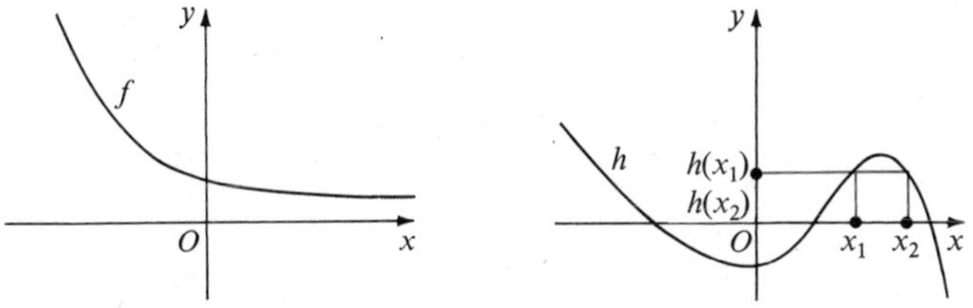

Graph of a one-to-one function f

Graph of a function h which is not one-to-one

Figure 1–17

In Figures 1–18(a) and (b), we show the mapping diagrams for two functions, f and h; f is one-to-one, while h is not.

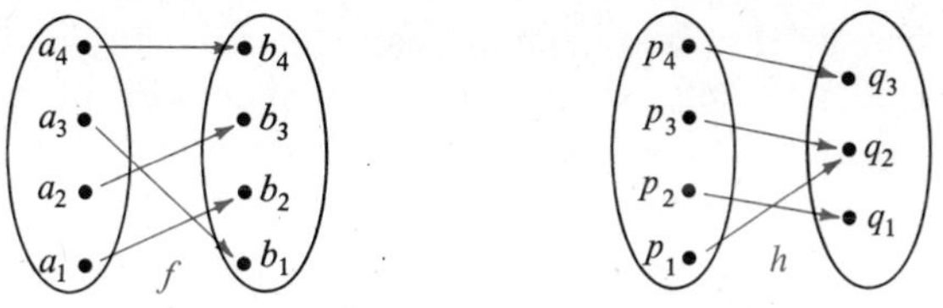

(a) (b)

Figure 1–18

Let us reverse the arrows in these diagrams to obtain Figures 1–19(a) and (b).

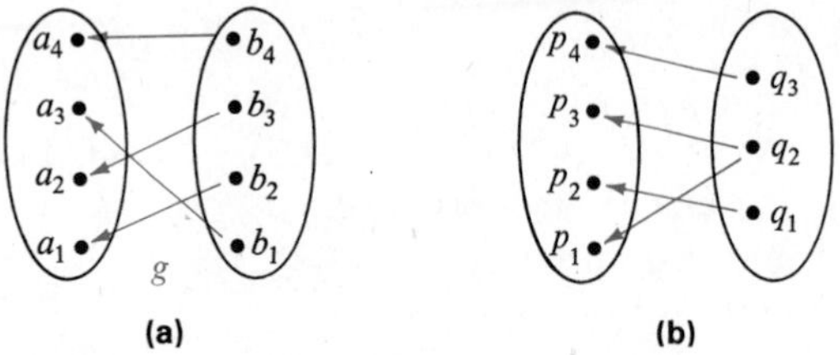

Figure 1–19

Notice that Figure 1–19(a) is the mapping diagram of a function g whose domain is the range of f and whose range is the domain of f. Figure 1–19(b), however, is *not* the mapping diagram of a function. The reversal of the arrows in the mapping diagram for f is equivalent to interchanging the first and second components of each ordered pair in f. If we do this for any *one-to-one* function f, we will get another function which we call the *inverse* of f.

> Let f be a one-to-one function. The **inverse** of f is the function $f^{-1} = \{(y, x): (x, y) \in f\}$.

Warning: The symbol f^{-1} for the inverse of f looks as if it might mean $\dfrac{1}{f}$; it does *not*. The inverse of a function has nothing to do with its reciprocal.

EXAMPLE 2. For $f = \{(1, -1), (2, 0), (3, 1)\}$, write out f^{-1} as a set of ordered pairs and find $f^{-1}(x)$ for every x in the domain of f^{-1}.

Solution: $f^{-1} = \{(-1, 1), (0, 2), (1, 3)\}$. The domain of f^{-1} is the set $\{-1, 0, 1\}$; $f^{-1}(-1) = 1, f^{-1}(0) = 2$, and $f^{-1}(1) = 3$.

We can see that for any one-to-one function f, the domain of f^{-1} is the range of f, and the range of f^{-1} is the domain of f; in symbols, $D_{f^{-1}} = R_f$ and $R_{f^{-1}} = D_f$.

If we interchange the components of an ordered pair, and then, in the resulting ordered pair, interchange the components again, we obtain the original ordered pair. Therefore the inverse of the inverse of a one-to-one function f is again f; in symbols, $(f^{-1})^{-1} = f$. To put this fact another way, if $g = f^{-1}$, then $g^{-1} = f$. Thus we may speak of two functions being inverses of each other.

You probably have the feeling that in some sense f^{-1} undoes whatever f does. That this is correct is the content of the following theorem:

Theorem 2.

Let f be a one-to-one function. Then $f^{-1}(f(x)) = x$ for every $x \in D_f$, and $f(f^{-1}(x)) = x$ for every $x \in R_f = D_{f^{-1}}$.

Proof

Let x be any member of D_f, and let $y = f(x)$. Then $(x, y) \in f$, and by the definition of an inverse function, $(y, x) \in f^{-1}$. Therefore $f^{-1}(y) = x$, and if we replace y by $f(x)$, we have $f^{-1}(f(x)) = x$.

To prove the second part of the theorem, we can apply the first part to the function $g = f^{-1}$ and use the fact that $g^{-1} = f$. Thus if x is any member of $D_g = D_{f^{-1}} = R_f$, we have

$$g^{-1}(g(x)) = x, \quad \text{or} \quad f(f^{-1}(x)) = x.$$

If we let $I' = \{(x, x)\colon x \in D_f\}$ and $I'' = \{(x, x)\colon x \in R_f\}$ be the identity functions having domains D_f and R_f, respectively, the conclusions of Theorem 2 can be written $f^{-1} \circ f = I'$ and $f \circ f^{-1} = I''$.

We can sometimes find a formula for the values of the inverse of a function if we are given a formula for the function.

EXAMPLE 3. If $f\colon x \to \dfrac{1}{x+1}$, find the domain of f^{-1} and a formula for $f^{-1}(x)$.

Solution: The values of f are given by

$$f(x) = \frac{1}{x+1}. \qquad (*)$$

From this formula, we see that 0 is not a value of f (a fraction names 0 only if its numerator is 0). But for any number $r \neq 0$, there is an x such that $f(x) = \dfrac{1}{x+1} = r$. Therefore the range of f is $\{x\colon x \neq 0\}$, and this set is the domain of f^{-1}.

Let x_1 and x_2 be any two members of D_f. Then if $f(x_1) = f(x_2)$, that is, if $\dfrac{1}{x_1+1} = \dfrac{1}{x_2+1}$, then $x_1 + 1 = x_2 + 1$, and $x_1 = x_2$. Hence, by the "contrapositive" form of the definition, f is one-to-one.

For any $x \in D_{f^{-1}}$, let $y = f^{-1}(x)$. Then, by Theorem 2,

$$f(y), \quad \text{or} \quad f(f^{-1}(x)), \text{ equals } x.$$

(*Solution continued*)

From (*), we have $f(y) = \dfrac{1}{y + 1}$, and therefore $\dfrac{1}{y+1} = x$.

Solving for y, we get $y = \dfrac{1 - x}{x}$. But $y = f^{-1}(x)$; hence

$$f^{-1}(x) = \frac{1 - x}{x}.$$

We might expect the graphs of a one-to-one function and its inverse to be related in some simple way. Let us look at an example.

EXAMPLE 4. If $f\colon x \to 2x - 4$, draw the graphs of f and f^{-1} in the same Cartesian plane.

Solution: Using the method of Example 3, we find that for all $x \in \mathcal{R}$

$$f^{-1}(x) = \tfrac{1}{2}x + 2$$

and

$$f^{-1}\colon x \to \tfrac{1}{2}x + 2.$$

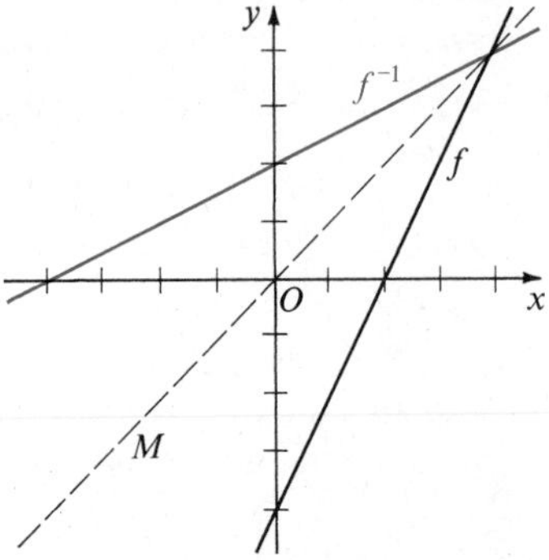

Since both f and f^{-1} are linear functions, their graphs are lines (see page 19). In the diagram at the right, the graph of f is shown in black and the graph of f^{-1} is shown in red.

In the diagram above, the graph of f^{-1} appears to be the mirror image of the graph of f if the dotted line $M\colon y = x$ (that is, the line M with equation $y = x$) is regarded as the mirror. We say that the graphs of f and f^{-1} are *symmetric* to each other with respect to the line M. (Note that M is the graph of the identity function I.)

Two points, P and Q, are **symmetric** with respect to a line K if K is the perpendicular bisector of the segment $\overline{PQ}$ (Figure 1–20). In a Cartesian

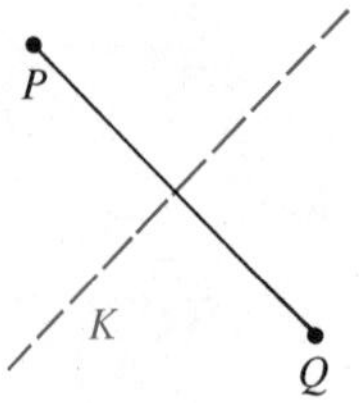

Figure 1–20

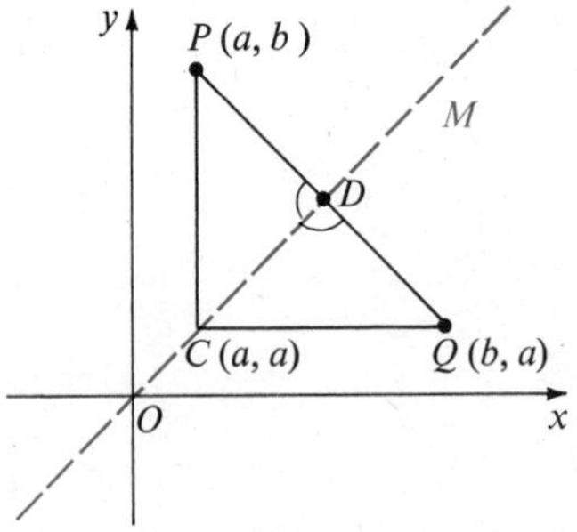

Figure 1–21

plane, the points $P(a, b)$ and $Q(b, a)$ are symmetric with respect to the line $M: y = x$. This can be shown by proving the triangles PCD and QCD in Figure 1–21 to be congruent (length $\overline{CP} = b - a =$ length $\overline{CQ}$, length $\overline{CD} =$ length $\overline{CD}$, and angle $PCD = 45° =$ angle QCD). From this it follows that the segments $\overline{DP}$ and $\overline{DQ}$ have equal length and that the two marked angles at D are equal and therefore are right angles. Thus M is the perpendicular bisector of the segment $\overline{PQ}$.

Two *sets* of points in a Cartesian plane are symmetric with respect to this line M if for every point (a, b) in one of the sets, the point (b, a) belongs to the other. (See Figure 1–22.)

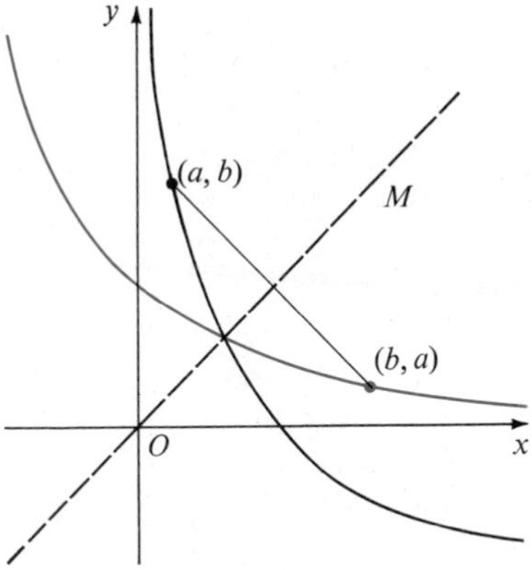

Figure 1–22

Now we can see that the graphs of two functions, f and g, which are inverses of each other are symmetric with respect to M. For if the point (a, b) is in the graph of f, then $(a, b) \in f$. Hence $(b, a) \in f^{-1} = g$, and therefore the point (b, a) is in the graph of g.

We can again use the idea of function machines to illustrate the discussion. If we run a function machine for a one-to-one function f backward, we obtain a machine for the function f^{-1}. This is shown schematically in Figure 1–23.

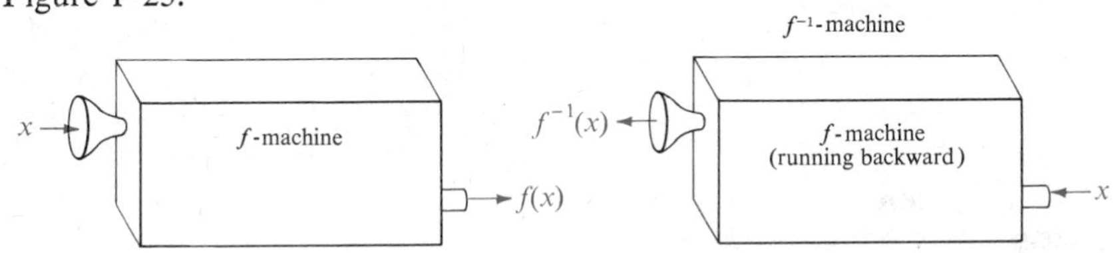

Figure 1–23

If a machine for a function which is *not* one-to-one were run backward, it would have a decision problem which would cause it to jam.

ORAL EXERCISES

In Exercises 1–17, decide whether or not f is one-to-one. If it is, find the domain and range of f^{-1} and find $f^{-1}(x)$ for each x in the domain of f^{-1}.

1. $f = \{(0, 0), (1, 2), (2, 4)\}$

2. $f = \{(0, 1), (1, 2), (2, 1)\}$

3. $f = \{(-1, 0), (2, -1), (0, 0)\}$

4. $f = \{(-1, 1), (0, 0), (1, -1)\}$

5. $f = \left\{(1, 1), \left(2, \frac{1}{2}\right), \left(3, \frac{1}{3}\right)\right\}$

6. $f = \{(x, 2x): x \in \{-1, 0, 1\}\}$

7. $f = \{(x, x^2): x \in \{-1, 0, 1\}\}$

8. $f = \{(x, x^2): x \in \{0, 1, 2\}\}$

9. $f = \{(x, |x|): x \in \{-2, 1, 3\}\}$

10. $f = \left\{\left(x, \frac{1}{x}\right): x \in \{-2, -1, 1, 2\}\right\}$

11.

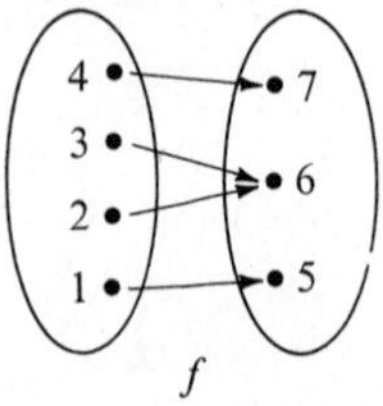

12.

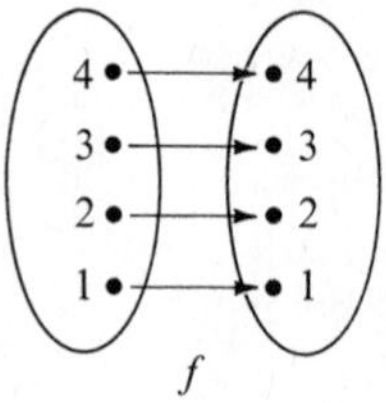

13.

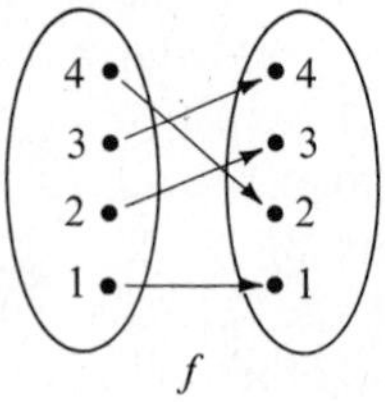

14.

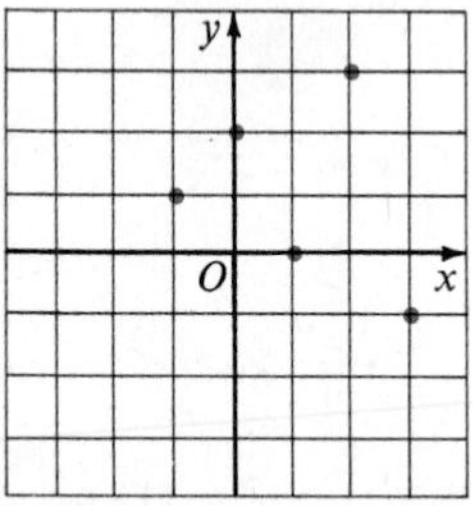

16.

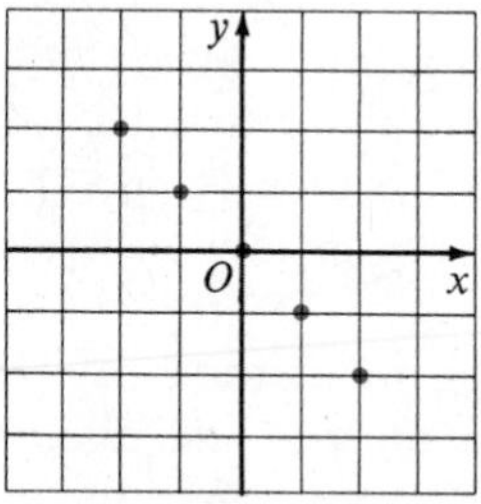

15.

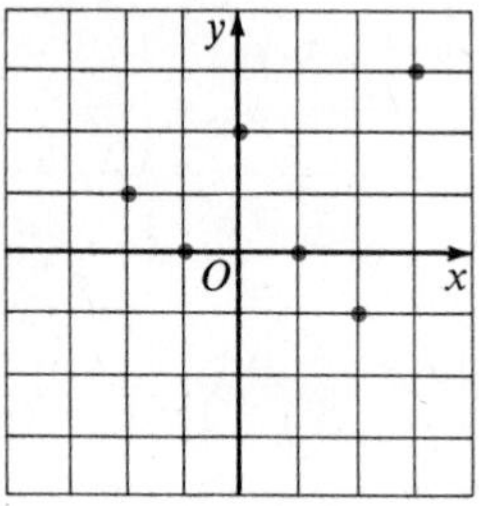

17.

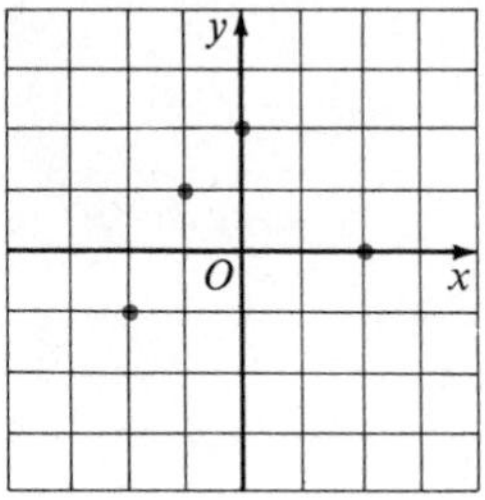

In Exercises 18–23, the graph of *f* is shown in black and the graph of *g* in red. Are *f* and *g* inverses of each other? Why or why not?

18.

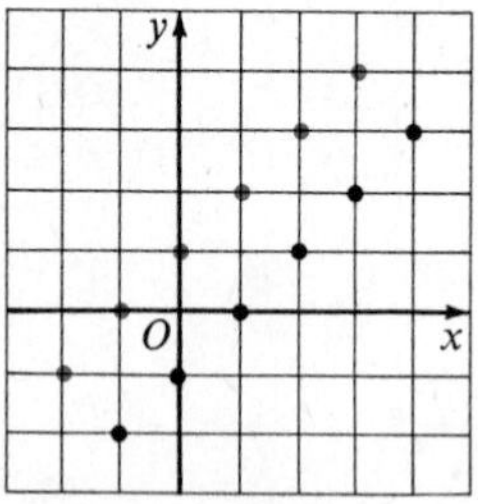

19.

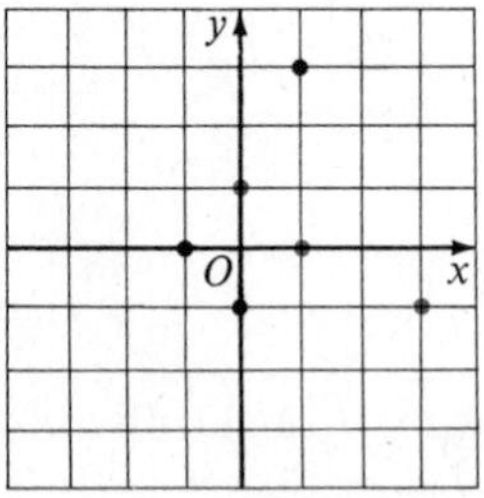

20.

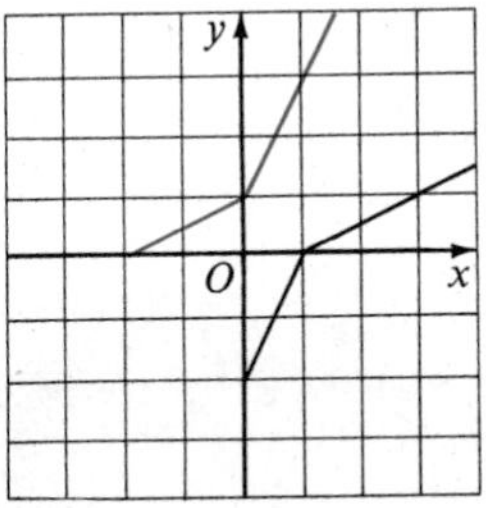

21.

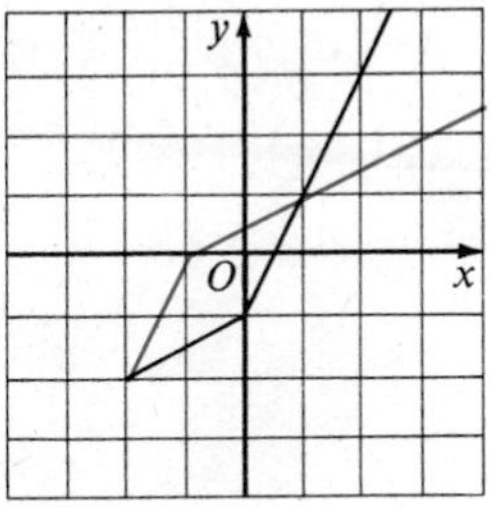

22.

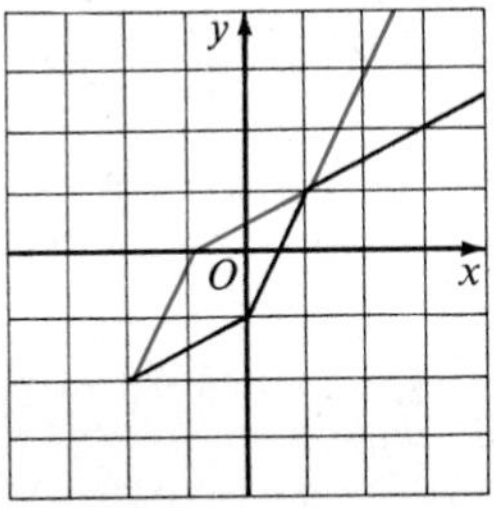

23.

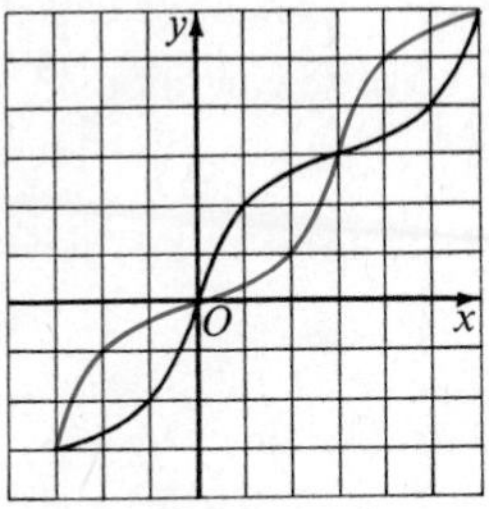

24. If $f^{-1} \circ f = f \circ f^{-1}$, what can you say about D_f and R_f?

25. If $f^{-1} \circ f = I$, what can you say about D_f?

WRITTEN EXERCISES

In Exercises 1–24, find the domain of f^{-1} and a formula for $f^{-1}(x)$.

A

1. $f: x \rightarrow x - 3$

2. $f: x \rightarrow x + 2$

3. $f: x \rightarrow 2x$

4. $f: x \rightarrow -2x$

5. $f: x \rightarrow 2x - 1$

6. $f: x \rightarrow 2x + 3$

7. $f: x \rightarrow \dfrac{1}{x}$

8. $f: x \rightarrow \dfrac{1}{x - 1}$

9. $f: x \rightarrow \dfrac{1}{2x + 1}$

10. $f: x \rightarrow \dfrac{x}{x + 1}$ $(R_f = \{x: x \neq 1\})$

11. $f: x \rightarrow \dfrac{x}{x - 1}$

12. $f: x \rightarrow x^3$

13. $f: x \rightarrow (x - 2)^3$

14. $f: x \rightarrow x^3 - 2$

15. $f: x \rightarrow x^{\frac{1}{3}}$

16. $f: x \rightarrow (x - 2)^{\frac{1}{3}}$

17. $f: x \rightarrow x^{\frac{1}{3}} - 2$

18. $f: x \rightarrow \dfrac{1}{x^3}$

B

19. $f: x \rightarrow \dfrac{b}{x}$ $(b \neq 0)$

20. $f: x \rightarrow \dfrac{1}{x + d}$

21. $f\colon x \to \dfrac{b}{x + d}$ $(b \neq 0)$

22. $f\colon x \to \dfrac{x}{x + d}$ $(d \neq 0)$

23. $f\colon x \to \dfrac{x + b}{x}$ $(b \neq 0)$

24. $f\colon x \to \dfrac{ax + b}{x}$ $(b \neq 0)$

Exercises 25–27 refer to the function $f\colon x \to \dfrac{ax + b}{cx - a}$, where $a^2 + bc \neq 0$.

C **25.** Find a formula for $f^{-1}(x)$.

26. Explain why f might be called "self-inversive."

27. Explain why the condition $a^2 + bc \neq 0$ is imposed.

Exercises 28–30 refer to the general **linear fractional** function $f\colon x \to \dfrac{ax + b}{cx + d}$, where $ad - bc \neq 0$.

28. Find a formula for $f^{-1}(x)$.

29. Verify that $(f \circ f^{-1})(x) = x$.

30. Explain why the condition $ad - bc \neq 0$ is imposed.

CHAPTER SUMMARY

1. In the ordered pair (x, y), x is called the **first component** and y the **second component.**
2. A **relation** is any set of ordered pairs. A **function** is a relation in which no two different ordered pairs have the same first component. Intuitively, we can say that a function associates with each member x of one set a unique member y of a second set. A symbol, such as x and y in the preceding sentence, which is used to represent any member of a specified set is called a **variable.**
3. A function that contains only a finite number of ordered pairs might be specified by listing its members. Otherwise, it might be described by means of **set-builder notation.** Two functions are **equal** if and only if they are the same set of ordered pairs.
4. The **domain** of a function f is the set of all first components of ordered pairs in f. The **range** of f is the set of all second components of ordered pairs in f.
5. If (x, y) is in f, then we write $y = f(x)$ (read "f of x"), and we call $f(x)$ the **value** of f at x. The function f might then be denoted by $x \to f(x)$.

6. Except when the contrary is stated, all functions occurring in this book have domains which are subsets of $\mathcal{R}$, and the domain of $f: x \to f(x)$ is taken to be the most inclusive subset of $\mathcal{R}$ for which the formula or rule for $f(x)$ produces a real number.

7. A function f might be regarded as a **mapping** from its domain to its range. If $f(a) = b$, we say that f **maps** a onto b, that the **image** of a under f is b, and that a is a **pre-image** of b under f.

8. The **Cartesian product** of $\mathcal{R}$ with itself, denoted by $\mathcal{R} \times \mathcal{R}$, is the set of all ordered pairs of real numbers. We use a **rectangular Cartesian coordinate system** to represent ordered pairs of real numbers. The components of an ordered pair are called the **coordinates** of the corresponding point; the first coordinate is the **abscissa** of the point, and the second is the **ordinate** of the point.

9. The **distance** between $P_1(x_1, y_1)$ and $P_2(x_2, y_2)$ is given by the **distance formula**

$$\text{dist}\,(P_1, P_2) = \sqrt{(x_2 - x_1)^2 + (y_2 - y_1)^2}.$$

10. For any points $P_1(x_1, y_1)$ and $P_2(x_2, y_2)$ with $x_2 \neq x_1$, the **slope** of the segment $\overline{P_1P_2}$ is given by

$$m = \frac{y_2 - y_1}{x_2 - x_1}.$$

Vertical segments have no slope; horizontal segments have slope 0. Segments that extend upward to the right have positive slope, while those that extend downward to the right have negative slope.

11. Two line segments are **parallel** or **perpendicular** if and only if they lie on lines which are respectively parallel or perpendicular. Two nonvertical segments having slopes m_1 and m_2, respectively, are

parallel if and only if $m_1 = m_2$,
perpendicular if and only if $m_1 m_2 = -1$.

To indicate that $m_1 m_2 = -1$, we say that m_1 and m_2 are **negative reciprocals** of each other.

12. If f is any function whose domain and range are subsets of $\mathcal{R}$, then the **graph** of f is $\{\text{point } (x, y)\colon\ (x, y) \in f\}$. The **graph of an equation** in two real variables is the set of all points (x, y) such that (x, y) is in the solution set of the equation. Thus the graph of the function f is the graph of the equation $y = f(x)$.

13. The abscissa of a point where a graph intersects the x-axis is called an ***x*-intercept** of the graph, and the ordinate of a point where the graph intersects the y-axis is called a ***y*-intercept** of the graph.

14. An equation of the form

$$Ax + By + C = 0,$$

where A, B, and C are real numbers and A and B are not both 0, is called a **linear equation.** The graph of any linear equation is a line, and every line is the graph of a linear equation. A function f is **linear** if there are numbers m and b such that $f\colon x \to mx + b$. The graph of any linear function is a nonvertical line, and every nonvertical line is the graph of a linear function.

15. Some special functions with which you should be familiar are the constant functions, the identity function, the absolute-value function, the greatest-integer function, and the signum (or sign) function.

16. For a relation to be a function, its graph must pass the **vertical-line test.** The graph of the equation $x^2 + y^2 = r^2$, $r > 0$, is the circle with center at the origin and radius r; this graph does not pass the vertical-line test.

17. Two **real-valued functions,** that is, functions whose ranges are subsets of $\mathcal{R}$, can be added, subtracted, multiplied, and divided. In each case, the domain of the resulting function is the intersection of the domains of the two original functions, except that for the quotient, any values in the intersection of the domains for which the denominator is zero must be excluded.

18. The system of all real-valued functions whose domains are $\mathcal{R}$ satisfies all the defining properties of a **commutative ring with unit element** (page 32). The system is not a **field** (page 33). Examples of fields are the system of rational numbers and the system of real numbers.

19. The **composition** of the function g with the function f is the function

$$g \circ f\colon x \to g(f(x)).$$

Its domain is the set $\{x\colon x \in D_f \text{ and } f(x) \in D_g\}$.

20. A function f is **one-to-one** if and only if for any two different members x_1 and x_2 of its domain, $f(x_1) \neq f(x_2)$. For a function to be one-to-one, its graph must pass the **horizontal-line test.** If f is a one-to-one function, then the **inverse** of f is the function $f^{-1} = \{(y, x)\colon (x, y) \in f\}$.

21. Two points, P and Q, are **symmetric** with respect to a line K if K is the perpendicular bisector of the segment $\overline{PQ}$. Two sets of points in a Cartesian plane are symmetric with respect to the line $M\colon y = x$ if for every point (a, b) in one of the sets, the point (b, a) is in the other. The graphs of any one-to-one function f and its inverse f^{-1} are symmetric with respect to M.

CHAPTER TEST

1–1

1. Find four members of each of the given relations and tell whether or not each relation is a function.

   a. $\{(x, x - 3): x \in \mathcal{R}\}$ c. $\{(0, y): y \in \mathcal{R}\}$

   b. $\{(x, 0): x \in \mathcal{R}\}$ d. $\{(x, x^2): x \in \mathcal{R}\}$

2. Which of the following pairs of functions are equal?

   a. $\{(1, 3), (2, 3), (3, 3)\}$; $\{(x, 3): x \in \{1, 2, 3\}\}$

   b. $\{(x^2, x^2 + 4): x \in \mathcal{R}\}$; $\{(x, x + 4): x \in \mathcal{R}\}$

1–2

3. Find the domain and range of each of these functions:

   a. $\{(x, x^2 - 1): x \in \mathcal{R}\}$

   b. $f: x \to \dfrac{x}{x^2 - 1}$

4. For the function $f: x \to 2x - 4$, find these values:

   a. $f(0)$ b. $f(2)$ c. $f(-1)$ d. $f(\frac{1}{2})$

1–3

5. a. For the points $P_1(1, 2)$, $P_2(4, 6)$, $P_3(8, 0)$, draw the segments $\overline{P_1P_2}$ and $\overline{P_2P_3}$.

   b. Find the length of $\overline{P_1P_2}$ and of $\overline{P_2P_3}$.

   c. Find the slope of $\overline{P_1P_2}$ and of $\overline{P_2P_3}$.

   d. Are $\overline{P_1P_2}$ and $\overline{P_2P_3}$ perpendicular? Why or why not?

1–4

6. For $-2 \leq x \leq 2$, graph the function described.

   a. $x \to |x| + 1$ c. $x \to x + |x|$

   b. $x \to |x + 1|$ d. $x \to 2x + 1$

1–5

7. For the functions $f = \{(-2, -3), (2, -2), (3, 1), (4, 0)\}$ and $g = \{(1, -2), (2, 3), (3, 0), (4, 3)\}$, write as sets of ordered pairs the functions $f + g$, $f - g$, fg, $\dfrac{f}{g}$, and g^2.

8. For the functions $f: x \to x + 2$ and $g: x \to x^2 - 4$, find the domain and a formula for the values of $f + g$, fg, and $\dfrac{f}{g}$.

1–6

9. For the functions $f: x \to 1 - x$ and $g: x \to \sqrt{x}$, find the domain and a formula for the values of $g \circ f$ and $f \circ g$.

1–7 **10.** For the function

$$f\colon x \rightarrow \frac{2x - 1}{3x + 4},$$

find the domain and a formula for the values of f^{-1}.

RECOMMENDED READINGS

MAY, KENNETH O., and VAN ENGEN, HENRY, "Relations and Functions," in *The Growth of Mathematical Ideas, Grades K-12* (Washington, D.C.: National Council of Teachers of Mathematics, 1959).

MCFADDEN, MYRA, MOORE, J. WILLIAM, and SMITH, WENDELL I., *Sets, Relations, and Functions: A Programmed Unit in Modern Mathematics* (New York: McGraw-Hill, Inc., 1963).

National Council of Teachers of Mathematics, *Graphs, Relations, and Functions* (Washington, D.C.: 1968).

School Mathematics Study Group, *Elementary Functions* (New Haven, Conn.: Yale University Press, 1961).

SELBY, SAMUEL M., and SWEET, LEONARD, *Sets — Relations — Functions* (New York: McGraw-Hill Inc., 1963).

Mathematics and Art

George David Birkhoff (1884–1944), one of the most outstanding of all American mathematicians, made a serious hobby of the mathematical theory of aesthetics. While realizing that a completely satisfactory theory of beauty can probably never be achieved, he nevertheless proposed as a simple quantitative *aesthetic measure* of any given object the ratio $\frac{N(R)}{N(E)}$, where $N(E)$ designates the number of elements in the object and $N(R)$ the number of relations between these elements. In his treatise *Aesthetic Measure,* he applied his theory with some interesting results to such diverse arts as ceramics, painting, poetry, and music.

Man's awareness of the relationship between mathematics and art dates back to ancient times. In the field of musical expression, an obvious example is the regular pattern of beats in a primitive rhythm. Another link between mathematics and music results from the discovery, attributed to Pythagoras, that two strings of the same material and under the same tension give a pleasing, restful effect when sounded together *provided* that their lengths are in the ratio of two small counting numbers, such as 2 and 3. Pythagoras was so strongly affected by this numerical observation that he founded his school of philosophy on a belief in the mystic powers of counting numbers. We now know, of course, that the pleasing effect results from the fact that the fundamental frequency of the sound waves emitted by a vibrating string is inversely proportional to the length of the string.

George David Birkhoff

Our present diatonic scale has evolved from the Greek sense of harmony in a succession of tones having simple frequency ratios between them. In the diatonic scale of C-major, for example, the ratios between the successive tones and the key tone C are as follows:

C	D	E	F	G	A	B	C
1	$\frac{9}{8}$	$\frac{5}{4}$	$\frac{4}{3}$	$\frac{3}{2}$	$\frac{5}{3}$	$\frac{15}{8}$	$\frac{2}{1}$

Since the human ear is not particularly offended by small variations in the relative frequencies, the exact intervals on the diatonic scale are slightly altered in modern keyboard instruments so as to permit playing in a number of different keys using a total of only twelve tones in each octave; this means that the same string has to serve for a number of slightly different tones.

Many mathematicians are deeply interested in art, and some of the most gifted artists have had mathematical talent as well. Few individuals, however, have ever achieved true greatness in both mathematics and art. The outstanding exception was Leonardo da Vinci (1452–1519). Generally acclaimed one of the world's greatest painters of all time, he was also an imaginative geometer and an accomplished physicist, anatomist, and scientific inventor — the prototype of the "Renaissance Man."

Mathematics is intimately related to the design arts of architecture, sculpture, painting, and drawing. This is particularly true of painting and drawing, where the problem of making two-dimensional representations of three-dimensional objects led to a mathematical theory of perspective and subsequently to the study of projective geometry and of descriptive geometry.

The model at the left is a reconstruction of the Parthenon, a Doric temple built in Athens in the 5th century B.C. The architects of the Parthenon used many geometric principles in its design; however, they departed from strict geometric exactness in a number of ways in order to increase the grace and beauty of the building.

The lines and the circle superimposed on the photograph of the Adoration of the Magi, *painted by Domenico Ghirlandaio in 1488, illustrate the underlying geometric structure of the work.*

Classical design artists often used subtle geometric arrangements of the elements in a composition to obtain a desired effect, as suggested in the photograph above. Many paintings, including Leonardo's famous *The Last Supper*, have been analyzed in the same way as this picture.

By contrast, twentieth-century arts such as painting, sculpture, and music, in their apparently wild, free, and abstract forms, might at first glance appear to be pulling away from the structural orderliness that most people associate with mathematics. The fact is, however, that mathematics and art remain as closely associated as ever. Actually, the arts have not become disorganized but have simply moved ahead to new patterns — patterns of "organized complexity." Mathematics, too, deals with organized complexity in today's social, industrial, and economic problems. To meet the challenges of these problems, mathematicians have had to develop many new approaches, including combinatorics, linear and dynamic programming, and the theory of games. In fact, mathematics has gone one step further, in that it now deals also with problems of "disorganized complexity" — for example, in insurance, gas dynamics, and atomic physics — through the application of statistical and probabilistic techniques.

READING LIST

BIRKHOFF, G. D., *Aesthetic Measure* (Cambridge, Mass.: Harvard University Press, 1933).

JANSON, H. W., *History of Art* (New York: Harry N. Abrams, Inc., 1964), especially p. 99 regarding the geometry of the Parthenon.

MAY, KENNETH O., *Mathematics and Art*, The Mathematics Teacher, Vol. 60, No. 6 (October 1967), pp. 568–572.

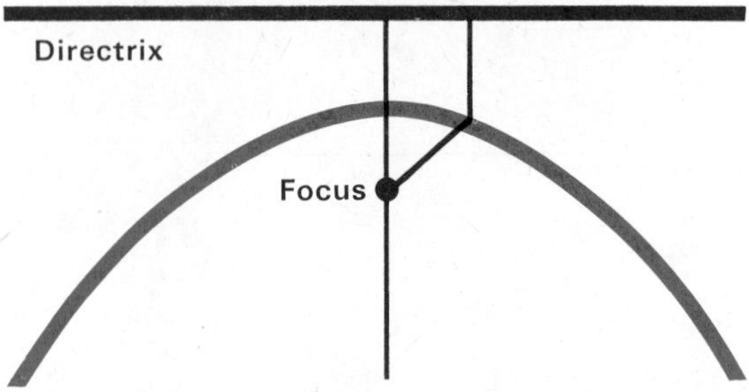

2

The water spouts from the fountains in the photograph above in parabolic arcs. A parabola is the set of points equidistant from a fixed line, the directrix, and a fixed point not on the line, the focus (see the diagram above).

Polynomial Functions

In this chapter, we shall first study two important special types of polynomial functions, linear and quadratic, in some detail. We shall then turn to a general consideration of polynomial functions and their properties.

■ Linear and Quadratic Functions

2–1 Lines and Linear Functions

In Section 1–4, we saw that the graph of any equation of the form

$$Ax + By + C = 0, \tag{1}$$

where A, B, and C are real numbers and not both A and B are 0, is a line, and, conversely, that every line is the graph of an equation of the form (1). For this reason, we called equations of the form (1) *linear equations.*

We saw further that the line is nonvertical if and only if $B \neq 0$, and that the equation can be written equivalently in the form

$$y = mx + b$$

if and only if $B \neq 0$. We called a function

$$f\colon x \rightarrow mx + b$$

a *linear function.* Thus the graph of every linear function is a nonvertical line and every nonvertical line is the graph of a linear function.

In Section 1–3, for any points $P_1(x_1, y_1)$ and $P_2(x_2, y_2)$ with $x_1 \neq x_2$, we defined the *slope* m of the segment $\overline{P_1P_2}$ by

$$m = \frac{y_2 - y_1}{x_2 - x_1}.$$

Suppose, now, that we have a nonvertical line

$$L\colon\ Ax + By + C = 0.$$

Since L is nonvertical, $B \neq 0$. If we let $P_1(x_1, y_1)$ and $P_2(x_2, y_2)$ be any two points of L, then we have

$$Ax_1 + By_1 + C = 0 \quad \text{and} \quad Ax_2 + By_2 + C = 0.$$

Subtracting the first of these equations from the second gives us

$$A(x_2 - x_1) + B(y_2 - y_1) = 0,$$

from which it follows, since $x_1 \neq x_2$, that

$$\text{slope } \overline{P_1P_2} = \frac{y_2 - y_1}{x_2 - x_1} = -\frac{A}{B}.$$

Since the number $-\dfrac{A}{B}$ is independent of P_1 and P_2, we have proved the unsurprising result that *all segments of a nonvertical line have the same slope.* This result enables us to speak of the *slope of a line:*

> The **slope of a nonvertical line** is the common value of the slopes of all its segments. A vertical line has no slope.

Thus we can find the slope of a line by calculating the slope of any one of its segments. For example, if L is the line passing through $P_1(4, -2)$ and $P_2(-1, -3)$, then the slope of L = slope $\overline{P_1P_2} = \dfrac{-3 - (-2)}{-1 - 4} = \dfrac{-1}{-5} = \dfrac{1}{5}$. We know, then, that every other segment of L also has slope $\frac{1}{5}$.

Suppose that we know the slope m of a nonvertical line L and a point $P_1(x_1, y_1)$ on L. If $P(x, y)$ is any other point on L, then

$$\text{slope } \overline{P_1P} = \frac{y - y_1}{x - x_1} = m,$$

and therefore

$$y - y_1 = m(x - x_1). \qquad (*)$$

Since this linear equation is satisfied by both P and $P_1(x_1, y_1)$, it is an equation of L. This is called the **point-slope form** of the equation of L.

EXAMPLE 1. Find an equation of the line L which passes through $P_1(2, 3)$ and $P_2(4, -2)$.

Solution: We first find the slope m of L by finding the slope of $\overline{P_1P_2}$: $m = \dfrac{-2 - 3}{4 - 2} = -\dfrac{5}{2}$. Using the point P_1 in the point-slope form, we get $y - 3 = -\frac{5}{2}(x - 2)$. This can be simplified to $5x + 2y - 16 = 0$.

Suppose the slope m and the y-intercept b of a line L are given. Then the point $(0, b)$ is on L, and we see from the point-slope form that an equation of L is $y - b = m(x - 0)$, or

$$y = mx + b.$$

This is the **slope-intercept form** of the equation.

The slope-intercept form suggests a way of finding the slope of a non-vertical line whose equation is given in the form $Ax + By + C = 0$. To find the slope of the line with equation $2x + 3y - 9 = 0$, for example, we solve the equation for y, getting $y = -\frac{2}{3}x + 3$. This equation is in the slope-intercept form, so we see immediately that the slope is $-\frac{2}{3}$ (and the y-intercept is 3).

For brevity, we shall sometimes refer to the line with equation $3x + 2y + 4 = 0$, for example, as the line $3x + 2y + 4 = 0$. We shall follow this practice with other geometric figures also. For example, we might speak of the circle $x^2 + y^2 = 1$ or the curve $y = \dfrac{1}{x}$.

Linear functions occur frequently in science and technology. For example, suppose that when one end of a coil spring is attached to the ceiling and a pan is hung from the other end, the length of the spring is 3 feet (Figure 2–1).

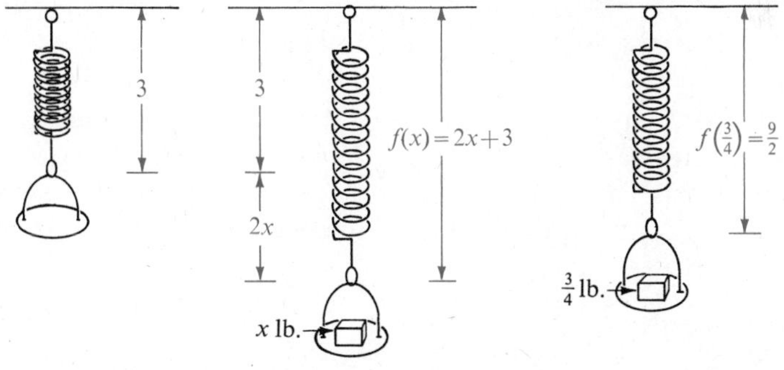

Figure 2–1

We may find by experiment that when an x-pound weight is placed in the pan, the spring is stretched $2x$ feet. The total length of the spring when an x-pound weight is in the pan is therefore $2x + 3$ feet. This gives rise to a *weight* $\rightarrow$ *length* linear function $f\colon x \rightarrow 2x + 3$. For another example, it is a physical fact that near the surface of the earth the velocity of an object moving vertically under the influence of gravity alone is (approximately) a linear function of time. That is, if v represents velocity and t represents time (in some convenient units), then there is a function $v\colon t \rightarrow mt + b$, where m and b are real numbers, which associates with each second, say, of time a definite velocity. (In saying that velocity is a function of time, we are using *function* in the "conversational" sense of Chapter 1. For brevity, we shall continue to do so when it seems appropriate. In such cases, however, it should be realized that the "conversational" description of the function can be translated into a mathematical one, as was done above.)

EXAMPLE 2. Ten seconds after a rifle bullet is fired vertically upward, its velocity is 1320 feet per second. After another 10 seconds, it is still going up and has velocity 1000 feet per second. Find

a. the *time* $\rightarrow$ *velocity* function;
b. the initial velocity at which the bullet was fired;
c. the time after firing at which the bullet has velocity zero (at the top of its flight).

Solution: We let t denote time (in seconds) and choose $t = 0$ to be the time of firing.

a. The required function is of the form $v\colon t \rightarrow mt + b$. Since $v(10) = 1320$ and $v(20) = 1000$, we have

$$m \cdot 10 + b = 1320 \quad \text{and} \quad m \cdot 20 + b = 1000.$$

We can determine m and b from these equations, obtaining $m = -32$ and $b = 1640$. Therefore the required function is $v\colon t \rightarrow -32t + 1640$.

b. Since the firing occurred when $t = 0$, the initial velocity of the bullet is $v(0) = 1640$ feet per second.

c. We want to find t_1 such that $v(t_1) = -32t_1 + 1640 = 0$. Solving, we obtain $t_1 = 51\frac{1}{4}$ seconds.

In Example 2, we can check that the velocity $v(t)$ is *negative* if $t > 51\frac{1}{4}$. The physical significance of this is that the bullet is then moving *downward*. The problem was set up in such a way that upward motion corresponds to positive velocity and downward motion to negative velocity.

ORAL EXERCISES

In Exercises 1–8, state the slope of the line which passes through the origin and the given point.

1. $(1, 3)$	**3.** $(-3, -9)$	**5.** $(1, -7)$	**7.** $(3, 2)$
2. $(4, 12)$	**4.** $(1, 7)$	**6.** $(3, 1)$	**8.** $(-2, 3)$

In Exercises 9–20, state the slope and *y*-intercept of the given line.

9. $y = 2x + 3$	**13.** $y = 4$	**17.** $y - x = 4$
10. $y = x - 3$	**14.** $y = \dfrac{x + 6}{2}$	**18.** $x - y = 4$
11. $y = 3 - x$	**15.** $2y = x + 2$	**19.** $3x - 2y = 0$
12. $y = 4x$	**16.** $y - 3 = 2x$	**20.** $2x + 3y + 6 = 0$

For each of the lines shown below, state the slope, the y-intercept, and an equation.

21.

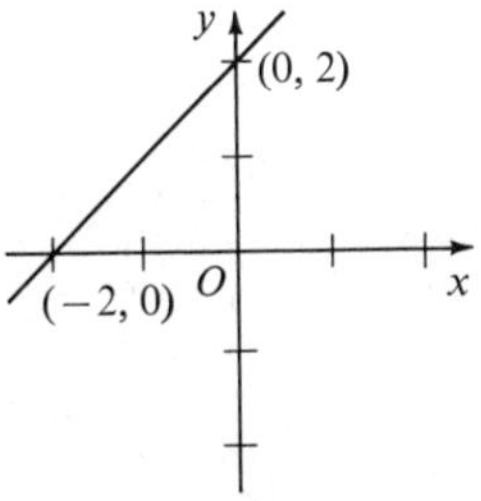

22.

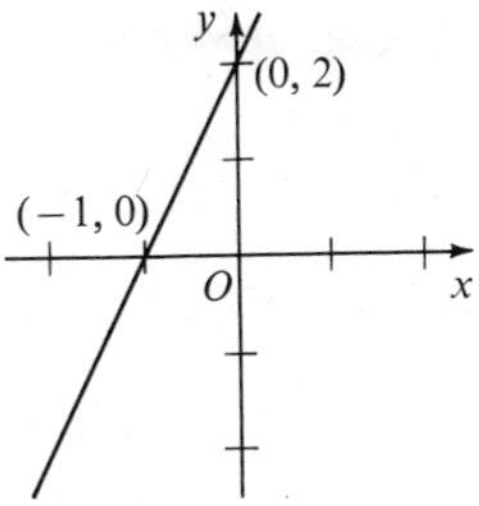

23.

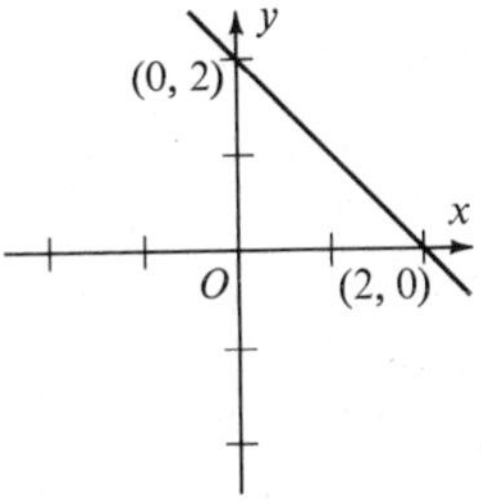

24.

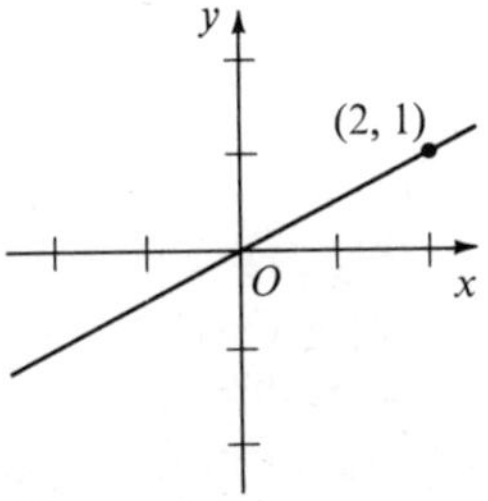

25.

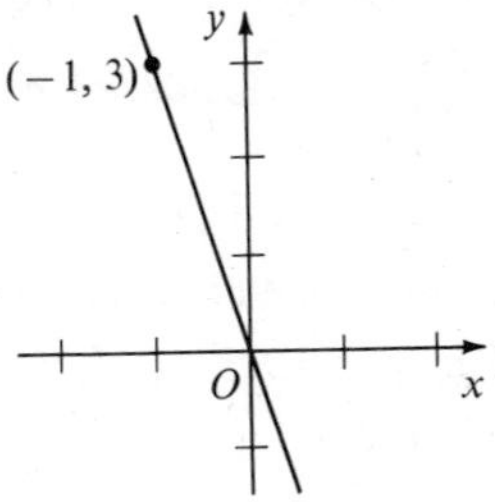

26.

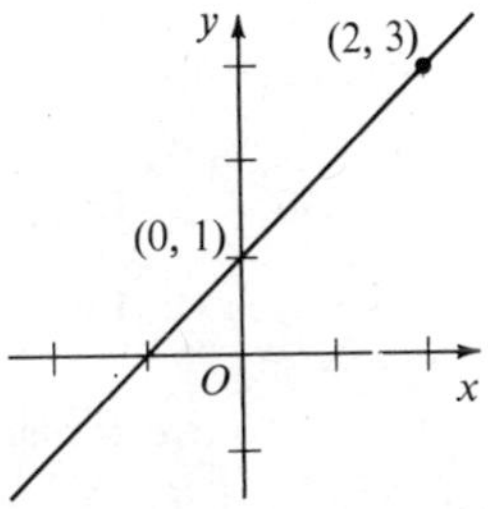

27. Suppose we know that a certain function f is linear. What is the least number of points on the graph of f we must know before we can find a formula for $f(x)$?

In Exercises 28–30, the given figure is part of a mapping diagram of a *linear* function f. State a formula for $f(x)$.

28.

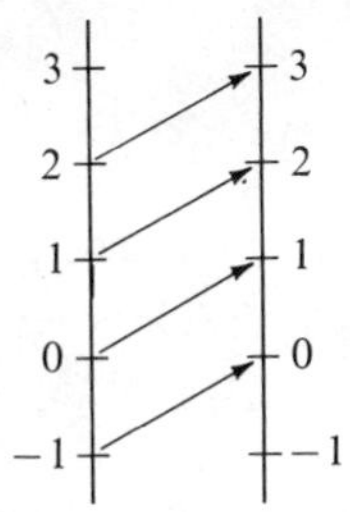

29.

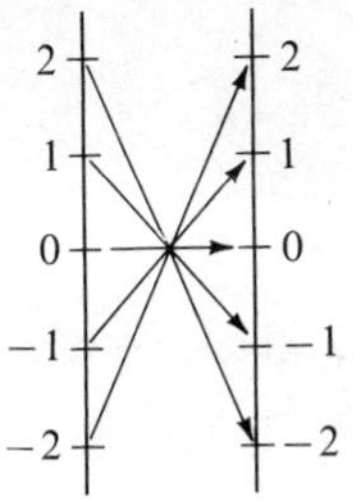

30.

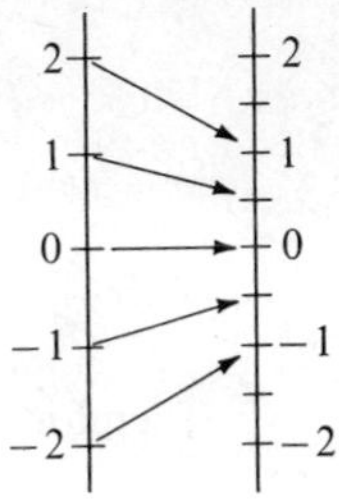

WRITTEN EXERCISES

In Exercises 1–12, certain characteristics of a line are given. Express an equation of the line in the form $Ax + By + C = 0$.

A

1. Slope 3, y-intercept -2.
2. Slope -1, y-intercept 3.
3. Slope 2, passes through $(-2, 0)$.
4. Slope $-\frac{1}{2}$, passes through $(1, 2)$.
5. Passes through $(-1, -1)$ and $(2, 3)$.
6. Passes through $(2, -1)$ and $(-3, -4)$.
7. Slope $\frac{2}{3}$, x-intercept $\frac{3}{2}$.
8. Slope -2, x-intercept $\frac{1}{2}$.
9. Has y-intercept -1, same slope as $y = 2x + 1$.
10. Has x-intercept 2, same slope as $x + 2y = 0$.
11. Same slope as $x + 3y = 2$, same y-intercept as $3x + y = 2$.
12. Same slope as $2x + 3y = 0$, same x-intercept as $3x + 2y = 6$.

In Exercises 13–18, draw the graph of the linear function f.

13. $f: x \to -x + 1$
14. $f: x \to 3(2 - x)$
15. $f: x \to \dfrac{x - 3}{3}$
16. $f: x \to -2x - 2$
17. $f = 2I \quad (I: x \to x)$
18. $f = 2I - 3$

In Exercises 19–22, find a formula for $f(x)$ if the graph of the linear function f

19. passes through the origin and $(2, 3)$.
20. passes through $(-2, 5)$ and $(5, -2)$.
21. passes through $(0, 1)$ and is parallel to the graph of $g: x \to \frac{1}{3}x$.
22. passes through $(0, 1)$ and is perpendicular to the graph of $g: x \to \frac{1}{3}x$.

In Exercises 23–28, find the inverse of the linear function f. Draw the graphs of f and f^{-1} in the same coordinate plane and label each.

EXAMPLE. $f: x \to 2x - 3$

Solution: Let $y = f^{-1}(x)$. Then

$x = f(y) = 2y - 3$. Thus

$$f^{-1}(x) = y = \frac{x + 3}{2}.$$

Therefore $f^{-1}: x \to \frac{1}{2}x + \frac{3}{2}$.

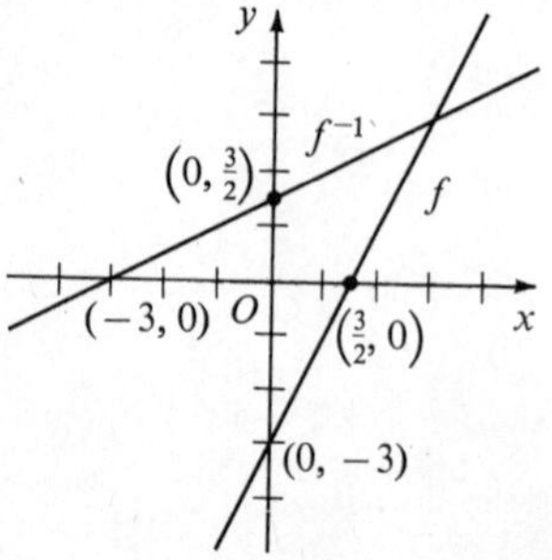

23. $f: x \to 3x$

24. $f: x \to -\frac{2}{3}x$

25. $f: x \to 2x + 1$

26. $f: x \to \frac{1}{3}x + 2$

27. $f: x \to \frac{2x + 1}{3}$

28. $f: x \to \frac{3}{4}(x + 3)$

In Exercises 29–33, find the function g ∘ f.

29. $f: x \to 2x,\ g: x \to x + 3$

30. $f: x \to x + 3,\ g: x \to 2x$

31. $f: x \to x - 3,\ g: x \to x + 3$

32. $f: x \to 2x - 1,\ g: x \to 3x + 2$

33. $f: x \to 2x - 1,\ g: x \to \frac{1}{2}(x + 1)$

B

34. Find the inverse of $f: x \to mx + b, m \neq 0$, thus proving that any nonconstant linear function has an inverse and that the inverse is a nonconstant linear function.

35. If $f: x \to mx + b$ and $g: x \to px + q$, find the function $g \circ f$, thus proving that the composition of linear functions is a linear function.

36. When a one-pound weight is suspended from the free end of a coil spring, the length of the spring is 5 feet. When an additional one-pound weight is suspended, the length is 7 feet. Find (**a**) the *weight* → *length* function, assuming that this function is linear, (**b**) the length of the spring when no weight is suspended from it, and (**c**) the total weight which must be suspended in order that the length be 8 feet.

37. The natural (unloaded) length of a coil spring is 20 inches. When a two-pound weight is suspended from the free end of the spring, its length is 30 inches. Find (**a**) the *weight* → *length* function, assuming that this function is linear, (**b**) the length of the spring when only a one-pound weight is suspended from it, and (**c**) the total weight which must be suspended in order that the length be 35 inches.

38. One second after a baseball is thrown vertically upward, its velocity is 96 feet per second. After one more second, it is still going up and has velocity 64 feet per second. Use the method of Example 2, page 58, to find

   a. the *time* → *velocity* function;
   b. the initial velocity with which the ball was thrown;
   c. the time after the ball was thrown at which it has velocity zero;
   d. the velocity of the ball $3\frac{1}{2}$ seconds after it was thrown (interpret the sign of the answer);
   e. the velocity of the ball 5 seconds after it was thrown (interpret the sign of the answer).

39. A rifle bullet is fired vertically upward (at time $t = 0$) with initial velocity 1600 feet per second. Twenty-five seconds later it is still going up and has velocity 800 feet per second. Use the method of Example 2, page 58, to find

   a. the *time* → *velocity* function;
   b. the velocity of the bullet 30 seconds after it was fired (interpret the sign of the answer);
   c. the velocity of the bullet one minute after it was fired (interpret the sign of the answer);
   d. the time in flight at which the bullet has velocity zero.

For Exercises 40–44, find a formula for $f(x)$ if the graph of the linear function f

40. passes through (2, 1) and has its x-intercept equal to its y-intercept.

41. passes through $(-3, 1)$ and has its x-intercept equal to its y-intercept.

42. has slope $-\frac{A}{B}$ and y-intercept $-\frac{C}{B}$ $(B \neq 0)$.

43. has slope $m \neq 0$ and x-intercept $-\frac{b}{m}$.

44. has x-intercept a and y-intercept b.

45. What are the x- and y-intercepts of the line

$$\frac{x}{a} + \frac{y}{b} = 1?$$

(This is the **intercept form** of the equation of a line.)

46. Show that the line passing through the points (x_1, y_1) and (x_2, y_2), $x_1 \neq x_2$, has equation

$$y - y_1 = \frac{y_2 - y_1}{x_2 - x_1}(x - x_1).$$

(This is the **two-point form** of the equation of a line.)

C **47.** Let $Ax + By + C = 0$ be an equation of a line L. The equation is said to be in **normal form** if and only if $A^2 + B^2 = 1$.

a. Show that

$$\frac{A}{\sqrt{A^2 + B^2}}x + \frac{B}{\sqrt{A^2 + B^2}}y + \frac{C}{\sqrt{A^2 + B^2}} = 0$$

is in normal form.

b. Show that the perpendicular distance p from the origin to L is

$$\frac{|C|}{\sqrt{A^2 + B^2}}.$$

(*Hint:* The lengths of the segments $\overline{OP}$ and $\overline{OQ}$ are $\left|\frac{C}{A}\right|$ and $\left|\frac{C}{B}\right|$, respectively. Find the length of $\overline{PQ}$. Then use the fact that the triangles POQ and PTO are similar.)

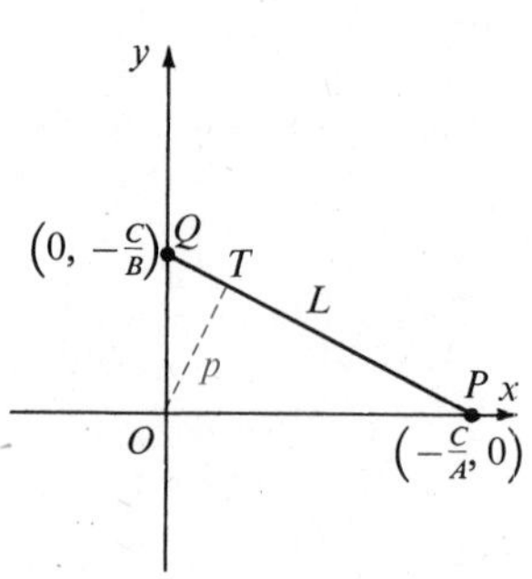

In Exercise 33, page 68, of the next section, it is shown that the perpendicular distance from any point $P_0(x_0, y_0)$ to L is

$$\left|\frac{Ax_0 + By_0 + C}{\sqrt{A^2 + B^2}}\right|.$$

2–2 Parallel and Perpendicular Lines (Optional)

In algebra courses, you learned methods for finding the solution set of a system of two linear equations in two variables. If you apply these methods to the three systems listed below, you will find the solution sets which are given below the systems. The graphs of the equations in each of the systems are shown in Figure 2–2.

System I	*System II*	*System III*
$2x + y - 4 = 0$	$2x + y - 4 = 0$	$2x + y - 4 = 0$
$x - y + 1 = 0$	$2x + y + 1 = 0$	$4x + 2y - 8 = 0$
Solution set = $\{(1, 2)\}$.	Solution set is empty.	Solution set = $\{(x, y)\colon y = 4 - 2x\}$.

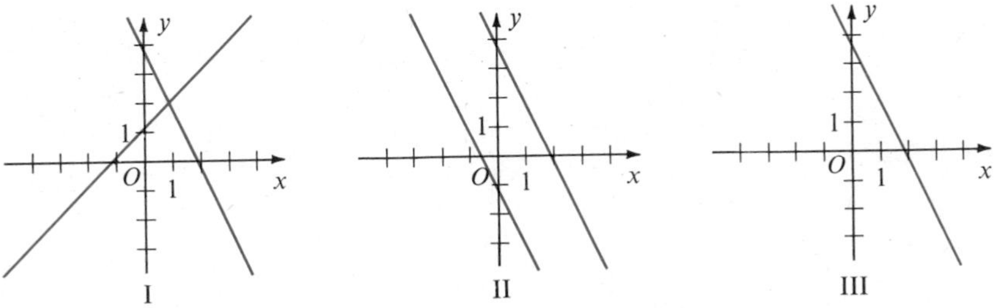

Figure 2–2

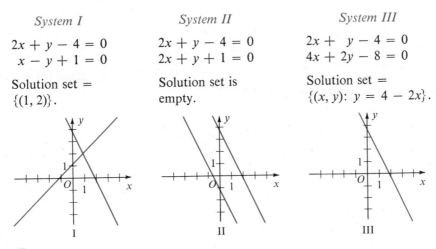

In System I, the equations have a *unique* common solution and their graphs intersect in just *one* point. In System II, the equations have *no* common solution, and their graphs do not meet at all; that is, the lines are *parallel.* In System III, the two equations are equivalent, and any solution of one is a solution of the other. Therefore they have *infinitely many* common solutions, and, in fact, their graphs coincide.

The analogy between the algebraic and geometric situations suggested by the examples above can be generalized. Let us consider lines

$$L_1 \text{ having equation } A_1x + B_1y + C_1 = 0$$

and

$$L_2 \text{ having equation } A_2x + B_2y + C_2 = 0.$$

A point is on *both* lines if and only if its coordinates satisfy *both* equations. Therefore L_1 and L_2 intersect in a single point, are parallel, or are coincident according as the system

$$\begin{aligned} A_1x + B_1y + C_1 &= 0 \\ A_2x + B_2y + C_2 &= 0 \end{aligned}$$

has, respectively, one, no, or infinitely many, common solutions.

EXAMPLE 1. Show that L_1: $4x - 2y + 3 = 0$ and L_2: $2x - y - 1 = 0$ are parallel.

Solution: Let us solve each equation of the system

$$4x - 2y + 3 = 0$$
$$2x - y - 1 = 0$$

for y to obtain the equivalent system

$$y = 2x + \tfrac{3}{2}$$
$$y = 2x - 1.$$

If there were a solution (x_0, y_0) of this system, then we would have $y_0 = 2x_0 + \frac{3}{2}$ and $y_0 = 2x_0 - 1$, so that $2x_0 + \frac{3}{2} = 2x_0 - 1$, or $\frac{3}{2} = -1$, which is not true. We see from this that the original system has *no* such common solution (x_0, y_0) and, therefore, that L_1 and L_2 are parallel.

Theorem 1.

Two (different) nonvertical lines L_1 and L_2 are parallel if and only if their slopes are equal.

Proof

We put the equations of the lines L_1 and L_2 into slope-intercept form:

$$L_1\colon\ y = m_1x + b_1$$
$$L_2\colon\ y = m_2x + b_2$$

We know that the slopes of L_1 and L_2 are m_1 and m_2, respectively. Now, L_1 and L_2 are parallel if and only if the system

$$y = m_1x + b_1$$
$$y = m_2x + b_2$$

has *no* solution.

To show that L_1 and L_2 are parallel only if $m_1 = m_2$, it is equivalent, and simpler, to show that if $m_1 \neq m_2$, then L_1 and L_2 are *not* parallel. If $m_1 \neq m_2$, then any of the various algebraic methods for solving the system above will yield the solution

$$\left(\frac{b_1 - b_2}{m_2 - m_1}, \frac{m_2b_1 - m_1b_2}{m_2 - m_1}\right).$$

Thus L_1 and L_2 are not parallel.

On the other hand, if $m_1 = m_2 = m$, say, then the system becomes

$$y = mx + b_1$$
$$y = mx + b_2$$

where $b_1 \neq b_2$ since L_1 and L_2 are different lines. We can see that this system has no solution. Hence L_1 and L_2 are parallel.

EXAMPLE 2. Is the line L_1: $52x + 37y + 67 = 0$ parallel to the line L_2 through $(-18, 11)$ and $(18, -40)$?

Solution: Putting the equation of L_1 into slope-intercept form,

$$y = -\tfrac{52}{37}x - \tfrac{67}{37},$$

we see that the slope of L_1 is $-\frac{52}{37}$. The slope of L_2 is

$$\frac{-40 - 11}{18 - (-18)} = -\frac{51}{36} = -\frac{17}{12}.$$

Therefore L_1 and L_2 are *not* parallel, because their slopes are *not* equal.

[A line L_1 and a line L_2 may have the same slope without being parallel (in the strict sense of the word): they may coincide. In order to simplify our terminology, however, we often consider coincident lines to be parallel.]

The following theorem gives us an algebraic test in terms of slopes to tell whether or not two (nonvertical) lines are perpendicular. (See page 15.) It is most easily proved using trigonometry. However, we shall give a proof which uses the Pythagorean Theorem and its converse: If the square of the length of one side of a triangle is equal to the sum of the squares of the lengths of the other two sides, then the triangle is a right triangle and the first of these three sides is its hypotenuse.

Theorem 2.

Let L_1 and L_2 be lines having slopes m_1 and m_2, respectively. Then L_1 and L_2 are perpendicular if and only if $m_1m_2 = -1$.

Proof

If L_1 and L_2 were parallel (or coincident), their slopes would be equal, and accordingly the product of their slopes would be nonnegative. Therefore, whether it is given that L_1 and L_2 are perpendicular, or whether it is

(Proof continued)

given that $m_1m_2 = -1$, we can conclude that L_1 and L_2 are not parallel (or coincident) and, hence, that they intersect in a single point.

Let $P(h, k)$ be the point of intersection of L_1 and L_2 (Figure 2–3). Then the equations of these lines in point-slope form are

$$L_1\colon\ y - k = m_1(x - h)$$

and

$$L_2\colon\ y - k = m_2(x - h).$$

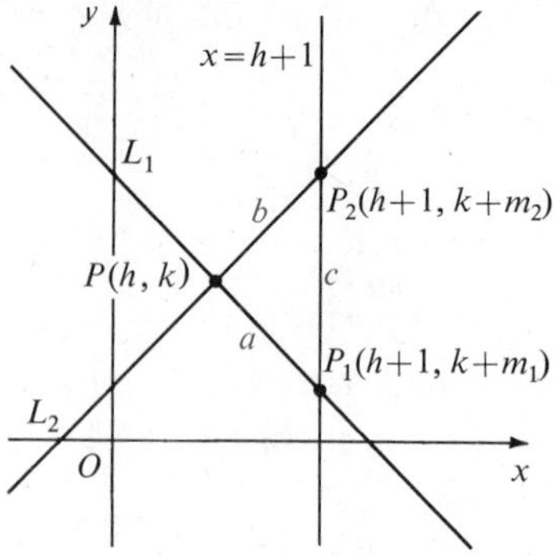

Figure 2–3

The vertical line $x = h + 1$ intersects L_1 in the point $P_1(h + 1, k + m_1)$ and L_2 in the point $P_2(h + 1, k + m_2)$. Let a, b, and c be the lengths of $\overline{PP_1}$, $\overline{PP_2}$, and $\overline{P_1P_2}$, respectively. Then, using the distance formula, we find

$$a^2 = [(h + 1) - h]^2 + [(k + m_1) - k]^2 = 1 + m_1^2,$$
$$b^2 = [(h + 1) - h]^2 + [(k + m_2) - k]^2 = 1 + m_2^2,$$
$$c^2 = [(k + m_2) - (k + m_1)]^2 = (m_2 - m_1)^2 = m_1^2 - 2m_1m_2 + m_2^2.$$

Now if L_1 and L_2 are perpendicular, then P_1PP_2 is a right triangle and, therefore, $c^2 = a^2 + b^2$, or $m_1^2 - 2m_1m_2 + m_2^2 = (1 + m_1^2) + (1 + m_2^2)$. This reduces to $-2m_1m_2 = 2$, or $m_1m_2 = -1$.

Conversely, if $m_1m_2 = -1$, then the expression for c^2 becomes

$$m_1^2 + 2 + m_2^2,$$

so we see that $c^2 = a^2 + b^2$. Therefore P_1PP_2 is a right triangle, and L_1 and L_2 are perpendicular.

EXAMPLE 3. Is the line L_1: $2x + 3y = 6$ perpendicular to the line L_2 which passes through $(-1, -1)$ and $(3, 5)$?

Solution: From the slope-intercept form, $y = -\frac{2}{3}x + 2$, of the equation of L_1, we see that its slope is $m_1 = -\frac{2}{3}$. The slope of L_2 is $m_2 = \dfrac{5 - (-1)}{3 - (-1)} = \dfrac{6}{4} = \dfrac{3}{2}$. Since $m_1m_2 = (-\frac{2}{3})(\frac{3}{2}) = -1$, L_1 and L_2 are perpendicular.

EXAMPLE 4. Find an equation of the line through $(2, -3)$ which is **(a)** parallel and **(b)** perpendicular to the line L: $2x + 5y = 6$.

Solution: The slope of L is $-\frac{2}{5}$.

a. The required line has slope $-\frac{2}{5}$ and passes through $(2, -3)$. Using the point-slope form, we have $y - (-3) = -\frac{2}{5}(x - 2)$, or $2x + 5y + 11 = 0$.

b. The required line has slope $\frac{5}{2}$. Using the point-slope form, we have $y - (-3) = \frac{5}{2}(x - 2)$, or $5x - 2y - 16 = 0$.

ORAL EXERCISES

In Exercises 1–12, a line is described. State the slope of any line which is (a) parallel and (b) perpendicular to the one described.

1. The line through (0, 0) having slope 2.
2. The line through (5, −2) having slope 2.
3. The line through (0, 0) having slope 1.
4. The line through (1, 2) having slope $-\frac{2}{3}$.
5. The line $y = 2x$.
6. The line $y = -x + 3$.
7. The line $y = \frac{1}{4}x - 2$.
8. The line $x - y = 0$.
9. The line through (0, 0) and (1, 3).
10. The line through (0, 0) and $(1, -\frac{1}{2})$.
11. The line through (0, 0) and (3, 6).
12. The line through (0, 0) and (−1, 2).

In Exercises 13–20, state whether the given lines are parallel, perpendicular, or neither parallel nor perpendicular.

13. $y = x$; $y = x + 2$
14. $y = \frac{1}{2}x$; $y = -2x$
15. $y = x$; $y = -x$
16. $y = 2x$; $y = -2x$
17. $y = 3x - 1$; $y = -\frac{1}{3}x - 1$
18. $y = 2x$; $y = \frac{1}{2}x$
19. $y = x + 2$; $x - y + 2 = 0$
20. $x + y = 0$; $x - y = 0$

WRITTEN EXERCISES

In Exercises 1–8, two lines are described. Determine whether they are parallel, perpendicular, or neither.

A

1. $x + 2y - 3 = 0$; $2x - y + 1 = 0$
2. $2x + 3y = 0$; $4x + 6y + 5 = 0$
3. $2x + 3y = 0$; $3x + 2y = 4$
4. $7x - 2y + 4 = 0$; the line through (4, 6) and (0, 8).
5. $5x + 2y - 4 = 0$; the line through (0, −4) and (10, 0).
6. The line through (1, −2) and (9, 3); the line through (−1, −4) and (4, 4).
7. The line through (1, −2) and (9, 3); the line through (−1, 4) and (4, −4).
8. The line through (6, −1) and (2, 5); the line through (0, 4) and (2, 1).

In Exercises 9–18, find an equation of the line through the given point which is (a) parallel and (b) perpendicular to the given line.

9. Point (0, 1), line $y = 2x + 3$.
10. Point (0, 2), line $y = x$.
11. Point (2, 1), line $y = -x + 1$.
12. Point $(-3, 0)$, line $y = \frac{1}{3}x + 2$.
13. Point (1, 1), line $x + 2y + 3 = 0$.
14. Point (3, 2), line $y - 2 = 0$.
15. Point $(-2, 5)$, line $5x - 2y = 4$.
16. Point $(0, -2)$, line through (0, 0) and (2, 5).
17. Point $(2, -3)$, line through $(-2, 0)$ and (0, 3).
18. Point $(-1, -2)$, line through $(-2, 4)$ and $(2, -5)$.

In Exercises 19–24, find the number t so that the line through the given points will be (a) parallel and (b) perpendicular to the line $x - 2y + 3 = 0$.

B **19.** $(0, 0), (1, t)$
20. $(0, 2), (2, t)$
21. $(3, -2), (4, t)$
22. $(0, 2), (t, t)$
23. $(1, 1), (t + 1, t - 1)$
24. $(t, t), (t + 1, 2t)$

In Exercises 25–30, find the number k so that the given line will be (a) parallel and (b) perpendicular to the line $x - 2y + 3 = 0$.

25. $y = kx + 2$
26. $y = k(x + 2)$
27. $kx - 2y = 3$
28. $x - ky + 1 = 0$
29. $(k + 1)x + ky + 2 = 0$
30. $(k + 2)x + (2k + 1)y + 5 = 0$

Exercises 31 and 32 refer to the nonvertical lines

$$L_1: A_1x + B_1y + C_1 = 0 \quad \text{and} \quad L_2: A_2x + B_2y + C_2 = 0.$$

C **31.** Show that L_1 and L_2 are parallel (or coincident) if and only if

$$\frac{A_1}{B_1} = \frac{A_2}{B_2}.$$

32. Show that L_1 and L_2 are perpendicular if and only if

$$A_1A_2 + B_1B_2 = 0.$$

Is this result valid without the assumption that the lines are nonvertical?

33. Show that the perpendicular distance k from any point $P_0(x_0, y_0)$ to the line $L: Ax + By + C = 0$ is

$$\left|\frac{Ax_0 + By_0 + C}{\sqrt{A^2 + B^2}}\right|.$$

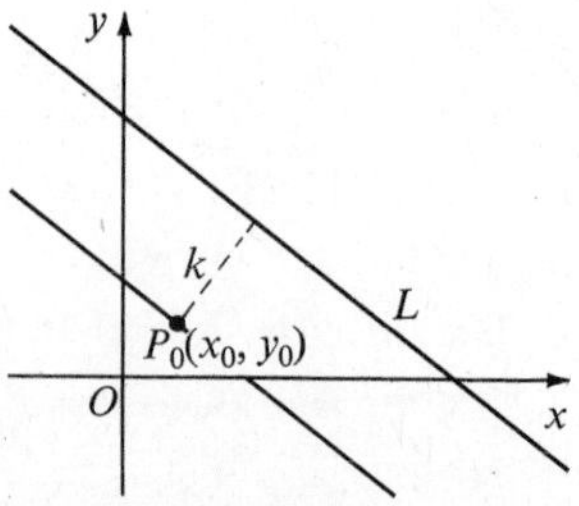

2–3 Quadratic Functions

Suppose an object is projected from the top of a 100-foot tower at an angle of 30° with the horizontal and with an initial velocity of 120 feet per second. (See Figure 2–4.) It can be verified experimentally that the approximate height of the object t seconds later is given by the formula

$$h(t) = 100 + 60t - 16t^2.$$

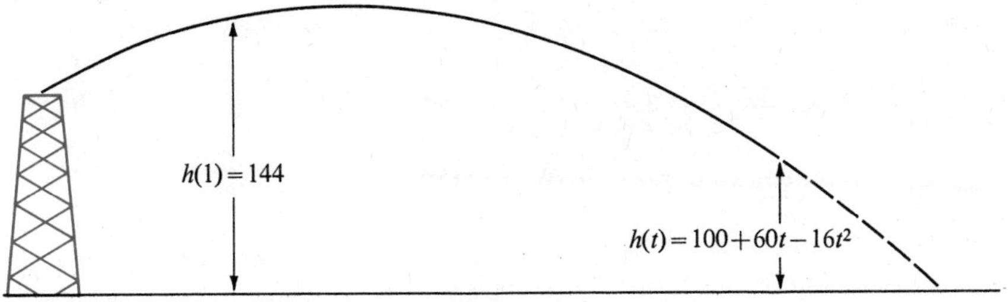

Figure 2–4

The *time* → *height* function

$$h: t \to 100 + 60t - 16t^2$$

is an example of a *quadratic* function.

A function f is **quadratic** if there are real numbers $a \neq 0$, b, and c such that

$$f(x) = ax^2 + bx + c.$$

Thus $f: x \to 2x^2 - 3x + 5$, $g: t \to t - t^2$, and $h: x \to x^2$ are quadratic functions, but $F: x \to 2x - 3$ is not.

EXAMPLE 1. In (**a**) and (**b**), plot at least six points of the graph of the given quadratic function. Then sketch the graph by drawing a smooth curve through these points.

a. $f: x \to 4x - x^2$ **b.** $g: x \to 6x^2 - 7x - 20$

Solution: We record the values of $f(x)$ and $g(x)$ for various values of x in tabular form:

x	0	1	2	3	4	5	−1
$f(x)$	0	3	4	3	0	−5	−5

x	0	1	2	3	−1	−2
$g(x)$	−20	−21	−10	13	−7	18

(*Solution continued*)

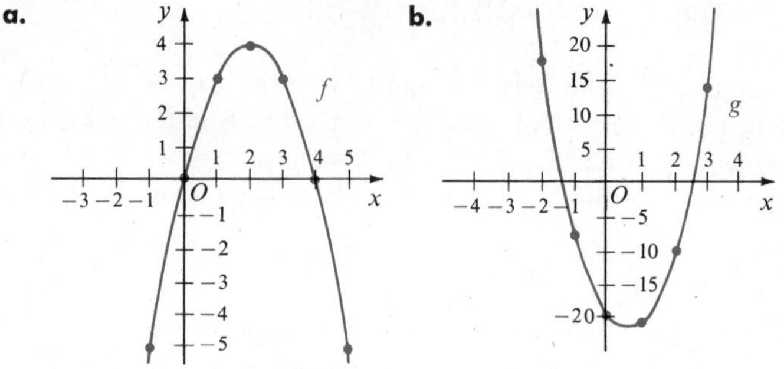

In (**b**), because of the relatively large values of g, we choose the unit of length on the vertical axis to be less than that on the horizontal axis. We then plot the points and draw a smooth curve through them, as shown.

The graphs of f and g in Example 1 are called *parabolas*. Parabolas will be defined and discussed in more detail in Section 2–4, where we shall see that the graph of every quadratic function is a parabola. The coefficient of x^2 in the expression for f is *negative*, and the parabola which is its graph opens *downward*. In the case of g, the coefficient of x^2 is *positive*, and the parabola opens *upward*.

A glance at the graph of the function f of Example 1(a), or at its table of values, shows us that the graph of f crosses the x-axis at (0, 0) and (4, 0), that is, that $f(0) = 0$ and $f(4) = 0$. Exactly where the graph of $g\colon x \to 6x^2 - 7x - 20$ of Example 1(b) crosses the x-axis is not as apparent, although the graph indicates that there are two such points. We can find them quite easily, however. Since we want the values of x for which $g(x) = 0$, we need only solve the quadratic equation $6x^2 - 7x - 20 = 0$. The quadratic expression can be factored to give $(2x - 5)(3x + 4) = 0$, from which we see that $g(x) = 0$ if $x = \frac{5}{2}$ or $x = -\frac{4}{3}$. The numbers $\frac{5}{2}$ and $-\frac{4}{3}$ are called the *zeros* of g.

> If f is any function and z is a number in the domain of f such that $f(z) = 0$, then z is a **zero** of f.

Thus the *zeros* of a *function* f are the same as the *roots* of the *equation* $f(x) = 0$, and are also the same as the *x-intercepts* of the *graph* of f.

To find the zeros of any quadratic function

$$f\colon x \to ax^2 + bx + c,$$

we need only solve the equation $ax^2 + bx + c = 0$. Using the familiar quadratic formula, we obtain

$$\frac{-b + \sqrt{b^2 - 4ac}}{2a} \quad \text{and} \quad \frac{-b - \sqrt{b^2 - 4ac}}{2a}.$$

Each of these expressions names a real number if and only if $b^2 - 4ac \geq 0$, so the graph of f intersects the x-axis only when this is true. Figure 2–5 illustrates how the graph of f (a) cuts the x-axis twice, (b) meets the x-axis at just one point, or (c) has no point on the x-axis, according as $b^2 - 4ac$ is greater than zero, equal to zero, or less than zero:

$f\colon x \to x^2 - 4x + 2$	$f\colon x \to x^2 - 4x + 4$	$f\colon x \to x^2 - 4x + 6$
$b^2 - 4ac = 8$	$b^2 - 4ac = 0$	$b^2 - 4ac = -8$
zeros of f: $2 \pm \sqrt{2}$	zero of f: 2	no real zeros of f

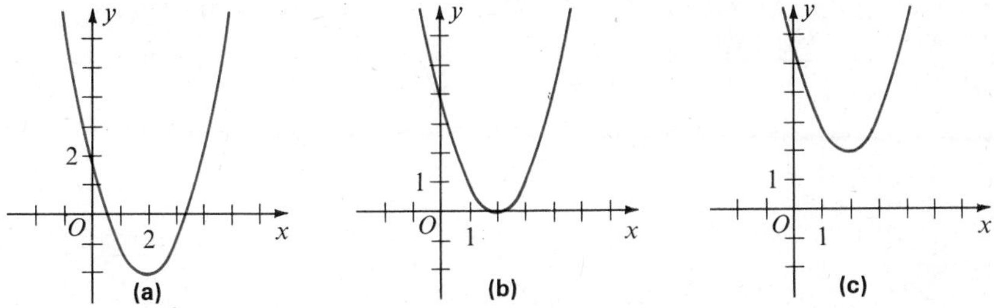

Figure 2–5

The graph of the quadratic function $f\colon x \to 2x^2 - 6x + 5$ is a parabola which opens upward and which therefore has a lowest point. This means that the function f has a least value, namely the ordinate of this point. We shall use the method of completing the square to find this least, or *minimum*, value of f. For any x,

$$\begin{aligned} f(x) &= 2x^2 - 6x + 5 \\ &= 2(x^2 - 3x) + 5 \\ &= 2(x^2 - 3x + \tfrac{9}{4}) + 5 - 2 \cdot \tfrac{9}{4} \\ &= 2(x - \tfrac{3}{2})^2 + \tfrac{1}{2} \end{aligned}$$

{We need $\frac{9}{4}$ inside the parentheses to complete the square and must compensate for it by subtracting $2 \cdot \frac{9}{4}$.

Since $(x - \frac{3}{2})^2$ is never negative, $f(x) \geq \frac{1}{2}$ for *all* x. Moreover, $f(\frac{3}{2}) = \frac{1}{2}$. Therefore $\frac{1}{2}$ is the minimum value of the function f, and the point $(\frac{3}{2}, \frac{1}{2})$ is the lowest point on the graph of f. Knowing this point is of considerable help in drawing the graph (Figure 2–6).

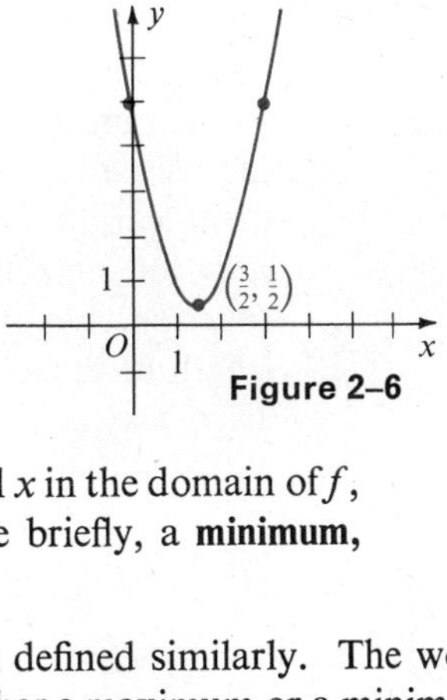

Figure 2–6

In general, we say:

> If for a given value t, $f(t) \leq f(x)$ for all x in the domain of f, then $f(t)$ is a **minimum value,** or, more briefly, a **minimum,** of f.

Maximum values, or **maxima,** of functions are defined similarly. The word ***extremum*** (plural: ***extrema***) is used to mean either a maximum or a minimum value. (Maxima and minima as we have defined them are sometimes called *absolute* maxima and minima. We shall discuss this in more detail in Chapter 4.)

Not every function has a minimum value: A quadratic function whose parabolic graph opens downward has a maximum but no minimum. Nonconstant linear functions have neither maxima nor minima. The finding of extrema is one of the important applications of differential calculus, which we shall study later. As we have seen, however, we may solve the problem for *quadratic* functions by purely algebraic methods. By applying the method of completing the square to the general quadratic function, we can prove the following (Exercise 28, page 75):

Theorem 3.

The function f: $x \to ax^2 + bx + c$, $a \neq 0$, has an extremum at $x = \dfrac{-b}{2a}$, and this extreme value is $f\left(\dfrac{-b}{2a}\right) = \dfrac{4ac - b^2}{4a}$. The extremum is a maximum or minimum according as $a < 0$ or $a > 0$.

There is no need to memorize the formula for the extreme value of the function: Since we know for what x this extremum occurs $\left(x = \dfrac{-b}{2a}\right)$, we can easily find the value of the function there by substitution in the quadratic expression.

EXAMPLE 2. A rectangular plot is to be enclosed by using part of an existing fence as one side and 120 feet of fencing for the other three sides. What is the greatest area which can be enclosed?

Solution: Our plan is to express the area of *any* rectangular plot which can be formed using the 120 feet of fencing as a function of some convenient variable x. We shall then find the maximum value of this function. Let us choose x to be the length of each of the sides perpendicular to the existing fence. Then the length of the side parallel to this fence must be $120 - 2x$, since the sum of the lengths of the three sides must be 120. For a given x, the dimensions of the plot are x and $120 - 2x$, and therefore its area is

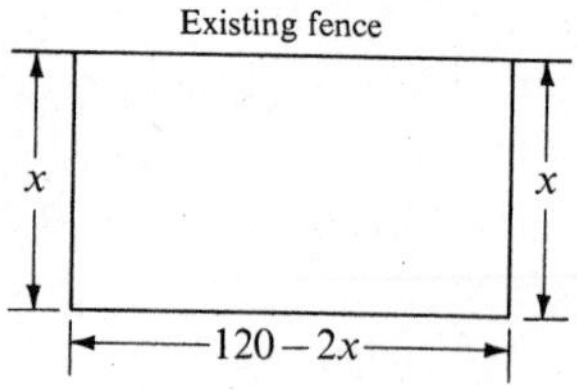

$$A(x) = x(120 - 2x) = 120x - 2x^2.$$

We wish, therefore, to find the maximum of the quadratic function $A\colon x \to 120x - 2x^2$. This can be done either by completing the square or by using Theorem 3, page 72, to find that the maximum of A occurs when $x = \dfrac{-120}{2(-2)} = 30$. Hence $A(30) = 120 \cdot 30 - 2 \cdot 30^2 = 1800$ square feet is the greatest area which can be enclosed. (We obtain as a by-product the fact that the dimensions of this largest plot are 30 feet by $120 - 2 \cdot 30$, or 60, feet.)

The physical conditions in Example 2 are such that x must be between 0 and 60. Therefore the graph of the function A is just the red part of the parabola shown in Figure 2–7. We see, however, that the maximum of the function A is the same as that of the quadratic function $x \to 120x - 2x^2$, since the maximum of the quadratic function happens to occur at a point of the domain of A.

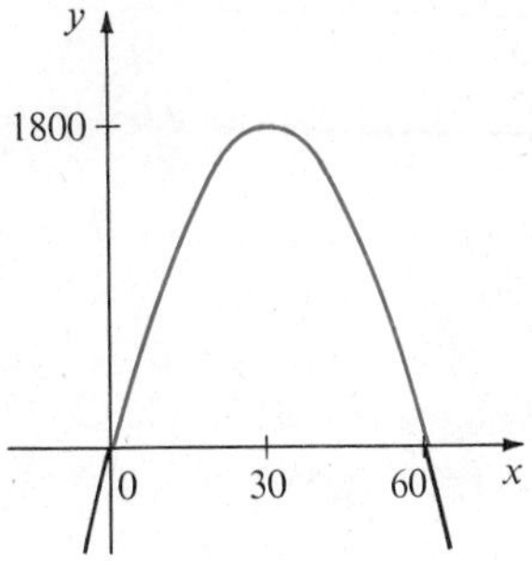

Figure 2–7

It is interesting to note in Example 2 that the maximum area is obtained by making the rectangle twice as long as it is wide. This would be true if the number, 120, of feet of fencing were replaced by any other number, c, of feet of fencing (see Exercise 24, page 74); the maximum area would be $\frac{c}{4} \cdot \frac{c}{2}$, or $\frac{c^2}{8}$, square feet.

ORAL EXERCISES

For each of the quadratic functions given in Exercises 1–14, state whether the graph opens upward or downward. If the function has real zeros, state what they are.

1. $f\colon x \to x^2$

2. $f\colon x \to 4x^2$

3. $f\colon x \to -2x^2$

4. $f\colon x \to x^2 - 1$

5. $f\colon x \to 1 - x^2$

6. $f\colon x \to x^2 + 1$

7. $f\colon x \to -x^2 - 1$

8. $f\colon x \to (x - 1)(x - 2)$

9. $f\colon x \to 4 - x^2$

10. $f\colon x \to (x - 2)(1 - x)$

11. $f\colon x \to x^2 - 2x$

12. $f\colon x \to x^2 + 2x$

13. $f\colon x \to x^2 - 2x + 1$

14. $f\colon x \to x^2 + 4x + 4$

15. Define *maximum value* of a function f.

WRITTEN EXERCISES

In Exercises 1–10, find at least six points of the graph of *f*. Then sketch the graph of *f* by drawing a smooth curve through these points. Remember that your graph must satisfy the vertical-line test. Use different units of length on the *x*- and *y*-axes if it seems appropriate. Then find the real zeros, if any, of each function.

A

1. $f: x \to x^2$
2. $f: x \to x^2 - 4$
3. $f: x \to 1 - x^2$
4. $f: x \to x^2 - 2x$
5. $f: x \to x^2 + 4x + 2$
6. $f: x \to x^2 - x - 2$
7. $f: x \to x^2 - 2x + 1$
8. $f: x \to x^2 + x + 1$
9. $f: x \to 2x^2 - x - 1$
10. $f: x \to (x + 2)(1 - x)$

In Exercises 11–20, (a) find the value of *x* for which the given function has its maximum or minimum. Then (b) find the extreme value of the function and (c) state whether it is a maximum or a minimum.

11. $f: x \to x^2$
12. $f: x \to 4 - x^2$
13. $f: x \to x^2 - 2x$
14. $f: x \to x^2 + 4x + 2$
15. $f: x \to x^2 + 3x$
16. $f: x \to 2 - x - x^2$
17. $f: x \to 1 - 6x + 9x^2$
18. $f: x \to |x|$
19. $f: x \to |x - 2|$
20. $f: x \to 2 - |x|$

B

21. After how many seconds does the object referred to in the first paragraph of this section hit the ground? What is the maximum height it attains?

22. A projectile is fired from the top of a tower standing on level ground. If the x-axis is taken to lie along the ground, the y-axis to pass through the firing point, and the xy-plane to contain the path of the projectile, then the path lies on the graph of the equation $y = 28 + x - \frac{1}{50}x^2$, where the units are feet. Find
    - **a.** the height of the tower;
    - **b.** where the projectile hits the ground;
    - **c.** the coordinates of the highest point of the path.
    - **d.** Draw a figure showing the path.

23. Work Example 2 of this section assuming that only 90 feet (instead of 120 feet) of fencing is available.

24. Work Example 2 of this section assuming that c feet (instead of 120 feet) of fencing is available.

C

25. A rectangular field is to be enclosed by a fence and divided into two smaller

rectangular fields by another fence. Find the dimensions of the field of greatest area which can be thus enclosed and partitioned with 1200 feet of fencing. (*Hint:* Express the area as a function of the x indicated in the figure.)

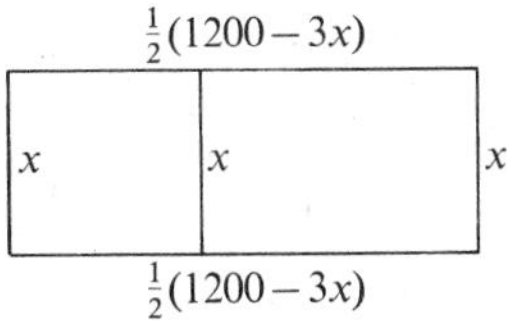

26. Find two numbers whose sum is 12 such that their product is as great as possible. What is this greatest product?

27. If the sum of two numbers is 12, what is the least value that the sum of their squares can attain?

28. Prove Theorem 3.

2–4 Parabolas (Optional)

Let us begin with an example:

EXAMPLE 1. Show that the set S of all points equidistant from the point $F(2, 1)$ and the horizontal line D: $y = 3$ is the graph of a quadratic function.

Solution: A point $P(x, y)$ is in S if and only if the distance from P to F,

$$\sqrt{(x-2)^2 + (y-1)^2},$$

is the same as the perpendicular distance from P to the line D, $|y - 3|$, that is, if and only if (since the steps are reversible)

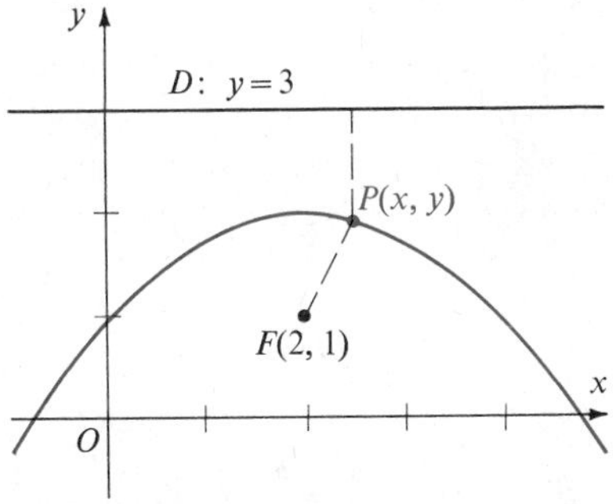

$$|y - 3| = \sqrt{(x-2)^2 + (y-1)^2},$$

or

$$y^2 - 6y + 9 = x^2 - 4x + 4 + y^2 - 2y + 1,$$

or

$$-4y = x^2 - 4x - 4,$$

or

$$y = -\tfrac{1}{4}x^2 + x + 1.$$

Therefore, S is the graph of the quadratic function

$$x \to -\tfrac{1}{4}x^2 + x + 1.$$

The set of all points equidistant from a fixed line and a fixed point not on this line is a **parabola.** (Although we referred to parabolas in the preceding section, we did not define them.) The fixed line is the **directrix** of the parabola, and the fixed point is its **focus.** Thus the set S in Example 1 is a parabola having as directrix the line $y = 3$ and as focus the point (2, 1).

By a method similar to that used in Example 1, we can show that every parabola whose directrix is a horizontal line is the graph of a quadratic function (Exercise 24, page 79). The converse is also true: The graph of every quadratic function is a parabola whose directrix is horizontal (Exercise 26, page 79). This is the fact we noted in Section 2–3.

It is clear from the definition that a parabola is symmetric with respect to the line through its focus perpendicular to its directrix. This line is the **axis,** or **axis of symmetry,** of the parabola. The point in which a parabola intersects its axis is its **vertex.** (See Figure 2–8.) In Example 1, the line $x = 2$ is the axis of the parabola, and the point (2, 2) is its vertex.

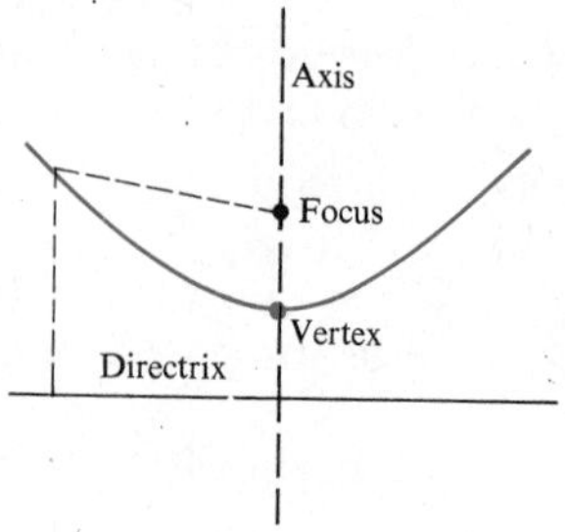

Figure 2–8

All parabolas are of the same *shape;* that is, each parabola is similar (in the manner indicated in Exercise 28, page 80) to each other parabola. The *size* depends on the distance between the focus and the directrix. The equation of a parabola takes on a particularly simple form if its *vertex* is the origin, and its axis is either horizontal or vertical. Suppose the focus of such a parabola is $F(p, 0)$, with $p \neq 0$. Then its directrix is the vertical line D: $x = -p$. A point $P(x, y)$ is on the parabola if and only if the distance from P to F is equal to the distance from P to D, that is, if and only if

$$(x - p)^2 + y^2 = (x + p)^2,$$
$$x^2 - 2px + p^2 + y^2 = x^2 + 2px + p^2,$$
$$y^2 = 4px.$$

Figure 2–9 shows the parabola $y^2 = 4px$ for a negative p. (Parabolas in the position just discussed are not, of course, the graphs of functions, since they do not pass the vertical-line test.)

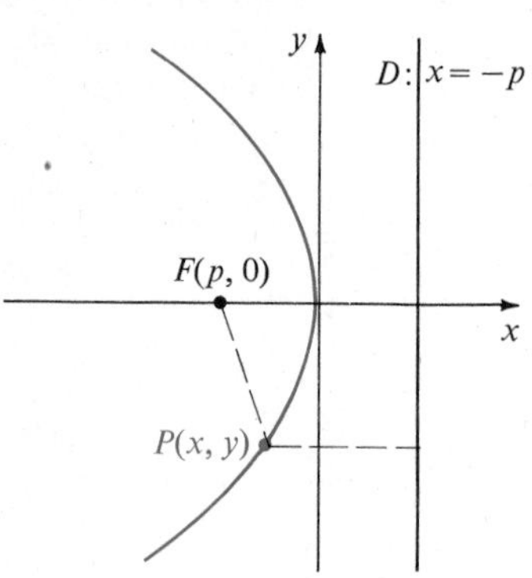

Figure 2–9

We have just proved the first part of the following theorem. The proof of the second part is a direct consequence of Exercise 25, page 79.

Theorem 4.

The parabola having focus $F(p, 0)$, $p \neq 0$, and directrix D: $x = -p$ has equation $y^2 = 4px$. The parabola having focus $F(0, p)$, $p \neq 0$, and directrix D: $y = -p$ has equation $x^2 = 4py$.

EXAMPLE 2. Find an equation of the parabola having the origin as vertex and the line $2y + 3 = 0$ as directrix.

Solution: Since the equation of the directrix can be written $y = -\frac{3}{2}$, we see that the second part of the theorem applies with $p = \frac{3}{2}$. Therefore the parabola has equation $x^2 = 4(\frac{3}{2})y$, or $x^2 = 6y$.

Warning: Do not apply the theorem unless the given data implies that the vertex of the parabola is the origin and the directrix is parallel to one of the coordinate axes.

EXAMPLE 3. A parabola having the origin as its vertex passes through the point $(2, -3)$. Find an equation of the parabola and its focus and directrix if its axis is (**a**) horizontal and (**b**) vertical.

Solution: **a.** Since the axis of the parabola is the x-axis, it has an equation of the form $y^2 = 4px$. Because the point $(2, -3)$ is on the parabola, we have $(-3)^2 = 4p(2)$, and therefore $p = \frac{9}{8}$. Thus the parabola has equation $y^2 = 4(\frac{9}{8})x$, or $y^2 = \frac{9}{2}x$, or $2y^2 - 9x = 0$. Its focus and directrix are, respectively, $(\frac{9}{8}, 0)$ and $x = -\frac{9}{8}$.

b. In this case, the parabola has an equation of the form $x^2 = 4py$, and we have $(2)^2 = 4p(-3)$. Thus $p = -\frac{1}{3}$, and the parabola has equation $x^2 = 4(-\frac{1}{3})y$, or $x^2 = -\frac{4}{3}y$, or $3x^2 + 4y = 0$. Its focus and directrix are $(0, -\frac{1}{3})$ and $y = -(-\frac{1}{3}) = \frac{1}{3}$.

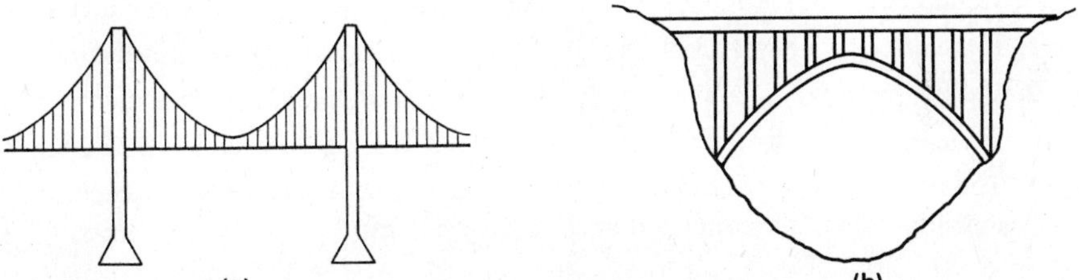

(a) (b)

Figure 2–10

Parabolas occur frequently in science and technology. For example, the supporting cables of a suspension bridge (ideally) hang in the form of part of a parabola [Figure 2–10(a)], and parabolic arches are often used in concrete bridges supported from below [Figure 2–10(b)]. A quite different occurrence is shown in Figure 2–11: If liquid in a cylindrical container is caused to rotate rapidly, a vertical cross section of the surface of the liquid is a parabolic arc.

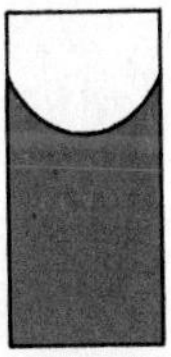

Figure 2–11

ORAL EXERCISES

The curves pictured in Exercises 1–6 are parabolas. In each case, either the focus F or the directrix D is given. State in each case the vertex, focus, and directrix, and, if you can, an equation of the parabola.

1.

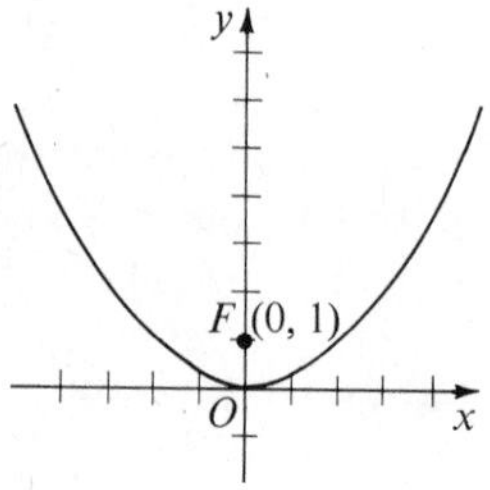

2.

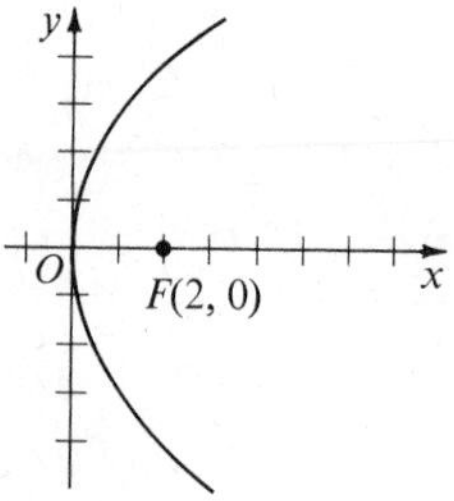

3.

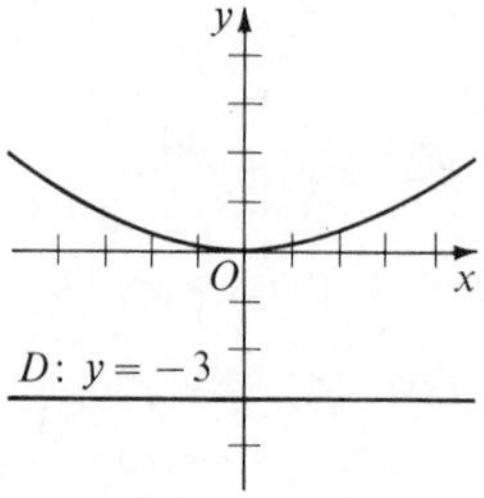

4.

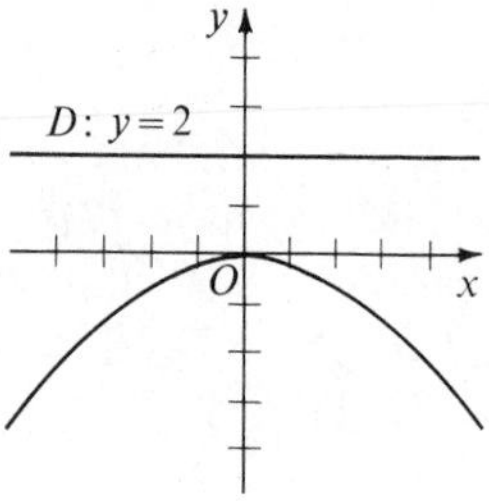

5.

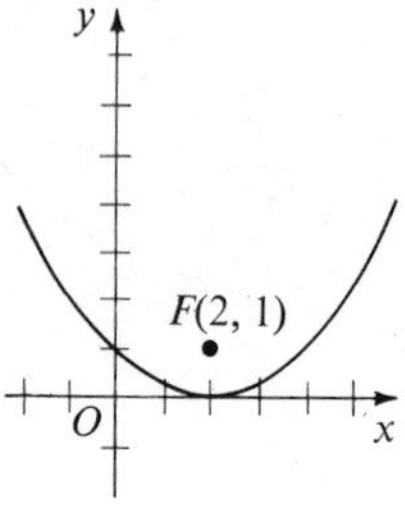

6.

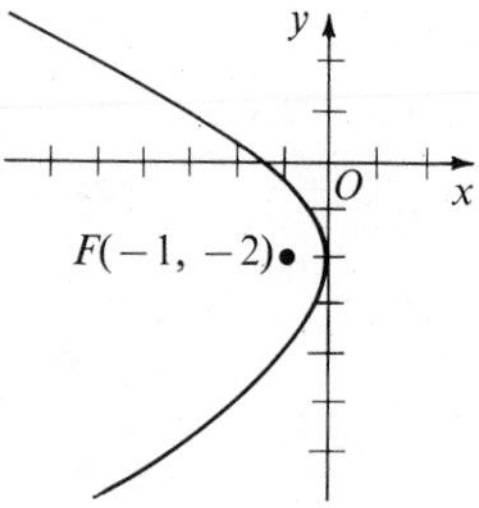

7. If the focus of a parabola is (3, 0) and the vertex is (0, 0), what is the directrix?

8. If the directrix of a parabola is $x = 2$ and the vertex is (0, 0), what is the focus?

9. If the directrix of a parabola is $y = 1$ and the focus is (0, 3), what is the vertex?

10. If the focus of a parabola is (2, 1) and the vertex is (2, 3), what is the directrix?

11. The parabola $y = x^2$ extends upward indefinitely. Does it also "spread out" indefinitely, or is it contained in some vertical strip?

WRITTEN EXERCISES

In Exercises 1–10, some information about a parabola having *the origin as vertex* is given. Find an equation of the parabola and its focus and directrix if these are not given.

A

1. Focus (1, 0).

2. Focus (−2, 0).

3. Directrix $y = 2$.

4. Directrix $x + 3 = 0$.

5. Directrix $2x = 5$.

6. Focus $(0, -3)$.

7. Axis vertical, passes through $(1, 2)$.

8. Axis horizontal, passes through $(1, 2)$.

9. Axis vertical, passes through $(-2, 3)$.

10. Axis horizontal, passes through $(-2, 3)$.

In Exercises 11–16, find the focus and directrix of the parabola whose equation is given and show them in a sketch of the graph.

11. $y^2 = 4x$	**13.** $y = x^2$	**15.** $x^2 + 8y = 0$
12. $y = \frac{1}{4}x^2$	**14.** $y^2 + 6x = 0$	**16.** $2x^2 + y = 0$

In Exercises 17–23, use the definition to find an equation of the parabola

B **17.** having focus $(0, 0)$ and directrix $y = 3$.

18. having focus $(0, 0)$ and directrix $x = -2$.

19. having focus $(0, 0)$ and vertex $(2, 0)$. (*Hint:* Find the directrix first.)

20. having focus $(0, 1)$ and vertex $(0, 3)$.

21. having vertex $(0, 2)$ and directrix $y = 3$.

22. having focus $(2, 1)$ and directrix $x = 0$.

23. having vertex $(-1, 2)$ and directrix $y = 4$.

24. Prove that if the directrix of a parabola is horizontal, then the parabola has an equation of the form $y = ax^2 + bx + c$, where $a \neq 0$. This implies that the parabola is the graph of a quadratic function $x \to ax^2 + bx + c$, thus establishing a statement made in the text. (*Hint:* Let the directrix be $y = d$ and the focus be (h, k), where $d \neq k$. Then use the method of Example 1.)

25. Prove that if a parabola has the point (h, k) as vertex and a horizontal directrix, then it has an equation of the form $(x - h)^2 = 4p(y - k)$. [*Hint:* Let the focus be $(h, k + p)$, where $p \neq 0$. Then the directrix is $y = k - p$. Apply the definition of a parabola and in subsequent simplifications keep the expressions $(x - h)$ and $(y - k)$ intact.]

C **26.** Show that the equation $y = ax^2 + bx + c$ $(a \neq 0)$ can be put into the form $(x - h)^2 = 4p(y - k)$. Explain how this can be used to prove that the graph of every quadratic function is a parabola.

27. Draw a horizontal line D and a point F, q units above D. Perform the following construction: **(a)** With F as center, draw a circle of any radius $r > \frac{1}{2}q$. **(b)** Draw a line parallel to D and r units above D. **(c)** Mark the points P_r and P_r' where the line intersects the circle. Repeat the construction for various values of r. Explain why all the points P_r and P_r' lie on the same parabola. (This construction enables us to find as many points as we please on a parabola when we are given its directrix and focus.)

28. Let p and q be positive numbers. Let P be the parabola having focus $(0, 0)$ and directrix $y = 2p$. Let Q be the parabola having focus $(0, 0)$ and directrix $y = 2q$.

a. Find equations of P and Q

b. Show that there is a constant k such that the point (kx, ky) is on Q if and only if the point (x, y) is on P.

(*Hint:* Try $k = \frac{q}{p}$.)

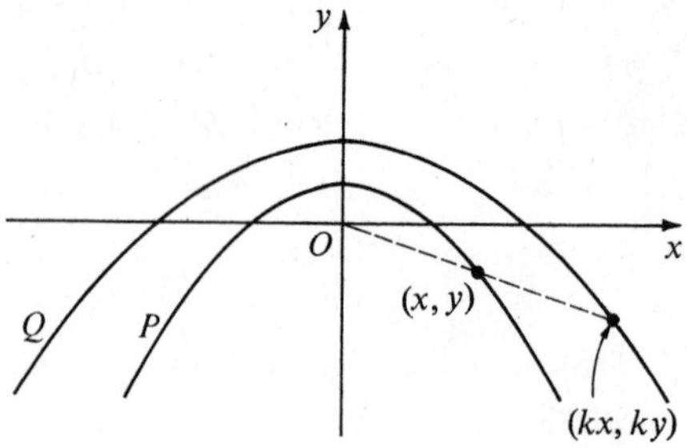

■ General Polynomial Functions

2–5 Polynomials and Their Arithmetic

For any nonnegative integer n, an expression of the form

$$a_0x^n + a_1x^{n-1} + \cdots + a_{n-1}x + a_n, \qquad a_0 \neq 0,$$

or the indicated sum of these same terms in any other order, is called a **polynomial of degree *n*** in the symbol x. The terms of a polynomial are ordinarily written with descending powers of x, as shown above.

If, as always in this book, $a_0, a_1, \ldots, a_{n-1}, a_n$ are all elements of the field $\mathcal{R}$ of real numbers, then the expression is said to be a **polynomial over** $\mathcal{R}$. (The results of this section are valid also for polynomials over any other field, for example, for polynomials over the field of rational numbers.) We call $a_0, a_1, \ldots, a_{n-1}, a_n$ the **coefficients,** a_0 the **leading coefficient,** and a_n the **constant term,** of the polynomial.

For example:

$4x^3 - 2x + \sqrt{3}$ has leading coefficient 4 and constant term $\sqrt{3}$. It is of degree 3 and is called a **cubic polynomial.**

$x^2 + 5x - 2$ has (understood) leading coefficient 1 and constant term -2. It is of degree 2 and is called a **quadratic polynomial.**

$-4x + 5$ has leading coefficient -4 and constant term 5. It is of degree 1 and is called a **linear polynomial.**

7 consists of only a constant term, 7. It is of degree 0 and is called a **constant polynomial.**

0 is also called a polynomial, namely the **zero polynomial,** but *no degree is assigned to it.*

Two polynomials in x are **equal** if and only if they are of the same degree and their coefficients of like powers of x are equal. For example, $2x + 3 = 3 + 2x$; but $2x + 3 \neq 3x + 2$, and $2x + 3 \neq x^2 + 2x + 3$.

As illustrated in the following example, sums, differences, and products of polynomials are defined in accordance with arithmetic procedures, or *algorithms*, with which you are assumed already to be familiar.

EXAMPLE 1. Determine (**a**) the sum, (**b**) the difference (second subtracted from first), and (**c**) the product, of the polynomials $4x^3 + 3x - 1$ and $2x^2 - x + 5$.

Solution: **a.**
$$\begin{aligned}
&(4x^3 + 3x - 1) + (2x^2 - x + 5)\\
&= (4 + 0)x^3 + (0 + 2)x^2 + (3 - 1)x + (-1 + 5)\\
&= 4x^3 + 2x^2 + 2x + 4
\end{aligned}$$

b.
$$\begin{aligned}
&(4x^3 + 3x - 1) - (2x^2 - x + 5)\\
&= (4x^3 + 3x - 1) + (-2x^2 + x - 5)\\
&= (4 + 0)x^3 + (0 - 2)x^2 + (3 + 1)x + (-1 - 5)\\
&= 4x^3 - 2x^2 + 4x - 6
\end{aligned}$$

c.
$$\begin{aligned}
&(4x^3 + 3x - 1)(2x^2 - x + 5)\\
&= 4x^3(2x^2 - x + 5) + 3x(2x^2 - x + 5)\\
&\qquad + (-1)(2x^2 - x + 5)\\
&= (8x^5 - 4x^4 + 20x^3) + (6x^3 - 3x^2 + 15x)\\
&\qquad + (-2x^2 + x - 5)\\
&= 8x^5 - 4x^4 + (20 + 6)x^3 + (-3 - 2)x^2\\
&\qquad + (15 + 1)x - 5\\
&= 8x^5 - 4x^4 + 26x^3 - 5x^2 + 16x - 5
\end{aligned}$$

You should be able to convince yourself by examples that the set of all polynomials over $\mathcal{R}$ with the operations of addition and multiplication is a commutative ring with unit element; see page 32. The zero polynomial and the constant polynomial 1 are the identity elements for addition and multiplication, respectively, in this ring.

In Section 2–6, we shall see that polynomials in x define functions. Accordingly, they are denoted by $P(x)$, $Q(x)$, and so on.

Division in the ring of polynomials over $\mathcal{R}$ rests on the following theorem.

Theorem 5.

If $P(x)$ is a polynomial of degree n over $\mathcal{R}$ and $S(x)$ is a polynomial of degree k, $0 \leq k \leq n$, over $\mathcal{R}$, then there exist unique polynomials $Q(x)$ and $R(x)$ over $\mathcal{R}$, where $Q(x)$ is of degree $n - k$ and $R(x)$ either is the zero polynomial or is of degree less than k, such that

$$P(x) = S(x)Q(x) + R(x).$$

Notice that the hypothesis of this theorem implies that neither $P(x)$ nor $S(x)$ is the zero polynomial.

We say that $Q(x)$ is the **quotient** and $R(x)$ is the **remainder,** when $P(x)$ is divided by $S(x)$. If $R(x) = 0$, so that $P(x) = S(x)Q(x)$, then $S(x)$ is said to be a **factor** of $P(x)$.

The familiar division algorithm for determining $Q(x)$ and $R(x)$ is illustrated in the following example. (A formal description of the algorithm, which we shall not give, would constitute a proof of Theorem 5.)

EXAMPLE 2. Determine the quotient $Q(x)$ and the remainder $R(x)$ when $8x^3 - 6x^2 + 3$ is divided by $2x^2 + x - 3$.

Solution:

$$\begin{array}{r@{\,}rrrr}
 & 4x & -\ 5 & & \\ \cline{2-5}
2x^2 + x - 3 \big) & 8x^3 & -\ 6x^2 & +\ 0x & +\ 3 \\
 & 8x^3 & +\ 4x^2 & -\ 12x & \\ \cline{2-4}
 & & -\ 10x^2 & +\ 12x & +\ 3 \\
 & & -\ 10x^2 & -\ 5x & +\ 15 \\ \cline{3-5}
 & & & 17x & -\ 12
\end{array}$$

Thus $Q(x) = 4x - 5$ and $R(x) = 17x - 12$.

Check: $(2x^2 + x - 3)(4x - 5) + (17x - 12)$

$$\begin{aligned}
&= (2x^2 + x - 3)(4x) + (2x^2 + x - 3)(-5) + (17x - 12) \\
&= 8x^3 + 4x^2 - 12x - 10x^2 - 5x + 15 + 17x - 12 \\
&= 8x^3 - 6x^2 + 3
\end{aligned}$$

If $S(x)$ is a linear polynomial of the form $x - a$, then the multiplication and subtraction steps of the division algorithm can be replaced by the multiplication and addition shorthand steps of *synthetic division.*

EXAMPLE 3. Find the quotient and remainder when $x^3 - 6x - 3$ is divided by $x + 2$.

Solution: Notice that $x + 2 = x - (-2)$.

$$\begin{array}{r|rrrr}
-2 & 1 & 0 & -6 & -3 \\
 & & -2 & 4 & 4 \\ \hline
 & 1 & -2 & -2 & 1 \\
 & \downarrow & \downarrow & \downarrow & \downarrow \\
\text{Quotient:} & x^2 & -2x & -2 & \\
\text{Remainder:} & & & & 1
\end{array}$$

Check: $(x + 2)(x^2 - 2x - 2) + 1$

$$\begin{aligned}
&= x(x^2 - 2x - 2) + 2(x^2 - 2x - 2) + 1 \\
&= x^3 - 2x^2 - 2x + 2x^2 - 4x - 4 + 1 \\
&= x^3 - 6x - 3.
\end{aligned}$$

It is often useful to express a polynomial $P(x)$ as a polynomial in $x - a$, that is, a polynomial in $x - a$ which, when interpreted as a polynomial in x, is equal to $P(x)$. This can be done by repeated applications of the synthetic-division process.

EXAMPLE 4. Express $2x^3 - 5x^2 - 4x + 1$ as a polynomial in $x - 3$.

Solution:

$$
\begin{array}{r|rrrr}
3 & 2 & -5 & -4 & 1 \\
 & & 6 & 3 & -3 \\
\hline
 & 2 & 1 & -1 & -2 \\
 & & 6 & 21 & \\
\hline
 & 2 & 7 & 20 & \\
 & & 6 & & \\
\hline
 & 2 & 13 & &
\end{array}
$$

$$2x^3 - 5x^2 - 4x + 1 = 2(x - 3)^3 + 13(x - 3)^2 + 20(x - 3) - 2$$

Checking the answer is left to you.

We can see why the extended synthetic-division process yields the desired result in the example above by noting that the successive applications give

$$
\begin{aligned}
2x^3 - 5x^2 - 4x + 1 &= (x - 3)\{2x^2 + x - 1\} - 2 \\
&= (x - 3)\{(x - 3)[2x + 7] + 20\} - 2 \\
&= (x - 3)\{(x - 3)[2(x - 3) + 13] + 20\} - 2 \\
&= 2(x - 3)^3 + 13(x - 3)^2 + 20(x - 3) - 2
\end{aligned}
$$

The multiplication and addition steps in the synthetic-division process can often be performed mentally. The computation in Example 4 then appears as follows:

$$
\begin{array}{r|rrrr}
3 & 2 & -5 & -4 & 1 \\
 & 2 & 1 & -1 & -2 \\
 & 2 & 7 & 20 & \\
 & 2 & 13 & &
\end{array}
$$

We shall henceforth use this abbreviated form.

ORAL EXERCISES

For the polynomials in Exercises 1–4, state (a) the leading coefficient, (b) the constant term, and (c) the degree of the polynomial. If the polynomial has no degree, so state.

1. $4x^3 - 2x + 6$

2. $2x - 3x^2$

3. 9

4. 0

In Exercises 5 and 6, which of the polynomials are equal?

5. $(3 + 2)x - \frac{7}{2}$, $5x - 3.5$, $3x - \frac{7}{2}$

6. $x^2 - 2x + 1$, 0, $x^3 - 2x + 1$, $x^2 - 2x$

In Exercises 7 and 8, state (a) the sum, (b) the difference, and (c) the product of the given polynomials.

7. $x^2 - 3x,\ x + 2$

8. $4x^4,\ x^4 - 1$

9. Use the polynomials in Exercise 7 or Exercise 8 to discuss the properties of polynomials over $\mathcal{R}$ corresponding to the fact that these polynomials form a commutative ring with unit element.

In Exercises 10 and 11, the synthetic division for $P(x) = (x - a)Q(x) + R$ is shown. In each case, what are (a) $P(x)$, (b) $x - a$, (c) $Q(x)$, and (d) R?

10. $\begin{array}{r|rrrr} 3 & 2 & -9 & 0 & 7 \\ \hline & 2 & -3 & -9 & -20 \end{array}$

11. $\begin{array}{r|rrrr} -2 & 1 & 0 & -4 & 0 \\ \hline & 1 & -2 & 0 & 0 \end{array}$

12. Is $x - a$ a factor of $P(x)$ **(a)** in Exercise 10 and **(b)** in Exercise 11? Why or why not?

13. Tell how the entries on the bottom line are determined for the synthetic division in **(a)** Exercise 10 and **(b)** Exercise 11.

In Exercises 14 and 15, the computation for expressing $P(x)$ as $T(x - a)$ is shown. In each case, state $P(x)$ and $T(x - a)$.

14. $\begin{array}{r|rrrr} -3 & 1 & 3 & 2 & 5 \\ \hline & 1 & 0 & 2 & -1 \\ & 1 & -3 & 11 & \\ & 1 & -6 & & \end{array}$

15. $\begin{array}{r|rrrr} 1 & 4 & -3 & 2 & -2 \\ \hline & 4 & 1 & 3 & 1 \\ & 4 & 5 & 8 & \\ & 4 & 9 & & \end{array}$

16. In Exercises 14 and 15, is $P(x) = T(x - a)$? Why or why not?

WRITTEN EXERCISES

In Exercises 1 and 2, determine a, b, c, and d so that the given polynomials are equal.

A

1. $(a + 1)x^3 - 3x^2 - cx + (d - c);\ x^3 + bx^2 + 2x - 3$

2. $(a - b)x^3 + (b - c)x^2 + (a + c)x - 1;\ 4x^2 + 2x + d$

In Exercises 3–6, for the given functions find (a) $P(x) + S(x)$, (b) $P(x) - S(x)$, (c) $P(x)S(x)$.

3. $P(x) = 4x^3 - 3x^2 + 2x - 2;\ S(x) = x^2 + x + 5$

4. $P(x) = x^4 + 4x - 3;\ S(x) = 2 - x + 4x^2$

5. $P(x) = x^3 - x + 1;\ S(x) = x^3 + x + 1$

6. $P(x) = x^4 + x^2 - 2;\ S(x) = x^4 - 1$

7–10. For the polynomials $P(x)$ and $S(x)$ in Exercises 3–6, find the polynomials $Q(x)$ and $R(x)$ referred to in Theorem 5 on page 81.

In Exercises 11 and 12, show that $S(x)$ is a factor of $P(x)$.

11. $P(x) = x^4 + 2x^3 - 3x - 6;\ S(x) = x^3 - 3$

12. $P(x) = x^4 + 2x^3 - 4x - 4;\ S(x) = x^2 + 2x + 2$

In Exercises 13–16, use synthetic division to find the quotient $Q(x)$ and the remainder R when the first polynomial is divided by the second.

13. $4x^3 - 3x^2 + x;\ x - 2$

14. $x^3 + 2x^2 + 3x + 4;\ x + 3$

15. $x^4 + 2;\ x + 2$

16. $1 + 2x - 4x^2 + x^4;\ x - 1$

In Exercises 17 and 18, determine a so that the second polynomial is a factor of the first.

B **17.** $x^4 + 5x^3 - 2x^2 + ax - 7;\ x - 2$

18. $x^5 - 2x + a;\ x + 2$

In Exercises 19 and 20, express the first polynomial as a polynomial in the second.

19. $x^3 - x^2 + 4x + 1;\ x - 3$

20. $x^4 + 5x^3 + 7x^2 - 3;\ x + 2$

Let $P(x)$, $S(x)$, and $T(x)$ be polynomials over $\mathcal{R}$. In Exercises 21–23, prove the given assertion.

C **21.** If $P(x)$ is a factor of $S(x)$ and $S(x)$ is a factor of $T(x)$, then $P(x)$ is a factor of $T(x)$.

22. If $P(x)$ is a factor of $S(x)$, then $P(x)$ is a factor of $S(x)T(x)$.

23. If $P(x)$ is a factor of $S(x)$ and of $T(x)$, and $S(x) + T(x)$ is not the zero polynomial, then $P(x)$ is a factor of $S(x) + T(x)$.

2–6 Polynomial Functions and Their Graphs

If x is a variable whose domain is a subset D of $\mathcal{R}$, and $P(x)$ is a polynomial over $\mathcal{R}$, then

$$\{(x, y)\colon\ y = P(x)\}, \qquad \text{or} \qquad P\colon x \to P(x),$$

is a **polynomial function** P whose domain is D and whose values are obtained by replacing x with various members of D. In accordance with the agreement on page 8, we shall ordinarily take $D = \mathcal{R}$.

Thus, for $D = \mathcal{R}$, the function

$$P\colon x \to x^3 - 4x^2 + 2$$

assigns to the real number 5 the real number

$$\begin{aligned} P(5) &= 5^3 - 4 \cdot 5^2 + 2 \\ &= 125 - 100 + 2, \quad \text{or} \quad 27, \end{aligned}$$

so that the ordered pair (5, 27) is in P.

If $P(x)$ is of degree n, then we say that $P: x \to P(x)$ is a **polynomial function of degree *n*.** For example, the nonconstant linear and the quadratic functions studied earlier in this chapter are also called polynomial functions of degree 1 and 2, respectively. Polynomials of degree 3, 4, and 5 are often called **cubic, quartic,** and **quintic polynomials,** respectively, and the corresponding functions are then called **cubic, quartic,** and **quintic functions.**

For a given polynomial $P(x)$ of degree n, $n \geq 1$, over $\mathcal{R}$, and for any $a \in \mathcal{R}$, an easy way to compute $P(a)$ can be found as follows: By Theorem 5 on page 81, we have

$$P(x) = (x - a)Q(x) + R,$$

where R is a constant. In particular, then,

$$\begin{aligned} P(a) &= (a - a)Q(a) + R \\ &= 0 \cdot Q(a) + R \\ &= R. \end{aligned}$$

Thus when $P(x)$ is divided by $x - a$, the remainder R is equal to $P(a)$. This result is called the **Remainder Theorem.**

Theorem 6.

If $P(x)$ is a polynomial of degree n, $n \geq 1$, over $\mathcal{R}$, and $a \in \mathcal{R}$, then the constant remainder when $P(x)$ is divided by $x - a$ is $P(a)$.

The remainder R, or $P(a)$, can be determined by synthetic division. Since $P(a)$ is also the number obtained by substituting a for x in $P(x)$, synthetic division is sometimes called *synthetic substitution.*

EXAMPLE. If $P(x) = x^4 - 5x^3 + 3x^2 - 2x + 18$, find $P(4)$

a. by direct substitution, and

b. by synthetic substitution.

Solution: **a.** $$\begin{aligned} P(4) &= 4^4 - 5 \cdot 4^3 + 3 \cdot 4^2 - 2 \cdot 4 + 18 \\ &= 256 - 320 + 48 - 8 + 18 \\ &= -6 \end{aligned}$$

b. $$\begin{array}{r|rrrrl} 4 & 1 & -5 & 3 & -2 & 18 \\ & 1 & -1 & -1 & -6 & -6 = P(4) \end{array}$$

For a given polynomial function $P: x \to P(x)$ and a given $a \in \mathcal{R}$, we can find the function value $P(a)$ as in the Example above and then can graph the point $(a, P(a))$ in a Cartesian plane. We shall see in Chapter 3 that the graph of a polynomial function with domain $\mathcal{R}$ is a smooth curve* without breaks containing the points $(a, P(a))$. We can often get a good idea of the general appearance of the curve by graphing several of its points. We should always be aware, however, that without further information we cannot determine a curve with certainty by plotting any finite number of its points (unless it is a line, of course). For example, consider the function

$$P: x \rightarrow x^4 - 2x^3 + x^2$$

for $x \in \mathcal{R}$. By synthetic substitution, we might determine values of $P(x)$ as shown in the table at the right. Graphing some of the corresponding points as shown in Figure 2–12(a), we might surmise that the graph has the appearance indicated in Figure 2–12(b). Note, however, that

x	$P(x)$
0	0
1	0
2	4
3	36
-1	4
-2	36

$$P(x) = x^4 - 2x^3 + x^2 = x^2(x - 1)^2.$$

Since $P(x)$ is the product of two squares, $P(x)$ is not negative for any $x \in \mathcal{R}$. The actual graph of the function is indicated in Figure 2–12(c).

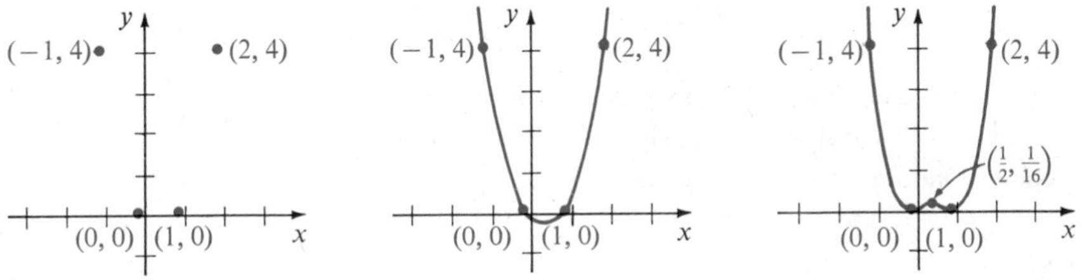

(a) (b) (c)

Figure 2–12

ORAL EXERCISES

In Exercises 1–8, for the given polynomial $P(x)$, state (a) $P(2)$, (b) $P(0)$, and (c) $P(-1)$.

1. $P(x) = x + 1$

2. $P(x) = 2x - 3$

3. $P(x) = ax + b$

4. $P(x) = 5$

5. $P(x) = x^2 - 1$

6. $P(x) = x^2 + x + 1$

7. $P(x) = (x - 1)(x - 2)$

8. $P(x) = (x - 2)(x + 1) + 1$

---

* A line is considered to be a curve.

9. The following computation shows the evaluation of $P(a)$ for a polynomial $P(x)$ and a constant a. State (**a**) $P(x)$, (**b**) a, and (**c**) $P(a)$.

$$\begin{array}{r|rrrr} 2 & 1 & 0 & -2 & 1 \\ & 1 & 2 & 2 & 5 \end{array}$$

WRITTEN EXERCISES

Use synthetic substitution to determine the indicated values.

$$P(x) = x^3 + 2x^2 - 5x + 1$$

A

1. $P(-3)$ **2.** $P(0)$ **3.** $P(1)$ **4.** $P(-1)$

$$S(x) = x^4 - 4x^3 + 2x - 5$$

5. $S(4)$ **6.** $S(\sqrt{2})$ **7.** $S(-1)$ **8.** $S(3)$

$$T = l^3 - l + 1$$

9. $T(0)$ **10.** $T(-5)$ **11.** $T(2)$ **12.** $T(\pi)$

$$U(x) = x^3 - (a + b + c)x^2 + (ab + bc + ca)x - abc$$

13. $U(a)$ **14.** $U(b)$ **15.** $U(c)$ **16.** $U(0)$

In Exercises 17–22, complete the table shown at the right for the given polynomial $P(x)$, sketch the graphs of the corresponding points, and draw a smooth curve through the graphed points.

x	P(x)
−2	?
−1	?
0	?
1	?
2	?

17. $P(x) = x^3 - 1$

18. $P(x) = 2x^3 - 3x$

19. $P(x) = x^3 + 2x^2 - 4x - 6$

20. $P(x) = x^3 - 2x + 1$

21. $P(x) = x^4 - x^2 - 7$

22. $P(x) = x^4 - 2x^2$

B

23. Show that if the graph of $P: x \to ax^6 + bx^4 + cx^2 + d$ contains the point (x_1, y_1), then it also contains the point $(-x_1, y_1)$.

24. Show that if the graph of $Q: x \to ax^7 + bx^5 + cx^3 + dx$ contains the point (x_1, y_1), then it also contains the point $(-x_1, -y_1)$.

C

25. On the basis of Exercise 23, state and prove a property of every polynomial function $P: x \to P(x)$ for which the expression $P(x)$ contains only even powers of x.

26. On the basis of Exercise 24, state and prove a property of every polynomial function $Q: x \to Q(x)$ for which the expression $Q(x)$ contains only odd powers of x.

2–7 Polynomial Equations

The graph of the polynomial function

$$P\colon x \to (x + 2)(x - 1)^2$$

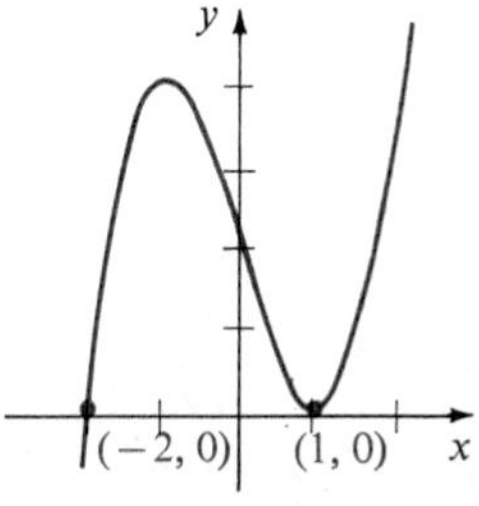

Figure 2–13

is shown in Figure 2–13. As defined on page 70, the zeros of P are the x-intercepts of the graph of P; that is, they are the roots -2 and 1 of the equation $P(x) = 0$.

In general, for any polynomial function P, the equation $P(x) = 0$ is called a **polynomial equation.** In this section, we shall be concerned with the zeros of polynomial functions, that is, with the roots of polynomial equations.

By the Remainder Theorem (page 86), the remainder R when a polynomial $P(x)$ of degree n, $n \geq 1$, over $\mathcal{R}$ is divided by $x - a$ is $P(a)$:

$$\begin{aligned} P(x) &= (x - a)Q(x) + R \\ &= (x - a)Q(x) + P(a). \end{aligned}$$

Further, by definition, $x - a$ is a factor of $P(x)$ if and only if $R = 0$. Therefore, $x - a$ is a factor of $P(x)$ if and only if $P(a) = 0$, that is, if and only if a is a zero of $P(x)$. This result is expressed in the following **Factor Theorem.**

Theorem 7.

If $P(x)$ is a polynomial of degree n, $n \geq 1$, over $\mathcal{R}$, and $a \in \mathcal{R}$, then $x - a$ is a factor of $P(x)$ if and only if a is a zero of $P(x)$.

EXAMPLE. Show that $x - 2$ is a factor of $P(x) = x^4 - 4x^3 + 7x^2 - 12x + 12$, so that $P(x) = (x - 2)Q(x)$. Then test whether or not $x - 2$ is a factor of $Q(x)$.

Solution:

$$\begin{array}{r|rrrrl} 2 & 1 & -4 & 7 & -12 & 12 \\ & 1 & -2 & 3 & -6 & 0 = P(2) \\ & 1 & 0 & 3 & 0 = Q(2) & \end{array}$$

Since $P(2) = 0$, $x - 2$ is a factor of $P(x)$:

$$P(x) = (x - 2)(x^3 - 2x^2 + 3x - 6).$$

Since $Q(2) = 0$, $x - 2$ is also a factor of $Q(x)$:

$$Q(x) = (x - 2)(x^2 + 3).$$

In the Example on page 89 we have

$$\begin{aligned} P(x) &= (x - 2)(x^3 - 2x^2 + 3x - 6) \\ &= (x - 2)(x - 2)(x^2 + 3) \\ &= (x - 2)^2(x^2 + 3). \end{aligned}$$

Since $x - 2$ is not also a factor of $x^2 + 3$, $x - 2$ is said to be a *factor of multiplicity* 2, or a *two-fold factor* of $P(x)$. In general, if $P(x) = (x - a)^m Q(x)$, and $x - a$ is not a factor of $Q(x)$, then $x - a$ is said to be a **factor of multiplicity m**, or an **m-fold factor**, of $P(x)$. We also say that a is a **zero of multiplicity m** of P.

The polynomial $P(x)$ of the Example on page 89 is a polynomial of degree 4. For any $a \neq 2$, $a \in \mathcal{R}$, you have $P(a) = (a - 2)^2(a^2 + 3)$, which is positive, and therefore $P(a) \neq 0$. Thus a polynomial function of degree 4 might have *fewer* than 4 zeros in $\mathcal{R}$. Similarly, a polynomial function of any degree n, $n > 1$, over $\mathcal{R}$ might have fewer than n zeros in $\mathcal{R}$. It can have *as many as n* zeros in $\mathcal{R}$, as the example $P\colon x \to P(x)$, where

$$P(x) = (x - 1)(x - 2) \cdots (x - n),$$

shows. The following theorem states, however, that it cannot have *more* than n zeros in $\mathcal{R}$.

Theorem 8.

If P is a polynomial function of degree n over $\mathcal{R}$, then P has at most n zeros in $\mathcal{R}$.

Proof

The degree n of a polynomial is a nonnegative integer, and we shall prove the theorem by mathematical induction* on n.

The conclusion of the theorem is true for $n = 0$, since by definition a polynomial of degree 0 is a nonzero constant. The conclusion is also true for $n = 1$, since the equation $a_0x + a_1 = 0$, with $a_0 \neq 0$, has only one solution in $\mathcal{R}$, namely $-\dfrac{a_1}{a_0}$.

Let k be a natural number for which the conclusion of the theorem is true, and let $P(x)$ be a polynomial over $\mathcal{R}$ of degree $k + 1$. If P has no zero in $\mathcal{R}$, then the conclusion of the theorem is true for P. If P has a zero, say a, in $\mathcal{R}$, then by the Factor Theorem, page 89, and Theorem 5, page 81,

$$P(x) = (x - a)Q(x),$$

*For a discussion of mathematical induction, see, for example, Dolciani and others, *Algebra and Trigonometry 2* (Houghton Mifflin Company, 1968), pp. 630-631.

where $Q(x)$ is a polynomial over $\mathcal{R}$ of degree k. If there is any zero b of P in $\mathcal{R}$, other than a, then $P(b) = (b - a)Q(b) = 0$; therefore, $Q(b) = 0$ since $b - a \neq 0$. Thus b is a zero of Q. Since $Q(x)$ is of degree k, by hypothesis Q has at most k zeros in $\mathcal{R}$, and hence P has at most $k + 1$ zeros in $\mathcal{R}$.

Consequently, by the principle of mathematical induction, the conclusion of the theorem is true for all nonnegative integers n.

Theorem 8 can be made more precise by counting multiplicities of zeros. For example, the polynomial

$$P(x) = (x - 1)^2(x + 2)^3(x^4 + 2x^2 + 1)$$

is of degree $2 + 3 + 4$, or 9; the sum of the multiplicities of the zeros of P in $\mathcal{R}$ is $2 + 3$, or 5; and $5 \leq 9$. In general:

> For a polynomial function of degree n, the sum of the multiplicities of the zeros of P in $\mathcal{R}$ is at most n.

ORAL EXERCISES

In Exercises 1–4, the given value a is a root of $P(x) = 0$ for the given polynomial $P(x)$. State a linear factor of $P(x)$.

1. $P(x) = x^3 - x^2 + 5x - 5$; $a = 1$
2. $P(x) = x^5 + 2x^4 + 3x + 6$; $a = -2$
3. $P(x) = x^4 - 3x^3 + 2x^2 + x$; $a = 0$
4. $P(x) = x^4 - 6x^3 + 11x^2 - 5x - 3$; $a = 3$

In Exercises 5–8, the second polynomial is a factor of the first polynomial, $P(x)$. State a root of $P(x) = 0$.

5. $P(x) = x^3 - x^2 + 5x - 5$; $x - 1$
6. $P(x) = x^3 + 3x^2 + 4x + 12$; $x + 3$
7. $P(x) = x^4 - x^3 - 5x^2 + 4x + 4$; $x + 2$
8. $P(x) = x^9 - 7x^4 + 3x^2$; x

In Exercises 9–11, state a polynomial $P(x)$ of the specified degree for which $P(x) = 0$ has the specified roots.

9. Degree 3; 3 roots in $\mathcal{R}$.
10. Degree 6; one root of multiplicity 2, and one of multiplicity 4, in $\mathcal{R}$.
11. Degree 4; no roots in $\mathcal{R}$.

WRITTEN EXERCISES

In Exercises 1–8, use the Factor Theorem to determine whether or not the second polynomial is a factor of the first.

A

1. $x^4 - 2x^3 + x^2 - x + 1;\ x - 1$
2. $x^4 - 2x^3 + x^2 - x + 1;\ x + 1$
3. $-3 + x^4 + 4x;\ x + 3$
4. $6 - 4x^2 + x^3;\ x - 2$
5. $x^4 - 2x^2 - 3;\ x + \sqrt{2}$
6. $x^4 - x^2 - 3;\ x - \sqrt{3}$
7. $2x^3 - 3x^2 + 4x + 2;\ x - 2$
8. $x^3 + 2x^2 - x - 7;\ x + 3$

In Exercises 9–12, show that the second polynomial is a multiple factor of the first, and determine its multiplicity.

B

9. $x^3 - x^2 - 8x + 12;\ x - 2$
10. $x^4 + 2x^3 - 2x - 1;\ x + 1$
11. $x^4 - 6x^2 + 9;\ x + \sqrt{3}$
12. $x^5 - 2x^4 - 6x^3 + 12x^2 + 9x - 18;\ x - \sqrt{3}$

C

13. Determine c and d so that $x + 2$ is a factor of multiplicity 2 of $x^3 + 3x^2 + cx + d$.
14. Prove that for every positive integer n, and every $a \in \mathcal{R}$, $x - a$ is a factor of $x^n - a^n$.
15. Prove that for every positive odd integer n, and for every $a \in \mathcal{R}$, $x + a$ is a factor of $x^n + a^n$.
16. Let $P(x)$ be a polynomial over $\mathcal{R}$, and let $a, b \in \mathcal{R}$, $a \neq b$, and let a be a root of multiplicity m of $P(x) = 0$, so that $P(x) = (x - a)^m Q(x)$. Show that b is a root of $P(x) = 0$ if and only if b is a root of $Q(x) = 0$.

2–8 Rational and Irrational Roots

For a given polynomial function $S: x \rightarrow S(x)$, and for any a in the domain of S, we have seen how we can use synthetic substitution to determine the corresponding value $S(a)$ in the range of S. In this section, we shall consider the inverse problem of determining the value or values in the domain of S corresponding to a given value k in the range of S.

The polynomial equation $S(x) = k$ is equivalent to $S(x) - k = 0$, that is, to the polynomial equation $P(x) = 0$, where $P(x) = S(x) - k$. Thus, determining the values of x for which $S(x) = k$ is equivalent to determining the *roots* of $P(x) = 0$. Accordingly, we shall concentrate on the problem of finding roots of polynomial equations.

If the coefficients of $P(x)$ are all rational numbers, then we can multiply by a common denominator to obtain an equivalent equation with integral coefficients. For example, $\frac{1}{2}x^2 + \frac{3}{5}x + \frac{1}{3} = 0$ is equivalent to $15x^2 + 18x + 10 = 0$. All the *rational* roots of such an equation can be found by means of the following **Rational Root Theorem.**

Theorem 9.

If $P(x) = a_0x^n + a_1x^{n-1} + \cdots + a_n$ $(a_0 \neq 0,\ a_n \neq 0)$ is a polynomial with integral coefficients, and if p and q are integers $(q \neq 0)$ such that the expression $\frac{p}{q}$ is in lowest terms and the number $\frac{p}{q}$ is a root of $P(x) = 0$, then p must be an integral factor of a_n, and q must be an integral factor of a_0.

The statement that $\frac{p}{q}$ is in lowest terms means that p and q have 1 as their greatest common factor in the set of integers; this condition is also expressed by saying that p and q have no common prime factor, or that p and q are **relatively prime.** For example, 14 and 15 are relatively prime since $14 = 2 \cdot 7$ and $15 = 3 \cdot 5$.

Before proving the theorem, let us consider an application.

EXAMPLE 1. Determine all rational roots of $3x^3 - 2x^2 + 2x + 1 = 0$.

Solution: By Theorem 9, if $\frac{p}{q}$ is a rational root in lowest terms, then p is a factor of 1 and q is a factor of 3. Thus $p \in \{1, -1\}$ and $q \in \{1, -1, 3, -3\}$, and the only rational numbers that need to be tested are $1, -1, \frac{1}{3}, -\frac{1}{3}$. Using synthetic substitution, we find:

	3	−2	2	1	
1	3	1	3	4	1 is not a root
−1	3	−5	7	−6	−1 is not a root
$\frac{1}{3}$	3	−1	$\frac{5}{3}$	$\frac{14}{9}$	$\frac{1}{3}$ is not a root
$-\frac{1}{3}$	3	−3	3	0	$-\frac{1}{3}$ is a root

Thus the only rational root is $-\frac{1}{3}$.

Proof of Theorem 9

If $\frac{p}{q}$ is a rational root, expressed in lowest terms, of $P(x) = 0$, then

$$a_0\left(\frac{p}{q}\right)^n + a_1\left(\frac{p}{q}\right)^{n-1} + \cdots + a_{n-1}\frac{p}{q} + a_n = 0.$$

Multiplying by q^n, we obtain

$$a_0p^n + a_1p^{n-1}q + \cdots + a_{n-1}pq^{n-1} + a_nq^n = 0, \qquad (*)$$

or

$$a_nq^n = -p(a_0p^{n-1} + a_1p^{n-2}q + \cdots + a_{n-1}q^{n-1}).$$

(Proof continued)

Notice that the left-hand member and the right-hand member of the last equation both name the same integer and that p is a factor of the right-hand member. Thus p must be a factor of the left-hand member. Since p and q have no common integral factors greater than 1, neither do p and q^n. Therefore all the prime factors of p are factors of a_n, so that p itself is a factor of a_n. [This argument uses the **Unique Factorization Theorem,** that (except for the order of the factors) every integer greater than 1 can be expressed as the product of prime numbers in exactly one way.]

We can show that q is a factor of a_0 by transforming (*) to

$$a_0p^n = -q(a_1p^{n-1} + \cdots + a_{n-1}pq^{n-2} + a_nq^{n-1})$$

and proceeding in a similar way (see Exercise 30, page 97).

If a is a root of $P(x) = 0$, so that $P(x) = (x - a)Q(x)$, then we can determine whether or not a is a *multiple* root by testing a in the **reduced equation** $Q(x) = 0$. Similarly, for any other value b we can determine whether or not b is a root of $P(x) = 0$ by testing b in $Q(x) = 0$, since $P(b) = (b - a)Q(b)$, $b - a \neq 0$, and, hence, $P(b) = 0$ if and only if $Q(b) = 0$.

EXAMPLE 2. For the equation $12x^5 + 8x^4 + 11x^3 + 7x^2 - x - 1 = 0$, determine all rational roots and their multiplicities.

Solution: If $\frac{p}{q}$ denotes a rational root in lowest terms, then p is a factor of -1 and q a factor of 12. Therefore, the only possible rational roots are $1, -1, \frac{1}{2}, -\frac{1}{2}, \frac{1}{3}, -\frac{1}{3}, \frac{1}{4}, -\frac{1}{4}, \frac{1}{6}, -\frac{1}{6}, \frac{1}{12}$, and $-\frac{1}{12}$.

	12	8	11	7	-1	-1	
1	12	20	31	38	37	36	1 is not a root
-1	12	-4	15	-8	7	-8	-1 is not a root
$\frac{1}{2}$	12	14	18	16	7	$\frac{5}{2}$	$\frac{1}{2}$ is not a root
$-\frac{1}{2}$	12	2	10	2	-2	0	$-\frac{1}{2}$ is a root
	12	2	10	2	-2		Reduced equation
	6	1	5	1	-1		Simplified (divide by 2)
$-\frac{1}{2}$	6	-2	6	-2	0		$-\frac{1}{2}$ is a root
	3	-1	3	-1			Reduced equation simplified
$-\frac{1}{2}$	3	$-\frac{5}{2}$	$\frac{17}{4}$	$-\frac{25}{8}$			$-\frac{1}{2}$ is not a root
$\frac{1}{3}$	3	0	3	0			$\frac{1}{3}$ is a root
	1	0	1				Reduced equation simplified

By Theorem 9, the only possible roots of the last reduced equation ($x^2 + 1 = 0$) are 1 and -1, which have already been tested. Therefore $-\frac{1}{2}$ is a root of multiplicity 2 (a **double root**) and $\frac{1}{3}$ is a root of multiplicity 1 (a **simple root**).

A polynomial with integral coefficients might have zeros in $\mathcal{R}$ that are not rational. Thus for $P(x) = x^3 + 2x^2 - x - 1$, by Theorem 9 the only possible rational roots of $P(x) = 0$ are 1 and -1.

	1	2	-1	-1	
1	1	3	2	1	1 is not a root
-1	1	1	-2	1	-1 is not a root

Hence there are no rational roots of $P(x) = 0$. Notice, however, that $P(0) = -1$, which is negative, while $P(1) = 1$, which is positive. Since, as was mentioned in Section 2–6, the graph of a polynomial function with domain $\mathcal{R}$ is a smooth curve without breaks, it seems intuitively clear, and in fact is true, that the graph of $P: x \to P(x)$ must cross the x-axis at least once between 0 and 1 (Figure 2–14). This illustrates the following **Location Principle.**

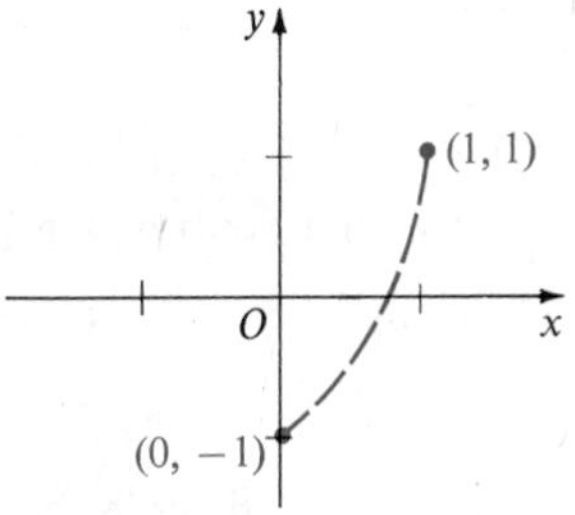

Figure 2–14

Theorem 10.

If P is a polynomial function with domain $\mathcal{R}$ and x_1 and x_2 are real numbers such that one of $P(x_1)$ and $P(x_2)$ is positive and the other negative, then P has at least one zero between x_1 and x_2.

This principle will be discussed further in Section 3–2, where we shall see that it holds for *any* function whose graph is an unbroken curve.

EXAMPLE 3. Determine all pairs of consecutive integers between which there are roots of $P(x) = 0$ for $P(x) = x^3 + 2x^2 - x - 1$.

Solution: We use synthetic substitution to compute values of $P(x)$.

	1	2	-1	-1
-3	1	-1	2	-7
-2	1	0	-1	1
-1	1	1	-2	1
0	1	2	-1	-1
1	1	3	2	1

(*Solution continued*)

Therefore there is at least one root between -3 and -2, at least one between -1 and 0, and at least one between 0 and 1. Since a polynomial equation of degree 3 can have at most 3 roots in $\mathcal{R}$, $P(x) = 0$ has exactly one root between -3 and -2, one between -1 and 0, and one between 0 and 1.

Notice that the three roots of $P(x) = 0$ in Example 3 are between -3 and -2, between -1 and 0, and between 0 and 1, and that by the Rational Root Theorem the only possible rational roots are -1 and 1. Hence all three of the roots must be irrational. Closer approximations to irrational roots will be discussed in Section 4–4.

ORAL EXERCISES

In Exercises 1–4, state a polynomial equation with integral coefficients which has the same roots as the given equation.

1. $4x^4 - 2x^3 + 3x + 1 = 8$
2. $\frac{2}{5}x^3 - 4x + 7 = 0$
3. $x^3 - \frac{1}{2}x^2 + 3x - \frac{1}{3} = 0$
4. $\frac{1}{3}x^4 - x + \frac{1}{2} = \frac{5}{2}$

In Exercises 5–8, state the possible rational roots of the given equation.

5. $4x^3 - 5x^2 + x - 1 = 0$
6. $x^3 + 2x^2 - 3x - 6 = 0$
7. $2x^3 - 3x^2 + 4x - 5 = 0$
8. $(x^4 - 3x^2 + 5)(7x^3 + x^2 - 1) = 0$

In Exercises 9 and 10, $P(x) = 0$ is a polynomial equation and $a < b$. Refer to the diagrams below in giving your answers.

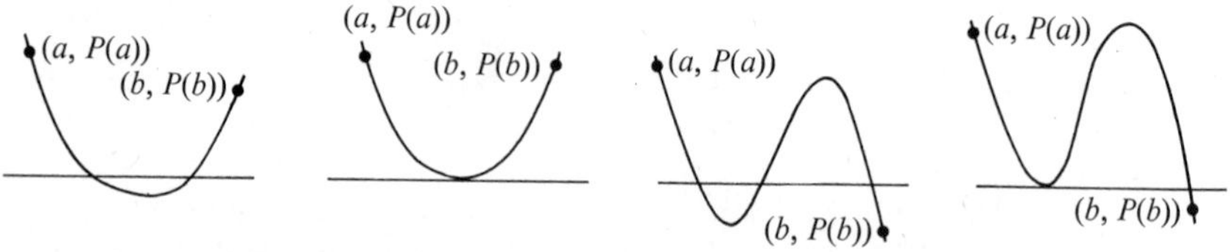

9. Suppose $P(a)$ and $P(b)$ are both positive or both negative.
   a. Is it true that $P(x) = 0$ cannot have a root between a and b?
   b. Do you think that $P(x) = 0$ might have an odd number of different roots between a and b?
10. Suppose one of $P(a)$ and $P(b)$ is positive and the other negative.
    a. Is it true that $P(x) = 0$ must have exactly one root between a and b?
    b. Do you think that $P(x) = 0$ might have an even number of different roots between a and b?

WRITTEN EXERCISES

In Exercises 1–12, determine all rational roots and their multiplicities for the given equation.

A

1. $2x^3 - 3x^2 - x + 12 = 0$
2. $3x^3 - 10x^2 + 7x + 10 = 0$
3. $x^4 - 3x^2 + 2x + 2 = 0$
4. $x^5 + x^4 - 2x - 3 = 0$
5. $x^3 - \frac{4}{3}x^2 - x + \frac{7}{3} = 1$
6. $x^3 + \frac{3}{4}x^2 - 4x - \frac{1}{2} = \frac{5}{2}$
7. $6x^4 - x^3 + 4x^2 - x - 2 = 0$
8. $2x^4 - 3x^3 - x^2 - 6x - 10 = 0$
9. $2x^5 + x^4 - 32x - 16 = 0$
10. $16x^5 + 48x^4 - x - 3 = 0$
11. $16x^5 - 16x^4 - 72x^3 + 72x^2 + 81x - 81 = 0$
12. $36x^4 - 181x^2 + 225 = 0$

In Exercises 13–16, determine all pairs of consecutive integers between which there are roots of the given polynomial equation.

13. $x^3 - 4x^2 - 4x + 17 = 0$
14. $x^3 - 4x^2 - 4x + 15 = 0$
15. $x^4 - 10x^2 + 8 = 0$
16. $x^4 - 10x^2 + 10 = 0$

B

17. Show that if the leading coefficient in a polynomial equation with integral coefficients is 1, then every rational root of the equation is an integer.
18. Show that if the constant term in a polynomial equation with integral coefficients is 1, then every rational root of the equation is the reciprocal of an integer.
19. By writing $(x - \sqrt{5})(x + \sqrt{5})$ as a polynomial in x and using the Rational Root Theorem, show that $\sqrt{5}$ is irrational.
20. By writing $(x + \sqrt{2} + \sqrt{3})(x + \sqrt{2} - \sqrt{3})(x - \sqrt{2} + \sqrt{3})(x - \sqrt{2} - \sqrt{3})$ as a polynomial in x, show that $\sqrt{2} + \sqrt{3}$ and $\sqrt{2} - \sqrt{3}$ are both irrational.

Show that each of the following numbers is irrational.

C

21. $2\sqrt{3}$
22. $-\sqrt{7}$
23. $1 + \sqrt{2}$
24. $3 - \sqrt{3}$
25. $\sqrt{3} - \sqrt{5}$
26. $\sqrt{5} + \sqrt{2}$
27. $\sqrt[3]{4}$
28. $1 - \sqrt[3]{2}$
29. $2 + 3\sqrt[4]{5}$
30. In Theorem 9, prove that q is a factor of a_0.

2–9 Number of Roots; Bounds on Roots

In this section, we shall further explore the problem of determining the roots of polynomial equations. In finding roots, we must sometimes use very short domain intervals.

EXAMPLE 1. Show that the equation $P(x) = 0$, where $P(x) = x^3 - 2x^2 - 9x + 19$, has three roots in $\mathcal{R}$ and determine three nonoverlapping intervals of length at most 1 such that each interval contains exactly one root.

x	$P(x)$
-4	-41
-3	1
-2	21
-1	25
0	19
1	9
2	1
3	1
4	15

Solution: Synthetic substitution yields the table shown at the right. Since $P(-4) = -41 < 0$ and $P(-3) = 1 > 0$, by the Location Principle there is at least one root between -4 and -3. The rough sketch shown below indicates that there might or might not be two roots between 2 and 3. A further application of synthetic substitution yields $P(2.5) = -0.375 < 0$. Since $P(2) > 0$ and $P(3) > 0$, we see from the Location Principle that there is at least one root between 2 and 2.5, and at least one root between 2.5 and 3. Since a polynomial equation of degree three can have at most three roots in $\mathcal{R}$, it follows that $P(x) = 0$ has exactly one root between -4 and -3, one between 2 and 2.5, and one between 2.5 and 3.

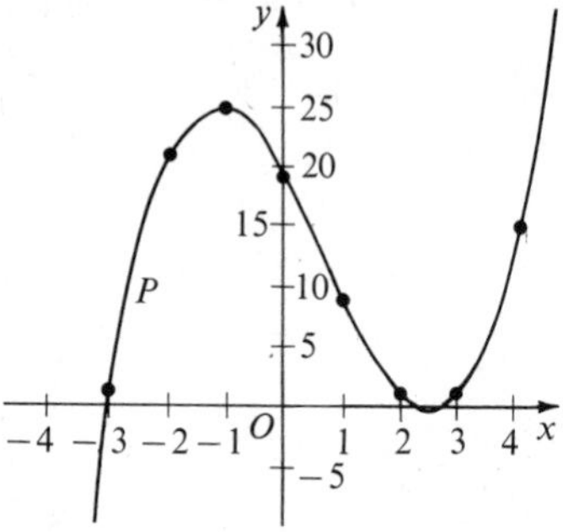

As we have seen, a polynomial equation of degree n might have fewer than n roots in $\mathcal{R}$. A result called *Descartes' Rule of Signs* is often useful in bounding the possible number of positive roots, the possible number of negative roots, and the possible total number of roots in $\mathcal{R}$. If a polynomial over $\mathcal{R}$ has terms in order of decreasing degree, and if one of two successive terms is positive and the other negative, then a **variation in sign** is said to occur. Thus

$$3x^5 - 2x^3 - x^2 + x + 3$$

$$\mathbf{1} \quad \mathbf{0} \quad \mathbf{1} \quad \mathbf{0}$$

$$1 + 1, \text{ or } 2, \text{ variations}$$

has two variations in sign. Descartes' Rule, which we accept here without proof, is as follows:

Theorem 11.

If $P(x)$ is a polynomial of degree n over $\mathcal{R}$, then the number of positive real roots (counting a root of multiplicity k, k times) of $P(x) = 0$ is equal to the number of variations in sign occurring in $P(x)$, or else is less than this number by a positive even integer.

Notice that every *negative* root of $P(x) = 0$ is a *positive* root of $P(-x) = 0$. For example, if $P(x) = x^2 + 2x$, then

$$P(-x) = (-x)^2 + 2(-x) = x^2 - 2x;$$

the roots of $P(x) = 0$ are -2 and 0, and the roots of $P(-x) = 0$ are 2 and 0. Thus you can also use Descartes' Rule of Signs to investigate the possible number of negative roots of $P(x) = 0$.

EXAMPLE 2. Use Descartes' Rule to determine **(a)** the possible number of positive roots and **(b)** the possible number of negative roots of $P(x) = 0$, where $P(x) = x^7 - x^5 + 2x^2 + 1$.

Solution: **a.** $P(x) = x^7 - x^5 + 2x^2 + 1$

$$\qquad 1 \quad 1 \quad 0$$

There are two variations in sign in $P(x)$, so there are either two or no positive roots of $P(x) = 0$.

b. $P(-x) = (-x)^7 - (-x)^5 + 2(-x)^2 + 1$

$$= -x^7 + x^5 + 2x^2 + 1$$

$$\qquad 1 \qquad 0 \qquad 0$$

There is just one variation in sign in $P(-x)$, so there is exactly one negative root of $P(x) = 0$.

Descartes' Rule of Signs allows us to find bounds for the *number* of positive roots and negative roots of $P(x) = 0$. We shall now indicate how to find bounds for the *magnitude* of the positive and negative roots of $P(x) = 0$. Thus in Example 3, page 100, we shall see that the equation $2x^3 - 5x^2 + x + 9 = 0$ has no root in $\mathcal{R}$ that is greater than 3 and no root in $\mathcal{R}$ that is less than -2. We say that 3 and -2 are **upper** and **lower bounds,** respectively, for the roots of this equation.

Theorem 12.

Let $P(x)$ be a polynomial of degree n, $n \geq 1$, over $\mathcal{R}$ with positive leading coefficient. Let M be a nonnegative real number and L a nonpositive real number. If the coefficients of the quotient and the remainder obtained on dividing $P(x)$ by $x - M$ are all nonnegative, then $P(x) = 0$ has no root in $\mathcal{R}$ that is greater than M. If the coefficients and remainder obtained on dividing $P(x)$ by $x - L$ are alternately nonnegative and nonpositive, then $P(x) = 0$ has no root in $\mathcal{R}$ that is less than L.

EXAMPLE 3. Find the least positive integer and the greatest negative integer that Theorem 12 shows to be upper and lower bounds for the roots in $\mathcal{R}$ of the equation $2x^3 - 5x^2 + x + 9 = 0$.

Solution: We use synthetic substitution with $x = 1, 2, 3, \ldots$ until an upper bound is reached, and then we use $x = -1, -2, -3, \ldots$ until a lower bound is reached.

	2	−5	1	9	
1	2	−3	−2	7	
2	2	−1	−1	7	
3	2	1	4	21	all nonnegative
−1	2	−7	8	1	
−2	2	−9	19	−29	alternating

Thus 3 is the integral upper bound and −2 is the integral lower bound.

To see why 3 is an upper bound in Example 3 above, notice that

$$P(x) = (x - 3)(2x^3 + x + 4) + 21.$$

For $x > 3$, observe that $x - 3$, $2x^3 + x + 4$, and 21 are all positive, so that $P(x) > 0$. Therefore, $P(x)$ cannot be 0 for any $x > 3$. In a similar way, we can see why −2 is a lower bound by noting that

$$P(x) = (x + 2)(2x^2 - 9x + 19) - 29$$

and that for $x < -2$, $x + 2$ is negative, $2x^2 - 9x + 19$ is positive, and −29 is negative. This argument illustrates the reasoning that can be used to prove Theorem 12 in general (Exercises 19 and 20, page 102).

ORAL EXERCISES

1. Explain why it is sometimes necessary to use very short domain intervals to determine the presence of zeros of polynomial functions.
2. Without using Descartes' Rule of Signs, tell how you know that the equation
$$x^9 + 5x^4 + 7x^3 + x + 2 = 0$$
has no positive roots.
3. Without using Descartes' Rule of Signs, tell how you know that the equation
$$x^6 - 4x^5 - 3x^3 + 6x^2 - x + 2 = 0$$
has no negative roots.
4. Without using Descartes' Rule of Signs, tell how you know that the equation
$$x^5 - 2x^4 + x^3 - 3x^2 + x - 2 = 0$$
has no negative roots.

In Exercises 5–8, use Descartes' Rule of Signs to determine (a) the possible number of positive roots and (b) the possible number of negative roots of $P(x) = 0$ for the given polynomial $P(x)$.

5. $P(x) = x^3 + 2x^2 + 3x - 4$
6. $P(x) = x^3 - 2x^2 - 3x - 4$
7. $P(x) = x^6 - 4x^5 + 2x^4 - 7x^3 + 2x^2 - x + 3$
8. $P(x) = x^7 + 4x^5 + 2x^3 + 3x$
9. Explain how you know that 2 is an upper bound for the roots in $\mathcal{R}$ of the equation
$$(x - 2)(x^2 + 2x + 5) + 7 = 0.$$
10. Explain how you know that -3 is a lower bound for the roots in $\mathcal{R}$ of the equation
$$(x + 3)(x^2 - 2x + 5) - 7 = 0.$$
11. Explain how you know that -9 is a lower bound for the roots in $\mathcal{R}$ of the equation
$$(x + 9)(x^3 - 4x^2 + 3x - 1) + 8 = 0.$$

WRITTEN EXERCISES

In Exercises 1 and 2, show that the given equation has three roots in $\mathcal{R}$ and determine three nonoverlapping intervals of length at most 1 such that each interval contains exactly one root.

A

1. $2x^3 - 3x^2 - 6x + 6 = 0$
2. $16x^3 + 24x^2 - 25x - 38 = 0$

In Exercises 3–8, find the possible number of positive roots and the possible number of negative roots of each equation.

3. $7x^3 - 15x^2 - 16x + 10 = 0$

4. $8x^3 + 9x^2 - 7x - 8 = 0$

5. $x^5 - x^3 + x + 3 = 0$

6. $x^4 + 3x^2 - 2 = 0$

7. $x^5 - x^2 + 2x - 1 = 0$

8. $x^6 + 2x^3 - x^2 + 4 = 0$

9–14. For the equations in Exercises 3–8, find the least positive integer and the greatest negative integer that Theorem 12 shows to be upper and lower bounds for the roots in $\mathcal{R}$ of the given equation.

In Exercises 15–18, show that the given equation has exactly one real root.

15. $x^5 + x^2 + 4 = 0$

16. $4x^5 - 3x^4 - x^2 - 2 = 0$

B **17.** $x^5 + 2x^4 + x^3 + 2x^2 + 3x + 6 = 0$

18. $2x^5 - 6x^4 + x^3 - 3x^2 + x - 3 = 0$

C **19.** Let $P(x)$ be a polynomial over $\mathcal{R}$ with positive leading coefficient, let M be a nonnegative real number, and let $P(x) = (x - M)Q(x) + R$. Prove that if the coefficients of $Q(x)$ are all nonnegative and $R \geq 0$, then $P(x) = 0$ can have no root in $\mathcal{R}$ that is greater than M.

20. Let $P(x)$ be a polynomial over $\mathcal{R}$ with positive leading coefficient, let L be a nonpositive real number, and let $P(x) = (x - L)Q(x) + R$. Prove that if the coefficients of $Q(x)$ and R are alternately nonnegative and nonpositive, then $P(x) = 0$ can have no root in $\mathcal{R}$ that is less than L.

CHAPTER SUMMARY

1. The **slope of a nonvertical line** is the common value of the slopes of all its segments. A vertical line has no slope.
2. The line passing through (x_1, y_1) and having slope m is represented by the **point-slope formula** $y - y_1 = m(x - x_1)$. The line having y-intercept b and slope m is represented by the **slope-intercept formula** $y = mx + b$.
3. Two nonvertical lines are *parallel* if and only if their slopes are equal. Two nonvertical lines are *perpendicular* if and only if their slopes are negative reciprocals of each other.
4. A function f is **quadratic** if and only if there are real numbers $a \neq 0$, b, and c such that $f(x) = ax^2 + bx + c$. The graph of a quadratic function opens upward if $a > 0$ and downward if $a < 0$.
5. If f is any function and z is a number in the domain of f such that $f(z) = 0$, then z is a **zero** of f. The *zeros of a function* f are the same as the

roots of the *equation* $f(x) = 0$ and are also the same as the *x-intercepts* of the *graph* of f.

6. If for a given value t, $f(t) \leq f(x)$ for all x in the domain of f, then $f(t)$ is a **minimum value,** or, more briefly, a **minimum,** of f. If the inequality is reversed, $f(t) \geq f(x)$, then $f(t)$ is a **maximum value,** or, more briefly, a **maximum,** of f. Maxima and minima are called **extrema** (singular: *extremum*).

7. Each quadratic function has exactly one extremum, which can be found by means of Theorem 3 (page 72).

8. The set of all points equidistant from a fixed line and a fixed point not on this line is a **parabola.** The fixed line is the **directrix** of the parabola, and the fixed point is its **focus.** The line through the focus perpendicular to the directrix is the **axis,** or **axis of symmetry,** of the parabola. The point in which a parabola intersects its axis is its **vertex.**

9. Equations of parabolas with vertex at the origin and axis either horizontal or vertical are given by Theorem 4 (page 76).

10. If in a **polynomial in** x **of degree** n**,**

$$a_0x^n + a_1x^{n-1} + \cdots + a_{n-1}x + a_n, \qquad a_0 \neq 0,$$

where n is a nonnegative integer, the **coefficients** $a_0, a_1, \ldots, a_{n-1}, a_n$ are all members of the field $\mathcal{R}$ of real numbers, then the polynomial is said to be a **polynomial over** $\mathcal{R}$. The **leading coefficient** is a_0, and the **constant term** is a_n. No degree is assigned to the **zero polynomial,** 0.

11. Two polynomials in x are **equal** if and only if they are of the same degree and their coefficients of like powers of x are equal. Polynomials are added, subtracted, and multiplied in accordance with familiar arithmetic **algorithms.** In each case, the result is a polynomial in x.

12. If $P(x)$ is a polynomial of degree n over $\mathcal{R}$ and $S(x)$ is a polynomial of degree k, $0 \leq k \leq n$, over $\mathcal{R}$, then (Theorem 5, page 81) we can write $P(x) = S(x)Q(x) + R(x)$, where $Q(x)$ is of degree $n - k$ and $R(x)$ either is the zero polynomial or is of degree less than k. We say that $Q(x)$ is the **quotient,** and $R(x)$ is the **remainder,** when $P(x)$ is **divided** by $S(x)$. If $R(x) = 0$, then $P(x) = S(x)\,Q(x)$, and $S(x)$ is said to be a **factor** of $P(x)$. If $S(x)$ is of the form $x - a$, then the quotient $Q(x)$ and remainder R can be determined by **synthetic division.**

13. If x is a variable whose domain is a subset D of $\mathcal{R}$, and $P(x)$ is a polynomial over $\mathcal{R}$, then $P\colon x \to P(x)$ is a **polynomial function** whose domain is D and whose values are obtained by replacing x with various members of D. By the **Remainder Theorem** (page 86), we can use synthetic division to determine $P(a)$ as the remainder when $P(x)$ is divided by $x - a$; for this reason, synthetic division is also called **synthetic substitution.**

14. If P is a polynomial function, then $P(x) = 0$ is called a **polynomial equation.** By the **Factor Theorem** (page 89), $x - a$ is a factor of $P(x)$ if and only if a is a root of $P(x) = 0$. If $P(x) = (x - a)^m Q(x)$, and $x - a$ is not a factor of $Q(x)$, then $x - a$ is said to be a **factor of multiplicity** $\boldsymbol{m}$, or an $\boldsymbol{m}$**-fold factor,** of $P(x)$. A polynomial function P of degree n over $\mathcal{R}$ has at most n zeros in $\mathcal{R}$; in fact, the sum of the multiplicities of the zeros of P in $\mathcal{R}$ is at most n.

15. If $P(x)$ is a polynomial with *integral* coefficients, then the rational roots of $P(x) = 0$ can be determined by means of the **Rational Root Theorem** (page 93). If $P(x) = (x - a)Q(x)$, then we can test a in the **reduced equation** $Q(x) = 0$ to see if a is a multiple root of $P(x) = 0$.

16. For a polynomial function P, the presence of at least one real zero, whether rational or irrational, in an interval can often be determined by means of the **Location Principle** (page 95). It is sometimes necessary, however, to use very short intervals to determine the presence of zeros.

17. We can determine bounds on the *number* and *magnitude*, respectively, of the real roots of a polynomial equation by means of **Descartes' Rule of Signs** (page 99) and **Theorem 12** (page 100).

CHAPTER TEST

2–1 **1.** Find an equation of the form $Ax + By + C = 0$ for each of the lines characterized.

a. Passes through $(2, -3)$, has slope 4.
b. Has slope -2, y-intercept 3.
c. Passes through $(-1, 3)$ and $(2, -4)$.
d. Has x-intercept -3, y-intercept 2.
e. Passes through $(1, 2)$, has the same slope as $x - 2y + 5 = 0$.

2–2 **2.** Find an equation of the line through $(2, -3)$ which is (**a**) parallel and (**b**) perpendicular to the line $3x - 4y + 2 = 0$.

2–3 **3.** Find at least six points on the graph of $f\colon x \to x^2 - x + 1$ and sketch the graph.

4. (**a**) Find the value of x for which $f\colon x \to 2 - 4x - 3x^2$ has its maximum or minimum. Then (**b**) find the extremum of f and (**c**) state whether this is a maximum or a minimum.

2–4 **5.** Find an equation of the parabola which has its vertex at the origin and

a. has its focus at (0, 4).
b. passes through (2, 1) and (2, −1).

2–5 **6.** Express $x^4 - 3x^3 + 3x^2 - 4$ as a polynomial in $(x - 2)$.

2–6 **7.** Find the points on the graph of

$$Q: x \to x^3 - 3x$$

having abscissas −2, −1, 0, 1, 2. Draw a smooth curve through these points.

2–7 **8.** Show that $x + 2$ is a multiple factor of

$$x^5 + 6x^4 + 10x^3 - 4x^2 - 24x - 16,$$

and determine is multiplicity.

2–8 **9.** For the equation

$$4x^5 - 8x^4 - 7x^3 - 11x^2 - 11x - 3 = 0,$$

determine all the rational roots and their multiplicities.

2–9 **10.** Using Descartes' Rule, determine the possible number of positive roots and the possible number of negative roots of

$$x^6 - 2x^5 + x^3 - 2 = 0.$$

11. Find the least positive integer and the greatest negative integer that Theorem 12 shows to be upper and lower bounds for the real roots of

$$x^4 - 2x^3 - 3x^2 - 15x - 3 = 0.$$

RECOMMENDED READINGS

BIRKHOFF, GARRETT, and MAC LANE, SAUNDERS, *A Survey of Modern Algebra*, revised edition (New York: The Macmillan Company, 1953).

PAIGE, LOWELL J., and SWIFT, J. DEAN, *Elements of Linear Algebra* (Boston: Ginn and Company, 1961).

SAWYER, W. W., *A Concrete Approach to Abstract Algebra* (San Francisco: W. H. Freeman and Company, 1959).

The Impact of Modern Computing Machines

Today, because of the widespread and varied use of electronic high-speed computers and the effect of these computers on our lives, we may be said to be living in the midst of the "Computer Revolution." The roots of this revolution can be traced back to the 1600's, but the most significant developments have been made in this century.

The article on "Calculating Machines" in the scholarly old eleventh edition of the *Encyclopaedia Britannica* (1910–11) begins with the statement that "instruments for the mechanical performance of numerical calculations, have in modern times come into ever-increasing use, not merely for dealing with large masses of figures in banks, insurance offices, etc., but also, as cash registers, for use on the counters of retail shops." It classifies computing machines as follows: (i) Addition machines; the first invented by Blaise Pascal (1642). (ii) Addition machines modified to facilitate multiplication; the first by G. W. Leibniz (1671). (iii) True multiplication machines; Léon Bollés (1888),Steiger (1894). (iv) Difference machines; Johann Helfrich von Müller (1786), Charles Babbage (1822). (v) Analytical machines; Babbage (1834). The article ends with a discussion of the harmonic analyzers of Lord Kelvin and others.

Some of the machines discussed above were digital computers; that is, they were machines in which numbers are represented as strings of digits (for example, in decimal or binary form). Others were analog devices, in which numbers are represented by physical quantities such as lengths, stretchings, and rotations. All, however, were mechanical rather than electronic. The analytical machines (v. above) were capable of mechanically performing integrations and solving differential equations such as you will be studying in this book.

In the 1920's, Vannevar Bush developed a greatly improved mechanical differential analyzer, and R. R. M. Mallock introduced an electronic machine for solving linear equations. Otherwise, except for minor routine improvements, the situation remained for some thirty-five years much as that described in the 1910–11 *Encyclopaedia* article cited above.

The first all-electronic digital computing machines were constructed during World War II. The brilliant mathematician John von Neumann (1903–1957) contributed many ideas for their design and construction, in particular the notion that base-two numerals representing instruction codes as well as data could be stored electronically; this eliminated the necessity of using masses of special wiring for each new problem. These machines were extraordinarily fast in comparison with any computers that had previously been developed, for they could perform an arithmetic operation in less than a thousandth of a second. Because of their vacuum-tube circuitry, however, these *first-generation* computers were subject to frequent break-down troubles, averaging about one per hour.

Second-generation computers, developed in the late 1950's, used transistorized, or solid-state, circuitry; they were much more reliable than the first-generation computers and at least ten times as fast. Now *third-* and *fourth-generation* computers, with integrated microcircuits and other technological improvements, have further drastically reduced component failure, and in comparison with second-generation computers they have again increased speed by a factor of at least ten.

These new computers have had a dramatic effect on business, industry, and scientific research. For example, they are used in processing bank checks, in governing automatic assembly lines, and in performing medical diagnosis and research; and they are essential in planning and controlling space exploration. Their full impact on our civilization has probably only begun to be fully realized. The Industrial Revolution made possible the enrichment of human life by releasing man from his former drudgery and by increasing the availability of food, clothing, and other commodities; the Computer Revolution is having a similar effect.

In the course of the search for design improvements which would further increase the capabilities of computing machines, scientists have "taught" these machines with considerable success to play such games as checkers and chess. They have also programmed the rudiments of musical composition — rhythm, harmony, melody, and so on — into computing machines on a probabilistic basis; then with the aid of random-number generators the machines have, in a sense, created their own musical compositions. Computers have also aided in the creation of graphic works of art, as illustrated on the cover of this book!

READING LIST

LOVIS, F. B., *Computers 1* and *2* (Boston: Houghton Mifflin Company, 1964).

MOTT-SMITH, JOHN, *Computers and Art*, The Arithmetic Teacher, Vol. 16, No. 3 (March, 1969), pp. 169–172.

PHILIPSON, MORRIS, ed., *Automation: Implications for the Future* (New York: Random House, Inc., 1962).

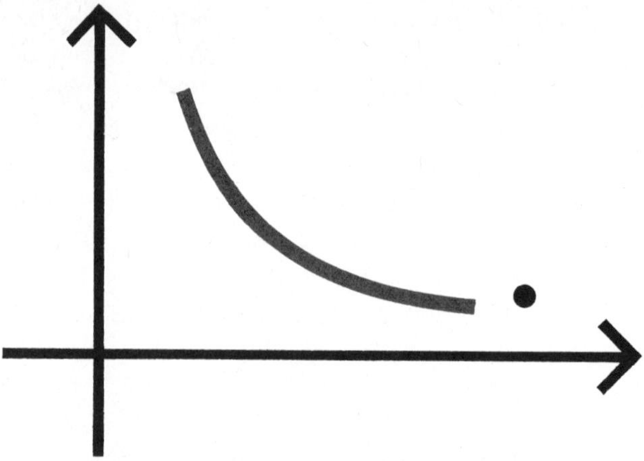

3

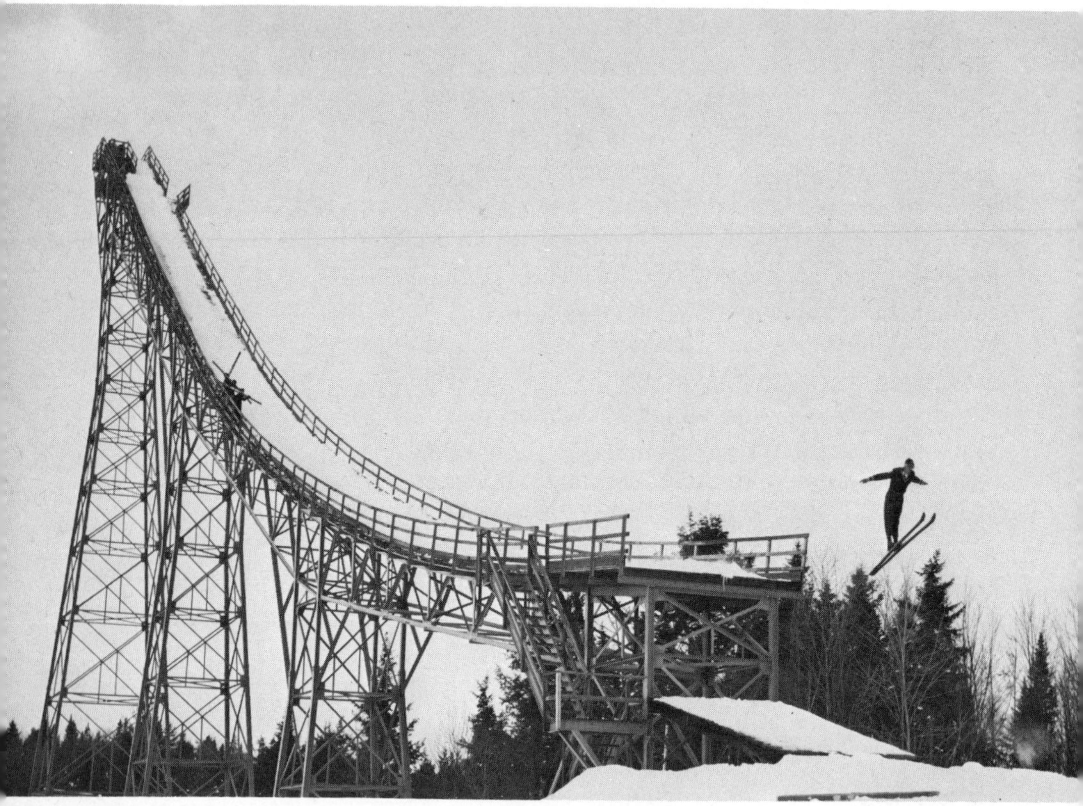

The ski jumper in the photograph above traces a smooth, continuous curve with his skis as he races down the steep jump (see the diagram above); then his skis leave the track and he sails into the air.

Introduction to Differential Calculus

In the seventeenth century, Newton, Leibniz, and others founded a new branch of mathematics which today we call *analysis*. Analysis, of which differential calculus is a part, differs from other main areas of mathematics in being based on the *limit concept*. The calculus makes possible the solution of many applied and theoretical problems which would be difficult or impossible to solve by other methods.

Limits and Continuity

3–1 The Limit Concept

Let us consider the behavior of the function

$$f\colon x \to x^2 - 1$$

when x is near 2. Now $f(2) = 2^2 - 1 = 3$; that is, the value of $f(x)$ is 3 when x is 2. What can we say about $f(x)$ if x is not 2 but is *close* to 2? The table at the right shows the value of $f(x)$ for some values of x near 2. In each case, the value of $f(x)$ is *close* to 3. We feel that this will be true for all values of x close to 2. We say that $f(x)$ *approaches* 3 *as* x *approaches* 2.

x	$f(x)$
1.9	2.61
2.1	3.41
1.99	2.9601
2.01	3.0401
1.999	2.996001
2.001	3.004001

Now let us consider the behavior of the function

$$g\colon x \to \begin{cases} x^2 - 1 & \text{if } x \neq 2 \\ 1 & \text{if } x = 2 \end{cases}$$

when x is near 2. Note that g has the same values as f except at 2. We must therefore conclude that if x is near 2, but not equal to 2, then $g(x)$ is near 3. An inspection of the graph of g (Figure 3–1) supports this conclusion. We say that $g(x)$ *approaches* 3 *as* x *approaches* 2, even though $g(2) \neq 3$. We also say that *the limit of* $g(x)$ *as* x *approaches* 2 is 3.

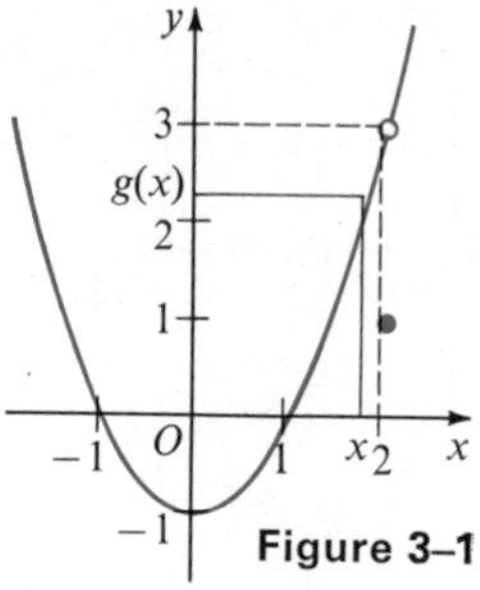

Figure 3–1

The domain of both of the functions we have considered is $\mathcal{R}$. Of course, this need not be the case. The domain of a function might, for example, be one of the following:

an *open interval*, like $\{x: 0 < x < 3\}$,
a *closed interval*, like $\{x: 0 \leq x \leq 3\}$,
an *open half-line*, like $\{x: x > 2\}$, or
a *closed half-line* (or *ray*), like $\{x: x \geq 2\}$.

In any case, in a limit situation, each "approaching variable" must represent numbers in the domain.

We are now ready to give a working definition of limit, based on intuition.

> Let f be a function having domain D, and let a be a number. If as x approaches a, $x \in D$, but does not take on the value a, $f(x)$ approaches some number b, then we call b the **limit of $f(x)$ as x approaches a,** and we write
>
> $$\lim_{x \to a} f(x) = b.$$

(The arrow in the "$x \to a$" part of the notation for limit is shorthand for the word "approaches." Notice in Example 1 below that arrows are used in two different ways. However, the "approaches" arrow always appears below "lim," so there should never be any confusion.)

EXAMPLE 1. Find $\lim_{x \to 2} f(x)$ for the function $f: x \to \dfrac{x^2 - 4}{x - 2}$.

Solution: Notice that f is *not defined* at 2 because if 2 is substituted for x in $\dfrac{x^2 - 4}{x - 2}$, the resulting expression, $\dfrac{0}{0}$, does not name a number. If $x \neq 2$, however, then

$$f(x) = \frac{x^2 - 4}{x - 2} = \frac{(x + 2)(x - 2)}{x - 2} = x + 2.$$

Now, the closer x is to 2, the closer $x + 2$ is to 4. Therefore,

$$\lim_{x \to 2} f(x) = 4.$$

You must realize that finding a limit is not a process of substitution. In Example 1, it is true that *after* we assumed $x \neq 2$ and *then* found that

$f(x) = x + 2$, we could obtain the number 4 by setting $x = 2$. But it is certainly illogical to assume $x \neq 2$ and then set $x = 2$. You should think of what $x + 2$ *approaches* as x *approaches* 2, rather than what $x + 2$ *is* when x *is* 2.

The graph of the function f of Example 1 is the line $y = x + 2$ with the point (2, 4) missing, as shown in Figure 3–2(a). Contrast the graph of f with the graph of $g: x \to x + 2$, the line shown in Figure 3–2(b). (Although $\lim_{x\to 2} g(x) = 4$, this is *not* because $g(2) = 4$.)

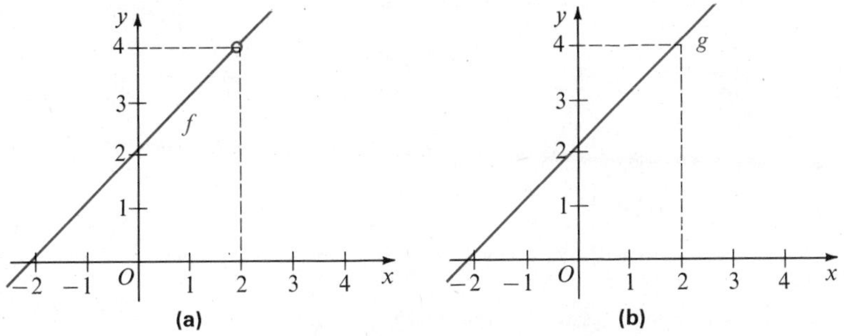

Figure 3–2

An example in which a limit fails to exist is provided by the function $G: x \to \operatorname{sgn} x$ [see Figure 3–3(a)], which was defined on page 21. $G(x) = \operatorname{sgn} x$ cannot approach any number b as x approaches 0 because for some values of x, as close to 0 as we please, $G(x)$ is 1, while for others, $G(x) = -1$. Therefore $\lim_{x\to 0} G(x)$ does not exist.

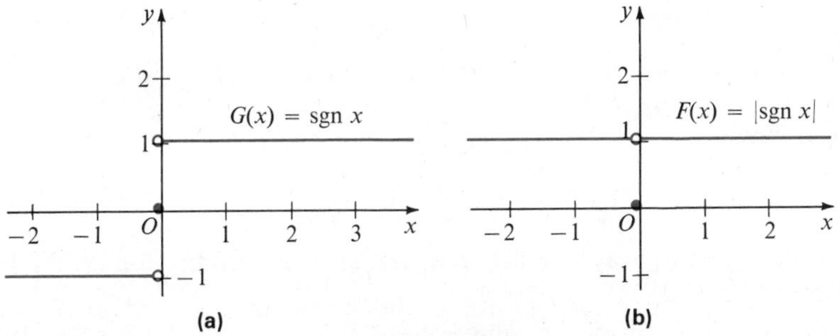

Figure 3–3

It can happen that $\lim_{x\to a} f(x) = b$ and that $f(a)$ exists, but that $b \neq f(a)$. For example, if $F: x \to |\operatorname{sgn} x|$, then $\lim_{x\to 0} F(x) = 1$, but $F(0) = 0$ [see Figure 3–3(b)]. For another example, if g is the function graphed in Figure 3–1, then $\lim_{x\to 2} g(x) = 3$, but $g(2) = 1$.

It is possible to give a precise definition of limit based on inequalities, one which does not use such words as "close," "near," or "approaches." On the basis of this definition, the properties of limits enumerated in the next theorem can be established. These properties (for example, "the limit of the sum of two functions is the sum of their limits") are quite easy to accept as being true, and we shall do so from now on.

Theorem 1.

Suppose $\lim_{x\to a} f(x)$ and $\lim_{x\to a} g(x)$ exist. Then

$$\lim_{x\to a} cf(x) = c\lim_{x\to a} f(x) \quad (c \text{ a constant}), \tag{C}$$

$$\lim_{x\to a} [f(x) + g(x)] = \lim_{x\to a} f(x) + \lim_{x\to a} g(x), \tag{S}$$

$$\lim_{x\to a} [f(x) - g(x)] = \lim_{x\to a} f(x) - \lim_{x\to a} g(x), \tag{D}$$

$$\lim_{x\to a} [f(x) \cdot g(x)] = \lim_{x\to a} f(x) \cdot \lim_{x\to a} g(x), \tag{Pr}$$

$$\lim_{x\to a} \frac{f(x)}{g(x)} = \frac{\lim_{x\to a} f(x)}{\lim_{x\to a} g(x)}. \tag{Q}$$

In (Q) we assume that $\lim_{x\to a} g(x) \neq 0$.

We are able to find limits of quite complicated functions with the help of Theorem 1 and some "special" limits. Using $\lim_{x\to a} x = a$ and part (Pr) of the theorem, we have

$$\lim_{x\to a} x^2 = \lim_{x\to a} (x \cdot x) = \lim_{x\to a} x \cdot \lim_{x\to a} x = a \cdot a = a^2.$$

Then we have

$$\lim_{x\to a} x^3 = \lim_{x\to a} (x^2 \cdot x) = \lim_{x\to a} x^2 \cdot \lim_{x\to a} x = a^2 \cdot a = a^3,$$

and so on. In this way, we arrive at the special formula for the "power function" $x \to x^n$:

$$\lim_{x\to a} x^n = a^n, \tag{Po}$$

where n is any positive integer.

If we consider the constant function $x \to b$, we see that

$$\lim_{x\to a} b = b. \tag{K}$$

EXAMPLE 2. Find $\lim_{x\to 2} \dfrac{3x^2}{x^3 + 4}$. At each step, indicate the "limit fact" being used.

Solution:

$$\lim_{x\to 2} x^2 = 2^2 = 4 \qquad \text{(Po)}$$

$$\lim_{x\to 2} 3x^2 = 3\lim_{x\to 2} x^2 = 3\cdot 4 = 12 \qquad \text{(C)}$$

$$\lim_{x\to 2} x^3 = 2^3 = 8 \qquad \text{(Po)}$$

$$\lim_{x\to 2} 4 = 4 \qquad \text{(K)}$$

$$\lim_{x\to 2} (x^3 + 4) = \lim_{x\to 2} x^3 + \lim_{x\to 2} 4 = 8 + 4 = 12 \qquad \text{(S)}$$

$$\lim_{x\to 2} \frac{3x^2}{x^3 + 4} = \frac{\lim_{x\to 2} 3x^2}{\lim_{x\to 2} (x^3 + 4)} = \frac{12}{12} = 1 \qquad \text{(Q)}$$

ORAL EXERCISES

1. State in your own words the meaning of $\lim_{x\to a} f(x) = b$.

The graphs of some functions are pictured below. Do you think that $\lim_{x\to 1} f(x)$ exists? If you think the limit does exist, state its value.

2.

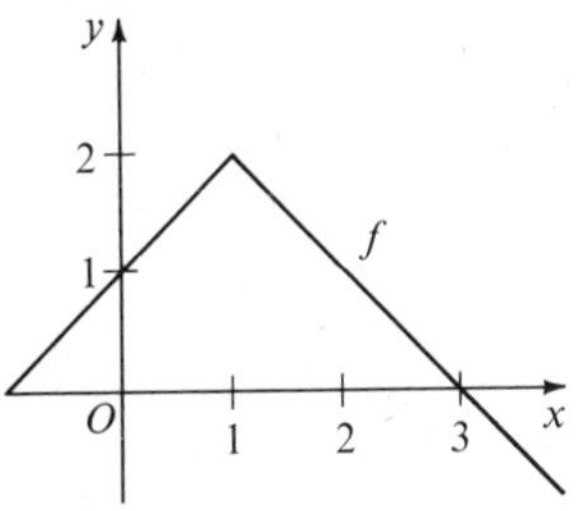

3.

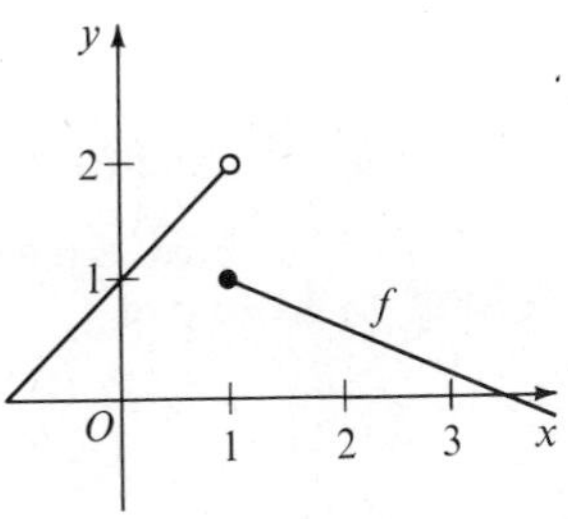

4.

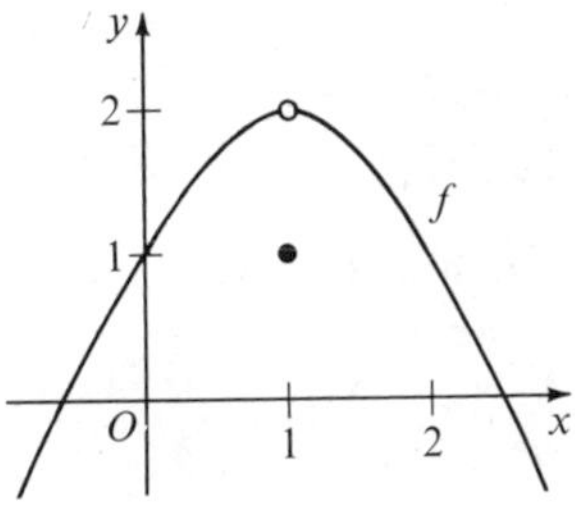

5.

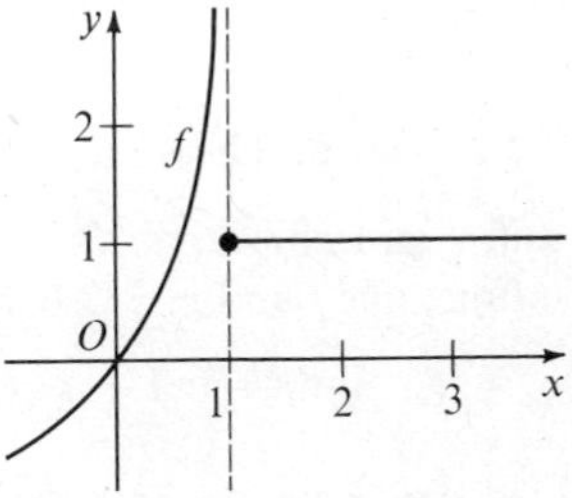

State the value of each of the following:

6. $\lim_{x\to 3} x$

7. $\lim_{x\to -2} x$

8. $\lim_{x\to 1} 2x$

9. $\lim_{x\to -1} (x + 1)$

10. $\lim_{x\to -2} x^2$

11. $\lim_{x\to -2} |x|$

12. Give a precise description of a function f having domain $\mathcal{R}$ such that $\lim_{x \to 2} f(x)$ does *not* exist.

WRITTEN EXERCISES

Use the limit facts (C), (S), (D), (Pr), (Q), (Po), and (K) to find each of the following limits. At each step, indicate what limit fact is being used (as in Example 2 on pages 112-113).

A

1. $\lim_{x \to 1} (x^2 + 2x)$
2. $\lim_{x \to 1} (3x - 2x^2)$
3. $\lim_{x \to 0} (x^3 + 4)$
4. $\lim_{x \to 0} (2 - x^3)$
5. $\lim_{x \to -1} (x^2 + x - 2)$
6. $\lim_{x \to -2} (x^2 + x - 2)$
7. $\lim_{x \to 2} \dfrac{x + 2}{x^3}$
8. $\lim_{x \to -1} \dfrac{x + 1}{x^2 + 1}$
9. $\lim_{x \to 1} \dfrac{x^2 - 2x}{x^2 + 2x}$
10. $\lim_{x \to 2} \dfrac{x^3 + x^2}{x^2 + 2}$
11. $\lim_{x \to 1} \dfrac{x - 1}{x^2 - 1}$
12. $\lim_{x \to 2} \dfrac{x^2 - 4}{x^2 - x - 2}$

Draw the graph of a function f such that $\lim_{x \to a} f(x)$ does *not* exist when a has the following values:

13. 1, 2, 3
14. $-1, 0, 1$

15. For what values of a does $\lim_{x \to a} [x]$ exist? (Recall the definition of $[x]$ given on page 20.)

B

16. Prove part (D) of Theorem 1, page 112, assuming parts (C) and (S).

17. If h and k are constants, then the function $hf + kg$ is a **linear combination** of the functions f and g. Use Theorem 1, page 112, to prove that

$$\lim_{x \to a} (hf(x) + kg(x)) = h \lim_{x \to a} f(x) + k \lim_{x \to a} g(x),$$

provided the limits on the right-hand side of the equation exist.

18. Give a precise formulation of a theorem which states that the limit of the sum of *three* functions is the sum of their limits. Prove the theorem using the (S) part of Theorem 1, page 112.

C

19. Prove formula (Po) on page 112, using mathematical induction.

3–2 Continuous Functions

In Example 2 of Section 3–1, we considered the function

$$f: x \to \frac{3x^2}{x^3 + 4}$$

and showed that

$$\lim_{x \to 2} f(x) = 1.$$

By direct substitution, we find that

$$f(2) = \frac{3 \cdot 2^2}{2^3 + 4} = 1.$$

Because

$$\lim_{x \to 2} f(x) = f(2),$$

we say that f is *continuous at* 2.

> Let a be a number in the domain of f. Then f is **continuous at a** if and only if
>
> $$\lim_{x \to a} f(x) = f(a).$$
>
> If f is continuous at each number of a subset S of its domain, then f is **continuous on S.** **A continuous function** is one which is continuous at each number of its domain.

EXAMPLE 1. Show that $f: x \to 3 - 2|x - 1|$ is continuous at 1.

Solution: By substitution, we have $f(1) = 3 - 2|1 - 1| = 3$. As x approaches 1, $x - 1$ approaches 0 and, therefore, $|x - 1|$ approaches 0. Then, using properties (C), (K), and (D) of Theorem 1 in Section 3–1, we see that

$$\lim_{x \to 1} f(x) = \lim_{x \to 1} 3 - 2 \lim_{x \to 1} |x - 1| = 3 - 2 \cdot 0 = 3.$$

Since $\lim_{x \to 1} f(x) = 3 = f(1)$, f is continuous at 1. (Actually, f is continuous on $\mathcal{R}$.)

Neither $G: x \to \text{sgn } x$ nor $F: x \to |\text{sgn } x|$ (see page 111) is continuous at 0. We observed that $\lim_{x \to 0} G(x)$ does not exist; existence of the limit is one of the requirements of continuity. On the other hand, F *does* have a limit as x approaches 0: $\lim_{x \to 0} F(x) = 1$. But since $F(0) = 0$, the limit is not the "right" number. The graphs of the functions F and G [Figures 3–3(a) and (b)] have breaks in them. This sort of thing cannot happen in the case of continuous functions.

Graphs of functions continuous on $\mathcal{R}$ are unbroken curves. Indeed, if a function is continuous at each point of an interval or half-line, then the corresponding part of its graph is an unbroken curve. (Note that we are using the word "curve" in the general sense. Thus a line segment, for example, is considered to be a curve.) Figure 3–4 shows the graphs of some continuous functions.

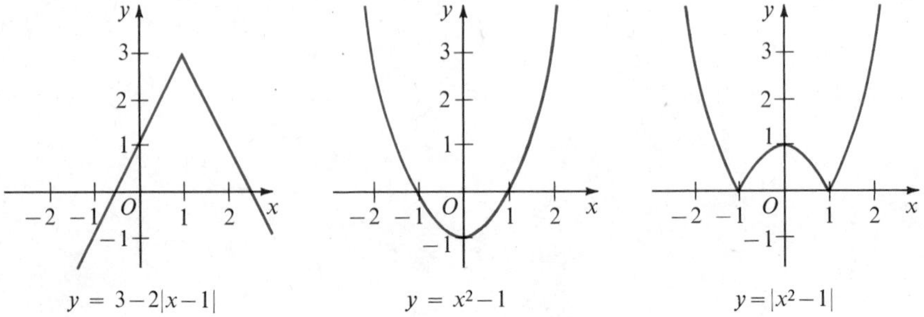

Figure 3–4

If we combine continuous functions arithmetically, the resulting function will be continuous, provided we take care to avoid zero denominators. We may prove this using Theorem 1 of Section 3–1.

Theorem 2.

Suppose f and g are continuous at a. Then cf (c a constant), $f + g$, $f - g$, and fg are continuous at a. If $g(a) \neq 0$, then $\dfrac{f}{g}$ is continuous at a.

Proof of the quotient case

By hypothesis,

$$\lim_{x \to a} f(x) = f(a) \quad \text{and} \quad \lim_{x \to a} g(x) = g(a) \neq 0.$$

Therefore, using the (Q) part of Theorem 1,

$$\lim_{x \to a} \left(\frac{f}{g}\right)(x) = \lim_{x \to a} \frac{f(x)}{g(x)} = \frac{\lim_{x \to a} f(x)}{\lim_{x \to a} g(x)} = \frac{f(a)}{g(a)} = \left(\frac{f}{g}\right)(a).$$

Most of the functions discussed in this book are continuous. For example, the special limits

$$\lim_{x \to a} x^n = a^n \quad \text{and} \quad \lim_{x \to a} b = b$$

let us know that the power functions $x \to x^n$ and the constant functions are continuous. Since polynomial functions are formed from these functions by multiplications and additions, Theorem 2 yields the following:

Corollary.

Every polynomial function is continuous.

EXAMPLE 2. Show that the function

$$\phi: x \to \frac{x^3 + 2x^2 - x - 6}{x^2 + x}$$

is continuous (at each number of its domain).

Solution: We see that $\phi = \dfrac{f}{g}$, where $f: x \to x^3 + 2x^2 - x - 6$ and $g: x \to x^2 + x$. Since f and g are polynomial functions, they are continuous (for all x), by the corollary to Theorem 2. Therefore, by Theorem 2, ϕ is continuous at every x for which $g(x) \neq 0$, that is, for all numbers except 0 and -1. But $\{x: x \neq 0 \text{ or } -1\}$ is the domain of ϕ, so ϕ is continuous at each number of its domain.

For the function ϕ of Example 2, we find that $\phi(1) = -2$ and $\phi(3) = 3$. Thus the points $(1, -2)$ and $(3, 3)$ are on the graph of ϕ. Let us consider the horizontal line $y = c$, where c is any number between $-2 = \phi(1)$ and $3 = \phi(3)$ [see Figure 3–5(a)]. We may not know just what the graph of

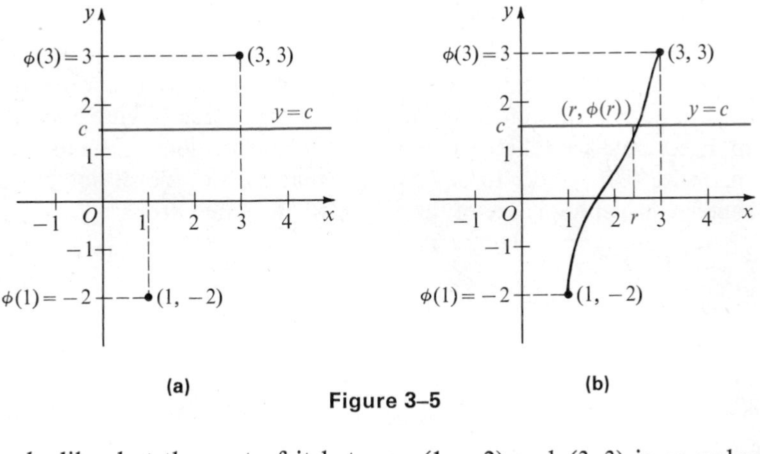

Figure 3–5

ϕ looks like, but the part of it between $(1, -2)$ and $(3, 3)$ is an unbroken curve because ϕ is continuous on the interval $\{x: 1 \leq x \leq 3\}$. Thus the graph of ϕ must intersect the line $y = c$ somewhere between $x = 1$ and $x = 3$, as indicated in Figure 3–5(b). That is, there is a number r between 1 and 3 such that $\phi(r) = c$. This behavior of ϕ illustrates an important property of functions that are continuous on an interval:

Theorem 3.

Let f be continuous on the interval $\{x\colon a \le x \le b\}$. Let c be any number between $f(a)$ and $f(b)$. Then there is a number r between a and b such that $f(r) = c$.

In other words, f "takes on" all values intermediate between $f(a)$ and $f(b)$. The property described in Theorem 3 is called the **Intermediate-Value Property.** (The theorem is proved in more advanced mathematics courses.)

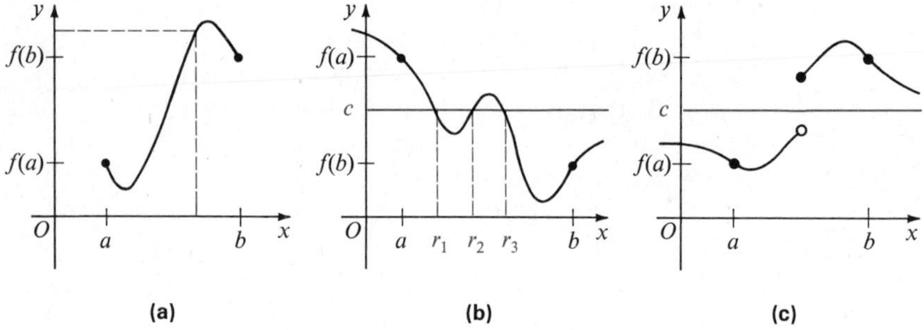

Figure 3–6

Notice that f may have values which are not between $f(a)$ and $f(b)$ [Figure 3–6(a)] and that a given value of c may be "taken on" more than once [Figure 3–6(b)]. If "continuous" is replaced by "defined" in the statement of Theorem 3, then the conclusion is not necessarily true [Figure 3–6(c)].

If in Theorem 3 we take f to be a polynomial function, $f(a)$ and $f(b)$ to have opposite signs, and c to be 0, we see that the Location Principle used in Chapter 2 is a special case of the Intermediate-Value Property.

ORAL EXERCISES

1. Does either of the following statements imply the other? Are the statements equivalent?

"$\lim\limits_{x\to a} f(x)$ exists." "f is continuous at a."

Discuss the continuity of the functions whose graphs are shown below.

2.

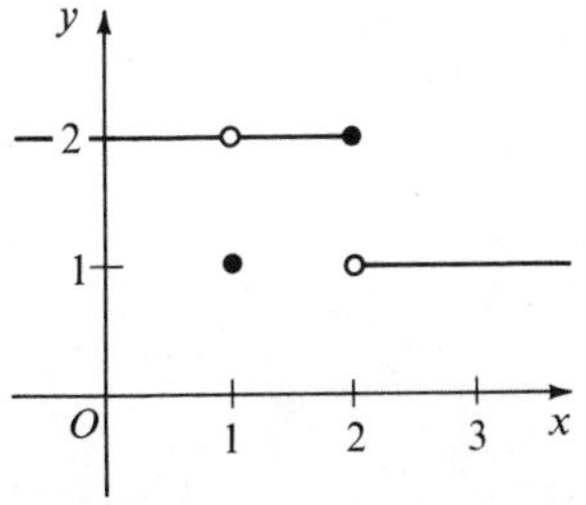

4.

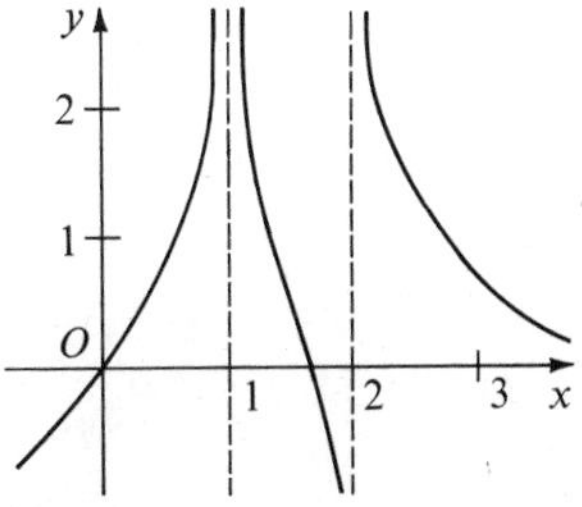

3.

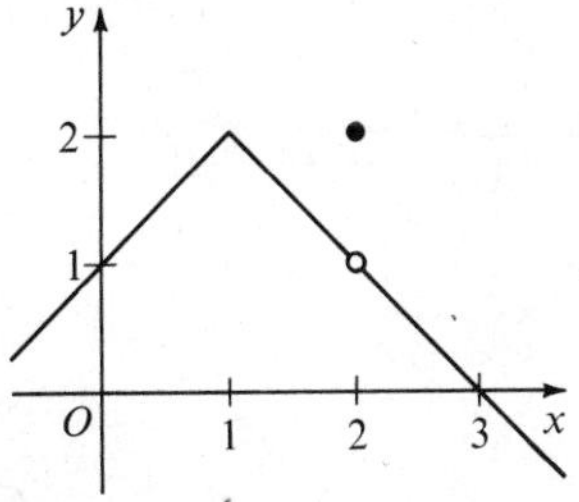

5.

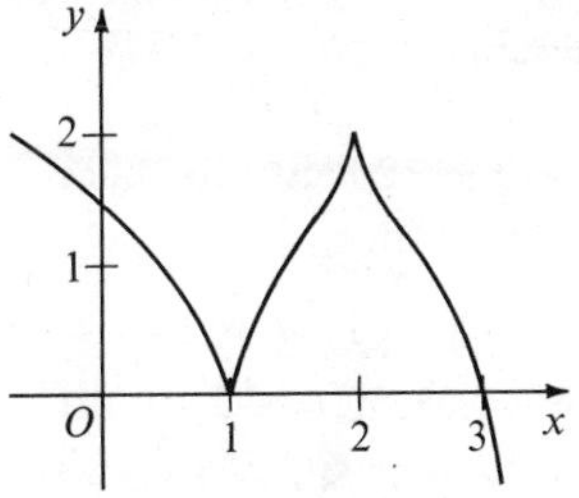

Discuss the truth or falsity of the following statements.

6. If f is known to be continuous at a, then we may evaluate $\lim_{x \to a} f(x)$ by substituting a for x in $f(x)$.

7. If when we substitute a for x in $f(x)$ we obtain $\lim_{x \to a} f(x)$, then f is continuous at a.

8. If when we substitute a for x in $f(x)$, the resulting expression does not name a number, then $\lim_{x \to a} f(x)$ does not exist.

WRITTEN EXERCISES

At what numbers, if any, do the following functions *fail* to be continuous?

A

1. $f\colon x \to x^4 + x^2 + 1$

2. $f\colon x \to x^2 - 4$

3. $f\colon x \to \dfrac{x}{x^2 + 4}$

4. $f\colon x \to \dfrac{x^2 - 1}{x^2 + 1}$

5. $f\colon x \to \operatorname{sgn}(x - 1)$

6. $f\colon x \to \operatorname{sgn}|x - 1|$

7. $f\colon x \to \begin{cases} x & \text{if } |x| \le 1 \\ 1 & \text{if } |x| > 1 \end{cases}$

8. $f\colon x \to \begin{cases} 1 & \text{if } |x| \le 1 \\ x & \text{if } |x| > 1 \end{cases}$

9. $f\colon x \to \begin{cases} x & \text{if } x \text{ is an integer} \\ -x & \text{if } x \text{ is not an integer} \end{cases}$

In Exercises 10, 11, and 12, draw the graph of a function defined on $\mathcal{R}$ which is not continuous at the given numbers but is continuous everywhere else.

10. 1, 2, 3 **11.** $-1, 0, 1$ **12.** $-1, -2, -3$

B **13.** Draw the graph of a function f having domain $\mathcal{R}$ such that $\lim_{x \to a} f(x)$ exists for every a, but such that f is not continuous at 2 and at -2.

Suppose that the functions f and g are continuous at a. Use Theorem 1, page 112, to prove the following:

14. $f + g$ is continuous at a.

15. $f - g$ is continuous at a.

16. fg is continuous at a.

17. Prove that any linear combination of continuous functions is continuous (see Exercise 17, page 114).

Exercises 18–22 illustrate Theorem 3, page 118, and the notation of that theorem is used. Find an r, given

18. $f: x \to x + 1$; $a = 1$, $b = 4$, $c = 3$

19. $f: x \to x^2$; $a = -2$, $b = 0$, $c = 1$

20. $f: x \to x^3 - 4x + 1$; $a = -3$, $b = 3$, $c = 1$

21. $f: x \to \dfrac{x+4}{x}$; $a = 1$, $b = 4$, $c = 3$

22. $f: x \to x^2$; $a = 0$, $b > 0$, $c = \frac{1}{2}[f(a) + f(b)]$

C **23.** Draw the graph of a function which is *not* continuous in an interval $\{x: a \leq x \leq b\}$, but which nevertheless has the Intermediate-Value Property with respect to this interval.

24. The quotient of two polynomial functions is a **rational function** provided the denominator is not the zero function. Show that a rational function is continuous at each number of its domain.

Differentiation

3–3 Slopes and Derivatives

We shall introduce the concept of *derivative* by considering the problem of describing the direction of a curve. Suppose we have a "smooth" curve S in a Cartesian plane, and we consider a point P on it (Figure 3–7). The curve S appears to have a definite direction at P: the direction of the line T which is tangent to S at P. It seems natural, therefore, to say that the *slope* of S at P is the same as the slope of T. We shall show how to find (actually, how to *define*) this slope (if it exists) for the case in which S is the graph of a function.

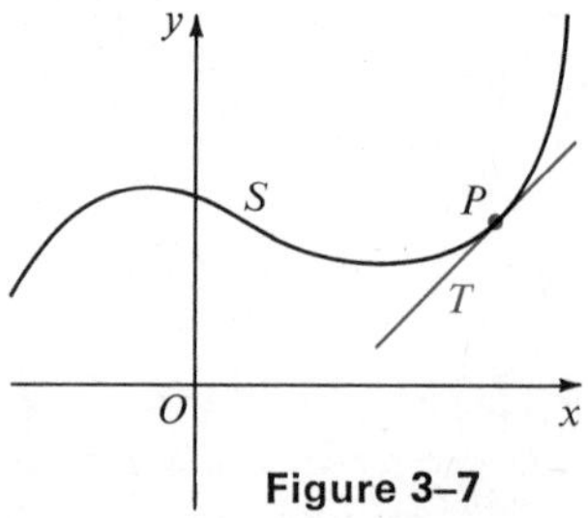

Figure 3–7

First, let us look at a specific example. Let S be the parabola which is the graph of the function

$$f\colon x \to x^2 - 2,$$

and consider the point $P(1, -1)$ on S (Figure 3–8). Let Q be any point of S different from P. If the abscissa of Q is x, then the ordinate of Q is $f(x) = x^2 - 2$. The slope of the line L_Q determined by $P(1, -1)$ and $Q(x, x^2 - 2)$ is

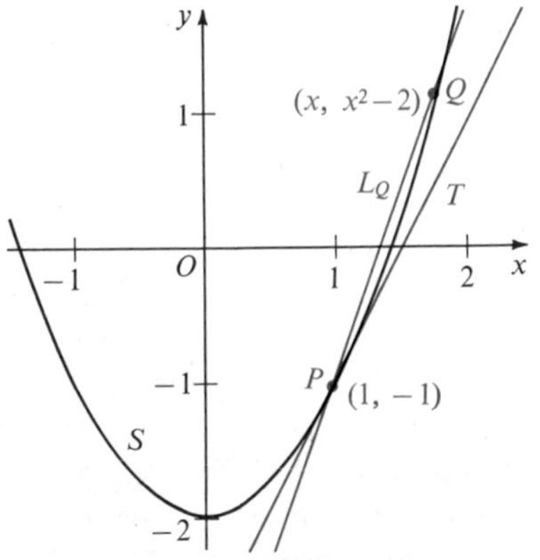

Figure 3–8

$$\frac{f(x) - f(1)}{x - 1} = \frac{(x^2 - 2) - (-1)}{x - 1}$$

$$= \frac{x^2 - 1}{x - 1} = x + 1 \quad (\text{since } x \neq 1).$$

It seems reasonable to assume that as Q approaches P along S, the slope of L_Q approaches what we would like the slope of S at P to be. Now as Q approaches P, the abscissa x of Q approaches 1. We therefore *define* the slope of S at P to be the number

$$\lim_{x \to 1} \frac{f(x) - f(1)}{x - 1} = \lim_{x \to 1} (x + 1) = 2.$$

At the same time, we *define* the tangent line T to S at P to be the line through P having slope 2. Thus (recall Equation (*) on page 56) an equation of T is

$$y - (-1) = 2(x - 1), \quad \text{or} \quad 2x - y = 3.$$

EXAMPLE 1. Using the methods employed above, (**a**) find the slope of the graph of $f\colon x \to x^2 - 2$ at the point P having abscissa a. Then (**b**) find an equation of the line tangent to the graph at $(-3, 7)$.

Solution: **a.** The point P has coordinates $(a, f(a))$, or $(a, a^2 - 2)$. If Q is a point of the graph different from P, then Q has coordinates $(x, f(x))$, or $(x, x^2 - 2)$, where $x \neq a$. The slope of the line determined by P and Q is

$$\frac{f(x) - f(a)}{x - a} = \frac{(x^2 - 2) - (a^2 - 2)}{x - a} = \frac{x^2 - a^2}{x - a} = x + a.$$

Therefore, the slope of the graph of f at P is

$$\lim_{x \to a} \frac{f(x) - f(a)}{x - a} = \lim_{x \to a} (x + a) = 2a.$$

(Solution continued)

b. By setting $a = -3$ in the expression just obtained, we find that the slope of the graph at $(-3, 7)$ is $2 \cdot (-3) = -6$. Therefore, an equation of the line tangent to the graph at $(-3, 7)$ is

$$y - 7 = -6[x - (-3)], \quad \text{or} \quad 6x + y + 11 = 0.$$

The method used above can be applied to a large variety of functions. Let f be any function and $P(a, f(a))$ be a point on its graph (Figure 3–9). Let $Q(x, f(x))$ be any point on the graph different from P. The slope of the line determined by P and Q is the so-called **difference quotient**

$$\frac{f(x) - f(a)}{x - a}.$$

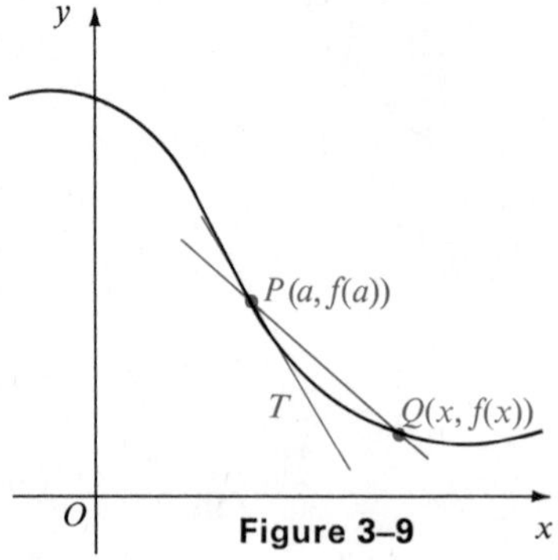

Figure 3–9

If this difference quotient approaches some number as Q approaches P, that is, if

$$\lim_{x \to a} \frac{f(x) - f(a)}{x - a} \tag{*}$$

exists, then this number is defined to be the **slope of the graph of f at the point $(a, f(a))$.**

Because the limit of the difference quotient (*) has many uses in addition to describing the direction of the graph of f, it has been given a name and a special notation:

> Let f be a function and a be a number in its domain. Then the **derivative of f at a** is the number
>
> $$f'(a) = \lim_{x \to a} \frac{f(x) - f(a)}{x - a},$$
>
> provided this limit exists.

The symbol $f'(a)$ is read "f prime of a."

EXAMPLE 2. For the function $f: x \to x^3$, find

a. the derivative of f at a;
b. the slope of the graph of f at $(\frac{2}{3}, \frac{8}{27})$.

Solution: **a.** The difference quotient is

$$\frac{f(x) - f(a)}{x - a} = \frac{x^3 - a^3}{x - a}$$
$$= \frac{(x - a)(x^2 + ax + a^2)}{x - a} = x^2 + ax + a^2.$$

Therefore,

$$f'(a) = \lim_{x \to a} \frac{f(x) - f(a)}{x - a} = \lim_{x \to a} (x^2 + ax + a^2)$$
$$= a^2 + a \cdot a + a^2 = 3a^2.$$

b. Since $f'(a)$ is the slope of the graph at $(a, f(a))$, the slope at $(\frac{2}{3}, \frac{8}{27})$ is $3 \cdot (\frac{2}{3})^2 = \frac{4}{3}$.

A function which has a derivative at a is said to be **differentiable at *a*.** If a function is differentiable at each number of a set, then it is said to be **differentiable on that set.** A **differentiable function** is one which is differentiable at each number of its domain. For example, the function $f\colon x \to x^3$ is differentiable because in Example 2(a) we showed that $f'(a)$ exists for every a in the domain $\mathcal{R}$ of f. The process of finding the derivative of a function is called **differentiation.**

EXAMPLE 3. Show that $f\colon x \to |x - 2|$ is not differentiable at 2.

Solution: The difference quotient is

$$\frac{f(x) - f(2)}{x - 2} = \frac{|x - 2| - |2 - 2|}{x - 2} = \frac{|x - 2|}{x - 2}.$$

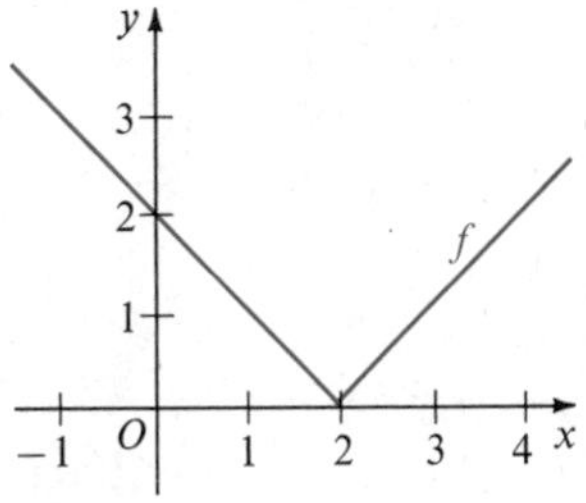

Because of the meaning of absolute value,

$$|x - 2| = x - 2 \quad \text{if} \quad x > 2,$$

and

$$|x - 2| = -(x - 2) \quad \text{if} \quad x < 2.$$

Therefore,

$$\frac{f(x) - f(2)}{x - 2} = \begin{cases} 1 & \text{if } x > 2 \\ -1 & \text{if } x < 2. \end{cases}$$

Hence $\lim_{x \to 2} \frac{f(x) - f(2)}{x - 2}$ does not exist. The nonexistence of the derivative of f at 2 shows up in its graph, which has a sharp corner at (2, 0).

Since the graph of a differentiable function has a well-defined tangent line at each point, it can have *no sharp corners;* and in light of the following theorem we may say: *The graph of a differentiable function* having as domain $\mathcal{R}$, a half-line, or an interval *is a smooth unbroken curve.*

Example 3 shows that a continuous function may fail to be differentiable. Every differentiable function, however, is continuous:

Theorem 4.

If the function f is differentiable at a, then f is continuous at a.

Proof

We wish to show that $\lim_{x \to a} f(x) = f(a)$. To do this, we first note that if $x \neq a$, then

$$f(x) = f(a) + \frac{f(x) - f(a)}{x - a} \cdot (x - a), \qquad (*)$$

because the right-hand side of the equation reduces algebraically to $f(x)$. Let us see what happens as x approaches a. Since $f(a)$ is a constant, $\lim_{x \to a} f(a) = f(a)$. Since f is differentiable at a,

$$\lim_{x \to a} \frac{f(x) - f(a)}{x - a} = f'(a).$$

Clearly, $\lim_{x \to a} (x - a) = 0$. Thus from (*), we have

$$\lim_{x \to a} f(x) = f(a) + f'(a) \cdot 0 = f(a).$$

EXAMPLE 4. For the function $f\colon x \to \dfrac{1}{x^2}$, find $f'(x)$, the derivative of f at x.

Solution: Since the symbol x is already being used, we use another symbol, z, say, in setting up the difference quotient: $\dfrac{f(z) - f(x)}{z - x}$. We regard x as fixed and let z approach x. We have

$$\frac{f(z) - f(x)}{z - x} = \frac{\frac{1}{z^2} - \frac{1}{x^2}}{z - x} = \frac{x^2 - z^2}{x^2 z^2 (z - x)}$$

$$= \frac{(x + z)(x - z)}{x^2 z^2 (z - x)} = -\frac{x + z}{x^2 z^2}.$$

Therefore,

$$f'(x) = \lim_{z \to x} \frac{f(z) - f(x)}{z - x} = \lim_{z \to x} \left(-\frac{x + z}{x^2 z^2} \right)$$

$$= -\frac{x + x}{x^2 x^2} = -\frac{2x}{x^4} = -\frac{2}{x^3}.$$

A variable, like z above, which does not appear after "passing to the limit" is called a **dummy variable.**

ORAL EXERCISES

The diagram below shows the graph of a function f. The red lines are tangent to the graph.

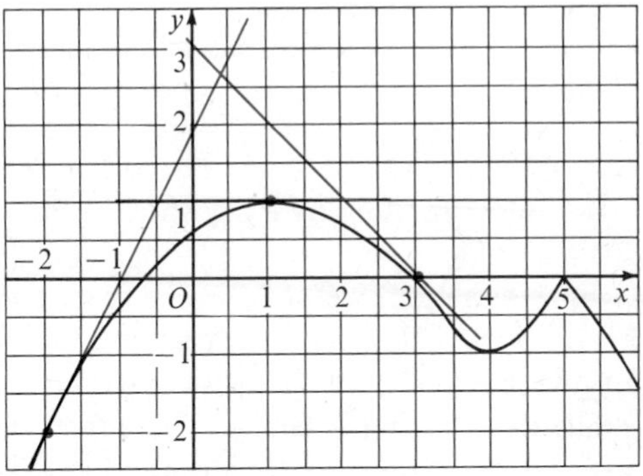

1. What is $f'(-2)$?
2. What is $f'(1)$?
3. What is $f'(3)$?
4. For what values of x is $f'(x) = 0$?
5. Does f appear to have a derivative at 5?
6. What algebraic sign does $f'(x)$ have if $-2 < x < 1$?
7. What algebraic sign does $f'(x)$ have if $1 < x < 4$?
8. Discuss the statement, "If a line intersects a curve in just one point, then the line is tangent to the curve."
9. Discuss the statement, "If a line is tangent to a curve, then the line intersects the curve in just one point."

WRITTEN EXERCISES

In Exercises 1–12, use the definition of a derivative to find f′(a) for an arbitrary number a in the domain of f.

A

1. $f\colon x \to x^2$
2. $f\colon x \to -x^2$
3. $f\colon x \to 4 - x^2$
4. $f\colon x \to 2x^2 + 3$
5. $f\colon x \to x^2 - x$
6. $f\colon x \to 4x - x^2$
7. $f\colon x \to 2x^3$
8. $f\colon x \to x^3 - x$
9. $f\colon x \to x^3 + x^2$
10. $f\colon x \to x^3 + x - 2$
11. $f\colon x \to \dfrac{1}{x}$
12. $f\colon x \to \dfrac{1}{x} - 1$

13–24. In Exercises 1–12, find **(a)** the slope of the graph of f at the point on it having abscissa 1 and **(b)** an equation of the tangent line at this point.

B

25. We know from Chapter 2 that the graph of the linear function $f\colon x \to mx + b$ is a line with slope m. By finding $f'(x)$, show that the slope of the graph *at each point* on it is m. (*Note:* You will find that the difference quotient has a constant value; its limit must be this constant.)

In Exercises 26–29, show that f fails to have a derivative at 0. Draw the graph of each function.

26. $f\colon x \to |x|$
27. $f\colon x \to |x| - 1$

C **28.** $f\colon x \to x + |x|$ **29.** $f\colon x \to |x| - x$

30. If $f\colon x \to \sqrt{x}$, find $f'(x)$ for $x > 0$. (*Hints:* Multiply numerator and denominator of the difference quotient $\dfrac{f(z) - f(x)}{z - x}$ by $\sqrt{z} + \sqrt{x}$. Use the fact that $\sqrt{z} \to \sqrt{x}$ as $z \to x$.) Does f have a derivative at 0?

31. If $f\colon x \to x|x|$, find **(a)** $f'(0)$, **(b)** $f'(x)$ for $x > 0$, and **(c)** $f'(x)$ for $x < 0$. Then **(d)** draw the graphs of the functions f and f' in the same coordinate plane.

3–4 Derivatives of Polynomial Functions

In this section, we prove some results which enable us to avoid the labor of using the definition every time we wish to find the derivative of a function. In giving proofs, we shall use the limit facts stated in Section 3–1 without explicitly referring to them. These facts were stated using x as the "dummy variable," but they are equally valid if some other symbol, like h or z, names the variable which is "doing the approaching."

The first result we shall prove enables us to find the derivative of the "power function" $f\colon x \to x^n$.

Theorem 5.

If $f(x) = x^n$, where n is a positive integer, then $f'(x) = nx^{n-1}$.

Proof

The difference quotient is

$$\frac{f(z) - f(x)}{z - x} = \frac{z^n - x^n}{z - x}.$$

We make a change of notation in order that we may use the binomial theorem: Let $h = z - x$. Then $z = x + h$, and the difference quotient takes the form

$$\begin{aligned}
&\frac{f(x+h) - f(x)}{h} \\
&= \frac{(x+h)^n - x^n}{h} \\
&= \frac{1}{h}\left[\left(x^n + nx^{n-1}h + \frac{n(n-1)}{2}x^{n-2}h^2 + \cdots + h^n\right) - x^n\right] \\
&= nx^{n-1} + \frac{n(n-1)}{2}x^{n-2}h + \cdots + h^{n-1}. \qquad (*)
\end{aligned}$$

As z approaches x, h approaches 0, and each term of (*) except the first approaches 0 because it contains h as a factor. Therefore,

$$f'(x) = \lim_{z \to x} \frac{f(z) - f(x)}{z - x} = \lim_{h \to 0} \frac{f(x + h) - f(x)}{h} = nx^{n-1}.$$

Thus, for example, if $f\colon x \to x^6$, then $f(x) = x^6$, and $f'(x) = 6x^{6-1} = 6x^5$. We leave as Exercise 20, page 130, the proof of the fact that *the derivative of a constant function is zero everywhere.*

The next two theorems state results we would expect to be true. The first asserts that the derivative of the sum of two functions is the sum of their derivatives.

Theorem 6.

If the functions f and g are differentiable at x, then the function $f + g$ is differentiable at x and $(f + g)'(x) = f'(x) + g'(x)$.

Proof

Let $s = f + g$. Then the difference quotient is

$$\frac{s(z) - s(x)}{z - x} = \frac{(f + g)(z) - (f + g)(x)}{z - x}$$
$$= \frac{[f(z) + g(z)] - [f(x) + g(x)]}{z - x}$$
$$= \frac{f(z) - f(x)}{z - x} + \frac{g(z) - g(x)}{z - x}.$$

By hypothesis,

$$\lim_{z \to x} \frac{f(z) - f(x)}{z - x} = f'(x) \quad \text{and} \quad \lim_{z \to x} \frac{g(z) - g(x)}{z - x} = g'(x).$$

Therefore,

$$\lim_{z \to x} \left[\frac{f(z) - f(x)}{z - x} + \frac{g(z) - g(x)}{z - x} \right] = \lim_{z \to x} \frac{s(z) - s(x)}{z - x} \text{ exists and}$$

$$s'(x) = (f + g)'(x) = f'(x) + g'(x).$$

The result in Theorem 6 extends, of course, to $(f + g + h)'(x)$, and so on.

The next theorem tells us that the derivative of a constant times a function is the constant times the derivative of the function. We leave its proof as Exercise 21, page 130.

Theorem 7.

If the function f is differentiable at x and c is a constant, then the function cf is differentiable at x and $(cf)'(x) = cf'(x)$.

For example, to find the derivative of $g\colon x \to 5x^6$, we mentally let $c = 5$ and $f(x) = x^6$, and then use Theorems 7 and 5:

$$g'(x) = (cf)'(x) = cf'(x) = 5 \cdot 6x^5 = 30x^5.$$

In a problem as simple as this, you should be able to write down the final answer immediately.

The results stated thus far in this section enable us to find the derivative of any polynomial function very easily. Thus if

$$p(x) = 2x^5 + x^4 - 3x^2 + 2x - 7,$$

then

$$\begin{aligned} p'(x) &= 2 \cdot 5x^4 + 4x^3 - 3 \cdot 2x + 2 \cdot 1 \\ &= 10x^4 + 4x^3 - 6x + 2. \end{aligned}$$

In general, if

$$f(x) = a_0x^n + a_1x^{n-1} + \cdots + a_{n-2}x^2 + a_{n-1}x + a_n,$$

then

$$f'(x) = na_0x^{n-1} + (n-1)a_1x^{n-2} + \cdots + 2a_{n-2}x + a_{n-1}.$$

EXAMPLE 1. For the polynomial function

$$f\colon x \to x^4 - 2x^3 - 3x^2 + 7x + 3,$$

find **(a)** $f(2)$ and **(b)** $f'(2)$.

Solution: **a.** Using synthetic substitution, we have

2	1	−2	−3	7	3
	1	0	−3	1	5 = $f(2)$

b. Since $f'(x) = 4x^3 - 6x^2 - 6x + 7$ is a polynomial, we may use synthetic substitution again:

2	4	−6	−6	7
	4	2	−2	3 = $f\,(2)$

Let us try the experiment of taking the coefficients of the quotient in Part (a) of Example 1 and substituting 2 synthetically:

2	1	0	−3	1
	1	2	1	3

It is not a coincidence that the remainder, 3, is $f'(2)$. We can combine the work just done with Part (a) of Example 1 as follows:

$$\begin{array}{r|rrrrl} 2 & 1 & -2 & -3 & 7 & 3 \\ & 1 & 0 & -3 & 1 & 5 = f(2) \\ & 1 & 2 & 1 & 3 = f'(2) & \end{array}$$

We shall indicate why this process works for the general third-degree polynomial function by considering

$$f\colon x \to a_0x^3 + a_1x^2 + a_2x + a_3, \quad a_0 \neq 0,$$

and its derivative

$$f'(x) = 3a_0x^2 + 2a_1x + a_2.$$

When the process is carried out using the number c, we obtain

$$\begin{array}{l|llll} c & a_0 & a_1 & a_2 & a_3 \\ & a_0 & a_0c + a_1 & a_0c^2 + a_1c + a_2 & a_0c^3 + a_1c^2 + a_2c + a_3 = f(c) \\ & a_0 & 2a_0c + a_1 & 3a_0c^2 + 2a_1c + a_2 = f'(c) & \end{array}$$

For polynomials in general, this "double division" process gives (see page 86)

$$\begin{aligned} f(x) &= (x - a)Q(x) + R = (x - a)Q(x) + f(a) \\ &= (x - a)[(x - a)Q_1(x) + R_1] + f(a), \end{aligned}$$

so that for $x \neq a$,

$$\frac{f(x) - f(a)}{x - a} = (x - a)Q_1(x) + R_1,$$

whence

$$\begin{aligned} f'(a) &= \lim_{x \to a} \frac{f(x) - f(a)}{x - a} = \lim_{x \to a} [(x - a)Q_1(x) + R_1] \\ &= [\lim_{x \to a} (x - a)] \cdot \lim_{x \to a} Q_1(x) + \lim_{x \to a} R_1 = 0 \cdot Q_1(a) + R_1 = R_1. \end{aligned}$$

This process may be used either to find the values of a polynomial function and its derivative for a given number or to check these values if they are obtained in some other way.

ORAL EXERCISES

In Exercises 1–12, $f(x)$ is given. Find $f'(x)$.

1. x^2
2. $3x^2$
3. 2
4. x
5. $2x + 3$
6. $2x^5 + 3$
7. $4 - x^2$
8. $x^2 + 2x$
9. $4x - x^2$
10. $x^3 - 2x^2$
11. $x^3 + 2x^2 + 3x + 4$
12. $x^{100} + 1$

13. What can you say about the derivative of a linear function?

14. What can you say about the derivative of a quadratic function?

WRITTEN EXERCISES

In Exercises 1–6, (a) find an expression for $f'(x)$. Then (b) for the given number a, find $f(a)$ and $f'(a)$ by two methods: direct substitution and the "double division" process.

A

1. $f\colon x \rightarrow x^2 + 2x + 3,\ a = -2$
2. $f\colon x \rightarrow 2 + 3x - x^2,\ a = 4$
3. $f\colon x \rightarrow x^3 + 3x^2 - 9x - 2,\ a = 2$
4. $f\colon x \rightarrow x^3 - 3x^2 + 6x - 8,\ a = 3$
5. $f\colon x \rightarrow x^4 + 4x^3 + 4x^2 - 7,\ a = 1$
6. $f\colon x \rightarrow x^4 + 4x^3 + 10,\ a = -2$

7–12. For the functions f in Exercises 1–6, find an equation of the line tangent to the graph of f at the point $(a, f(a))$.

B

13–18. For the functions f in Exercises 1–6, find the coordinates of the point(s) on the graph of f, if any, at which the tangent line is horizontal.

19. Carry out the details of the proof of Theorem 5 for $n = 5$.

20. Prove that the derivative of a constant function is zero.

21. Prove Theorem 7.

22. For the general quartic function $f\colon x \rightarrow a_0x^4 + a_1x^3 + a_2x^2 + a_3x + a_4$,
    a. find $f'(x)$;
    b. find $f(c)$ and $f'(c)$ by direct substitution;
    c. verify that the "double division" process for finding $f(c)$ and $f'(c)$ works in this case.

C

23. Let f be a differentiable function. Find an equation for the line tangent to the graph of f at the point $(a, f(a))$.

24. Find equations of two lines passing through $(0, 1)$ and tangent to the graph of $f\colon x \rightarrow x^2 - 3x + 5$. (*Hint:* Use Exercise 23.)

25. Prove that if f and g are differentiable at x, then $(f - g)'(x) = f'(x) - g'(x)$.

In Exercises 26 and 27, assume that f is a polynomial function.

26. Prove that if f' is a nonzero constant function, then f is a nonconstant linear function.

27. Prove that if f' is a nonconstant linear function, then f is a quadratic function.

28. Use the fact that

$$z^n - x^n = (z - x)(z^{n-1} + z^{n-2}x + z^{n-3}x^2 + \cdots + zx^{n-2} + x^{n-1})$$

to prove Theorem 5.

29. Show that if $f\colon x \to (ax + b)^n$, then $f'(x) = na(ax + b)^{n-1}$. (*Hint:* After setting up the difference quotient, use the identity given in Exercise 28, with $(az + b)$ replacing z and $(ax + b)$ replacing x.)

3–5 Graphs of Polynomial Functions

Although we shall graph only polynomial functions in this section, the definitions, theorems, and many of the methods used apply to all differentiable functions.

We know that the graph of a function which is differentiable on $\mathcal{R}$ is an unbroken curve which has a tangent line at each point. Let f be such a function and let c be a real number. Then one of the following is true:

1. $f'(c) > 0$. In this case, the tangent line at the point $(c, f(c))$ has *positive* slope, and therefore the part of the graph near $(c, f(c))$ *rises* as x increases. Figure 3–10 shows some possibilities. Note that in Part (c) the curve *crosses* its tangent at $(c, f(c))$.

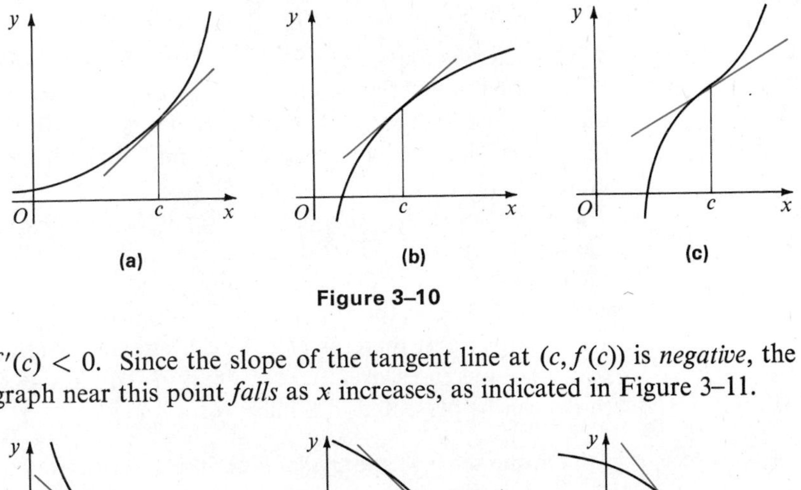

Figure 3–10

2. $f'(c) < 0$. Since the slope of the tangent line at $(c, f(c))$ is *negative*, the graph near this point *falls* as x increases, as indicated in Figure 3–11.

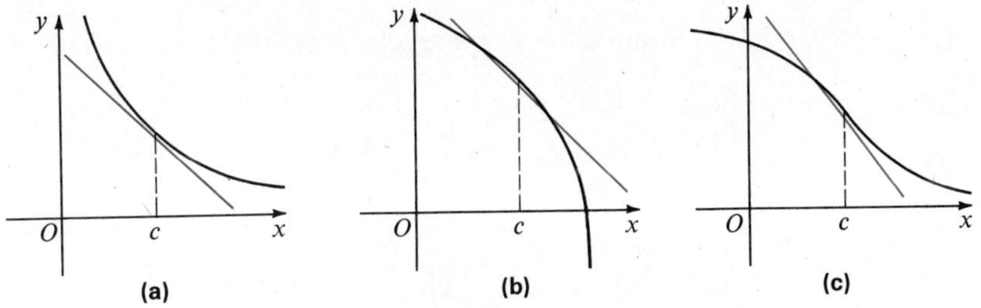

Figure 3–11

3. $f'(c) = 0$. In this case the tangent line at $(c, f(c))$ is *horizontal*, and the point $(c, f(c))$ is called a **critical point** of the graph. Figure 3–12 shows some possibilities for the behavior of the graph near a critical point.

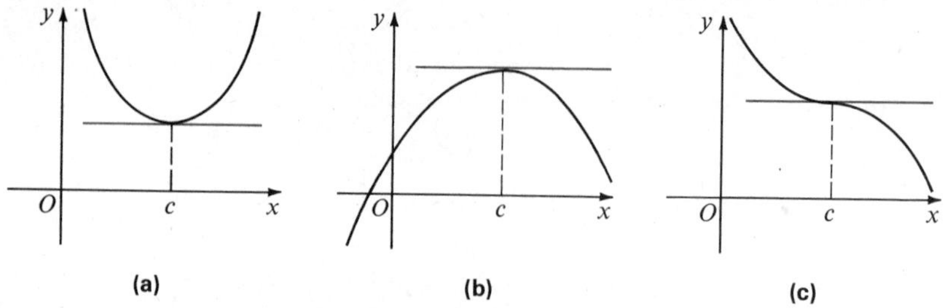

Figure 3–12

The next example illustrates how we may use these ideas in graphing a polynomial function.

EXAMPLE 1. For the function

$$f: x \to x^3 - 3x^2 + 1,$$

a. find the critical points of the graph;
b. find where the graph rises and where it falls;
c. draw the graph.

Solution: **a.** $f'(x) = 3x^2 - 6x = 3x(x - 2)$. The abscissas of the critical points are the zeros of the derivative function f', that is, 0 and 2. Therefore, the critical points are (0, 1) and (2, −3), as you see by substituting 0 and 2 for x in the formula for f.

b. The abscissas of the critical points separate the x-axis into the sets $\{x: x < 0\}$, $\{x: 0 < x < 2\}$, and $\{x: x > 2\}$. On each of these sets, $f'(x)$ is either always positive or always negative. If $x < 0$, for example, both factors of $(3x)(x - 2)$ are negative, and therefore $f'(x) > 0$, and the graph of f rises as x increases over the set $\{x: x < 0\}$. The answer to (**b**) can be presented in tabular form:

On the set	the sign of $f'(x)$ is	and the graph of f
$\{x: x < 0\}$	positive	rises
$\{x: 0 < x < 2\}$	negative	falls
$\{x: x > 2\}$	positive	rises

c. The graph of f may be drawn using a very short table of values. The first two entries, the critical point data, are the most important. The remaining entries are included to obtain information about the x-intercepts.

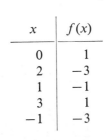

x	$f(x)$
0	1
2	-3
1	-1
3	1
-1	-3

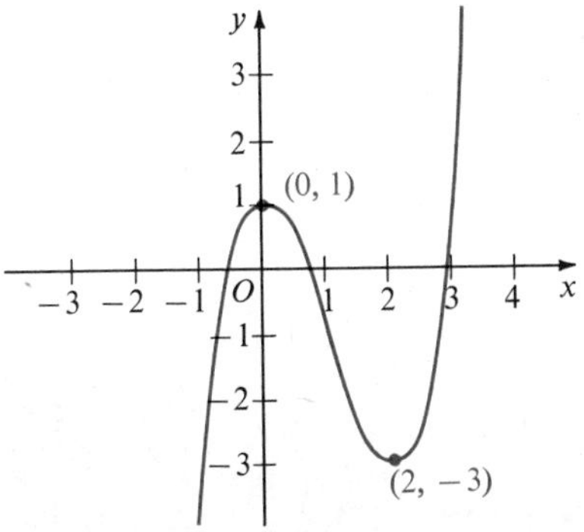

In Example 1, the critical point (0, 1) is higher than other *nearby* points of the graph. It is called a *relative maximum point*, and the function f is said to have a *relative maximum*, $f(0) = 1$, when $x = 0$. Similarly, f has a *relative minimum*, $f(2) = -3$, when $x = 2$.

More precisely, a function f has a **relative maximum,** $f(c)$, at c if there are numbers a and b, $a < c$ and $b > c$, such that $f(x) \leq f(c)$ whenever $a < x < b$. A function f has a **relative minimum,** $f(c)$, at c if there are numbers a and b, $a < c$ and $b > c$, such that $f(x) \geq f(c)$ whenever $a < x < b$.

Graphical evidence strongly suggests the truth of the next theorem; an analytic proof is indicated in Exercises 18 and 19, pages 136–137.

Theorem 8.

If the differentiable function f is defined on both sides of c and has a relative extremum at c, then $f'(c) = 0$.

It may happen that $f'(c) = 0$ but that f does not have a relative extremum at c.

EXAMPLE 2. For the function $f: x \rightarrow x^4 - 4x^3 + 10$,

a. find the critical points of the graph;
b. find where the graph rises and where it falls;
c. draw the graph;
d. determine the relative maxima and minima of the function.

Solution: In (**a**), (**b**), and (**c**), we use the method of Example 1.

a. $f'(x) = 4x^3 - 12x^2$
$\quad = 4x^2(x - 3).$

Therefore, $f'(x) = 0$ if $x = 0$ or $x = 3$, and the critical points are (0, 10) and (3, -17).

(Solution continued)

b.

On the set	the sign of $f'(x)$ is	and the graph of f
$\{x: x < 0\}$	negative	falls
$\{x: 0 < x < 3\}$	negative	falls
$\{x: x > 3\}$	positive	rises

c.

x	$f(x)$
0	10
3	−17
1	7
2	−6
4	10

These are the most important entries. (0 and 3)

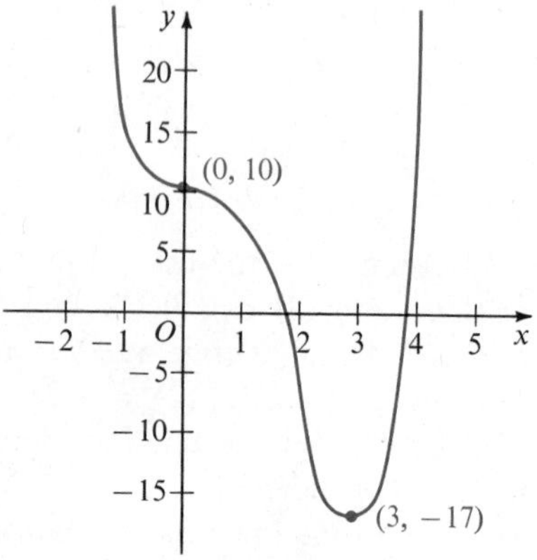

The general shape of the graph can be determined by plotting the two critical points and using the information in (**b**). The last three entries in the table of values were included to gain information about the x-intercepts.

d. We see from the graph that f has a relative minimum, −17, at 3. The function has *no* relative maxima. (We notice that the critical point (0, 10) is not a relative extremum.)

In Section 4–1, we shall give some nongraphical tests for relative maxima and minima.

When we formalize the idea of a rising or falling graph, we obtain the concept of an increasing or decreasing function: A function f is **increasing** on an interval or half-line S if for any two numbers x_1 and x_2 of S with $x_1 < x_2$, we have $f(x_1) < f(x_2)$; f is **decreasing** on S if for any two numbers x_1 and x_2 of S with $x_1 < x_2$, we have $f(x_1) > f(x_2)$. (See Figure 3–13.)

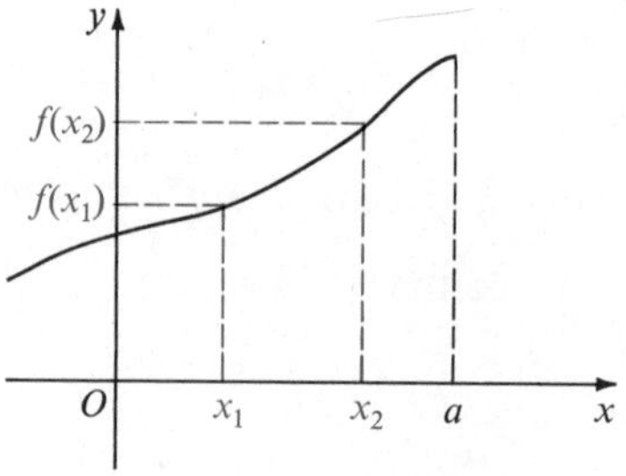

f is increasing on the half-line $\{x: x<a\}$

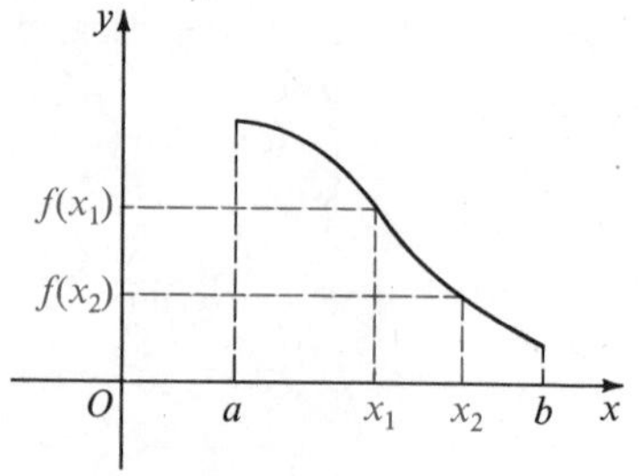

f is decreasing on the interval $\{x: a<x<b\}$

Figure 3–13

Graphical evidence suggests that the following is true (see Exercises 21 and 22, page 137).

Theorem 9.

If $f'(x) > 0$ on an interval or half-line S, then f is increasing on S. If $f'(x) < 0$ on S, then f is decreasing on S.

In Example 2, f is decreasing on the half-line $\{x: x < 0\}$ and on the interval $\{x: 0 < x < 3\}$. It is also decreasing on the entire half-line $\{x: x < 3\}$ even though $f'(0) = 0$. It is increasing on the half-line $\{x: x > 3\}$.

ORAL EXERCISES

The graphs of some functions f are shown below. Assume that all critical points have *integer* coordinates. In each case,

a. give the coordinates of the critical points;
b. give the relative maximum and relative minimum values of f;
c. describe the sets on which f is increasing and on which f is decreasing.

1.

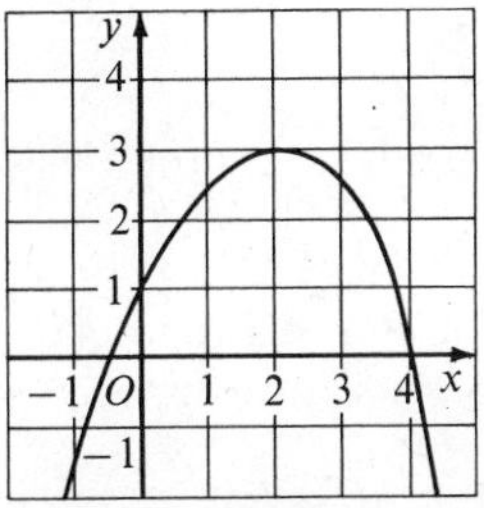

2.

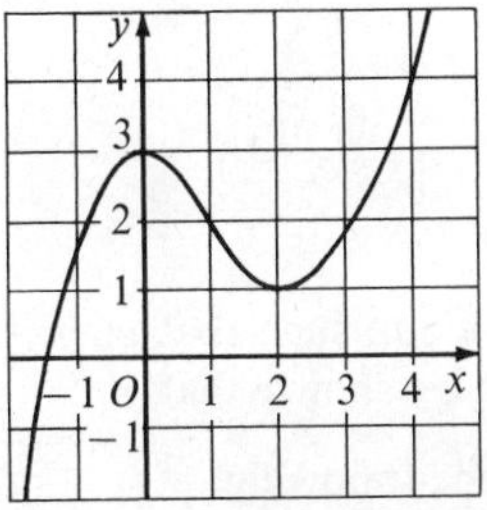

3.

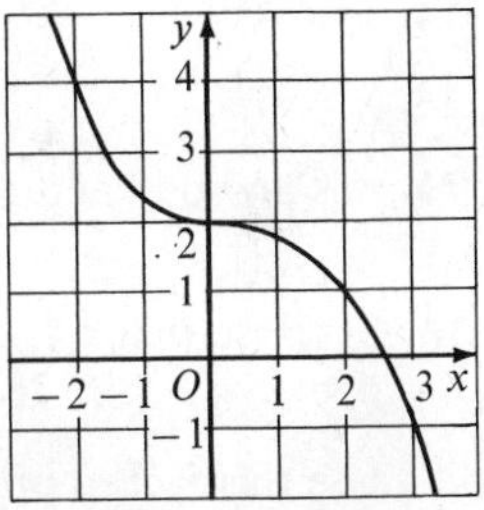

4.

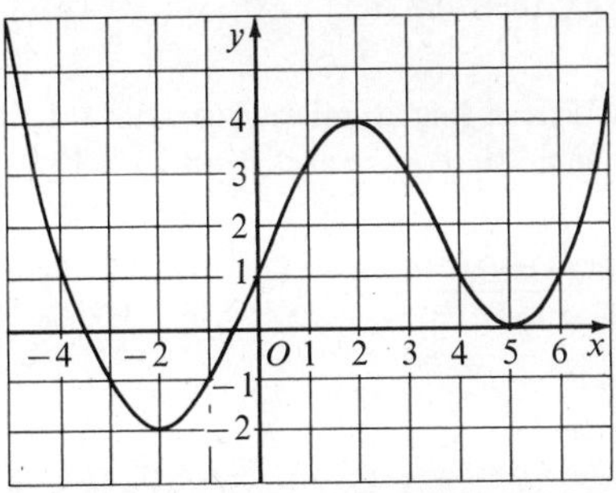

5.

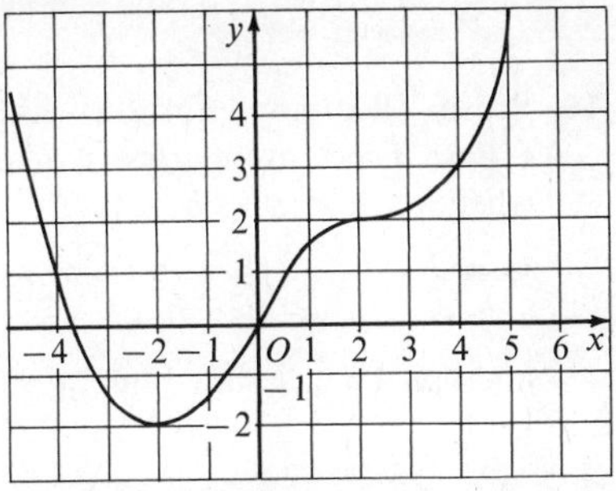

WRITTEN EXERCISES

For each of the functions given in Exercises 1–10,

a. find the critical points of the graph;
b. find where the graph rises and where it falls;
c. draw the graph of the function;
d. find the relative maxima and minima of the function, and where these occur.

A

1. $f\colon x \to x^2 - 1$
2. $f\colon x \to 2x - x^2$
3. $f\colon x \to x^3 - 3x$
4. $f\colon x \to x^3 + 3x^2 - 1$
5. $f\colon x \to x^3 + x$
6. $f\colon x \to x^3 + 1$
7. $f\colon x \to x^3 - x^2 - x$
8. $f\colon x \to x^4 - 4x^2$
9. $f\colon x \to x^4 - 4x$
10. $f\colon x \to x^4 + 4x^3 + 7$

B

11. Sketch the graph of a function which is differentiable on $\mathcal{R}$ and has a relative minimum which is greater than one of its relative maxima.
12. What is the greatest number of relative extrema that a polynomial function of degree n, $n > 0$, can have? Explain.
13. Explain why the graph of every polynomial function of even degree must have at least one critical point.

Find a polynomial function of degree n whose graph has no critical points if

14. $n = 3$
15. $n = 5$
16. n is any odd natural number

C

17. Suppose that g is a function such that $g(x) \geq 0$ if $a < x < c$, and $g(x) \leq 0$ if $c < x < b$. It can be shown that if $\lim_{x \to c} g(x)$ exists, then $\lim_{x \to c} g(x) = 0$.

    Use this fact to prove the following:

    If h is a function such that $h(x) \leq 0$ if $a < x < c$, $h(x) \geq 0$ if $c < x < b$, and $\lim_{x \to c} h(x)$ exists, then $\lim_{x \to c} h(x) = 0$.

18. Prove Theorem 8 for the case in which f has a relative maximum at c. (*Hint:* There are numbers a and b such that $a < c < b$ and $f(x) \leq f(c)$ whenever $a < x < b$. Let

$$g(x) = \frac{f(x) - f(c)}{x - c}$$

and use the fact stated in Exercise 17.)

19. Prove Theorem 8 for the case in which f has a relative minimum at c.

20. The following theorem is known as the **Law of the Mean:**

> Suppose the function f is continuous on $\{x: a \le x \le b\}$ and differentiable on $\{x: a < x < b\}$. Then there is a number c between a and b such that
>
> $$f'(c) = \frac{f(b) - f(a)}{b - a}.$$

a. The points $(a, f(a))$ and $(b, f(b))$ are on the graph of f. What is the slope of the line segment joining them?

b. What is the slope of the line tangent to the graph of f at the point $(c, f(c))$?

c. Supply the missing words in the following geometrical interpretation of the conclusion of the Law of the Mean and draw a sketch:

> There is a point on the graph of f between $A(a, f(a))$ and $B(b, f(b))$ at which the line __?__ to the graph is __?__ to the segment $\overline{AB}$.

21. Suppose $f'(x) > 0$ on an interval or half-line S. Let x_1 and x_2 be any two numbers of S such that $x_1 < x_2$. Show that $f(x_1) < f(x_2)$. (*Hint:* Use the Law of the Mean (see Exercise 20) with $a = x_1$ and $b = x_2$.)

22. Exercise 21 proves one part of Theorem 9. Prove the other part.

3–6 Higher Derivatives; Convexity

The expression $f'(x)$ for the derivative of a function f at x may be used to define a new function

$$f': x \to f'(x).$$

The function f' is the **derivative** (or **derived**) **function** of f. Thus the derivative function of

$$f: x \to x^4 + 2x^2 + 3$$

is

$$f': x \to 4x^3 + 4x.$$

It is often the case in practice that the derivative function f' of a given function f is itself differentiable. Its derivative $(f')'(x)$ is denoted by $f''(x)$ and is the **second derivative** of f at x. We may continue this process to define the derivatives of higher *order.* Thus

$$f''' = (f'')', \quad f^{\text{iv}} = (f''')', \quad f^{\text{v}} = (f^{\text{iv}})', \text{ and so on.}$$

Notice that we use lower-case Roman letters for the superscripts in derivatives of orders higher than the third. The general notation for the nth derivative of f is $f^{(n)}$.

EXAMPLE 1. Find the derivatives of all orders of the function

$$f\colon x \to x^4 + 2x^3 - 5x + 6.$$

Solution: Since $f(x) = x^4 + 2x^3 - 5x + 6$, we have

$$f'(x) = 4x^3 + 6x^2 - 5,$$
$$f''(x) = 12x^2 + 12x,$$
$$f'''(x) = 24x + 12,$$
$$f^{\text{iv}}(x) = 24,$$
$$f^{\text{v}}(x) = 0.$$

Derivatives of orders higher than the fifth all exist and are 0.

Other Notations for Derivatives. The symbol D is often used to stand for the phrase "the derivative of." Thus $Df = f'$ and $Df(x) = f'(x)$. We sometimes write as a subscript to the D the name of the variable being used; for example, $D_x x^5 = 5x^4$ and $D_t t^5 = 5t^4$. The last equation is read "the derivative with respect to t of t^5 is $5t^4$."

The symbol $D(Df)$ for the second derivative f'' is shortened to $D^2 f$. The third, fourth, . . . derivatives of f are denoted by $D^3 f$, $D^{\text{iv}} f$, ...

The symbol $\dfrac{d}{dx}$ is used to mean the same thing as D_x, that is, "the derivative with respect to x of." For example, $\dfrac{d}{dx}x^5 = 5x^4$, and, in general, $\dfrac{d}{dx}f(x) = f'(x)$. This notation is most frequently used when a single symbol, like y, is used for the value of a function. In this case, we write $\dfrac{dy}{dx}$ instead of $\dfrac{d}{dx}y$. Thus if $y = x^5$, then $\dfrac{dy}{dx} = 5x^4$. In this notation, the second derivative $\dfrac{d}{dx}\left(\dfrac{dy}{dx}\right)$ is written as $\dfrac{d^2y}{dx^2}$ (note the placement of the superscripts), the third derivative as $\dfrac{d^3y}{dx^3}$, and so on.

If we have $y = f(x)$, then we often use y' for $f'(x)$, y'' for $f''(x)$, and so on.

In this book we shall seldom use derivatives of orders higher than the second. Second derivatives may be used in studying the graphs of functions, as described below.

A segment G of the graph of a function is **convex downward** (or **concave upward**) if given any two points P and Q of G, every point of G between P and Q lies *below* the chord $\overline{PQ}$ (Figure 3–14). A segment G is **convex**

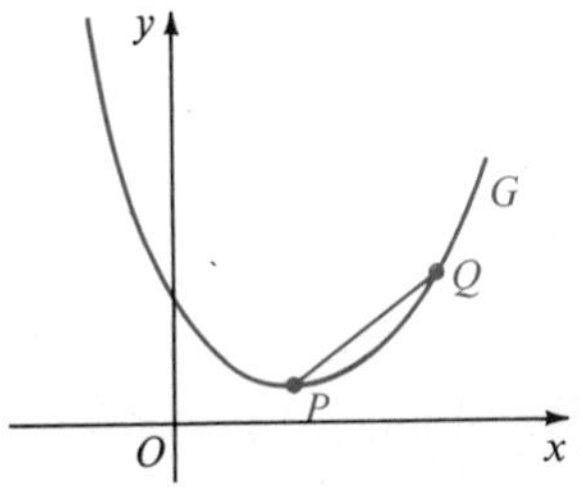

G is convex downward

Figure 3–14

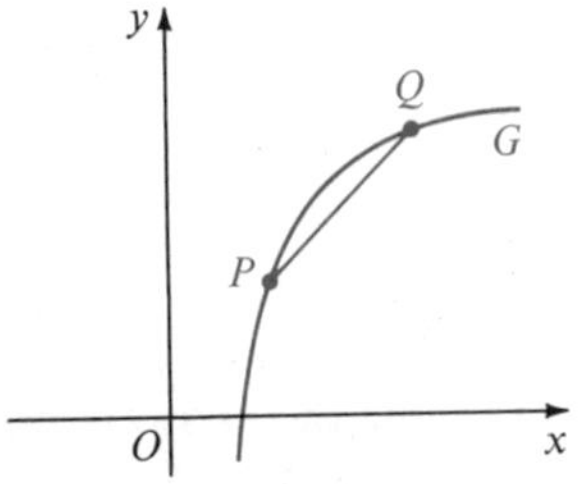

G is convex upward

Figure 3–15

upward (or **concave downward**) if given any two points P and Q of G, every point of G between P and Q lies *above* the chord $\overline{PQ}$ (Figure 3–15).

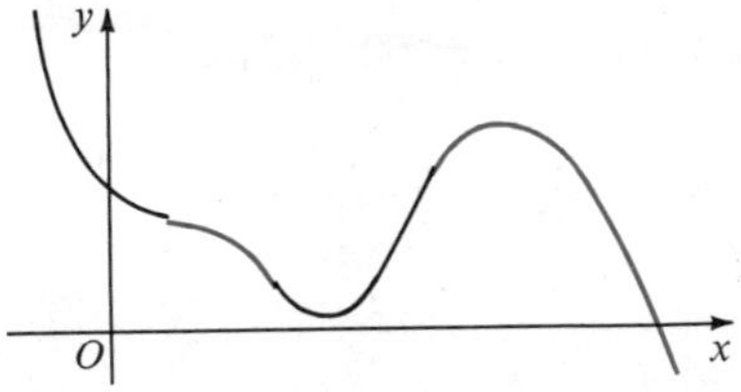

Figure 3–16

In Figure 3–16, the black portions of the graph are convex downward, and the red portions are convex upward.

Suppose that on an interval or half-line, a function f has a *positive* second derivative f''. Since $f'' = (f')'$, this means that the function f' is increasing, by Theorem 9. Now, the values of f' give the slope of the graph of f, and if you draw a curve in such a way that its slope increases, you will find that it is convex downward (try it). This experiment suggests the truth of the following theorem. (See Exercises 22 and 23, page 142.)

Theorem 10.

If $f''(x) > 0$ on an interval or half-line S, then the graph of f is convex downward on S. If $f''(x) < 0$ on S, then the graph of f is convex upward on S.

A point P on a graph is an **inflection point** if the graph is convex downward on an interval adjacent to P on one side and convex upward on an interval adjacent to P on the other side. In Figure 3–16, the points where the red and black parts of the graph join are inflection points. It can be shown that if $(c, f(c))$ is an inflection point, then $f''(c) = 0$, provided f'' is continuous at c. It is possible, however, that $f''(c) = 0$ even though $(c, f(c))$ is *not* an inflection point.

EXAMPLE 2. For the function

$$f\colon x \to x^4 - 4x^3 + 10$$

of Example 2, Section 3–5, page 133, find

a. where the graph is convex downward and where it is convex upward;

b. the coordinates of the inflection points.

Solution: Since

$$f'(x) = 4x^3 - 12x^2,$$

we have

$$f''(x) = 12x^2 - 24x = 12x(x - 2).$$

a. Therefore,

On the set	the sign of $f''(x)$ is	and the graph of f is
$\{x\colon x < 0\}$	positive	convex downward
$\{x\colon 0 < x < 2\}$	negative	convex upward
$\{x\colon x > 2\}$	positive	convex downward

b. The abscissas of the inflection points are 0 and 2, and thus the inflection points are (0, 10) and (2, −6).

Figure 3–17 shows the graph of a function f in black and the graph of its derivative function f' in red. Notice that whenever the graph of f has a critical point, the graph of f' has an x-intercept; and whenever the graph of f has an inflection point, the graph of f' has a critical point. Notice also that when the graph of f is falling, the graph of f' is on or below the x-axis. It is an interesting and edifying exercise to start with the graph of a function and then to sketch the graph of its derivative function using the considerations noted above.

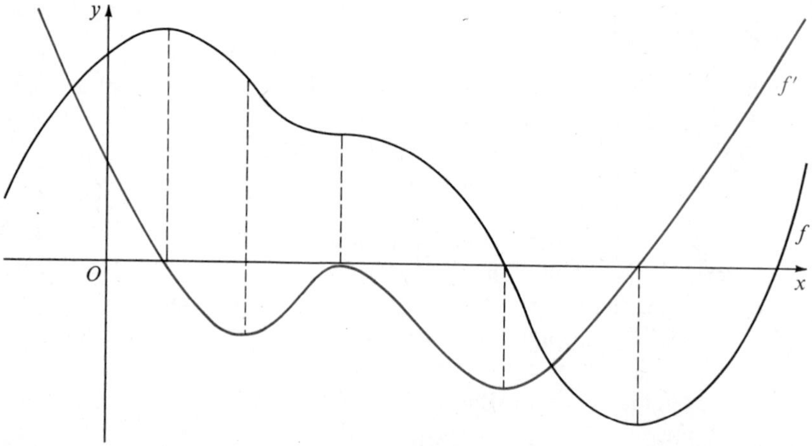

Figure 3–17

ORAL EXERCISES

In Exercises 1–6, (a) give the coordinates of the inflection points, assuming that these are integers, and (b) describe where the graph is convex downward and where it is convex upward.

1.
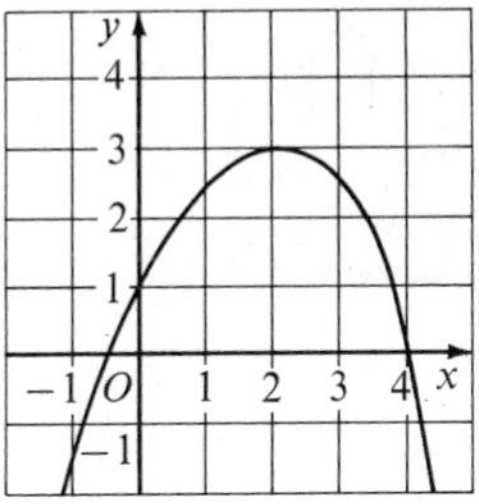

4.
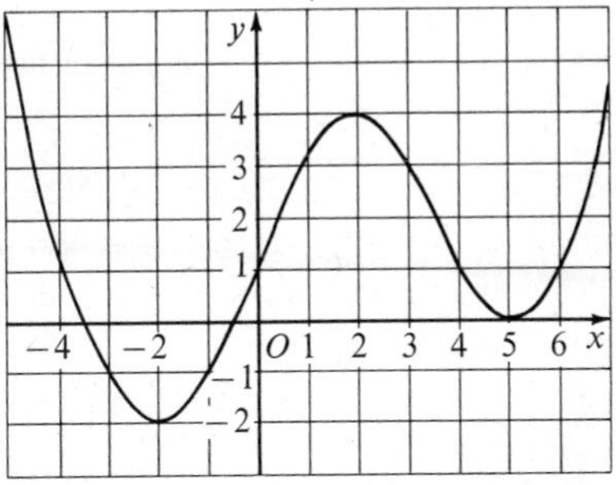

2.
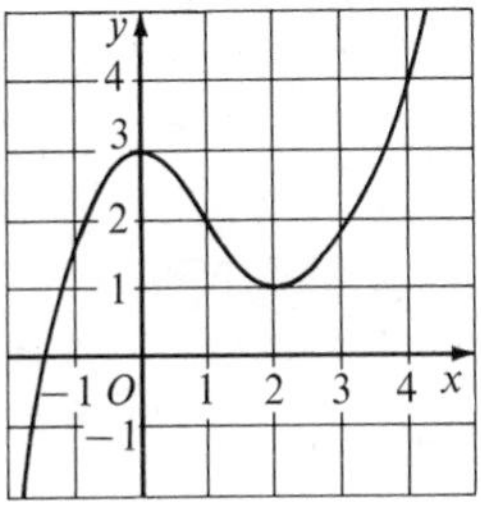

5.
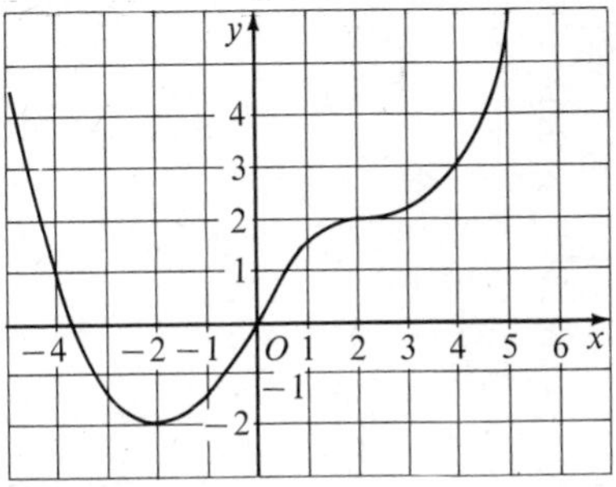

3.
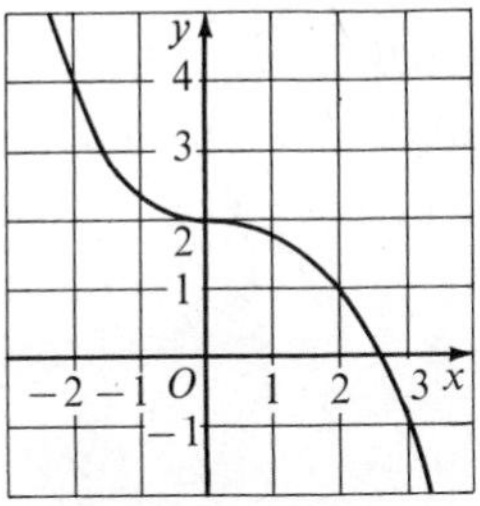

6.
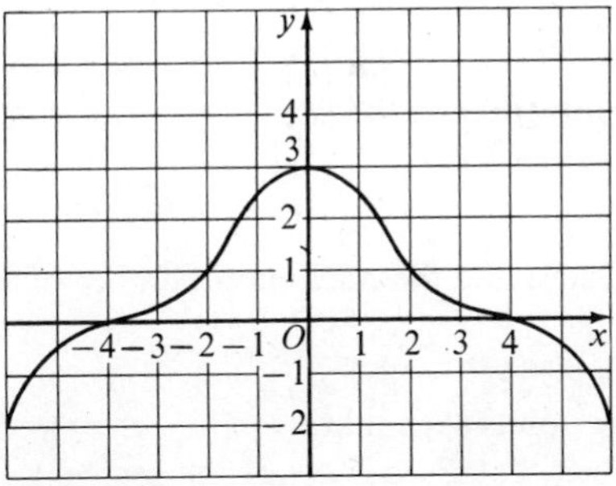

Exercises 7–12 have to do with the function

$$f\colon x \to x^3.$$

Tell whether each statement about f is true or false.

7. $f'(x) = 3x^2$

8. $f'\colon x \to 3x^2$

9. $\dfrac{d}{dx} f(x) = 3x^2$

10. $f'(2) = 12$

11. $\dfrac{d}{dx} f(2) = 12$

12. $D_x f(2) = 0$

WRITTEN EXERCISES

In Exercises 1 and 2, find all the nonzero derivatives of the given polynomial function.

A

1. $g: x \to x^4 - 4x^3 + 6x^2 - 4x + 1$
2. $g: x \to x^5$

The functions in Exercises 3–10 are the same as those in Exercises 3–10 of Section 3–5, page 136.

a. Find where the graph is convex downward and where it is convex upward.
b. Find the coordinates of the inflection points.
c. Redraw the graph done earlier, this time showing the features found in (a) and (b).

3. $f: x \to x^3 - 3x$
4. $f: x \to x^3 + 3x^2 - 1$
5. $f: x \to x^3 + x$
6. $f: x \to x^3 + 1$
7. $f: x \to x^3 - x^2 - x$
8. $f: x \to x^4 - 4x^2$
9. $f: x \to x^4 - 4x$
10. $f: x \to x^4 + 4x^3 + 7$

11–16. Reproduce the graph of the function f given in Oral Exercises 1–6 (using a larger scale). Then, in the same coordinate plane, sketch the graph of the function f'.

17. Given $g: x \to x^4$, find $g''(0)$. Determine whether or not the graph of g has an inflection point at $(0, 0)$.

In Exercises 18–21, Q is a polynomial function of degree n.

B

18. Show that in the case $n = 2$, the graph of Q has no inflection points.
19. Show that in the case $n = 3$, the graph of Q has exactly one inflection point.
20. Show that if n is odd, $n > 1$, then the graph of Q has at least one inflection point.
21. Determine the maximum number of inflection points on the graph of Q.

C

22. Let $P_1(x_1, y_1)$, $P_2(x_2, y_2)$, and $P_3(x_3, y_3)$ be points such that $x_1 < x_2 < x_3$ and also such that P_2 lies *above* the segment $\overline{P_1P_3}$. Prove that

$$\text{slope } \overline{P_1P_2} > \text{slope } \overline{P_2P_3}.$$

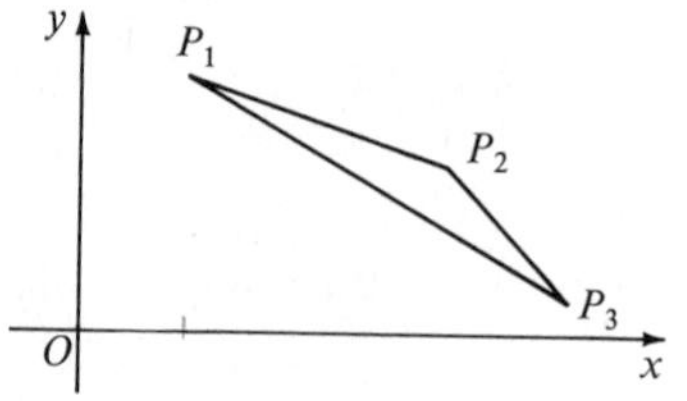

23. Prove the first part of Theorem 10. [*Hint:* Since $f''(x) > 0$ on S, f' is increasing on S, by Theorem 9. If we suppose that the graph is not convex downward, then there must be points P_1, P_2, and P_3 satisfying the conditions of Exercise 22. Use the Law of the Mean, Exercise 20, page 137, to show that there are two numbers, t_1 and t_2, of S such that $t_1 < t_2$ but $f'(t_1) > f'(t_2)$.]

CHAPTER SUMMARY

1. Let f be a function having domain D, and let a be a number. If as x approaches a, $x \in D$, but does not take on the value a, $f(x)$ approaches some number b, then **b is the limit of $f(x)$ as x approaches a,** and we write

$$\lim_{x \to a} f(x) = b.$$

2. The informal definition given above can be made precise, and the following properties of limits can be proved:

Suppose $\lim_{x \to a} f(x) = A$ and $\lim_{x \to a} g(x) = B$. Then

$$\lim_{x \to a} cf(x) = cA \qquad (c \text{ a constant})$$

$$\lim_{x \to a} [f(x) \pm g(x)] = A \pm B$$

$$\lim_{x \to a} [f(x)\, g(x)] = AB$$

$$\lim_{x \to a} \frac{f(x)}{g(x)} = \frac{A}{B} \qquad (\text{assuming } B \neq 0)$$

3. A function f is **continuous** at a number a of its domain if and only if

$$\lim_{x \to a} f(x) = f(a).$$

4. Suppose f and g are continuous at a. Then cf (c a constant), $f + g$, $f - g$, and fg are continuous at a. If $g(a) \neq 0$, then $\frac{f}{g}$ is continous at a. In particular, every polynomial function is continuous.
5. If a function is continuous at each point of an interval or half-line, then the corresponding part of its graph is an *unbroken curve.*
6. The **Intermediate-Value Theorem:** Let f be continuous on the interval $\{x\colon a \leq x \leq b\}$. Let c be any number between $f(a)$ and $f(b)$. Then there is a number r between a and b such that $f(r) = c$.
7. Let f be a function and a be a number in its domain. The **derivative of f at a** is the number

$$f'(a) = \lim_{x \to a} \frac{f(x) - f(a)}{x - a}$$

provided this limit exists.

8. The number $f'(a)$ is the **slope of the graph of f at the point $(a, (f(a))$.**
9. A function which has a derivative at a is **differentiable at a,** and a **differentiable function** is one which is differentiable at each number of its domain.

10. If the function f is differentiable at a, then f is continuous at a. The graph of a differentiable function having as domain $\mathcal{R}$, a half-line, or an interval is a *smooth unbroken curve.*

11. If $f(x) = x^n$, where n is a natural number, then $f'(x) = nx^{n-1}$.

12. If f and g are differentiable and c is a constant, then

$$(cf)'(x) = cf'(x) \qquad \text{and} \qquad (f + g)'(x) = f'(x) + g'(x).$$

13. A function f has a **relative maximum,** $f(c)$, at c if $f(c) \geq f(x)$ for all x near c. **Relative minimum** is defined similarly. Suppose that f is a differentiable function defined on both sides of c and that f has a relative **extremum** (maximum or minimum) at c. Then $(c, f(c))$ is a **critical point,** that is, $f'(c) = 0$.

14. A function f is **increasing** on an interval or half-line S if for any two numbers x_1 and x_2 in S with $x_1 < x_2$, we have $f(x_1) < f(x_2)$. If $f'(x) > 0$ for all x in S, then f is increasing on S. [A similar definition and theorem exist for **decreasing** functions.]

15. If the **derivative function** $f'\colon x \to f'(x)$ of f is itself differentiable, then its derivative $(f')'(x) = f''(x)$ is the **second derivative** of f at x. Derivatives of higher order are defined similarly.

16. A segment G of the graph of a function f is **convex downward** (or **concave upward)** if for any two points P and Q of G, the part of G between P and Q lies *below* the chord $\overline{PQ}$. If $f''(x) > 0$ for each x in an interval or half-line S, then the graph of f is convex downward on S. [A similar definition and theorem exist for functions that are **convex upward.]** A point P on a graph is an **inflection point** if the graph is convex downward on an interval adjacent to P on one side and convex upward on an interval adjacent to P on the other side.

CHAPTER TEST

3–1 **1.** Find $\lim_{x \to 2} \dfrac{x^2 + 2}{x}$. At each step indicate which of the limit facts (C), (S), (D), (Pr), (Q), (Po), and (K) you are using.

3–2 **2.** Draw the graph of the function f described at the right. At what numbers, if any, does f fail to be continuous?

$$f(x) = \begin{cases} x & \text{if } x < 1 \\ 2 - x & \text{if } 1 \leq x \leq 2 \\ 1 & \text{if } x > 2 \end{cases}$$

3–3 **3.** Use the definition of a derivative to find $f'(a)$ if $f\colon x \to \dfrac{x + 1}{x}$.

3–4 4. Find an equation of the line tangent to the graph of $f\colon x \to x^3 - 2x^2 - 2x$ at the point $(2, f(2))$.

5. Find a quadratic function f such that $f'(x) = 2x + 3$.

3–5 6. For the function $f\colon x \to x^4 - 6x^2$, find **(a)** the critical points
3–6 of the graph, **(b)** where the graph rises and where it falls, **(c)** where the graph is convex downward and where it is convex upward, and **(d)** the coordinates of the inflection points. Then **(e)** draw the graph.

3–6 7. Suppose that the point $(a, f(a))$ on the graph of f is both a critical point and an inflection point. What can you say about the graph of f' at $x = a$?

RECOMMENDED READINGS

HIGHT, DONALD W., *The Limit Concept in the SMSG Revised Sample Textbooks*, The Mathematics Teacher, Vol. 57, No. 4 (April, 1964), pp. 194–199.

SAWYER, W. W., *What Is Calculus About?* (New York: Random House, Inc., 1961).

Development of Differential Calculus

The basic notion in differential calculus is that of a *derivative function* f' of a given function f whose graph is a smooth curve. The value $f'(a)$, for an a in the domain of f and f', is the slope of the graph of f at the point $(a, f(a))$. Once this slope is known, the tangent line to the curve at that point can be determined, as we saw in the chapter we have just completed.

Even in ancient times mathematicians were interested in the problem of finding tangents to curves. Archimedes (287?–212 B.C.), who undoubtedly was one of the most extraordinarily gifted and versatile mathematicians who ever lived, actually used the methods of differential calculus to construct the tangent line at any point on a certain spiral, called the spiral of Archimedes. This spiral, shown below, is the curve traced by a point which, starting at the endpoint of a ray, moves with uniform speed along the ray while the ray rotates with uniform angular speed about its endpoint.

Further progress in differential calculus had to await the discovery, made independently some 2000 years later by René Descartes (1596–1650) and Pierre de Fermat (1601–1665), of *analytic*, or *coordinate*,

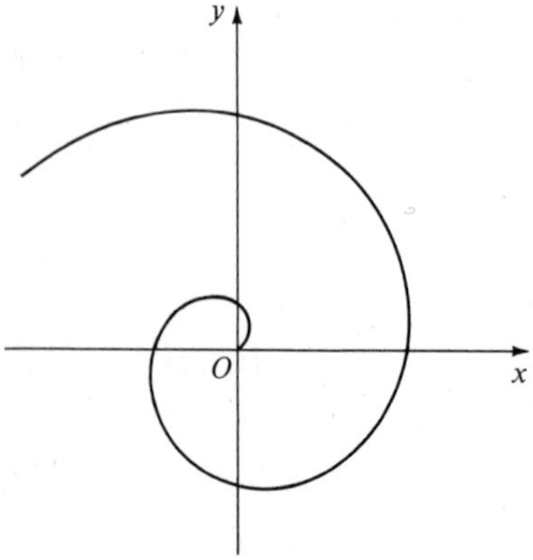

Archimedes

Isaac Newton

Gottfried Wilhelm von Leibniz

geometry. To find the extrema of a function f, Fermat determined the slope of the tangent line to the graph of f at each of its points, essentially as we did in Section 3–5.

Other mathematicians and scientists also made relevant contributions, but it is generally considered that the systematic development of calculus was begun independently by Isaac Newton (1642–1727) and Gottfried Wilhelm von Leibniz (1646–1716). There was a bitter controversy for many years as to which of these two extremely talented men deserved credit for inventing this new subject. Newton made his discoveries first; but Leibniz published his results first. Newton had the advantage of being acquainted with Fermat's work and of having as his teacher Dr. Isaac Barrow (1630–1677), who also was concerned with the problem of drawing tangents to curves; Leibniz was largely self-taught. Newton's reasoning probably was sounder; but it is Leibniz's notation $\frac{dy}{dx}$ for the derivative rather than Newton's $\dot{y}$ that is most commonly used today.

For $y = f(x)$, Leibniz started with the nonzero difference $x - a$, which he denoted by Δx (read "delta x" or "the change in x"), and the corresponding $\Delta y = f(x) - f(a)$. He then formed the difference quotient

$$\frac{\Delta y}{\Delta x} = \frac{f(x) - f(a)}{x - a},$$

just as we did in Section 3–3. For example, if $y = f(x) = 2x$, then

$$\frac{\Delta y}{\Delta x} = \frac{2x - 2a}{x - a} = \frac{2(x - a)}{x - a}.$$

It is quite clear today that we are concerned only with the value of the right-hand member of the equation, which is 2, so that

$$\lim_{\Delta x \to 0} \frac{\Delta y}{\Delta x} = \lim_{\Delta x \to 0} 2 = 2;$$

but Leibniz and many of his followers were obsessed with the consideration of the ultimate fate of the denominator, Δx, and of the numerator, Δy, of the left-hand member, $\frac{\Delta y}{\Delta x}$. Of course, both Δx and Δy simply have limit 0 as Δx approaches 0. Leibniz and his followers, however, seem to have felt that Δx and Δy do not really approach 0 but instead approach some strange "infinitely small quantities," or "infinitesimals," or "differentials," which were denoted by dx and dy, respectively. Bishop George Berkeley (1685–1753), who found this reasoning obscure, poked fun at it by calling dx and dy "ghosts of departed quantities." The "ultimate ratio" of these "differentials," however, was considered to be an ordinary number, and thus Leibniz wrote

$$\frac{dy}{dx} = f'(a).$$

He called $\frac{dy}{dx}$ a "differential quotient."

There is no reason why the derivative should not be denoted $\frac{dy}{dx}$, as long as we understand the limiting process that is involved. The notation is quite brief, convenient, and an aid to memory. For example (see Chapter 4), we have the formulas

$$\frac{dy}{dx} = \frac{dy}{du} \cdot \frac{du}{dx} \quad \text{and} \quad \frac{dy}{dx} \cdot \frac{dx}{dy} = 1,$$

which suggest that "differentials" may be treated like ordinary numbers.

As a matter of fact, while "differentials" as "infinitely small quantities" simply do not exist and the notion has been entirely discredited, the term "differential," denoted by dx or dy, is used today in a thoroughly legitimate mathematical way. Namely, dx and Δx are now used interchangeably, so that $dx = x - a$. Then dy is defined by

$$dy = f'(a)\, dx.$$

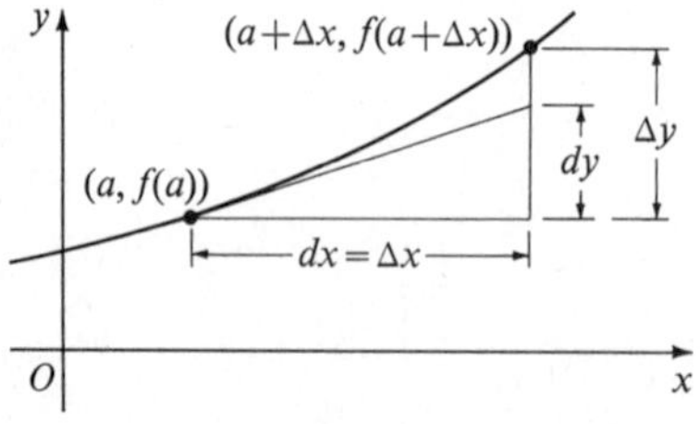

As indicated in the diagram at the left, dy accordingly denotes the change corresponding to dx or Δx in the function value of the function whose graph is the tangent to the curve at the point $(a, f(a))$.

The diagram on page 148 suggests that if $|\Delta x|$ is small, then dy is a good approximation to Δy. Thus if $y = x^2$, then

$$\Delta y = (a + \Delta x)^2 - a^2$$
$$= a^2 + 2a\,\Delta x + (\Delta x)^2 - a^2$$
$$= 2a\,\Delta x + (\Delta x)^2,$$

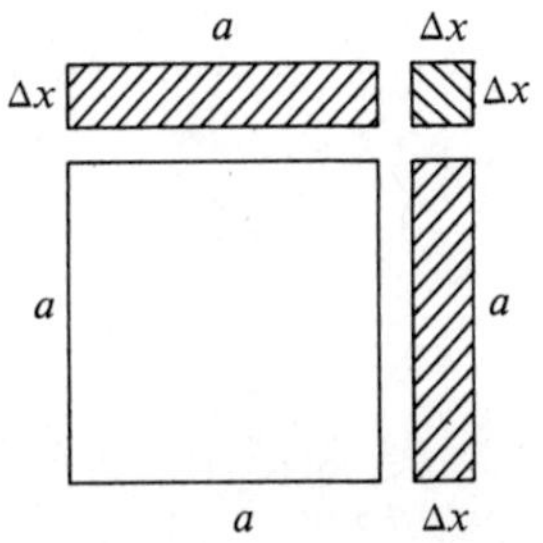

as illustrated in the diagram at the right, and

$$dy = f'(a)\,\Delta x$$
$$= 2a\,\Delta x.$$

For example, if $a = 10$ and $\Delta x = 0.1$, then

$$\Delta y = (10.1)^2 - 10^2$$
$$= 2.01,$$

and

$$dy = 20 \times 0.1$$
$$= 2.$$

Differential calculus now rests on an entirely rigorous mathematical basis. The subject has been essential in physics ever since Newton's fundamental work on rates of change (see Section 4–3). Soon it furnished basic methods in other physical sciences, and now it is indispensable in life and social sciences also.

READING LIST

APOSTOL, TOM M., *Calculus*, Vol. 1 (New York: Blaisdell Publishing Company, 1961).

BELL, E. T., *Men of Mathematics* (New York: Simon and Schuster, Inc., 1961).

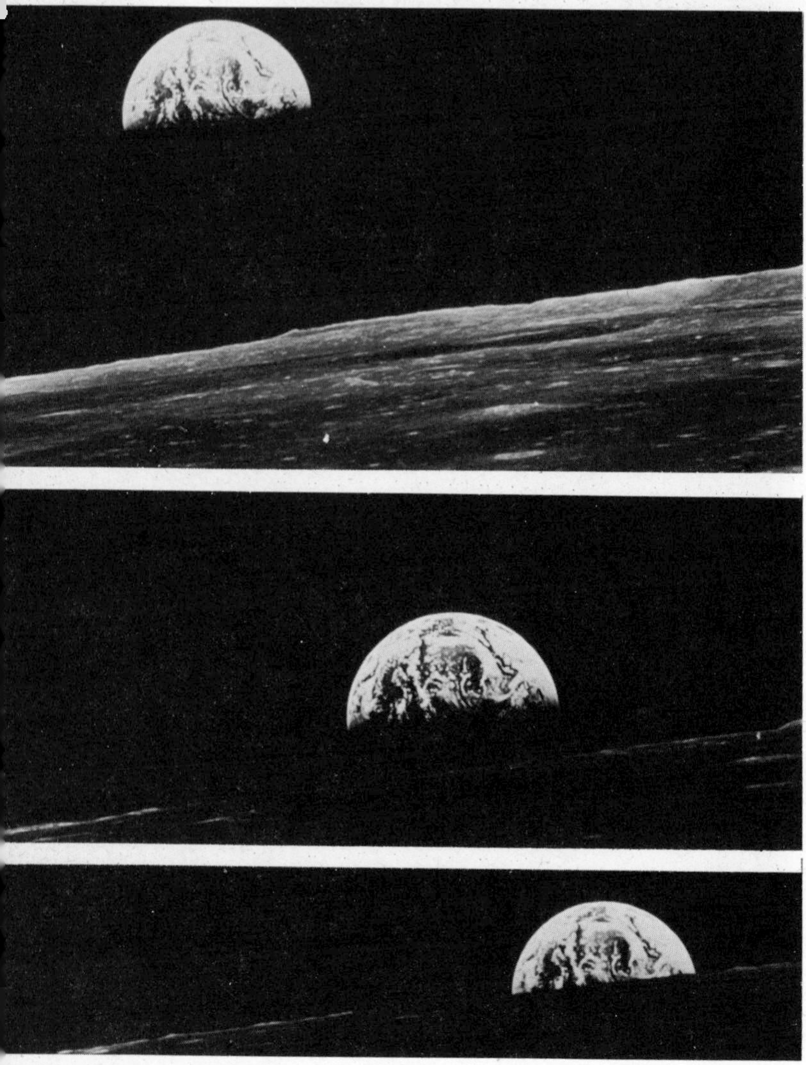

4

Differential calculus has many applications in astronomy and space exploration; for example, in the mathematical derivation or application of physical principles such as Kepler's laws of planetary motion or Newton's law of gravitation. The diagram at the right illustrates Kepler's law that the planets move in elliptical orbits having the Sun as focus. The photographs above, taken from the Apollo 10 Lunar Module, show the Earth rising above the horizon of the Moon.

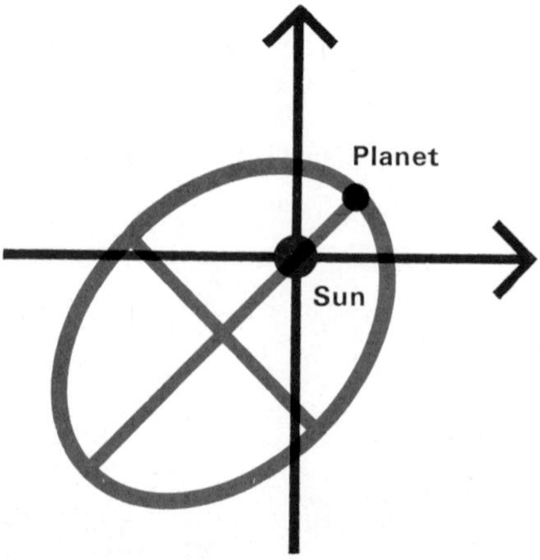

Applications of Differential Calculus

In this chapter, we shall indicate some ways in which differential calculus can be used to solve physical and geometric problems. We shall also develop some theory which will enable us to differentiate a larger class of functions and thereby extend the range of applications.

Maxima and Minima

4–1 Tests for Maxima and Minima

In applications, we often must find relative maxima and relative minima of functions. Theorem 8 of Section 3–5 provides us with a way to begin the search for the relative extrema of a differentiable function f: We find the zeros of f'. Suppose c is one of these zeros, so that $f'(c) = 0$. We shall give some tests to help determine whether $f(c)$ is a relative maximum, a relative minimum, or neither, without having to draw the graph of f.

The first test uses the *definition* of relative maxima and relative minima and consists essentially of comparing $f(c)$ with $f(x)$ for values of x near c (that is, values of x in some open interval containing c). This comparison can be made by considering the sign of $f(x) - f(c)$. If $f(x) - f(c) \geq 0$, for example, then $f(c) \leq f(x)$, and $f(c)$ is a relative minimum.

The f-test.

Suppose $f'(c) = 0$.

If $f(x) \leq f(c)$ for all x near c, then $f(c)$ is a relative maximum of f.

If $f(x) \geq f(c)$ for all x near c, then $f(c)$ is a relative minimum of f.

This test is easy to remember if we think of the graphical situation. For example:

If we have

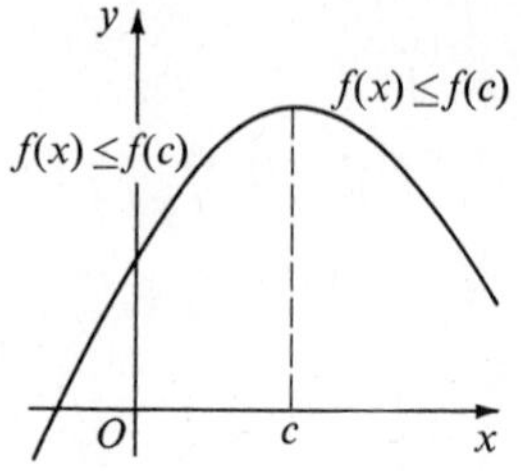

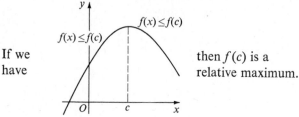

then $f(c)$ is a relative maximum.

EXAMPLE 1. Find the relative maxima and relative minima of

$$f\colon x \to x^3 - 3x^2 - 9x + 8.$$

Solution: $f'(x) = 3x^2 - 6x - 9 = 3(x + 1)(x - 3)$. Therefore the zeros of f' are -1 and 3. We want to determine the sign of $f(x) - f(c)$ for $c = -1$ and $c = 3$ so that we can apply the f-test. To do this, we shall first find an expression for $f(x) - f(c)$. By the Remainder Theorem, we have

$$f(x) = (x - c)q(x) + f(c),$$

or

$$f(x) - f(c) = (x - c)q(x). \tag{1}$$

We can find the product on the right-hand side of (1) by dividing $f(x)$ by $x - c$ to determine $q(x)$. We use synthetic division. For $c = -1$, we have

$$\begin{array}{r|rrrl} -1 & 1 & -3 & -9 & 8 \\ \hline & 1 & -4 & -5 & 13 = f(-1) \end{array}$$

Thus
$f(x) - f(-1) = (x + 1)(x^2 - 4x - 5) = (x + 1)^2(x - 5)$.
For x near -1, $(x + 1)^2 \geq 0$ and $x - 5 < 0$. Therefore,

$$f(x) - f(-1) \leq 0, \qquad \text{or} \qquad f(x) \leq f(-1),$$

and $f(-1) = 13$ is a relative maximum.
For $c = 3$, we have

$$\begin{array}{r|rrrl} 3 & 1 & -3 & -9 & 8 \\ \hline & 1 & 0 & -9 & -19 = f(3) \end{array}$$

Thus $f(x) - f(3) = (x - 3)(x^2 - 9) = (x - 3)^2(x + 3)$.
For x near 3, $(x - 3)^2 \geq 0$ and $x + 3 > 0$. Therefore,

$$f(x) - f(3) \geq 0, \qquad \text{or} \qquad f(x) \geq f(3),$$

and $f(3) = -19$ is a relative minimum.

The next test uses the idea of a function increasing or decreasing on an interval and the fact that the sign of the derivative detects such behavior (Theorem 9, Section 3–5, page 135). See Exercises 28 and 29, page 158.

The f′-test.

Suppose $f'(c) = 0$.

If $f'(x) > 0$ for all x near c on the left (i.e., all x near c and less than c) and $f'(x) < 0$ for all x near c on the right, then $f(c)$ is a relative maximum of f.

If $f'(x) < 0$ for all x near c on the left and $f'(x) > 0$ for all x near c on the right, then $f(c)$ is a relative minimum of f.

This test, too, is easy to remember if we think of the graphical situation. For example:

If we have

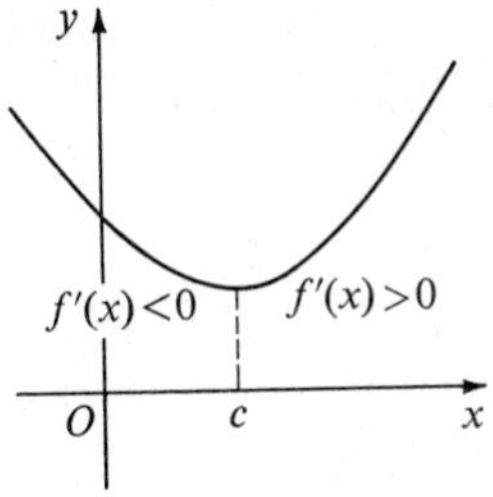

then $f(c)$ is a relative minimum.

EXAMPLE 2. Find the relative maxima and relative minima of

$$f: x \to x^4 - 6x^2 - 8x + 7.$$

Solution: $f'(x) = 4x^3 - 12x - 8 = 4(x + 1)^2(x - 2)$. Therefore the zeros of f' are 2 and -1. If x is near 2 and less than 2, then $x - 2 < 0$ and $(x + 1)^2 > 0$; hence $f'(x) < 0$. If x is near 2 and greater than 2, then $x - 2 > 0$ and $(x + 1)^2 > 0$; hence $f'(x) > 0$. Therefore, by the f'-test, $f(2) = -17$ is a relative minimum.

If x is near (but not equal to) -1, then $f'(x) < 0$ because $x - 2 < 0$ and $(x + 1)^2 > 0$. Therefore f is decreasing on both sides of -1, and $f(-1)$ is *neither* a relative maximum *nor* a relative minimum. The graph of f appears at the right. It is the curve pictured in Example 2 on page 134, moved 1 unit to the left.

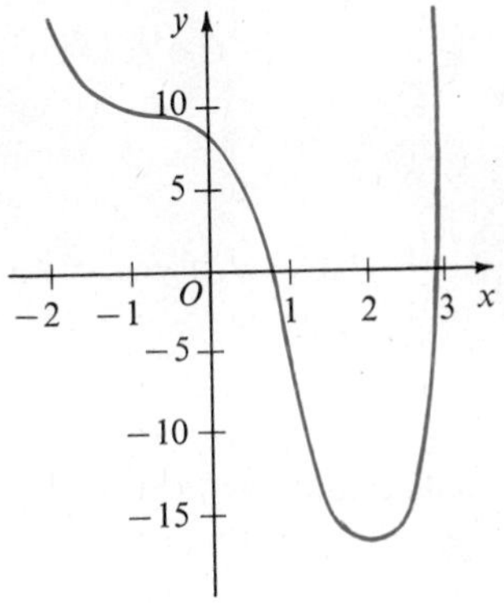

Suppose we know, concerning a differentiable function f, that $f'(c) = 0$ and $f''(c) > 0$. Since f'' is the derivative of f', the difference quotient for $f''(c)$ is

$$\frac{f'(x) - f'(c)}{x - c} = \frac{f'(x) - 0}{x - c} = \frac{f'(x)}{x - c}.$$

As x approaches c, $\dfrac{f'(x)}{x - c}$ approaches the *positive* number $f''(c)$. Therefore, for x near c, $\dfrac{f'(x)}{x - c}$ itself must be positive. This means that the numerator and denominator of $\dfrac{f'(x)}{x - c}$ must have the *same sign*. Hence,

$$f'(x)\begin{cases} < 0 & \text{if } x < c \\ > 0 & \text{if } x > c \end{cases} \quad \text{for } x \text{ near } c.$$

By the f'-test, therefore, $f(c)$ is a relative minimum.

The argument just given proves half of the next test (often called the **Second-Derivative Test**). The proof of the other half is similar. (See Exercise 27, page 158.)

The f″-test.

Suppose $f'(c) = 0$.

If $f''(c) < 0$, then $f(c)$ is a relative maximum of f.

If $f''(c) > 0$, then $f(c)$ is a relative minimum of f.

EXAMPLE 3. Find the relative maxima and relative minima of

$$f\colon x \to x^4 + 2x^3 - 2x^2 + 5.$$

Solution: $f'(x) = 4x^3 + 6x^2 - 4x = 2x(2x - 1)(x + 2)$;

$f''(x) = 12x^2 + 12x - 4.$

The zeros of f' are -2, 0, and $\frac{1}{2}$.

Since $f'(-2) = 0$ and $f''(-2) > 0$, $f(-2) = -3$ is a relative minimum. Since $f'(0) = 0$ and $f''(0) < 0$, $f(0) = 5$ is a relative maximum. Since $f'(\frac{1}{2}) = 0$ and $f''(\frac{1}{2}) > 0$, $f(\frac{1}{2}) = 4\frac{13}{16}$ is a relative minimum.

If $f'(c) = 0$ and $f''(c) = 0$, the f''-test gives *no* information; $f(c)$ may be a relative maximum, a relative minimum, or neither (see Exercise 26, page 158).

The number $f(c)$ is an **absolute maximum** of f if and only if $f(c) \geq f(x)$ for *all* x in the domain of f (not just x's near c). Similarly, $f(c)$ is an

absolute minimum of f if and only if $f(c) \leq f(x)$ for *all* x in the domain of f. If a function has an absolute maximum, then this must be the greatest of its relative maxima. A function need not have an absolute maximum or minimum, however. In Section 3–5, the function of Example 2 has an absolute minimum but no absolute maximum, while the function of Example 1 has neither.

The following fact is often useful in finding absolute extrema:

> If a continuous function f whose domain is an interval, a half-line, or $\mathcal{R}$ has just *one* relative extremum, $f(c)$, then $f(c)$ is an absolute extremum.

To prove this fact, we use an indirect argument. That is, we assume that f has just one relative extremum, $f(c)$, but that $f(c)$ is not an absolute extremum. If $f(c)$ is a relative maximum, for example, then according to our assumption there is some a in the domain of f such that $f(c) < f(a)$. The graphical situation at a and near c is as indicated in Figure 4–1(a).

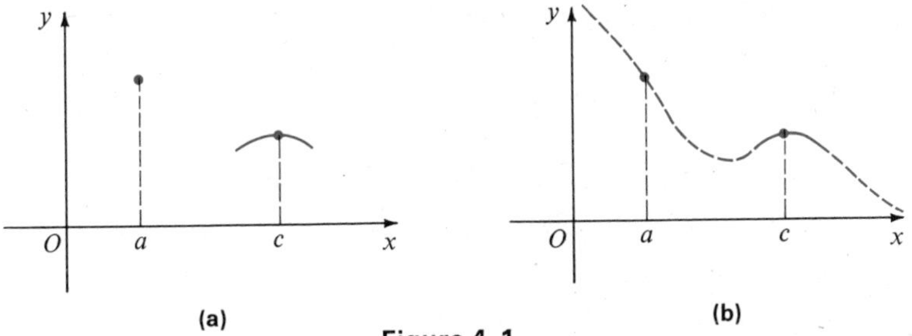

Figure 4–1

Because f is defined between a and c, f must have a relative minimum between a and c, as suggested by Figure 4–1(b). This is impossible, however, because $f(c)$ is the only relative extremum. Hence our assumption that $f(c)$ is not an absolute extremum must be false, and we can conclude that $f(c)$ is an *absolute* maximum.

In the next example, we shall use the following facts:

If $f\colon x \to \dfrac{1}{x}$, then $f'(x) = -\dfrac{1}{x^2}$ (Exercise 11, page 125).

If $f\colon x \to \dfrac{1}{x^2}$, then $f'(x) = -\dfrac{2}{x^3}$ (Example 4, Section 3–3, page 124).

EXAMPLE 4. What is the least value the sum of the square and the reciprocal of a positive number can attain?

Solution: Consider the function f defined on the half-line $\{x\colon x > 0\}$ by

$$f(x) = x^2 + \frac{1}{x} \quad (x > 0).$$

(Solution continued)

We are asked to find the absolute minimum of f.

$$f'(x) = 2x - \frac{1}{x^2}.$$

Therefore, $f'(x) = 0$ if and only if $2x = \frac{1}{x^2}$, or $2x^3 = 1$, or $x = 2^{-\frac{1}{3}}$. It is easy to show, using the f''-test, that $f(2^{-\frac{1}{3}})$ is a relative minimum:

$$f''(x) = 2 + \frac{2}{x^3}; \quad f''(2^{-\frac{1}{3}}) = 2 + \frac{2}{2^{-1}} = 2 + 4 > 0.$$

Since $f(2^{-\frac{1}{3}})$ is the only relative extremum of f,

$$f(2^{-\frac{1}{3}}) = (2^{-\frac{1}{3}})^2 + \frac{1}{2^{-\frac{1}{3}}} = 2^{-\frac{2}{3}} + 2^{\frac{1}{3}} = 2^{-\frac{2}{3}}(1 + 2) = 3 \cdot 2^{-\frac{2}{3}}$$

is the absolute minimum of f.

We have noted that a way to begin the search for the extrema of a function f is to find the zeros of f'. We must realize, however, that this procedure may not detect all of the extrema. Other extrema might occur (1) at points where the function is not differentiable or (2) at endpoints of the domain of the function. These points must be considered separately.

EXAMPLE 5. Find the absolute maximum and absolute minimum of the function

$$f: x \to |x - 2| + 1 \qquad (0 \le x \le 3).$$

Solution: Since $|x - 2| = 2 - x$ if $x < 2$, and $|x - 2| = x - 2$ if $x \ge 2$, we have

$$f(x) = \begin{cases} 3 - x & \text{if } 0 \le x < 2 \\ x - 1 & \text{if } 2 \le x \le 3. \end{cases}$$

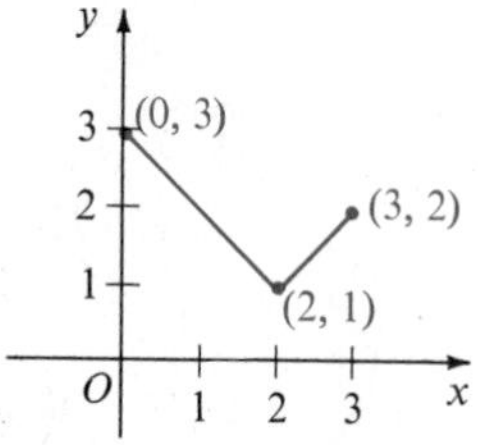

Therefore,

$$f'(x) = \begin{cases} -1 & \text{if } 0 \le x < 2 \\ 1 & \text{if } 2 < x \le 3 \end{cases}$$

and f is not differentiable at 2. Since $f'(x)$ is never 0, the extrema of f must occur either at a point where f is not differentiable or at an endpoint of the domain of f. Testing these, we find $f(2) = 1$, $f(0) = 3$, and $f(3) = 2$. Therefore the absolute maximum is 3 (at $x = 0$), and the absolute minimum is 1 (at $x = 2$). Note that f has a *relative* maximum at $x = 3$.

Situations similar to the one in Example 5 can occur even in nature. Consider an object which weighs one pound at the surface of the earth, (approximately) 4000 miles from the center of the earth. It can be shown, using Newton's law of gravitation, that if $g(x)$ is the weight in pounds of this object when it is x thousands of miles from the center of the earth, then

$$g(x) = \begin{cases} \dfrac{x}{4} & \text{if } 0 \leq x \leq 4 \\[2ex] \dfrac{16}{x^2} & \text{if } 4 < x. \end{cases}$$

The graph of g is shown in Figure 4–2. Note that neither the maximum nor the minimum of g occurs when $g'(x)$ is zero.

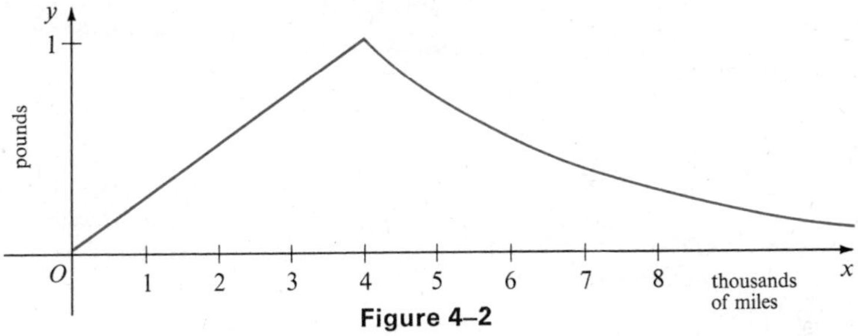

Figure 4–2

ORAL EXERCISES

In your own words, state

1. the f-test for a maximum.
2. the f-test for a minimum.
3. the f'-test for a maximum.
4. the f'-test for a minimum.
5. the f''-test for a maximum.
6. the f''-test for a minimum.

WRITTEN EXERCISES

Find the relative maxima and relative minima of each of the following functions using the f-test. Pattern your work after Example 1, page 152.

A

1. $f: x \to x^3 - 6x^2 + 9x + 9$
2. $f: x \to x^3 + x^2 - x$
3. $f: x \to x^3 + 6x^2 + 12x + 13$
4. $f: x \to 8 - x^4$
5. $f: x \to x^4 - 8x^2 + 8$
6. $f: x \to x^4 + 4x^3 - 16x$

7–12. Work Exercises 1–6 using the f'-test.

13–18. Work Exercises 1–6 using the f''-test insofar as this test is applicable. If the test is not applicable, so state.

Find the absolute maximum and the absolute minimum of each of the following functions.

19. $f: x \to x^2, \ -1 \le x \le 2$

20. $f: x \to x^2, \ 1 \le x \le 2$

21. $f: x \to x + 2|x|, \ -1 \le x \le 1$

22. $f: x \to |x| - 2|x - 1|, \ -1 \le x \le 2$

B **23.** Find the relative maximum and the relative minimum values of the function $f: x \to x + \dfrac{1}{x}\cdot$ Use the f''-test.

24. What is the least value the sum of the square of a positive number and the square of its reciprocal can attain?

25. If the product of two positive numbers is c, what is the least value the sum of their squares can attain?

C **26.** This exercise illustrates the remark following the solution to Example 3 on page 154.

a. If $f: x \to x^3$, find $f'(0)$ and $f''(0)$. Does f have a relative extremum at 0?
b. If $g: x \to x^4$, find $g'(0)$ and $g''(0)$. Does g have a relative extremum at 0?
c. Find a function h such that $h'(0) = 0$ and $h''(0) = 0$ and such that h has a relative maximum at 0.

27. Complete the proof of the f''-test (page 154).

28. Suppose that $f'(c) = 0, f'(x) > 0$ if $a < x < c$, and $f'(x) < 0$ if $c < x < b$. Let z be any number in the interval $\{x: a < x < b\}$. If $c < z < b$, we may use the Law of the Mean (Exercise 20, page 137) to conclude that there is a number u between c and z such that $\dfrac{f(z) - f(c)}{z - c} = f'(u)$, or

$$f(z) - f(c) = (z - c)f'(u). \qquad (*)$$

Then $z - c > 0$ and $f'(u) < 0$ (because $c < u < b$). Hence the product on the right-hand side of (*) is negative, and therefore $f(z) - f(c) < 0$, or $f(c) > f(z)$. Carry out an argument similar to the one just given to show that $f(c) > f(z)$ in the case $a < z < c$. This proves half of the f'-test.

29. Prove the other half of the f'-test (see Exercise 28).

4–2 Applications of Maxima and Minima

A variety of physical, geometric, and economic problems require that some quantity be made as large or as small as possible. We can often apply calculus to the solution of such problems.

EXAMPLE 1. A box is to be made from a rectangular piece of cardboard 15 by 24 inches by cutting equal squares out of the corners and folding up the flaps. Find the dimensions for which the box will have the greatest volume.

Solution: 1. We see that this is an extremum problem because some quantity, namely, the volume V of the box, is to be maximized.

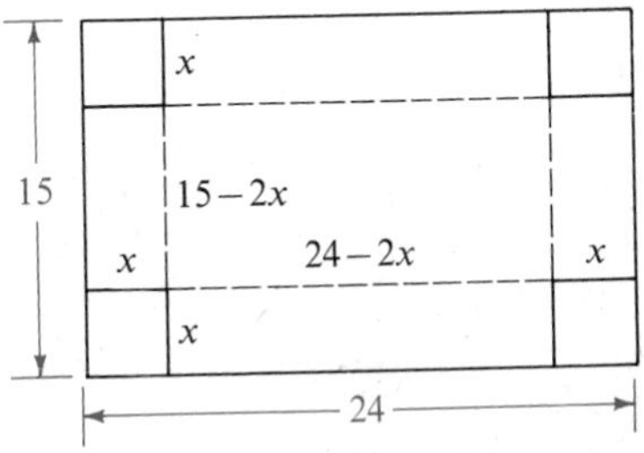

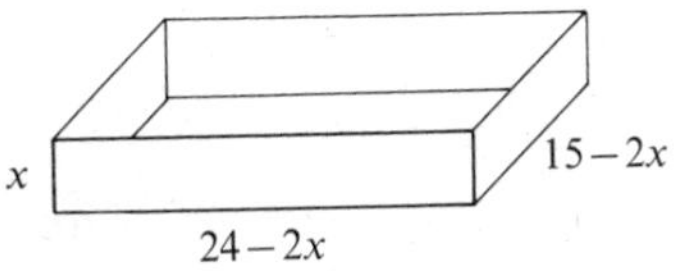

2. Let x be the length in inches of the sides of the cut-out squares. Then the lengths of the fold lines are $15 - 2x$ and $24 - 2x$ inches, and the dimensions of the resulting box are x by $15 - 2x$ by $24 - 2x$ inches. The volume V of the box is given by

$$\begin{aligned} V = f(x) &= x(15 - 2x)(24 - 2x) \\ &= 4x^3 - 78x^2 + 360x. \qquad (*) \end{aligned}$$

We have therefore expressed the quantity V to be maximized as a function of the variable x. Although the expression (*) is a polynomial, we must restrict the domain of the function f to the interval $0 \leq x \leq \frac{15}{2}$ because of physical limitations† on the size of x.

3. $f'(x) = 12x^2 - 156x + 360 = 12(x - 3)(x - 10)$.

Therefore $f'(x) = 0$ if $x = 3$ or $x = 10$. No meaningful result can be produced by $x = 10$, because 10 is not in the domain of f. Since

$$f''(x) = 24x - 156,$$

we have

$$f''(3) = 72 - 156 < 0,$$

and by the f''-test, $f(3) = 486$ is a relative maximum.

4. The function f is differentiable throughout, but we must consider the possibility that the greatest value of f occurs at an endpoint of its domain. Since $f(0) = 0$ and $f(\frac{15}{2}) = 0$, this is not the case.

5. The dimensions in inches of the box of greatest volume are therefore x, $15 - 2x$, and $24 - 2x$ for $x = 3$; that is, 3, 9, and 18 inches.

---

† We *are allowing* boxes having a zero dimension; it sometimes simplifies matters to consider such "degenerate cases." Whether or not they would be accepted as solutions to a practical problem depends on the particular problem.

The steps used in the solution of Example 1 may be taken as a pattern to follow in solving other applied extremum problems:

1. Study the statement of the problem carefully and identify the quantity to be maximized or minimized. Assign this quantity a name, for example, y.
2. Express y as a function of some variable: for example, $y = f(x)$. (The choice of x will sometimes be dictated by the nature of the problem. In other cases, choose it in any convenient way. A sketch will often be helpful at this stage.) Note any restrictions on x, that is, on the domain of f, which are imposed by the problem.
3. Use calculus to find the relative maxima or minima of f.
4. Check to see if f attains its greatest or least value at a point where f is not differentiable or at an endpoint of its domain.
5. Give the answer asked for in the problem (usually this is either the maximum or minimum value of f or the x which produces this value).

EXAMPLE 2. At noon an ocean liner steaming due west at 20 knots observes on its radar a ship which is 50 nautical miles dead ahead and proceeding due north at 10 knots. Assuming that each ship maintains its speed and course, find when they will be closest together. (*Note:* 1 knot = 1 nautical mile per hour $\doteq$ 1.15 statute miles per hour.)

Solution: 1. The quantity to be minimized is the distance d between the ocean liner, L, and the other ship, S.

2. With the help of a sketch, we can express d as a function of t, the time in hours after noon. Using the Pythagorean Theorem, we find

$$d^2 = (10t)^2 + (50 - 20t)^2.$$

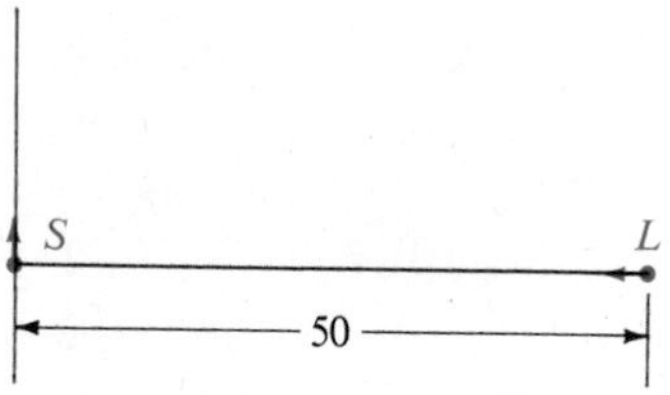

The situation at noon.

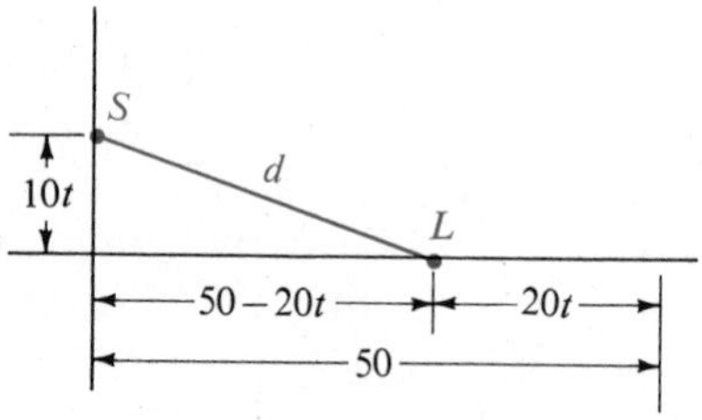

The situation t hours later.

Since $d \geq 0$, by minimizing d^2 we will also minimize d,

so we let $d^2 = f(t) = 100(t^2 + 25 - 20t + 4t^2)$
$$= 500(t^2 - 4t + 5).$$

The domain of f is $\{t\colon t \geq 0\}$.

3. $f'(t) = 500(2t - 4)$.
   Therefore $f'(t) = 0$ if $t = 2$. We can check to see that $f(2)$ is actually a minimum by using the f'-test or f''-test.
4. The function f is differentiable throughout its domain. Since $f(0) = 2500$, while $f(2) = 500$, the minimum does not occur at the endpoint, 0, of the domain of f.
5. Therefore the ships are closest together when $t = 2$, that is, at 2 P.M. (At that time they are $\sqrt{500}$, or approximately 22.36, nautical miles apart.)

It is often convenient, in Step 2, first to express the quantity to be maximized or minimized in terms of more than one variable. Before proceeding with Step 3, however, all but one of these variables must be eliminated. The following example illustrates this procedure.

EXAMPLE 3. A box of volume 32 cubic feet having a square base and no top is to be constructed from material costing $1 per square foot. Find the dimensions of such a box for which the cost of material is least.

Solution: 1. The quantity to be minimized is the cost of material, or, what amounts to the same thing, the surface area A of the box.

2. If, as indicated in the figure at the right, we let the length in feet of each edge of the square base be x and the height in feet be y, then

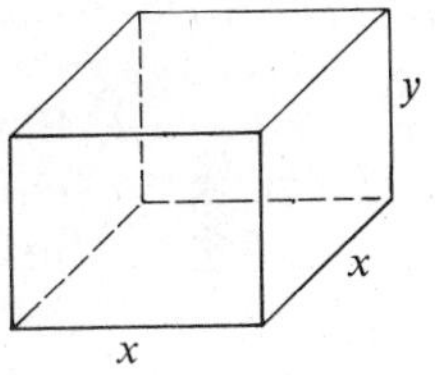

$$A = x^2 + 4xy.$$

In order to eliminate one of the variables, we observe that the volume of the box is $x \cdot x \cdot y = x^2y$, and therefore $x^2y = 32$, or

$$y = \frac{32}{x^2}. \qquad (*)$$

Hence

$$A = f(x) = x^2 + 4x \cdot \left(\frac{32}{x^2}\right) = x^2 + 128 \cdot \frac{1}{x}.$$

The domain of f is $\{x\colon x > 0\}$.

(*Solution continued*)

3. $$\frac{dA}{dx} = f'(x) = 2x + 128\left(-\frac{1}{x^2}\right) = \frac{2(x^3 - 64)}{x^2}.$$

Therefore, $f'(x) = 0$ if $x^3 = 64$, or $x = 4$. The f'-test shows that $f(4)$ is a relative minimum.

4. The function f is differentiable throughout its domain, and its domain has no endpoints. Since f has only one relative extremum, $f(4)$ is an absolute minimum by the observation made on page 155.

5. Knowing $x = 4$, we can find y from (*): $y = \dfrac{32}{4^2} = 2$.

Therefore the required dimensions are 4 feet, 4 feet, and 2 feet.

Another type of problem which can be attacked by means of calculus is that of finding the point (or points) on a given curve closest to a given point not on the curve.

EXAMPLE 4. Find the point on the parabola $2y = x^2$ which is closest to (4, 1).

Solution: 1. The quantity to be minimized is the distance d from (4, 1) to a variable point on the parabola $2y = x^2$. It is equivalent and somewhat easier to minimize d^2 instead of d.

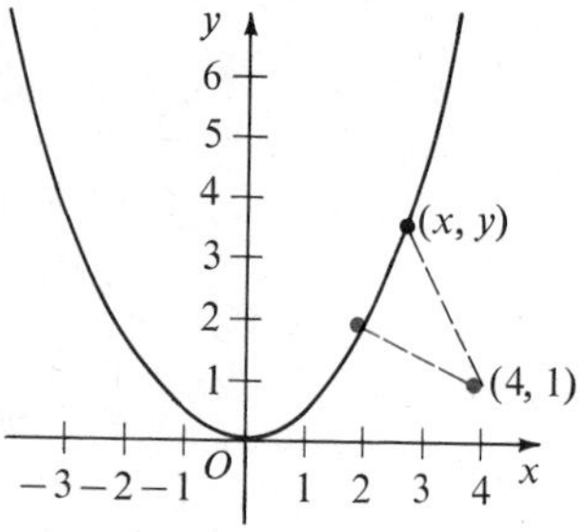

2. Using the distance formula, we find

$$d^2 = (x - 4)^2 + (y - 1)^2.$$

Since (x, y) must satisfy the equation $2y = x^2$, we can eliminate y to get

$$\begin{aligned} d^2 &= f(x) \\ &= (x - 4)^2 + \left(\frac{x^2}{2} - 1\right)^2 \\ &= \frac{x^4}{4} - 8x + 17. \end{aligned}$$

The domain of f is all of $\mathcal{R}$.

3. $f'(x) = x^3 - 8$ and $f''(x) = 3x^2$. Therefore $f'(x) = 0$ if $x = 2$. Since $f''(2) > 0$, f has a minimum at 2.

4. The function f is differentiable throughout its domain, and its domain has no endpoints.

5. The point of the parabola $2y = x^2$ having abscissa 2 is (2, 2), which is the required point.

ORAL EXERCISES

In Exercises 1–8, discuss the given statements relative to the following problem: Determine the least possible cost for fencing a rectangular plot of 200 square feet if material costs \$3 per foot for one side and \$1 per foot for the other three sides.

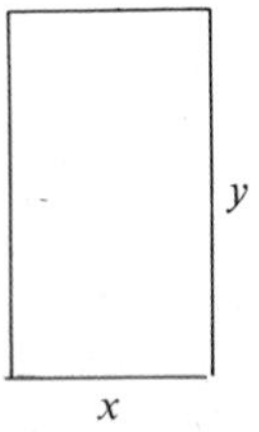

1. $C = 4x + 2y$
2. $xy = 200$
3. $C = f(x) = 4x + \dfrac{400}{x}$
4. $f'(x) = 4 - \dfrac{400}{x^2}$
5. $f'(x) = 0$ if $x = 10$
6. $f''(10) > 0$
7. $y = 20$
8. $C = 80$

WRITTEN EXERCISES

In Exercises 1–4, find two numbers whose sum is 12 which satisfy the stated condition. (*Hint:* Let the numbers be x and 12 − x.)

A

1. Their product is maximum.
2. The sum of their squares is minimum.
3. The product of one of the numbers and the square of the other is maximum.
4. The product of one of the numbers and the cube of the other is maximum.
5. A rectangular plot of ground is to be enclosed by using part of a long existing fence as one side and 120 feet of fencing for the other three sides. What is the greatest area which can be enclosed? (You may recall that we solved this exercise by algebraic methods in Chapter 2.)
6. Two hundred and forty feet of fencing are to be used to enclose a rectangular plot of ground and to separate it into two parts by means of a fence parallel to one of the sides. What is the greatest area which can be enclosed?

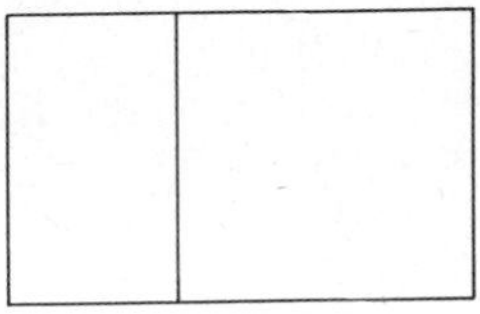

Ex. 6

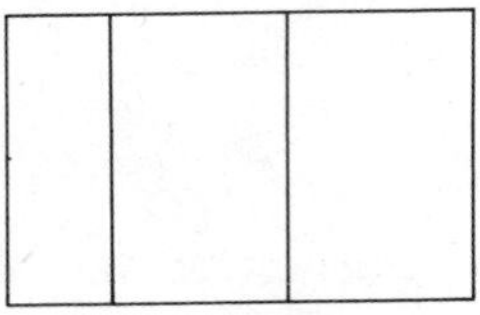

Ex. 7

7. Work Exercise 6 if the plot is to be separated into three parts by two fences parallel to one of the sides.
8. A rectangular plot of ground of area 1350 square feet is to be enclosed by fencing and separated into two parts by a fence parallel to one of the sides. What is the least length of fencing which can be used to do this?

9. Work Exercise 8 if the plot is to be separated into three parts by two fences parallel to one of the sides.

B 10. An open box is to be made from a square piece of cardboard 12 inches on a side by cutting equal squares out of the corners and folding up the flaps. Find the dimensions and volume of the box having the greatest volume.

11. Work Exercise 10 if the square of cardboard is a inches on a side.

12. At noon Ship A, steaming east at 10 knots, is 130 nautical miles due north of Ship B, which is steaming north at 15 knots. When will the ships be closest together?

13. Work Exercise 12 if the speed of Ship A is 15 knots and that of Ship B is 10 knots.

14. It is desired to construct an open rectangular box having square ends and volume 36 cubic feet. What should the dimensions be in order that the surface area be least?

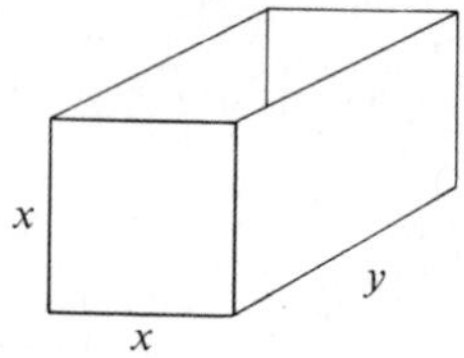

15. An open rectangular box having a square base and volume 64 cubic feet is to be built of materials costing \$2 per square foot for the base and \$1 per square foot for the sides. Find the most economical dimensions.

In Exercises 16–19, use the method of Example 4, page 162, to find the point on the line L which is closest to the point P.

16. L: $3x - y + 10 = 0$; $P(0, 0)$

17. L: $x + 2y = 5$; $P(0, 0)$

18. L: $2x - y = 3$; $P(-2, 3)$

19. L: $3x - 2y + 6 = 0$; $P(1, 2)$

20. Find the point of the parabola $y = x^2$ which is closest to the point $(3, 0)$.

21. Find the point of the curve $y = x^3$ which is closest to the point $(4, 0)$. (*Note:* The required point must have positive abscissa.)

22. Find the point on the parabola $6x = y^2$ which is closest to P.

a. $P(4, 0)$ **b.** $P(3, 0)$ **c.** $P(2, 0)$ **d.** $P(-1, 0)$

Further Applications

4–3 The Derivative as a Rate of Change

We shall begin by studying the motion of a point P which is moving on a line*. Two things are basic to this study: *time* and the *position* of the moving point P at each instant of time.

---

* We can study the motion of a material object, a car on a straight road, for example, by studying the motion of one of its points, its center of gravity, say.

Time may be measured, say in seconds, by taking any convenient instant to be time 0. To describe the position of P, we introduce a coordinate system on the line of motion, choosing some fixed point as the origin, 0. Then at any time t, the position of P is given by its coordinate, s, which is therefore a function of t:

$$s = f(t).$$

This equation is the **law of motion** of P.

Suppose P is moving in such a way that its law of motion is

$$s = f(t) = 8t - t^2,$$

where t is measured in seconds and s in feet. At each instant of time, P is moving with some definite velocity which, however, is different at different times. We shall discuss the velocity of P when $t = 2$, at which time the position of P is $f(2) = 12$. One second later, when $t = 3$, the position of P is $f(3) = 15$. During this second, the position of P changed by $f(3) - f(2) = 15 - 12 = 3$ feet, and therefore the *average rate of change of position with respect to time* is

$$\frac{\text{change in position}}{\text{change in time}} = \frac{f(3) - f(2)}{3 - 2} = \frac{15 - 12}{1} = 3 \text{ feet per second.}$$

This is the **average velocity** of P over the time interval from $t = 2$ to $t = 3$ and may be taken as an approximation to the velocity when $t = 2$.

We shall get a better approximation if we take a shorter time interval, say from $t = 2$ to $t = 2.1$. Over this time interval, the average velocity is

$$\frac{\text{change in position}}{\text{change in time}} = \frac{f(2.1) - f(2)}{2.1 - 2} = \frac{12.39 - 12}{0.1}$$

$$= \frac{0.39}{0.1} = 3.9 \text{ feet per second.}$$

Rather than repeat these calculations for shorter and shorter time intervals, let us consider the time interval from $t = 2$ to $t = z$. Then the average rate of change of position with respect to time is

$$\frac{\text{change in position}}{\text{change in time}} = \frac{f(z) - f(2)}{z - 2}.$$

The closer z is to 2, the better this average velocity approximates the velocity of P at $t = 2$, which we therefore take to be

$$\lim_{z \to 2} \frac{f(z) - f(2)}{z - 2}.$$

This limit is the derivative of f at 2, $f'(2)$. Since

$$f'(t) = 8 - 2t,$$

the velocity of P at 2 is $f'(2) = 4$ feet per second.

There is nothing special about time 2, however, so we conclude that for the point P, moving according to the law of motion

$$s = f(t) = 8t - t^2,$$

the velocity of P at *any* time t is

$$v = f'(t) = 8 - 2t.$$

We note that $v = f'(t)$ is *positive* if $t < 4$. This means (Theorem 9, Section 3–5, page 135) that $s = f(t)$ is *increasing;* therefore, if the s-axis is directed horizontally to the right, then P is moving to the *right* when $t < 4$. When $t > 4$, P is moving to the *left* because $v = f'(t) < 0$ for $t > 4$. At the instant $t = 4$, the velocity of P is 0, and P is momentarily at rest. The motion of P is indicated schematically in Figure 4–3.

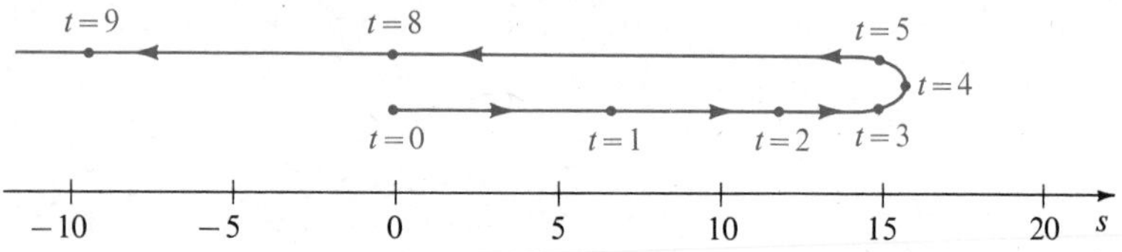

Figure 4–3

In general, if a point P is moving on a line in such a way that its law of motion is

$$s = f(t),$$

then the **velocity** of P at time t is

$$v = \frac{ds}{dt} = f'(t).$$

Just as *velocity* is the rate of change of *position* with respect to time, *acceleration* is the rate of change of *velocity* with respect to time. Thus the **acceleration** of P at time t is

$$a = \frac{dv}{dt} = f''(t).$$

In the example we considered above, we saw that $v = f'(t) = 8 - 2t$, and therefore $a = f''(t) = -2$.

EXAMPLE 1. The law of motion of a point P moving on an s-axis directed horizontally to the right is $s = t^3 - 6t^2 + 9t \quad (t \geq 0)$. Find

a. the velocity of P at time t;
b. the acceleration of P at time t;
c. the positions of P when P is at rest. Then
d. indicate the motion of P in a diagram similar to Figure 4–3.

Solution: The position function f of P is given by

$$s = f(t) = t^3 - 6t^2 + 9t.$$

a. $v = f'(t) = 3t^2 - 12t + 9.$
b. $a = f''(t) = 6t - 12.$
c. Since $v = 3t^2 - 12t + 9 = 3(t - 1)(t - 3)$, $v = 0$ when $t = 1$ and when $t = 3$. The position of P when $t = 1$ is $f(1) = 4$. The position of P when $t = 3$ is $f(3) = 0$.
d. If $t < 1$, then $v > 0$, and P is moving to the right.
If $1 < t < 3$, then $v < 0$, and P is moving to the left.
If $t > 3$, then $v > 0$, and P is moving to the right.

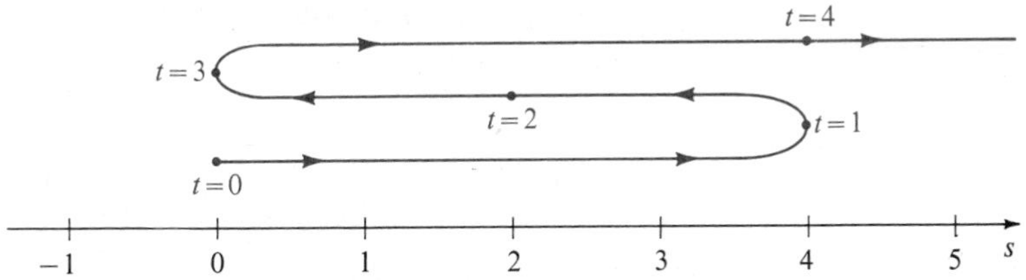

In considering laws of motion, $s = f(t)$, we have been interpreting $\frac{ds}{dt} = f'(t)$ as the rate of change of position with respect to time, that is, the *rate of change of s with respect to t*. We may extend this interpretation to the general case, $y = f(x)$, where x and y do not necessarily represent time and position:

If $y = f(x)$, then $\frac{dy}{dx}$, or $f'(x)$, is the **rate of change** of y with respect to x.

EXAMPLE 2. If A is the area of a circle of radius r inches, find the rate of change of A with respect to r when $A = 16\pi$ square inches.

Solution: We use the well-known expression for the area of a circle as a function of its radius:

$$A = f(r) = \pi r^2.$$

The rate of change of A with respect to r, for $r > 0$, is

$$\frac{dA}{dr} = f'(r) = 2\pi r.$$

When $A = 16\pi$, we have $\pi r^2 = 16\pi$, or $r = 4$. The required rate of change is therefore

$$f'(4) = 8\pi \text{ square inches per inch.}$$

This result can be interpreted as follows: If when $A = 16\pi$ (or $r = 4$) we increase r by a small amount, h inches, then A increases by about $8\pi h$ ($\doteq 25h$) square inches. Note that in increasing the radius from 4 to $4 + h$ inches, we are adding to the circle a band, or ring, of "width" h inches and "length" 8π inches (Figure 4–4); it is reasonable, therefore, that its area be about $8\pi h$ square inches.

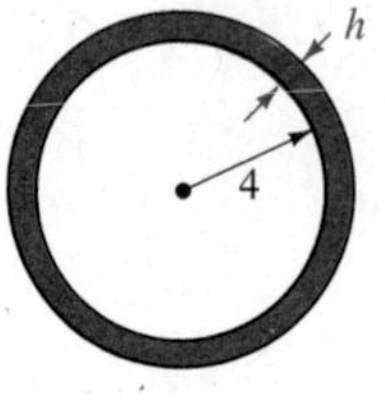

Figure 4–4

ORAL EXERCISES

1. If a ball is thrown vertically upward, is it at rest at any time before it hits the ground?
2. How would you define the *average acceleration* of a moving point over a time interval from $t = t_1$ to $t = t_2$?

At time $t = 0$, a moving point P has position $s = 0$ and velocity $v = 3$. When $t = 2$, P has position $s = 8$ and velocity $v = 1$.

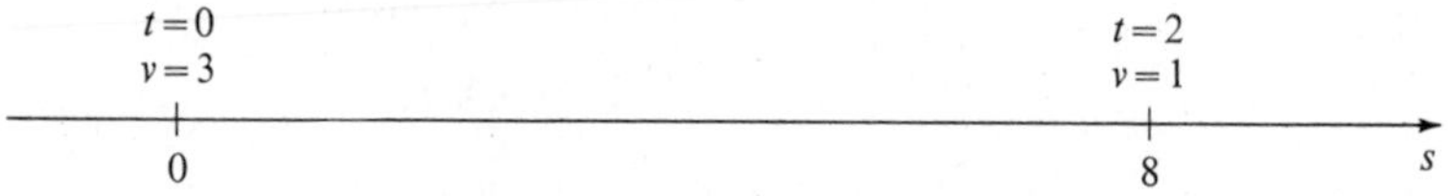

Answer the following questions about the motion of P during the time interval from $t = 0$ to $t = 2$.

3. What is the average velocity of P?
4. Could the velocity of P be negative at any time?
5. Must the acceleration of P be positive at some time?
6. Must the acceleration of P be negative at some time?
7. What is the average acceleration of P?

WRITTEN EXERCISES

In Exercises 1–6, the law of motion of a moving point P is given. Find

a. the velocity of P at time t;
b. the acceleration of P at time t;
c. the positions of P when P is at rest.
d. Indicate the motion of P in a diagram similar to Figure 4–3.

A

1. $s = t^2 - 6t$
2. $s = 2 + 6t - t^2$
3. $s = t^3 - 6t^2 + 9t$
4. $s = 12t^2 - t^3 - 36t$
5. $s = t^3 - 6t^2 + 12t$
6. $s = t^4 - 8t^3 + 22t^2 - 24t$

In Exercises 7–16, a geometrical figure is named first, and then two quantities associated with the figure are given. Find the rate of change of the first of these quantities with respect to the second for the given figure.

7. Square	Area	Length of an edge
8. Square	Perimeter	Length of an edge
9. Sphere	Volume	Radius
10. Sphere	Surface area	Radius
11. Circle	Circumference	Radius
12. Circle	Area	Diameter
13. Cube	Volume	Length of an edge
14. Cube	Surface area	Length of an edge
15. Equilateral triangle	Perimeter	Length of an edge
16. Equilateral triangle	Area	Length of an edge

4–4 Newton's Method

Very often in applied work, roots of equations or, equivalently, zeros of functions are needed. In textbooks, it is usually arranged that the exact values of these are easy to find (in order that the points being illustrated by the problem not be obscured by computation). In "real life," however, these exact values are seldom attainable, and approximation methods must be used. We shall discuss a method for approximating the zeros of functions which, although it was discovered by Newton, is well adapted to use on modern high-speed computers.

We shall introduce Newton's method by considering an example. We know that the polynomial function

$$g: x \rightarrow x^3 - 3x - 1$$

has at least one zero between 1 and 2 because $g(1) < 0$ and $g(2) > 0$. Since g has no rational zeros, however, finding the exact values of its zeros is not easy.

The graph of g is shown in Figure 4–5. From it we see that g has one zero, r, between 1 and 2, and two negative zeros. We shall show how to get successively better approximations to the zero r.

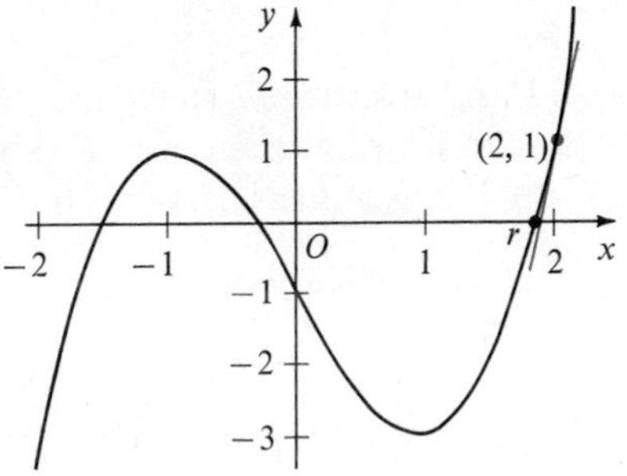

Figure 4–5

Since r appears to be quite close to 2, we may regard $x_1 = 2$ as a first approximation to r. Figure 4–5 suggests that the x-intercept, x_2, of the line tangent to the graph of g at $(x_1, g(x_1)) = (2, 1)$ is a *better* approximation to r.

Since $g'(x) = 3x^2 - 3$, the slope of the tangent line at (2, 1) is $g'(2) = 9$, and an equation of the line is

$$y - 1 = 9(x - 2), \quad \text{or} \quad 9x - y = 17.$$

The x-intercept, x_2, of this line (found by setting $y = 0$) is

$$x_2 = \tfrac{17}{9} \doteq 1.89;$$

this is the second approximation to r. Figure 4–6 (which shows a distorted portion of the graph of g near the zero r) suggests how we could repeat the process, using x_2 in place of x_1, to find the third approximation, x_3.

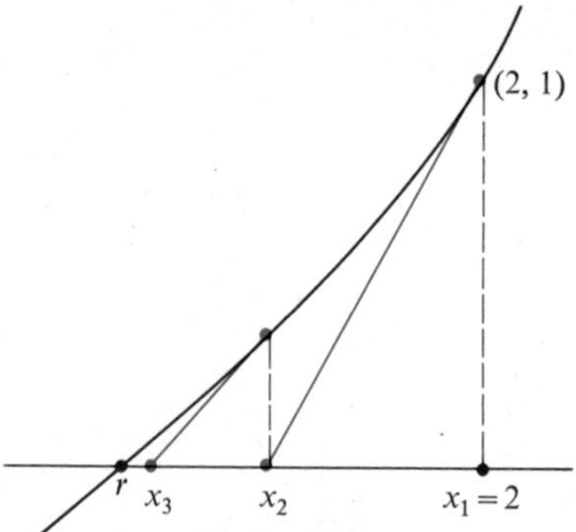

Figure 4–6

Suppose now that we have found the nth approximation, x_n, to a zero r of a differentiable function f. The line tangent to the graph of f at $(x_n, f(x_n))$ has slope $f'(x_n)$. (See Figure 4–7.) Therefore the equation of this tangent line is

$$y - f(x_n) = f'(x_n)(x - x_n). \quad (*)$$

We take the x-intercept, x_{n+1}, of this line as the $(n + 1)$st approximation to r. To find this x-intercept, we set $y = 0$ in (*), obtaining

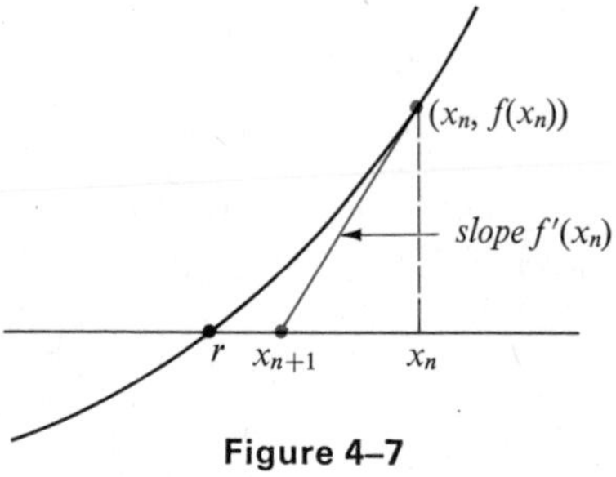

Figure 4–7

$$0 - f(x_n) = f'(x_n)(x - x_n),$$

or

$$x = x_{n+1} = \frac{f'(x_n)x_n - f(x_n)}{f'(x_n)}.$$

Thus, provided $f'(x_n) \neq 0$,

$$x_{n+1} = x_n - \frac{f(x_n)}{f'(x_n)}.$$

This is the *recursion formula*† of Newton's Method.

We shall illustrate the use of this formula by continuing the example at the beginning of the section.

EXAMPLE 1. Approximate the positive zero of

$$g\colon x \to x^3 - 3x - 1$$

to four decimal places.

---

† That is, a formula which gives each term of a sequence, beyond the first, in terms of its predecessor.

Solution: Again we choose for our first approximation $x_1 = 2$. Then $x_2 = x_1 - \dfrac{g(x_1)}{g'(x_1)}$. We may find $g(x_1)$ and $g'(x_1)$ by the "double division" process (page 129).

$$\begin{array}{r|rrrl} x_1 = 2 & 1 & 0 & -3 & -1 \\ & 1 & 2 & 1 & 1 = g(x_1) \\ & 1 & 4 & 9 = g'(x_1) & \end{array}$$

Hence $x_2 = 2 - \frac{1}{9} = \frac{17}{9} \doteq 1.89$.

Then $x_3 = x_2 - \dfrac{g(x_2)}{g'(x_2)}$.

$$\begin{array}{r|rrrl} x_2 = 1.89 & 1 & 0 & -3 & -1 \\ & 1 & 1.89 & 0.5721 & 0.08127 \doteq g(x_2) \\ & 1 & 3.78 & 7.7163 = g'(x_2) & \end{array}$$

Hence $x_3 \doteq 1.89 - \dfrac{0.08127}{7.7163} \doteq 1.89 - 0.0105 = 1.8795$.

Then $x_4 = x_3 - \dfrac{g(x_3)}{g'(x_3)}$.

$$\begin{array}{r|rrrl} x_3 = 1.8795 & 1 & 0 & -3 & -1 \\ & 1 & 1.8795 & 0.53252 & 0.00087 \doteq g(x_3) \\ & 1 & 3.7590 & 7.59756 \doteq g'(x_3) & \end{array}$$

Hence $x_4 \doteq 1.8795 - \dfrac{0.00087}{7.59756} \doteq 1.8795 - 0.0001 = 1.8794$.

Further applications of Newton's formula cause no change in the fourth decimal place, so we take 1.8794 as the desired approximation.

In using Newton's Method, a good working rule is to retain at each intermediate step about twice as many decimal places as in the preceding step.

Some care must be exercised in the choice of the first approximation, x_1, to a zero r of a function f. If the graph of f has a critical point or an inflection point whose abscissa lies between r and x_1 or x_2, Newton's Method may fail, as illustrated in Figure 4–8.

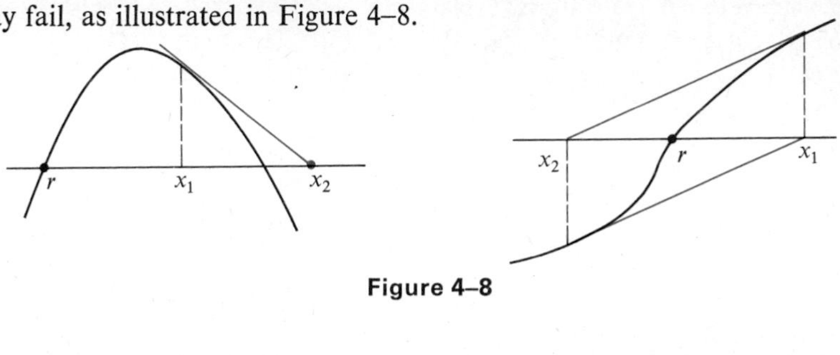

Figure 4–8

EXAMPLE 2. Find $\sqrt[3]{3.842}$ to three decimal places.

Solution: The problem is equivalent to approximating the zero of the function f, where

$$f(x) = x^3 - 3.842.$$

Since $f'(x) = 3x^2$, the recursion formula of Newton's Method is

$$x_{n+1} = x_n - \frac{x_n^3 - 3.842}{3x_n^2}.$$

(Because the critical point and the inflection point of the graph of f have abscissa 0, the difficulties referred to on page 171 will not occur if x_1 and x_2 are positive.)

Letting $x_1 = 1.5$ (a rough guess), we find

$$x_2 = 1.5 - \frac{(1.5)^3 - 3.842}{3(1.5)^2} = 1.5 + \frac{0.467}{6.75} \doteq 1.569,$$

$$x_3 = 1.569 - \frac{(1.569)^3 - 3.842}{3(1.569)^2} \doteq 1.569 - 0.0028 = 1.5662.$$

Further iterations (repetitions of the process) do not affect the third decimal place. Therefore, $\sqrt[3]{3.842} \doteq 1.566$.

ORAL EXERCISES

1. Referring to the figure at the right, explain geometrically how starting with an initial approximation $x_1 = 2$ to the solution of $f(x) = 0$, Newton's Method would yield $x_2 = 1$ as a second approximation.

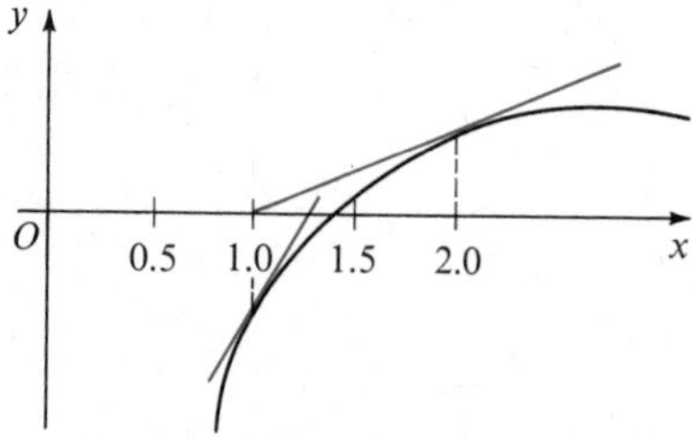

2. Repeat Exercise 1, starting with $x_2 = 1$ and explaining how the next approximation would be obtained.
3. Referring to the figure above, explain why

$$\frac{0 - f(x_1)}{x_2 - x_1} = f'(x_1)$$

and therefore

$$x_2 = x_1 - \frac{f(x_1)}{f'(x_1)}.$$

4. What is the recursion formula of Newton's Method?

WRITTEN EXERCISES

Use Newton's Method to find the indicated root to three decimal places.

A

1. $\sqrt{2}$
2. $\sqrt{5}$
3. $\sqrt[3]{-4}$
4. $\sqrt[3]{2}$
5. $\sqrt[3]{-2.664}$
6. $\sqrt[4]{8.642}$

Use Newton's Method to find the indicated zero of the given function to three decimal places.

7. $f: x \to x^3 - 3x + 1$, between 0 and 1
8. $f: x \to x^3 - 3x + 1$, between -2 and -1
9. $f: x \to x^3 + 2x - 4$, the only zero
10. $f: x \to x^4 + 2x^2 - 2$, the positive zero
11. Find the abscissa of the point of intersection of the graphs of $y = x^3$ and $2x + y = 2$.

B

12. Show that if a is positive, the recursion formula of Newton's Method for approximating $\sqrt{a}$ can be written in the form

$$x_{n+1} = \frac{1}{2}\left(x_n + \frac{a}{x_n}\right).$$

13. Show that for any real number a, the recursion formula of Newton's Method for approximating $\sqrt[3]{a}$ can be written in the form

$$x_{n+1} = \frac{1}{3}\left(2x_n + \frac{a}{x_n^2}\right).$$

C

14. Find a form of the Newton's Method recursion formula, similar to those in Exercises 12 and 13, for approximating $\sqrt[k]{a}$, $a > 0$, k a positive integer.

■ Techniques of Differentiation

4–5 Derivatives of Products and Quotients

In this section and in the next, we shall consider some theorems about differentiation which will be useful in solving applied problems.

Because the derivative of the sum of two functions is the sum of their derivatives, we might be tempted to think that the derivative of the product of two functions is the product of their derivatives. The following example shows that this is *not* true.

Let $f: x \to x^3$ and $g: x \to x^2$. Then $fg: x \to x^3 \cdot x^2$, or $fg: x \to x^5$, and therefore the derivative of the product is

$$(fg)'(x) = 5x^4.$$

Since $f'(x) = 3x^2$ and $g'(x) = 2x$, the product of the derivatives is

$$f'(x) \cdot g'(x) = 3x^2 \cdot 2x = 6x^3.$$

Therefore $(fg)'(x) \neq f'(x) \cdot g'(x)$.

The correct formula for the derivative of the product of two functions is the *Product Rule* given in the next theorem.

Theorem 1.

If the functions f and g are differentiable at x, then fg is differentiable at x and

$$(fg)'(x) = f(x)g'(x) + f'(x)g(x).$$

Proof

The difference quotient is

$$\frac{(fg)(z) - (fg)(x)}{z - x} = \frac{f(z)g(z) - f(x)g(x)}{z - x}$$

$$= \frac{f(z)g(z) - f(z)g(x) + f(z)g(x) - f(x)g(x)}{z - x} \qquad (1)$$

$$= f(z)\frac{g(z) - g(x)}{z - x} + \frac{f(z) - f(x)}{z - x}\, g(x). \qquad (2)$$

To arrive at (1), we use the trick of adding and subtracting the same quantity, $f(z)g(x)$, in the numerator; doing this does not change the value of the fraction. To get from (1) to (2), we split the fraction into two fractions and factor.

Now, by hypothesis, f and g are differentiable at x, so that

$$\lim_{z \to x} \frac{g(z) - g(x)}{z - x} = g'(x) \quad \text{and} \quad \lim_{z \to x} \frac{f(z) - f(x)}{z - x} = f'(x).$$

Since f is differentiable at x, f is continuous at x by Theorem 4, page 124. Therefore, by the definition of continuity,

$$\lim_{z \to x} f(z) = f(x).$$

Hence, by the properties of limits, fg is differentiable at x and

$$(fg)'(x) = \lim_{z \to x} \frac{(fg)(z) - (fg)(x)}{z - x} = f(x)g'(x) + f'(x)g(x).$$

EXAMPLE 1. Find the derivative of the function

$$\phi: x \to (x^3 + 1)(x^2 + 4)$$

by two methods.

First Method: If we let $f(x) = x^3 + 1$ and $g(x) = x^2 + 4$, we see that

$$\phi(x) = f(x) \cdot g(x) = (fg)(x).$$

Since f and g are differentiable, by Theorem 1 we have

$$\begin{aligned}\phi'(x) &= (fg)'(x) = f(x)g'(x) + f'(x)g(x)\\ &= (x^3 + 1)2x + 3x^2(x^2 + 4)\\ &= 5x^4 + 12x^2 + 2x.\end{aligned}$$

Second Method: If we multiply the binomials $f(x)$ and $g(x)$ together, we get

$$\phi(x) = x^5 + 4x^3 + x^2 + 4.$$

The derivative of this polynomial function is

$$\phi'(x) = 5x^4 + 12x^2 + 2x.$$

We shall find the Product Rule more useful when we have a greater variety of functions to work with.

EXAMPLE 2. Assume that if $f: x \to \sqrt{x}$, then $f'(x) = \dfrac{1}{2\sqrt{x}}$ (see Exercise 30, page 126). Find the derivative of $\phi: x \to \sqrt{x}\,(x^2 + 1)$ for $x > 0$.

Solution: Taking $f(x) = \sqrt{x}$ and $g(x) = x^2 + 1$, we have

$$\phi(x) = f(x) \cdot g(x) = (fg)(x).$$

Therefore

$$\begin{aligned}\phi'(x) &= (fg)'(x) = f(x)g'(x) + f'(x)g(x)\\ &= \sqrt{x}(2x) + \frac{1}{2\sqrt{x}}(x^2 + 1) \qquad (*)\\ &= \frac{4x^2 + (x^2 + 1)}{2\sqrt{x}} = \frac{5x^2 + 1}{2\sqrt{x}}.\end{aligned}$$

After a little practice with product problems, you should be able to identify the factors $f(x)$ and $g(x)$ *mentally* and proceed directly to the (*) step.

The next theorem gives us the *Quotient Rule* for finding the derivative of the quotient of two functions.

Theorem 2.

If the functions f and g are differentiable at x and $g(x) \neq 0$, then $\frac{f}{g}$ is differentiable at x and

$$\left(\frac{f}{g}\right)'(x) = \frac{f'(x)g(x) - f(x)g'(x)}{[g(x)]^2}.$$

We can prove Theorem 2 using the following two steps:

First we prove that

$$\left(\frac{1}{g}\right)'(x) = -\frac{g'(x)}{[g(x)]^2}. \tag{R}$$

(This formula for the derivative of the reciprocal of a function is useful in its own right.) Then we think of the quotient $\frac{f}{g}$ as $f \cdot \left(\frac{1}{g}\right)$ and use Theorem 1 and (R). The details are left as Exercises 24 and 25, page 178.

EXAMPLE 3. Find $\phi'(x)$ if

a. $\phi\colon x \to \dfrac{x^3}{x^2 + 1}$ **b.** $\phi\colon x \to \dfrac{1}{mx + b}$

Solution: **a.** If we let $f(x) = x^3$ and $g(x) = x^2 + 1$, then

$$\phi(x) = \frac{f(x)}{g(x)} = \left(\frac{f}{g}\right)(x).$$

Since f and g are differentiable and $g(x)$ is never 0, by Theorem 2 we have

$$\phi'(x) = \left(\frac{f}{g}\right)'(x) = \frac{f'(x)g(x) - f(x)g'(x)}{[g(x)]^2}$$

$$= \frac{3x^2(x^2 + 1) - x^3(2x)}{(x^2 + 1)^2} \tag{*}$$

$$= \frac{x^4 + 3x^2}{(x^2 + 1)^2}.$$

(You should assign $f(x)$ and $g(x)$ mentally, so that (*) is the first step actually written down.)

b. Thinking of $mx + b$ as being $g(x)$ and using (R), we have

$$\phi'(x) = -\frac{m}{(mx + b)^2}.$$

ORAL EXERCISES

1. Complete the statement: "The derivative of the product of two functions is the first times the derivative of the second plus . . . ."

2. Give statements similar to the one in Exercise 1 for the derivative of **(a)** the reciprocal of a function and **(b)** the quotient of two functions.

3. If $f'(x) = \alpha(x)$ and $g'(x) = \beta(x)$, what is $(fg)'(x)$?

4. If $f'(x) = \alpha(x)$, $g'(x) = \beta(x)$, and $g(x) \neq 0$, what is $\left(\frac{f}{g}\right)'(x)$?

WRITTEN EXERCISES

In Exercises 1–4, find y' by two methods (see Example 1, page 175).

A

1. $y = x^2(x^2 + 1)$

2. $y = (x + 2)(x^2 + 1)$

3. $y = (x^2 + 1)(x^2 + x)$

4. $y = (x^3 + 1)(x^2 + 2x + 3)$

In Exercises 5–16, find $\phi'(x)$. If fractions are involved, express the answer as a single fraction in simple form with no radicals in the denominator. (You may use the fact that $\frac{d}{dx}\sqrt{x} = \frac{1}{2\sqrt{x}}$ when needed.)

5. $\phi: x \rightarrow x\sqrt{x}$

6. $\phi: x \rightarrow x^2\sqrt{x}$

7. $\phi: x \rightarrow (x + 1)\sqrt{x}$

8. $\phi: x \rightarrow x(\sqrt{x} + 1)$

9. $\phi: x \rightarrow \frac{1}{1 - x}$

10. $\phi: x \rightarrow \frac{1}{x^2 + 1}$

11. $\phi: x \rightarrow \frac{x + 1}{x - 1}$

12. $\phi: x \rightarrow \frac{x - 1}{x + 1}$

13. $\phi: x \rightarrow \frac{x + 1}{\sqrt{x}}$

14. $\phi: x \rightarrow \frac{x^2 + 1}{\sqrt{x}}$

15. $\phi: x \rightarrow \frac{x^2 + 1}{x + 1}$

16. $\phi: x \rightarrow \frac{x + 1}{x^2 + 1}$

In Exercises 17–20, find an equation of the line tangent to the given curve at the given point.

17. $y = \frac{1}{x}$; $(1, 1)$

18. $y = \frac{1}{x^2}$; $(2, \frac{1}{4})$

19. $y = \dfrac{1}{\sqrt{x}}$; $(4, \frac{1}{2})$

20. $y = \dfrac{x+1}{x}$; $(-1, 0)$

In the remaining exercises, assume that the functions involved are differentiable.

B **21.** Use Theorem 1 to show that if $y = [f(x)]^2$, then $y' = 2f(x)f'(x)$.

22. Show that

$$\frac{d}{dx}(uvw) = uv\frac{dw}{dx} + uw\frac{dv}{dx} + vw\frac{du}{dx}.$$

C **23.** Use Theorem 1 to prove by mathematical induction that $\dfrac{d}{dx}x^n = nx^{n-1}$ for all positive integers n.

24. Prove formula (R) of the text. [*Hint:* Set up and simplify the difference quotient

$$\frac{\dfrac{1}{g(z)} - \dfrac{1}{g(x)}}{z - x}.$$

Then use $\lim\limits_{z \to x} \dfrac{g(z) - g(x)}{z - x} = g'(x)$ and $\lim\limits_{z \to x} g(z) = g(x)$.]

25. Prove Theorem 2 using the method suggested in the text. (See Exercise 24.)

26. Prove that $\dfrac{d}{dx}x^n = nx^{n-1}$ if n is a *negative* integer. (*Hint:* Let $m = -n$. Then m is a positive integer, and $x^n = x^{-m} = \dfrac{1}{x^m}$. Now use (R) and Theorem 5, page 126.)

27. Prove that $\dfrac{d}{dx}x^{n+\frac{1}{2}} = (n + \frac{1}{2})x^{(n+\frac{1}{2})-1}$ if n is an integer.

$\left(\textit{Hint: } x^{n+\frac{1}{2}} = x^n x^{\frac{1}{2}} = x^n\sqrt{x}, \text{ and you may use the fact that } \dfrac{d}{dx}\sqrt{x} = \dfrac{1}{2\sqrt{x}}.\right)$

28. Let r be a zero of the polynomial function f. Then by the Factor Theorem, $f(x) = (x - r)g(x)$.

a. Find $f'(x)$.

b. Show that if r is a multiple zero of f, then r is a zero of f'.

c. Show that the converse of the statement in (**b**) is true.

d. Formulate the results (**b**) and (**c**) as a theorem.

4–6 The Chain Rule

In this section, you will learn how to find the derivative of the composition of two functions and will, as a consequence, be able to differentiate many functions to which the formulas developed thus far cannot be directly applied. At this point you should reread Section 1–6, in which the concept of composition was introduced.

Suppose we wish to find the derivative of

$$\phi: x \to \sqrt{x^2 + 1}.$$

In Example 4 of Section 1–6, we showed that

$$\phi = g \circ f,$$

where

$$f: x \to x^2 + 1 \quad \text{and} \quad g: x \to \sqrt{x}.$$

That is,

$$\phi(x) = (g \circ f)(x) = g(f(x)) = g(x^2 + 1) = \sqrt{x^2 + 1}.$$

We can find the derivatives of both f and g:

$$f'(x) = 2x \quad \text{and} \quad g'(x) = \frac{1}{2\sqrt{x}}.$$

The next theorem (whose proof we defer; see pages 182–183 and Exercise 21, page 184) enables us to use these derivatives to find the derivative of ϕ.

Theorem 3.

If f is differentiable at x, g is differentiable at $f(x)$, and $\phi = g \circ f$, then ϕ is differentiable at x and

$$\phi'(x) = (g \circ f)'(x) = g'(f(x)) \cdot f'(x).$$

In our example, we have $f'(x) = 2x$, and since $g'(x) = \dfrac{1}{2\sqrt{x}}$, we have

$$g'(f(x)) = \frac{1}{2\sqrt{f(x)}} = \frac{1}{2\sqrt{x^2 + 1}}.$$

Thus, using Theorem 3, we get

$$\phi'(x) = \frac{1}{2\sqrt{x^2 + 1}} \cdot 2x = \frac{x}{\sqrt{x^2 + 1}}.$$

The formula for $(g \circ f)'(x)$ given in Theorem 3 is commonly known as the *Chain Rule*.

EXAMPLE 1. If $\phi = g \circ f$, where $f: x \to x^3 + 3x + 1$ and $g: x \to x^{10}$, find $\phi'(x)$.

Solution: We have $f'(x) = 3x^2 + 3$, $g'(x) = 10x^9$, and $g'(f(x)) = 10[f(x)]^9 = 10(x^3 + 3x + 1)^9$. Both f and g are differentiable on $\mathcal{R}$. Therefore, using Theorem 3, we have

$$\begin{aligned} \phi'(x) &= 10(x^3 + 3x + 1)^9 \cdot (3x^2 + 3) \\ &= 30(x^2 + 1)(x^3 + 3x + 1)^9. \end{aligned}$$

In Example 1, $\phi(x) = g(f(x)) = (x^3 + 3x + 1)^{10}$. We have therefore solved the problem

"If $\phi\colon x \to (x^3 + 3x + 1)^{10}$, find $\phi'(x)$"

and its equivalent,

$$\text{“If } y = (x^3 + 3x + 1)^{10}, \text{ find } \frac{dy}{dx}.\text{”} \qquad (*)$$

Had Example 1 been stated in either of these forms, however, we would first have had to identify the functions f and g before applying Theorem 3.

Looking at (*), we might well reason as follows:

We have

$$y = u^{10}, \text{ where } u = x^3 + 3x + 1.$$

We can easily find the derivatives $\frac{dy}{du}$ and $\frac{du}{dx}$:

$$\frac{dy}{du} = 10u^9 \quad \text{and} \quad \frac{du}{dx} = 3x^2 + 3.$$

How do we put these together to obtain $\frac{dy}{dx}$? The next theorem, a paraphrase of Theorem 3, tells us to multiply them:

$$\frac{dy}{dx} = \frac{dy}{du}\cdot\frac{du}{dx} = 10u^9 \cdot (3x^2 + 3) = 10(x^3 + 3x + 1)^9(3x^2 + 3).$$

Theorem 3′.

If $y = g(u)$ and $u = f(x)$, then

$$\frac{dy}{dx} = \frac{dy}{du}\cdot\frac{du}{dx}$$

provided the derivatives on the right-hand side of the equation exist.

We can show that the result in Theorem 3′ is consistent with Theorem 3 as follows: From $y = g(u)$, we have $\frac{dy}{du} = g'(u)$; and from $u = f(x)$, we have $\frac{du}{dx} = f'(x)$. We also have $y = g(u) = g(f(x)) = (g \circ f)(x)$. Hence, using Theorem 3, we have

$$\frac{dy}{dx} = (g \circ f)'(x) = g'(f(x)) \cdot f'(x) = g'(u) \cdot f'(x) = \frac{dy}{du}\cdot\frac{du}{dx},$$

as stated in Theorem 3′.

EXAMPLE 2. If $\phi: x \to \sqrt{a^2 - x^2}$, find $\phi'(x)$.

Solution: Let $y = \phi(x) = \sqrt{a^2 - x^2}$. We can "break down" this rather complicated expression by letting $u = a^2 - x^2$. Then we have

$$y = \sqrt{u} \quad \text{and} \quad u = a^2 - x^2.$$

These are easily differentiated:

$$\frac{dy}{du} = \frac{1}{2\sqrt{u}} \quad \text{and} \quad \frac{du}{dx} = -2x.$$

Using Theorem 3′, we have

$$\phi'(x) = \frac{dy}{dx} = \frac{dy}{du} \cdot \frac{du}{dx} = \frac{1}{2\sqrt{u}} \cdot (-2x) = \frac{-x}{\sqrt{u}} = \frac{-x}{\sqrt{a^2 - x^2}}.$$

(The "intermediate variable" u was introduced only as a convenience and should not appear in the final answer. After you have had enough practice, you can omit it altogether.)

The result of Example 2 is the third one of the following frequently used formulas:

$$\frac{d}{dx}\sqrt{x^2 + a^2} = \frac{x}{\sqrt{x^2 + a^2}}, \quad \frac{d}{dx}\sqrt{x^2 - a^2} = \frac{x}{\sqrt{x^2 - a^2}},$$

$$\frac{d}{dx}\sqrt{a^2 - x^2} = \frac{-x}{\sqrt{a^2 - x^2}}.$$

The derivations of the other two are left as Exercises 13 and 14, page 183.

EXAMPLE 3. Determine the area of the trapezoid of greatest area which can be inscribed in a semicircle of radius a, as shown in the figure at the right.

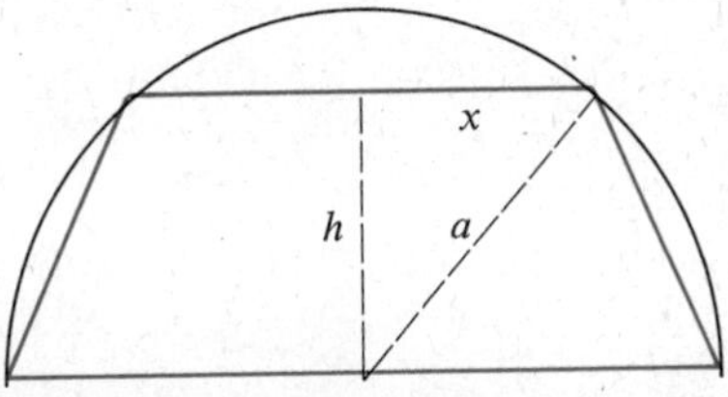

Solution: (The numbered steps follow the pattern established in Section 4–2 for the solution of extremum problems.)

1. The quantity to be maximized is the area A of the trapezoid.
2. We can express A in terms of either h, the height of the trapezoid, or x, half the length of the shorter of the parallel sides; it is easier to do the latter. The lengths of the parallel sides are then $2x$ and $2a$, and $h = \sqrt{a^2 - x^2}$ by the Pythagorean Theorem. Hence

   $A = f(x) = \frac{1}{2}(2x + 2a)\sqrt{a^2 - x^2} = (x + a)\sqrt{a^2 - x^2}.$

   The domain of f is $\{x: 0 \le x \le a\}$.

(Solution continued)

3. Using the formula for the derivative of a product (Theorem 1, page 174) and the result of Example 2, we find that

$$\frac{dA}{dx} = f'(x) = (x + a)\frac{-x}{\sqrt{a^2 - x^2}} + \sqrt{a^2 - x^2}$$

$$= \frac{(a - 2x)(a + x)}{\sqrt{a^2 - x^2}}. \qquad (*)$$

The expression (*) is zero if $x = -a$ or $x = \frac{a}{2}$. However, since $-a$ is not in the domain of f, the only zero of f' is $\frac{a}{2}$, and

$$f\left(\frac{a}{2}\right) = \left(\frac{a}{2} + a\right)\sqrt{a^2 - \left(\frac{a}{2}\right)^2} = \frac{3\sqrt{3}}{4}a^2$$

is seen, with the help of the f'-test, to be a relative maximum.

4. The function f is differentiable at all interior points of its domain. Because $f(0) = a^2 < \frac{3\sqrt{3}}{4}a^2$ and $f(a) = 0$, the maximum value of A does not occur at an endpoint of the domain of f.
5. Therefore the required area is $\frac{3\sqrt{3}}{4}a^2$.

Now that we have considered several examples, we shall turn to the proof of Theorem 3. The plausibility of Theorem 3

> If f is differentiable at x and g is differentiable at $f(x)$, then $g \circ f$ is differentiable at x and
>
> $$(g \circ f)'(x) = g'(f(x)) \cdot f'(x).$$

can be seen from the following argument:

If $z \neq x$ and $f(z) \neq f(x)$, we have

$$\frac{g(f(z)) - g(f(x))}{z - x} = \frac{g(f(z)) - g(f(x))}{f(z) - f(x)} \cdot \frac{f(z) - f(x)}{z - x}, \qquad (1)$$

or, letting $a = f(x)$ and $b = f(z)$ in the first factor of the product in (1),

$$\frac{(g \circ f)(z) - (g \circ f)(x)}{z - x} = \frac{g(b) - g(a)}{b - a} \cdot \frac{f(z) - f(x)}{z - x}. \qquad (2)$$

As z approaches x, $f(z)$ approaches $f(x)$ [because f is continuous at x], and therefore b approaches a. Thus, taking the limit as z approaches x in (2), we see that $g \circ f$ is differentiable at x and

$$(g \circ f)'(x) = g'(a) \cdot f'(x) = g'(f(x)) \cdot f'(x).$$

The argument given above fails to prove Theorem 3 only because it might happen that $f(z) = f(x)$ for infinitely many z's arbitrarily close to x (Equation (1) is not then valid). A proof which is valid in all cases is indicated in Exercise 21, page 184.

ORAL EXERCISES

Use the Chain Rule to explain the following results.

1. $\frac{d}{dx} u^n = nu^{n-1} \frac{du}{dx}$

2. $\frac{d}{dx}(4x - 5)^{100} = 100(4x - 5)^{99}(4)$

3. $\frac{d}{dx}(x^2 + 3x - 1)^7 = 7(x^2 + 3x - 1)^6(2x + 3)$

4. $\frac{d}{dx}\left(\frac{x}{x^2 + 1}\right)^{10} = 10\left(\frac{x}{x^2 + 1}\right)^9 \frac{(x^2 + 1)(1) - x(2x)}{(x^2 + 1)^2}$

WRITTEN EXERCISES

Find $\frac{dy}{dx}$ in two ways: (a) by putting the right-hand side of each equation in standard polynomial form and then differentiating and (b) by using Theorem 3′ with u representing the quantity inside parentheses.

A

1. $y = (x + 1)^3$
2. $y = (2x - 3)^2$
3. $y = (x^2 + 1)^2$
4. $y = (1 - x^2)^3$
5. $y = (x^2 + 2x + 4)^2$
6. $y = (x^2 + 2x)^4$

Find $(g \circ f)'(x)$.

7. $f: x \to x + 2,\ g: x \to x^4$
8. $f: x \to 1 - x,\ g: x \to x^3$
9. $f: x \to 1 - x^2,\ g: x \to \frac{1}{x}$
10. $f: x \to x^2 + 1,\ g: x \to \frac{1}{x}$

Find $\phi'(x)$.

11. $\phi: x \to (2x + 1)^{10}$ (*Hint:* Let $y = \phi(x)$, $u = 2x + 1$. Then $y = u^{10}$. Use Theorem 3′.)
12. $\phi: x \to (x^2 + 1)^{10}$
13. $\phi: x \to \sqrt{x^2 + a^2}$ } (See Example 2, page 181.)
14. $\phi: x \to \sqrt{x^2 - a^2}$ }
15. $\phi: x \to \sqrt{x^2 + 2x}$
16. $\phi: x \to \sqrt{3x - x^3}$

B **17.** Find the area of the isosceles triangle of greatest area which can be inscribed in a circle of radius a, as shown below. (*Hint:* Express the area in terms of x.)

18. Find the radius and height of the right circular cylinder of greatest lateral (curved) area which can be inscribed in a sphere of radius a, as shown below.

19. Find the radius and height of the right circular cone of greatest lateral area which can be inscribed in a sphere of radius a. (*Hint:* Express the area, πrs, in terms of the x shown in the figure below.)

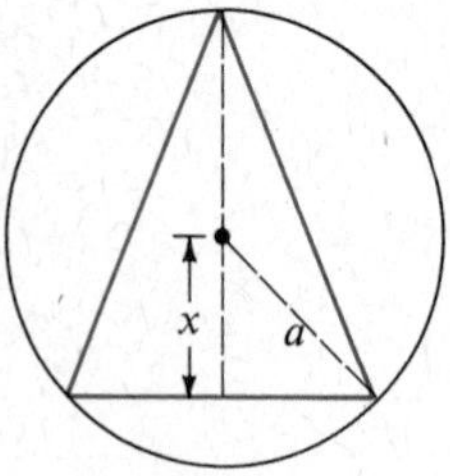

Ex. 17

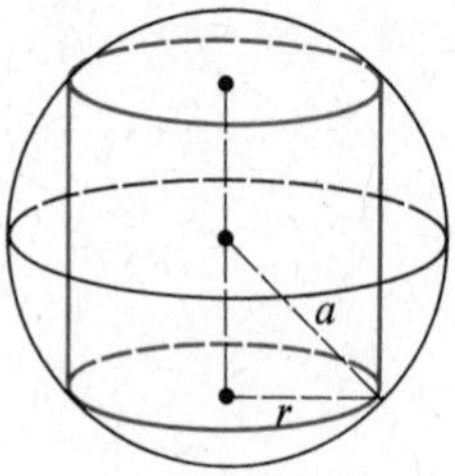

Ex. 18

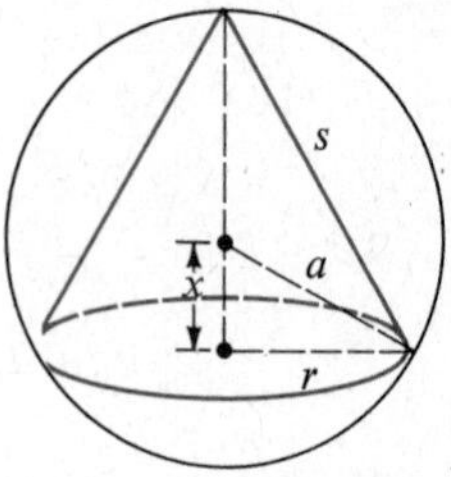

Ex. 19

20. A man in a rowboat at P, 2 miles from the nearest point, A, of a straight shore, wishes to reach a point B on the shore, 4 miles from A, in the least possible time. If he can row 3 m.p.h. and run 5 m.p.h., how far from A should he land? (*Hint:* Referring to the figure, express the distance from P to Q in terms of x; then find how long it takes to row from P to Q. Add to this the time it takes to run from Q to B, and minimize the resulting function of x.)

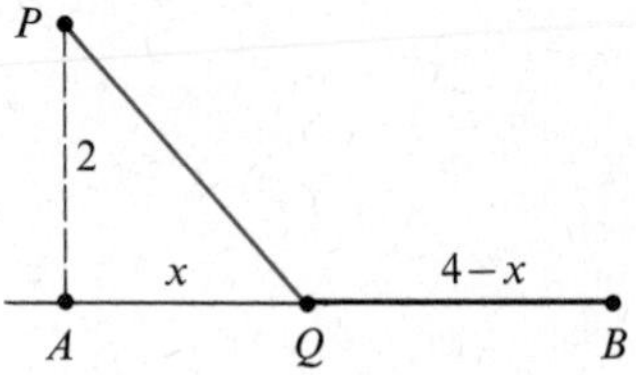

C **21.** (Proof of Theorem 3) Let $f(x) = a$, and define a new function h as follows:

$$h(u) = \begin{cases} \dfrac{g(u) - g(a)}{u - a} - g'(a) & \text{if } u \neq a \\ 0 & \text{if } u = a. \end{cases}$$

a. Show that because $\lim_{u \to a} \dfrac{g(u) - g(a)}{u - a} = g'(a)$, we have

$$\lim_{u \to a} h(u) = 0.$$

b. Show that

$$g(u) - g(a) = (u - a)[h(u) + g'(a)]$$

is valid for $u \neq a$ and for $u = a$.

c. In (**b**), let $u = f(z)$ and replace a by $f(x)$. Show that for $z \neq x$,

$$\frac{g(f(z)) - g(f(x))}{z - x} = \frac{f(z) - f(x)}{z - x}[h(f(z)) + g'(f(x))].$$

d. Let z approach x. Explain why $f(z)$ approaches $f(x) = a$, and why $h(f(z))$ approaches 0.

e. Use (**c**) and (**d**) to obtain $(g \circ f)'(x) = f'(x) \cdot g'(f(x))$.

4–7 Related Rates; Implicit Differentiation

The Chain Rule is often useful in determining the rate of change of one of two related quantities when the rate of change of the other is given. This situation occurs frequently when the quantities are physically or geometrically related.

EXAMPLE 1. Hydrogen is being pumped into a spherical balloon at the rate of 100 cubic feet per minute. At what rate is the radius of the balloon increasing when the radius is **(a)** 10 feet? **(b)** 20 feet?

Solution: Here we have a *time* $(t) \longrightarrow$ *volume* (V) function, with $\frac{dV}{dt} = 100$, a *radius* $(r) \longrightarrow$ *volume* function defined by $V = \frac{4}{3}\pi r^3$, and a *time* $\longrightarrow$ *radius* function. We are required to find $\frac{dr}{dt}$ when $r = 10$ and when $r = 20$. By the Chain Rule,

$$\frac{dV}{dt} = \frac{dV}{dr} \cdot \frac{dr}{dt}.$$

Since $\frac{dV}{dt} = 100$ and

$$\frac{dV}{dr} = \frac{d}{dr}\left(\tfrac{4}{3}\pi r^3\right) = 4\pi r^2,$$

we have

$$\frac{dr}{dt} = \frac{\frac{dV}{dt}}{\frac{dV}{dr}} = \frac{100}{4\pi r^2} \quad (r \neq 0).$$

When $r = 10$,

$$\frac{dr}{dt} = \frac{100}{4\pi \cdot 100} = \frac{1}{4\pi} \doteq 0.08.$$

When $r = 20$,

$$\frac{dr}{dt} = \frac{100}{4\pi \cdot 400} = \frac{1}{16\pi} \doteq 0.02.$$

Hence the radius is increasing at approximately **(a)** 0.08 feet per minute when $r = 10$ and **(b)** 0.02 feet per minute when $r = 20$.

The Chain Rule is also useful when two quantities are related by an equation that is either impossible or inconvenient to solve for one of the quantities in terms of the other. The equation is said to define one of the quantities **implicitly** in terms of the other.

EXAMPLE 2. If $x^2 + y^2 = 25$, find $\frac{dy}{dx}$ at $(x, y) = (3, 4)$.

Solution 1: The equation $x^2 + y^2 = 25$ defines two functions,

$$f: x \to \sqrt{25 - x^2}$$

and

$$g: x \to -\sqrt{25 - x^2}.$$

Since we are interested in the point (3, 4), we choose the first of these. Thus we have

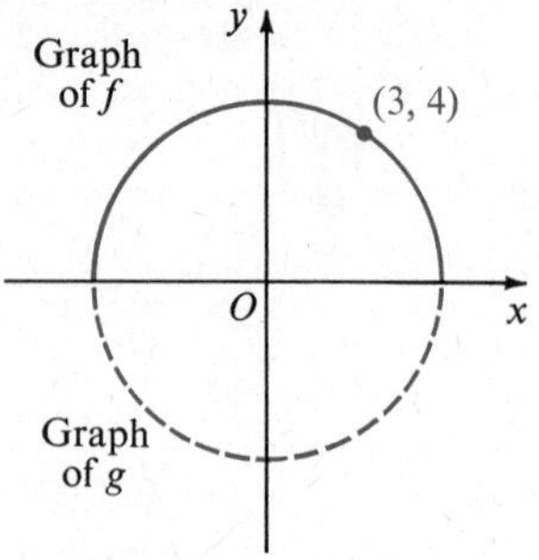

$$y = f(x) = \sqrt{25 - x^2}.$$

The Chain Rule, with $y = \sqrt{u}$ and $u = 25 - x^2$, gives

$$\frac{dy}{dx} = \frac{dy}{du} \cdot \frac{du}{dx} = f'(x) = \frac{-x}{\sqrt{25 - x^2}},$$

which at $(x, y) = (3, 4)$ becomes

$$\frac{dy}{dx} = f'(3) = \frac{-3}{\sqrt{25 - 9}} = \frac{-3}{\sqrt{16}} = \frac{-3}{4}.$$

Solution 2: Since $x^2 + y^2 = 25$, we have

$$\frac{d}{dx}(x^2 + y^2) = \frac{d}{dx}(25),$$

or

$$\frac{d}{dx}(x^2) + \frac{d}{dx}(y^2) = 0. \qquad (*)$$

By the Chain Rule,

$$\frac{d}{dx}(y^2) = \frac{d}{dy}(y^2) \cdot \frac{dy}{dx} = 2y\frac{dy}{dx}.$$

Hence (*) becomes

$$2x + 2y\frac{dy}{dx} = 0,$$

so that

$$\frac{dy}{dx} = -\frac{x}{y} \quad (y \neq 0).$$

At $(x, y) = (3, 4)$, this gives

$$\frac{dy}{dx} = -\frac{3}{4}.$$

In Solution 2 above we found $\frac{dy}{dx}$ by *implicit differentiation*.

EXAMPLE 3. A 10-foot ladder is leaning against a wall. The foot of the ladder slips and moves outward from the wall at the rate of 3 feet per second. At what rate is the top of the ladder moving down the wall when it is 8 feet from the floor?

Solution: We introduce coordinate axes as shown. We are concerned with functions $t \to x$ and $t \to y$, where $\frac{dx}{dt}$ is given to be 3 and $\frac{dy}{dt}$ is to be found. If the foot of the ladder is at $(x, 0)$ and the top is at $(0, y)$, then by the Pythagorean Theorem we have $x^2 + y^2 = 100$, so that

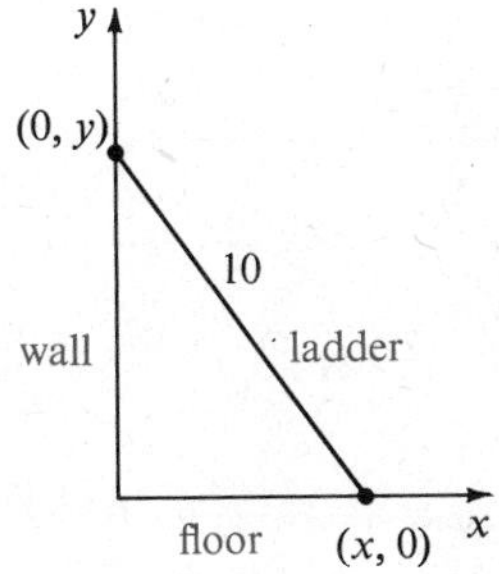

$$\frac{d}{dt}(x^2 + y^2) = \frac{d}{dt}(100), \qquad \text{or} \qquad \frac{d}{dt}(x^2) + \frac{d}{dt}(y^2) = 0.$$

Using the Chain Rule, we have

$$2x\frac{dx}{dt} + 2y\frac{dy}{dt} = 0,$$

or

$$\frac{dy}{dt} = -\frac{x}{y}\frac{dx}{dt} = -\frac{x}{y} \cdot 3.$$

When $y = 8$, we have $x = 6$, and

$$\frac{dy}{dt} = -\frac{6}{8} \cdot 3 = -\frac{9}{4} = -2\tfrac{1}{4}.$$

Thus the top of the ladder is moving *down* the wall at the rate of $2\frac{1}{4}$ feet per second when $y = 8$.

ORAL EXERCISES

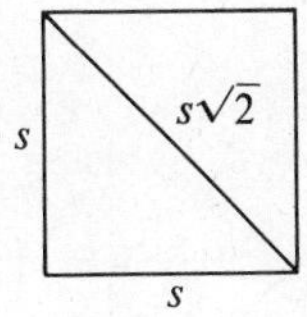

1. Each side of a square figure is increasing at the rate of 3 feet per second. At what rate is the diagonal increasing?
2. In Exercise 1, at what rate is the perimeter increasing?
3. In Exercise 1, at what rate is the area $A = s^2$ increasing when each side is of length 5 feet?
4. The diameter of a circular figure is increasing at the rate of 6 feet per minute. At what rate is the radius increasing?
5. In Exercise 4, at what rate is the circumference increasing?
6. In Exercise 4, at what rate is the area increasing when the diameter has length 2 feet?

WRITTEN EXERCISES

In Exercises 1–6, the graph of the given equation passes through the given point. Find the slope of the graph at the point.

A

1. $x^2 + y^3 + 4x - y = 0$; $(0, 0)$

2. $x^3 - 2y^2 + 3x + 4y = 0$; $(0, 0)$

3. $-x^2 + y^3 + 5y^2 - 2 = 0$; $(4, -3)$

4. $2x - x^2 + y^3 - y = 0$; $(2, 1)$

5. $x^4 + xy + y^4 = 19$; $(1, 2)$

[*Hint:* By the Product Rule, $\frac{d}{dx}(xy) = x\frac{dy}{dx} + y$.]

6. $x^3 - y^2 + 2x^2y^3 = 2$; $(1, 1)$
[*Hint:* By the Product Rule and the Chain Rule,

$$\frac{d}{dx}(x^2y^3) = x^2\frac{d}{dx}(y^3) + y^3\frac{d}{dx}(x^2) = x^2 \cdot 3y^2\frac{dy}{dx} + y^3 \cdot 2x.]$$

B

7. A cube of metal is being heated, and the volume is expanding at the rate of 6 cubic centimeters per hour. At what rate per hour is an edge of the cube increasing when the volume is 1000 cubic centimeters?

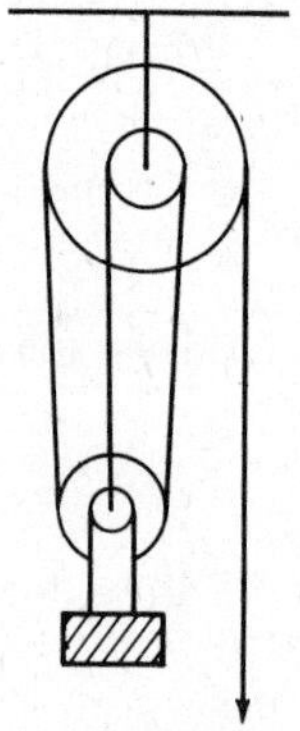

Ex. 8

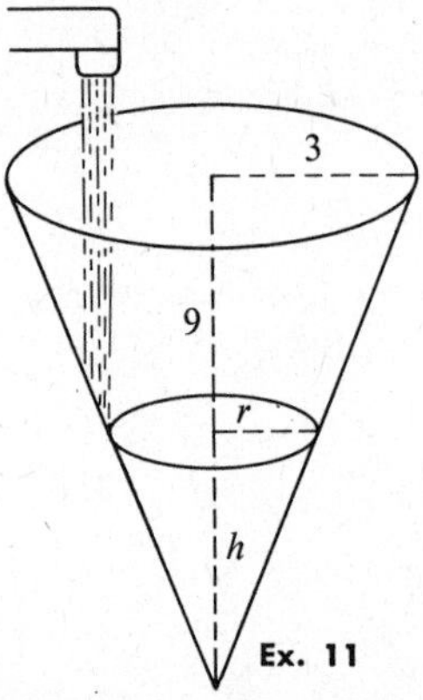

Ex. 11

8. For the pulley arrangement shown in the diagram above, at what rate is the weight rising if the rope is being hauled in at the rate of 60 feet per minute?

C

9. A boy who is 5 feet táll is walking at the rate of 6 feet per second directly away from a street light at the top of a pole that is 15 feet high. At what rate is his shadow lengthening?

10. A ship steaming at the rate of 20 knots (nautical miles per hour) parallel to a straight coast line and 10 nautical miles at sea is directly out from a man standing on the shore at 2 P.M. At what rate is the distance between the ship and the man increasing at 3 P.M.?

11. Water is flowing into a right circular conical tank 9 feet high and 6 feet across the top (see the diagram on page 188) at the rate of 2 cubic feet per minute. At what rate is the water level rising when the water is 3 feet deep? [*Hint:* Use similar triangles and the formula $V = \frac{1}{3}\pi r^2 h$.]

12. Sand is falling onto the ground at the rate of 10 cubic feet per second to form a right circular conical pile whose height is always one-fourth the diameter of its base. Find the rate at which the height of the pile is increasing at the moment it is 5 feet high.

CHAPTER SUMMARY

1. Three tests for relative maxima are:

The f-test. If $f'(c) = 0$ and $f(x) \leq f(c)$ for all x near c, then $f(c)$ is a relative maximum of f.

The f′-test. If $f'(c) = 0$ and $f'(x) > 0$ for all x near c on the left and $f'(x) < 0$ for all x near c on the right, then $f(c)$ is a relative maximum of f.

The f″-test. If $f'(c) = 0$ and $f''(c) < 0$, then $f(c)$ is a relative maximum of f.

Corresponding tests for relative minima are obtained by reversing each inequality.

2. The number $f(c)$ is an **absolute maximum [minimum]** of f if and only if $f(c) \geq f(x)$ [$f(c) \leq f(x)$] for *all* x in the domain of f. In applications, it is usually absolute extrema that are required. A pattern to follow in such extremum problems is given on page 160.

3. If $y = f(x)$, then $\dfrac{dy}{dx}$, or $f'(x)$, is the **rate of change** of y with respect to x. If s gives the position at time t of a point P moving on a line, then $s = f(t)$ is the **law of motion** of P, $v = \dfrac{ds}{dt} = f'(t)$ is the **velocity** of P, and $a = \dfrac{dv}{dt} = f''(t)$ is the **acceleration** of P.

4. **Newton's Method** for approximating a zero r of a differentiable function f consists of making a careful guess to obtain a first approximation x_1 to r, and then applying the *recursion formula*

$$x_{n+1} = x_n - \frac{f(x_n)}{f'(x_n)}$$

repeatedly, first with $n = 1$ to produce x_2, then with $n = 2$ to produce x_3, and so on, until the desired degree of accuracy has been achieved.

5. Suppose f and g are differentiable at x. Then fg is differentiable at x, and

$$(fg)'(x) = f(x)\,g'(x) + f'(x)\,g(x). \qquad \text{(Product Formula)}$$

If $g(x) \neq 0$, then $\frac{f}{g}$ is differentiable at x and

$$\left(\frac{f}{g}\right)'(x) = \frac{f'(x)\,g(x) - f(x)\,g'(x)}{[g(x)]^2}. \qquad \text{(Quotient Formula)}$$

6. If f is differentiable at x and g is differentiable at $f(x)$, then $g \circ f$ is differentiable at x, and

$$(g \circ f)'(x) = g'(f(x)) \cdot f'(x). \qquad \text{(Chain Rule)}$$

In other words, if y is a differentiable function of u and u is a differentiable function of x, then

$$\frac{dy}{dx} = \frac{dy}{du} \cdot \frac{du}{dx}. \qquad \text{(Chain Rule)}$$

The chain rule is often useful in determining the rate of change of one of two related quantities when the rate of change of the other is given. It is also useful in finding rates of change by *implicit differentiation.*

CHAPTER TEST

4–1 **1.** Find the relative maxima and relative minima of the function

$$f\colon x \to x^3 + 3x^2 + 3$$

using (**a**) the f-test, (**b**) the f'-test, and (**c**) the f''-test.

4–2 **2.** Forty-eight square feet of sheet metal are to be used in making a rectangular box having a square base and open top. What should the dimensions be in order that the volume of the box be as large as possible?

4–3 **3.** The law of motion of a moving point P is

$$s = t^3 - 9t^2 + 15t.$$

Find (**a**) the velocity of P at time t, (**b**) the acceleration of P at time t, and (**c**) the positions of P when P is at rest. Then (**d**) in a diagram, indicate the motion of P.

4–4 **4.** Take $x_1 = -1.2$ as a first approximation to the real zero of

$$f\colon x \to x^3 + 2.$$

Use Newton's Method to find a second approximation, x_2, to three decimal places.

4–5 **5.** If $f(x) = \dfrac{x^2 - 1}{x^2 + 1}$, find $f'(x)$.

6. If f and g are functions such that $f' = g$ and $g' = f$, find $(f^2 - g^2)'$.

4–6 **7.** Find $\dfrac{d}{dx}\sqrt{x^3 + a^3}$.

4–7 **8.** Find the slope of the graph of

$$x^3 + 3xy + y^3 = 1$$

at the point $(2, -1)$.

RECOMMENDED READINGS

BECKENBACH, EDWIN, and BELLMAN, RICHARD, *An Introduction to Inequalities* (New York: Random House, Inc., 1961).

COURANT, RICHARD, and ROBBINS, HERBERT, *What is Mathematics?* (New York: Oxford University Press, 1941).

Mathematics and Atomic Energy

In 1905 a brilliant 26-year-old physicist named Albert Einstein published a revolutionary paper describing his theory of relativity, in which he showed how physical measurement depends on the observer as well as on what is being observed. One of the most startling conclusions that Einstein deduced mathematically from the basic postulates of his theory was that mass and energy are interchangeable and that mass is simply a form of energy. This mass-energy equivalence is expressed mathematically in the well-known Einstein equation $\Delta E = \Delta mc^2$ (or simply $E = mc^2$), where ΔE is the amount of energy change associated with a change, Δm, in the mass of an object, and c is the velocity of light, approximately 3×10^{10} centimeters per second.

At first, the notion that mass can be converted into energy, and vice versa, seemed to contradict two long-held basic principles of physical science: mass cannot be created or destroyed; energy cannot be created or destroyed. If, however, mass is regarded as stored energy, then according to Einstein the two separate laws of conservation can be replaced with a single law of conservation of mass-energy: In any physical or chemical process, the total amount of energy involved, including its mass equivalent, remains constant.

Since the factor c^2 in Einstein's equation is so large, one can see that the conversion of even a tiny amount of matter should produce an enormous yield of energy. For example, the energy obtained from the complete conversion of 1 gram of mass would be equal to that produced by burning 3,000,000,000 grams of coal!

The discovery that vast amounts of energy could be released from the nuclei of atoms had its beginnings in Becquerel's discovery in 1896 of

Albert Einstein (ca. 1912)

The linear accelerator shown at the right provides protons with an energy of 50 million electron-volts.

the strange radiation emitted spontaneously from the element uranium. It was not then recognized, however, that this was an example in nature of mass actually being converted into energy through the phenomenon called *radioactive decay* (which we shall discuss in Chapter 6 of this book). Ernest Rutherford and his followers then began to experiment with bombarding atoms with rays from radioactive substances in order to investigate the structure of the atomic nucleus. In more recent years, scientists have devised powerful "atom smashers" such as the cyclotron and the linear accelerator which impart enormous velocities to subatomic particles before directing them at nuclei. In the process, new isotopes have been formed, new particles created or discovered, and corresponding amounts of energy released.

In 1938, just before the outbreak of World War II, two German scientists, Otto Hahn and Lise Meitner, bombarded the heavy metal uranium with neutrons and were amazed to discover that in doing so they had split the uranium atom roughly in half. They noted also that the process released an astonishing amount of energy. They named this new phenomenon *atomic fission.* Moreover, their mathematical calculations confirmed the fact that for the first time neutrons had been emitted from a target substance during its bombardment with neutrons. This suggested the exciting possibility of setting up a *chain reaction* in which the neutrons released by one atom might bombard other atoms and cause them to split. In this way a very large number of atoms might break down in a very short time, releasing tremendous quantities of energy.

While such a yield of atomic energy would have much constructive potential, unfortunately it could also be put to violently destructive use in the form of an atomic bomb. Deeply concerned with the prospect that either Hitler or Mussolini might soon have access to such a horrifying weapon, Enrico Fermi, the Nobel prize-winning Italian physicist, persuaded Einstein to contact President Roosevelt and urge a crash program in atomic research. Fermi himself directed the construction of the first successful *nuclear reactor* to produce fission energy by a controlled chain reaction. In all, it required four years of feverish work under the supervision of the leading scientific minds in the country (many of them refugees from Hitler's rule) to conquer the technical difficulties of producing an atomic bomb.

Another nuclear process, which gives off even more energy than that produced by uranium fission, is the one called *fusion.* This occurs when two or more light nuclei, such as those of hydrogen atoms, are combined to form a single heavier nucleus. Since the positively charged protons of one nucleus strongly repel those of another, a substance must be heated to extremely high temperatures — on the order of several million degrees — in order that its atoms will have the kinetic energy to overcome this force, so that some may fuse.

Temperatures in the sun are high enough that the sun's hydrogen nuclei are constantly being fused to form helium, with the resulting release of enormous amounts of energy that we call *thermonuclear power.* The temperatures obtained in a nuclear fission reaction also are sufficient to enable fusion to occur. The hydrogen bomb offers an illustration of the destructive violence that can be achieved when suitable fusion materials are combined with a uranium or plutonium fission bomb.

Since World War II, scientists have been largely concerned with harnessing the power of the atom for peaceful uses. Thus nuclear fission reactors are used to produce radioisotopes, such as radioactive cobalt, which are widely used in medical diagnosis and in the treatment of cancer and other diseases.

The experimental nuclear reactor shown at the left provides intense beams of neutrons for nuclear research.

Electric power is provided by a nuclear reactor at the San Onofre Generating Station in California.

Moreover, the heat from a nuclear reactor can be used to run an electric power plant. A likely source of atomic power in the future will be the thermonuclear power obtained from a successful *fusion reactor.* Leading scientists in laboratories all over the world are today trying to devise a method of obtaining the slow, controlled release of nuclear energy from the process of atomic fusion.

READING LIST

FERMI, LAURA, *Atoms for the World* (Chicago: University of Chicago Press, 1957).

HODGSON, PETER E., *Nuclear Physics in Peace and War* (New York: Hawthorn Books, Inc., 1961).

HUGHES, DONALD J., *On Nuclear Energy: Its Potential for Peacetime Uses* (Cambridge, Mass.: Harvard University Press, 1957).

JUNGK, ROBERT, *Brighter Than a Thousand Suns* (New York: Harcourt, Brace and World, Inc., 1958).

LAPP, RALPH E., *Atoms and People* (New York, Harper and Co., 1956).

WENDT, GERALD, *You and the Atom* (New York: Whiteside Press, 1956).

5

The Gateway Arch (photograph above) on the bank of the Mississippi River in St. Louis, Missouri, commemorates the westward expansion of the United States. It is built in the shape of an inverted catenary that has been weighted at the ends to produce a slightly more pointed arch. A catenary, the shape assumed by a perfectly flexible chain hanging freely from two supports (see the diagram at the right), is defined by an equation of the form $y=\frac{a}{2}\left(e^{\frac{x}{a}}+e^{-\frac{x}{a}}\right)$.

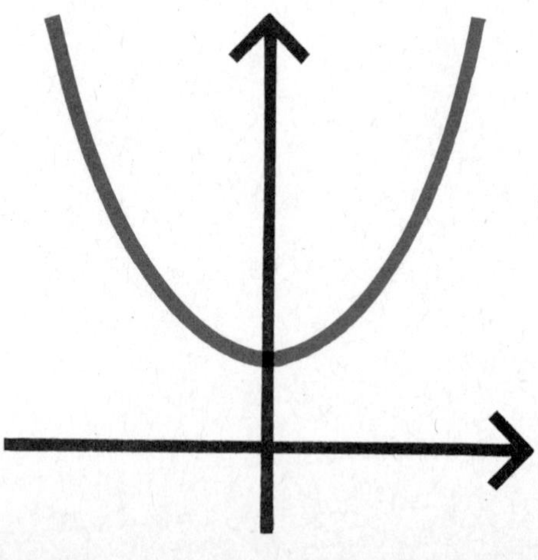

The Natural Logarithm and Natural Exponential Functions

The primary purpose of this chapter is to introduce two of the most important functions in all of mathematics, the natural logarithm function and the natural exponential function. Of the various ways to define these functions — none of them particularly easy — we have chosen a geometrical method. The logarithm and exponential functions as defined will at first bear little resemblance to the ones to which you may be accustomed; this discrepancy will be eliminated in Chapter 6. The development of the theory in the present chapter is essentially independent of the first section, which is included primarily for review of technique.

■ Preliminaries

5–1 Rational Exponents

In the **exponential expression p^q**, the number p is called the **base** and q, the **exponent.** One of the principal goals of this chapter is to define the value of p^q, where p is *positive* and q is *any* real number. Once we have done this, we shall have at our disposal one of the most important classes of functions in pure and applied mathematics, the *exponential functions*

$$x \to a^x \quad (x \in \mathcal{R},\ a > 0),$$

as well as the *power functions*

$$x \to x^a \quad (x > 0,\ a \in \mathcal{R}).$$

In your earlier work, you have undoubtedly seen definitions of a^n, where a is a real number and n is an integer.

You have probably also seen definitions of a^r, where a is a positive real number and r is any *rational* number, that is, r is the quotient of two integers. In the interest of completeness, we shall recall these definitions below.

If n is a positive integer, for any real number a we may define a^n inductively by

$$a^1 = a \quad \text{and} \quad a^n = a \cdot a^{n-1} \quad \text{if } n > 1.$$

On the basis of this definition, we can prove, for example, that

$$a^m \cdot a^n = a^{m+n} \quad \text{and} \quad (a^m)^n = a^{mn}. \qquad (*)$$

Formulas (*) lead us to define

$$a^0 = 1 \quad (a \neq 0)$$

and for n a negative integer

$$a^n = \frac{1}{a^{-n}} \quad (a \neq 0),$$

because if we do, (*) will hold for any integers m and n: positive, negative, or zero. (Notice that if n is negative, $-n$ is positive, so that a^{-n} is meaningful.)

In defining a^r, where r is rational, we require $a > 0$. Let m and n, $n > 0$, be integers such that $r = \dfrac{m}{n}$. Then by definition,

$$a^r = a^{\frac{m}{n}} = (\sqrt[n]{a})^m.$$

By $\sqrt[n]{a}$ we mean the unique *positive* number c such that $c^n = a$. *Note 1:* We require $a > 0$ because if $a < 0$ and n is even, no such c exists; for example, there is no positive — or real — number c such that $c^2 = -2$. *Note 2:* The value of a^r depends only on a and r and not on the particular representation of r as the quotient of integers; thus if $r = \dfrac{m}{n}$ and $r = \dfrac{h}{k}$ $(n, k > 0)$, then $(\sqrt[n]{a})^m = (\sqrt[k]{a})^h$.

EXAMPLE 1. Evaluate $4^{-\frac{3}{2}}$.

Solution: $4^{-\frac{3}{2}} = 4^{\frac{-3}{2}} = (\sqrt[2]{4})^{-3} = 2^{-3} = \dfrac{1}{2^3} = \dfrac{1}{8}\cdot$

Thus far, we have given meaning to a^r, where a is a positive real number and r is any *rational* number. There remains the problem of defining what we mean by $3^{\sqrt{2}}$ or 10^{π} or, in general, a^x, where a is a positive real number and x is an *irrational* number. In Sections 5–2 through 5–5 we shall develop the necessary background so that in Section 6–1 we can give this general definition and can prove that the following "laws of exponents" hold for any positive real numbers a and b and any real numbers x and y:

$$a^x a^y = a^{x+y} \qquad \frac{a^x}{a^y} = a^{x-y}$$

$$(ab)^x = a^x b^x \qquad \left(\frac{a}{b}\right)^x = \frac{a^x}{b^x}$$

$$(a^x)^y = a^{xy}$$

If $a \neq 1$ and $a^x = a^y$, then $x = y$.

If $x \neq 0$ and $a^x = b^x$, then $a = b$.

For the time being, we shall assume the validity of these results. (It would be possible to prove them for *rational* values of x and y on the basis of the definitions given above.)

EXAMPLE 2. Express each of the following as a fraction which does not involve negative exponents, and simplify where possible.

a. $\left(\dfrac{a^0b^2c^{-3}}{c}\right)^{-\frac{1}{2}}$ $(a, b, c > 0)$

b. $\dfrac{x^{-2} + y^{-2}}{x^{-1} + y^{-1}}$ $(x, y \neq 0)$

Solution: **a.** $$\left(\frac{a^0b^2c^{-3}}{c}\right)^{-\frac{1}{2}} = \left(\frac{1 \cdot b^2 \cdot \frac{1}{c^3}}{c}\right)^{\frac{-1}{2}} = \left(\frac{b^2}{c^4}\right)^{\frac{-1}{2}} = \left(\sqrt[2]{\frac{b^2}{c^4}}\right)^{-1}$$

$$= \left(\frac{b}{c^2}\right)^{-1} = \frac{1}{\frac{b}{c^2}} = \frac{c^2}{b}.$$

b. $$\frac{x^{-2} + y^{-2}}{x^{-1} + y^{-1}} = \frac{\frac{1}{x^2} + \frac{1}{y^2}}{\frac{1}{x} + \frac{1}{y}} = \frac{\frac{y^2 + x^2}{x^2y^2}}{\frac{y + x}{xy}} = \frac{y^2 + x^2}{xy(y + x)}.$$

In Chapters 3 and 4, we proved the formula

$$\frac{d}{dx}x^r = rx^{r-1}$$

for r any *integer* (Theorem 5, page 126, and Exercise 26, page 178). We may use the methods of Section 4–6 to prove that the formula is valid when r is any *rational* number: Let $r = \dfrac{m}{n}$, where m and n are integers, $n > 0$, and let

$$u = x^r = x^{\frac{m}{n}}$$

We wish to show that $\dfrac{du}{dx} = rx^{r-1}$. Let

$$y = u^n.$$

Then by Theorem 3′, page 180,

$$\frac{dy}{dx} = \frac{dy}{du} \cdot \frac{du}{dx}. \qquad (*)$$

Now $\frac{dy}{du} = nu^{n-1}$, and since $y = u^n = x^m$, $\frac{dy}{dx} = mx^{m-1}$. Substituting into (*), we have

$$mx^{m-1} = nu^{n-1} \cdot \frac{du}{dx}.$$

Therefore,

$$\frac{du}{dx} = \frac{mx^{m-1}}{nu^{n-1}} = \frac{mux^{m-1}}{nu^n}.$$

Since $u = x^{\frac{m}{n}}$,

$$\frac{du}{dx} = \frac{mx^{\frac{m}{n}}x^{m-1}}{nx^m} = \frac{m}{n}x^{\frac{m}{n}}x^{-1} = \frac{m}{n}x^{\frac{m}{n}-1} = rx^{r-1},$$

as was to be shown.

EXAMPLE 3. Find $f'(x)$ if **(a)** $f\colon x \to \sqrt[3]{x^2}$; **(b)** $f\colon x \to \frac{1}{\sqrt{1 - x^2}}$.

Solution: **a.** $f(x) = \sqrt[3]{x^2} = (\sqrt[3]{x})^2 = x^{\frac{2}{3}}$;

$$f'(x) = \tfrac{2}{3}x^{\frac{2}{3}-1} = \tfrac{2}{3}x^{-\frac{1}{3}} = \frac{2}{3x^{\frac{1}{3}}}.$$

b. Let $y = f(x) = \frac{1}{\sqrt{1 - x^2}} = (1 - x^2)^{-\frac{1}{2}}$.

Let $u = 1 - x^2$. Then $y = u^{-\frac{1}{2}}$. By Theorem 3′, page 180, we have

$$f'(x) = \frac{dy}{dx} = \frac{dy}{du} \cdot \frac{du}{dx} = (-\tfrac{1}{2}u^{-\frac{3}{2}}) \cdot (-2x)$$

$$= \frac{x}{u^{\frac{3}{2}}} = \frac{x}{(1 - x^2)^{\frac{3}{2}}}.$$

ORAL EXERCISES

Simplify each expression.

1. $2^0 + 3^0$
2. $(2 + 3)^0$
3. $4^{\frac{1}{2}}$
4. $4^{\frac{3}{2}}$
5. $4^{-\frac{1}{2}}$
6. $8^{\frac{1}{3}}$
7. $8^{-\frac{1}{3}}$
8. $8^{\frac{2}{3}}$
9. $(\frac{3}{2})^{-1}$

10. $(\frac{3}{2})^2$
11. $(\frac{3}{2})^{-2}$
12. $(17^2)^{\frac{1}{2}}$
13. $(17^n)^{\frac{1}{n}}$
14. $(\frac{1}{2})^{-1} + (\frac{1}{4})^{-1}$
15. $(\frac{1}{2} + \frac{1}{4})^{-1}$
16. $2^2 \cdot 2^{-2}$
17. $2^3 \cdot 2^{-2}$
18. $2^{\frac{3}{2}} \cdot 2^{\frac{1}{2}}$
19. $(-8)^{\frac{1}{3}}$
20. $(-1)^{\frac{1}{3}}$
21. $(-8)^{-\frac{1}{3}}$

WRITTEN EXERCISES

In Exercises 1–14, write the given expression as a single fraction in lowest terms, using only positive exponents and no radicals. Assume that all literal symbols name positive numbers.

A

1. $(x^2y^{-3})^{-1}$
2. $\dfrac{2^{-1}r^{-2}s}{3r^2s^3}$
3. $\dfrac{(-r^2s)^3}{(2rs^{-1})^2}$
4. $\dfrac{(-r^2s)^{-3}}{(2rs^{-1})^{-2}}$
5. $\sqrt{4x^2y^{-4}}$
6. $\dfrac{x}{\sqrt{x^{-3}}}$
7. $\dfrac{x^{-2} - y^{-2}}{x^{-1} - y^{-1}}$
8. $\dfrac{x^{-2} - y^{-2}}{x^{-1} + y^{-1}}$
9. $(r + s)^{-1} - r^{-1} - s^{-1}$
10. $1 + r^{-1} - (1 + r)^{-1}$
11. $\sqrt{x^{-2} + y^{-2}}$
12. $(x^{-2} + y^{-2})^{-\frac{1}{2}}$
13. $\left(\dfrac{1 - x}{1 + x}\right)^{-\frac{1}{2}} \cdot \dfrac{1}{(1 + x)^2}$
14. $\left(\dfrac{1 - x}{1 + x}\right)^{-\frac{3}{2}} \cdot \dfrac{1}{1 + x}$

In Exercises 15–18, find an x which satisfies the given equation.

15. $2^x = 2^{2x-1}$
16. $3^{x-1} = 9$
17. $3^x = 9^{x+1}$
18. $2^{x+1} = 8^x$

In Exercises 19–29, find an expression for $f'(x)$.

19. $f\colon x \to \sqrt[3]{x}$
20. $f\colon x \to \sqrt{x^3}$

B

21. $f\colon x \to \dfrac{1}{\sqrt{x}}$
22. $f\colon x \to \dfrac{1}{\sqrt[3]{x^2}}$
23. $f\colon x \to \sqrt[3]{2x^2}$
24. $f\colon x \to \sqrt[3]{\dfrac{27}{x}}$

25. $f: x \to \sqrt{2x+1}$ [*Hint:* Let $y = f(x) = \sqrt{2x+1}$ and $u = 2x + 1$. Then $y = \sqrt{u}$. Follow the method of Example 3(b).]

26. $f: x \to \sqrt{2-x}$

27. $f: x \to \sqrt[3]{3x+2}$

28. $f: x \to \sqrt{x^2+1}$

29. $f: x \to \sqrt{1-x^2}$

5–2 Areas Under the Curve $y = \frac{1}{x}$

The main objective of this chapter and the next, as indicated on page 197, is to define and study two important classes of functions: logarithmic and exponential. These two types of functions are closely related, and either type can be defined in terms of the other. You have perhaps seen the common logarithm defined in terms of the exponential function having base 10. A standard definition of $\log_{10} y$ is that it is the power to which 10 must be raised to give y; that is, $\log_{10} y = x$ if and only if $10^x = y$. To make this definition, however, we must know what 10^x means when x is irrational, and you will recall that we have not yet defined exponential expressions with irrational exponents.

Since defining and discussing irrational exponents is difficult, we shall take the opposite approach of first defining a certain kind of logarithmic function, called the *natural logarithm function*, and then defining exponential and other logarithmic functions in terms of this natural logarithm function. The definition of the natural logarithm function will lean heavily on certain remarkable properties of areas under the curve $y = \frac{1}{x}$, and the remainder of this section is devoted to a study of these properties.

Let g be the function whose domain is $\{x\colon x > 0\}$ and whose value at $x > 0$ is $g(x) = \frac{1}{x}$. Thus, for example, $g(1) = 1$, $g(3) = \frac{1}{3}$, and $g(\frac{2}{5}) = \frac{5}{2}$. Since $g'(x) = -\frac{1}{x^2}$, the slope of the graph of g is always negative. Further, since $g''(x) = \frac{2}{x^3}$, which is positive for $x > 0$, the graph of g is convex downward.

Moreover, for large values of x, $g(x)$ is near zero. Similarly, for values of x near zero, $g(x)$ is large.

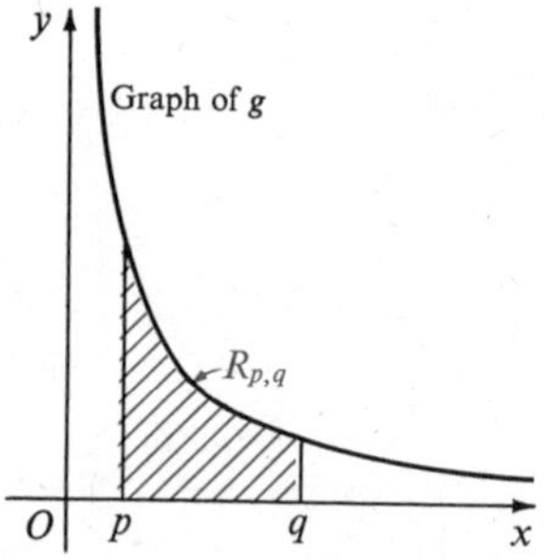

Figure 5–1

The graph of g is shown in Figure 5–1.

If p and q are numbers such that $0 < p \leq q$, then a certain region $R_{p,q}$

is bounded by parts of the x-axis, the curve $y = g(x) = \dfrac{1}{x}$, and the vertical lines $x = p$ and $x = q$. (See Figure 5–1.) In set-builder notation,

$$R_{p,q} = \left\{\text{point } (x, y)\text{: } p \le x \le q \text{ and } 0 \le y \le \frac{1}{x}\right\}.$$

We shall let $A(p, q)$ be the area of the region $R_{p,q}$ and shall refer to it as *the area under the curve* $y = \dfrac{1}{x}$ *from* p *to* q. If $p = q$, then $A(p, q) = 0$ because then the region $R_{p,q}$ collapses to a line segment, which has area zero. If $p < q$, then $A(p, q)$ is a positive number.

A method for approximating the number $A(p, q)$ is suggested by Figure 5–2 for the case $A(1, 3)$. In Figure 5–2(a), the region $R_{1,3}$ *is contained in* the union of the four rectangular regions whose top edges are shown in red.

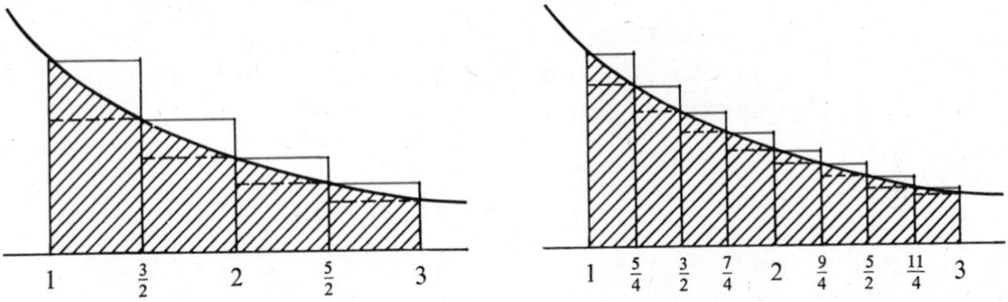

Figure 5–2

The base of each of the four rectangles has length $\frac{1}{2}$, and the heights of the rectangles are, from left to right, 1, $\frac{2}{3}$, $\frac{1}{2}$, and $\frac{2}{5}$. The areas of the rectangular regions, therefore, are $\frac{1}{2}$, $\frac{1}{3}$, $\frac{1}{4}$, and $\frac{1}{5}$, respectively, and we see that

$$A(1, 3) = \text{Area of } R_{1,3} < \tfrac{1}{2} + \tfrac{1}{3} + \tfrac{1}{4} + \tfrac{1}{5}.$$

On the other hand, the region $R_{1,3}$ *contains* the union of the four rectangular regions whose top edges are dotted lines. In this case, the rectangles have heights $\frac{2}{3}$, $\frac{1}{2}$, $\frac{2}{5}$, and $\frac{1}{3}$, respectively; therefore the areas of the rectangular regions are $\frac{1}{3}$, $\frac{1}{4}$, $\frac{1}{5}$, and $\frac{1}{6}$, respectively. Thus

$$A(1, 3) = \text{Area of } R_{1,3} > \tfrac{1}{3} + \tfrac{1}{4} + \tfrac{1}{5} + \tfrac{1}{6}.$$

Hence we have

$$0.950 \doteq \tfrac{1}{3} + \tfrac{1}{4} + \tfrac{1}{5} + \tfrac{1}{6} < A(1, 3) < \tfrac{1}{2} + \tfrac{1}{3} + \tfrac{1}{4} + \tfrac{1}{5} \doteq 1.283.$$

If we repeat this procedure using two sets of eight rectangles each (see Figure 5–2(b)), we find that

$$1.020 \doteq \tfrac{1}{5} + \tfrac{1}{6} + \tfrac{1}{7} + \tfrac{1}{8} + \tfrac{1}{9} + \tfrac{1}{10} + \tfrac{1}{11} + \tfrac{1}{12} < A(1, 3)$$
$$< \tfrac{1}{4} + \tfrac{1}{5} + \tfrac{1}{6} + \tfrac{1}{7} + \tfrac{1}{8} + \tfrac{1}{9} + \tfrac{1}{10} + \tfrac{1}{11} \doteq 1.187.$$

The procedure may be repeated using more and more rectangles until the upper and lower estimates of $A(1, 3)$ are as close together as desired. (Even with eight rectangles of each kind, the average of these estimates,

$$\tfrac{1}{2}(1.020 + 1.187) \doteq 1.103$$

is quite close to the actual value of $A(1, 3)$, which can be shown to be 1.099 to three decimal places.)

The limits of the upper and lower estimates as the number of rectangles increases without bound and the lengths of the bases of the rectangles approach zero actually are equal. Moreover, as suggested in Figure 5–3, these limits are independent of the way the x-interval $(1, 3)$ or, in general, the x-interval (p, q) is separated into subintervals *provided the maximum length of the subintervals approaches* 0. In *integral calculus*, in fact, the area $A(p, q)$ is *defined* to be this common limit and is denoted $\int_p^q \frac{1}{x}\,dx$ (read "the integral from p to q of one over x with respect to x" or simply "the integral from p to q of one over $x\,dx$"). Thus you have $A(p, q) = \int_p^q \frac{1}{x}\,dx$. Any other symbol might equally well be used for x here, so that, for example, $A(p, q) = \int_p^q \frac{1}{t}\,dt$.

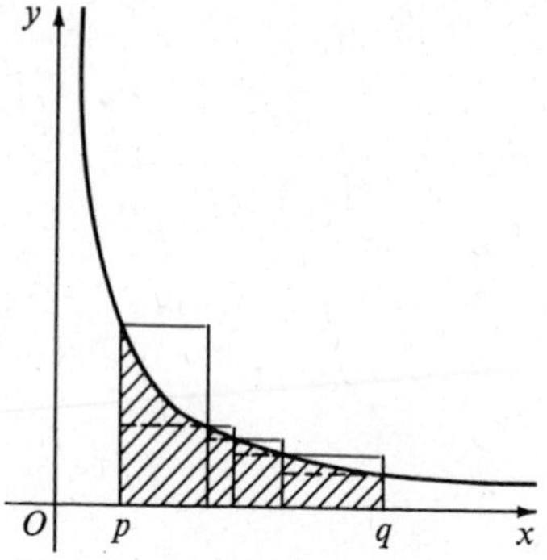

Figure 5–3

An important property of the "area function" A (see Exercise 21, page 207) can be established using the method of "approximating rectangles" discussed above.

Property A–1.

If $0 < p \leq q$ and $r > 0$, then $A(p, q) = A(rp, rq)$.

Some numerical examples of Property A–1 are:

$A(1, 2) = A(3 \cdot 1, 3 \cdot 2) = A(3, 6)$ (See Figure 5–4(a).)

$A(2, 3) = A(\tfrac{1}{4} \cdot 2, \tfrac{1}{4} \cdot 3) = A(\tfrac{1}{2}, \tfrac{3}{4})$ (See Figure 5–4(b).)

$A(\tfrac{1}{2}, 2) = A(2 \cdot \tfrac{1}{2}, 2 \cdot 2) = A(1, 4)$ (See Figure 5–4(c).)

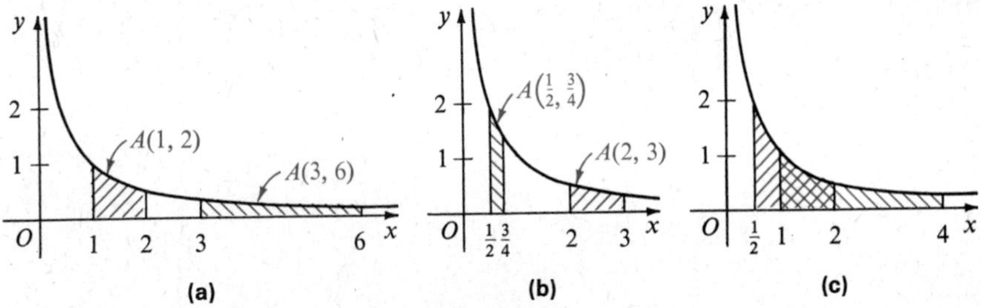

In each case, the hatched area
is equal to the hatched area

Figure 5–4

A method of proof of Property A–1 is suggested by Figure 5–5, in which the case $A(1, 2) = A(3, 6)$ is depicted. Shown in the figure are sets of "approximating rectangles" for the regions $R_{1,2}$ and $R_{3,6}$, with the same

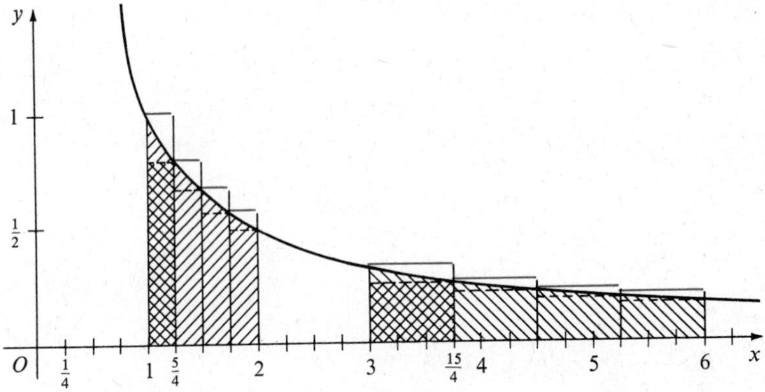

Figure 5–5

number of rectangles in each set. Although corresponding rectangular regions for $R_{1,2}$ and $R_{3,6}$ have different shapes, their *areas* are equal because a given rectangle for $R_{3,6}$ is 3, or r, times as wide and $\frac{1}{3}$, or $\frac{1}{r}$, times as high as the corresponding one for $R_{1,2}$. For example, the leftmost "lower" rectangle for $R_{1,2}$ has base $\frac{1}{4}$ and height $\frac{4}{5}$, while the leftmost "lower" rectangle for $R_{3,6}$ has base $3 \cdot \frac{1}{4} = \frac{3}{4}$ and height $\frac{1}{3} \cdot \frac{4}{5} = \frac{4}{15}$. Since $\frac{1}{4} \cdot \frac{4}{5} = \frac{3}{4} \cdot \frac{4}{15}$, the areas of the two rectangular regions are equal. Therefore, the lower estimates for $A(1, 2)$ and $A(3, 6)$ are equal. We can show in this way that to *any* estimate for either $A(1, 2)$ or $A(3, 6)$ there corresponds an estimate for the other which has equal value. Thus we conclude that $A(1, 2) = A(3, 6)$.

EXAMPLE 1. For what value of x is each of the following true?

a. $A(1, x) = A(2, 5)$;
b. $A(x, 1) = A(2, 3)$;
c. $A(2, x) = A(\frac{1}{2}, 2)$.

Solution: **a.** $A(2, 5) = A(\frac{1}{2} \cdot 2, \frac{1}{2} \cdot 5) = A(1, \frac{5}{2}) = A(1, x)$ if $x = \frac{5}{2}$.
b. $A(2, 3) = A(\frac{1}{3} \cdot 2, \frac{1}{3} \cdot 3) = A(\frac{2}{3}, 1) = A(x, 1)$ if $x = \frac{2}{3}$.
c. $A(\frac{1}{2}, 2) = A(4 \cdot \frac{1}{2}, 4 \cdot 2) = A(2, 8) = A(2, x)$ if $x = 8$.

Suppose two plane regions R_1 and R_2 have areas A_1 and A_2, respectively, and that the area of $R_1 \cap R_2$ is zero. Then it is intuitively clear that the area of $R_1 \cup R_2$ is $A_1 + A_2$. If we apply this fact to regions of the type we are considering, we have

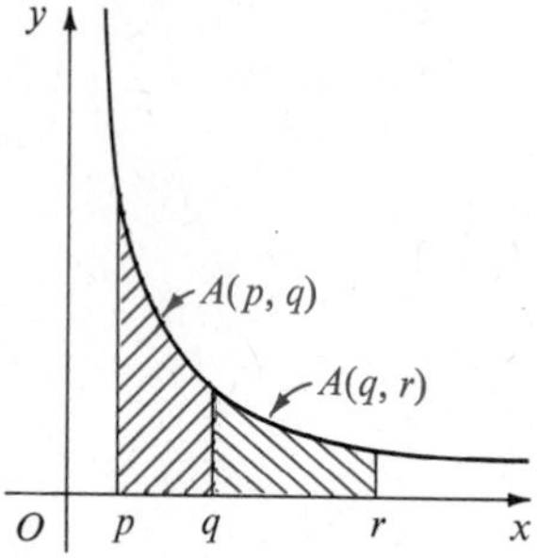

Figure 5–6

Property A–2.

If $0 < p \leq q \leq r$, $A(p, r) = A(p, q) + A(q, r)$.

(See Figure 5–6, in which $A(p, r)$ is the area of the total shaded region.)

EXAMPLE 2. Assuming that $A(1, 2) = 0.69$ and $A(1, 3) = 1.10$, find

a. $A(\frac{1}{2}, 3)$; **b.** $A(1, 9)$.

Solution: **a.** By Property A–1, $A(\frac{1}{2}, 1) = A(\frac{1}{2} \cdot 1, \frac{1}{2} \cdot 2) = A(1, 2) = 0.69$.
By Property A–2, $A(\frac{1}{2}, 3) = A(\frac{1}{2}, 1) + A(1, 3) = 0.69 + 1.10 = 1.79$.
b. By Property A–1, $A(3, 9) = A(3 \cdot 1, 3 \cdot 3) = A(1, 3) = 1.10$.
By Property A–2, $A(1, 9) = A(1, 3) + A(3, 9) = 1.10 + 1.10 = 2.20$.

ORAL EXERCISES

In Exercises 1–6, state equations of the four curves, portions of which bound the regions named.

1. $R_{1,2}$
2. $R_{\frac{1}{2},3}$
3. $R_{a,b}$
4. $R_{1,2} \cup R_{2,3}$
5. $R_{\frac{1}{2},1} \cup R_{1,2}$
6. $R_{1,2} \cup R_{2,3} \cup R_{3,4}$

In Exercises 7–20, state whether the first of the numbers named is less than, equal to, or greater than the second.

7. $A(1, 2)$; $A(1, 3)$

8. $A(\frac{1}{2}, 1)$; $A(\frac{1}{3}, 1)$

9. $A(1, 3)$; $A(1, 2) + A(2, 3)$

10. $A(\frac{1}{2}, 1)$; $A(1, 2)$

11. $A(1, 3)$; $A(2, 5)$

12. $A(\frac{1}{3}, 1)$; $A(1, 2)$

13. 1; $A(1, 2)$

14. 1; $A(\frac{1}{2}, 1)$

15. $\frac{1}{2}$; $A(\frac{1}{2}, 1)$

16. 5; $A(1, 6)$

17. $1 + \frac{1}{2}$; $A(1, 3)$

18. $\frac{1}{2} + \frac{1}{3}$; $A(1, 3)$

19. $1 + \frac{1}{2} + \frac{1}{3}$; $A(1, 4)$

20. $\frac{1}{2} + \frac{1}{3} + \frac{1}{4}$; $A(1, 4)$

21. On page 204, A is referred to as a function, the "area function." Define this function A precisely by describing **(a)** the domain of A and **(b)** the value of A at each member of its domain.

Complete and read the statements in Exercises 22–27.

22. $\int_2^4 \frac{1}{x}\,dx = A(\_\_, 4)$

23. $\int_{\_\_}^3 \frac{1}{x}\,dx = A(1, \_\_)$

24. $\int_1^3 \frac{1}{x}\,dx \doteq 1.0\_\_\ \_\_$

25. $\int_2^5 \frac{1}{x}\,dx = \int_6^{\_\_} \frac{1}{x}\,dx$

26. $\int_3^5 \frac{1}{x}\,dx + \int_5^6 \frac{1}{x}\,dx = \int_{\_\_}^6 \frac{1}{x}\,dx$

27. $\int_4^6 \frac{1}{x}\,dx \_\_ \int_4^7 \frac{1}{x}\,dx$

WRITTEN EXERCISES

In Exercises 1–10, determine the value of x which makes the statement true.

A

1. $A(1, x) = A(2, 6)$

2. $A(2, x) = A(4, 12)$

3. $A(1, x) = A(\frac{1}{3}, 1)$

4. $A(1, x) = A(\frac{1}{2}, 2)$

5. $\int_x^1 \frac{1}{t}\,dt = \int_2^4 \frac{1}{t}\,dt$

6. $\int_1^{x+1} \frac{1}{t}\,dt = \int_2^6 \frac{1}{t}\,dt$

7. $\int_x^{x+1} \frac{1}{t}\,dt = \int_4^6 \frac{1}{t}\,dt$

8. $\int_x^{x+1} \frac{1}{t}\,dt = \int_{\frac{1}{3}}^{\frac{1}{2}} \frac{1}{t}\,dt$

9. $A(1, x) = A(p, q)$ $(p < q)$

10. $A(x, x + 1) = A(p, q)$ $(p < q)$

B **11. a.** Draw a figure (similar to Figure 5–2) showing the region $R_{1,5}$ and the two sets of four rectangles each.

b. Calculate the sum of the areas of the "upper" rectangular regions.

c. Calculate the sum of the areas of the "lower" rectangular regions.

d. Relate the answers in **(b)** and **(c)** to the number $A(1, 5)$, or $\int_1^5 \frac{1}{x}\,dx$, by means of inequalities.

e. The average of the numbers found in **(b)** and **(c)** is an approximation to $A(1, 5)$, or $\int_1^5 \frac{1}{x}\,dx$. Find it.

12. Repeat Exercise 11 using two sets of eight rectangles each.

13. Repeat Exercise 11 for the region $R_{1,2}$.

14. Repeat Exercise 12 for the region $R_{1,2}$.

15. To four decimal places,

$$A(1, 5) = \int_1^5 \frac{1}{x}\,dx = 1.6094 \quad \text{and} \quad A(1, 2) = \int_1^2 \frac{1}{x}\,dx = 0.6932.$$

The approximations you found in the **(e)** parts of Exercises 11–14 are too large. Use graphical evidence to explain why this is true.

■ The Functions L and E

5–3 The Natural Logarithm Function

We are now in a position to define the **natural logarithm function,** which, for the present, we shall denote by L. The definition of L is:

$$L(x) = \begin{cases} A(1, x) & \text{if } x \geq 1 \\ -A(x, 1) & \text{if } 0 < x < 1, \end{cases}$$

where A is the "area function" introduced in Section 5–2 (see Figure 5–7). The domain of L is $\{x: x > 0\}$. (We shall show later that the range of L is $\mathbb{R}$.)

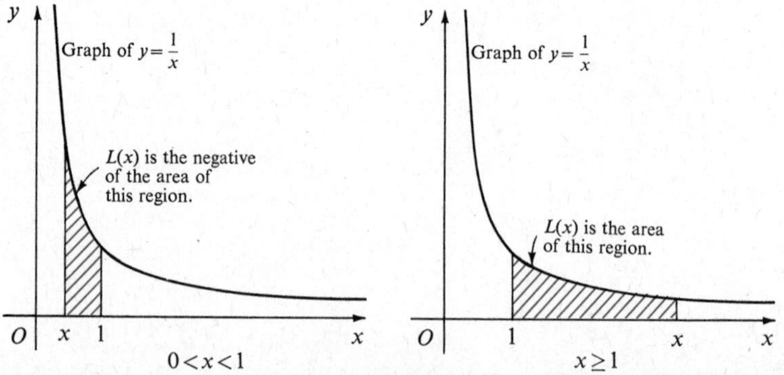

Figure 5–7

Since $A(1, 1) = 0$, we have $L(1) = 0$. Moreover, $L(x) > 0$ if $x > 1$, and $L(x) < 0$ if $0 < x < 1$. As a result of work done in Section 5–2 (pages 203–204, and Exercises 12 and 14 on page 208), we have $L(2) = A(1, 2) \doteq 0.69$, $L(3) \doteq 1.10$, and $L(5) \doteq 1.61$.

The following is easy to prove:

Property AL.

If $0 < p \leq q$, then $A(p, q) = L(q) - L(p)$.

For example, if $0 < p < 1 \leq q$ (Figure 5–8), then $L(p) = -A(p, 1)$ and $L(q) = A(1, q)$. Using Property A–2, we have

$$\begin{aligned} A(p, q) &= A(p, 1) + A(1, q) \\ &= -L(p) + L(q) \\ &= L(q) - L(p). \end{aligned}$$

The proofs of the two remaining cases, $0 < p \leq q < 1$ and $1 \leq p \leq q$, are left as exercises (page 213).

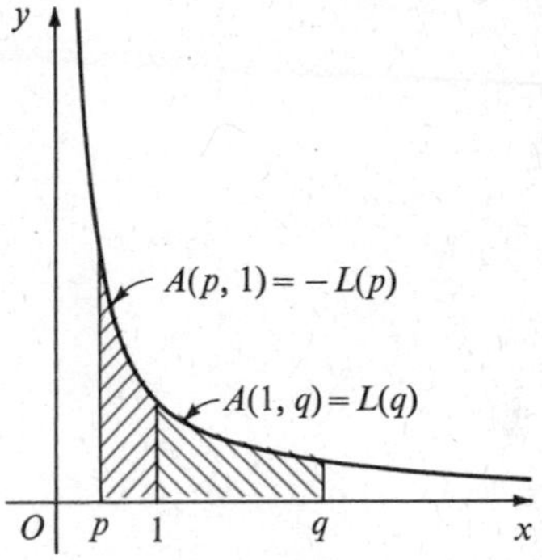

Figure 5–8

Lemma.*

If $x > 0$, then $L\left(\frac{1}{x}\right) = -L(x)$.

Proof

Suppose $x > 1$. Then $0 < \frac{1}{x} < 1$, and we have

$$\begin{aligned} L\left(\frac{1}{x}\right) &= -A\left(\frac{1}{x}, 1\right) && \text{Definition of } L \\ &= -A\left(x \cdot \frac{1}{x}, x \cdot 1\right) && \text{Property A–1} \\ &= -A(1, x) \\ &= -L(x) && \text{Definition of } L \end{aligned}$$

The proof for the case $0 < x \leq 1$ is left as an exercise (page 213).

---

* A theorem whose principal use is in proving other theorems is sometimes called a **lemma.**

As a consequence of the Lemma we have, for example,

$$L(0.5) = L(\tfrac{1}{2}) = -L(2) \doteq -0.69$$

and

$$L(0.2) = L(\tfrac{1}{5}) = -L(5) \doteq -1.61.$$

Although we have not yet defined the *common logarithm*, $\log_{10}$, you are probably familiar with some of its properties from earlier work. The next theorem shows that the natural logarithm has many of the properties of the common logarithm.

Theorem 1.

Let x and y be positive numbers and r be a rational number. Then

$$\text{L–1.} \quad L(xy) = L(x) + L(y)$$

$$\text{L–2.} \quad L\left(\frac{y}{x}\right) = L(y) - L(x)$$

$$\text{L–3.} \quad L(x^r) = rL(x).$$

Proof of L–1

Case 1: At least one of x and y is ≥ 1.
Suppose $y \geq 1$. Then $x \leq xy$, and by Property AL, we have

$$A(x, xy) = L(xy) - L(x).$$

On the other hand, using Property A–1 and the definition of L, we have

$$A(x, xy) = A(1, y) = L(y).$$

Equating the two expressions for $A(x, xy)$, we have

$$L(xy) - L(x) = L(y), \quad \text{or} \quad L(xy) = L(x) + L(y).$$

Case 2: Both x and y are <1.
Then $\frac{1}{x} > 1$, $\frac{1}{y} > 1$, and $\frac{1}{xy} > 1$. By Case 1, we have

$$L\left(\frac{1}{xy}\right) = L\left(\frac{1}{x}\cdot\frac{1}{y}\right) = L\left(\frac{1}{x}\right) + L\left(\frac{1}{y}\right).$$

Applying the Lemma to this equation, we get

$$-L(xy) = -L(x) - L(y), \quad \text{or} \quad L(xy) = L(x) + L(y).$$

Proof of L–2

Using L–1 and the Lemma, we have

$$L\left(\frac{y}{x}\right) = L\left(y \cdot \frac{1}{x}\right) = L(y) + L\left(\frac{1}{x}\right) = L(y) - L(x).$$

Proof of L–3

Since $L(x^0) = L(1) = 0$, L–3 holds when $r = 0$. We shall next use mathematical induction to prove L–3 in the case where $r = n$, a positive integer.

The proposition $L(x^n) = nL(x)$ is certainly true when $n = 1$. Suppose the proposition is true when $n = k$, that is, suppose that

$$L(x^k) = kL(x) \text{ is true.} \qquad (*)$$

We wish to prove the proposition is true when $n = k + 1$. We have

$$\begin{aligned} L(x^{k+1}) &= L(x \cdot x^k) \\ &= L(x) + L(x^k) && \text{By L–1} \\ &= L(x) + kL(x) && \text{By } (*) \\ &= (k + 1)L(x). \end{aligned}$$

Therefore the proposition is true for $n = k + 1$, and the proof by induction is complete.

If $r = n$, a *negative* integer, then $-n$ is a *positive* integer, and we have

$$\begin{aligned} L(x^n) &= L\left(\frac{1}{x^{-n}}\right) \\ &= -L(x^{-n}) && \text{By the Lemma} \\ &= -[(-n)L(x)] && \text{By L–3 for positive integral exponents} \\ &= nL(x). \end{aligned}$$

Thus far we have proved L–3 for r any integer.

If $r = \frac{1}{n}$, the reciprocal of a positive integer, then by L–3 for positive integral exponents,

$$nL\left(x^{\frac{1}{n}}\right) = L\left(\left(x^{\frac{1}{n}}\right)^n\right) = L(x).$$

Thus

$$L\left(x^{\frac{1}{n}}\right) = \frac{1}{n}L(x).$$

Finally, let $r = \frac{m}{n}$, where m and n are integers and n is positive. Then, using previously proved parts of L–3,

$$L(x^r) = L\left(x^{\frac{m}{n}}\right) = L\left(\left(x^{\frac{1}{n}}\right)^m\right) = mL\left(x^{\frac{1}{n}}\right)$$
$$= m \cdot \frac{1}{n} L(x) = \frac{m}{n} L(x) = rL(x).$$

As a consequence of Theorem 1, we see that it is possible to use natural logarithms for computational purposes. This is seldom done, however, because the "characteristic-mantissa" scheme of common logarithms is not available. Tables of natural logarithms have been prepared; a very short three-place one is given below.

Table of Natural Logarithms

x	$L(x)$	x	$L(x)$	x	$L(x)$
1.5	0.405	4.5	1.504	7.5	2.015
2.0	0.693	5.0	1.609	8.0	2.079
2.5	0.916	5.5	1.705	8.5	2.140
3.0	1.099	6.0	1.792	9.0	2.197
3.5	1.253	6.5	1.872	9.5	2.251
4.0	1.386	7.0	1.946	10.0	2.303

EXAMPLE. Use the table of natural logarithms to find

a. $L(0.5)$;

b. $L(20.0)$;

c. the area under the curve $y = \frac{1}{x}$ from 0.5 to 20.0.

Solution: **a.** $L(0.5) = L(\frac{1}{2}) = -L(2) = -0.693.$

b. $L(20) = L(2) + L(10) = 0.693 + 2.303 = 2.996.$

c. $A(0.5, 20.0) = \int_{0.5}^{20.0} \frac{1}{x}\,dx = L(20.0) - L(0.5)$

$= 2.996 - (-0.693) = 3.689.$

ORAL EXERCISES

1. Complete the statement: "The natural logarithm of the reciprocal of a positive number is . . . ."
2. State Properties L–1, L–2, and L–3 in words.
3. Give three real numbers r for which the equation given in Property L–3 has not yet been proved.

WRITTEN EXERCISES

In Exercises 1–21, use the short table of natural logarithms given on page 212 to find the specified numbers.

A

1. $L(30)$
2. $L(15)$
3. $L(\frac{2}{3})$
4. $L(\frac{2}{15})$
5. $L(\frac{16}{3})$
6. $L(49)$
7. $L(\sqrt{2})$
8. $L(\sqrt[3]{4})$
9. $L(\sqrt{15})$
10. $L(\frac{1}{16})$
11. $L(0.7)$
12. $L(20{,}000)$
13. $L(0.02)$
14. $L(0.00002)$
15. $L(\sqrt[3]{0.002})$
16. $A(2, 5.5)$
17. $A(\frac{1}{5}, 10)$
18. $A(\frac{1}{5}, \frac{1}{3})$
19. $\int_{15}^{30} \frac{1}{x}\, dx$
20. $\int_{0.7}^{\sqrt{2}} \frac{1}{x}\, dx$
21. $\int_{\frac{2}{3}}^{1} \frac{1}{x}\, dx$

B

22. There are 18 entries in the short table of natural logarithms given on page 212. Three of these were given in Section 5–2:

$$L(2) \doteq 0.693 \qquad L(3) \doteq 1.099 \qquad L(5) \doteq 1.609.$$

Nine of the remaining 15 entries can be calculated using these three. Do so.

C

23. Prove Property AL for the case $0 < p \leq q < 1$.
24. Prove Property AL for the case $1 \leq p \leq q$.
25. Prove the Lemma on page 209 for the case $0 < x \leq 1$.

5–4 Further Properties of the Natural Logarithm Function

Next we shall find the derivative of the natural logarithm function. To do this, we shall use the following fact about the area under the curve $y = \frac{1}{x}$ from p to q: If $0 < p < q$, then

$$\frac{1}{q}(q - p) < A(p, q) < \frac{1}{p}(q - p). \qquad (*)$$

[Note that the first and third terms of (*) can be interpreted as the areas of rectangular regions respectively contained in, and containing, the region $R_{p,q}$ (see Figure 5–9).]

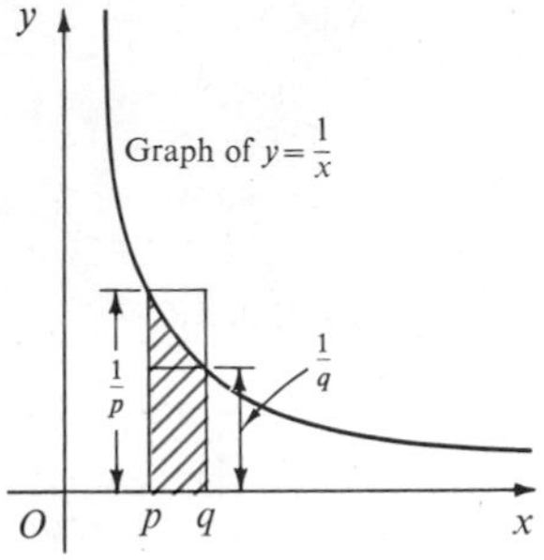

Figure 5–9

To find $L'(a)$ for any $a > 0$, we consider the difference quotient

$$\frac{L(z) - L(a)}{z - a}, \quad z \neq a.$$

If $z < a$, by Property AL (page 209) we have

$$L(a) - L(z) = A(z, a).$$

Therefore, using (*) on page 213 with $p = z$ and $q = a$, we see that

$$\frac{1}{a}(a - z) < L(a) - L(z) < \frac{1}{z}(a - z).$$

Hence, dividing by the positive number $a - z$, we obtain

$$\frac{1}{a} < \frac{L(a) - L(z)}{a - z} < \frac{1}{z},$$

or

$$\frac{1}{a} < \frac{L(z) - L(a)}{z - a} < \frac{1}{z}.$$

If $a < z$, we can show in a similar way that

$$\frac{1}{z} < \frac{L(z) - L(a)}{z - a} < \frac{1}{a}.$$

Therefore the difference quotient, $\frac{L(z) - L(a)}{z - a}$, is always between $\frac{1}{z}$ and $\frac{1}{a}$; and since $\frac{1}{z}$ approaches $\frac{1}{a}$ as z approaches a, we have

$$L'(a) = \lim_{z \to a} \frac{L(z) - L(a)}{z - a} = \frac{1}{a}.$$

Thus $L'(a)$ exists for every a in the domain $\{x: x > 0\}$ of L, and we have therefore proved

Theorem 2.

The natural logarithm function L is differentiable and, therefore, continuous, and

$$L'(x) = \frac{1}{x}, \quad x > 0.$$

EXAMPLE 1. Find the slope of the graph of L at the point $(x, L(x))$ for the following values of x:

a. $\frac{1}{10}$; **b.** $\frac{1}{2}$; **c.** 1; **d.** 2; **e.** 10.

Solution: **a.** $L'(\frac{1}{10}) = \dfrac{1}{\frac{1}{10}} = 10;$ **b.** $L'(\frac{1}{2}) = \dfrac{1}{\frac{1}{2}} = 2;$

c. $L'(1) = \frac{1}{1} = 1;$ **d.** $L'(2) = \frac{1}{2};$ **e.** $L'(10) = \frac{1}{10}.$

EXAMPLE 2. If $f\colon x \to L\left(\dfrac{1}{\sqrt{x}}\right)$, find $f'(x)$.

Solution: Since $\dfrac{1}{\sqrt{x}} = x^{-\frac{1}{2}}$, by Property L–3 (Theorem 1, page 210) we have

$$f(x) = L\left(\frac{1}{\sqrt{x}}\right) = L(x^{-\frac{1}{2}}) = -\tfrac{1}{2}L(x).$$

Therefore,

$$f'(x) = -\tfrac{1}{2}L'(x) = -\frac{1}{2}\cdot\frac{1}{x} = -\frac{1}{2x}.$$

Since $L'(x) = \dfrac{1}{x}$ is positive for $x > 0$, we see that the function L is *increasing* on $\{x\colon x > 0\}$. Moreover, $L''(x) = -\dfrac{1}{x^2}$ is negative for $x > 0$; therefore the graph of L is convex upward. This fact, or an inspection of the formula $L'(x) = \dfrac{1}{x}$ itself, shows that although L is increasing, it is increasing more and more slowly as x becomes greater and greater.

The facts noted above, together with a short table of values, enable us to draw the graph of L quite accurately (Figure 5–10, page 216). The second line of the table below can be constructed from three values of L which we already know,

$$L(2) \doteq 0.69, \qquad L(3) \doteq 1.10, \qquad L(5) \doteq 1.61,$$

by using the properties of L listed in Theorem 1 (page 210). For example,

$$L(\tfrac{3}{4}) = L(3) - L(2^2) = L(3) - 2L(2) \doteq 1.10 - 2(0.69) = -0.28.$$

x	$\frac{1}{4}$	$\frac{1}{2}$	$\frac{3}{4}$	1	$\frac{3}{2}$	2	$\frac{5}{2}$	3	4	5
$L(x)$	−1.38	−0.69	−0.28	0	0.41	0.69	0.92	1.10	1.38	1.61
$L'(x)$	4	2	$\frac{4}{3}$	1	$\frac{2}{3}$	$\frac{1}{2}$	$\frac{2}{5}$	$\frac{1}{3}$	$\frac{1}{4}$	$\frac{1}{5}$

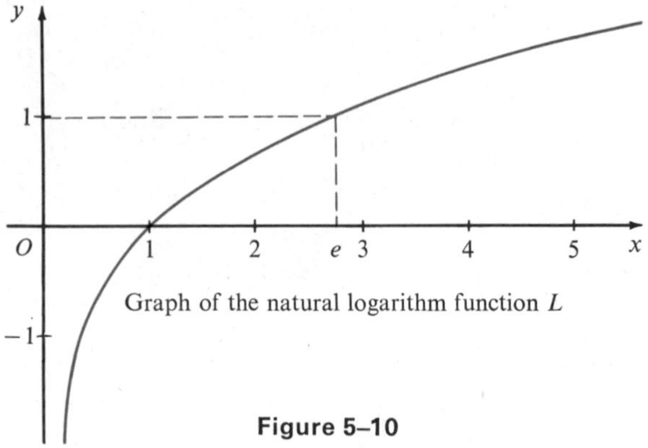

Figure 5–10

Theorem 3.

For every real number r, there is a unique positive number c such that

$$L(c) = r.$$

Proof

Suppose $r > 0$. No matter how large r is, there is an integer $k > r$. We have shown (page 209) that $L(3) > 1$. Therefore, using Property L–3, we have $L(3^k) = kL(3) > k > r$. On the other hand, $L(1) = 0 < r$. Thus

$$L(1) < r < L(3^k).$$

Now, since L is continuous, by the Intermediate-Value Property (Theorem 3, Chapter 3, page 118) there is a number c (between 1 and 3^k) such that

$$L(c) = r.$$

Since L is an increasing function, there is only one such number c.

The proof in the case $r < 0$ is similar. Of course, if $r = 0$, then $c = 1$.

From Theorem 3, we see that there is a unique number whose natural logarithm is 1. This number is universally denoted by e. Thus e is defined by the formula

$$L(e) = 1.$$

The number e, called, for reasons which will appear later, the **base of natural logarithms,** is one of the most important numbers in all of mathematics and its applications. Since $L(2.5) < 1$ and $L(3.0) > 1$, e lies between 2.5 and 3.0. Its value to five decimal places is 2.71828.

EXAMPLE 3. Find the point P such that the line tangent to the graph of L at P passes through (0, 1).

Solution: Let the abscissa of P be a. Then the ordinate of P is $L(a)$, and the slope of the graph at P is $L'(a) = \frac{1}{a}$. An equation of the tangent line, therefore, is

$$y - L(a) = \frac{1}{a}(x - a).$$

Since this line is to pass through (0, 1), we must have

$$1 - L(a) = \frac{1}{a}(0 - a), \quad \text{or} \quad L(a) = 2.$$

We know from Theorem 3, page 216, that there is precisely one number a such that $L(a) = 2$. To find it, we use the fact that since $L(e) = 1$, $L(e^2) = 2L(e) = 2$. Thus $a = e^2$, and P is the point $(e^2, L(e^2)) = (e^2, 2)$.

ORAL EXERCISES

State (a) which number should replace the question mark in order that the point lie on the graph of L, and
(b) the slope of the graph of L at this point.

1. (1, ?)
2. (?, 1)
3. (?, 0)
4. (e, ?)
5. (e^4, ?)
6. (?, 3)

WRITTEN EXERCISES

In Exercises 1–8, find $f'(x)$.

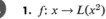

A

1. $f\colon x \to L(x^2)$
2. $f\colon x \to L(x^4)$
3. $f\colon x \to L\left(\frac{1}{x}\right)$
4. $f\colon x \to L\left(\frac{1}{x^2}\right)$
5. $f\colon x \to L(\sqrt{x})$
6. $f\colon x \to L(\sqrt[3]{x})$
7. $f\colon x \to L\left(\frac{1}{\sqrt[3]{x}}\right)$
8. $f\colon x \to L\left(\sqrt[3]{\frac{1}{x^2}}\right)$

9. Find an equation of the line tangent to the graph of L at its x-intercept.

In Exercises 10–13, find the point P such that the line tangent to the graph of L at P passes through the given point.

10. (0, 0)
11. (0, 3)
12. (0, −2)
13. (0, c)

In Exercises 14–17, find an equation of the line which has slope m and is tangent to the graph of L.

B **14.** $m = e$

15. $m = e^2$

16. $m = \frac{1}{e}$

17. $m = \frac{1}{e^2}$

18. Draw the graph of $f: x \to L(|x|)$.

C **19.** Consider the function $f: x \to xL(x) \quad (x > 0)$.

a. Find $f'(x)$. (*Hint:* Use the Product Rule.)

b. Find $f''(x)$.

c. Find the critical point of the graph of f and determine whether it is a maximum or a minimum point.

d. Where is the graph convex upward? convex downward?

e. Sketch the graph of f. (You may use the unproved fact that $\lim_{x \to 0} xL(x) = 0$.)

20. Repeat Exercise 19 for the function $g: x \to \frac{L(x)}{x} \quad (x > 0)$.

21. Prove directly that L is continuous at every $a > 0$. [*Hint:* Use (*) on page 213 to show that if $0 < z \neq a$, then

$$\frac{1}{z}(z - a) < L(z) - L(a) < \frac{1}{a}(z - a).$$

Show that $\lim_{z \to a} [L(z) - L(a)] = 0$ and that therefore $\lim_{z \to a} L(z) = L(a)$.]

5–5 The Natural Exponential Function

Theorem 3 of Section 5–4 is the assertion that the natural logarithm function L is a one-to-one function with domain $\mathcal{R}^+ = \{x: x > 0\}$ and range $\mathcal{R}$, the set of all real numbers. We shall now consider the inverse function L^{-1} of L. The existence of L^{-1} is a consequence of matters discussed in Section 1–7, which you should reread at this time.

We shall denote L^{-1} by E and call it, for reasons which will appear later, the **natural exponential function.** The domain of E is $\mathcal{R}$ (the range of L), the range of E is $\mathcal{R}^+$ (the domain of L), and

$$E(x) = y \quad \text{if and only if} \quad L(y) = x. \tag{I}$$

For example,

$$E(0) = 1 \quad \text{because} \quad L(1) = 0,$$
$$E(1) = e \quad \text{because} \quad L(e) = 1,$$
$$E(2) = e^2 \quad \text{because} \quad L(e^2) = 2L(e) = 2,$$
$$E(-1) = \frac{1}{e} \quad \text{because} \quad L\left(\frac{1}{e}\right) = -L(e) = -1.$$

From (I), or from Theorem 2 of Section 1–7, we have

$$L(E(u)) = u \qquad \text{for any real number } u, \tag{II}$$

$$E(L(v)) = v \qquad \text{for any positive number } v. \tag{III}$$

We can now establish two properties of the function E:

Theorem 4.

Let u and v be any real numbers. Then

E–1. $E(u) \cdot E(v) = E(u + v)$,

E–2. $\dfrac{E(u)}{E(v)} = E(u - v)$.

Proof

To prove Property E–1, we use Property L–1 (Theorem 1, page 210) with $x = E(u)$ and $y = E(v)$ to obtain

$$L[E(u) \cdot E(v)] = L[E(u)] + L[E(v)] = u + v. \tag{*}$$

Note that in the second step we used (II) twice. By the definition of E [that is, (I) with $x = u + v$ and $y = E(u) \cdot E(v)$], or by (III), (*) is equivalent to

$$E(u) \cdot E(v) = E(u + v).$$

The proof of Property E–2 is similar and is left as an exercise (page 222).

In Section 1–7, we showed that if two functions are inverses of each other, then their graphs are symmetric with respect to the line $y = x$. We may, therefore, obtain the graph of E by reflecting the graph of L in the line $y = x$ (Figure 5–11).

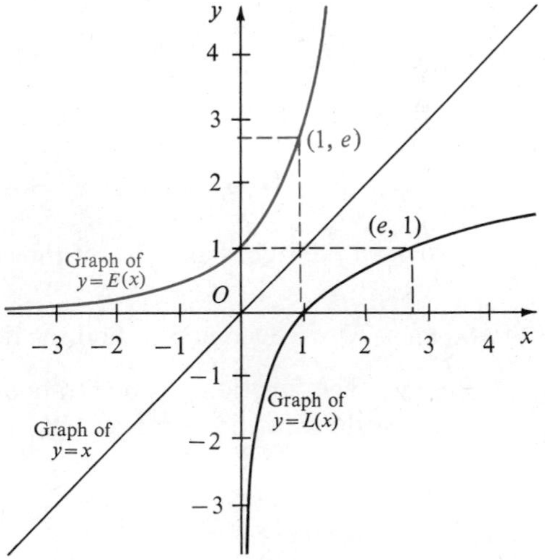

Figure 5–11

The fact that two functions, f and g, which are inverses of each other have graphs which are symmetric with respect to the line $y = x$ enables us to find a relationship between their derivatives. Let u be a number in the domain of g, and let $v = g(u)$. Then the point (u, v) is on the graph of g, and therefore the point (v, u) is on the graph of f. (See Figure 5–12.) Suppose that f has a nonzero derivative at v. Then there is a line H which is tangent to the graph of f at (v, u), and its slope is $f'(v)$. Let K be the line symmetric to H with respect to the line $y = x$. The slopes of H and K are reciprocals of each other (see Exercise 16, page 222), and therefore

$$\text{slope of } K = \frac{1}{f'(v)}.$$

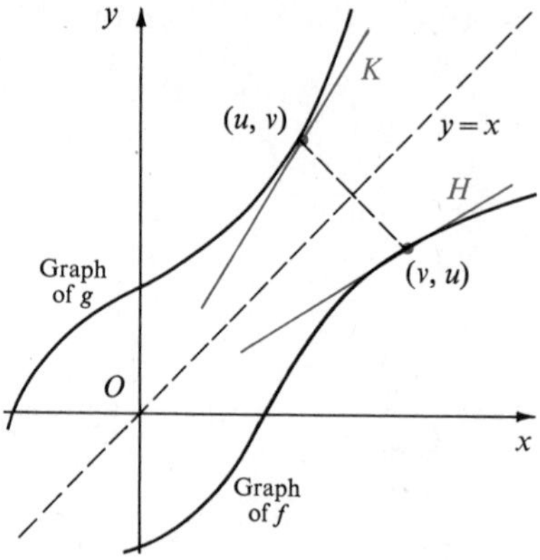

Figure 5–12

By appealing to geometric symmetry, we conclude that K is tangent to the graph of g at (u, v), and therefore

$$\text{slope of } K = g'(u).$$

Equating the two expressions for the slope of K, we have

$$g'(u) = \frac{1}{f'(v)},$$

or since $v = g(u)$,

$$g'(u) = \frac{1}{f'(g(u))}.$$

We therefore have the following:

Theorem 5.

If the functions f and g are inverses of each other, then

$$g'(x) = \frac{1}{f'(g(x))}$$

provided the right-hand side of the equation is meaningful.

EXAMPLE 1. Use Theorem 5 to find the derivative of $g: x \to \sqrt{x}$.

Solution: The function g is one-to-one and has the set $\{x: x \geq 0\}$ as its domain and its range. The inverse of g is the function f having $\{x: x \geq 0\}$ as domain and values $f(x) = x^2$. Since $f'(x) = 2x$, $f'(g(x)) = 2g(x) = 2\sqrt{x}$. Therefore,

$$g'(x) = \frac{1}{f'(g(x))} = \frac{1}{2\sqrt{x}}.$$

Note that this formula is meaningful only if $x > 0$.

As a corollary to Theorem 5, we have an important and perhaps surprising fact about the function E: *It is its own derivative.*

Corollary. $$E'(x) = E(x).$$

Proof

We use Theorem 5 with $g = E$ and $f = L$. Since $L'(x) = \frac{1}{x}$ by Theorem 2, page 214, we have

$$L'(E(x)) = \frac{1}{E(x)}.$$

Therefore, by Theorem 5,

$$E'(x) = \frac{1}{L'(E(x))} = E(x).$$

EXAMPLE 2. Find **(a)** $E'(1)$, **(b)** $E''(1)$, and **(c)** $E'''(1)$.

Solution: **a.** $E'(x) = E(x)$; therefore $E'(1) = E(1) = e$.

b. $E''(x) = \frac{d}{dx}E'(x) = \frac{d}{dx}E(x) = E(x)$; therefore $E''(1) = e$.

c. $E'''(x) = \frac{d}{dx}E''(x) = \frac{d}{dx}E(x) = E(x)$; therefore $E'''(1) = e$.

ORAL EXERCISES

Restate each of the following using the function E.

1. $L(a) = b$ **2.** $2L(a) = b$ **3.** $L(a) + L(b) = c$

Restate each of the following using the function L.

4. $E(a) = b$ **5.** $E(a) \cdot E(b) = c$ **6.** $E(a) = cE(b)$

Describe the domain and the range of each of the following functions.

7. $L \circ E$ **8.** $E \circ L$ **9.** $E \cdot L$

WRITTEN EXERCISES

In Exercises 1–5, find an equation of the line tangent to the graph of E at the point whose abscissa is given.

A

1. 0 2. 1 3. 2 4. -1 5. a

In Exercises 6–9, find the inverse, f, of g. Then use the method of Example 1 to find $g'(x)$. Check your result by using the formula for $\frac{d}{dx} x^r$ (r rational).

6. $g: x \to \sqrt[3]{x}$
7. $g: x \to x^{\frac{1}{5}}$
8. $g: x \to x^{\frac{1}{4}}$
9. $g: x \to \dfrac{1}{\sqrt{x}}$

B

10. Find an equation of the line tangent to the graph of E which passes through the point $(c, 0)$. Show that the slope of this line is $E(c + 1)$.

In Exercises 11 and 12, find $f'(x)$, $f''(x)$, $f'''(x)$, $f^{\text{iv}}(x)$, and $f^{\text{v}}(x)$.

11. $f: x \to xE(x)$
12. $x \to x^2E(x)$

C

13. Use the results of Exercise 11 to guess at a formula for the nth derivative, $f^{(n)}(x)$, of the function $f: x \to xE(x)$. Use mathematical induction to prove the validity of the formula.
14. Find, and prove the validity of, a formula for the nth derivative, $f^{(n)}(x)$, of the function $f: x \to x^2E(x)$. (See Exercise 12.)
15. Prove Property E–2, page 219.
16. Let H be the graph of the linear function

$$f: x \to mx + b \qquad (m \neq 0),$$

and let K be the graph of f^{-1}. Show that

$$f^{-1}: x \to \frac{1}{m}x - \frac{b}{m}$$

and that therefore the slopes of H and K are reciprocals of each other.

CHAPTER SUMMARY

1. The definition of exponential expressions with rational exponents is made in such a way that the exponential laws for positive integral exponents remain true. If $a > 0$, and m and n are integers with $n > 0$, then $a^{\frac{m}{n}}$ is the mth power of the positive nth root of a.

2. For $0 < p \leq q$, $A(p, q)$ denotes the area of the region lying between the lines $x = p$ and $x = q$, above the x-axis, and below the graph of $y = \frac{1}{x}$. Integral-calculus notation for $A(p, q)$ is $\int_p^q \frac{1}{x}\,dx$. If $0 < p \leq q \leq r$ and $k > 0$, then

$$\text{A–1.} \quad A(p, q) = A(kp, kq)$$
$$\text{A–2.} \quad A(p, q) + A(q, r) = A(p, r).$$

3. The **natural logarithm function,** denoted (in this chapter) by L, is defined by the formula

$$L(x) = \begin{cases} A(1, x) & \text{if } x \geq 1 \\ -A(x, 1) & \text{if } 0 < x < 1. \end{cases}$$

The domain of L is $\{x: x > 0\}$.

4. The function L satisfies the following **laws of logarithms:** If x and y are positive numbers and r is a rational number, then

$$\text{L–1.} \quad L(xy) = L(x) + L(y)$$
$$\text{L–2.} \quad L\left(\frac{y}{x}\right) = L(y) - L(x)$$
$$\text{L–3.} \quad L(x^r) = rL(x).$$

5. The natural logarithm function L is differentiable, hence continuous, and $L'(x) = \frac{1}{x}$ $(x > 0)$.

6. The natural logarithm function L has range $\mathcal{R}$. The **base of natural logarithms,** e, is defined by the equation $L(e) = 1$.

7. The natural logarithm function L is increasing; therefore it is one-to-one and thus has an *inverse function*, E (the notation E is restricted to this chapter and part of the next). The function E is the **natural exponential function.** Because L and E are inverses of each other, they satisfy

$$L(E(u)) = u \quad \text{for any real number } u,$$
$$E(L(v)) = v \quad \text{for any positive number } v.$$

8. The exponential function E satisfies the laws

$$\text{E–1.} \quad E(x) \cdot E(y) = E(x + y),$$
$$\text{E–2.} \quad \frac{E(y)}{E(x)} = E(y - x).$$

9. If the functions f and g are inverses of each other, then

$$g'(x) = \frac{1}{f'(g(x))}$$

provided the right-hand side of the equation is meaningful.

10. The exponential function E is its own derivative; that is, $E'(x) = E(x)$ for all real numbers x.

CHAPTER TEST

5–1 **1.** Express as a single fraction in lowest terms without the use of negative exponents or radicals.

a. $\dfrac{(2ab^{-1})^{-2}}{(-a^2b)^{-3}}$ **b.** $\dfrac{1}{\sqrt{a^{-2}+b^{-2}}}$ $(a, b > 0)$

5–2 **2.** Determine the value of x which makes the statement true:

a. $A(1, 3) + A(3, 6) = A(1, x)$

b. $A(1, 3) = A(3, x)$

c. $A(x, 2) = A(1, 3)$

d. $\int_1^3 \frac{1}{t}\,dt = \int_2^x \frac{1}{t}\,dt$

5–3 **3.** If $L(2) = a$ and $L(5) = b$, find each of the following in terms of a and b.

a. $L(10)$ **c.** $L(25)$ **e.** $A(2, 5)$

b. $L(100)$ **d.** $L(12.5)$ **f.** $\int_2^5 \frac{1}{x}\,dx$

5–4 **4.** Find $f'(x)$ if **(a)** $f(x) = L\left(\frac{1}{x^2}\right)$ and **(b)** $f(x) = L\left(\frac{2}{x}\right)$.

5. Find an equation of the line tangent to the graph of L at the point having ordinate 1. (Leave your answer in terms of e.)

5–5 **6.** Let $f(x) = L(2x)$ and $g(x) = \frac{1}{2}E(x)$.

a. Find $f(g(x))$.

b. Find $g(f(x))$ if $x > 0$.

c. What do the results of **(a)** and **(b)** imply about the functions f and g?

7. Find $f'(x)$ for **(a)** $f: x \to \dfrac{E(x)}{x}$; **(b)** $f: x \to E(2L(x))$; and **(c)** $f: x \to L(2E(x))$.

RECOMMENDED READINGS

Courant, Richard, and Robbins, Herbert, *What is Mathematics?* (New York: Oxford University Press, 1941).

Menger, Karl, *Methods of Presenting e and π*, American Mathematical Monthly, Vol. 52, No. 1 (January, 1945), pp. 28–33.

Development of Integral Calculus

In the essay at the end of Chapter 3, it was stated that Archimedes applied the methods of differential calculus (thus anticipating its "official" invention by some 2000 years) in showing how to construct the tangent line at each point of a certain spiral. To a much greater extent, Archimedes used the methods of *integral calculus*, as described below.

A geometric problem of antiquity was that of "squaring the circle," that is, of constructing by means of straightedge and compass alone a square region with area exactly equal to that of a given circular region. Archimedes did not solve this problem; indeed, the construction is now known to be *impossible*. It was not until 1882, though, that the impossibility of the construction was finally established when the German mathematician Ferdinand Lindemann proved that π is a *transcendental* irrational number.

Archimedes did, however, succeed in solving the problem of "squaring" a region bounded by an arc of a *parabola*. His result is the following:

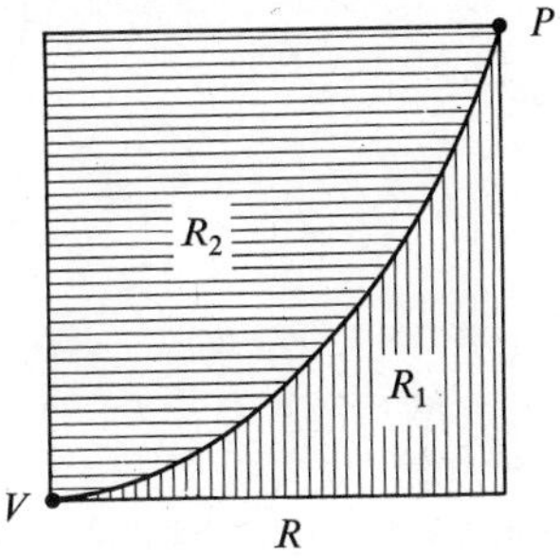

Let R be a rectangular region with two of its opposite vertices the vertex, V, and another point, P, of a parabola, and with one side on the axis of the parabola, as indicated in the diagram at the right. Then *the areas A_1 and A_2 of the regions R_1 and R_2 into which the parabola separates R are in the ratio* $\dfrac{A_1}{A_2} = \dfrac{1}{2}$.

We can use modern notation to obtain Archimedes' result, as follows:

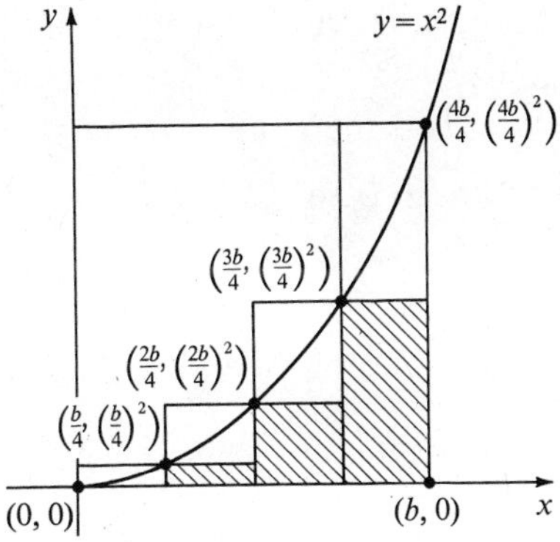

Suppose the parabola is the graph of the equation $y = x^2$, and let the opposite vertices of R be $(0, 0)$ and (b, b^2), as indicated in the diagram at the right. Since the height of R is b^2 and the length of its base is b, its area A is given by $A = b^2 \cdot b$, or $A = b^3$. Thus we can establish Archimedes' result by showing that the area A_1 of the region R_1 below the parabola is $A_1 = \dfrac{b^3}{3}$.

Separating the interval $\{x: 0 \leq x \leq b\}$ into n congruent subintervals each of length $\Delta x = \frac{b}{n}$ (illustrated in the diagram with $n = 4$), we see that the area A_1 of R_1 is greater than the sum of the areas of the shorter (shaded) rectangular regions (one of them is degenerate, with height 0) and is less than the sum of the areas of the taller (their lower portions shaded) rectangular regions:

$$0 \cdot \left(\frac{b}{n}\right) + \left(\frac{b}{n}\right)^2 \cdot \left(\frac{b}{n}\right) + \left(\frac{2b}{n}\right)^2 \cdot \left(\frac{b}{n}\right) + \cdots + \left(\frac{(n-1)b}{n}\right)^2 \cdot \left(\frac{b}{n}\right)$$
$$\leq A_1 \leq \left(\frac{b}{n}\right)^2 \cdot \left(\frac{b}{n}\right) + \left(\frac{2b}{n}\right)^2 \cdot \left(\frac{b}{n}\right) + \cdots + \left(\frac{nb}{n}\right)^2 \cdot \left(\frac{b}{n}\right), \tag{1}$$

or

$$[1^2 + 2^2 + \cdots + (n-1)^2] \cdot \left(\frac{b}{n}\right)^3 \leq A_1 \leq [1^2 + 2^2 + \cdots + n^2] \cdot \left(\frac{b}{n}\right)^3. \tag{2}$$

You may be familiar with the formula

$$1^2 + 2^2 + \cdots + k^2 = \frac{k(k+1)(2k+1)}{6}$$

for the sum of the squares of the first k counting numbers; if not, you can establish it by mathematical induction.

Substituting from this formula in (2), we obtain

$$\frac{(n-1)n(2n-1)}{6} \cdot \left(\frac{b}{n}\right)^3 \leq A_1 \leq \frac{n(n+1)(2n+1)}{6} \cdot \left(\frac{b}{n}\right)^3,$$

or

$$\left(1 - \frac{1}{n}\right)\left(2 - \frac{1}{n}\right) \cdot \frac{b^3}{6} \leq A_1 \leq \left(1 + \frac{1}{n}\right)\left(2 + \frac{1}{n}\right) \cdot \frac{b^3}{6}. \tag{3}$$

It should be intuitively clear from the diagram on page 225 that if n is quite large, then the two estimates of A_1 in (3), one from below and the other from above, differ by very little; in fact, if you imagine the unshaded upper rectangles to be shifted horizontally to form one tall rectangle against the y-axis, you can see that the two estimates differ by the area of a rectangular region of height b^2 and length of base $\Delta x = \frac{b}{n}$, that is, by $\frac{b^3}{n}$.

Taking the limit as n increases indefinitely, and accordingly Δx and $\frac{1}{n}$ approach 0, in (3), we obtain the desired result:

$$\frac{b^3}{3} \leq A_1 \leq \frac{b^3}{3}, \qquad \text{or} \qquad A_1 = \frac{b^3}{3}.$$

To denote sums such as those in (1), we often use the Greek capital letter Σ (sigma). Thus, recalling that $\frac{b}{n} = \Delta x$, we write (1) as

$$\sum_{j=0}^{n-1} \left(\frac{jb}{n}\right)^2 \Delta x \leq A_1 \leq \sum_{j=1}^{n} \left(\frac{jb}{n}\right)^2 \Delta x,$$

reading "$\sum_{j=1}^{n}$ . . ." as "the sum from $j = 1$ to $j = n$ of . . . ."

The method just used to find the area under the parabola $y = x^2$ can be generalized as follows: For a continuous function f defined by $y = f(x)$ for $a \leq x \leq b$, we separate the interval $\{x: a \leq x \leq b\}$ into n congruent subintervals each of length $\Delta x = \frac{b - a}{n}$ (we take the lengths of the subintervals to be equal only for convenience), choose points $x_1, x_2, \ldots, x_n$ in the successive subintervals, and then form the sum $\sum_{j=1}^{n} f(x_j)\Delta x$. As we illustrated with $f(x) = x^2$ and with the interval $\{x: 0 \leq x \leq b\}$, as n increases indefinitely and accordingly Δx approaches 0, this sum has a unique limit. This limit is called the *integral*, or the *definite integral*, from a to b of $f(x)$ with respect to x.

As was the case with differential calculus, Newton and Leibniz are credited with the systematic development of integral calculus. Just as Leibniz invented the standard notation $\frac{d}{dx} f(x)$ for the derivative,

$$\frac{d}{dx} f(x) = \lim_{\Delta x \to 0} \frac{\Delta f(x)}{\Delta x},$$

so did he invent the standard symbol for the integral. Namely, he replaced the difference symbol Δ with d, just as in the symbol for the derivative, and he replaced the summation symbol $\sum$ with S, which we now write in stylized form as $\int$:

$$\int_a^b f(x)\, dx = \lim_{\substack{\Delta x \to 0 \\ (n \to \infty)}} \sum_{j=1}^{n} f(x_j)\, \Delta x.$$

Today, integral calculus provides some of the most useful methods in the applications of mathematical analysis. Whenever it is desirable to think of a physical quantity as the limit of a sum, we represent the quantity as an integral. The quantity might, for example, be the hydrostatic force of water against a dam, where the pressure (the force per unit of area) increases with the depth; or it might be the amount of work, and accordingly the amount of fuel, necessary to accomplish an interplanetary space flight.

READING LIST

BERS, LIPMAN, *Calculus* (New York: Holt, Rinehart, and Winston, Inc., 1969).

NIVEN, IVAN, *Numbers: Rational and Irrational* (New York: Random House, Inc., 1961).

6

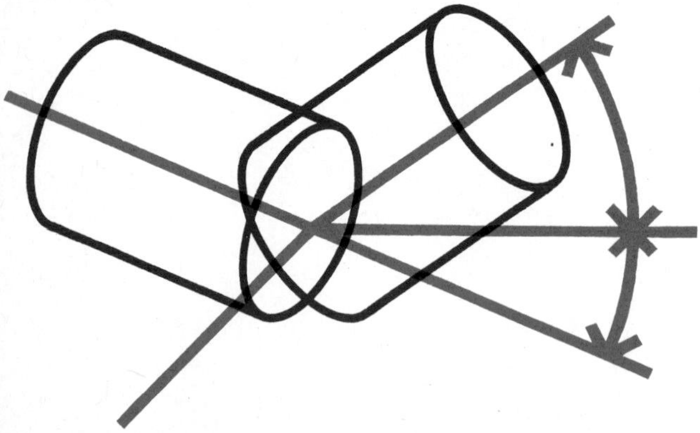

A cat's ability to right itself after being dropped upside down may help future astronauts maneuver in space. Scientists have formulated differential equations predicting the amount of overturning that the cat achieves by bending forward, to one side, backward, to the other side, and then forward again (diagram at the left). These equations are then used to produce computer-drawn diagrams of the cat's movements that can be copied by a gymnast on a trampoline (dressed as an astronaut in the photographs).

General Logarithmic and Exponential Functions; Applications

In this chapter, we use the foundations laid in Chapter 5 to give precise definitions of the general exponential and logarithmic functions and to develop some of their most important properties. We discuss how some applied problems can be formulated in terms of *differential equations,* and we solve an important class of these equations with the help of exponential functions.

Basic Properties, Graphs, and Derivatives

6–1 The General Exponential and Logarithmic Functions

Let a be any positive number and r be any *rational* number. By Property L–3 (Theorem 1, Chapter 5, page 210), we know that $L(a^r) = rL(a)$. Therefore, we have

$$E(rL(a)) = E(L(a^r)) = a^r,$$

where, in the second step, we used $E(L(v)) = v$ with $v = a^r$ (see (III), page 219).

The result

$$a^r = E(rL(a)) \qquad (*)$$

has been *proved* only for rational numbers r. (Indeed, we have not even defined a^r if r is irrational.) Notice, however, that the *right-hand* side of (*) is meaningful even if r is irrational. Thus we may *define* the general exponential function in terms of it:

Let a be positive and x be any real number. Then

$$a^x = E(xL(a)).$$

For example, we have $3^{\sqrt{2}} = E(\sqrt{2}\,L(3)) \doteq E(1.41 \times 1.10) \doteq E(1.55)$, and $(\sqrt{2})^{\pi} = E(\pi L(\sqrt{2})) = E(\pi \times \frac{1}{2} \times L(2)) \doteq E(3.14 \times \frac{1}{2} \times 0.69) \doteq E(1.08)$. It is possible to calculate values of a^x from the definition by using tables of values of the functions L and E, but there are easier ways to do this. The importance of the definition is that it removes all doubts about what a^x *means.*

Notice that the result (*) on the preceding page guarantees that the definition of a^x just given coincides when x is rational with the one given in Section 5–1.

Notice also that if we take the base a of the exponential expression a^x to be the number e, then we have

$$e^x = E(xL(e)) = E(x),$$

since, by the definition of e, $L(e) = 1$. It is because $E(x) = e^x$ that we called E an *exponential function.* The notation e^x, rather than $E(x)$, is almost always used, but we shall continue to use the latter in the proofs below for ease of reference.

Properties L–1, L–2, and L–3 referred to below are those of Theorem 1, Chapter 5, page 210, and Properties E–1 and E–2 are those of Theorem 4, Chapter 5, page 219.

We note first that by the definition of E [(I) on page 218], the defining equation

$$a^x = E(xL(a))$$

is equivalent to

$$\text{L–3}'. \qquad L(a^x) = xL(a).$$

This is an extension of L–3 to any real exponent.

We shall now prove that the laws of exponents stated in Section 5–1 are valid.

Theorem 1.

Let a and b be any positive numbers, and let x and y be any real numbers. Then

$$a^x a^y = a^{x+y}, \qquad \frac{a^x}{a^y} = a^{x-y},$$

$$(ab)^x = a^x b^x, \qquad \left(\frac{a}{b}\right)^x = \frac{a^x}{b^x},$$

$$(a^x)^y = a^{xy}.$$

If $a \neq 1$ and $a^x = a^y$, then $x = y$.

If $x \neq 0$ and $a^x = b^x$, then $a = b$.

Proof

$a^x a^y = E(xL(a)) \cdot E(yL(a))$	Definition of a^x and a^y
$= E[xL(a) + yL(a)]$	Property E–1
$= E[(x + y)L(a)]$	Distributive law
$= a^{x+y}$	Definition of a^{x+y}
$\left(\frac{a}{b}\right)^x = E\left[xL\left(\frac{a}{b}\right)\right]$	Definition of $\left(\frac{a}{b}\right)^x$
$= E[x(L(a) - L(b))]$	Property L–2
$= E[xL(a) - xL(b)]$	Distributive law
$= \frac{E(xL(a))}{E(xL(b))}$	Property E–2
$= \frac{a^x}{b^x}$	Definition of a^x and b^x
$(a^x)^y = E(yL(a^x))$	Definition of $(a^x)^y$
$= E[y(xL(a))]$	Property L–3′
$= E[(xy)L(a)]$	Associative and commutative laws
$= a^{xy}$	Definition of a^{xy}

Suppose $a \neq 1$ and $a^x = a^y$. This equation is equivalent to

$$E(xL(a)) = E(yL(a)).$$

Since the function E is one-to-one, we have

$$xL(a) = yL(a).$$

Because $a \neq 1$, $L(a) \neq 0$, and therefore $x = y$.

The proofs of the remaining three laws are left as exercises (Exercises 27–29, page 235).

EXAMPLE 1. Let a be a positive number different from 1, and let b be a positive number. Show that there is a constant k such that $b^x = a^{kx}$ for all real x.

Solution: Assuming for the moment that such a k exists, we have

$$L(b^x) = L(a^{kx}).$$

Using L–3′, we find that

$$xL(b) = kxL(a), \quad \text{or (if } x \neq 0\text{)} \quad k = \frac{L(b)}{L(a)}.$$

Therefore if k exists, it must be $\frac{L(b)}{L(a)}$. We now verify that

(*Solution continued*)

$k = \dfrac{L(b)}{L(a)}$ does indeed have the desired property:

$$a^{\frac{L(b)}{L(a)}x} = E\left[\left(\frac{L(b)}{L(a)}x\right) \cdot L(a)\right] = E(xL(b)) = b^x \text{ for all real } x.$$

Now let a be any positive number different from 1, and let x be any positive number. Then

$$a^{\frac{L(x)}{L(a)}} = E\left(\frac{L(x)}{L(a)} \cdot L(a)\right) = E(L(x)) = x.$$

That is, if we raise a to the power $\dfrac{L(x)}{L(a)}$, we obtain x. This fact suggests the following definition:

> Let a be a positive number different from 1, and let x be any positive number. Then the **logarithm of x to the base a** is
>
> $$\log_a x = \frac{L(x)}{L(a)}.$$

EXAMPLE 2. Use the table on page 212 to find

a. $\log_{10} 2$. Find also
b. $\log_{10} 200$, and
c. $\log_{10} 0.2$.

Solution: **a.** $\log_{10} 2 = \dfrac{L(2)}{L(10)} \doteq \dfrac{0.693}{2.303} \doteq 0.301.$

(This result may be checked by using a table of common (base 10) logarithms. A five-place table gives $\log_{10} 2 = 0.30103$.)

b. $$\log_{10} 200 = \frac{L(200)}{L(10)} = \frac{L(10^2 \times 2)}{L(10)} = \frac{2L(10) + L(2)}{L(10)}$$
$$= 2 + \frac{L(2)}{L(10)} \doteq 2 + 0.301 = 2.301.$$

c. $$\log_{10} 0.2 = \frac{L(0.2)}{L(10)} = \frac{L(10^{-1} \times 2)}{L(10)} = \frac{-L(10) + L(2)}{L(10)}$$
$$= -1 + \frac{L(2)}{L(10)} \doteq -1 + 0.301 = -0.699.$$

(It is often convenient for computational purposes to use the form $\log_{10} 0.2 = -1 + 0.301 = 9.301 - 10$.)

Notice that

$$\log_e x = \frac{L(x)}{L(e)} = L(x).$$

It is for this reason that we called L a *logarithmic function* and e the *base of natural logarithms.*

The *natural* logarithm $\log_e x$ is denoted by

$$\log x \quad \text{or} \quad \ln x.$$

In *computational* work, $\log x$ is often used to mean $\log_{10} x$, the *common* logarithm of x. From this point on in your study of mathematics, however, $\log x$ will almost always mean the *natural* logarithm of x unless the contrary is explicitly stated. The reason for this is that the natural logarithm is used almost exclusively because of its important theoretical advantages over logarithms to bases other than e. In particular,

$$\frac{d}{dx}\log x = L'(x) = \frac{1}{x}$$

by Theorem 2, Chapter 5, page 214. As we shall see, formulas for derivatives of logarithms to other bases are more complicated.

It is an easy matter to prove the following "standard" properties of logarithms.

Theorem 2.

If $a > 0$, $a \neq 1$, $x > 0$, $y > 0$, and z is any real number, then

$$\begin{aligned} \log_a xy &= \log_a x + \log_a y, \\ \log_a \frac{x}{y} &= \log_a x - \log_a y, \\ \log_a x^z &= z \log_a x. \end{aligned}$$

To prove the first part of the theorem, for example, we note that

$$\begin{aligned} \log_a xy &= \frac{L(xy)}{L(a)} && \text{Definition of } \log_a xy \\ &= \frac{L(x) + L(y)}{L(a)} && \text{Property L–1} \\ &= \frac{L(x)}{L(a)} + \frac{L(y)}{L(a)} \\ &= \log_a x + \log_a y && \text{Definition of } \log_a x \text{ and } \log_a y \end{aligned}$$

The proofs of the other two parts are left as exercises (Exercises 30 and 31, page 235).

There is a "change of base" formula which enables us to find logarithms of numbers to any base b if we know logarithms of numbers to some base a:

If $a > 0$, $a \neq 1$, $b > 0$, $b \neq 1$, and $x > 0$, then

$$\log_b x = \frac{\log_a x}{\log_a b}.$$

To prove that this formula is correct, we note that

$$\log_a x = \frac{L(x)}{L(a)} = \frac{L(x)}{L(b)} \cdot \frac{L(b)}{L(a)} = \log_b x \cdot \log_a b.$$

The desired result is obtained by dividing by $\log_a b$.

ORAL EXERCISES

Using the *definition* of a^x, explain why

1. $1^x = 1$ for all $x \in \mathbb{R}$.
2. $a^0 = 1$ for all $a > 0$.
3. Why was the condition $a \neq 1$ imposed in the definition of $\log_a x$?
4. The graphs of all the functions $x \to a^x$ $(a > 0)$ pass through the same point. What point is it?
5. The graphs of all the functions $x \to \log_a x$ $(a > 0, a \neq 1, x > 0)$ pass through the same point. What point is it?
6. Give the domain and range of the function $x \to \log_a x$ $(a > 0, a \neq 1)$.
7. Give the domain and range of the function $x \to a^x$ $(a > 0, a \neq 1)$.
8. Let a be a positive number different from 1. For what value of x is it true that

$$a^{\log_a x} = \log_a a^x?$$

WRITTEN EXERCISES

In Exercises 1–16, find the exact value of the given quantity.

A

1. $\log_2 8$
2. $\log_3 9$
3. $\log_{\frac{1}{2}} 2$
4. $\log_{\frac{1}{3}} 9$
5. $\log_{\frac{1}{2}} \frac{1}{8}$
6. $\log_{\frac{1}{100}} \frac{1}{10}$
7. $2^{\log_2 3}$
8. $3^{\log_3 \frac{1}{2}}$
9. $(\frac{1}{2})^{\log_2 5}$
10. $3^{\log_{\frac{1}{3}} 5}$
11. $3^{2 \log_3 4}$
12. $3^{\frac{1}{2} \log_3 4}$
13. $2^{(\log_2 3 + \log_2 5)}$
14. $2^{(\log_2 3 - \log_2 5)}$
15. $3^{\log_2 6} \cdot 3^{\log_2 \frac{1}{3}}$
16. $2^{\log_3 18} \cdot 2^{\log_3 \frac{1}{2}}$

In Exercises 17 and 18, find how the given pairs of numbers are related.

B **17.** $\log_a b$, $\log_b a$ **18.** $\log_a x$, $\log_{\frac{1}{a}} x$

In Exercises 19–22, use the table on page 212 to find approximate values of the given quantities.

19. $\log_2 3$ **21.** $\log_4 \frac{1}{5}$

20. $\log_3 2$ **22.** $\log_{\frac{1}{3}} 4$

In Exercises 23–26, use the table on page 212 to find *k* so that the equations hold for all x.

23. $3^x = 2^{kx}$ **25.** $(\frac{1}{4})^x = 5^{kx}$

24. $2^x = 3^{kx}$ **26.** $(\sqrt{2})^x = (\frac{1}{2})^{kx}$

In Exercises 27–29, *a* and *b* are positive numbers and x and *y* are any real numbers.

C **27.** Prove that $\dfrac{a^x}{a^y} = a^{x-y}$.

28. Prove that $(ab)^x = a^x b^x$.

29. Prove that if $x \neq 0$ and $a^x = b^x$, then $a = b$.

If $x > 0$, $y > 0$, $a > 0$, $a \neq 1$, and $z \in \mathcal{R}$, prove that

30. $\log_a \dfrac{x}{y} = \log_a x - \log_a y$

31. $\log_a x^z = z \log_a x$

6–2 Graphs of Logarithmic and Exponential Functions

The graphs of the logarithmic functions

$$x \rightarrow \log_a x \quad (a > 0, a \neq 1, x > 0)$$

can be constructed easily from the graph of L. For example, in the case of the function

$$x \rightarrow \log_{10} x,$$

we use the definition of $\log_a x$ (page 232) to get

$$\log_{10} x = \frac{L(x)}{L(10)} \doteq \frac{L(x)}{2.303} \doteq 0.434L(x).$$

Thus we need only multiply the ordinate of a point on the graph of L by 0.434 to obtain the ordinate of the point on the graph of $x \rightarrow \log_{10} x$ which has the same abscissa (see Figure 6–1 on the next page).

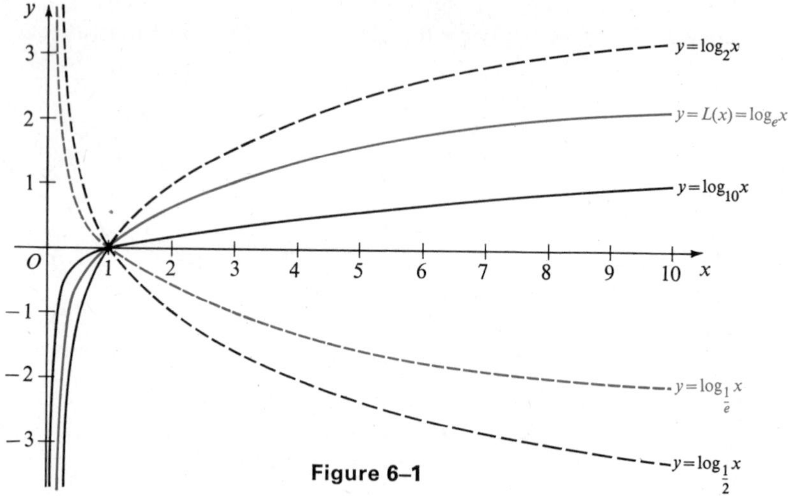

Figure 6–1

Figure 6–1 shows examples of graphs of

$$x \longrightarrow \log_a x$$

for cases where $a > e$, $e > a > 1$, and $1 > a > 0$, namely $a = 10$, 2, and $\frac{1}{2}$ and $\frac{1}{e}$, respectively. Notice the positions of these graphs relative to the graph of L.

Since E and L, that is,

$$x \longrightarrow e^x \quad \text{and} \quad x \longrightarrow \log_e x,$$

are inverses of each other, it probably comes as no surprise that the functions

$$x \longrightarrow a^x \quad \text{and} \quad x \longrightarrow \log_a x$$

are also inverses of each other (if $a > 0$ and $a \neq 1$). Since the functions are one-to-one, we can show this by observing that the following statements are equivalent:

$$v = a^u,$$

$$v = E(uL(a)),$$

$$L(v) = uL(a),$$

$$u = \frac{L(v)}{L(a)},$$

$$u = \log_a v.$$

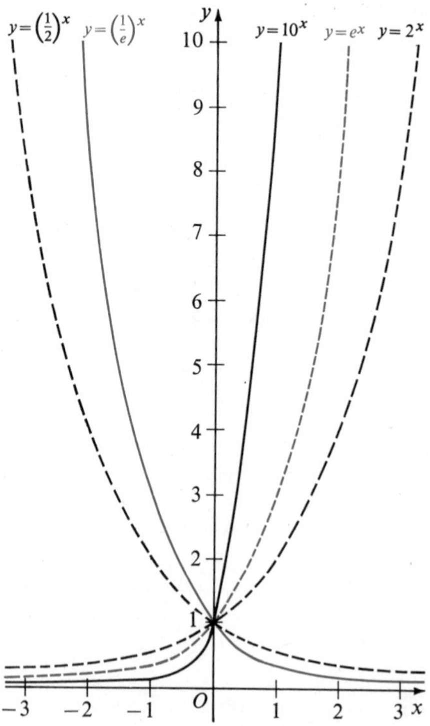

Figure 6–2

Consequently, the graph of the function

$$x \to a^x$$

may be obtained from the graph of

$$x \to \log_a x$$

(which we already know how to construct) by reflecting the latter in the line $y = x$. Figure 6–2 shows the result of reflecting the curves of Figure 6–1 in the line $y = x$. Notice that the curves labeled $y = \left(\frac{1}{2}\right)^x$ and $y = \left(\frac{1}{e}\right)^x$ are also the graphs of $y = 2^{-x}$ and $y = e^{-x}$, respectively.

The graphs of $y = a^x$ $(a > 0)$ and $y = a^{-x}$ are symmetric to each other with respect to the y-axis (Figure 6–3). This is true because (u, v) satisfies one of the equations if and only if $(-u, v)$ satisfies the other, and the points (u, v) and $(-u, v)$ are reflections of each other in the y-axis.

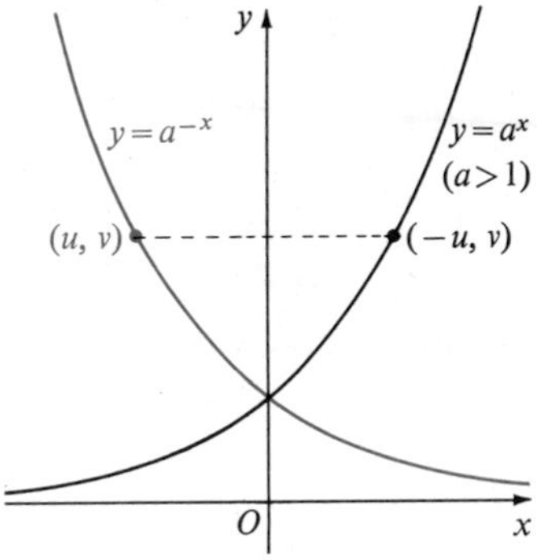

Figure 6–3

Because of the definition of a^x,

$$a^x = E(xL(a)) = e^{(\log a)x},$$

we see that any exponential expression can be written in the form e^{kx}, and this is the form most frequently used in both applications and theory. A practical way of graphing the equation

$$y = e^{kx}$$

is to take advantage of the fact that the graphs of all exponential functions have the same general shape and to draw such a curve through the points $(0, 1)$ and $(1, e^k)$. This has been done for various values of k in Figure 6–4.

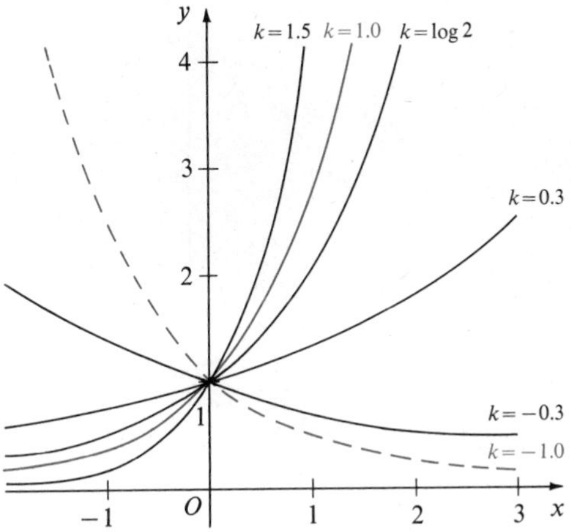

Figure 6–4

In applications, we often meet functions of the form

$$x \to ce^{kx},$$

where c is usually positive but k can be either positive or negative. The graph of

$$y = ce^{kx}$$

can be constructed from the graph of $y = e^{kx}$ by multiplying each ordinate by the factor c. Figure 6–5 shows the graph of the function

$$x \to 2e^{-0.3x}.$$

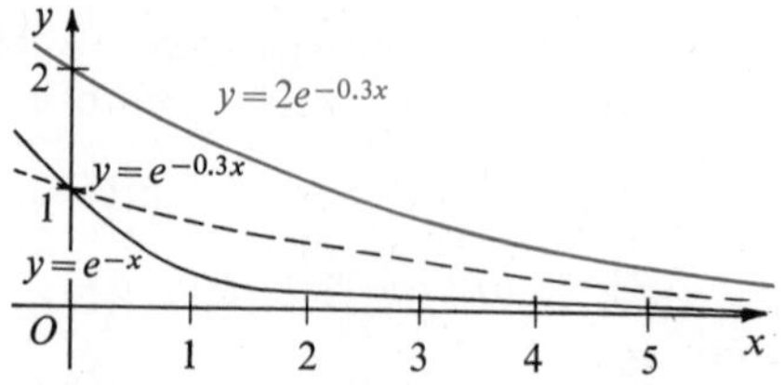

Figure 6–5

Certain combinations of exponential functions occur frequently enough to have been given names. Two of these are the **hyperbolic cosine** and the **hyperbolic sine,** abbreviated cosh and sinh, respectively, and defined by

$$\cosh x = \frac{e^x + e^{-x}}{2} \quad \text{and} \quad \sinh x = \frac{e^x - e^{-x}}{2}.$$

EXAMPLE. Graph the function $x \to \cosh x$.

Solution: The equation $y = \cosh x = \dfrac{e^x + e^{-x}}{2}$ may be written as $y = y_1 + y_2$, where $y_1 = \frac{1}{2}e^x$ and $y_2 = \frac{1}{2}e^{-x}$. We graph the latter two equations; then for each x, we determine the corresponding y by graphical *addition of ordinates* as indicated in the diagram below.

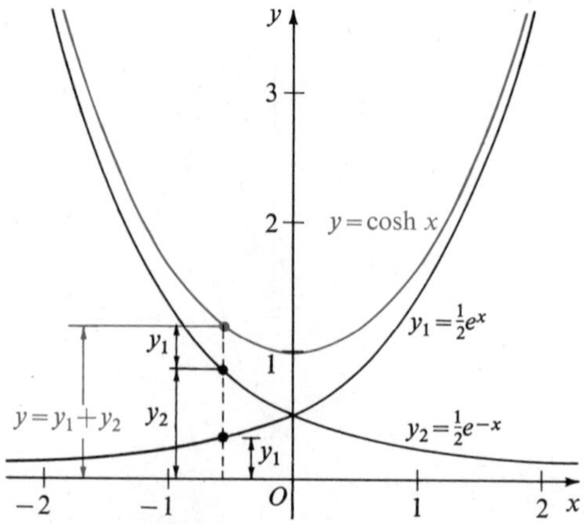

ORAL EXERCISES

Read each of the following sentences aloud, choosing the correct word or symbol from the alternatives provided.

1. The graph of $y = \log_a x$ goes (up/down) to the right for all $a > 1$.
2. The graph of $y = \log_a x$ goes (up/down) to the right for all positive $a < 1$.
3. The graph of $y = a^x$ goes (up/down) to the right for all $a > 1$.
4. The graph of $y = a^x$ goes (up/down) to the right for all positive $a < 1$.
5. The graph of $y = \log_a x$ is convex (upward/downward) for all $a > 1$.
6. The graph of $y = \log_a x$ is convex (upward/downward) for all positive $a < 1$.
7. The graph of $y = a^x$ is convex (upward/downward) for all $a > 0$, $a \neq 1$.
8. $\cosh x = \dfrac{e^x(+/-)e^{-x}}{2}$
9. $\sinh x = \dfrac{e^x(+/-)e^{-x}}{2}$

WRITTEN EXERCISES

In Exercises 1–4, draw the graphs of the functions *E*, *f*, and *g* in the same Cartesian plane.

A

1. $f\colon x \to 2e^x;\ g\colon x \to 3e^x$
2. $f\colon x \to e^{-x};\ g\colon x \to 2e^{-x}$
3. $f\colon x \to \frac{1}{2}e^x;\ g\colon x \to e^{\frac{1}{2}x}$
4. $f\colon x \to \frac{1}{2}e^{-x};\ g\colon x \to e^{-\frac{1}{2}x}$
5. Find the coordinates of the point of intersection of the graphs of f and g in Exercise 3.
6. Find the coordinates of the point of intersection of the graphs of f and g in Exercise 4.
7. Give reasons to show that the statements opposite Figure 6–2 on page 236 are equivalent.

In Exercises 8–11, draw the graphs of the functions *L*, *f*, and *g* in the same Cartesian plane.

8. $f\colon x \to \log 2x;\ g\colon x \to \log x^2$
9. $f\colon x \to \log ex;\ g\colon x \to \log x^e$
10. $f\colon x \to \log_3 x;\ g\colon x \to \log_{\frac{1}{3}} x$
11. $f\colon x \to \log_{e^2} x;\ g\colon x \to \log_{\sqrt{e}} x$

B

12. Draw the graph of the function $x \to \sinh x$.
13. Show that $\sinh x < \cosh x < e^x$ for $x > 0$.
14. Show that cosh is an even function and that sinh is an odd function, that is, that $\cosh(-x) = \cosh x$ and $\sinh(-x) = -\sinh x$.

6–3 Derivatives of Logarithmic and Exponential Functions

Since for $a > 0$, $a \neq 1$, and $x > 0$, $\log_a x = \dfrac{L(x)}{L(a)} = \dfrac{1}{\log a} \log x$, and $\dfrac{d}{dx} \log x = \dfrac{1}{x}$, we see that

$$\frac{d}{dx} \log_a x = \frac{1}{\log a} \cdot \frac{1}{x}.$$

We can use the change-of-base formula, page 234 (with $b = e$ and $x = a$), to rewrite this in the form

$$\frac{d}{dx} \log_a x = (\log_a e) \cdot \frac{1}{x}.$$

We can use Theorem 5 of Chapter 5 (page 220) and the fact that $x \rightarrow a^x$ and $x \rightarrow \log_a x$ are inverse functions to show that for $a > 0$, $a \neq 1$,

$$\frac{d}{dx} a^x = (\log a) \cdot a^x.$$

EXAMPLE 1. Find **(a)** $\dfrac{d}{dx} \log_{10} x$; **(b)** $\dfrac{d}{dx} 10^x$.

Solution: **a.** $\dfrac{d}{dx} \log_{10} x = (\log_{10} e) \cdot \dfrac{1}{x} \doteq \dfrac{0.434}{x}.$

b. $\dfrac{d}{dx} 10^x = (\log 10) \cdot 10^x \doteq 2.303 \cdot 10^x.$

When we contrast the results of Example 1 with

$$\frac{d}{dx} \log x = \frac{1}{x} \quad \text{and} \quad \frac{d}{dx} e^x = e^x,$$

one advantage of using the base e for logarithms and exponential expressions becomes apparent.

Theorem 3.

Let f be a differentiable function whose range is contained in $\{x : x > 0\}$. Then

$$\frac{d}{dx} \log f(x) = \frac{f'(x)}{f(x)}.$$

Proof

Let $\phi(x) = \log f(x)$ and $g(x) = \log x$. Then

$$\phi(x) = g(f(x)) = (g \circ f)(x).$$

By the Chain Rule (Chapter 4, Theorem 3, page 179), we have

$$\phi'(x) = g'(f(x)) \cdot f'(x).$$

Since $g'(x) = \dfrac{1}{x}$, we have $g'(f(x)) = \dfrac{1}{f(x)}$, and therefore

$$\frac{d}{dx} \log f(x) = \phi'(x) = \frac{1}{f(x)} \cdot f'(x).$$

The proof of the next theorem is similar (see Exercise 19, page 243).

Theorem 4.

Let f be a differentiable function. Then

$$\frac{d}{dx} e^{f(x)} = e^{f(x)} \cdot f'(x).$$

The results of Theorems 3 and 4 are often given, for differentiable functions u of x, as

$$\frac{d}{dx} \log u = \frac{1}{u} \frac{du}{dx} \quad \text{and} \quad \frac{d}{dx} e^u = e^u \frac{du}{dx}.$$

EXAMPLE 2. Find **(a)** $\dfrac{d}{dx} e^{kx}$; **(b)** $\dfrac{d}{dx} \log \sqrt{x^2 + 1}$.

Solution: **a.** $\dfrac{d}{dx} e^{kx} = e^{kx} \dfrac{d}{dx}(kx) = e^{kx} \cdot k = ke^{kx}$.

b. $\log \sqrt{x^2 + 1} = \log (x^2 + 1)^{\frac{1}{2}} = \frac{1}{2} \log (x^2 + 1)$. Therefore,

$$\frac{d}{dx} \log \sqrt{x^2 + 1} = \frac{1}{2} \frac{d}{dx} \log (x^2 + 1)$$
$$= \frac{1}{2}\left(\frac{1}{x^2 + 1}\right) \cdot \frac{d}{dx}(x^2 + 1)$$
$$= \frac{1}{2}\left(\frac{1}{x^2 + 1}\right)(2x)$$
$$= \frac{x}{x^2 + 1}.$$

We can use Theorem 4 to extend the formula

$$\frac{d}{dx} x^r = rx^{r-1}$$

(proved earlier, first for r an integer, then for r rational) to *any* real exponent, a.

If $x > 0$, then $x^a = e^{a \log x}$, and therefore

$$\frac{d}{dx} x^a = \frac{d}{dx} e^{a \log x}$$
$$= \left(e^{a \log x}\right) \frac{d}{dx} (a \log x),$$
$$\frac{d}{dx} x^a = x^a \cdot a \cdot \frac{1}{x} = ax^{a-1}.$$

ORAL EXERCISES

1. In Theorem 3, why did we impose the condition that the range of f be contained in $\{x: x > 0\}$? Why was no such condition necessary in Theorem 4?

In Exercises 2–13, a formula for $f(x)$ is given. Find $f'(x)$ mentally.

2. x^π
3. e^{2x}
4. e^{10x}
5. $e^{\frac{x}{2}}$
6. e^{-x}
7. e^{-2x}
8. $\log 2x$
9. $\log (x + 2)$
10. $\log x^2$
11. $\log \sqrt{x}$
12. $\log x^{-1}$
13. $\log \frac{2}{x}$

WRITTEN EXERCISES

In Exercises 1–8, find the derivative of the given function. Use the table on page 212 to approximate the logarithm which occurs.

A

1. $x \to 2^x$
2. $x \to 5^x$
3. $x \to (\sqrt{2})^x$
4. $x \to (\sqrt{5})^x$
5. $x \to (0.5)^x$
6. $x \to (0.2)^x$
7. $x \to \log_2 x$
8. $x \to \log_5 x$

In Exercises 9–16, use Theorem 3 or Theorem 4 to find $f'(x)$. In exercises involving *log*, use properties of the logarithm to simplify $f(x)$ before differentiating.

9. $f(x) = \log \sqrt[3]{x^2 + 1}$
10. $f(x) = \log \frac{1}{x^2 + 1}$
11. $f(x) = e^{x^2}$
12. $f(x) = e^{-x^2}$
13. $f(x) = e^{1-x}$
14. $f(x) = e^{2x-1}$
15. $f(x) = \log (x\sqrt{x^2 + 1})$
16. $f(x) = \log \left(\frac{\sqrt{x^2 + 1}}{x}\right)$

B

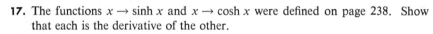

17. The functions $x \to \sinh x$ and $x \to \cosh x$ were defined on page 238. Show that each is the derivative of the other.

18. Find a formula for the nth derivative, $f^{(n)}(x)$, of f if

a. $f: x \to \sinh x$; **b.** $f: x \to \cosh x$.

19. Prove Theorem 4, page 241.

C

20. Prove the formula $\frac{d}{dx} a^x = (\log a)a^x$ by using Theorem 5, Chapter 5 (page 220), and the fact that $g: x \to a^x$ and $f: x \to \log_a x$ are inverse functions.

21. Prove the formula of Exercise 20 by using Theorem 4 (page 241) and the fact that $a^x = e^{x \log a}$.

22. Prove the formula $\frac{d}{dx} e^{kx} = ke^{kx}$ by writing e^{kx} in the form $(e^k)^x$ and using the formula of Exercise 20.

23. Find the inverse function of $g: x \to e^{kx}$. Then use Theorem 5, Chapter 5 (page 220), to prove that $g'(x) = ke^{kx}$.

■ Antiderivatives and Differential Equations

6–4 Antiderivatives

It often is necessary to find a function g whose derivative is a given function f. We can sometimes do this by reversing a derivative formula that we happen to know or to have seen. For example, given

$$f: x \to \frac{x}{x^2 + 1},$$

we see by Example 2(b) of Section 6–3 that if we take

$$g: x \to \log \sqrt{x^2 + 1},$$

then $g' = f$. We call g an *antiderivative* of f.

In general:

> The function g is an **antiderivative** of the function f if f and g have the same domain D and $g'(x) = f(x)$ for all x in D.

The term **indefinite integral** is also used for *antiderivative*. [In Chapter 5, we briefly studied the (definite) integral $\int_p^q f(x)\,dx$, but only for $f(x) = \frac{1}{x}$. The definite integral was further discussed in the essay at the end of that chapter, and a relationship between the definite and indefinite integrals will be indicated in the essay at the end of Chapter 8.]

EXAMPLE 1. Find an antiderivative of (**a**) $f: x \to e^{kx}$ and (**b**) $f: x \to a^x$.

Solution: **a.** In Example 2(a) of Section 6–3, we found that $\frac{d}{dx} e^{kx} = ke^{kx}$. From this result we note that, for $k \neq 0$,

$$\frac{d}{dx}\left(\frac{1}{k} e^{kx}\right) = \frac{1}{k} \cdot ke^{kx} = e^{kx}.$$

Therefore $g: x \to \frac{1}{k} e^{kx}$ is an antiderivative of $f: x \to e^{kx}$.

b. From the formula for the derivative of a^x (page 240), we see that, for $a > 0$, $a \neq 1$,

$$\frac{d}{dx}\left(\frac{1}{\log a} a^x\right) = \frac{1}{\log a} \cdot (\log a)a^x = a^x.$$

Therefore $g: x \to \frac{1}{\log a} a^x$ [or $x \to (\log_a e)a^x$] is an antiderivative of $f: x \to a^x$.

If g is an antiderivative of f, then so is g + c, where c is any constant. For example, since $\frac{d}{dx} \log \sqrt{x^2 + 1} = \frac{x}{x^2 + 1}$, each of the functions $x \to \log \sqrt{x^2 + 1} + 1$, $x \to \log 3\sqrt{x^2 + 1}$, and $x \to \frac{1 + \log (x^2 + 1)}{2}$ is an antiderivative of $x \to \frac{x}{x^2 + 1}$. (Check to see that this is so.)

On the other hand, *if g is one antiderivative of f, and h is any antiderivative of f, then* $h = g + c$ for some constant c. We can show this using the fact that *if the derivative of a function is the zero function, then the given function is a constant function* (see Exercise 16, page 247): Since g and h are antiderivatives of f, we have $g' = f$ and $h' = f$. Therefore,

$$(h - g)' = h' - g' = f - f = 0,$$

and there is a constant c such that

$$h - g = c, \quad \text{or} \quad h = g + c.$$

The notation $\int f(x)\, dx$ is used to denote the "most general" antiderivative of f, that is, to express all antiderivatives of f. Thus we see from Example 1 that

$$\int e^{kx}\, dx = \frac{1}{k} e^{kx} + c \quad (k \neq 0), \tag{I}$$

and

$$\int a^x\, dx = (\log_a e)a^x + c \quad (a > 0, a \neq 1). \tag{II}$$

The arbitrary constant c appearing in such formulas is known as a **constant of integration.**

From the derivative formula $\frac{d}{dx} x^{a+1} = (a + 1)x^a$, we see that if $a \neq -1$,

$$\frac{d}{dx}\left(\frac{1}{a+1} x^{a+1}\right) = x^a.$$

This is equivalent to the formula

$$\int x^a \, dx = \frac{x^{a+1}}{a+1} + c \quad (a \neq -1). \tag{III}$$

To extend (III) to the case $a = -1$, we use

$$\frac{d}{dx} \log x = \frac{1}{x} = x^{-1} \quad (x > 0). \tag{*}$$

This result is valid only for $x > 0$, because the domain of log is $\{x: x > 0\}$. If $x < 0$, then $-x > 0$ and $\log(-x)$ is defined. (See Figure 6–6.) Using Theorem 3, page 240, with $f(x) = -x$, we see that (for $x < 0$)

$$\frac{d}{dx} \log(-x) = \frac{-1}{-x} = \frac{1}{x} = x^{-1}. \tag{†}$$

Since $|x| = x$ if $x > 0$, and $|x| = -x$ if $x < 0$, formulas (*) and (†) can be combined to give

$$\frac{d}{dx} \log |x| = \frac{1}{x} = x^{-1},$$

which is equivalent to

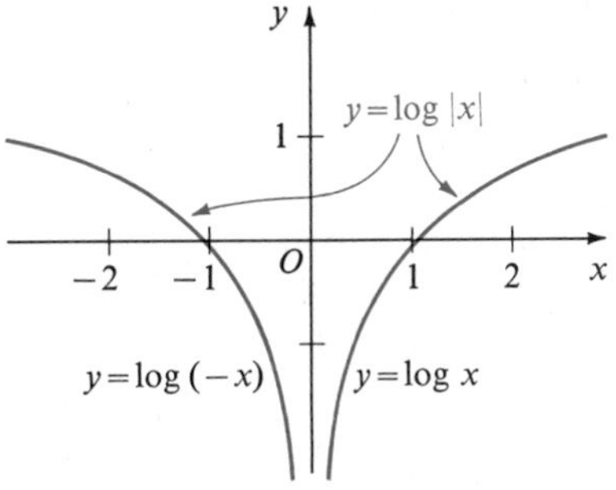

Figure 6–6

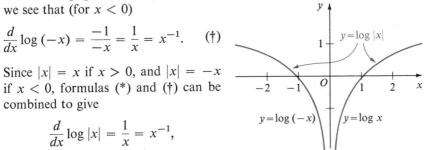

$$\int x^{-1} \, dx = \int \frac{1}{x} \, dx = \log |x| + c \quad (x \neq 0). \tag{IV}$$

Formulas (I)–(IV) are examples of what are usually called *integral formulas,* and *tables of integrals* containing hundreds and even thousands of such formulas have been prepared.

Since the derivative of the sum of a finite number of functions is the sum of their derivatives, we can find an antiderivative of a finite sum of functions by adding together antiderivatives of the individual functions. Moreover, if a is a constant, then $\int af(x)\,dx = a\int f(x)\,dx$. These facts, together with formula (III), enable us to find antiderivatives of all polynomial functions.

EXAMPLE 2. Find **(a)** $\int (x^3 + 3x^2 + 4x + 2)\, dx$;

(b) $\int \frac{x^2 + 1}{x}\, dx$ (for $x \neq 0$).

Solution: **a.** $\int (x^3 + 3x^2 + 4x + 2)\,dx$

$$= \int x^3\,dx + 3\int x^2\,dx + 4\int x\,dx + 2\int x^0\,dx$$

$$= \frac{x^4}{4} + 3\cdot\frac{x^3}{3} + 4\cdot\frac{x^2}{2} + 2\cdot\frac{x^1}{1} + c$$

$$= \frac{x^4}{4} + x^3 + 2x^2 + 2x + c.$$

b. $\int \frac{x^2+1}{x}\,dx = \int \left(x + \frac{1}{x}\right) dx$

$$= \int x\,dx + \int \frac{1}{x}\,dx = \frac{x^2}{2} + \log|x| + c.$$

ORAL EXERCISES

Use formulas (I), (III), and (IV) to find these antiderivatives:

1. $\int x\,dx$

2. $\int x^3\,dx$

3. $\int x^{-1}\,dx$

4. $\int e^x\,dx$

5. $\int e^{2x}\,dx$

6. $\int e^{-x}\,dx$

7. $\int \frac{2}{x}\,dx$

8. $\int x^{\frac{1}{2}}\,dx$

9. $\int \sqrt{x}\,dx$

WRITTEN EXERCISES

In Exercises 1–10, find the indicated antiderivatives.

A

1. $\int (x^3 + x^2 + x + 1)\,dx$

2. $\int (4x^3 + 3x^2 + 2x + 1)\,dx$

3. $\int \left(x + \frac{1}{x}\right) dx$

4. $\int \frac{x^3+1}{x}\,dx$

5. $\int \frac{x^2+x+1}{x^2}\,dx$

6. $\int (x^3 + x + x^{-1} + x^{-3})\,dx$

7. $\int 2^x\,dx$

8. $\int 10^x\,dx$

9. $\int \sinh x\,dx$

10. $\int \cosh x\,dx$

(*Hint:* For Exercises 9 and 10, Exercise 17, page 243, is helpful.)

In Exercises 11–14, find $g'(x)$. (The Product Rule of Section 4–5, page 174, will be needed.) Use the result obtained to give an integral (antiderivative) formula.

B

11. $g(x) = xe^x - x$

12. $g(x) = x \log x - x$

13. $g(x) = \frac{1}{2} \log \frac{x-1}{x+1}$

14. $g(x) = \frac{1}{2} \log \frac{1+x}{1-x}$

15. Find the domains of the functions defined in Exercises 13 and 14.

C

16. Use the Law of the Mean (Exercise 20, page 137) to prove that if ϕ is a function such that $\phi'(x) = 0$ for all $x \in \mathcal{R}$, then ϕ is a constant function.

6–5 Differential Equations

We often have information about the derivative (or second derivative, and so forth) of a function and wish to find the function.

EXAMPLE 1. Find the function whose graph has the following properties: (1) its slope at each point is twice the abscissa of the point, and (2) it passes through (2, 1).

Solution: Since the slope is given by $\frac{dy}{dx}$, the properties may be stated in the form

(1′) $\frac{dy}{dx} = 2x$, (2′) $y = 1$ when $x = 2$.

We wish to find a function f such that if $y = f(x)$, then conditions (1′) and (2′) are satisfied. In terms of f, the conditions become

(1″) $f'(x) = 2x$, (2″) $f(2) = 1$.

From (1″) we see that f is an antiderivative of the function $x \to 2x$. Since one antiderivative of $x \to 2x$ is $x \to x^2$, and since *every* antiderivative of $x \to 2x$ differs from this one by a constant, we have

$$f(x) = \int 2x\,dx = x^2 + c.$$

For each c, the resulting function f satisfies (1″). Of all these functions, we wish to determine the one which satisfies condition (2″):

$$f(2) = 2^2 + c = 4 + c = 1;\ \text{therefore, } c = -3.$$

Thus the required function is $f: x \to x^2 - 3$.

Equation (1′) appearing on the preceding page,

$$\frac{dy}{dx} = 2x,$$

is an example of a **differential equation,** that is, an equation which involves two variables and a derivative or derivatives of one of these variables with respect to the other. The function $f\colon x \to x^2 - 3$ is a **solution** of this differential equation, because if $y = f(x) = x^2 - 3$, then $\dfrac{dy}{dx} = 2x$. For each constant c, the function $x \to x^2 + c$ is a solution of the differential equation, and since *every* solution is of this form, the function

$$x \to x^2 + c$$

is called the **general solution** of $\dfrac{dy}{dx} = 2x$. (Informally, we say briefly that the *expression* $x^2 - 3$ is a solution, and that $x^2 + c$ is the general solution, of the differential equation.)

In most applications involving differential equations, we want only some particular solution. We often find the general solution first, however, as in Example 1.

Differential equations often arise in motion problems (see Section 4–3).

EXAMPLE 2. A point is moving on a line, the s-axis, in such a way that when its position measured in feet is s, its velocity measured in feet per second is $-2s$. When $t = 0$, the position of the point is $s = 10$. Find **(a)** the position of the point at time t and **(b)** at what time it is 5 units from 0.

Solution: **a.** Because the velocity is given by $\dfrac{ds}{dt}$, the motion is described by the differential equation

$$\frac{ds}{dt} = -2s, \tag{1}$$

together with the "initial condition"

$$s = 10 \quad \text{when} \quad t = 0. \tag{2}$$

In view of work done in Section 6–3, we know that

$$\frac{d}{dt}e^{-2t} = -2e^{-2t}.$$

Hence if c is any constant and $s = ce^{-2t}$, we have

$$\frac{ds}{dt} = c\frac{d}{dt}e^{-2t} = -2(ce^{-2t}) = -2s.$$

That is, for any c,

$$s = ce^{-2t} \tag{3}$$

is a solution of the differential equation

$$\frac{ds}{dt} = -2s. \tag{1}$$

[It can be shown (see Exercise 10, page 257) that every solution of (1) is of the form (3), so (3) is the general solution of (1).]

We use condition (2) to pick out the solution we want: Substituting $t = 0$ and $s = 10$ into (3), we have

$$10 = ce^0, \quad \text{or} \quad c = 10.$$

Therefore the answer is

$$s = 10e^{-2t} \text{ feet.}$$

b. To find the value of t for which $s = 5$, we must solve the equation

$$5 = 10e^{-2t}, \quad \text{or} \quad e^{-2t} = \tfrac{1}{2}.$$

This equation is equivalent to

$$\log e^{-2t} = \log \tfrac{1}{2}, \quad \text{or} \quad -2t = \log \tfrac{1}{2} = -\log 2.$$

Therefore, using the table on page 212,

$$t = \frac{\log 2}{2} \doteq \frac{0.693}{2} = 0.347 \text{ seconds.}$$

To find the *law of motion of a point moving on a vertical line under the influence of gravity*, we introduce an s-coordinate system on the line, as in Section 4–3. We choose the origin at any convenient point, the surface of the earth, say, and direct the line upward. Then the acceleration a of the point is a negative constant,* $-g$. Let the initial ($t = 0$) position and initial velocity of the point be s_0 and v_0, respectively.

If we use primes to denote differentiation with respect to t, we have

$$v = s' \quad \text{and} \quad a = v' = s''.$$

The motion of the point is then described by the differential equation

$$s'' = -g, \tag{†}$$

together with the initial conditions

$$s = s_0 \quad \text{and} \quad v = v_0 \quad \text{when} \quad t = 0.$$

---

* Provided that air resistance and variations in gravity are neglected. If distance is measured in feet and time in seconds, then $g \doteq 32$. If distance is measured in centimeters and time in seconds, then $g \doteq 980$.

We rewrite (†) on the preceding page as

$$v' = -g$$

and antidifferentiate to find that

$$v = \int (-g)\, dt = -gt + c_1.$$

We evaluate the constant c_1 by substituting $t = 0$ and $v = v_0$ to obtain

$$v_0 = c_1.$$

Thus

$$v = s' = -gt + v_0.$$

Antidifferentiating again, we have

$$s = \int (-gt + v_0)\, dt = -\tfrac{1}{2}gt^2 + v_0t + c_2.$$

Substituting $t = 0$ and $s = s_0$, we have $s_0 = c_2$. Therefore the law of motion is

$$s = -\tfrac{1}{2}gt^2 + v_0t + s_0.$$

ORAL EXERCISES

State the general solution of each of the following differential equations.

1. $\dfrac{dy}{dx} = 0$
2. $\dfrac{dy}{dx} = 5$
3. $\dfrac{dy}{dx} = x^3$
4. $\dfrac{dy}{dx} = \dfrac{1}{x}$
5. $\dfrac{dy}{dx} = 2x - 1$
6. $\dfrac{dy}{dx} = e^x$
7. $\dfrac{dy}{dx} = e^{-2x}$
8. $\dfrac{dy}{dx} = \dfrac{1}{x^2} + x^2$

State the particular solution of each of the following differential equations, given that $y = 2$ when $x = 1$.

9. $\dfrac{dy}{dx} = 0$
10. $\dfrac{dy}{dx} = 3$
11. $\dfrac{dy}{dx} = \dfrac{1}{x}$
12. $\dfrac{dy}{dx} = x$

WRITTEN EXERCISES

In Exercises 1–6, find a function f whose graph passes through the given point and has the specified slope at each point (x, y) on the graph.

A

1. Point $(0, -1)$, slope $2x$.
2. Point $(0, 0)$, slope $-2x$.
3. Point $(3, 9)$, slope x^2.
4. Point $(1, 0)$, slope $1 - x$.
5. Point $(0, 2)$, slope y.
6. Point $(0, 1)$, slope $2y$.

In Exercises 7–14, a formula for the velocity v of a point P moving on the s-axis is given, together with its initial position.

(a) Find the law of motion of P.
(b) Indicate the motion of P for $t \geq 0$, using a diagram similar to Figure 4–3, page 166.

7. $v = 4 - 2t$; $s = 0$ when $t = 0$.
8. $v = 2t - 6$; $s = 0$ when $t = 0$.
9. $v = 2t - 2$; $s = 1$ when $t = 0$.
10. $v = 2 - t$; $s = 2$ when $t = 0$.
11. $v = t^2 - 4t + 3$; $s = 0$ when $t = 0$.
12. $v = (t - 1)^3$; $s = 0$ when $t = 0$.
13. $v = -2s$; $s = 1$ when $t = 0$.
14. $v = s$; $s = -1$ when $t = 0$.

In Exercises 15–18, a formula for the acceleration a of a point P moving on the s-axis is given, together with its initial position and initial velocity.

(a) Find the law of motion of P.
(b) Indicate the motion of P, using a diagram similar to Figure 4–3, page 166.

B

15. $a = -6$; $s = 0$ and $v = 12$ when $t = 0$.
16. $a = 2$; $s = 5$ and $v = -6$ when $t = 0$.
17. $a = 6t - 12$; $s = 0$ and $v = 9$ when $t = 0$.
18. $a = 6t - 6$; $s = 0$ and $v = 2$ when $t = 0$.

C

19. In studying the motion of a point dropped (with initial velocity zero) from a point O above the surface of the earth, we can choose the s-axis to be directed *downward* and to have origin at O. In this case the differential equation and initial conditions are

$$s'' = g; \; s = 0 \text{ and } v = 0 \text{ when } t = 0.$$

a. Find the law of motion of the point.
b. Express the velocity v in terms of the distance s that the point has fallen.

20. Show that each of the following is a solution of the differential equation $y'' - y = 0$:

a. $y = e^x$, **b.** $y = e^{-x}$, **c.** $y = \sinh x$, **d.** $y = \cosh x$.

21. **a.** Show that $y = ce^{-ax}$ is a solution of the differential equation $y'' - a^2y = 0$.
b. Find three other solutions of $y'' - a^2y = 0$. (*Hint:* Let Exercise 20 be your guide.)

6–6 Natural Growth and Decay

The differential equation

$$\frac{dy}{dx} = ky \tag{N}$$

arises in many important applications, some of which we shall consider below. We first verify that for any constant c,

$$y = ce^{kx} \tag{S}$$

is a solution of (N):

$$\frac{dy}{dx} = c\frac{d}{dx}e^{kx} = cke^{kx} = k(ce^{kx}) = ky.$$

Moreover, we can show (see Exercise 10, page 257) that every solution of (N) is of the form (S).

We shall now consider some phenomena leading to differential equations of the form (N).

Radioactive Decay. Radioactive substances such as radium, uranium, and all the elements created since 1940 share the property that each of them decays (decomposes) at a rate proportional to the amount present.

If z grams of a radioactive substance are present at time t, then the decay property is described by the differential equation

$$\frac{dz}{dt} = kz, \tag{1}$$

where the negative proportionality constant k depends on the particular substance (and the units being used). If z_0 grams are present at time $t = 0$, then we have the initial condition

$$z = z_0 \quad \text{when} \quad t = 0. \tag{2}$$

Since (1) is of the form (N), its general solution is

$$z = ce^{kt}.$$

Using (2), we find that $z_0 = ce^0 = c$, so that

$$z = z_0e^{kt} \tag{3}$$

is the particular solution of (1) which satisfies (2).

The length of time it takes half of the substance to disappear is called the **half-life** of the substance. It can be found by solving the equation

$$\tfrac{1}{2}z_0 = z_0e^{kt}, \quad \text{or} \quad e^{kt} = \tfrac{1}{2},$$

for t. Since the latter equation does not involve z_0, we see that the half-life is independent of the amount originally present.

EXAMPLE 1. A physicist has 12 grams of radioactive bismuth, which has a half-life of 5 days. Find how much of the substance will be present after

a. 15 days;
b. t days.
c. How long will it take 2 grams of the substance to disappear?

Solution: The amount present at time t is, by (3),

$$z = 12e^{kt}.$$

Since the half-life is 5 days,

$$6 = 12e^{k\cdot 5}, \quad \text{or} \quad (e^k)^5 = \tfrac{1}{2}, \quad \text{or} \quad e^k = (\tfrac{1}{2})^{\frac{1}{5}}.$$

a. Setting $t = 15$, we have

$$z = 12e^{k\cdot 15} = 12(e^k)^{15} = 12[(\tfrac{1}{2})^{\frac{1}{5}}]^{15}$$
$$= 12(\tfrac{1}{2})^3 = 1.5 \text{ grams.}$$

b. For any t, we have

$$z = 12e^{kt} = 12(e^k)^t = 12[(\tfrac{1}{2})^{\frac{1}{5}}]^t = 12(\tfrac{1}{2})^{\frac{t}{5}},$$

or

$$z = 12\cdot 2^{-\frac{t}{5}}. \qquad (*)$$

[Alternatively, we may solve $e^k = (\tfrac{1}{2})^{\frac{1}{5}}$ for k. Taking natural logarithms, we have

$$k = \log e^k = \log(\tfrac{1}{2})^{\frac{1}{5}} = \tfrac{1}{5}\log\tfrac{1}{2} = -\tfrac{1}{5}\log 2.$$

Therefore, using the table on page 212, we have

$$z = 12e^{kt} = 12e^{(-\frac{1}{5}\log 2)t} \doteq 12e^{-0.139t}.]$$

c. When 2 grams have disappeared, the amount present is $z = 10$. Putting this into (*), we have

$$10 = 12\cdot 2^{-\frac{t}{5}}, \quad \text{or} \quad 2^{-\frac{t}{5}} = \tfrac{5}{6}, \quad \text{or} \quad 2^{\frac{t}{5}} = \tfrac{6}{5} = 1.2.$$

Therefore, taking common logarithms (page 342), we have

$$\log_{10} 2^{\frac{t}{5}} = \log_{10} 1.2, \quad \text{or} \quad \frac{t}{5}\log_{10} 2 = \log_{10} 1.2.$$

Thus $t = 5\cdot\dfrac{\log_{10} 1.2}{\log_{10} 2} \doteq 5\cdot\dfrac{0.0792}{0.3010} \doteq 1.316$ days.

Population Growth. Let us consider the growth of a population containing a large number of individuals — for example, a culture of bacteria. The size of the population, that is, the number of individuals comprising it, is, of course, a natural number n at any time t. If the population is large enough, however, we can approximate the actual situation by a *mathematical model* in which we allow n to assume any positive real value.

Under ideal conditions (ample food, space, and so forth), a large population increases at a rate approximately proportional to its size. Thus, if n is the size of a given population at time t, and the size when $t = 0$ is n_0, we have the differential equation

$$\frac{dn}{dt} = kn, \tag{1'}$$

(where, in a healthy population, the proportionality constant k is positive) and the initial condition

$$n = n_0 \quad \text{when} \quad t = 0. \tag{2'}$$

By analogy with the radioactive decay problem, we see that

$$n = n_0 e^{kt} \tag{3'}$$

is the solution of (1′) which satisfies (2′).

When we compare (1) and (1′) with (N), we see why equations of the form

$$\frac{dy}{dx} = ky$$

are called the **differential equations of natural growth or decay** (depending on the sign of k) and why their solutions,

$$y = y_0 e^{kx},$$

are called **laws of natural growth or decay.** Thus natural growth is exponential growth.

EXAMPLE 2. In 1950 the population of a city was 80,000, and in 1960 it was 100,000. Assuming the law of natural growth, find the population (**a**) in 1980 and (**b**) in 1900.

Solution: Let us measure time t in years and let $t = 0$ be 1950. If n is the population at time t, we have

$$n = ce^{kt},$$

$$n = 80{,}000 \quad \text{when} \quad t = 0,$$

$$n = 100{,}000 \quad \text{when} \quad t = 10.$$

Substituting $t = 0$ and $n = 80{,}000$ yields $c = 80{,}000$. Hence

$$n = 80{,}000e^{kt}.$$

Substituting $t = 10$ and $n = 100{,}000$ yields

$$100{,}000 = 80{,}000e^{k \cdot 10}, \quad \text{or} \quad e^k = (\tfrac{5}{4})^{\frac{1}{10}}.$$

Therefore,

$$n = 80{,}000(e^k)^t = 80{,}000(\tfrac{5}{4})^{\frac{t}{10}}.$$

a. Setting $t = 30$, we find that the population in 1980 will be

$$n = 80{,}000(\tfrac{5}{4})^3 = 156{,}250.$$

b. Setting $t = -50$, we find that the population in 1900 was

$$n = 80{,}000(\tfrac{5}{4})^{-5} \doteq 26{,}214.$$

Newton's Law of Cooling. This law is the assertion that the rate of change of temperature of a body is proportional to the difference in temperatures of the body and the surrounding medium. If T is the temperature of the body at time t and A is the (constant) temperature of the surrounding medium, then we have

$$\frac{dT}{dt} = k(T - A), \qquad (\dagger)$$

where the proportionality constant k is negative.

We can express this differential equation in the form (N) by letting $u = T - A$ be the temperature difference. Since

$$\frac{du}{dt} = \frac{d}{dt}(T - A) = \frac{dT}{dt},$$

($\dagger$) can be written

$$\frac{du}{dt} = ku.$$

EXAMPLE 3. A cup of coffee surrounded by air at 70°F takes 10 minutes to cool from 190°F to 150°F. How much time will it take it to cool from 150°F to 120°F?

Solution: We measure time t in minutes and let $t = 0$ be the time when the coffee is at 190°F. Then we let T be the temperature of the coffee at time t and let $u = T - 70$.

We have the differential equation

$$\frac{du}{dt} = ku$$

and the conditions

$$u = 120 \text{ when } t = 0 \quad \text{and} \quad u = 80 \text{ when } t = 10.$$

(Solution continued)

The general solution of the differential equation is

$$u = ce^{kt}.$$

Using the two conditions, we obtain

$$u = 120e^{kt}$$

and

$$80 = 120e^{k \cdot 10}, \quad \text{or} \quad e^k = (\tfrac{2}{3})^{\frac{1}{10}},$$

so that

$$u = 120(\tfrac{2}{3})^{\frac{t}{10}}.$$

To find when $u = 120 - 70 = 50$, we solve the equation

$$50 = 120(\tfrac{2}{3})^{\frac{t}{10}}, \quad \text{or} \quad (\tfrac{2}{3})^{\frac{t}{10}} = \tfrac{5}{12},$$

by taking common logarithms:

$$\frac{t}{10} \log_{10} \tfrac{2}{3} = \log_{10} \tfrac{5}{12}$$

$$t = 10 \frac{\log_{10} \frac{5}{12}}{\log_{10} \frac{2}{3}} = 10 \frac{\log_{10} \frac{12}{5}}{\log_{10} \frac{3}{2}}$$

$$= 10 \frac{\log_{10} 2.4}{\log_{10} 1.5} \doteq 10 \frac{0.3802}{0.1761} \doteq 21.59.$$

It therefore takes the coffee $21.59 - 10$, or about 11.6, minutes to cool from 150°F to 120°F.

ORAL EXERCISES

1. Is the differential equation describing radioactive decay an approximate mathematical model, or does it represent the physical situation exactly?

2. Discuss whether or not a mathematical formulation of a physical situation ever represents it exactly.

3. Using equation (†) on page 255 and recalling that $k < 0$, state the sign of the rate of change of temperature of the body **(a)** if it is warmer and **(b)** if it is cooler than the surrounding medium.

4. If the half-life of a radioactive substance is 10 years, what fraction of an amount present now will be left

a. 20 years from now?

b. 40 years from now?

WRITTEN EXERCISES

A

1. The half-life of radium is (about) 1620 years.

a. How much of a sample of 4 grams will be left 1000 years from now?
b. In how many years will only 1 gram be left?

2. A sample of 1 gram of radioactive lead is made using a cyclotron. At the end of one hour, 0.2118 grams remain. Find the half-life of radioactive lead to the nearest tenth of a minute.

3. Find a formula for the half-life h of a radioactive substance in terms of the proportionality constant k.

4. Find a formula for the amount z of a radioactive substance present at time t in terms of t, the original amount z_0, and the half-life h.

5. The population of a culture of bacteria doubles every 40 minutes. How long will it take the population to increase from one million to three million?

6. At noon there were one million bacteria present in a culture, and at 2 P.M. there were six million. How many were present in the culture at 1 P.M.?

B

7. The population of a city doubles every s years. Express the number n of inhabitants of the city t years after 1900 in terms of t, s, and the population n_0 in 1900.

8. A thermometer reading 20°F is brought into a room in which the air temperature is 70°F. One minute later the thermometer reads 40°F. Find

a. a formula giving the thermometer reading t minutes after it was brought into the room, and
b. the reading when $t = 5$.

9. When sugar is placed in water, it dissolves at a rate proportional to the amount still undissolved.

a. Express this fact in the form of a differential equation.
b. One kilogram of sugar is placed in a tank of water at a certain time ($t = 0$). Ten minutes later, 60% of the sugar has dissolved. How long after the sugar was placed in the tank will 95% of it have dissolved?

10. Let f be any function which satisfies the differential equation

$$\frac{dy}{dx} = ky,$$

so that $f'(x) = kf(x)$.

a. Show that $\frac{d}{dx}[e^{-kx}f(x)] = 0$ for all $x \in \mathcal{R}$.
b. What kind of function is $\phi: x \to e^{-kx}f(x)$? (See Exercise 16, page 247.)
c. Deduce that f is of the form $x \to ce^{kx}$.

CHAPTER SUMMARY

1. The general **exponential** and **logarithmic functions** are *defined* in terms of the functions L and E of Chapter 5:

$$a^x = E(xL(a)) \qquad a > 0,\ x \in \mathcal{R}$$

$$\log_a x = \frac{L(x)}{L(a)} \qquad a > 0,\ a \neq 1,\ x > 0.$$

In particular, $e^x = E(x)$ and $\log_e x = L(x)$. Usually $\log_e$ is written log.

2. The following **laws of exponents** can be proved: Let a and b be positive numbers. Then

$$a^x a^y = a^{x+y}, \qquad \frac{a^x}{a^y} = a^{x-y},$$

$$(ab)^x = a^x b^x, \qquad \left(\frac{a}{b}\right)^x = \frac{a^x}{b^x},$$

$$(a^x)^y = a^{xy}.$$

If $a \neq 1$ and $a^x = a^y$, then $x = y$.
If $x \neq 0$ and $a^x = b^x$, then $a = b$.

3. We have the following **laws of logarithms**: If $a > 0$, $a \neq 1$, $x > 0$, $y > 0$, and z is any real number, then

$$\log_a xy = \log_a x + \log_a y,$$

$$\log_a \frac{x}{y} = \log_a x - \log_a y,$$

$$\log_a x^z = z \log_a x.$$

4. The change-of-base formula for logarithms is $\log_b x = \dfrac{\log_a x}{\log_a b}$.

5. The functions $x \to a^x$ and $x \to \log_a x$ $(a > 0,\ a \neq 1)$ are inverses of each other. We have

$$a^{\log_a x} = x \quad \text{for } x > 0$$

$$\log_a a^x = x.$$

6. The **hyperbolic sine** and **hyperbolic cosine** functions are defined, respectively, by the formulas

$$\sinh x = \frac{e^x - e^{-x}}{2} \quad \text{and} \quad \cosh x = \frac{e^x + e^{-x}}{2}.$$

7. We have

$$\frac{d}{dx}a^x = (\log a)a^x, \qquad \frac{d}{dx}e^x = e^x,$$

$$\frac{d}{dx}\log_a x = (\log_a e)\frac{1}{x}, \qquad \frac{d}{dx}\log x = \frac{1}{x}.$$

8. If u is a differentiable function of x, then

$$\frac{d}{dx}e^u = e^u\frac{du}{dx} \quad \text{and} \quad \frac{d}{dx}\log u = \frac{1}{u}\frac{du}{dx}.$$

9. The function g is an **antiderivative** of the function f if f and g have the same domain D and $g'(x) = f(x)$ for all x in D. Any two antiderivatives of a given function differ only by a constant.

10. Some useful integral formulas are

$$\int x^n\,dx = \frac{x^{n+1}}{n+1} + c \quad \text{if } n \neq -1,$$

$$\int x^{-1}\,dx = \log|x| + c \quad (x \neq 0),$$

$$\int e^{kx}\,dx = \frac{1}{k}e^{kx} + c \quad (k \neq 0),$$

$$\int a^x\,dx = (\log_a e)a^x + c \quad (a > 0, a \neq 1).$$

11. A **differential equation** is one which involves two variables and a derivative or derivatives of one of these with respect to the other. Many phenomena lead to the differential equation

$$\frac{dy}{dx} = ky, \tag{N}$$

the equation of **natural growth** or **decay,** depending on whether $k > 0$ or $k < 0$. The general solution of (N) is

$$y = ce^{kx},$$

where c is a constant.

RECOMMENDED READINGS

CLARK, RONALD J., ed., *Radioactive Decay*, Supplementary and Enrichment Series, SMSG (Pasadena, California: A. C. Vroman, Inc., 1965).

SCHIFFER, MAX M., *Applied Mathematics in the High School*, Studies in Mathematics, Vol. X, SMSG (Pasadena, California: A. C. Vroman, Inc., 1963).

CHAPTER TEST

6–1 **1.** Find the exact value of each of the following:

a. $\log_a a^3$; **b.** $\log_a \frac{1}{a}$; **c.** $\log_{\frac{1}{a}} a^2$.

2. Find the exact value of each of the following:

a. $3^{\log_3 2 + \log_3 4}$; **b.** $3^{\log_2 12 - \log_2 3}$.

6–2 **3.** Sketch in the same Cartesian plane the graphs of

a. $y = 3^x$ and $y = 3^{-x}$;

b. $y = \log_3 x$ and $y = \log_{\frac{1}{3}} x$.

6–3 **4.** Find $f'(x)$ if

a. $f(x) = (\sqrt{3})^x$; **b.** $f(x) = \log_{\frac{1}{2}} x$.

5. Find $f'(x)$ if

a. $f(x) = (\sqrt{e})^{4x}$; **b.** $f(x) = \log (x^2\sqrt{1 + x})$.

6–4 **6.** Find the indicated antiderivative (for $x \neq 0$):

$$\int \frac{x^2 + x + 1}{x} dx.$$

7. Find $\frac{d}{dx}(x^2 - 2x + 2)e^x$ and use the result to give an integral formula.

6–5 **8.** Find a function whose graph passes through the point (2, 0) and has slope $1 - 2x$ at each point (x, y) of the graph.

6–6 **9.** At noon there were 10^5 bacteria present in a culture, and at 2 P.M. there were 3×10^5 present. How many were present at **(a)** 1 P.M.? **(b)** 3 P.M.?

Mathematics and Archaeology

In 1960 the American scientist Willard F. Libby received the Nobel prize for his discovery of an ingenious method for dating archaeological relics by measuring their radioactive-carbon content.

The investigations which led to radiocarbon dating had their origin before World War I in the quest for information about possible effects of cosmic radiation on the earth and in its atmosphere. By 1930 the noted physicist Arthur Compton had established that these mysterious rays from outer space actually consist of ordinary atoms of the chemical elements moving at tremendous speeds, some almost as great as the speed of light. The energy of such high-speed particles is of course immense, in the multibillion electron-volt range. Since it was far beyond laboratory capability at that time to reproduce such high-energy reactions, it was impossible to predict with any certainty the likely effects when these fast-moving atoms bombard our atmosphere.

The first breakthrough came in 1939 with the discovery that primary cosmic rays produce a shower of secondary particles as they first strike the molecules in the earth's atmosphere. The secondary neutrons released by the primary bombardment were found to have energies in the million electron-volt range, which happened to be within the capability of laboratory experimentation.

Among the many relics found in caves overlooking the Dead Sea were 2,000-year-old scroll fragments containing passages from Exodus and Psalms.

Once experiments could be performed, it was found that the oxygen in the air is largely inert to neutron bombardment, but the abundant nitrogen isotope N^{14} reacts to form the unstable radioactive isotope of carbon C^{14}. This radioactive carbon then disintegrates into N^{14} at a rate steadily proportionate to the amount present.

Scientists feel safe in assuming that cosmic rays have been bombarding the earth's atmosphere with their present intensity for at least several million years, and that an equilibrium state between the rate of formation and disintegration of radioactive carbon has long since been reached everywhere on earth.

Both ordinary and radioactive carbon atoms in the air react with oxygen molecules to form a mildly radioactive mixture of carbon dioxides. Since all plants absorb carbon dioxide in order to live, and all animals live directly or indirectly off plants, it follows that all living organisms contain a small amount of radiocarbon. The proportion of C^{14} to ordinary carbon, C^{12}, is the same in all living things. Libby determined this ratio to be 10^{-12} parts of C^{14} to one part of C^{12}.

As soon as an organism dies, the radiocarbon-disintegration process takes over completely because the organism is no longer replenishing its content of C^{14} by ingesting carbon dioxide. The decay rate of a radioactive substance is usually expressed in terms of its half-life (see Section 6–6), that is, the time required for half of the atoms in a sample to disintegrate. Libby's experiments showed that radiocarbon has a half-life of about 5600 years.

An archaeologist examines and carefully reconstructs one of the Dead Sea Scrolls. One of these restored documents is shown at the right.

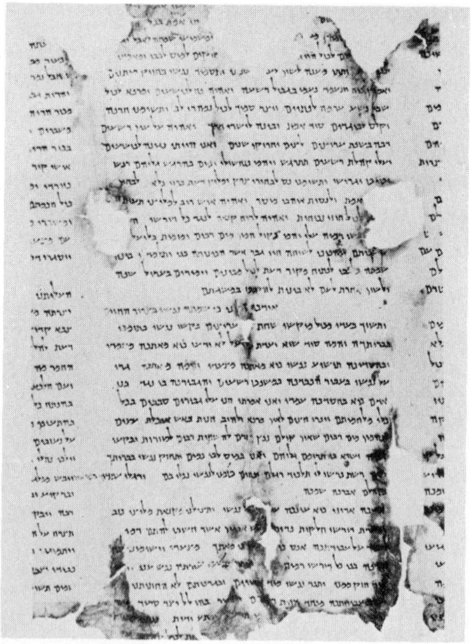

A geologist burns a sample of charcoal in the process of radiocarbon dating.

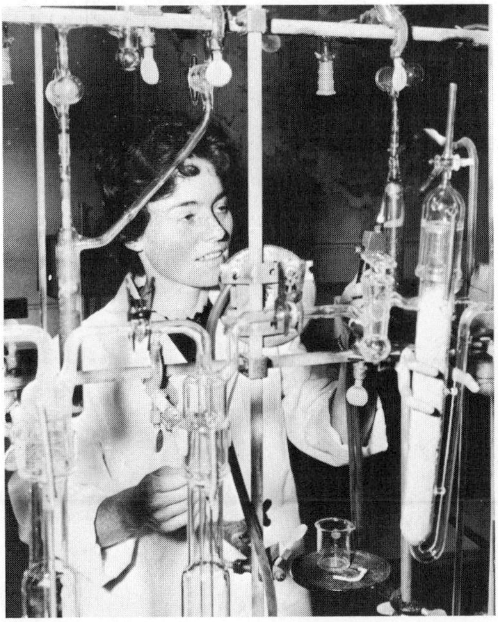

To determine the age of any once-living relic, a sample of it is burned to form carbon dioxide. Then by finding the ratio of C^{14} to C^{12} in this carbon-dioxide sample and comparing it with the known ratio, 10^{-12} to 1, in a living organism, one can determine the percentage of radiocarbon that has disappeared in the given specimen. From the known half-life of C^{14}, one can then calculate how long ago the specimen died.

This procedure has made it possible to date with reasonable accuracy many interesting archaeological remains of once-living things, such as mummies, wooden implements, cloth, and leather. A particularly exciting example was Libby's dating of the linen wrappings around the Dead Sea Scrolls.

The same methods, applied to uranium decay, can be used to determine the age of rocks.

In recent years, many radioactivity laboratories have come into operation, providing new insights into the geological age of the earth and of the things that have lived on it.

READING LIST

BALDWIN, GORDON C., *Calendars to the Past: How Science Dates Archaeological Ruins* (New York: W. W. Norton & Company, Inc., 1967).

LIBBY, WILLARD F., *Radiocarbon Dating* (Chicago: The University of Chicago Press, 1955).

SCHOENWETTER, JAMES, *How Old Is It?* (Santa Fe: Museum of New Mexico Press, 1965).

7

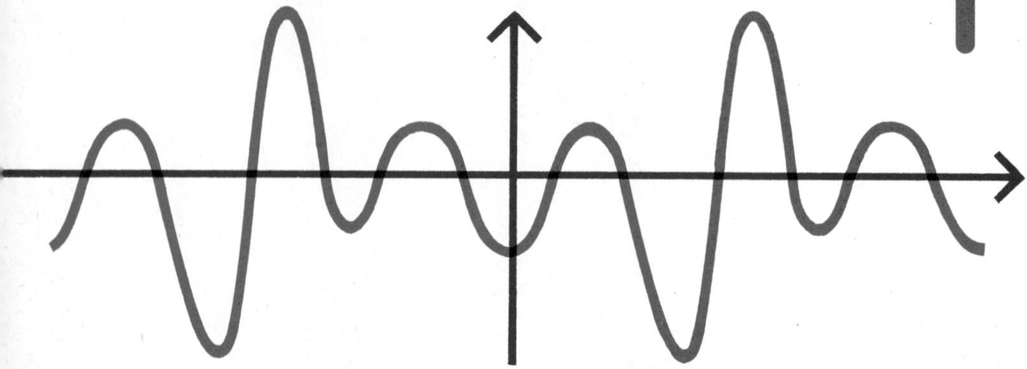

The periodic oscillations of a vibrating drumhead or a musical sound produced by a saxophone or trumpet can be described by equations involving sines and cosines. The diagram above shows the graph of a sound made by a trumpet.

The Circular Functions Sine and Cosine

Many physical phenomena repeat in regular patterns or periods. For example, the seasons of the year follow each other in a recurring cycle, and the voltage in an alternating-current circuit oscillates between positive and negative values. Basic tools in the study of such periodic phenomena are sine and cosine, two of the six circular functions we shall study in this chapter and the next.

■ Definitions and Basic Properties

7–1 Preliminaries

As one might expect, the definition of circular functions involves a circle. We take a Cartesian coordinate system in a plane and consider the circle C having center at the origin and radius 1, as shown in Figure 7–1. Because we wish to reserve x and y for another purpose, we shall name the horizontal axis the u-axis, and the vertical axis the v-axis. By using the distance formula (page 13), we can see that if (u, v) is a point on C, then

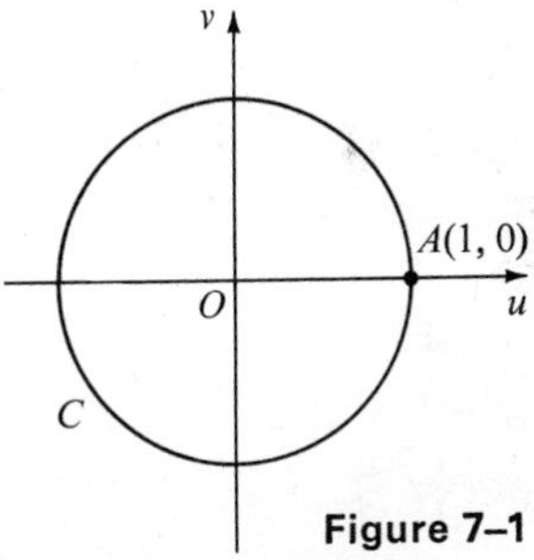

Figure 7–1

$$\sqrt{(u-0)^2 + (v-0)^2} = 1,$$

and conversely. Hence $u^2 + v^2 = 1$ is an equation of C.

Let A be the point $(1, 0)$. Given any real number x, we locate a point P_x on C according to the following rule:

> If $x \geq 0$, start from A and measure off x units *along the circle C* in a *counterclockwise* direction. The point reached is P_x.
>
> If $x < 0$, start from A and measure off $|x|$ units *along the circle C* in a *clockwise* direction. The point reached is P_x.

(We are assuming that each arc of C has a definite length. In your further studies of calculus, you will examine the problem of defining arc length.)

Figure 7–2 suggests a way of visualizing the procedure just described: We think of the vertical line $u = 1$ as being an x-axis directed upward, with origin at $A(1, 0)$ and with the same unit of measure as on the u- and v-axes. We imagine that this x-axis is flexible, so that it can be wound around the circle C. When this is done, we see that with each real number x there is associated a definite point P_x on C. We therefore have a function $x \rightarrow P_x$ whose domain is $\mathcal{R}$ and whose range is C. Figure 7–3 shows P_x for several values of x.

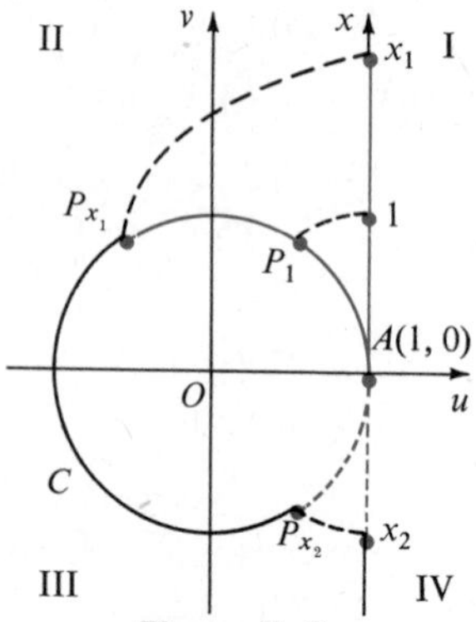

Figure 7–2

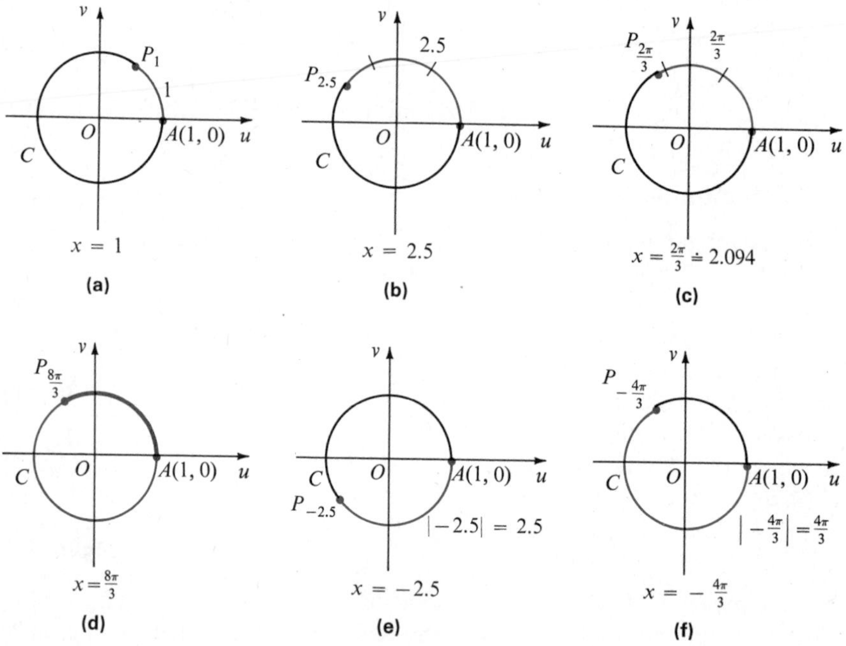

Figure 7–3

For some numbers x, specifically certain rational multiples of π, P_x is quite easy to locate. For example, the arc from $A(1, 0)$ to the point $(0, 1)$ is one-fourth of the circumference of C, and therefore has length $\frac{1}{4} \cdot 2\pi = \frac{\pi}{2}$. Thus $P_{\frac{\pi}{2}}$ is the point $(0, 1)$.

EXAMPLE 1. Find the coordinates of $P_{\frac{\pi}{6}}$.

Solution: For brevity, we denote $P_{\frac{\pi}{6}}$ by P; we let its coordinates be (h, k). Then we let Q be the point $(h, -k)$ and B be $(0, 1)$. By symmetry, we see that the lengths of the arcs $\widehat{QA}$ and $\widehat{AP}$ are equal. Therefore

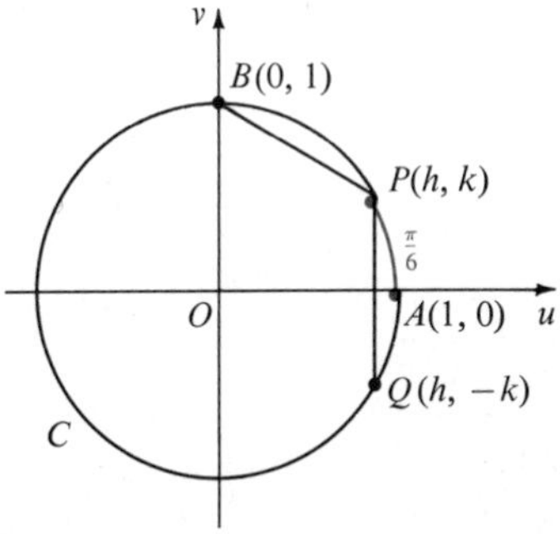

$$\text{length } \widehat{QP} = \frac{\pi}{6} + \frac{\pi}{6} = \frac{\pi}{3}.$$

Since the length of $\widehat{AB}$ is $\frac{\pi}{2}$,

and since

$$\text{length } \widehat{PB} = \text{length } \widehat{AB} - \text{length } \widehat{AP},$$
$$\text{length } \widehat{PB} = \frac{\pi}{2} - \frac{\pi}{6} = \frac{\pi}{3}.$$

Because congruent arcs of a circle subtend congruent chords,

$$\text{length } \overline{QP} = \text{length } \overline{PB},$$

or

$$2k = \sqrt{(h - 0)^2 + (k - 1)^2}.$$

From this we have

$$4k^2 = h^2 + k^2 - 2k + 1. \qquad (*)$$

Since (h, k) is on C, $h^2 + k^2 = 1$, and (*) becomes

$$4k^2 = 1 - 2k + 1,$$

from which we have

$$2k^2 + k - 1 = (2k - 1)(k + 1) = 0.$$

Therefore $k = \frac{1}{2}$ or $k = -1$. Since P is in the first quadrant, we discard the possibility that $k = -1$. Thus $k = \frac{1}{2}$; and therefore, since $h > 0$,

$$h = \sqrt{1 - k^2} = \sqrt{1 - \tfrac{1}{4}} = \frac{\sqrt{3}}{2}.$$

Hence $P_{\frac{\pi}{6}}$ is the point $\left(\frac{\sqrt{3}}{2}, \frac{1}{2}\right)$.

The circle C is symmetric with respect to the u-axis, the v-axis, and the line $u = v$. We may take advantage of these facts to find the coordinates of several points of C if we know the coordinates of one point. Figure 7–4, page 268, suggests how this may be done.

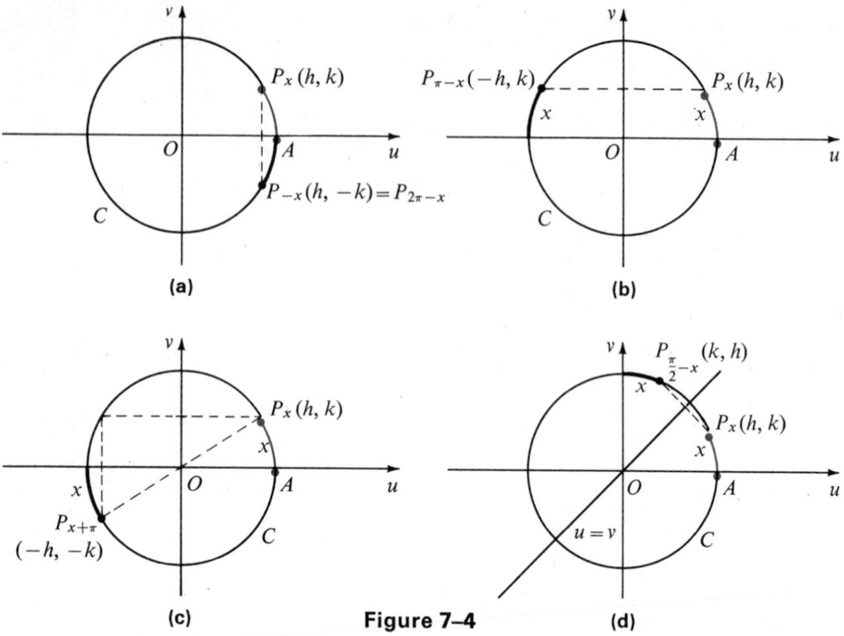

Figure 7–4

EXAMPLE 2. Find the coordinates of (**a**) $P_{\frac{\pi}{3}}$, (**b**) $P_{\frac{2\pi}{3}}$, (**c**) $P_{-\frac{\pi}{3}}$, and (**d**) $P_{\frac{5\pi}{3}}$.

Solution: **a.** From Example 1, $P_{\frac{\pi}{6}}$ has coordinates $\left(\frac{\sqrt{3}}{2}, \frac{1}{2}\right)$. Since $P_{\frac{\pi}{3}} = P_{\frac{\pi}{2}-\frac{\pi}{6}}$, $P_{\frac{\pi}{3}}$ and $P_{\frac{\pi}{6}}$ are symmetric with respect to the line $u = v$, and we see [Figure 7–4(d)] that $P_{\frac{\pi}{3}}$ has coordinates $\left(\frac{1}{2}, \frac{\sqrt{3}}{2}\right)$.

b. Since $P_{\frac{2\pi}{3}} = P_{\pi-\frac{\pi}{3}}$, we use (**a**) to find that $P_{\frac{2\pi}{3}}$ has coordinates $\left(-\frac{1}{2}, \frac{\sqrt{3}}{2}\right)$. [See Figure 7–4(b).]

c. Using (**a**), we find that $P_{-\frac{\pi}{3}}$ has coordinates $\left(\frac{1}{2}, -\frac{\sqrt{3}}{2}\right)$. [See Figure 7–4(a).]

d. Since $P_{\frac{5\pi}{3}} = P_{\frac{2\pi}{3}+\pi}$, we use (**b**) to find that $P_{\frac{5\pi}{3}}$ has coordinates $\left(-\left(-\frac{1}{2}\right), -\frac{\sqrt{3}}{2}\right) = \left(\frac{1}{2}, -\frac{\sqrt{3}}{2}\right)$.

[See Figure 7–4(c).]

It is clear that we can have $P_{x_1} = P_{x_2}$ even though $x_1 \neq x_2$ [see the results of parts (c) and (d) of Example 2]. In other words, the function $x \to P_x$ is *not* one-to-one.

It is often convenient to call a number x a **first-quadrant number** if P_x lies in Quadrant I, a **second-quadrant number** if P_x lies in Quadrant II, and so on. For example, $\frac{5\pi}{3}$ and $-\frac{\pi}{3}$ are both fourth-quadrant numbers. If P_x lies on an axis, then x is not a quadrant number.

ORAL EXERCISES

If (a, b) is in Quadrant I, in which quadrant is each of the following?

1. $(-a, b)$ **2.** $(a, -b)$ **3.** $(-a, -b)$ **4.** (b, a)

If (a, b) is in Quadrant IV, in which quadrant is each of the following?

5. $(-a, b)$ **6.** $(a, -b)$ **7.** $(-a, -b)$ **8.** (b, a)

State the quadrant of each of the following numbers.

9. 1 **11.** 3 **13.** −1 **15.** −3

10. 2 **12.** 4 **14.** −2 **16.** −4

If (a, b) is on C: $u^2 + v^2 = 1$, state whether each of the following points must, may, or cannot, be on C.

17. $(-a, b)$ **20.** $(2a, 2b)$ **23.** $(a^2 + b^2, 0)$

18. (b, a) **21.** $(-a, -b)$ **24.** $(a^2 + b^2, a^2 + b^2)$

19. $(a, 0)$ **22.** $(-b, -a)$

Give the coordinates of P_x for the given value of x.

25. $x = 0$ **27.** $x = -\pi$ **29.** $x = \frac{\pi}{2}$ **31.** $x = \frac{3\pi}{2}$

26. $x = \pi$ **28.** $x = 3\pi$ **30.** $x = -\frac{\pi}{2}$ **32.** $x = 100\pi$

33. If $P_{x_1} = P_{x_2}$, what can be said of the number $x_2 - x_1$?

WRITTEN EXERCISES

In Exercises 1–6, find the quadrant of the given number (n denotes an integer).

A **1.** $\frac{17\pi}{4}$ **3.** $(2n + 1)\pi + \frac{\pi}{6}$ **5.** $\frac{8n + 1}{4}\pi$

2. $\frac{10\pi}{3}$ **4.** $(2n + 1)\pi - \frac{\pi}{6}$ **6.** $\frac{12n + 5}{6}\pi$

In Exercises 7–12, find the missing coordinate of P_x.

7. $P_x(\frac{3}{5}, ?), 0 < x < \frac{\pi}{2}$

8. $P_x(?, \frac{3}{5}), 0 < x < \frac{\pi}{2}$

9. $P_x(-\frac{5}{13}, ?), \frac{\pi}{2} < x < \pi$

10. $P_x(-\frac{12}{13}, ?), \pi < x < \frac{3\pi}{2}$

11. $P_x\left(?, -\frac{1}{\sqrt{10}}\right), -\frac{\pi}{2} < x < 0$

12. $P_x\left(?, \frac{3}{\sqrt{10}}\right), -\frac{3\pi}{2} < x < -\pi$

B **13–18.** For the x in Exercises 7–12, find the coordinates of

a. P_{-x}, **b.** $P_{\pi-x}$, **c.** $P_{x+\pi}$, **d.** $P_{\frac{\pi}{2}-x}$.

19. Find the coordinates of $P_{\frac{\pi}{4}}$.

20. Complete the following table. (*Hint:* Use the result of Exercise 19.)

x	0	$\frac{\pi}{6}$	$\frac{\pi}{4}$	$\frac{\pi}{3}$	$\frac{\pi}{2}$	$\frac{2\pi}{3}$	$\frac{3\pi}{4}$	$\frac{5\pi}{6}$	π
P_x	$(1, 0)$	$\left(\frac{\sqrt{3}}{2}, \frac{1}{2}\right)$	?	?	?	$\left(-\frac{1}{2}, \frac{\sqrt{3}}{2}\right)$	?	?	?

x	$\frac{7\pi}{6}$	$\frac{5\pi}{4}$	$\frac{4\pi}{3}$	$\frac{3\pi}{2}$	$\frac{5\pi}{3}$	$\frac{7\pi}{4}$	$\frac{11\pi}{6}$	2π
P_x	?	?	?	?	?	?	?	?

7–2 The Sine and Cosine Functions

We shall now define the most important two of the six circular functions. These are the **sine** and **cosine** functions, which are abbreviated sin and cos, respectively. If P_x is the point on the circle C: $u^2 + v^2 = 1$ which corresponds to the number x (as described in Section 7–1), then

$$\textbf{sin}: x \rightarrow \textbf{ordinate of } P_x$$

$$\textbf{cos}: x \rightarrow \textbf{abscissa of } P_x.$$

Thus (Figure 7–5) if x is any real number and P_x is the point (u, v), we have

$$\sin x = v \quad \text{and} \quad \cos x = u.$$

The *domain* of both sin and cos is $\mathcal{R}$; and since the range of $x \rightarrow P_x(u, v)$ is C, the *range* of both sin and cos is the interval $\{z: -1 \leq z \leq 1\}$.

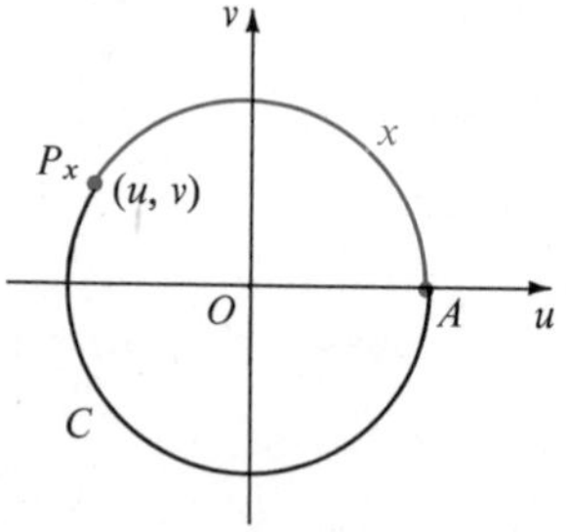

Figure 7–5

Since the coordinates of $P_{\frac{\pi}{3}}$ are $\left(\frac{1}{2}, \frac{\sqrt{3}}{2}\right)$ by Example 2, page 268, we have $\sin\frac{\pi}{3} = \frac{\sqrt{3}}{2}$ and $\cos\frac{\pi}{3} = \frac{1}{2}$. From the same example, we see that $\sin\frac{2\pi}{3} = \frac{\sqrt{3}}{2}$, $\cos\frac{2\pi}{3} = -\frac{1}{2}$, $\sin\frac{5\pi}{3} = -\frac{\sqrt{3}}{2}$, and $\cos\frac{5\pi}{3} = \frac{1}{2}$.

Exercise 20, page 270, enables us to construct Table 1. You should be able to call the entries in this table to mind readily. Notice that the sines and cosines of the second-, third-, and fourth-quadrant numbers in the first column differ only in sign from sines and cosines of $\frac{\pi}{6}$, $\frac{\pi}{4}$, and $\frac{\pi}{3}$. If you know these first-quadrant entries, you can obtain the others by mentally using symmetry considerations.

From the definition of sin and cos, we observe this important fact:

> For any number x, the coordinates of P_x are $(\cos x, \sin x)$.

Suppose x is a second-quadrant number (for example, $\frac{\pi}{2} < x < \pi$, $\frac{5\pi}{2} < x < 3\pi$, or $-\frac{3\pi}{2} < x < -\pi$). Then P_x $(\cos x, \sin x)$ is in the second quadrant and therefore has negative abscissa and positive ordinate. Thus $\cos x < 0$ and $\sin x > 0$. The algebraic signs of $\sin x$ and $\cos x$ according to the quadrant of x are indicated below.

Quadrant of x	$\sin x$	$\cos x$
First	Positive	Positive
Second	Positive	Negative
Third	Negative	Negative
Fourth	Negative	Positive

Table 1

x	$\sin x$	$\cos x$
0	0	1
$\frac{\pi}{6}$	$\frac{1}{2}$	$\frac{\sqrt{3}}{2}$
$\frac{\pi}{4}$	$\frac{\sqrt{2}}{2}$	$\frac{\sqrt{2}}{2}$
$\frac{\pi}{3}$	$\frac{\sqrt{3}}{2}$	$\frac{1}{2}$
$\frac{\pi}{2}$	1	0
$\frac{2\pi}{3}$	$\frac{\sqrt{3}}{2}$	$-\frac{1}{2}$
$\frac{3\pi}{4}$	$\frac{\sqrt{2}}{2}$	$-\frac{\sqrt{2}}{2}$
$\frac{5\pi}{6}$	$\frac{1}{2}$	$-\frac{\sqrt{3}}{2}$
π	0	-1
$\frac{7\pi}{6}$	$-\frac{1}{2}$	$-\frac{\sqrt{3}}{2}$
$\frac{5\pi}{4}$	$-\frac{\sqrt{2}}{2}$	$-\frac{\sqrt{2}}{2}$
$\frac{4\pi}{3}$	$-\frac{\sqrt{3}}{2}$	$-\frac{1}{2}$
$\frac{3\pi}{2}$	-1	0
$\frac{5\pi}{3}$	$-\frac{\sqrt{3}}{2}$	$\frac{1}{2}$
$\frac{7\pi}{4}$	$-\frac{\sqrt{2}}{2}$	$\frac{\sqrt{2}}{2}$
$\frac{11\pi}{6}$	$-\frac{1}{2}$	$\frac{\sqrt{3}}{2}$
2π	0	1

Since P_x (cos x, sin x) is on the circle C: $u^2 + v^2 = 1$, we must have

$$(\cos x)^2 + (\sin x)^2 = 1.$$

Therefore:

Theorem 1.

For every real number x,

$$\sin^2 x + \cos^2 x = 1.$$

Notice that to avoid the use of parentheses, we have written $\sin^2 x$ for $(\sin x)^2$ and $\cos^2 x$ for $(\cos x)^2$.

EXAMPLE 1. Given that $\cos x = \frac{3}{5}$, find $\sin x$ if

a. $0 < x < \frac{\pi}{2}$; **b.** $\frac{3\pi}{2} < x < 2\pi$.

Solution: From Theorem 1, $\sin^2 x = 1 - \cos^2 x = 1 - (\frac{3}{5})^2 = \frac{16}{25}$. Therefore $\sin x = \frac{4}{5}$ or $\sin x = -\frac{4}{5}$.

a. Since x is a first-quadrant number, $\sin x > 0$. Therefore $\sin x = \frac{4}{5}$.

b. Since x is a fourth-quadrant number, $\sin x < 0$. Therefore $\sin x = -\frac{4}{5}$.

In Section 7–1, we saw that if P_x is the point (u, v), then, because C is

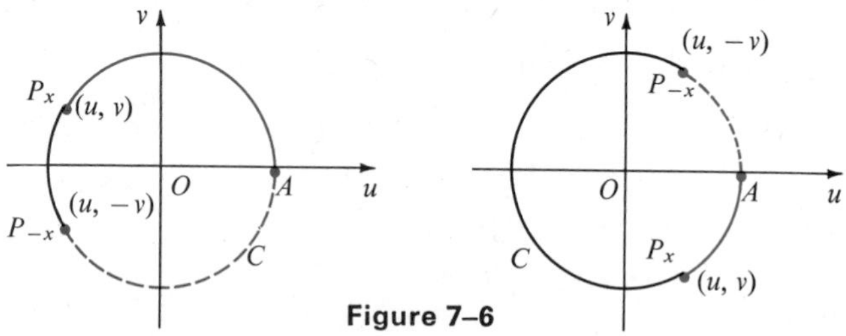

Figure 7–6

symmetric with respect to the u-axis, P_{-x} is the point $(u, -v)$. (See Figure 7–6.) From this we have:

Theorem 2.

For every real number x,

$$\sin(-x) = -\sin x \quad \text{and} \quad \cos(-x) = \cos x.$$

Thus, for the number x of Example 1(b), $\cos(-x) = \cos x = \frac{3}{5}$, and $\sin(-x) = -\sin x = -(-\frac{4}{5}) = \frac{4}{5}$.

From Theorem 2, we see that the function

$$f: x \to \sin x \quad \text{has the property} \quad f(-x) = -f(x).$$

Any function f such that $f(-x) = -f(x)$ for each x in its domain is called an **odd function.** We also see that

$$g: x \to \cos x \quad \text{has the property} \quad g(-x) = g(x).$$

Any function having this property for each x in its domain is called an **even function.** Thus sin is an odd function and cos is an even function. You may recall (Exercise 14, page 239) that sinh is an odd function and cosh is an even function. Other examples of odd functions and even functions are $P: x \to P(x)$ and $Q: x \to Q(x)$, where $P(x)$ and $Q(x)$ are polynomials over $\mathcal{R}$ that contain, respectively, only odd powers of x and only even powers of x; see Exercises 23–26, page 88, and Example 2(a) below.

EXAMPLE 2. Determine whether the following functions are odd, even, or neither.

a. $f: x \to x^3 - 4x$;
b. $f: x \to x^2 - 4x$;
c. $f: x \to x^2 + x \sin x$;
d. $f: x \to g(x) \cdot h(x)$, where g is even and h is odd.

Solution: **a.** $f(-x) = (-x)^3 - 4(-x) = -x^3 + 4x = -(x^3 - 4x) = -f(x)$. Therefore f is odd.
b. $f(-x) = (-x)^2 - 4(-x) = x^2 + 4x \neq \pm f(x)$. Therefore f is neither odd nor even.
c. $f(-x) = (-x)^2 + (-x)\sin(-x) = x^2 - x(-\sin x) = x^2 + x \sin x = f(x)$. Therefore f is even.
d. $f(-x) = g(-x) \cdot h(-x) = g(x) \cdot [-h(x)] = -[g(x) \cdot h(x)] = -f(x)$. Therefore f is odd.

Since the length of the circumference of C is 2π, and since $x + 2\pi n$ (n an integer) and x differ by an integral multiple of 2π, we have $P_{x+2\pi n} = P_x$. Hence we have the following:

Theorem 3.

For every real number x and every integer n,

$$\sin(x + 2\pi n) = \sin x \quad \text{and} \quad \cos(x + 2\pi n) = \cos x.$$

EXAMPLE 3. Find (**a**) $\cos \dfrac{100\pi}{3}$ and (**b**) $\sin \dfrac{4n+1}{2}\pi$ (n an integer).

Solution: **a.** $\dfrac{100\pi}{3} = 33\pi + \frac{1}{3}\pi = 32\pi + \dfrac{4\pi}{3} = \dfrac{4\pi}{3} + 2\pi \cdot 16.$

$$\text{Therefore } \cos \frac{100\pi}{3} = \cos\left(\frac{4\pi}{3} + 2\pi \cdot 16\right)$$
$$= \cos \frac{4\pi}{3} = -\frac{1}{2}.$$

b. $\dfrac{4n+1}{2}\pi = (2n + \frac{1}{2})\pi = \dfrac{\pi}{2} + 2\pi n.$

$$\text{Therefore } \sin \frac{4n+1}{2}\pi = \sin\left(\frac{\pi}{2} + 2\pi n\right) = \sin \frac{\pi}{2} = 1.$$

Equations such as

$$\cos^2 x + \sin^2 x = 1,$$
$$x^2 - 1 = (x-1)(x+1),$$
$$\log e^x = x,$$

which are true for *all* $x \in \mathcal{R}$, are called **identities** (over $\mathcal{R}$). Equations like

$$\frac{x^2-1}{x-1} = x + 1$$

and

$$e^{\log x} = x$$

are not meaningful for all values of x but *are true whenever both sides of the equation are defined.* We agree to call such equations **identities** as well.

For example, by subtracting $\sin^2 x$ from both members of the identity

$$\cos^2 x + \sin^2 x = 1,$$

we obtain the identity

$$\cos^2 x = 1 - \sin^2 x,$$

or

$$\cos^2 x = (1 - \sin x)(1 + \sin x).$$

For values of x where neither $\cos x = 0$ nor $(1 - \sin x) = 0$, we may divide both members by $\cos x\,(1 - \sin x)$ to obtain still another identity,

$$\frac{\cos x}{1 - \sin x} = \frac{1 + \sin x}{\cos x}.$$

Another example of such an identity is found in Exercise 30, page 276.

ORAL EXERCISES

Without referring to Table 1 on page 271, give sin x and cos x for each of the following values of x.

1. 0 **3.** $\frac{\pi}{2}$ **5.** $-\frac{\pi}{2}$ **7.** $-\pi$ **9.** 99π

2. π **4.** 2π **6.** $\frac{3\pi}{2}$ **8.** -4π **10.** 100π

Give the quadrant of x if

11. $\sin x > 0$ and $\cos x > 0$.

12. $\sin x < 0$ and $\cos x < 0$.

13. $\sin x < 0$ and $\cos x > 0$.

14. $\sin x > 0$ and $\cos x < 0$.

State whether or not there is a value of x which satisfies *both* equations.

15. $\sin x = 1$
$\cos x = -1$

16. $\sin x = -1$
$\cos x = 0$

17. $\sin x = \frac{1}{2}$
$\cos x = \frac{1}{2}$

18. $\sin x = \frac{1}{\sqrt{2}}$
$\cos x = \frac{1}{\sqrt{2}}$

19. $\sin x = \sqrt{a}$
$\cos x = \sqrt{1 - a}$ $(0 \leq a \leq 1)$

20. $\sin x = \cos 2$
$\cos x = \sin 2$

WRITTEN EXERCISES

In Exercises 1–8, use Table 1 on page 271 (if necessary) to evaluate sin x and cos x for the given value of x.

A

1. $-\frac{\pi}{4}$

2. $-\frac{4\pi}{3}$

3. $\frac{13\pi}{6}$

4. $\frac{13\pi}{3}$

5. $-\frac{100\pi}{3}$

6. $\frac{101\pi}{4}$

7. $\frac{6n + 4}{3}\pi$, n an integer

8. $\frac{6n - 4}{3}\pi$, n an integer

In Exercises 9–20, find the least positive solution of the equation.

9. $\sin 2x = \frac{1}{2}$

10. $\cos 2x = \frac{1}{2}$

11. $\sin 2x = -1$

12. $\cos 4x = 0$

13. $\cos \frac{x}{10} = \frac{\sqrt{3}}{2}$

14. $\sin \frac{x}{6} = -\frac{\sqrt{3}}{2}$

15. $\cos (x + \pi) = -\frac{\sqrt{2}}{2}$

16. $\sin \left(x + \frac{\pi}{2}\right) = -\frac{\sqrt{2}}{2}$

17. $\sin (x + 4\pi) = \frac{1}{2}$

18. $\cos (x - 6\pi) = \frac{1}{2}$

19. $\cos (x + 3\pi) = 0$

20. $\sin (x - 3\pi) = 1$

In Exercises 21–26, find cos *x*.

21. $\sin x = \frac{3}{5}$, x a first-quadrant number

22. $\sin x = \frac{1}{\sqrt{10}}$, x a second-quadrant number

23. $\sin x = \frac{5}{13}, \frac{\pi}{2} < x < \frac{3\pi}{2}$

24. $\sin x = -\frac{5}{13}, 0 < x < \frac{3\pi}{2}$

B **25.** $\sin x = -\frac{1}{3}, |x| < \frac{\pi}{2}$

26. $\sin x = a, a > 0, |x - \pi| < \frac{\pi}{2}$

27. Prove that the product of two even functions is an even function.

28. Prove that the product of two odd functions is an even function.

C **29.** Prove or disprove the following statement: If the product of two functions, f and g, is an even function, then either both f and g are even functions or both f and g are odd functions.

30. Show that if x is not an integral multiple of π, then

$$\frac{\sin x}{1 + \cos x} = \frac{1 - \cos x}{\sin x}.$$

7–3 Trigonometric Functions, Radian Measure (Optional)

The *circular* functions sin and cos are closely related to the *trigonometric* functions bearing the same names. The latter, however, have as domains the set of all *angles*, rather than numbers.

The word "angle" has two related meanings in mathematics. In (Euclidean) geometry, an **angle** is defined to be the union of two noncollinear rays with a common endpoint. In trigonometry, an **angle** (sometimes for distinction called a **directed angle**) more often is defined to be an ordered pair (R_1, R_2) of rays having a common endpoint, together with a *rotation* of R_1 into R_2. We call the common endpoint the **vertex** of the angle, R_1 the **initial side** of the angle, and R_2 the **terminal side.** The rotation can be indicated by a curved arrow, as shown in Figure 7–7.

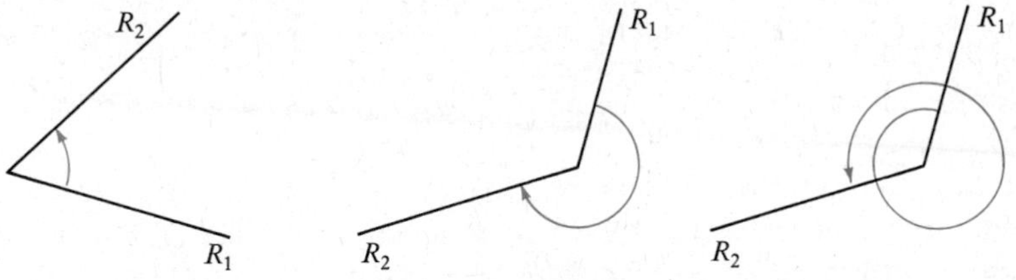

Figure 7–7

In much geometrical work, the angles which interest us appear in polygons, as in Figure 7–8. We often name such angles by symbols like $\angle BAC$, where B, A, and C are consecutive vertices of the polygon. By $\angle BAC$ we shall mean an angle such that $\overline{AB}$ is a subset of the initial side and $\overline{AC}$ is a subset of the terminal side. In the interest of brevity, we frequently use such symbols as $\angle\alpha$ or simply α to name angles.

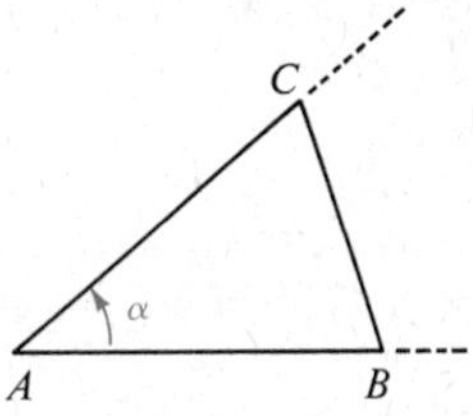

Figure 7–8

Let θ be an angle situated in a plane in which a counterclockwise sense of rotation has been chosen to be positive. Introduce a (u, v)-coordinate system in such a way that the positive u-axis coincides with the initial side R_1 of θ and the positive v-axis is a positive right-angle rotation from the positive u-axis (Figure 7–9). The curved arrow indicating the rotation of R_1 into the terminal side R_2 of θ determines a "directed" arc of C: $u^2 + v^2 = 1$. The initial point of this arc is $A(1, 0)$, and the terminal point is the point P of intersection of R_2 and C.

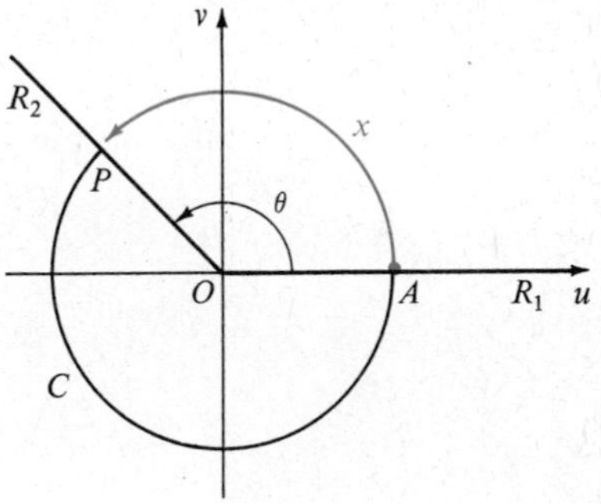

Figure 7–9

We may use the directed length x of the arc $\widehat{AP}$ as a *measure* of the angle θ. (The number x is negative if the arc is directed in a clockwise sense.) The number x is the **radian measure** of θ; in symbols,

$$m^R\theta = x.$$

Thus if ϕ is the right angle shown in Figure 7–10, we have

$$m^R\phi = \frac{\pi}{2}. \qquad (*)$$

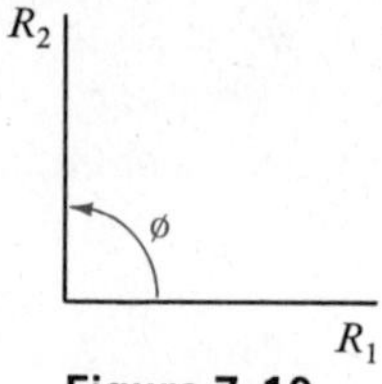

Figure 7–10

We define the **trigonometric sine** and **cosine** of an *angle* θ by

$$\sin\theta = \sin m^R\theta \quad \text{and} \quad \cos\theta = \cos m^R\theta,$$

where the *sin* and *cos* appearing on the right-hand sides of the equations are *circular* functions.

In computational work, it is customary to use *degree measure* of angles rather than radian measure: Given an angle θ, introduce a (u, v)-coordinate system as in Figure 7–9, and divide the circumference of C into 360 equal parts. The **degree measure** of θ, $m°\theta$, is the number of these parts contained in the arc $\widehat{AP}$ if the arc is directed counterclockwise and is the negative of this number if the arc is directed clockwise. Thus for the right angle ϕ of Figure 7–10, we have

$$m°\phi = 90. \qquad (\dagger)$$

For more precise measurement, $\frac{1}{60}$ of a degree is called a **minute** (written 1′); and $\frac{1}{60}$ of a minute is called a **second** (written 1″).

Radian and degree measures are proportional, that is, there is a number k such that for any angle θ,

$$m°\theta = k \cdot m^R\theta.$$

We can use (*) and (†) to determine k by setting $\theta = \phi$ in the equation above:

$$m°\phi = k \cdot m^R\phi, \quad \text{or} \quad 90 = k \cdot \frac{\pi}{2},$$

so that $k = \dfrac{180}{\pi}$. Therefore, for any angle θ,

$$m°\theta = \frac{180}{\pi} m^R\theta \quad \text{and} \quad m^R\theta = \frac{\pi}{180} m°\theta.$$

For example, an angle having radian measure 1 has degree measure

$$\frac{180}{\pi} \doteq 57.2958.$$

An angle is often indicated by naming the amount of its rotation. Thus if $m°\theta = 30$, we may write cos 30° for $\cos\theta$. That is, cos 30° means the (trigonometric) cosine of an angle whose degree measure is 30. The superscript ° is used to specify that *degree* measure is being used, just as the abbreviation *ft.* following a numeral is used to specify that *foot* measure is being used.

If $m^R\theta = \frac{\pi}{4}$, we could write $\sin \frac{\pi}{4}^R$ for $\sin \theta$. However, because $\sin \frac{\pi}{4}^R = \sin \frac{\pi}{4}$, the superscript ^{R} ordinarily is not used. When the measure of an angle is given as a numerical symbol without a superscript, for example, as 30 or $\frac{\pi}{6}$, it is to be understood that *radian* measure is being used, unless otherwise indicated.

EXAMPLE. The degree *or* radian measure of an angle θ is given in each of (**a**)–(**d**) below. Find the *other* measure in each case.

a. 30 **b.** 30° **c.** $\frac{\pi}{6}$ **d.** 0.0174533

Solution: **a.** $m°\theta = \frac{180}{\pi} m^R\theta = \frac{180}{\pi} \cdot 30 \doteq 1718.87$

b. $m^R\theta = \frac{\pi}{180} m°\theta = \frac{\pi}{180} \cdot 30 = \frac{\pi}{6}$

c. $m°\theta = \frac{180}{\pi} \cdot \frac{\pi}{6} = 30$

d. $m°\theta = \frac{180}{\pi} \cdot (0.0174533) \doteq 1.00000$

Figure 7–11 shows a central angle θ of a circle K of radius r. C is the circle of radius 1 concentric with K. Let s and x be, respectively, the lengths of the arcs of K and C subtended by θ. Then x is the *radian* measure of θ, that is, $x = m^R\theta$. From similar figures, we have the proportion $\frac{s}{r} = \frac{x}{1}$. Therefore,

$$s = rx, \quad \text{or} \quad s = r \cdot m^R\theta.$$

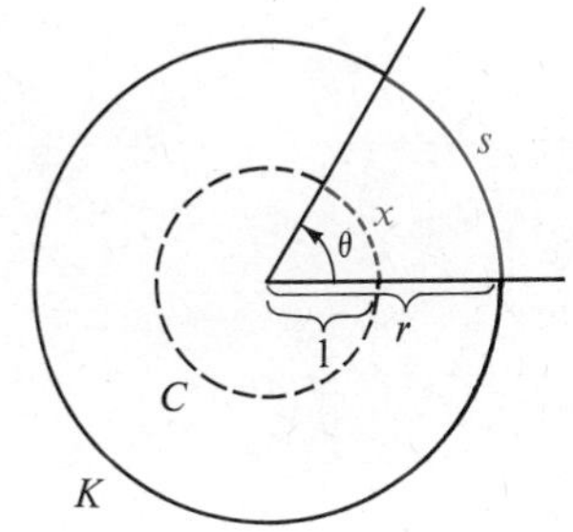

Figure 7–11

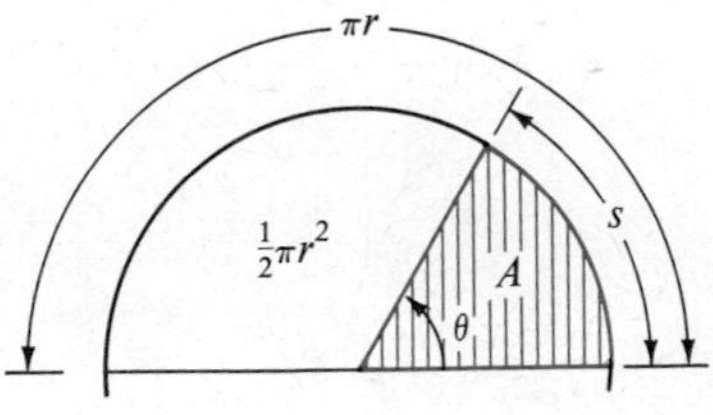

Figure 7–12

A **sector** of a circle is a region bounded by a central angle θ of the circle and the arc subtended by θ. (See Figure 7–12.) A semicircular region is an example of a sector of a circle. We can express the area A of any sector in terms of the radius r of the circle and either the length s of the subtended arc or the radian measure of θ: Since the area of a semicircular region is $\frac{1}{2}\pi r^2$ and the length of the arc that bounds it is πr, from Figure 7–12 we have the proportion

$$\frac{A}{\frac{1}{2}\pi r^2} = \frac{s}{\pi r}.$$

From this we obtain

$$A = \tfrac{1}{2}rs, \quad \text{or} \quad A = \tfrac{1}{2}r^2 m^{\text{R}}\theta.$$

ORAL EXERCISES

The first measure listed is a measure of an angle θ. State which, if either, of the other two measures is also a measure of θ.

1. π; $180°$, $-180°$
2. 0; 2π, $0°$
3. $90°$; $-270°$, $\frac{3\pi}{2}$
4. $180°$; $-\pi$, 3π
5. $270°$; $-90°$, $\frac{3\pi}{2}$
6. $-\frac{\pi}{2}$; $270°$, $-90°$
7. $\frac{\pi}{4}$; $45°$, $2\pi + \frac{\pi}{4}$
8. $60°$; $\frac{\pi}{6}$, $\frac{\pi}{3}$
9. $-135°$; $\frac{5\pi}{4}$, $-\frac{3\pi}{4}$
10. $\frac{2\pi}{3}$; $\frac{8\pi}{3}$, $120°$

WRITTEN EXERCISES

A

1. Reproduce the following table and complete it.

$m^{\text{R}}\theta$	0	$\frac{\pi}{6}$	?	$\frac{\pi}{3}$	$\frac{\pi}{2}$	?	?	$\frac{5\pi}{6}$	π	$\frac{7\pi}{6}$	?	?	$\frac{3\pi}{2}$	?
$m°\theta$	?	?	45	?	?	120	135	?	?	?	225	240	?	360
$\sin\theta$	?	?	?	?	?	?	?	?	?	?	?	?	?	?
$\cos\theta$	?	?	?	$\frac{1}{2}$	?	?	?	?	?	?	?	?	?	?

2. Find the degree measures of the angles whose radian measures are

a. -1; **b.** 10; **c.** $\frac{1}{10}$; **d.** 2; **e.** $-\frac{1}{2}$.

3. A wheel turns at 200 revolutions per minute (r.p.m.). Through how many radians does a spoke of the wheel turn in one hour? Through how many degrees?

In Exercises 4–12, θ is a central angle of a circle of radius r, s is the length of the arc subtended by θ, and A is the area of the sector determined by θ. Find the missing numbers.

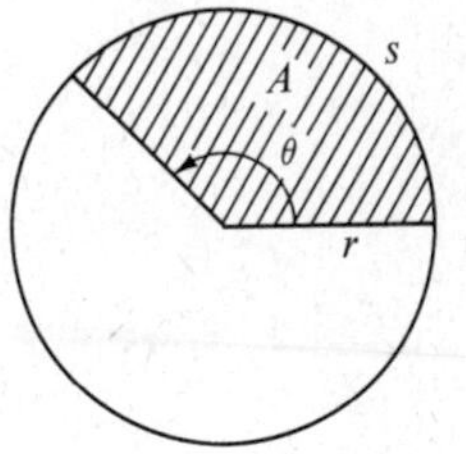

4. $r = 2,\ m^R\theta = \frac{\pi}{4},\ s = ?,\ A = ?$

5. $r = 4,\ m^\circ\theta = 135,\ s = ?,\ A = ?$

6. $r = 4,\ s = 3\pi,\ m^R\theta = ?,\ m^\circ\theta = ?,\ A = ?$

7. $r = \frac{1}{\pi},\ s = \frac{1}{2},\ m^R\theta = ?,\ m^\circ\theta = ?,\ A = ?$

8. $m^R\theta = \frac{\pi}{3},\ s = \pi,\ r = ?,\ A = ?$

9. $r = 1,\ s = 1,\ m^R\theta = ?,\ m^\circ\theta = ?,\ A = ?$

10. $m^\circ\theta = 150,\ s = 10\pi,\ r = ?,\ A = ?$

11. $m^\circ\theta = 30,\ A = 3\pi,\ r = ?,\ s = ?$

12. $A = 10,\ s = 5,\ m^R\theta = ?,\ m^\circ\theta = ?,\ r = ?$

■ Graphs and Identities

7–4 Graphs of sin and cos

If we graph the points $(x, \sin x)$ for the values of x and $\sin x$ given in the table on page 271 $\left(\text{using } \frac{\sqrt{2}}{2} \doteq 0.707 \text{ and } \frac{\sqrt{3}}{2} \doteq 0.866\right)$, we obtain the points shown in red in Figure 7–13. In Section 8–1 we shall show that sin is a differentiable function. Therefore its graph is an unbroken curve with no sharp corners. The smooth curve drawn through the red points is a fairly accurate sketch of the graph of $x \to \sin x$ for $0 \le x \le 2\pi$.

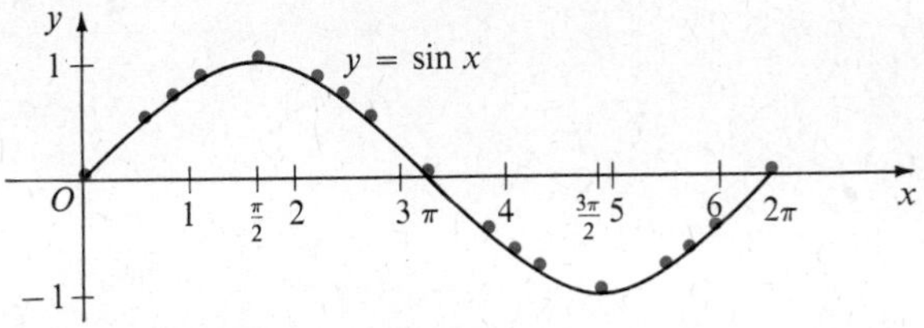

Figure 7–13

In a similar way (Figure 7–14), we can obtain a sketch of the graph of $x \to \cos x$ for $0 \leq x \leq 2\pi$.

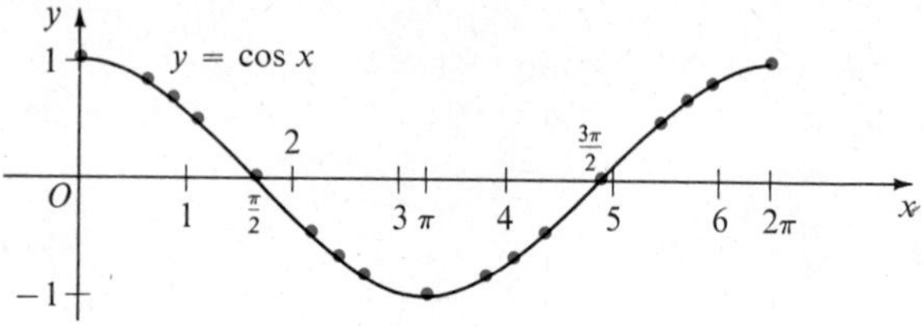

Figure 7–14

To obtain the graphs of $x \to \sin x$ and $x \to \cos x$ for values of x outside the interval $0 \leq x \leq 2\pi$, that is, $\{x: 0 \leq x \leq 2\pi\}$, we shall use the fact that sin and cos are *periodic*.

A function f is **periodic** if there is a number p, $p \neq 0$, such that for every x in its domain, $x + p$ and $x - p$ are in its domain, and

$$f(x + p) = f(x).$$

The number p is a **period** of f. We see that

$$f(x + 2p) = f((x + p) + p) = f(x + p) = f(x),$$

and indeed we can show (Exercises 26 and 27, page 287) that for every integer n and every x in the domain of f,

$$f(x + np) = f(x).$$

If there is a *least positive* number p that is a period of f, then p is called the **fundamental period** of f. Ordinarily, when we say that f has period p, we imply that p is the fundamental period of f.

If f has period p and, as shown in red in Figure 7–15, we have the part of the graph of f in the interval $0 \leq x < p$ (or in any such interval of length p), then we can construct the graph everywhere:

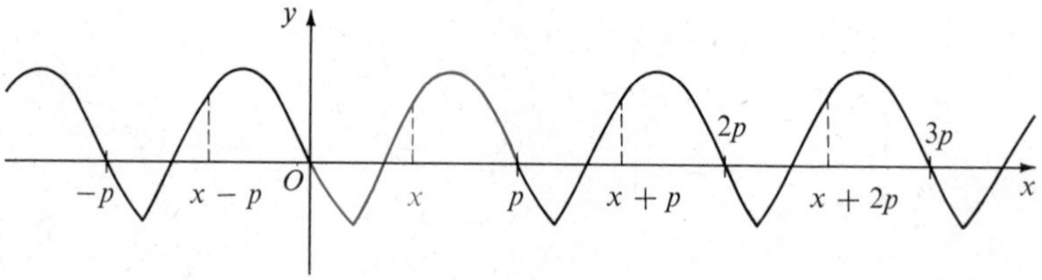

Figure 7–15

The part of the graph of $y = f(x)$ for $a \leq x < a + p$ is called a **cycle** of the graph; it is also called the graph of a cycle of the function f.

EXAMPLE 1. The function f has period 2, and in the interval $0 \leq x < 2$, $f(x) = x - 1$. Draw the graph of f in the interval $-3 \leq x \leq 7$.

Solution: The part of the graph of f for $0 \leq x < 2$ is a subset of the line $y = x - 1$, and is shown in red in the diagram below. The rest of the graph is obtained by moving this cycle rigidly to the right and to the left distances which are integral multiples of 2.

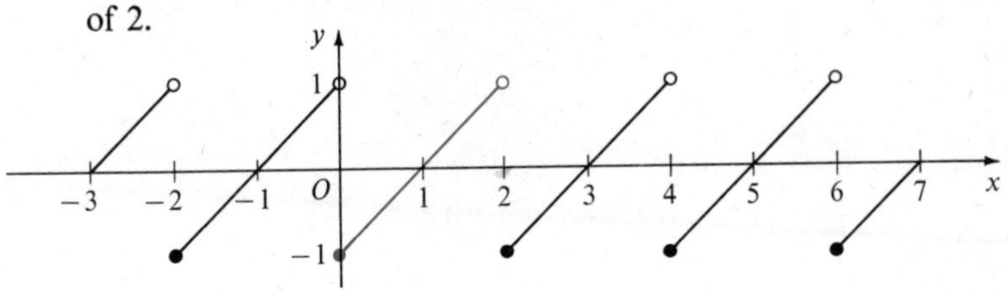

Since for every $x \in \mathcal{R}$, $\sin(x + 2\pi) = \sin x$ and $\cos(x + 2\pi) = \cos x$ (Theorem 3, page 273), we see that both sin and cos have 2π as a period. (This actually is their least positive, or fundamental, period. To see that sin, for example, has no period less than 2π, we have only to note that $\sin\frac{\pi}{2} = 1$, while for $0 < k < 2\pi$ we have $\sin\left(\frac{\pi}{2} + k\right) < 1$; since $\sin\left(\frac{\pi}{2} + k\right) \neq \sin\frac{\pi}{2}$, sin does not have k as a period.)

The graphs of sin and cos (see Figure 7–16) can therefore be constructed from Figures 7–13 and 7–14 by the method illustrated above:

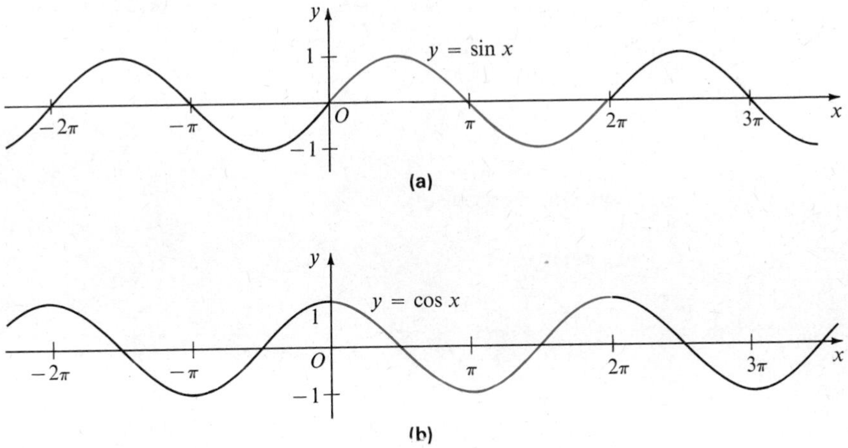

Figure 7–16

Let us determine the fundamental period p for the function $x \to \sin kx$ $(k > 0)$. For this function, the requirement $f(x + p) = f(x)$ becomes

$$\sin k(x + p) = \sin kx,$$

or

$$\sin (kx + kp) = \sin kx,$$

and this holds for all x if $kp = 2\pi$, but for no value of kp less than 2π. Therefore

$$p = \frac{2\pi}{k},$$

and this is the fundamental period for $\sin kx$. Likewise, the function $x \to \cos kx$ $(k > 0)$ has fundamental period $\dfrac{2\pi}{k}$.

EXAMPLE 2. Graph **(a)** $x \to \sin 3x$ and **(b)** $x \to \cos \dfrac{\pi}{4} x$.

Solution: **a.** The period is $\dfrac{2\pi}{3}$. As x increases from 0 to $\dfrac{2\pi}{3}$, $3x$ increases from 0 to 2π, and therefore $\sin 3x$ runs through a complete cycle of sin values. The diagram below includes the (dotted) graph of $x \to \sin x$ for comparison.

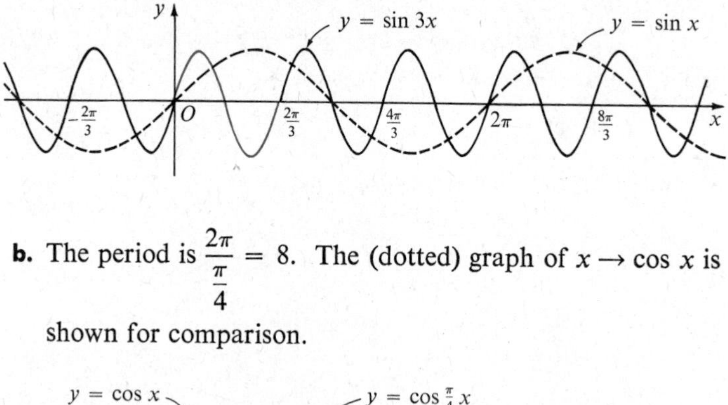

b. The period is $\dfrac{2\pi}{\frac{\pi}{4}} = 8$. The (dotted) graph of $x \to \cos x$ is shown for comparison.

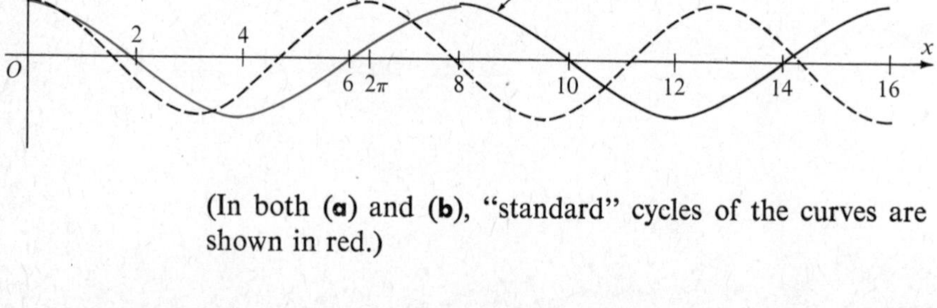

(In both **(a)** and **(b)**, "standard" cycles of the curves are shown in red.)

In functions of the form

$$x \to A \sin kx \quad \text{or} \quad x \to A \cos kx,$$

the number $|A|$ is called the **amplitude.** (In applications, A is usually positive.)

EXAMPLE 3. Graph the function $x \to 2 \cos \frac{\pi}{2} x$.

Solution: We first graph the function $x \to \cos \frac{\pi}{2} x$, whose amplitude is 1 and whose period is $\dfrac{2\pi}{\frac{\pi}{2}} = 4$ (dotted curve shown below). We can then obtain the required curve by (graphically) multiplying each ordinate by 2.

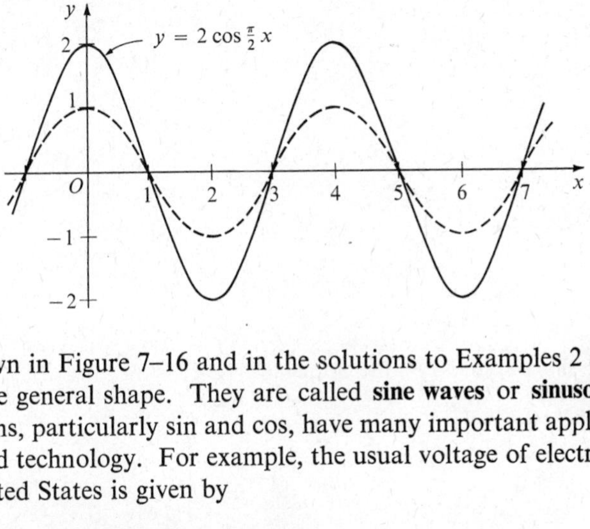

The graphs shown in Figure 7–16 and in the solutions to Examples 2 and 3 all have the same general shape. They are called **sine waves** or **sinusoids.**

Periodic functions, particularly sin and cos, have many important applications in science and technology. For example, the usual voltage of electrical circuits in the United States is given by

$$V = 115 \sin 120\pi t,$$

where t is time measured in seconds. Since

$$\sin 120\pi(t + \tfrac{1}{60}) = \sin (120\pi t + 2\pi) = \sin 120\pi t,$$

the period of the $t \to V$ function is $\frac{1}{60}$ second. Hence the voltage goes from a maximum of 115 volts to a minimum of -115 volts and back again to 115 volts in $\frac{1}{60}$ of a second, and we say that we have 60-cycle current. We shall consider some more applications later, after developing more analytic techniques.

ORAL EXERCISES

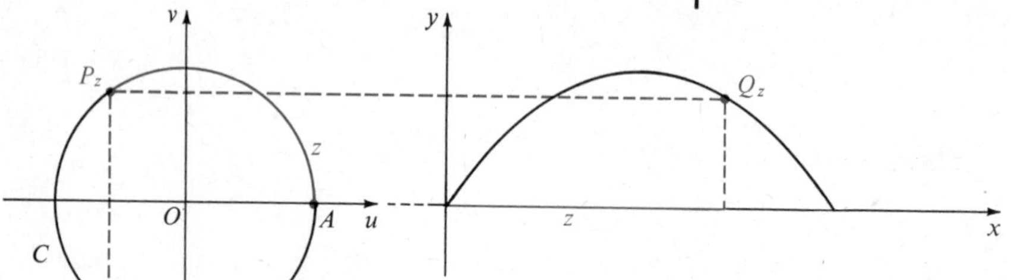

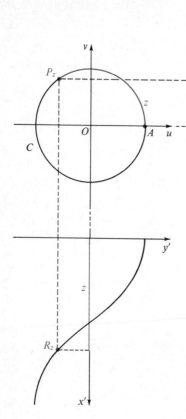

The figure shows three coordinate systems in a plane: a (u, v)-, an (x, y)-, and an (x', y')-system; the units of length are the same in all three. For any point P_z on $C: u^2 + v^2 = 1$, points Q_z and R_z are located as indicated.

Express in terms of z:

1. The (u, v)-coordinates of P_z.
2. The (x, y)-coordinates of Q_z.
3. The (x', y')-coordinates of R_z.
4. What is an (x, y)-equation of the curve traced out by Q_z as P_z traces out C?
5. What is an (x', y')-equation of the curve traced out by R_z as P_z traces out C?

Give the amplitude and (fundamental) period of each of the following functions:

6. $x \to 2 \cos x$
7. $x \to \cos 2x$
8. $x \to 2 \sin \pi x$
9. $x \to \pi \sin \pi x$
10. $x \to 3 \cos \dfrac{x}{2}$
11. $x \to \cos \dfrac{\pi x}{3}$

WRITTEN EXERCISES

In Exercises 1–8, find a function of the form $x \to A \sin kx$ having the given characteristics:

A

1. Amplitude 3, period 2π.
2. Amplitude $\frac{1}{2}$, period 2π.
3. Amplitude 2, period π.
4. Amplitude 4, period 4π.
5. Amplitude 2, period 3.
6. Amplitude $\frac{1}{2}$, period $\frac{1}{2}$.
7. Amplitude 10, period $\frac{1}{10}$.
8. Amplitude 10, period 100.

In Exercises 9–20, draw at least two complete cycles of the graph of the given function.

9. $x \to \sin 2x$

10. $x \to \cos 2x$

11. $x \to 3 \sin 2x$

12. $x \to 2 \cos 2x$

13. $x \to \cos \frac{x}{2}$

14. $x \to \sin \frac{x}{3}$

15. $x \to 3 \cos \frac{x}{2}$

16. $x \to 2 \sin \frac{x}{3}$

17. $x \to 2 \cos 2\pi x$

18. $x \to \frac{1}{2} \sin 3\pi x$

19. $x \to 10 \sin \frac{\pi x}{10}$

20. $x \to 3 \cos \frac{\pi x}{3}$

B **21.** The function f has period 2, and $f(x) = |x|$ if $-1 \le x \le 1$. Draw the graph of $x \to f(x)$ for $-3 \le x \le 7$.

22. The function f has period 1, and $f(x) = x$ if $0 \le x < 1$. Draw the graph of $x \to f(x)$ for $-1 \le x < 4$.

23. The function f is even (see page 273) and has period 2, and $f(x) = x$ if $0 \le x \le 1$. Draw the graph of $x \to f(x)$ for $-4 \le x \le 6$.

24. Prove that cos has no positive period less than 2π.

25. Prove that the function $x \to \cos kx$ $(k > 0)$ has fundamental period $\frac{2\pi}{k}$.

C **26.** Prove, using mathematical induction, that if f has period p, then $f(x + np) = f(x)$ for every natural number n.

27. Use Exercise 26 to prove that if f has period p, then $f(x + np) = f(x)$ for every integer n. [*Hint:* For $n < 0$, let $n = -m$. Then use the fact that $x = x - mp + mp = (x + np) + mp$.]

7–5 Some Important Identities

The identities in the next theorem are called the sum and difference formulas for sin and cos.

Theorem 4.

If x and y are real numbers, then

$$\sin(x + y) = \sin x \cos y + \cos x \sin y \quad (1)$$

$$\sin(x - y) = \sin x \cos y - \cos x \sin y \quad (2)$$

$$\cos(x + y) = \cos x \cos y - \sin x \sin y \quad (3)$$

$$\cos(x - y) = \cos x \cos y + \sin x \sin y \quad (4)$$

For example, since we know the values of sin and cos for $x = \frac{\pi}{4}$ and $y = \frac{\pi}{3}$ (Table 1, page 271), we find, using (1) and (3), that

$$\sin\frac{7\pi}{12} = \sin\left(\frac{\pi}{4} + \frac{\pi}{3}\right) = \sin\frac{\pi}{4}\cos\frac{\pi}{3} + \cos\frac{\pi}{4}\sin\frac{\pi}{3}$$
$$= \frac{\sqrt{2}}{2}\cdot\frac{1}{2} + \frac{\sqrt{2}}{2}\cdot\frac{\sqrt{3}}{2} = \frac{1}{4}(\sqrt{2} + \sqrt{6}) \doteq 0.9659;$$
$$\cos\frac{7\pi}{12} = \cos\left(\frac{\pi}{4} + \frac{\pi}{3}\right) = \cos\frac{\pi}{4}\cos\frac{\pi}{3} - \sin\frac{\pi}{4}\sin\frac{\pi}{3}$$
$$= \frac{\sqrt{2}}{2}\cdot\frac{1}{2} - \frac{\sqrt{2}}{2}\cdot\frac{\sqrt{3}}{2} = \frac{1}{4}(\sqrt{2} - \sqrt{6}) \doteq -0.2588.$$

In establishing Theorem 4, it is convenient to prove (3) first: Locate the points A, P_x, P_{x+y}, and P_{-y} on C: $u^2 + v^2 = 1$. (See Figure 7–17.) By the rule (page 265) for locating P_{x+y}, an arc from A to P_{x+y} has length $|x + y|$. Moreover, the corresponding arc of C from P_{-y} to P_x has length $|x - (-y)|$, or $|x + y|$. Because congruent arcs of a circle subtend congruent chords, we have

$$\text{length } \overline{AP_{x+y}} = \text{length } \overline{P_{-y}P_x}. \qquad (*)$$

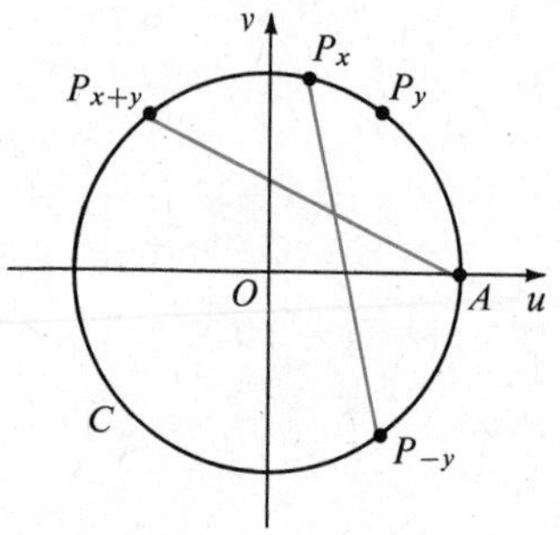

Figure 7–17

The coordinates of the points appearing in (*) are

A: (1, 0) $\qquad P_{x+y}$: $(\cos(x + y), \sin(x + y))$

P_x: $(\cos x, \sin x)$ $\qquad P_{-y}$: $(\cos(-y), \sin(-y)) = (\cos y, -\sin y)$

If we use the distance formula, (*) becomes, after squaring,

$$[\cos(x + y) - 1]^2 + [\sin(x + y) - 0]^2$$
$$= [\cos x - \cos y]^2 + [\sin x + \sin y]^2.$$

When we expand the squares of the binomials and replace combinations of the form $\sin^2 z + \cos^2 z$ by 1, we obtain

$$-2\cos(x + y) + 2 = 2 - 2\cos x\cos y + 2\sin x\sin y,$$

or

$$\cos(x + y) = \cos x\cos y - \sin x\sin y. \qquad (3)$$

Applying formula (3) to the numbers x and $-y$, we have

$$\cos(x + (-y)) = \cos x\cos(-y) - \sin x\sin(-y)$$
$$= \cos x\cos y - \sin x\cdot(-\sin y).$$

From this we obtain

$$\cos (x - y) = \cos x \cos y + \sin x \sin y. \tag{4}$$

Formulas (1) and (2) follow from (3) and (4) with the help of the following result:

Corollary.

For any real number z,

$$\cos \left(\frac{\pi}{2} - z\right) = \sin z, \tag{5}$$

$$\sin \left(\frac{\pi}{2} - z\right) = \cos z. \tag{6}$$

Proof

To prove (5), we use (4) with $x = \frac{\pi}{2}$ and $y = z$:

$$\begin{aligned}\cos \left(\frac{\pi}{2} - z\right) &= \cos \frac{\pi}{2} \cos z + \sin \frac{\pi}{2} \sin z \\ &= 0 \cdot \cos z + 1 \cdot \sin z = \sin z.\end{aligned}$$

We obtain (6) by replacing z by $\frac{\pi}{2} - z$ in (5):

$$\cos \left(\frac{\pi}{2} - \left(\frac{\pi}{2} - z\right)\right) = \sin \left(\frac{\pi}{2} - z\right),$$

or

$$\cos z = \sin \left(\frac{\pi}{2} - z\right).$$

[In geometry, two angles, α and β, are **complementary** if their sum is a right angle. If the *radian* measure of α is z, then the *radian* measure of β is $\frac{\pi}{2} - z$. By the Corollary above, $\sin \alpha = \cos \beta$ (*trigonometric* functions). It is for this reason that sine and cosine are called **cofunctions.**]

We can now prove (1) of Theorem 4:

$$\begin{aligned}\sin (x + y) &= \cos \left(\frac{\pi}{2} - (x + y)\right) = \cos \left(\left(\frac{\pi}{2} - x\right) - y\right) \\ &= \cos \left(\frac{\pi}{2} - x\right) \cos y + \sin \left(\frac{\pi}{2} - x\right) \sin y \\ &= \sin x \cos y + \cos x \sin y.\end{aligned}$$

The proof of (2) is left as an exercise (Exercise 18, page 292).

EXAMPLE 1. Let x be a second-quadrant number with $\sin x = \frac{3}{5}$. Find (**a**) $\sin 2x$; (**b**) $\cos 2x$; (**c**) the quadrant of $2x$.

Solution: Since x is a second-quadrant number, $\cos x < 0$. Therefore

$$\cos x = -\sqrt{1 - \sin^2 x} = -\sqrt{1 - (\tfrac{3}{5})^2} = -\sqrt{\tfrac{16}{25}} = -\tfrac{4}{5}.$$

a. $\sin 2x = \sin (x + x) = \sin x \cos x + \cos x \sin x$
$= 2 \sin x \cos x = 2 \cdot \frac{3}{5} \cdot (-\frac{4}{5}) = -\frac{24}{25}.$

b. $\cos 2x = \cos (x + x) = \cos x \cos x - \sin x \sin x$
$= \cos^2 x - \sin^2 x = (-\frac{4}{5})^2 - (\frac{3}{5})^2 = \frac{7}{25}.$

c. Since $\sin 2x < 0$ and $\cos 2x > 0$, $2x$ is a fourth-quadrant number.

In the process of solving Example 1, we derived two important identities (called, using trigonometric terminology, *double-angle formulas*):

$$\mathbf{\sin 2x = 2 \sin x \cos x} \qquad (7)$$

$$\mathbf{\cos 2x = \cos^2 x - \sin^2 x} \qquad (8)$$

$$\mathbf{= 1 - 2 \sin^2 x} \qquad (8')$$

$$\mathbf{= 2 \cos^2 x - 1} \qquad (8'')$$

(Forms (8′) and (8″) follow from (8) and the formula $\sin^2 x + \cos^2 x = 1$.)

Many other identities can be derived from those already proved. For example, a (so-called) *half-angle formula* for $\sin \frac{z}{2}$ can be obtained from (8′) by letting $x = \frac{z}{2}$:

$$\cos \left(2 \cdot \frac{z}{2}\right) = \cos z = 1 - 2 \sin^2 \frac{z}{2}.$$

Therefore

$$\sin^2 \frac{z}{2} = \frac{1 - \cos z}{2},$$

or

$$\mathbf{\sin \frac{z}{2} = \pm \sqrt{\frac{1 - \cos z}{2}}}.$$

The quadrant of $\frac{z}{2}$ must be known in order to decide which sign to use. (It is not enough to know the quadrant of z. For example, $z_1 = \frac{5\pi}{4}$ and $z_2 = -\frac{3\pi}{4}$ are both third-quadrant numbers; but $\frac{z_1}{2}$ is a second-quadrant number and $\frac{z_2}{2}$ is a fourth-quadrant number, so that $\sin \frac{z_1}{2}$ is positive while $\sin \frac{z_2}{2}$ is negative.)

Formula (8″) can be used similarly to show that

$$\cos \frac{z}{2} = \pm \sqrt{\frac{1 + \cos z}{2}}.$$

EXAMPLE 2. Find $\sin \frac{z}{2}$ if **(a)** $z = \frac{7\pi}{6}$ and **(b)** $z = -\frac{5\pi}{6}$.

Solution: We have $\cos \frac{7\pi}{6} = -\frac{\sqrt{3}}{2}$ and $\cos\left(-\frac{5\pi}{6}\right) = -\frac{\sqrt{3}}{2}$.

a. $\sin \frac{z}{2} = \sin \frac{7\pi}{12} = +\sqrt{\frac{1 - \left(-\frac{\sqrt{3}}{2}\right)}{2}} = \frac{1}{2}\sqrt{2 + \sqrt{3}}.$

b. $\sin \frac{z}{2} = \sin\left(-\frac{5\pi}{12}\right) = -\sqrt{\frac{1 - \left(-\frac{\sqrt{3}}{2}\right)}{2}}$

$= -\frac{1}{2}\sqrt{2 + \sqrt{3}}.$

WRITTEN EXERCISES

Formulas (5) and (6) of the corollary on page 289 are examples of **reduction formulas.** In Exercises 1–10, determine whether the given expression is equal to sin x, −sin x, cos x, or −cos x to obtain more reduction formulas.

A

1. $\sin\left(\frac{\pi}{2} + x\right)$

2. $\cos\left(\frac{\pi}{2} + x\right)$

3. $\sin(\pi + x)$

4. $\cos(\pi + x)$

5. $\sin(\pi - x)$

6. $\cos(\pi - x)$

7. $\sin\left(\frac{3\pi}{2} + x\right)$

8. $\cos\left(\frac{3\pi}{2} + x\right)$

9. $\sin\left(\frac{3\pi}{2} - x\right)$

10. $\cos\left(\frac{3\pi}{2} - x\right)$

11. Find $\sin \frac{\pi}{12}$ and $\sin \frac{5\pi}{12}$.

12. Find $\cos \frac{\pi}{12}$ and $\cos \frac{5\pi}{12}$.

13. There are six integral multiples of $\frac{\pi}{12}$, other than $\frac{\pi}{12}$ and $\frac{5\pi}{12}$, between 0 and 2π which do not appear in Table 1, page 271. Find the sine and cosine of these by reducing each to plus or minus a function of $\frac{\pi}{12}$ or $\frac{5\pi}{12}$.

In Exercises 14–17, find (a) $\sin 2x$, (b) $\cos 2x$, (c) $\sin \frac{x}{2}$, and (d) $\cos \frac{x}{2}$.

14. $\sin x = \frac{12}{13}, 0 < x < \frac{\pi}{2}$

15. $\cos x = -\frac{4}{5}, \frac{\pi}{2} < x < \pi$

16. $\cos x = \frac{1}{10}, -\frac{\pi}{2} < x < 0$

17. $\sin x = -\frac{2}{3}, -\pi < x < -\frac{\pi}{2}$

B

18. Prove formula (2) of Theorem 4, page 287.

19. Prove that $\cos \frac{z}{2} = \pm\sqrt{\frac{1 + \cos z}{2}}$.

20. Express $\sin 3x$ as a polynomial in $\sin x$.
[*Hint:* $\sin 3x = \sin (2x + x)$; use formulas (1), (7), and (8)].

21. Express $\cos 3x$ as a polynomial in $\cos x$.

22. Show that $\sin x \sin y = \frac{1}{2}[\cos (x - y) - \cos (x + y)]$.
(*Hint:* Reduce the right-hand side of the equation to the left.)

C

23. Find formulas similar to the one in Exercise 22 for **(a)** $\cos x \cos y$ and **(b)** $\sin x \cos y$.

24. In the formula of Exercise 22, let $x - y = a$ and $x + y = b$. Solve for x and y to obtain $x = \frac{a + b}{2}$ and $y = -\frac{a - b}{2}$. Then show that

$$\cos a - \cos b = -2 \sin \frac{a + b}{2} \sin \frac{a - b}{2}.$$

25. Obtain formulas similar to the one in Exercise 24 for **(a)** $\sin a + \sin b$, **(b)** $\sin a - \sin b$, and **(c)** $\cos a + \cos b$.

26. Near the beginning of this section we found that $\sin \frac{7\pi}{12} = \sin \left(\frac{\pi}{4} + \frac{\pi}{3}\right) = \frac{1}{4}(\sqrt{2} + \sqrt{6})$, and in Example 2(a) we found that $\sin \frac{7\pi}{12} = \sin \left(\frac{1}{2} \cdot \frac{7\pi}{6}\right) = \frac{1}{2}\sqrt{2 + \sqrt{3}}$. Explain the apparent discrepancy.

27. Obtain formulas (5) and (6) on page 289 directly from a consideration of Figure 7–4(d), page 268.

7–6 The General Sine Wave

To graph the function

$$x \to \sin\left(x - \frac{\pi}{3}\right),$$

we note that as x increases from $\frac{\pi}{3}$ to $\frac{7\pi}{3}$, $x - \frac{\pi}{3}$ increases from 0 to 2π. Therefore a "standard" cycle of $y = \sin\left(x - \frac{\pi}{3}\right)$ occurs in the interval $\frac{\pi}{3} \le x \le \frac{7\pi}{3}$. Notice from Figure 7–18 that the graph of $y = \sin\left(x - \frac{\pi}{3}\right)$ can be obtained by shifting, or *translating*, the graph of $y = \sin x$ to the *right* $\frac{\pi}{3}$ units.

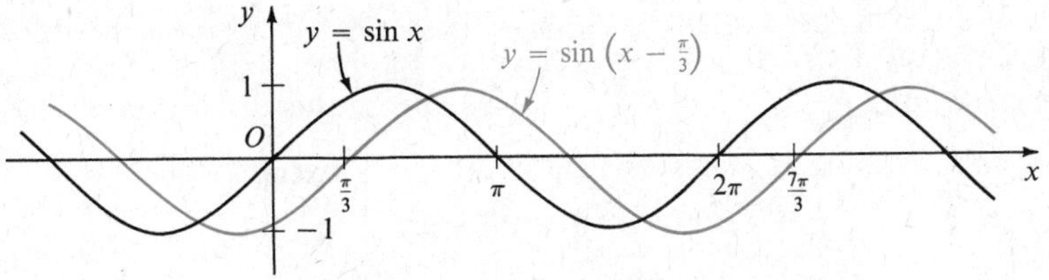

Figure 7–18

In the case of the function

$$x \to \sin\left(x + \frac{\pi}{3}\right),$$

a "standard" cycle occurs in the interval $-\frac{\pi}{3} \le x \le \frac{5\pi}{3}$. The graph of $y = \sin\left(x + \frac{\pi}{3}\right)$ is the same as that of $y = \sin x$ except that it is translated $\frac{\pi}{3}$ units to the *left*. (See Figure 7–19.)

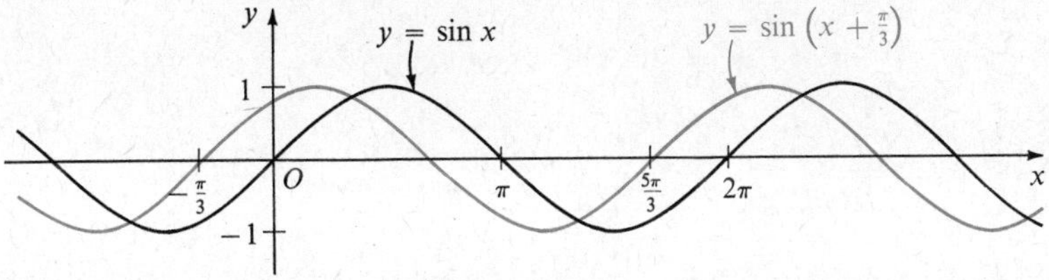

Figure 7–19

The situations considered on page 293 can be generalized: Let f be any function, and consider the curves

$$G: y = f(x) \qquad \text{and} \qquad H: y = f(x - d),$$

where d is a positive number. It is clear that if $P(a, b)$ is any point, then $Q(a + d, b)$ is the point d units to the right of P [Figure 7–20(a)]. Thus if

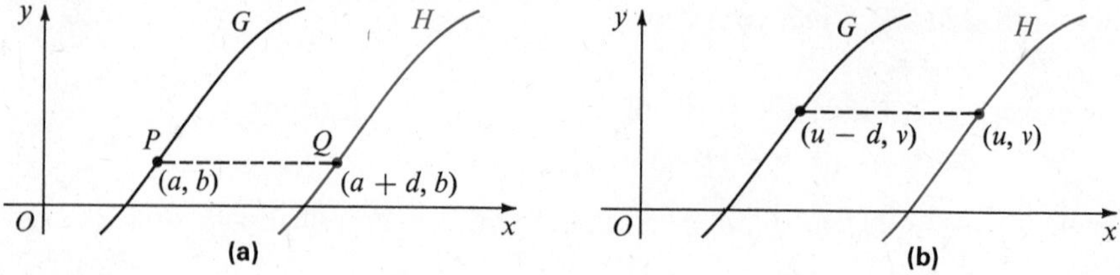

Figure 7–20

$P(a, b)$ is any point on G, so that $b = f(a)$, then $b = f((a + d) - d)$, and therefore $Q(a + d, b)$ is on H. Conversely, if (u, v) is any point on H [Figure 7–20(b)], then $v = f(u - d)$, and therefore $(u - d, v)$ is on G. But (u, v) is d units to the right of $(u - d, v)$. From this discussion we see that

H: $y = f(x - d)$ can be obtained by translating
G: $y = f(x)$ to the right d units.

If the number d is *negative*, then we translate $|d|$ units to the *left*.

EXAMPLE 1. Graph the function $g: x \to 2 \cos\left(\frac{\pi}{2} x - \frac{\pi}{4}\right)$.

Solution: We have $g(x) = 2 \cos \frac{\pi}{2} (x - \frac{1}{2})$. This suggests that we consider the function $f: x \to 2 \cos \frac{\pi}{2} x$. Since $f(x - \frac{1}{2}) = 2 \cos \frac{\pi}{2} (x - \frac{1}{2}) = g(x)$, we can obtain the graph of g by translating the graph of f to the right $\frac{1}{2}$ unit. (The graph of f appears on page 285 and is reproduced in black below.)

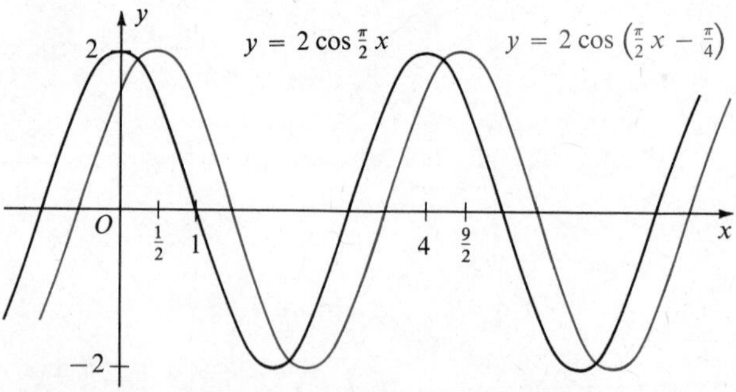

The function $g: x \rightarrow 2 \cos\left(\frac{\pi}{2}x - \frac{\pi}{4}\right)$ has period $\frac{2\pi}{\frac{\pi}{2}} = 4$, and it has amplitude 2. The number $-\frac{\pi}{4}$ is called the *initial phase.*

The graph of a function of either of the types

$$x \rightarrow A \sin(kx - h)$$

and

$$x \rightarrow A \cos(kx - h),$$

where $A > 0$ and $k > 0$, is called a **sine wave** or **sinusoid.** These functions and their graphs have (fundamental) **period** $\frac{2\pi}{k}$, **amplitude** A, **phase** $kx - h$, and **initial phase** $-h$. Figure 7–21 shows how the numbers A, k, and h determine the graph of $x \rightarrow A \sin(kx - h)$.

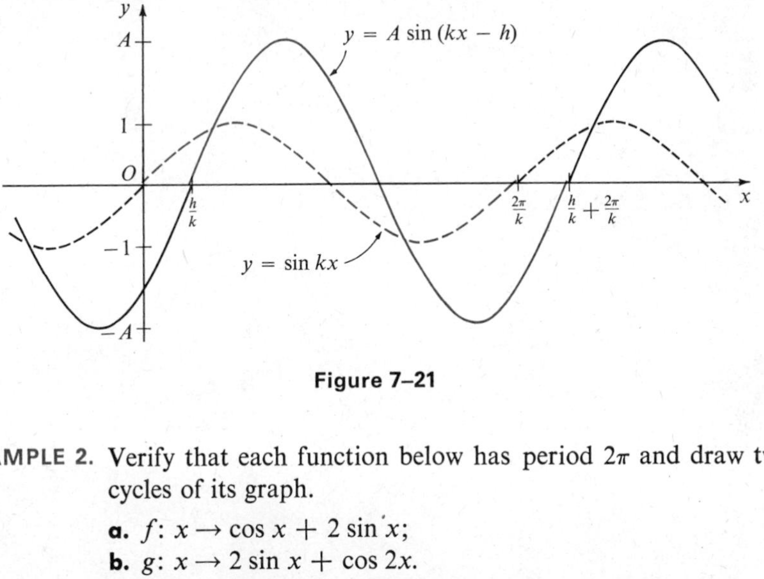

Figure 7–21

EXAMPLE 2. Verify that each function below has period 2π and draw two cycles of its graph.

a. $f: x \rightarrow \cos x + 2 \sin x$;

b. $g: x \rightarrow 2 \sin x + \cos 2x$.

Solution: **a.** $f(x + 2\pi) = \cos(x + 2\pi) + 2 \sin(x + 2\pi)$
$= \cos x + 2 \sin x = f(x)$.

To graph f, we first graph

$$f_1: x \rightarrow \cos x \quad \text{and} \quad f_2: x \rightarrow 2 \sin x.$$

Since $f(x) = f_1(x) + f_2(x)$, we can obtain the graph of f by adding ordinates, as shown on page 296.

(*Solution continued*)

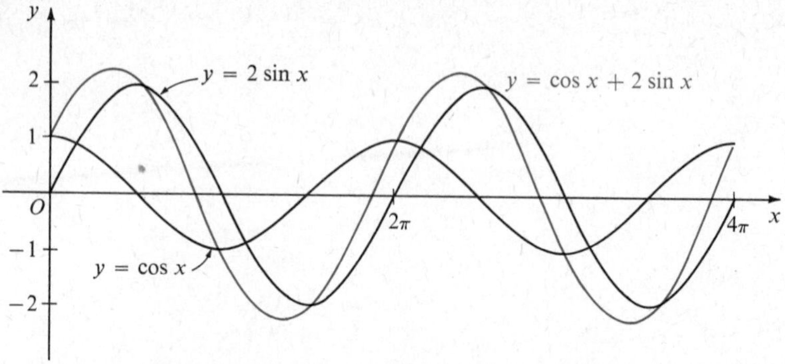

b. $g(x + 2\pi) = 2 \sin (x + 2\pi) + \cos 2(x + 2\pi)$
$= 2 \sin x + \cos (2x + 4\pi)$
$= 2 \sin x + \cos 2x = g(x).$

We first graph

$$g_1: x \to 2 \sin x \qquad \text{and} \qquad g_2: x \to \cos 2x,$$

and then we add ordinates. The graph of g is shown in red below.

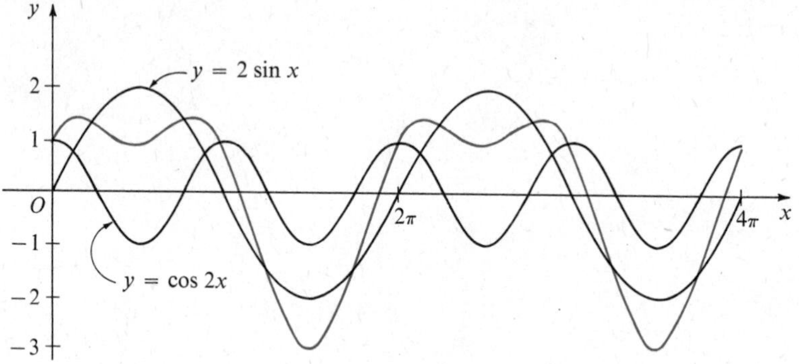

We shall show that the graph of

$$y = f(x) = 1 \cdot \cos x + 2 \cdot \sin x$$

given in Example 2(a) is a sine wave (just as it appears to be). In the equation above, we multiply and divide by the square root of the sum of the squares of the coefficients of sin x and cos x, $\sqrt{2^2 + 1^2} = \sqrt{5}$, to obtain

$$f(x) = \sqrt{5}\left[\frac{1}{\sqrt{5}} \cos x + \frac{2}{\sqrt{5}} \sin x\right]. \qquad (*)$$

Since $\left(\frac{2}{\sqrt{5}}\right)^2 + \left(\frac{1}{\sqrt{5}}\right)^2 = 1$, the point $\left(\frac{2}{\sqrt{5}}, \frac{1}{\sqrt{5}}\right)$ is on the unit circle C, and therefore is the point P_h for some number h. That is,

$$\cos h = \frac{2}{\sqrt{5}} \quad \text{and} \quad \sin h = \frac{1}{\sqrt{5}}.$$

We may therefore rewrite (*) as

$$f(x) = \sqrt{5}\,[\sin h \cos x + \cos h \sin x].$$

Using identity (1) of Theorem 4, page 287, we have

$$f(x) = \sqrt{5}\sin(h + x) = \sqrt{5}\sin(x + h),$$

so the graph of f is a sine wave of amplitude $\sqrt{5}$.

There are tables which enable us to approximate h numerically. Since $\sin h = \frac{1}{\sqrt{5}} \doteq 0.4472$, such a table gives $h \doteq 0.464$. Therefore, since $\sqrt{5} \doteq 2.236$,

$$f(x) \doteq 2.236 \sin(x + 0.464),$$

or, using $\sin z = \cos\left(z - \frac{\pi}{2}\right)$ with $z = x + 0.464$,

$$f(x) \doteq 2.236 \cos(x - 1.107).$$

The method used above can be adapted (Exercises 16 and 17, page 298) to show that the sum of any two sine-wave functions *having equal periods* is again a sine-wave function. This is not true if the periods are different, as Example 2(b) shows.

ORAL EXERCISES

For each of the following, state (a) the period, (b) the amplitude, (c) the phase, and (d) the initial phase.

1. $x \to 2\sin(x - 1)$

2. $x \to \cos\left(2x - \frac{\pi}{2}\right)$

3. $x \to \cos 2(x - 1)$

4. $x \to 3\sin \pi(x + 1)$

5. $x \to \frac{1}{2}\sin 2\pi x$

6. $x \to 4\cos(4x + 4)$

7. Explain why the graph of $y = \cos x$ is a sine wave.

WRITTEN EXERCISES

In Exercises 1–10, draw at least two cycles of the graph of f.

A

1. $f: x \to \sin\left(x - \frac{\pi}{4}\right)$
2. $f: x \to \cos\left(x + \frac{\pi}{4}\right)$
3. $f: x \to \cos(2x - 1)$
4. $f: x \to \sin\left(2x - \frac{\pi}{3}\right)$
5. $f: x \to 2\sin\left(\pi x + \frac{\pi}{3}\right)$
6. $f: x \to 2\cos \pi(x - 1)$
7. $f: x \to \sin x + \sin 2x$
8. $f: x \to \cos x + \cos 2x$
9. $f: x \to \frac{1}{2}\sin x + \cos 2x$
10. $f: x \to 2\cos x + \sin 2x$

In Exercises 11–14, (a) put each equation into one of the forms $y = A \sin (kx - h)$ or $y = A \cos (kx - h)$ and (b) draw at least two cycles of the graph.

B

11. $y = \sin x + \cos x$
12. $y = \sin x - \cos x$
13. $y = \sqrt{3}\sin x - \cos x$
14. $y = \sin x + \sqrt{3}\cos x$

C

15. Show that the equation

$$y = A \sin (kx - h) \tag{1}$$

can be put into the form

$$y = B \sin kx + C \cos kx. \tag{2}$$

16. Show that the equation

$$y = B \sin kx + C \cos kx \tag{2}$$

can be put into the form

$$y = A \sin (kx - h). \tag{1}$$

Hint: Begin by multiplying and dividing the right-hand side of (2) by $A = \sqrt{B^2 + C^2}$. Observe that the point $\left(\frac{B}{A}, -\frac{C}{A}\right)$ is on $u^2 + v^2 = 1$, so that there is a number h such that P_h is this point. Then

$$\sin h = -\frac{C}{A} \quad \text{and} \quad \cos h = \frac{B}{A}.$$

17. Show that the equation

$$y = A_1 \sin (kx - h_1) + A_2 \sin (kx - h_2)$$

can be put into form (2) of Exercise 16. (Since it can then be put into form (1), this shows that the sum of any two sine-wave functions having the same period is again a sine-wave function.)

CHAPTER SUMMARY

1. To each real number x we make correspond a unique point P_x on the unit circle C: $u^2 + v^2 = 1$, as follows: Starting from the point $A(1, 0)$, measure $|x|$ units along C, counterclockwise if $x > 0$, clockwise if $x < 0$; the point reached is P_x.

2. The **circular functions sine** and **cosine,** abbreviated sin and cos, respectively, are defined by the formulas

$$\sin x = \text{ordinate of } P_x,$$
$$\cos x = \text{abscissa of } P_x.$$

3. For every real number x, $\sin^2 x + \cos^2 x = 1$.

4. The function sin is **odd,** cos is **even.** In symbols,

$$\sin(-x) = -\sin x, \quad \cos(-x) = \cos x.$$

5. The **trigonometric sine** and **cosine** of an angle θ may be defined by

$$\sin \theta = \sin m^{R}\theta \quad \text{and} \quad \cos \theta = \cos m^{R}\theta,$$

where $m^{R}\theta$ is the **radian measure** of θ and the *sin* and *cos* appearing on the right-hand sides of the equations are *circular* functions.

6. The functions sin and cos are **periodic** and have **(fundamental) period** 2π. That is, 2π is the least positive value of p such that

$$\sin(x + p) = \sin x \quad \text{and} \quad \cos(x + p) = \cos x$$

for all $x \in \mathcal{R}$. For any integer n and all $x \in \mathcal{R}$,

$$\sin(x + 2\pi n) = \sin x \quad \text{and} \quad \cos(x + 2\pi n) = \cos x.$$

7. The sum and difference formulas for sin and cos are

$$\sin(x \pm y) = \sin x \cos y \pm \cos x \sin y,$$
$$\cos(x \pm y) = \cos x \cos y \mp \sin x \sin y.$$

Many other identities can be derived from these. For example:

$$\sin 2x = 2 \sin x \cos x \quad \text{or} \quad \cos 2x = \cos^2 x - \sin^2 x.$$

8. Graphs of functions of the form

$$x \to A \sin(kx - h) \quad \text{or} \quad x \to A \cos(kx - h),$$

where $A > 0$ and $k > 0$, are called **sine waves** or **sinusoids.** These functions and their graphs have **(fundamental) period** $\frac{2\pi}{k}$, **amplitude** A, **phase** $kx - h$, and **initial phase** $-h$.

CHAPTER TEST

7–1 **1.** For a certain number x, $-\frac{\pi}{2} < x < 0$, the point P_x on the unit circle C has abscissa $\frac{4}{5}$. Find **(a)** the ordinate of P_x and **(b)** the coordinates of $P_{x-\frac{\pi}{2}}$.

7–2 **2.** Given that x is a third-quadrant number with $\sin x = -\frac{5}{13}$, find **(a)** $\cos x$, **(b)** $\sin\left(x+\frac{\pi}{2}\right)$, **(c)** $\cos\left(x+\frac{\pi}{2}\right)$, **(d)** $\sin(x+\pi)$, and **(e)** $\sin(x + 20\pi)$.

7–3 **3.** In a circle of radius 2, θ is a central angle, s is the length of the arc subtended by θ, and A is the area of the sector determined by θ.

a. If $m°\theta = 120$, find s and A.
b. If $A = 6$, find $m^R\theta$ and s.

7–4 **4.** Find an equation of a sine wave having **(a)** amplitude 3 and period 1, **(b)** amplitude 2 and period $\frac{\pi}{2}$.

5. Draw two complete cycles of the graph of $f\colon x \to 2\cos \pi x$.

7–5 **6.** If $\cos x = -\frac{3}{5}$ and $\pi < x < 2\pi$, find $\sin 2x$, $\cos 2x$, $\sin\frac{x}{2}$, and $\cos\frac{x}{2}$.

7–6 **7.** The graph of $f\colon x \to 2\cos \pi x + \sin \pi x$ is a sinusoid.

a. Draw two cycles of the graph.
b. Find its amplitude.

RECOMMENDED READINGS

Commission on Mathematics, *Appendices to the Report of the Commission on Mathematics* (New York: College Entrance Examination Board, 1959).

TROYER, ROBERT, *Rotations, Angles, and Trigonometry*, The Mathematics Teacher, Vol. 61, No. 2 (February, 1968), pp. 123–129.

WOOTON, WILLIAM, BECKENBACH, EDWIN F., and DOLCIANI, MARY P., *Modern Trigonometry* (Boston: Houghton Mifflin Company, 1966).

Socio-biomathematics

Throughout recorded history, mathematics has been applied with remarkable success in the physical sciences. We are now witnessing the development of exciting, promising, and already significantly productive applications of mathematics in the social and biological sciences as well.

The possibilities of medical analysis have been vastly extended by the coming of the computer age, and the medical and communication aspects of space travel have made new demands and opened new areas of investigation. Increasingly, these and other current developments are forcing social and life scientists into mathematics classrooms and are enticing mathematicians into scientific laboratories and libraries, thus creating a new breed of scientists, the socio-biomathematicians.

Probability and *statistics* have, of course, been applied for many years in the life and social sciences. *Linear programming* and the *theory of games*, on the other hand, were not developed until the middle third of the present century. Originally created to solve economic problems, these new fields are today widely applied to scientific management in government and industry.

Linear programming is concerned with determining extrema of linear expressions under linear-inequality constraints — for example, finding the minimum of the expression $3x + 2y$ under the constraints $x \geq 0$, $y \geq 0$, $y \geq 5 - x$, and $y \geq 7 - 2x$.

The theory of games, which deals with situations in which there are opposing interests, provides mathematical methods for solving problems such as the following: Suppose it is agreed that Tom must pay John *one* of the numbers of dollars shown in the matrix at the right. Tom chooses the row and *at the same time* John chooses the column. Tom naturally would like to keep the amount low, while John would like to make it high. How should each decide what choice to make?

$$\begin{array}{cc} & \text{John} \\ \text{Tom} & \begin{bmatrix} 0 & 2 \\ 3 & 1 \end{bmatrix} \end{array}$$

Mathematical models — for example, models of traffic flow or weather patterns — based on past observations are analyzed by computers to bring about improvements or to predict future happenings. Similarly, models of complex biological entities such as the human respiratory system are used in medical research — for instance, in studying adaptability for long periods of time to the unfamiliar conditions of space travel.

Combinatorial mathematics is employed, for example, in the microbiological study of the genetic code; and one of its branches, *graph theory*, is extensively applied to transportation problems and the study of the communication process of the human nervous system.

Differential equations, such as the equation of natural growth or decay,

$$\frac{dy}{dt} = ky,$$

(see Section 6–6) occur frequently in the life and social sciences.

Let us now consider a slightly more complicated mathematical situation involving an ecological process, that is, a process concerning the interrelationship between living organisms and their environment. Suppose that there are r rabbits in a certain locality at a certain time and that the rabbit population is happily growing in accordance with the differential equation

$$\frac{dr}{dt} = kr,$$

with $k > 0$, when suddenly the environment is altered by the invasion of a pack of f predator foxes! The foxes take up permanent residence, and $\frac{dr}{dt}$ is changed as a result of the fact that a number of rabbits are killed by the foxes. It seems safe to assume that this number is proportional to the product rf of the number of rabbits and the number of foxes, so that now

$$\frac{dr}{dt} = kr - lrf, \tag{A}$$

with $l > 0$. If there were no rabbits to feed on, then the fox population would die out,

$$\frac{df}{dt} = -mf,$$

with $m > 0$; but the number of kills helps the fox population grow, so that actually

$$\frac{df}{dt} = -mf + nrf, \tag{B}$$

with $n > 0$.

We can now see how the ecological pattern will fluctuate. By equation (B), we have $\frac{df}{dt} > 0$ as long as $r > \frac{m}{n}$, so that the number of foxes increases. By equation (A), however, as soon as f becomes greater than $\frac{k}{l}$, we have $\frac{dr}{dt} < 0$, and the number of rabbits decreases. As a result, we see from equation (B) that the rate of increase of the fox population is slowed until, when r becomes less than $\frac{m}{n}$, we have $\frac{df}{dt} < 0$, and the fox population actually begins to decrease. Continuing, we see that, unless the rabbit and fox populations happen to be $\frac{m}{n}$ and $\frac{k}{l}$, respectively, each of the two populations alternately increases and decreases. One way in which this might occur is illustrated in the figure at the right, in which nature repeats periodically. It might happen, however, that the graph of the two populations would either spiral in toward a limiting oval or toward the point $\left(\frac{m}{n}, \frac{k}{l}\right)$, as illustrated, or out toward a

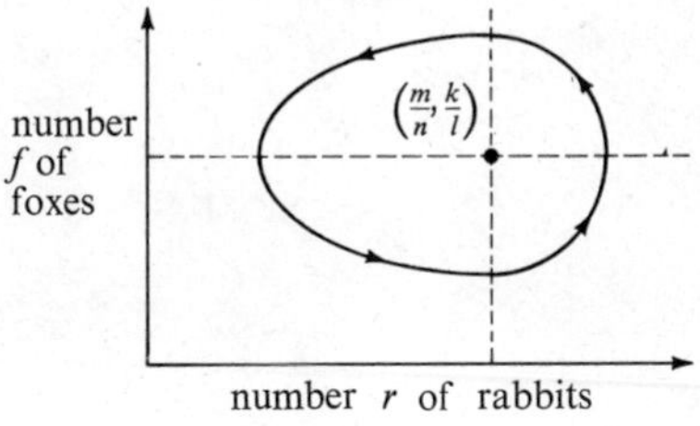

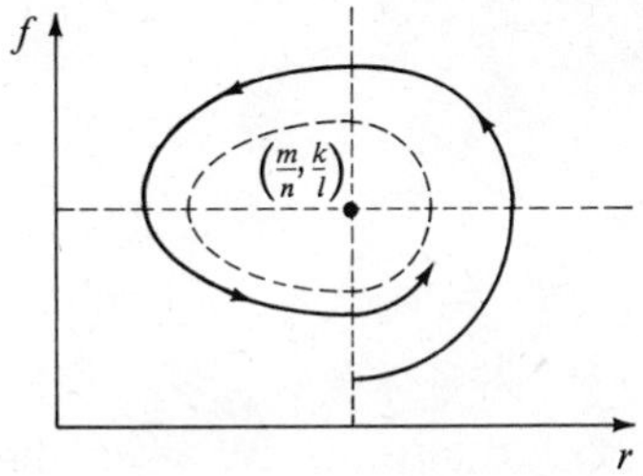

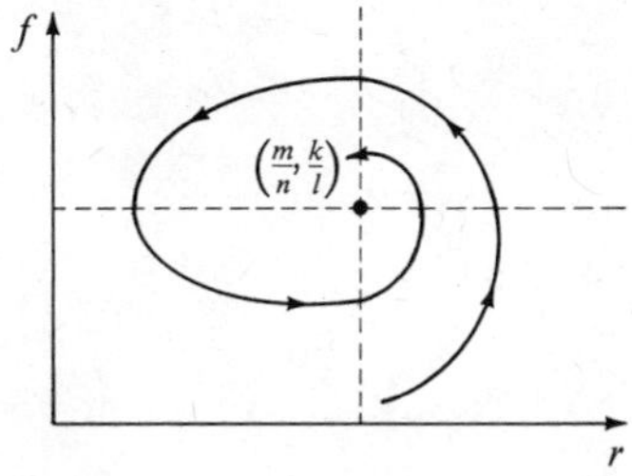

limiting oval or to a point indicating the extermination of one of them, as shown below.

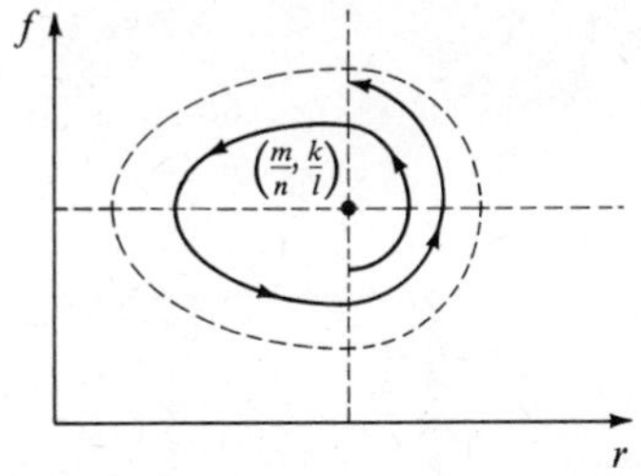

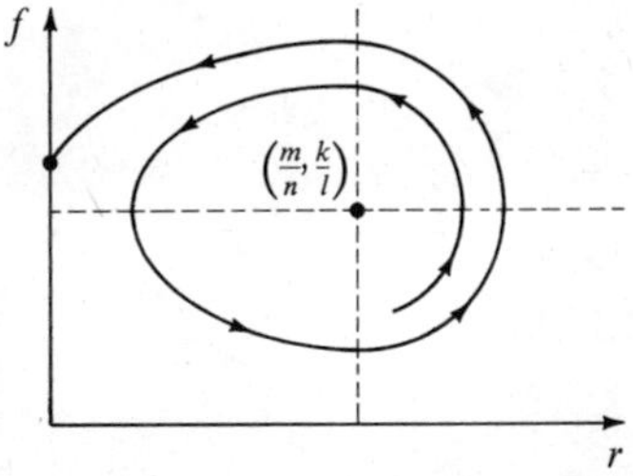

READING LIST

BECKENBACH, EDWIN F., ed., *Applied Combinatorial Mathematics* (New York: John Wiley and Sons, Inc., 1964).

BECKENBACH, EDWIN F., and TOMPKINS, CHARLES B., eds., *Communication Concepts: Interpersonal, Intrapersonal, and Mathematical* (New York: John Wiley and Sons, Inc., 1970).

COMMITTEE ON SUPPORT OF RESEARCH IN THE MATHEMATICAL SCIENCES and GEORGE A. W. BOEHM, eds., *The Mathematical Sciences: A Collection of Essays* (Cambridge, Mass.: The M.I.T. Press, 1969).

8

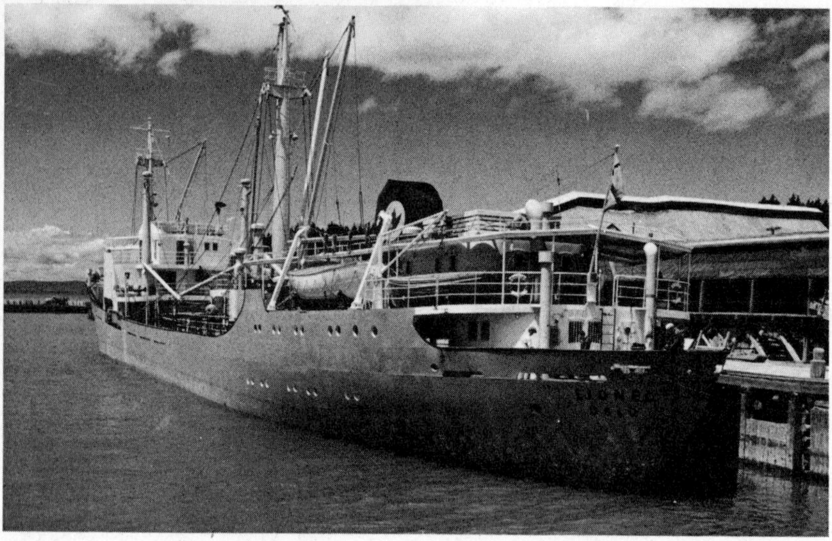

The mathematical analysis of periodic phenomena, such as the rise and fall of the tides, depends on sine-wave functions. In the Bay of Fundy, between New Brunswick and Nova Scotia, Canada, the daily tidal range often exceeds 20 feet (see the photographs and diagram above), and sometimes reaches 50 feet.

Circular Functions: Derivatives; Other Functions

In this chapter, we develop the calculus of the sine and cosine functions and that of the remaining four circular functions. Inverse circular functions are introduced and studied. The chapter concludes with an application to simple harmonic motion.

8–1 Continuity and Differentiability

We begin the discussion by showing that the sine function is continuous at 0, that is, that

$$\lim_{x\to 0} \sin x = \sin 0,$$

or, since $\sin 0 = 0$, that

$$\lim_{x\to 0} \sin x = 0.$$

Suppose $0 < x < \frac{\pi}{2}$. Then (recall the definition of P_x on page 265) we know that $P_x(\cos x, \sin x)$ is in the first quadrant (see Figure 8–1). If M is the foot of the perpendicular dropped from P_x to the u-axis, then

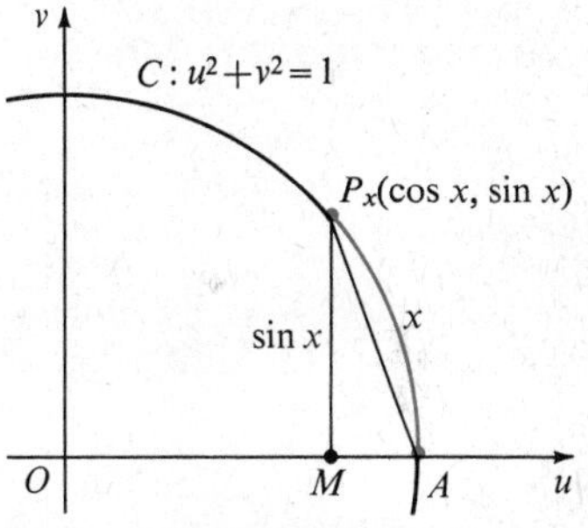

Figure 8–1

$$\text{length } \overline{MP_x} = \text{ordinate of } P_x = \sin x.$$

From geometry, we have

$$\sin x = \text{length } \overline{MP_x} < \text{length } \overline{AP_x} < \text{length } \widehat{AP_x} = x.$$

Since $\sin x > 0$ in the first quadrant, we therefore have

$$0 < \sin x < x \qquad \left(0 < x < \frac{\pi}{2}\right). \tag{A}$$

If $-\frac{\pi}{2} < x < 0$, and $z = -x$, then $0 < z < \frac{\pi}{2}$. Therefore, by inequality (A), page 305,

$$0 < \sin z < z,$$

or

$$0 < \sin(-x) < -x,$$

or (by Theorem 2 of Chapter 7, page 272)

$$0 < -\sin x < -x.$$

If we multiply each term of this inequality by -1, we must reverse its sense. Therefore,

$$0 > \sin x > x \qquad \left(-\frac{\pi}{2} < x < 0\right). \tag{B}$$

From (A) and (B), we see that for all x such that $x \neq 0$ and $-\frac{\pi}{2} < x < \frac{\pi}{2}$, *sin x is between* 0 *and x.* Therefore, as x approaches 0, $\sin x$ must also approach 0. That is,

$$\lim_{x \to 0} \sin x = 0 = \sin 0, \tag{1}$$

and the function sin is continuous at 0.

If $-\frac{\pi}{2} < x < \frac{\pi}{2}$, $x \neq 0$, then x is either a first- or a fourth-quadrant number, and therefore $\cos x > 0$. Hence from $\sin^2 x + \cos^2 x = 1$, we obtain

$$\cos x = +\sqrt{1 - \sin^2 x} \qquad \left(-\frac{\pi}{2} < x < \frac{\pi}{2}\right). \tag{C}$$

As x approaches 0, $\sin x$ approaches 0 by (1), and therefore $1 - \sin^2 x$ approaches 1. Thus, from (C),

$$\lim_{x \to 0} \cos x = 1, \tag{2}$$

or, since $\cos 0 = 1$,

$$\lim_{x \to 0} \cos x = \cos 0.$$

That is, the function cos is continuous at 0.

That sin and cos are continuous *everywhere* can be proved directly with the help of (1) and (2) [Exercises 23 and 24, page 312]; but we shall obtain the continuity of these functions as a by-product of their differentiability, which will be established in Theorem 1, page 309. To prove this theorem, we shall need the following important limits:

$$\lim_{x \to 0} \frac{\sin x}{x} = 1 \quad (3) \qquad\qquad \lim_{x \to 0} \frac{\cos x - 1}{x} = 0 \quad (4)$$

(Notice that neither of the functions $x \to \dfrac{\sin x}{x}$ or $x \to \dfrac{\cos x - 1}{x}$ is defined at 0; if we substitute 0 for x, we obtain in both cases a symbol that does not name a number.)

To prove (3), we first suppose that $0 < x < \dfrac{\pi}{2}$. Then by (A) on page 305 we have, on dividing by the positive number x,

$$\frac{\sin x}{x} < 1. \qquad \text{(D)}$$

We locate P_x on C and draw vertical lines through P_x and A, determining the points M and Q shown in Figure 8–2. The sector OAP_x (the region bounded by the radii $\overline{OA}$ and $\overline{OP_x}$ of C and the arc $\widehat{AP_x}$ of C) *is contained in* the triangular region OAQ. Therefore,

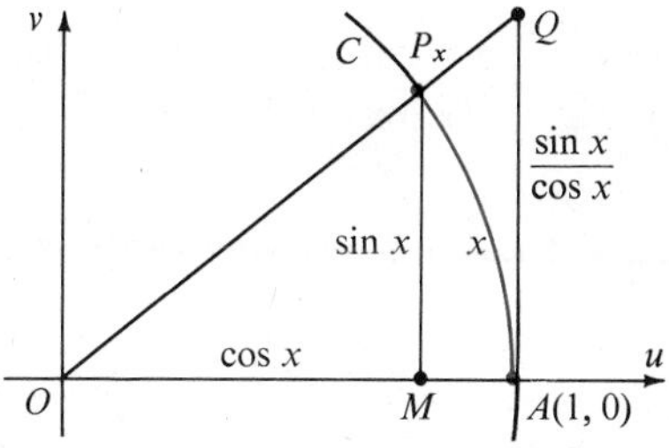

Figure 8–2

$$\text{area sector } OAP_x < \text{area triangular region } OAQ. \qquad \text{(E)}$$

We can express these areas in terms of x: As we saw in Section 7–3, the area of a sector of a circle of radius r is $\frac{1}{2}rs$, where s is the length of the circular arc forming part of the boundary of the sector. Therefore, since the radius of C is 1 and the length of $\widehat{AP_x}$ is x,

$$\text{area sector } OAP_x = \tfrac{1}{2} \cdot 1 \cdot x = \tfrac{1}{2}x.$$

Since P_x is the point $(\cos x, \sin x)$, length $\overline{OM} = \cos x$ and length $\overline{MP_x} = \sin x$. Using the fact that triangles OAQ and OMP_x are similar, and therefore that the lengths of corresponding sides are proportional, we have

$$\frac{\text{length } \overline{AQ}}{\text{length } \overline{OA}} = \frac{\text{length } \overline{MP_x}}{\text{length } \overline{OM}} = \frac{\sin x}{\cos x},$$

or

$$\text{length } \overline{AQ} = \frac{\sin x}{\cos x}.$$

Therefore

$$\text{area triangular region } OAQ = \frac{1}{2} \cdot 1 \cdot \frac{\sin x}{\cos x} = \frac{1}{2}\,\frac{\sin x}{\cos x}.$$

Inequality (E) can accordingly be written

$$\frac{1}{2}x < \frac{1}{2}\,\frac{\sin x}{\cos x},$$

or, when we multiply by the positive number $\frac{2 \cos x}{x}$ $\left(\text{recall that } 0 < x < \frac{\pi}{2}\right)$,

$$\cos x < \frac{\sin x}{x}.$$

Combined with the inequality (D) on page 307, this gives

$$\cos x < \frac{\sin x}{x} < 1. \tag{F}$$

Thus far we have assumed $0 < x < \frac{\pi}{2}$. If we have $-\frac{\pi}{2} < x < 0$, then $0 < -x < \frac{\pi}{2}$, and by (F),

$$\cos(-x) < \frac{\sin(-x)}{-x} < 1.$$

By Theorem 2, Chapter 7, page 272, this reduces to

$$\cos x < \frac{-\sin x}{-x} < 1,$$

or

$$\cos x < \frac{\sin x}{x} < 1.$$

Thus we see that (F) holds for all x such that $-\frac{\pi}{2} < x < \frac{\pi}{2}$, $x \neq 0$.

By (2), page 306, $\lim_{x \to 0} \cos x = 1$; and, of course, $\lim_{x \to 0} 1 = 1$. Since the first and third members of (F) both approach 1 as x approaches 0, the middle member must also approach 1; that is,

$$\lim_{x \to 0} \frac{\sin x}{x} = 1.$$

To prove (4), page 306, we notice that from $\sin^2 x + \cos^2 x = 1$ we have

$$\cos^2 x - 1 = -\sin^2 x, \quad \text{or} \quad (\cos x + 1)(\cos x - 1) = -\sin^2 x.$$

Therefore for $-\frac{\pi}{2} < x < \frac{\pi}{2}$, $x \neq 0$,

$$\frac{\cos x - 1}{x} = \frac{-\sin^2 x}{x(\cos x + 1)} = -\frac{\sin x}{x} \cdot \frac{\sin x}{\cos x + 1}.$$

Since the limit as x approaches 0 of each factor on the right exists, we can use properties of limits and (1), (2), and (3) to obtain

$$\lim_{x \to 0} \frac{\cos x - 1}{x} = -\lim_{x \to 0} \frac{\sin x}{x} \cdot \lim_{x \to 0} \frac{\sin x}{\cos x + 1} = -1 \cdot \frac{0}{1 + 1} = 0.$$

We are now ready to prove the following:

Theorem 1.

The functions sin and cos are differentiable and therefore continuous. Moreover,

$$\frac{d}{dx}\sin x = \cos x \tag{5}$$

and

$$\frac{d}{dx}\cos x = -\sin x. \tag{6}$$

Proof

In finding the derivative of the function $f\colon x \rightarrow \cos x$ at the number x, we must consider the difference quotient

$$\frac{f(z) - f(x)}{z - x} = \frac{\cos z - \cos x}{z - x}.$$

We let $t = z - x$. Then $z = t + x$, and as z approaches x, t approaches 0. We have

$$\begin{aligned}\frac{\cos z - \cos x}{z - x} &= \frac{\cos(t + x) - \cos x}{t} \\ &= \frac{\cos t \cos x - \sin t \sin x - \cos x}{t} \qquad [(3), \text{page } 287] \\ &= \frac{\cos t - 1}{t}\cdot \cos x - \frac{\sin t}{t}\cdot \sin x.\end{aligned}$$

Thus, noting that the limits as t approaches 0 of both factors of each term on the right exist, and using (3) and (4) with t in place of x, we obtain

$$\begin{aligned}\frac{d}{dx}\cos x = f'(x) &= \lim_{z\to x}\frac{f(z) - f(x)}{z - x} = \lim_{z\to x}\frac{\cos z - \cos x}{z - x} \\ &= \lim_{t\to 0}\frac{\cos(t + x) - \cos x}{t} \\ &= \left(\lim_{t\to 0}\frac{\cos t - 1}{t}\right)\cdot \cos x - \left(\lim_{t\to 0}\frac{\sin t}{t}\right)\cdot \sin x \\ &= 0\cdot \cos x - 1\cdot \sin x = -\sin x,\end{aligned}$$

as desired.

Two methods of proving the remaining part of the theorem, that

$$\frac{d}{dx}\sin x = \cos x, \tag{5}$$

are indicated in Exercises 25 and 26, page 312.

Since $\dfrac{d}{dx}(-\cos x) = -\dfrac{d}{dx}\cos x = -(-\sin x) = \sin x$, we have the integral formula (recall Section 6–4)

$$\int \sin x\, dx = -\cos x + c.$$

From (5), we also have

$$\int \cos x\, dx = \sin x + c.$$

EXAMPLE 1. Find $\dfrac{dy}{dx}$ if (**a**) $y = \cos kx$ and (**b**) $y = \sin^2 x$.

Solution: **a.** $y = \cos u$, where $u = kx$. By the Chain Rule (Theorem 3′, Chapter 4, page 180), we have

$$\frac{dy}{dx} = \frac{dy}{du}\cdot\frac{du}{dx} = (-\sin u)\cdot k = -k \sin kx.$$

b. $y = u^2$, where $u = \sin x$. Hence

$$\frac{dy}{dx} = \frac{dy}{du}\cdot\frac{du}{dx} = 2u\cdot\cos x = 2\sin x\cos x.$$

An alternative solution of (**b**) uses (**a**) and formula (8′), page 290: $\cos 2x = 1 - 2\sin^2 x$. Thus

$$y = \sin^2 x = \tfrac{1}{2} - \tfrac{1}{2}\cos 2x,$$

and

$$\frac{dy}{dx} = -\frac{1}{2}\frac{d}{dx}\cos 2x = -\tfrac{1}{2}(-2\sin 2x) = \sin 2x.$$

That the two answers are equal can be seen from formula (7), page 290.

EXAMPLE 2. Find the relative maxima and relative minima of

$$f\colon x \to 2\sin x + \cos 2x$$

in the interval $0 \le x \le 2\pi$.

Solution:
$$\begin{aligned} f'(x) &= 2\cos x - 2\sin 2x \\ &= 2\cos x - 2\cdot 2\sin x\cos x \\ &= 2\cos x\,(1 - 2\sin x). \end{aligned}$$

Therefore $f'(x) = 0$ if $\cos x = 0$ or if $\sin x = \tfrac{1}{2}$, that is, if $x = \dfrac{\pi}{2}$ or $\dfrac{3\pi}{2}$, or if $x = \dfrac{\pi}{6}$ or $\dfrac{5\pi}{6}$.

$$f''(x) = -2\sin x - 4\cos 2x.$$

Since $f''\left(\frac{\pi}{2}\right) = -2 \sin \frac{\pi}{2} - 4 \cos \pi = -2 + 4 = 2 > 0$, we see by the Second-Derivative Test (page 154) that

$$f\left(\frac{\pi}{2}\right) = 2 \sin \frac{\pi}{2} + \cos \pi = 1$$

is a relative minimum of f. Similarly, $f\left(\frac{3\pi}{2}\right) = -3$ is a relative minimum, while $f\left(\frac{\pi}{6}\right) = \frac{3}{2}$ and $f\left(\frac{5\pi}{6}\right) = \frac{3}{2}$ are relative maxima. (The graph of f is shown in Example 2(b), page 296.)

ORAL EXERCISES

In Exercises 1–3, it is given that the function $f: x \rightarrow f(x)$ is such that $|f(x)| \leq |x|$ for all $x \in \mathcal{R}$.

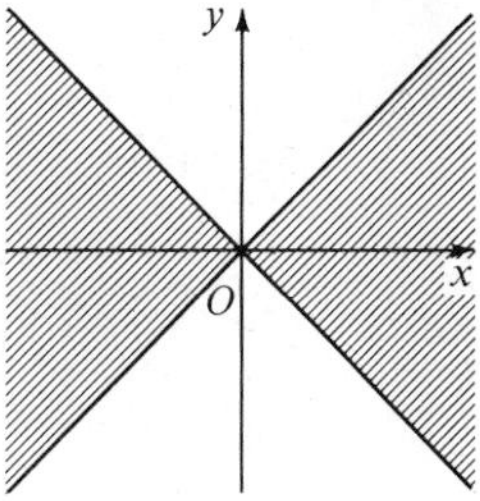

1. Explain why the graph of f must lie in the shaded region indicated in the diagram at the right.
2. Explain why f must be continuous at 0.
3. Describe an example showing that f is not necessarily continuous at x_0 if $x_0 \neq 0$.

In Exercises 4–9, $f(x)$ is given. State $f'(x)$.

4. $\sin x$
5. $\cos x$
6. $\sin x + \cos x$
7. $\sin x - \cos x$
8. $2 \sin x$
9. $\sin 2x$

WRITTEN EXERCISES

In Exercises 1–10, $f(x)$ is given; find $f'(x)$.

A

1. $\cos x \sin x$
2. $\cos^2 x - \sin^2 x$
3. $\cos^2 x + \sin^2 x$
4. $x \sin x$
5. $x \cos x$
6. $e^x \sin x$
7. $e^x \cos x$
8. $\log \sin x$
9. $\log \cos x$
10. $\sin x \log \sin x$

In Exercises 11–14, find the derivative, and use your result to state an integral formula.

11. $\frac{d}{dx}(x \sin x + \cos x)$

12. $\frac{d}{dx}(-x \cos x + \sin x)$

13. $\frac{d}{dx}(\frac{1}{2} \sin x \cos x + \frac{1}{2}x)$

14. $\frac{d}{dx}(-\frac{1}{2} \sin x \cos x + \frac{1}{2}x)$

In Exercises 15–18, for each of the points whose abscissas are given, find an equation of the line tangent to the curve at that point.

B **15.** $y = \sin x;\quad x = 0, \pi, 2\pi$

16. $y = \cos x;\quad x = 0, \pi, 2\pi$

17. $y = \cos 2x;\quad x = 0, \frac{\pi}{2}, \pi$

18. $y = \sin \frac{x}{2};\quad x = 0, \pi, 2\pi$

In Exercises 19–22, find the relative maxima and relative minima of the given function in the interval $0 \le x \le 2\pi$.

19. $f: x \to \cos 2x - 2 \cos x$

20. $f: x \to \cos 2x - 2 \sin x$

21. $f: x \to \sin 2x - 2 \sin x$

22. $f: x \to \sin 2x - 2 \cos x$

(21, 22) *Hint:* If the f''-test fails, use the f'-test.

23. Use Theorem 4 of Chapter 7, page 287, and formulas (1) and (2), page 306, to show that sin is continuous for all $x \in \mathcal{R}$.

24. Use Theorem 4 of Chapter 7, page 287, and formulas (1) and (2), page 306, to show that cos is continuous for all $x \in \mathcal{R}$.

C **25.** Prove that $\frac{d}{dx} \sin x = \cos x$ by using the fact that $\sin x = \cos\left(\frac{\pi}{2} - x\right)$ and the formula for the derivative of cos.

26. Prove that $\frac{d}{dx} \sin x = \cos x$ by letting $f: x \to \sin x$ and following the pattern of the proof of the part of Theorem 1 given in the text.

27. Illustrate the inequalities (A) and (B) on pages 305 and 306 by graphing $x \to \sin x$ and $x \to x$ for $-\frac{\pi}{2} < x < \frac{\pi}{2}$ in the same coordinate plane.

28. **a.** Draw the graph of $g: x \to \frac{\sin x}{x}$ for $-\pi \le x \le \pi, x \ne 0$.

b. Include the graphs of $f: x \to \cos x$ and $h: x \to 1 \left(-\frac{\pi}{2} < x < \frac{\pi}{2}\right)$ in your answer to (**a**), thus illustrating graphically the inequality (F) on page 308.

29. Find an expression for the nth derivative $f^{(n)}(x)$ if (**a**) $f(x) = \sin x$ and (**b**) $f(x) = \cos x$.

8–2 The Other Circular Functions

In addition to the sine and cosine, there are four other circular functions: the **tangent, cotangent, secant,** and **cosecant,** abbreviated tan, ctn (or cot), sec, and csc, respectively. These are defined in terms of sin and cos as follows:

$$\tan x = \frac{\sin x}{\cos x} \qquad \sec x = \frac{1}{\cos x} \qquad \text{(provided } \cos x \neq 0\text{)}$$

$$\text{ctn } x = \frac{\cos x}{\sin x} \qquad \csc x = \frac{1}{\sin x} \qquad \text{(provided } \sin x \neq 0\text{)}$$

Since $\cos x = 0$ if x is any odd multiple of $\frac{\pi}{2}$, the domains of tan and sec do not contain such numbers. Similarly, since $\sin x = 0$ if x is any even multiple of $\frac{\pi}{2}$, that is, any integral multiple of π, the domains of ctn and csc do not contain these numbers. The table below gives the domains and ranges of the four functions:

Function	Domain	Range
tan	$\left\{x: x \neq \frac{n\pi}{2}, n \text{ an odd integer}\right\}$	$\mathcal{R}$
ctn	$\{x: x \neq n\pi, n \text{ an integer}\}$	$\mathcal{R}$
sec	$\left\{x: x \neq \frac{n\pi}{2}, n \text{ an odd integer}\right\}$	$\{y: \lvert y\rvert \geq 1\}$
csc	$\{x: x \neq n\pi, n \text{ an integer}\}$	$\{y: \lvert y\rvert \geq 1\}$

To see that the range of sec, for example, is as given in the table, suppose that $y = \sec x$ is any member of the range of sec. Then since $|\cos x| \leq 1$, we have

$$|y| = |\sec x| = \left|\frac{1}{\cos x}\right| = \frac{1}{|\cos x|} \geq 1.$$

Conversely, if y is any number such that $|y| \geq 1$, then $y \geq 1$ or $y \leq -1$, and $-1 \leq \frac{1}{y} \leq 1$. Thus (recall the graph of cos) there is an x such that $\cos x = \frac{1}{y}$; for this x, $\sec x = \frac{1}{\cos x} = y$. Hence y is in the range of sec.

Using the definitions of tan, ctn, sec, and csc, we can supply the entries in the last four columns of Table 2 on page 314. A dash in Table 2 indicates that the corresponding x is not in the domain of the function.

Table 2

x	$\sin x$	$\cos x$	$\tan x$	$\text{ctn } x$	$\sec x$	$\csc x$
0	0	1	0	—	1	—
$\frac{\pi}{6}$	$\frac{1}{2}$	$\frac{\sqrt{3}}{2}$	$\frac{\sqrt{3}}{3}$	$\sqrt{3}$	$\frac{2\sqrt{3}}{3}$	2
$\frac{\pi}{4}$	$\frac{\sqrt{2}}{2}$	$\frac{\sqrt{2}}{2}$	1	1	$\sqrt{2}$	$\sqrt{2}$
$\frac{\pi}{3}$	$\frac{\sqrt{3}}{2}$	$\frac{1}{2}$	$\sqrt{3}$	$\frac{\sqrt{3}}{3}$	2	$\frac{2\sqrt{3}}{3}$
$\frac{\pi}{2}$	1	0	—	0	—	1
$\frac{2\pi}{3}$	$\frac{\sqrt{3}}{2}$	$-\frac{1}{2}$	$-\sqrt{3}$	$-\frac{\sqrt{3}}{3}$	-2	$\frac{2\sqrt{3}}{3}$
$\frac{3\pi}{4}$	$\frac{\sqrt{2}}{2}$	$-\frac{\sqrt{2}}{2}$	-1	-1	$-\sqrt{2}$	$\sqrt{2}$
$\frac{5\pi}{6}$	$\frac{1}{2}$	$-\frac{\sqrt{3}}{2}$	$-\frac{\sqrt{3}}{3}$	$-\sqrt{3}$	$-\frac{2\sqrt{3}}{3}$	2
π	0	-1	0	—	-1	—
$\frac{7\pi}{6}$	$-\frac{1}{2}$	$-\frac{\sqrt{3}}{2}$	$\frac{\sqrt{3}}{3}$	$\sqrt{3}$	$-\frac{2\sqrt{3}}{3}$	-2
$\frac{5\pi}{4}$	$-\frac{\sqrt{2}}{2}$	$-\frac{\sqrt{2}}{2}$	1	1	$-\sqrt{2}$	$-\sqrt{2}$
$\frac{4\pi}{3}$	$-\frac{\sqrt{3}}{2}$	$-\frac{1}{2}$	$\sqrt{3}$	$\frac{\sqrt{3}}{3}$	-2	$-\frac{2\sqrt{3}}{3}$
$\frac{3\pi}{2}$	-1	0	—	0	—	-1
$\frac{5\pi}{3}$	$-\frac{\sqrt{3}}{2}$	$\frac{1}{2}$	$-\sqrt{3}$	$-\frac{\sqrt{3}}{3}$	2	$-\frac{2\sqrt{3}}{3}$
$\frac{7\pi}{4}$	$-\frac{\sqrt{2}}{2}$	$\frac{\sqrt{2}}{2}$	-1	-1	$\sqrt{2}$	$-\sqrt{2}$
$\frac{11\pi}{6}$	$-\frac{1}{2}$	$\frac{\sqrt{3}}{2}$	$-\frac{\sqrt{3}}{3}$	$-\sqrt{3}$	$\frac{2\sqrt{3}}{3}$	-2
2π	0	1	0	—	1	—

The graphs of tan, ctn, sec, and csc are shown in Figure 8–5 on page 316. To indicate how these graphs can be obtained, we shall consider the graph of the tangent function in some detail.

We note first that tan has period π: For any x,

$$\tan(x+\pi) = \frac{\sin(x+\pi)}{\cos(x+\pi)} = \frac{-\sin x}{-\cos x} = \tan x.$$

Thus if we know the graph of tan in the interval $-\frac{\pi}{2} < x < \frac{\pi}{2}$, we can obtain the rest of the graph by moving this cycle rigidly to the right and left distances which are integral multiples of π.

To draw the graph of tan in the interval $0 \leq x < \frac{\pi}{2}$, we first locate the points given in the table below.

x	0	$\frac{\pi}{6}$	$\frac{\pi}{4}$	$\frac{\pi}{3}$
$\tan x$	0	$\frac{\sqrt{3}}{3} \doteq 0.577$	1	$\sqrt{3} \doteq 1.732$

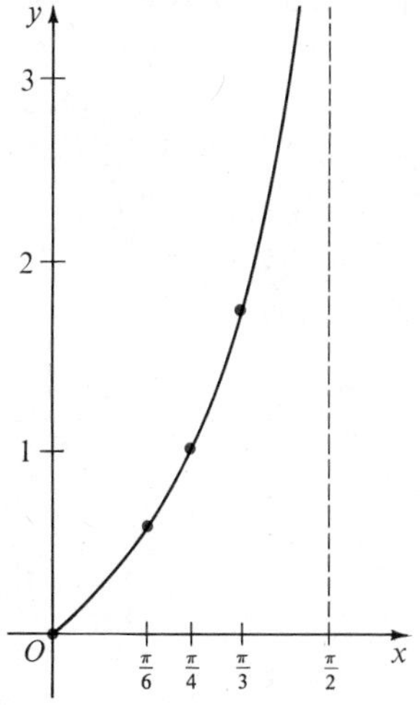

Figure 8–3

Next we observe that as x approaches $\frac{\pi}{2}$, $\sin x$ approaches 1 and $\cos x$ approaches 0. Therefore the values of

$$\tan x = \frac{\sin x}{\cos x}$$

are large when x is near $\frac{\pi}{2}$. We conclude that the graph has the appearance shown in Figure 8–3. [We know that the graph is a smooth curve because tan is a differentiable function, being the quotient of the differentiable functions sin and cos (see page 176).]

Since

$$\tan(-x) = \frac{\sin(-x)}{\cos(-x)} = \frac{-\sin x}{\cos x} = -\tan x,$$

tan is an odd function. We can therefore obtain the part of the graph of tan for $-\frac{\pi}{2} < x \leq 0$ by "reflecting in the origin" the part for $0 \leq x < \frac{\pi}{2}$, as shown in Figure 8–4. Now that we have the graph of tan in the interval $-\frac{\pi}{2} < x < \frac{\pi}{2}$, we can use the periodicity of tan to obtain the

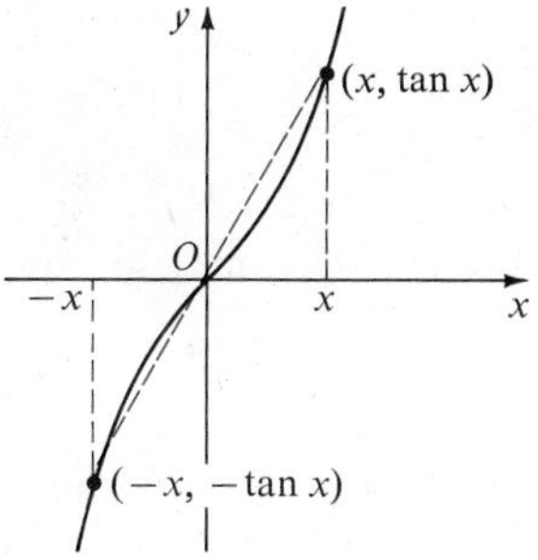

Figure 8–4

graph shown in Figure 8–5(a). It is evident from the graph that tan has no positive period less than π; hence π is its fundamental period.

The function ctn is related to tan by

$$\operatorname{ctn} x = \frac{\cos x}{\sin x} = \frac{\sin\left(\frac{\pi}{2} - x\right)}{\cos\left(\frac{\pi}{2} - x\right)} = \tan\left(\frac{\pi}{2} - x\right).$$

Its graph is shown in Figure 8–5(b).

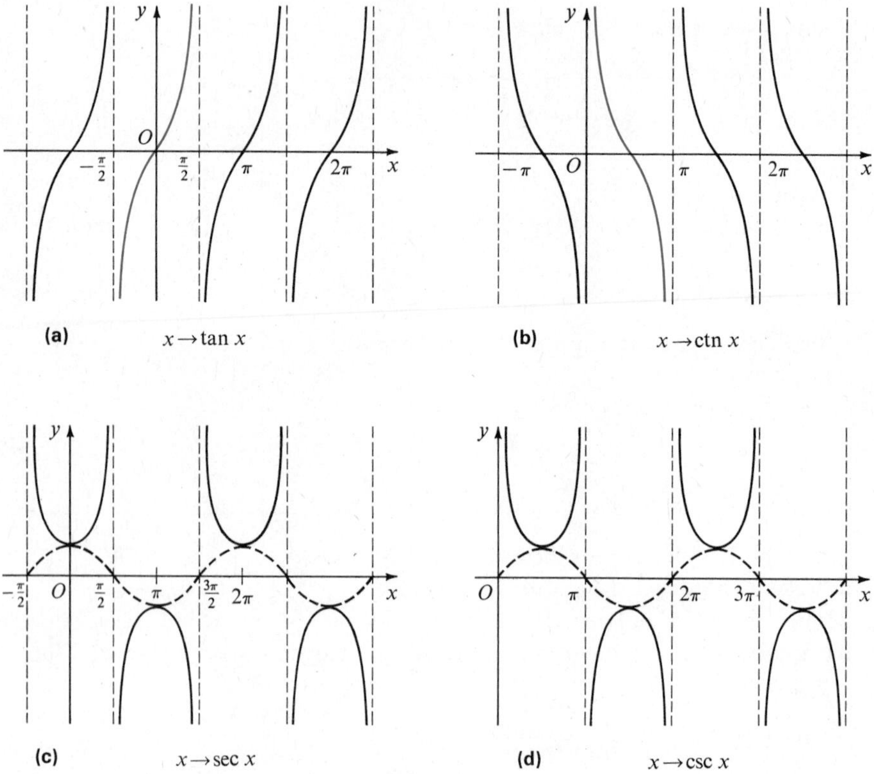

Figure 8–5

The graphs of sec and csc are shown in Figures 8–5(c) and (d), respectively. The dotted graphs in these figures are those of cos and sin, respectively. They are shown because of their reciprocal relationship, $\frac{1}{\cos x} = \sec x$, $\frac{1}{\sin x} = \csc x$, with the graphs of sec and csc.

A few of the many identities involving the functions tan, ctn, sec, and csc are noted below. From the "quadratic" identity $\sin^2 x + \cos^2 x = 1$, we have (provided $\cos x \neq 0$)

$$\frac{\sin^2 x}{\cos^2 x} + \frac{\cos^2 x}{\cos^2 x} = \frac{1}{\cos^2 x}, \quad \text{or} \quad \left(\frac{\sin x}{\cos x}\right)^2 + 1 = \left(\frac{1}{\cos x}\right)^2.$$

From this we obtain the first of the following additional "quadratic" identities:

$$\mathbf{\tan^2 x + 1 = \sec^2 x} \quad (1) \qquad\qquad \mathbf{1 + ctn^2 x = \csc^2 x} \quad (2)$$

The proof of (2) is left as an exercise (Exercise 1, page 319).

We can derive sum and difference formulas for tan and ctn using those for sin and cos. For example,

$$\tan(x + y) = \frac{\sin(x + y)}{\cos(x + y)} = \frac{\sin x \cos y + \cos x \sin y}{\cos x \cos y - \sin x \sin y}.$$

If we divide numerator and denominator by $\cos x \cos y$, we have

$$\tan(x + y) = \frac{\dfrac{\sin x}{\cos x} + \dfrac{\sin y}{\cos y}}{1 - \dfrac{\sin x \sin y}{\cos x \cos y}},$$

or

$$\mathbf{\tan(x + y) = \frac{\tan x + \tan y}{1 - \tan x \tan y}}. \qquad (3)$$

Similarly (Exercise 5, page 319),

$$\mathbf{ctn(x + y) = \frac{ctn\, x\, ctn\, y - 1}{ctn\, y + ctn\, x} = \frac{1 - \tan x \tan y}{\tan x + \tan y}}. \qquad (4)$$

It is not difficult to derive formulas for the derivatives of the functions tan, ctn, sec, and csc. To find the derivative of $f: x \to \text{ctn}\, x$, for example, we use the quotient formula (Theorem 2, Chapter 4, page 176).

Since $f(x) = \text{ctn}\, x = \dfrac{\cos x}{\sin x}$, for all values of x for which $\sin x \neq 0$ we have

$$\begin{aligned} f'(x) &= \frac{\sin x \dfrac{d}{dx}(\cos x) - \cos x \dfrac{d}{dx}(\sin x)}{(\sin x)^2} \\ &= \frac{\sin x(-\sin x) - \cos x(\cos x)}{(\sin x)^2} \\ &= \frac{-(\sin^2 x + \cos^2 x)}{(\sin x)^2} = \frac{-1}{(\sin x)^2} = -\csc^2 x. \end{aligned}$$

The remaining three of the four formulas listed below can be derived in a similar way (Exercises 2, 3, and 4, page 319).

$$\frac{d}{dx}\tan x = \sec^2 x \tag{5}$$

$$\frac{d}{dx}\operatorname{ctn} x = -\csc^2 x \tag{6}$$

$$\frac{d}{dx}\sec x = \sec x \tan x \tag{7}$$

$$\frac{d}{dx}\csc x = -\csc x \operatorname{ctn} x \tag{8}$$

EXAMPLE. Show that if $y = \log \tan x$, then $y' = 2 \csc 2x$.

Solution: $y = \log u$, where $u = \tan x$. By the Chain Rule (Theorem 3′, Chapter 4, page 180),

$$y' = \frac{dy}{dx} = \frac{dy}{du}\cdot\frac{du}{dx} = \frac{1}{u}\sec^2 x = \frac{1}{\tan x}\sec^2 x$$

$$= \frac{\cos x}{\sin x}\cdot\frac{1}{\cos^2 x} = \frac{1}{\sin x \cos x}$$

$$= \frac{2}{2 \sin x \cos x} = \frac{2}{\sin 2x} = 2 \csc 2x.$$

ORAL EXERCISES

1. Because $\tan x = \dfrac{1}{\operatorname{ctn} x}$ and $\operatorname{ctn} x = \dfrac{1}{\tan x}$, the tangent and cotangent are called *reciprocal* functions. Give two more pairs of reciprocal circular functions.
2. How many cycles of tan are shown in Figure 8–5(a)?
3. How many cycles of ctn are shown in Figure 8–5(b)?
4. How many cycles of sec are shown in Figure 8–5(c)?
5. How many cycles of csc are shown in Figure 8–5(d)?
6. Give the algebraic sign of $\tan x$ if x is a first- (second-, third-, fourth-) quadrant number.
7. Repeat Exercise 6 for $\operatorname{ctn} x$.
8. Repeat Exercise 6 for $\sec x$.
9. Repeat Exercise 6 for $\csc x$.

WRITTEN EXERCISES

In Exercises 1–5, prove the indicated formula of this section. For what values of x is the formula valid?

A **1.** (2) **2.** (5) **3.** (7) **4.** (8) **5.** (4)

In Exercises 6–12, simplify, reducing each expression to a real number or to a multiple of a value of one of the circular functions. State any restrictions on the variable involved.

6. $\sin x \cdot \cos x \cdot \tan x \cdot \operatorname{ctn} x \cdot \sec x \cdot \csc x$

7. $\sin 2x \cdot \csc 2x$

8. $\cos \frac{x}{2} \sec \frac{x}{2}$

9. $\sin 2x \cdot \csc x$

10. $\sin 2x \cdot \sec x$

11. $\sin x (\tan x + \operatorname{ctn} x)$

12. $\cos x (\operatorname{ctn} x + \tan x)$

13. Express the other five circular functions in terms of sin.

14. Express the other five circular functions in terms of cos.

Prove the identities in Exercises 15–20.

15. $\tan x + \operatorname{ctn} x = \sec x \csc x$

16. $\sin x (\sec x - \csc x) = \tan x - 1$

B **17.** $\dfrac{1}{1 + \sin x} + \dfrac{1}{1 - \sin x} = 2 \sec^2 x$

18. $\dfrac{1 + \sin x}{\cos x} + \dfrac{\cos x}{1 + \sin x} = 2 \sec x$

19. $\dfrac{\tan x + 1}{\operatorname{ctn} x + 1} = \dfrac{\sec x}{\csc x}$

20. $\dfrac{\tan^3 x + 1}{\tan x + 1} = \sec^2 x - \tan x$

21. Prove the formulas in **(a)** and **(b)** and deduce a "half-angle" formula from each:

(a) $\dfrac{\sin 2x}{1 + \cos 2x} = \tan x$

(b) $\dfrac{\sin 2x}{1 - \cos 2x} = \operatorname{ctn} x$

$\left[\textit{Hint: } \text{Let } x = \dfrac{z}{2}. \right]$

22. Express $\tan 2x$ in terms of $\tan x$.

23. Express $\operatorname{ctn} 2x$ in terms of $\operatorname{ctn} x$.

In Exercises 24–31, $f(x)$ is given. Find $f'(x)$ and reduce it to either a value of one of the circular functions or the square of such a value.

C **24.** $-x - \dfrac{\cos x}{\sin x}$

25. $\dfrac{\sin x - x\cos x}{\cos x}$

26. $\dfrac{x}{2} + \dfrac{\sin 2x}{4}$

27. $\dfrac{x}{2} - \dfrac{\sin 2x}{4}$

28. $\log(\sec x + \tan x)$

29. $\log(\csc x - \operatorname{ctn} x)$

30. $\log \tan\left(\dfrac{x}{2} + \dfrac{\pi}{4}\right)$

31. $\log \tan \dfrac{x}{2}$

8–3 Inverse Circular Functions

The function $x \to \sin x$ is *not* one-to-one (nor are any of the other circular functions). In other words, there are horizontal lines which intersect the graph of $x \to \sin x$ in more than one point. Actually, every horizontal line of the form $y = a$, where $|a| \leq 1$, intersects the graph of $x \to \sin x$ in infinitely many points. (See Figure 8–6.) However, the *subset* of the graph of

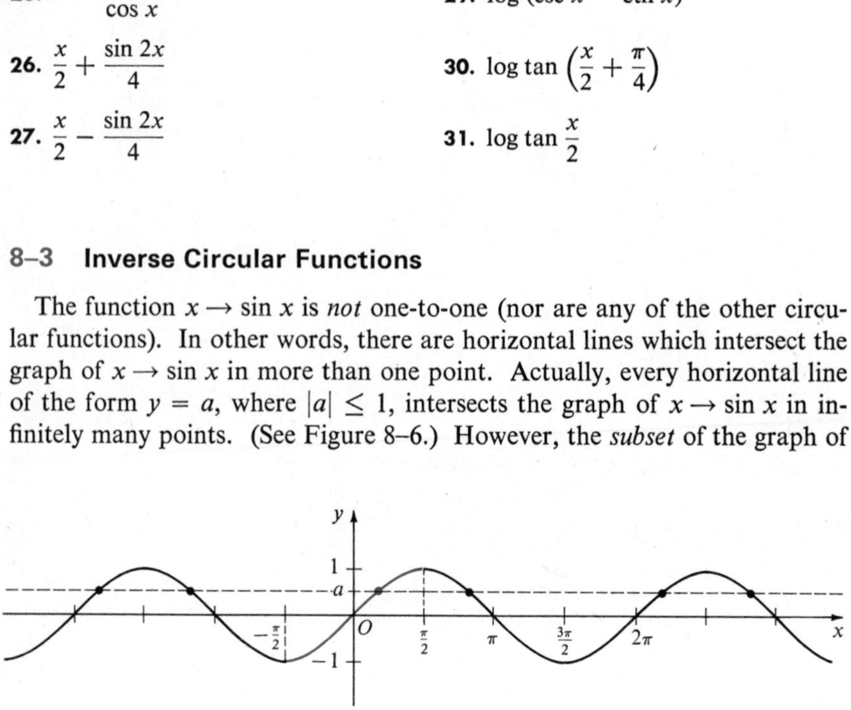

Figure 8–6

$x \to \sin x$ for which $-\dfrac{\pi}{2} \leq x \leq \dfrac{\pi}{2}$ is intersected by each horizontal line in at most one point.

Corresponding to this *subset* of the graph is the **subfunction**

$$\left\{(x, \sin x)\colon -\frac{\pi}{2} \leq x \leq \frac{\pi}{2}\right\}$$

of sin. We shall name this function *Sin.* Thus Sin has domain

$$\left\{x\colon -\frac{\pi}{2} \leq x \leq \frac{\pi}{2}\right\}$$

and range $\{y\colon -1 \leq y \leq 1\}$; and for each x in the domain of Sin, $\operatorname{Sin} x = \sin x$.

Since the function Sin is one-to-one, it has an inverse function Sin^{-1} (recall Section 1–7). The *domain* of Sin^{-1} is $\{x\colon -1 \leq x \leq 1\}$, the range of Sin; and the *range* of Sin^{-1} is $\left\{y\colon -\frac{\pi}{2} \le y \le \frac{\pi}{2}\right\}$, the domain of Sin. Figures 8–7(a) and (c) show the graphs of Sin and Sin^{-1}. Because Sin and

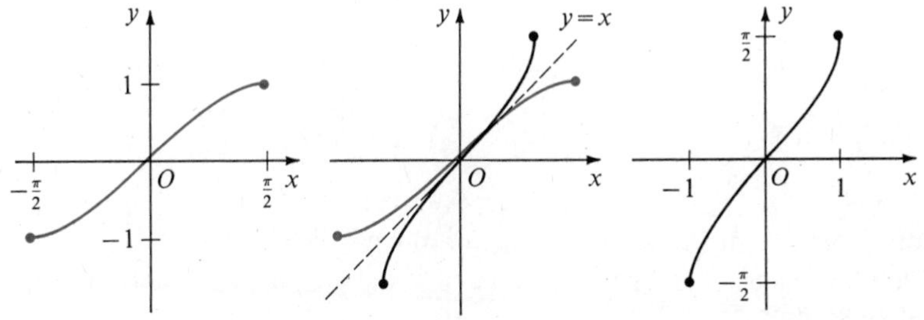

(a) $x \to \text{Sin}\,x$ **(b)** **(c)** $x \to \text{Sin}^{-1}\,x$

Figure 8–7

Sin^{-1} are inverse functions, their graphs are symmetric with respect to the line $y = x$ [Figure 8–7(b)].

The function $x \to \text{Sin}^{-1}\,x$ is called the **inverse sine function.** Notice that there is a certain degree of arbitrariness in the definition of Sin and Sin^{-1}. The interval $\frac{\pi}{2} \le x \le \frac{3\pi}{2}$, for example, could have been used for the domain of Sin and, therefore, the range of Sin^{-1}. However, the interval $-\frac{\pi}{2} \le x \le \frac{\pi}{2}$ is always used, and values in this range are called the **principal values** of the inverse sine function.

By Theorem 2, Chapter 1, page 41, we have

$$\text{Sin}\,(\text{Sin}^{-1}\,x) = x \qquad \text{if } -1 \le x \le 1, \tag{1}$$

$$\text{Sin}^{-1}\,(\text{Sin}\,x) = x \qquad \text{if } -\frac{\pi}{2} \le x \le \frac{\pi}{2}. \tag{2}$$

EXAMPLE 1. Find **(a)** $\text{Sin}^{-1}\,(-\frac{1}{2})$, **(b)** $\text{Sin}\,(\text{Sin}^{-1}\,(-\frac{1}{2}))$, **(c)** $\sin\,(\text{Sin}^{-1}\,(-\frac{1}{2}))$, **(d)** $\text{Sin}^{-1}\left(\text{Sin}\left(-\frac{\pi}{6}\right)\right)$, and **(e)** $\text{Sin}^{-1}\left(\sin\frac{11\pi}{6}\right)$.

Solution: **a.** Because $\sin\left(-\frac{\pi}{6}\right) = -\frac{1}{2}$, and $-\frac{\pi}{2} \le -\frac{\pi}{6} \le \frac{\pi}{2}$ (that is, $-\frac{\pi}{6}$ is in the domain of Sin), we have $\text{Sin}\left(-\frac{\pi}{6}\right) = -\frac{1}{2}$. Hence $\text{Sin}^{-1}\left(-\frac{1}{2}\right) = -\frac{\pi}{6}$.

(*Solution continued*)

b. By (1), $\text{Sin}\,(\text{Sin}^{-1}\,(-\tfrac{1}{2})) = -\tfrac{1}{2}$.

c. Using (**a**), we have $\sin\,(\text{Sin}^{-1}\,(-\tfrac{1}{2})) = \sin\left(-\dfrac{\pi}{6}\right) = -\tfrac{1}{2}$.

d. By (2), $\text{Sin}^{-1}\left(\text{Sin}\left(-\dfrac{\pi}{6}\right)\right) = -\dfrac{\pi}{6}$.

e. Using (**a**), we have

$$\text{Sin}^{-1}\left(\sin\frac{11\pi}{6}\right) = \text{Sin}^{-1}\left(-\frac{1}{2}\right) = -\frac{\pi}{6}.$$

Note from Example 1(e) that it is *not* always true that $\text{Sin}^{-1}\,(\sin x) = x$. On the other hand, it *is* true that $\sin\,(\text{Sin}^{-1}\,x) = x$, provided, of course, that $-1 \leq x \leq 1$.

When we come to the definition of the **inverse cosine function,** Cos^{-1}, we can no longer use the principal-value interval $-\dfrac{\pi}{2} \leq x \leq \dfrac{\pi}{2}$ because $x \rightarrow \cos x$ is not one-to-one in this interval. We use instead the interval $0 \leq x \leq \pi$ [Figure 8–8(a)]. Thus we define Cos to be the function with

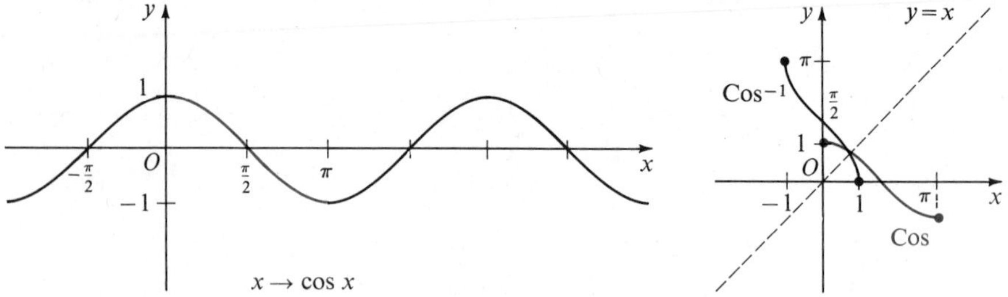

(a) **Figure 8–8** (b)

domain $\{x\colon 0 \leq x \leq \pi\}$ whose values are given by $\text{Cos}\,x = \cos x$, and then we define Cos^{-1} to be the inverse of this function. The *domain* of Cos^{-1} is $\{x\colon -1 \leq x \leq 1\}$, and the *range* of Cos^{-1} is $\{y\colon 0 \leq y \leq \pi\}$. We can obtain the graph of Cos^{-1} by reflecting the graph of Cos in the line $y = x$ [Figure 8–8(b)].

By Theorem 2, page 41, we have

$$\text{Cos}\,(\text{Cos}^{-1}\,x) = x \qquad \text{if } -1 \leq x \leq 1, \tag{3}$$

$$\text{Cos}^{-1}\,(\text{Cos}\,x) = x \qquad \text{if } 0 \leq x \leq \pi. \tag{4}$$

EXAMPLE 2. Write as an equivalent expression not involving circular or inverse circular functions.

a. $\sin\,(\text{Cos}^{-1}\,x) \quad (-1 \leq x \leq 1)$

b. $\text{Cos}^{-1}\,(\sin x) \quad \left(-\dfrac{\pi}{2} \leq x \leq \dfrac{\pi}{2}\right)$

Solution: **a.** We let $u = \text{Cos}^{-1} x$. Since the range of Cos^{-1} is the set $\{y: 0 \leq y \leq \pi\}$, we know that $0 \leq u \leq \pi$. Then we have

$$\text{Cos } u = \text{Cos } (\text{Cos}^{-1} x),$$

or, using the definition of Cos and (3),

$$\cos u = x.$$

Therefore

$$\sin u = +\sqrt{1 - \cos^2 u} \quad (\text{since } 0 \leq u \leq \pi)$$
$$= +\sqrt{1 - x^2},$$

and

$$\sin (\text{Cos}^{-1} x) = \sqrt{1 - x^2}.$$

b. We let $z = \text{Cos}^{-1} (\sin x)$. Then

$$\text{Cos } z = \text{Cos } (\text{Cos}^{-1} (\sin x))$$
$$= \sin x$$
$$= \cos \left(\frac{\pi}{2} - x\right).$$

From $-\frac{\pi}{2} \leq x \leq \frac{\pi}{2}$, we have $0 \leq \frac{\pi}{2} - x \leq \pi$; therefore, $\cos \left(\frac{\pi}{2} - x\right) = \text{Cos} \left(\frac{\pi}{2} - x\right)$. Thus $\text{Cos } z = \text{Cos} \left(\frac{\pi}{2} - x\right)$, and since Cos is one-to-one, we can conclude that

$$z = \frac{\pi}{2} - x.$$

Therefore

$$\text{Cos}^{-1} (\sin x) = \frac{\pi}{2} - x \quad \left(-\frac{\pi}{2} \leq x \leq \frac{\pi}{2}\right).$$

Referring to Figure 8–5(a), page 316, where the graph of $x \rightarrow \tan x$ is shown, we see that the "branch" of the graph colored red is intersected by each horizontal line in just one point. Therefore if we define the function Tan to be $\left\{(x, \tan x): -\frac{\pi}{2} < x < \frac{\pi}{2}\right\}$, then Tan is one-to-one and has an inverse, Tan^{-1}, called the **inverse tangent function.** The *domain* of Tan^{-1} is $\mathbb{R}$, and the (principal-value) *range* of Tan^{-1} is $\left\{y: -\frac{\pi}{2} < y < \frac{\pi}{2}\right\}$.

The **inverse cotangent function** is defined similarly. Its domain is $\mathbb{R}$ and its (principal-value) range is $\{y: 0 < y < \pi\}$. The graphs of Tan^{-1} and

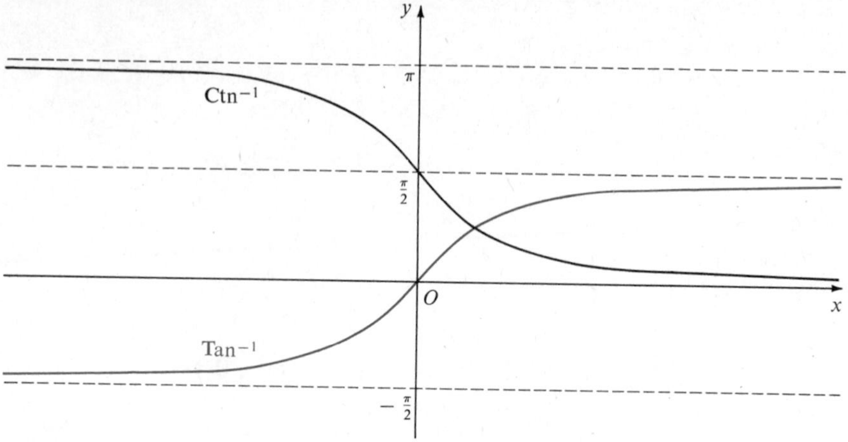

Figure 8–9

Ctn^{-1} are shown in Figure 8–9. The *inverse secant* and *inverse cosecant* functions are seldom used and will not be discussed here.

Next we shall consider the derivatives of the inverse circular functions. We shall begin by using Theorem 5, Chapter 5, page 220, concerning the derivatives of inverse functions, to show that the function

$$f: x \to \text{Cos}^{-1} x$$

is differentiable for $-1 < x < 1$ and to find its derivative. The inverse of f is

$$g: x \to \text{Cos}\, x,$$

and since $g(x) = \text{Cos}\, x = \cos x$, provided $0 \le x \le \pi$, we have $g'(x) = -\sin x$. Therefore

$$g'(f(x)) = -\sin(\text{Cos}^{-1} x) = -\sqrt{1 - x^2},$$

by the result of Example 2(a). Thus for $-1 < x < 1$, that is, for $1 - x^2 > 0$,

$$\frac{d}{dx}\text{Cos}^{-1} x = f'(x) = \frac{1}{g'(f(x))} = -\frac{1}{\sqrt{1 - x^2}}.$$

For the sake of variety, we shall use a different method to find the derivative of Tan^{-1} (assuming that this derivative exists). We let

$$y = \text{Tan}\, u \qquad \text{and} \qquad u = \text{Tan}^{-1} x.$$

By the Chain Rule (Theorem 3′, page 180), we have

$$\frac{dy}{dx} = \frac{dy}{du}\cdot\frac{du}{dx} = \sec^2 u \cdot \frac{du}{dx}.$$

Since $y = \text{Tan}(\text{Tan}^{-1} x) = x$, $\dfrac{dy}{dx} = 1$. Thus $1 = \sec^2 u \cdot \dfrac{du}{dx}$, and

$$\frac{d}{dx}\,\mathrm{Tan}^{-1}\,x = \frac{du}{dx} = \frac{1}{\sec^2 u} = \frac{1}{1 + \tan^2 u}$$

$$= \frac{1}{1 + [\tan\,(\mathrm{Tan}^{-1}\,x)]^2} = \frac{1}{1 + x^2}.$$

The derivation of the remaining two of the four formulas listed below are left as exercises (Exercises 17 and 18, page 326).

$$\frac{d}{dx}\,\mathrm{Sin}^{-1}\,x = \frac{1}{\sqrt{1 - x^2}} \quad (5) \qquad \frac{d}{dx}\,\mathrm{Tan}^{-1}\,x = \frac{1}{1 + x^2} \quad (7)$$

$$\frac{d}{dx}\,\mathrm{Cos}^{-1}\,x = \frac{-1}{\sqrt{1 - x^2}} \quad (6) \qquad \frac{d}{dx}\,\mathrm{Ctn}^{-1}\,x = \frac{-1}{1 + x^2} \quad (8)$$

Much of the importance of the inverse circular functions stems from the indefinite-integral formulas

$$\int \frac{1}{\sqrt{1 - x^2}}\,dx = \mathrm{Sin}^{-1}\,x + c \quad \text{and} \quad \int \frac{1}{1 + x^2}\,dx = \mathrm{Tan}^{-1}\,x + c,$$

which are equivalent to (5) and (7), respectively.

EXAMPLE 3. Show that $\mathrm{Tan}^{-1}\,x + \mathrm{Ctn}^{-1}\,x = \frac{\pi}{2}$.

Solution: We consider the function

$$f\colon x \to \mathrm{Tan}^{-1}\,x + \mathrm{Ctn}^{-1}\,x.$$

Using (7) and (8), we see that

$$f'(x) = \frac{1}{1 + x^2} + \frac{-1}{1 + x^2} = 0.$$

Since a function whose derivative is 0 for all x is a constant function (Exercise 16, page 247),

$$f(x) = \mathrm{Tan}^{-1}\,x + \mathrm{Ctn}^{-1}\,x = C$$

for some constant C. To determine C, we set $x = 0$:

$$f(0) = \mathrm{Tan}^{-1}0 + \mathrm{Ctn}^{-1}0 = 0 + \frac{\pi}{2} = C.$$

Hence

$$\mathrm{Tan}^{-1}\,x + \mathrm{Ctn}^{-1}\,x = \frac{\pi}{2}.$$

Note: Two other systems of notation for the inverse circular functions are in common use. One of these employs $\sin^{-1}$ for Sin^{-1}, $\cos^{-1}$ for Cos^{-1}, and so on. The other uses arcsin for Sin^{-1}, arccos for Cos^{-1}, and so on. Sometimes still another system, with Arcsin for Sin^{-1}, Arccos for Cos^{-1}, and so forth, is used.

ORAL EXERCISES

Give the value of each of the following:

1. $\text{Sin}^{-1} 0$
2. $\text{Cos}^{-1} 0$
3. $\text{Tan}^{-1} 0$
4. $\text{Ctn}^{-1} 0$
5. $\text{Sin}^{-1} 1$
6. $\text{Cos}^{-1} 1$
7. $\text{Tan}^{-1} 1$
8. $\text{Ctn}^{-1} 1$
9. $\text{Sin}^{-1} (-1)$
10. $\text{Cos}^{-1} (-1)$
11. $\text{Tan}^{-1} (-1)$
12. $\text{Ctn}^{-1} (-1)$

Which, if any, of the inverse circular functions are

13. periodic?
14. even?
15. odd?

(Use graphical evidence in answering these questions.)

WRITTEN EXERCISES

In Exercises 1–10, give the numerical value of the given expression.

A

1. $\text{Sin}^{-1} (-\frac{1}{2})$
2. $\text{Cos}^{-1} (-\frac{1}{2})$
3. $\text{Ctn}^{-1} \frac{1}{\sqrt{3}} - \text{Tan}^{-1} \frac{1}{\sqrt{3}}$
4. $\text{Tan}^{-1} (-\sqrt{3}) - \text{Ctn}^{-1} (-\sqrt{3})$
5. $\text{Sin}^{-1} \left(\sin \frac{3\pi}{4}\right)$
6. $\text{Cos}^{-1} \left(\cos \left(-\frac{\pi}{3}\right)\right)$
7. $\sin (\text{Cos}^{-1} 0)$
8. $\cos (\text{Sin}^{-1} 0)$
9. $\sin (\text{Cos}^{-1} \frac{3}{5})$
10. $\cos \left(\text{Sin}^{-1} (-\frac{5}{13})\right)$

In Exercises 11–16, write the given expression as an equivalent expression which does not involve circular or inverse circular functions.

11. $\cos (\text{Sin}^{-1} x) \quad -1 \le x \le 1$
12. $\tan (\text{Ctn}^{-1} x)$

B

13. $\text{Sin}^{-1} (\cos x) \quad 0 \le x \le \pi$
14. $\text{Ctn}^{-1} (\tan x) \quad -\frac{\pi}{2} < x < \frac{\pi}{2}$
15. $\cos (2 \text{ Cos}^{-1} x) \quad -1 \le x \le 1$
16. $\tan (2 \text{ Tan}^{-1} x)$
17. Derive formula (5) on page 325.
18. Derive formula (8) on page 325.

In Exercises 19–24, $f(x)$ is given. Find $f'(x)$.

19. $\text{Cos}^{-1} 2x$

20. $\text{Sin}^{-1} 3x$

21. $\text{Tan}^{-1} \frac{x}{2}$

22. $\text{Ctn}^{-1} \frac{x}{4}$

23. $\text{Ctn}^{-1} \frac{1}{x}$

24. $\text{Tan}^{-1} \frac{1}{x}$

In Exercises 25 and 26, prove the given integral formula by differentiating the expression on the right-hand side of the equation.

25. $\displaystyle\int \frac{1}{a^2 + x^2}\, dx = \frac{1}{a} \text{Tan}^{-1} \frac{x}{a} + c$

26. $\displaystyle\int \frac{1}{\sqrt{a^2 - x^2}}\, dx = \text{Sin}^{-1} \frac{x}{a} + c$

27. Prove that Sin^{-1} is an odd function.

28. Prove that Tan^{-1} is an odd function.

29. Express $\text{Cos}^{-1}(-x)$, $|x| \leq 1$, in terms of $\text{Cos}^{-1} x$.

30. Express $\text{Ctn}^{-1}(-x)$ in terms of $\text{Ctn}^{-1} x$.

C 31. a. Show that $\text{Tan}^{-1} \frac{1}{x} = \begin{cases} \text{Ctn}^{-1} x & \text{if } x > 0, \\ \text{Ctn}^{-1} x - \pi & \text{if } x < 0. \end{cases}$

b. Graph the function $x \to \text{Tan}^{-1} \frac{1}{x}$.

32. Graph the function $f: x \to \text{Sin}^{-1}(\sin x)$.
(Note that f has domain $\mathcal{R}$ and period 2π.)

8–4 Periodic Motion

Many phenomena in nature and technology are, or are caused by, motions which repeat themselves over regular periods of time and which are, therefore, called *periodic*. Among these are the motion of the earth relative to the sun and the consequent succession of the seasons, the vibration of a drumhead and the resulting sound, and the motion of electrons in a wire carrying an alternating current. In this section we shall indicate very briefly how periodic phenomena can be studied with the help of the circular functions sin and cos.

The **period** of a periodic motion is the time required for the completion of one full cycle. The reciprocal of this number, that is, the number of cycles completed in unit time, is the **frequency** of the motion. For example, a satellite which circles the earth in two hours (the period) has a frequency of $\frac{1}{2}$ revolution, or cycle, per hour, or 12 cycles per day.

Uniform Circular Motion. Perhaps the simplest periodic motion is that of a point P which travels at a constant speed around a circle of given radius b ($b > 0$). In such a case, P is said to be traveling with **uniform circular motion.** Let us introduce an (x, y)-coordinate system with origin O at the center of the circle, as shown in Figure 8–10. We let θ be the radian measure of angle BOP, where B is the point $(b, 0)$. Recalling the definitions of sine

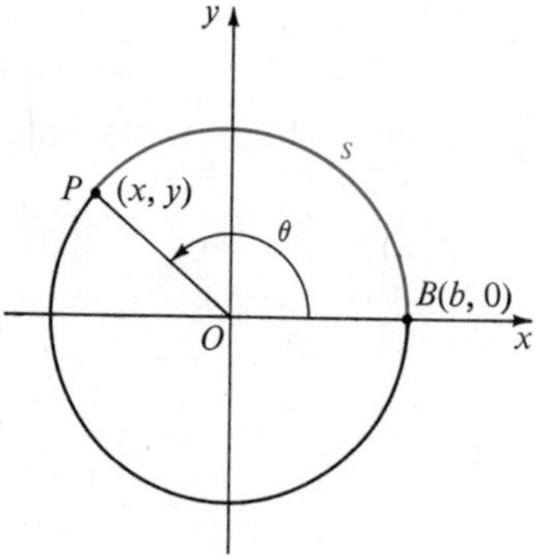

Figure 8–10

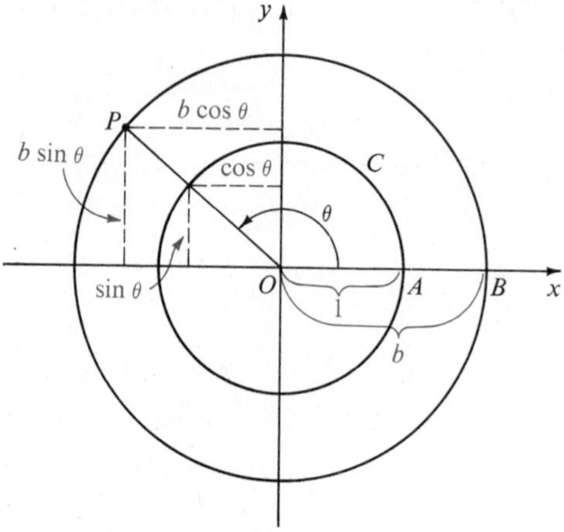

Figure 8–11

and cosine, we can see from Figure 8–11 that the coordinates of P are

$$x = b\cos\theta, \qquad y = b\sin\theta. \tag{A}$$

The length of the arc subtended by angle BOP is $s = b\theta$ (see page 279), so that s is a function of θ. Further, in the uniform motion of P around the circle, θ is a function of time t. Therefore the rates of change of s and θ with respect to t are connected through the Chain Rule by the equation

$$\frac{ds}{dt} = \frac{ds}{d\theta}\cdot\frac{d\theta}{dt} = b\frac{d\theta}{dt}, \quad \text{or} \quad \frac{ds}{dt} = b\omega,$$

where $\frac{ds}{dt}$ and $\omega = \frac{d\theta}{dt}$ are constants. The number $\left|\frac{ds}{dt}\right|$ is the speed of P in its path, and $|\omega|$ is the **angular speed** of P in radians per unit time. (Note that if P is traveling in a clockwise sense around the circle, then θ is decreasing and hence $\frac{ds}{dt}$ and ω are negative.)

From $\frac{d\theta}{dt} = \omega$, we have, by antidifferentiation,

$$\theta = \omega t + \theta_0, \tag{B}$$

where θ_0 is a constant (Figure 8–12). Upon setting $t = 0$, we see that θ_0 is the radian

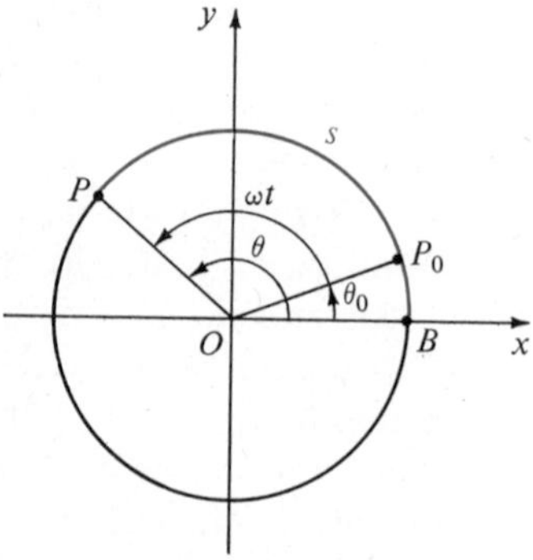

Figure 8–12

measure of angle BOP_0, where P_0 is the position of P at time $t = 0$. Using (B), we may rewrite (A) as

$$x = b \cos (\omega t + \theta_0), \qquad y = b \sin (\omega t + \theta_0). \tag{1}$$

These equations constitute the *law of motion* of P (recall Section 4–3).

Angular speed is often given in such units as revolutions per minute (r.p.m.) or degrees per hour. In formulas (1), however, we take ω to be in *radians* per unit time to simplify differentiation formulas (page 331).

We see from (1) that the period of the motion of P is $\frac{2\pi}{|\omega|}$ and the frequency is $\frac{|\omega|}{2\pi}$.

EXAMPLE 1. A point starts at $(0, -4)$ and travels counterclockwise around the circle $x^2 + y^2 = 16$. Find its law of motion (**a**) if its speed is 2 units per minute and (**b**) if its angular speed is 3 r.p.m.

Solution: **a.** The radius b of the circle is 4, and θ_0 may be taken to be $-\frac{\pi}{2}$, as indicated in the diagram at the right. From $\frac{ds}{dt} = b\omega$, we find that $2 = 4\omega$, or $\omega = \frac{1}{2}$. Substituting in equations (1), we have

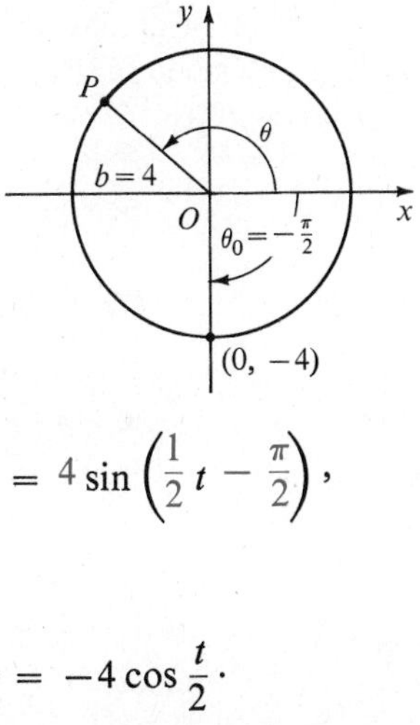

$$x = 4 \cos \left(\frac{1}{2} t - \frac{\pi}{2}\right), \qquad y = 4 \sin \left(\frac{1}{2} t - \frac{\pi}{2}\right),$$

or, by (4) and (2), page 287,

$$x = 4 \sin \frac{t}{2}, \qquad y = -4 \cos \frac{t}{2}.$$

b. The constants b and θ_0 are as in (**a**). Since the point travels 2π radians in one revolution, $\omega = 3 \cdot 2\pi = 6\pi$ radians per minute. Therefore, by (1),

$$x = 4 \cos \left(6\pi t - \frac{\pi}{2}\right), \qquad y = 4 \sin \left(6\pi t - \frac{\pi}{2}\right),$$

or

$$x = 4 \sin 6\pi t, \qquad y = -4 \cos 6\pi t.$$

Simple Harmonic Motion. Let Q be the projection on a line L of a point P which is describing uniform circular motion (Figure 8–13). Then Q oscillates back and forth on an interval of L in **simple harmonic motion.** The midpoint of the interval is the **mean,** or **central,** position of the motion, and the distance from the mean position to an endpoint of the interval is the **amplitude.**

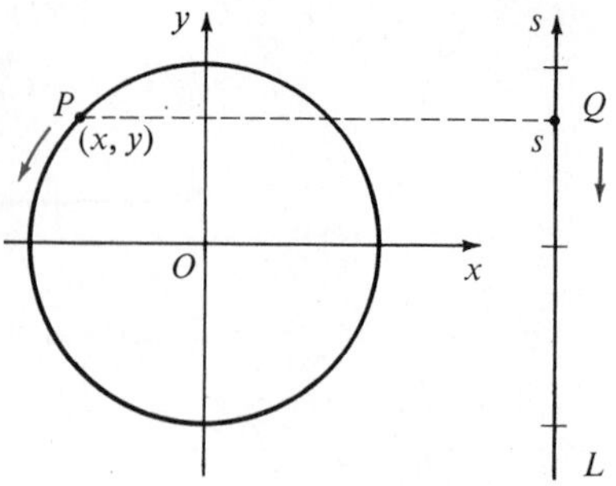

Figure 8–13

By introducing coordinate systems as indicated in Figure 8–13, with the y-axis parallel to L, we may assume that the law of motion of P is given by the two equations in (1), page 329, and we may assume also that the coordinate s of Q on L is equal to the ordinate y of P. Thus, by the second equation in (1), page 329, the law of motion of a point describing simple harmonic motion may be taken to be

$$s = b \sin(\omega t + \theta_0). \tag{2}$$

(The motion of Q may be considered to be the projection of uniform circular motion described in the *counterclockwise* sense; thus we may assume $\omega > 0$.)

In terms of the constants b, ω, and θ_0, we have

$$\text{period} = \frac{2\pi}{\omega}, \qquad \text{amplitude} = b,$$

$$\text{frequency} = \frac{\omega}{2\pi}, \qquad \text{initial phase} = \theta_0.$$

EXAMPLE 2. A point P is describing simple harmonic motion with amplitude 4 feet and frequency 6 cycles per second. Find a law of motion of P if P is at an endpoint of its path at time $t = 0$.

Solution: We choose coordinate systems as in Figure 8–13. Then we need only determine the constants b, ω, and θ_0 which appear in (2). We have amplitude $= b = 4$; and frequency $= \frac{\omega}{2\pi} = 6$, or $\omega = 12\pi$. Thus (2) becomes

$$s = 4 \sin(12\pi t + \theta_0).$$

When $t = 0$, we have $s = 4 \sin \theta_0$. We wish this number to be ± 4, so we choose θ_0 to be an odd multiple of $\frac{\pi}{2}$, for example, $\frac{\pi}{2}$ itself. We obtain

$$s = 4 \sin\left(12\pi t + \frac{\pi}{2}\right).$$

Figure 8–14 illustrates the relation between

(**a**) the uniform circular motion

$$x = 2\cos\left(4\pi t - \frac{\pi}{3}\right), \qquad y = 2\sin\left(4\pi t - \frac{\pi}{3}\right);$$

(**b**) the simple harmonic motion

$$s = 2\sin\left(4\pi t - \frac{\pi}{3}\right); \quad \text{and}$$

(**c**) the graph of the $t \to s$ function described in (**b**) (recall Section 7–6).

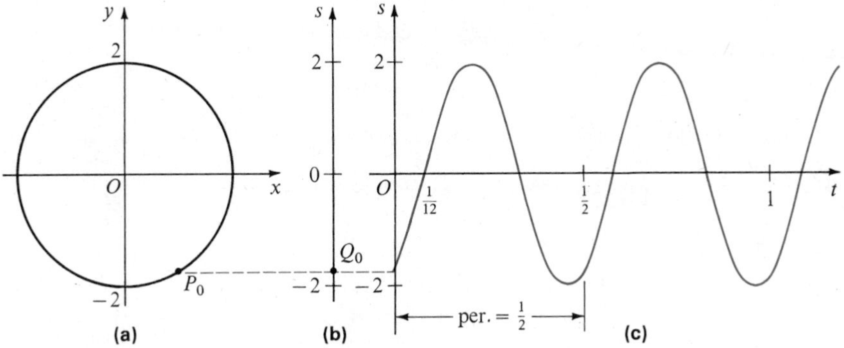

Figure 8–14

Returning to the general case,

$$s = b\sin(\omega t + \theta_0), \tag{2}$$

we see that the velocity (see page 166) of the point describing this simple harmonic motion is

$$v = \frac{ds}{dt} = b\omega\cos(\omega t + \theta_0), \tag{3}$$

and its acceleration (see page 166) is

$$a = \frac{dv}{dt} = -b\omega^2\sin(\omega t + \theta_0). \tag{4}$$

ORAL EXERCISES

An angular speed of 120 r.p.m. is the same as:

1. __?__ radians per minute

2. __?__ radians per second

3. __?__ degrees per second

In Exercises 4–6, a law for a uniform circular motion is given. State (a) the radius of the circle, (b) the period of the motion, (c) the frequency of the motion, and (d) the position of the moving point when $t = 0$.

4. $x = 3 \cos 2t,\ y = 3 \sin 2t$

5. $x = \cos\left(\pi t + \frac{\pi}{2}\right),\ y = \sin\left(\pi t + \frac{\pi}{2}\right)$

6. $x = -2 \sin 3t,\ y = 2 \cos 3t$

WRITTEN EXERCISES

In Exercises 1–6, a point which is at P_0 when $t = 0$ travels around the circle at a constant speed in the indicated direction with $\frac{ds}{dt}$ or ω as indicated. Find equations for the law of motion. Specify the units used for t and for x and y.

A

1.

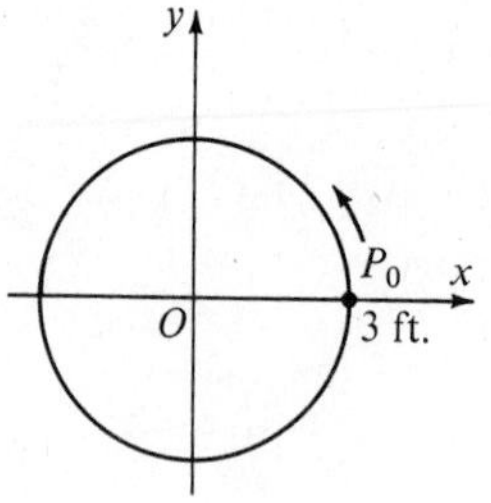

a. $\frac{ds}{dt} = 2$ feet per minute

b. $\omega = 4$ r.p.m.

2.

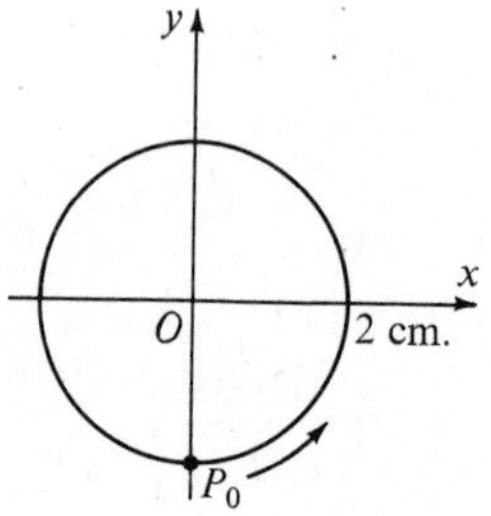

a. $\frac{ds}{dt} = 2$ centimeters per second

b. $\omega = 1$ radian per second

3.

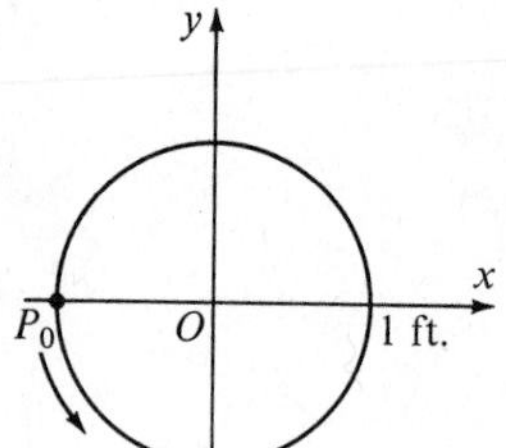

a. $\frac{ds}{dt} = 1$ inch per minute

b. $\omega = 10$ degrees per hour

4.

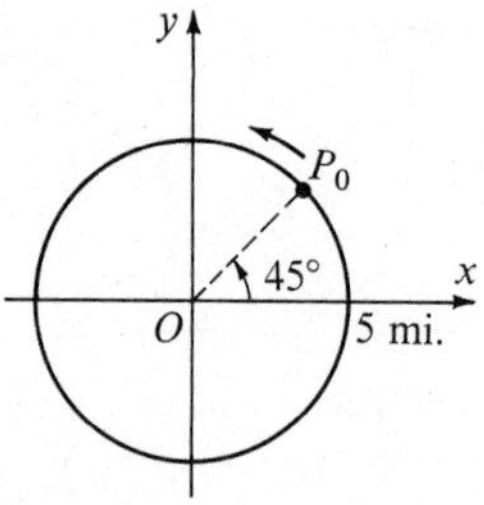

a. $\frac{ds}{dt} = 60$ m.p.h.

b. $\omega = \frac{1}{2}$ rev. per hour

5.

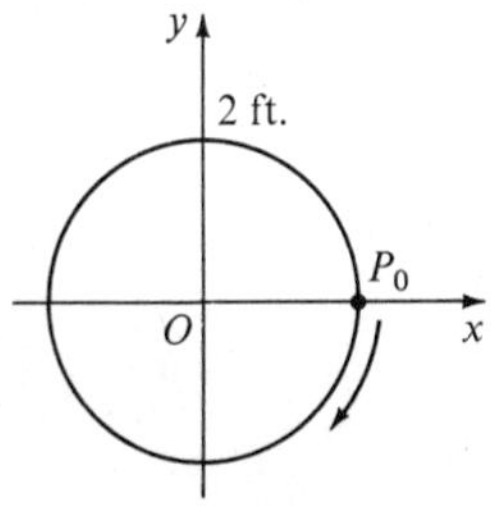

a. $\left|\frac{ds}{dt}\right| = 10$ feet per minute

b. $|\omega| = 10$ r.p.m.

6.

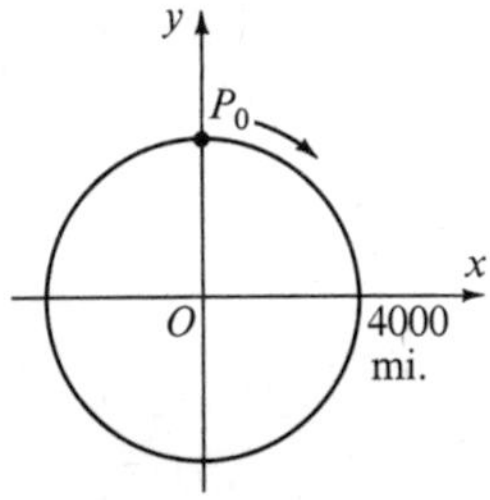

a. $\left|\frac{ds}{dt}\right| = 18{,}000$ m.p.h.

b. $|\omega| = 12$ rev. per day

In Exercises 7 and 8, some information is given about the simple harmonic motion described by a point *P*. Find an equation for the law of motion of *P*.

7. Amplitude 2 feet; period 8π seconds; P is at an endpoint of its path when $t = 0$.

8. P oscillates over an interval 6 centimeters long with frequency 6 cycles per second and is at the mean position when $t = 0$.

9. Show that for simple harmonic motion

$$v^2 = \omega^2(b^2 - s^2).$$

[*Hint:* Use Equations (2) and (3), page 331.]

10. Show that for simple harmonic motion

$$a = -\omega^2 s,$$

and therefore

$$s'' + \omega^2 s = 0. \qquad \text{(C)}$$

[*Hint:* Use Equations (2) and (4), page 331. Equation (C) is sometimes called the **harmonic oscillator equation.** This exercise shows that (2) is a solution of (C), and it can be shown that every solution of (C) is of the form (2).]

11. Show the following about simple harmonic motion:

a. The speed $|v|$ is greatest when the point is at the mean position ($s = 0$), and is then equal to ωb. [*Hint:* Use the result of Exercise 9.]

b. The magnitude of the acceleration $|a|$ is greatest when the point is at an endpoint of its path and is then equal to $\omega^2 b$. [*Hint:* Use the result of Exercise 10.]

EXAMPLE. A point Q is moving in simple harmonic motion. When Q is 8 feet from the mean position, its speed is 3 feet per second and the magnitude of its acceleration is 2 feet per second per second. Find (**a**) the period and (**b**) the amplitude.

Solution: At a certain instant, we must have $s = 8$, $v = 3$, $a = -2$.
[Since $a = -\omega^2 s$ (Exercise 10, above), displacement and acceleration have opposite signs.]

(*Solution continued*)

a. Substituting in $a = -\omega^2 s$, we have

$$-2 = -\omega^2 \cdot 8, \quad \text{or} \quad \omega = \tfrac{1}{2}.$$

From this, we see that the period $= \dfrac{2\pi}{\omega} = 4\pi$ seconds.

b. Substituting in $v^2 = \omega^2(b^2 - s^2)$ [see Exercise 9, page 333], we get

$$3^2 = (\tfrac{1}{2})^2(b^2 - 8^2).$$

From this, it follows that the amplitude $= b = 10$ feet.

In Exercises 12–16, a point P is describing simple harmonic motion.

B **12.** The amplitude of the motion is 8 feet, and the maximum acceleration of P is 32 feet per second per second. Find the frequency.

13. When P is 8 centimeters from the mean position, its speed is 18 centimeters per second; and the maximum speed of P is 30 centimeters per second. Find the amplitude and the frequency.

14. The maximum speed of P is 10 feet per second, and the period is one minute. Find the amplitude.

15. At what portion of its maximum speed is P traveling when it is halfway from the mean position to an endpoint of its path?

16. Where is P when it is traveling at half its maximum speed?

C **17.** The law of motion of a point is given by

$$s = a \cos kt + b \sin kt.$$

Show that the point is describing simple harmonic motion and find the amplitude and the period of the motion. [*Hint:* See Exercise 16, page 298.]

18. Suppose it were possible to drill a hole through the earth, passing through its center. It can be shown that if a ball were to be dropped into the hole, it would (approximately) describe simple harmonic motion with amplitude equal to the radius of the earth (about 4000 miles). Find the period of the motion of the ball. (The magnitude of the acceleration at the surface of the earth is about 32 feet per second per second.)

CHAPTER SUMMARY

1. The circular functions **tangent, cotangent, secant,** and **cosecant** are defined in terms of the sine and cosine functions by

$$\tan x = \frac{\sin x}{\cos x} \qquad \sec x = \frac{1}{\cos x} \qquad (\text{provided } \cos x \neq 0)$$

$$\operatorname{ctn} x = \frac{\cos x}{\sin x} \qquad \csc x = \frac{1}{\sin x} \qquad (\text{provided } \sin x \neq 0)$$

2. Among the identities involving these functions are

$$\tan^2 x + 1 = \sec^2 x \qquad \text{and} \qquad 1 + \operatorname{ctn}^2 x = \csc^2 x.$$

3. All six circular functions are differentiable, and

$$\frac{d}{dx}\sin x = \cos x \qquad \frac{d}{dx}\cos x = -\sin x$$

$$\frac{d}{dx}\tan x = \sec^2 x \qquad \frac{d}{dx}\operatorname{ctn} x = -\csc^2 x$$

$$\frac{d}{dx}\sec x = \sec x \tan x \qquad \frac{d}{dx}\csc x = -\csc x \operatorname{ctn} x.$$

4. We obtain the one-to-one subfunction Sin of sin by restricting the domain of sin to the interval $-\frac{\pi}{2} \leq x \leq \frac{\pi}{2}$. Sin has an inverse function Sin^{-1}, the **inverse sine function.** Thus,

$$y = \text{Sin}^{-1} x \quad \text{if and only if} \quad \sin y = x \;\text{ and }\; -\frac{\pi}{2} \leq y \leq \frac{\pi}{2}.$$

Using similar methods we can define the inverse circular functions Cos^{-1}, Tan^{-1}, and Ctn^{-1}. For these we have:

$$y = \text{Cos}^{-1} x \quad \text{if and only if} \quad \cos y = x \;\text{ and }\; 0 \leq y \leq \pi,$$

$$y = \text{Tan}^{-1} x \quad \text{if and only if} \quad \tan y = x \;\text{ and }\; -\frac{\pi}{2} < y < \frac{\pi}{2},$$

$$y = \text{Ctn}^{-1} x \quad \text{if and only if} \quad \operatorname{ctn} y = x \;\text{ and }\; 0 < y < \pi.$$

5. The derivatives of the inverse circular functions are given by the formulas

$$\frac{d}{dx}\text{Sin}^{-1} x = \frac{1}{\sqrt{1 - x^2}} \qquad \frac{d}{dx}\text{Tan}^{-1} x = \frac{1}{1 + x^2}$$

$$\frac{d}{dx}\text{Cos}^{-1} x = -\frac{1}{\sqrt{1 - x^2}} \qquad \frac{d}{dx}\text{Ctn}^{-1} x = -\frac{1}{1 + x^2}.$$

6. A point P which is moving at constant speed around a circle is said to be describing **uniform circular motion.** If Q is the projection on a line L of such a point P, then Q describes **simple harmonic motion.** The law of motion of Q may be taken to be

$$s = b \sin(\omega t + \theta_0), \qquad \omega > 0,$$

where s is the coordinate of Q on L.

CHAPTER TEST

8–1 **1.** Find the first, second, third, and fourth derivatives of

$$f\colon x \to \sin x.$$

What do you think the 43rd derivative of f is?

2. Show that if $y = e^x \sin x$, then

$$\frac{d^2y}{dx^2} - 2\frac{dy}{dx} + 2y = 0.$$

8–2 **3.** Find a formula for $\tan 3x$ in terms of $\tan x$.

4. Show that

$$\frac{d}{dx}\log(\tan x + \operatorname{ctn} x) = \tan x - \operatorname{ctn} x.$$

8–3 **5.** Give the numerical value of

a. $\operatorname{Sin}^{-1}\left(\sin\frac{3\pi}{4}\right)$ **b.** $\sin\left(\operatorname{Cos}^{-1}\left(-\frac{1}{2}\right)\right)$

6. Find $\frac{d}{dx}(x\operatorname{Tan}^{-1}x - \log\sqrt{1+x^2})$ and use the result to state an integral formula.

8–4 **7.** A point travels with speed 6 feet per second in a counterclockwise direction around the circle $x^2 + y^2 = 8$ (x and y measured in feet). When $t = 0$, the point is at (2, 2). Find equations for the law of motion.

8. A point is describing simple harmonic motion according to the law

$$s = 5\sin(3t + 2).$$

Find (**a**) the amplitude, (**b**) the period, and (**c**) the frequency. (**d**) What is the first time after $t = 0$ that the point is at the mean position?

RECOMMENDED READINGS

DUBISCH, ROY, ed., *Circular Functions*, Supplementary and Enrichment Series, SMSG (Pasadena, California: A. C. Vroman, Inc., 1964).

PÓLYA, GEORGE, *Mathematical Methods in Science*, Studies in Mathematics, Vol. XI, SMSG (Pasadena, California: A. C. Vroman, Inc., 1963).

The Fundamental Theorem of Calculus

In Chapter 3 we defined the *derivative* of a function f as follows:

$$f'(x) = \frac{d}{dx} f(x) = \lim_{z \to x} \frac{f(z) - f(x)}{z - x}.$$

Then in the essay following Chapter 5, using a somewhat more complicated limiting process, we introduced the *integral* of a function f over an interval $a \leq x \leq b$: $\int_a^b f(x)\,dx$. The two concepts have the geometrical interpretations indicated below. Leibniz and Newton discovered independently

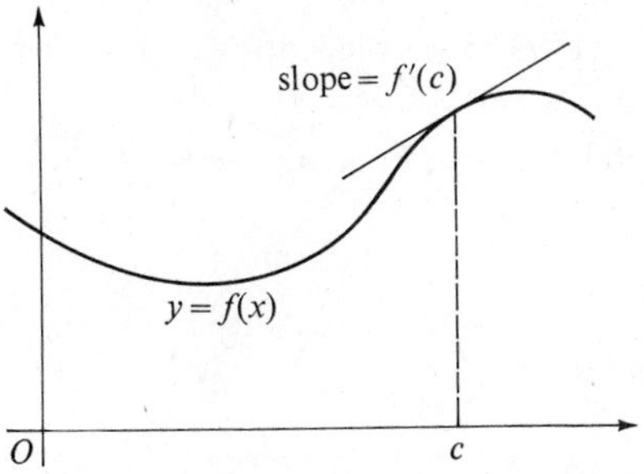

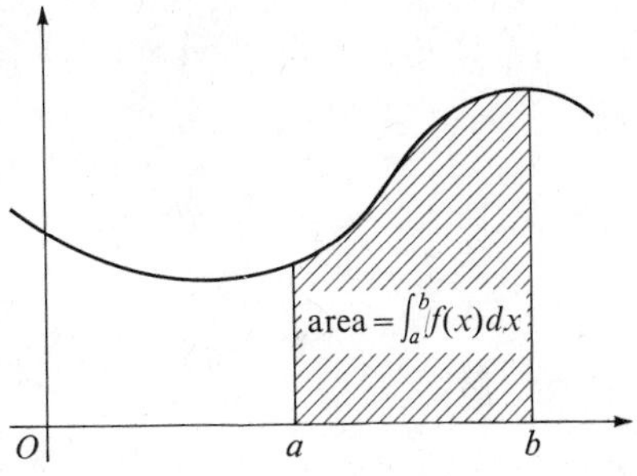

that these concepts are related in a way which allows each to be used in the study of the other and permits the development of the calculus as a unified whole.

This relationship is expressed in the Fundamental Theorem of Calculus; to discuss it, let us consider a function f continuous on $a \leq x \leq b$. Now define a new function F on $a \leq x \leq b$ by integrating f, not from a to the fixed number b, but rather from a to x, where x is a variable. To avoid using x as this variable and also as the variable appearing in the symbol $f(x)\,dx$, we use t in the latter and define F by

$$F(x) = \int_a^x f(t)\,dt. \tag{1}$$

This integral can be interpreted as the area of the region bounded by the t-axis, the curve $y = f(t)$, and the lines $t = a$ and $t = x$, as shown at the left, below.

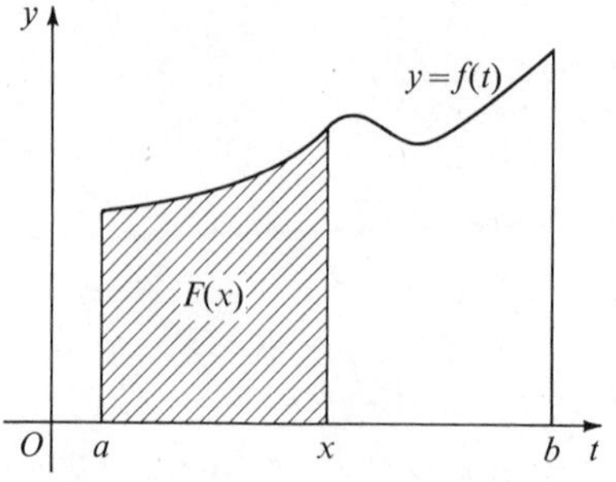

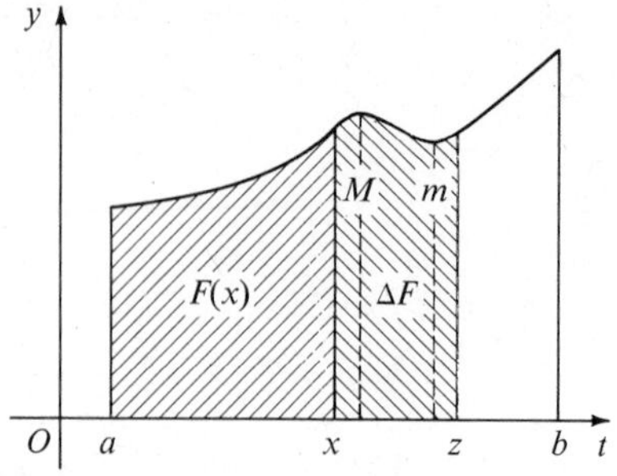

The Fundamental Theorem of Calculus asserts that $F'(x) = f(x)$. Using other notation, we have

$$\frac{d}{dx}\int_a^x f(t)\,dt = f(x).$$

Notice that the left-hand member involves *both* integration and differentiation.

To see why $F'(x) = f(x)$ for the function F defined by (1), notice in the figure at the right, above, that $\Delta F = F(z) - F(x)$ is the area of the region shaded with segments slanting downward to the right. Notice also that the value of ΔF lies between $m(z - x)$ and $M(z - x)$, where m and M are the least and greatest values, respectively, of f in the interval from x to z. Thus we have $m(z - x) \leq F(z) - F(x) = M(z - x)$, or

$$m \leq \frac{F(z) - F(x)}{z - x} \leq M.$$

Since f is continuous, both m and M approach $f(x)$ as z approaches x. Therefore, by definition of derivative,

$$F'(x) = \lim_{z \to x} \frac{F(z) - F(x)}{z - x} = f(x).$$

[Geometrically, this means that the rate of change, with respect to x, of the area under the graph of f is equal, for each x, to the ordinate $f(x)$.]

The result just proved enables us to give an affirmative answer to the question: Given a function f continuous on $a \leq x \leq b$, does f necessarily have an *antiderivative* function F such that $F'(x) = f(x)$? The result also reveals why we use the term "indefinite integral" as a synonym for "antiderivative" and use the symbol $\int f(x)\,dx$ for the most general antiderivative of f (see pages 243 and 244). Using the fact that any two antiderivatives of a given function differ by a constant, we have

$$\int f(x)\,dx = \int_a^x f(t)\,dt + c.$$

For example, if we did not know an antiderivative of $f\colon x \to x^2$, we could perform an *integration* as in the essay at the end of Chapter 5 to show that

$$\int_0^x t^2\,dt = \frac{x^3}{3}$$

and would therefore have

$$\int x^2\,dx = \frac{x^3}{3} + c.$$

This method is of mostly theoretical interest and is seldom used in practice.

A second part of the Fundamental Theorem of Calculus provides us with a very useful way of evaluating $\int_a^b f(x)\,dx$ provided we know any antiderivative G of f. Since the antiderivative $G(x)$ and $\int_a^x f(t)\,dt$ differ by a constant, we have

$$\int_a^x f(t)\,dt = G(x) + c. \tag{2}$$

It is natural to define $\int_a^a f(t)\,dt$ to be 0, hence if we substitute a for x in (2), we obtain

$$0 = G(a) + c, \quad \text{or} \quad c = -G(a).$$

Therefore,

$$\int_a^x f(t)\,dt = G(x) - G(a).$$

Now substitute b for x:

$$\int_a^b f(t)\,dt = G(b) - G(a).$$

Since t is a "dummy variable" we may replace it by any symbol not already appearing. Thus

$$\int_a^b f(x)\,dx = G(b) - G(a),$$

where G is any antiderivative of f.

Putting together the results proved above, we have the complete

Fundamental Theorem of Calculus:

Let f be continuous on $a \leq x \leq b$, and define F by

$$F(x) = \int_a^x f(t)\,dt.$$

Then F is an antiderivative of f; that is, $F'(x) = f(x)$. Moreover, if G is *any* antiderivative of f, then

$$\int_a^b f(x)\,dx = G(b) - G(a).$$

To illustrate the use of this theorem in evaluating integrals, consider

$$\int_1^3 \left(x + \frac{1}{x}\right) dx.$$

Using the antiderivative formulas on page 245, we see that an antiderivative of $f(x) = x + \dfrac{1}{x}$ is $G(x) = \dfrac{x^2}{2} + \log|x|$. Therefore,

$$\int_1^3 \left(x + \frac{1}{x}\right) dx = \left(\frac{3^2}{2} + \log 3\right) - \left(\frac{1^2}{2} + \log 1\right) = 4 + \log 3.$$

Both differential and integral calculus are used in solving the variety of engineering problems that arise in the construction and operation of dams and their powerplants.

From the impetus given by Newton and Leibniz, calculus has developed and is continuing to develop as one of the most basic intellectual tools for dealing with the complex problems of today's scientific and industrial society.

READING LIST

APOSTOL, TOM M., *Calculus*, Vol. 1 (New York: Blaisdell Publishing Company, 1961).

School Mathematics Study Group, *Calculus of Elementary Functions* (Pasadena, California: A. C. Vroman, Inc., 1969).

COMPREHENSIVE REVIEW

Chapters 1 and 2. Functions and Polynomials

1. Given the functions $f: x \to 1 - 2x$ and $g: x \to x^2$, find formulas for:

a. $(f + g)(x)$ **b.** $(fg)(x)$ **c.** $(f \circ g)(x)$ **d.** $(g \circ f)(x)$ **e.** $f^{-1}(x)$

2. Graph each of the following functions:

a. $x \to |2 - x|$ **b.** $x \to 2 - |x|$ **c.** $x \to |2 - |x||$

3. Given the line L: $2x - 3y = 6$. Find an equation of the line which passes through $(2, -1)$ and:

***a.** is parallel to L, ***b.** is perpendicular to L,

c. passes through the point where L crosses the x-axis.

4. For the function $f: x \to 5 + 4x - x^2$, find (**a**) the zeros of f and (**b**) without using calculus, the greatest value of f.

5. Determine all the rational roots of the equation

$$4x^5 + 8x^4 + x^3 - 5x^2 - x + 1 = 0$$

and their multiplicities.

6. Find all the *real* roots of the equation $4x^7 + x^4 + 3 = 0$ and explain how you know you have found them all.

Chapters 3 and 4. Differential Calculus

7. Use the definition of the derivative to find $f'(a)$ if

$$f(x) = \frac{x}{x + 2}.$$

8. Draw the graph of the function $f: x \to x^3 - 6x^2 + 9x$ after first finding the coordinates of its relative maximum and minimum, and inflection points.

9. Find the points of the parabola $y = x^2$ which are closest to the point $\left(0, \frac{9}{2}\right)$.

10. Find the rate of change of (**a**) the volume, and (**b**) the surface area of a sphere with respect to its diameter.

11. Find $f'(x)$ if (**a**) $f(x) = \dfrac{1 - x^2}{1 + x^2}$, (**b**) $f(x) = \dfrac{1}{\sqrt{1 - x^2}}$

12. Find an equation of the line which is tangent to the graph of $x^3 + 3x^2y - y^3 = 3$ at the point $(1, -2)$.

Chapters 5 and 6. Logarithmic and Exponential Functions

13. Determine the value of x which makes the statement true:

a. $\int_3^9 \frac{1}{t}\,dt = \int_x^6 \frac{1}{t}\,dt$ **b.** $\int_1^x \frac{1}{t}\,dt = 3$

14. Given that $\log 4 = p$ and $\log 5 = q$, find in terms of p and q:

a. $\log 20$ **b.** $\log 2$ **c.** $\log 0.2$ **d.** $\int_4^5 \frac{1 + x^2}{x}\,dx$

15. Find $f'(x)$ if (**a**) $f(x) = \left(\frac{1}{e}\right) 2x$, (**b**) $\log x \sqrt{1 + x^2}$.

16. Find a function whose graph passes through $(0, 1)$ and has slope at (x, y) equal to (**a**) $-2x$, (**b**) $-2y$.

Chapters 7 and 8. Circular and Inverse Circular Functions

17. **a.** Find the period of the graph of $f: x \to \cos \pi x - \sin \pi x$.

b. Draw two complete cycles of the graph of f.

18. If $\sin x = -\frac{4}{5}$ and $\frac{3\pi}{2} < x < 2\pi$, find:

a. $\sin 2x$ **b.** $\cos 2x$ **c.** $\sin \frac{x}{2}$ **d.** $\cos \frac{x}{2}$

19. Find the relative maximum and relative minimum of $f: x \to 2 \cos x + \cos 2x$ in the interval $0 \leq x < 2\pi$.

***20.** The graph of the function $f: x \to \cos (2 \operatorname{Cos}^{-1} x)$ is part of a parabola. Draw the graph after first finding an equation of the parabola.

---

* Optional

COMMON LOGARITHMS OF NUMBERS*

x	0	1	2	3	4	5	6	7	8	9
10	0000	0043	0086	0128	0170	0212	0253	0294	0334	0374
11	0414	0453	0492	0531	0569	0607	0645	0682	0719	0755
12	0792	0828	0864	0899	0934	0969	1004	1038	1072	1106
13	1139	1173	1206	1239	1271	1303	1335	1367	1399	1430
14	1461	1492	1523	1553	1584	1614	1644	1673	1703	1732
15	1761	1790	1818	1847	1875	1903	1931	1959	1987	2014
16	2041	2068	2095	2122	2148	2175	2201	2227	2253	2279
17	2304	2330	2355	2380	2405	2430	2455	2480	2504	2529
18	2553	2577	2601	2625	2648	2672	2695	2718	2742	2765
19	2788	2810	2833	2856	2878	2900	2923	2945	2967	2989
20	3010	3032	3054	3075	3096	3118	3139	3160	3181	3201
21	3222	3243	3263	3284	3304	3324	3345	3365	3385	3404
22	3424	3444	3464	3483	3502	3522	3541	3560	3579	3598
23	3617	3636	3655	3674	3692	3711	3729	3747	3766	3784
24	3802	3820	3838	3856	3874	3892	3909	3927	3945	3962
25	3979	3997	4014	4031	4048	4065	4082	4099	4116	4133
26	4150	4166	4183	4200	4216	4232	4249	4265	4281	4298
27	4314	4330	4346	4362	4378	4393	4409	4425	4440	4456
28	4472	4487	4502	4518	4533	4548	4564	4579	4594	4609
29	4624	4639	4654	4669	4683	4698	4713	4728	4742	4757
30	4771	4786	4800	4814	4829	4843	4857	4871	4886	4900
31	4914	4928	4942	4955	4969	4983	4997	5011	5024	5038
32	5051	5065	5079	5092	5105	5119	5132	5145	5159	5172
33	5185	5198	5211	5224	5237	5250	5263	5276	5289	5302
34	5315	5328	5340	5353	5366	5378	5391	5403	5416	5428
35	5441	5453	5465	5478	5490	5502	5514	5527	5539	5551
36	5563	5575	5587	5599	5611	5623	5635	5647	5658	5670
37	5682	5694	5705	5717	5729	5740	5752	5763	5775	5786
38	5798	5809	5821	5832	5843	5855	5866	5877	5888	5899
39	5911	5922	5933	5944	5955	5966	5977	5988	5999	6010
40	6021	6031	6042	6053	6064	6075	6085	6096	6107	6117
41	6128	6138	6149	6160	6170	6180	6191	6201	6212	6222
42	6232	6243	6253	6263	6274	6284	6294	6304	6314	6325
43	6335	6345	6355	6365	6375	6385	6395	6405	6415	6425
44	6435	6444	6454	6464	6474	6484	6493	6503	6513	6522
45	6532	6542	6551	6561	6571	6580	6590	6599	6609	6618
46	6628	6637	6646	6656	6665	6675	6684	6693	6702	6712
47	6721	6730	6739	6749	6758	6767	6776	6785	6794	6803
48	6812	6821	6830	6839	6848	6857	6866	6875	6884	6893
49	6902	6911	6920	6928	6937	6946	6955	6964	6972	6981
50	6990	6998	7007	7016	7024	7033	7042	7050	7059	7067
51	7076	7084	7093	7101	7110	7118	7126	7135	7143	7152
52	7160	7168	7177	7185	7193	7202	7210	7218	7226	7235
53	7243	7251	7259	7267	7275	7284	7292	7300	7308	7316
54	7324	7332	7340	7348	7356	7364	7372	7380	7388	7396

*Mantissas, decimal points omitted. Characteristics are found by inspection.

COMMON LOGARITHMS OF NUMBERS

x	0	1	2	3	4	5	6	7	8	9
55	7404	7412	7419	7427	7435	7443	7451	7459	7466	7474
56	7482	7490	7497	7505	7513	7520	7528	7536	7543	7551
57	7559	7566	7574	7582	7589	7597	7604	7612	7619	7627
58	7634	7642	7649	7657	7664	7672	7679	7686	7694	7701
59	7709	7716	7723	7731	7738	7745	7752	7760	7767	7774
60	7782	7789	7796	7803	7810	7818	7825	7832	7839	7846
61	7853	7860	7868	7875	7882	7889	7896	7903	7910	7917
62	7924	7931	7938	7945	7952	7959	7966	7973	7980	7987
63	7993	8000	8007	8014	8021	8028	8035	8041	8048	8055
64	8062	8069	8075	8082	8089	8096	8102	8109	8116	8122
65	8129	8136	8142	8149	8156	8162	8169	8176	8182	8189
66	8195	8202	8209	8215	8222	8228	8235	8241	8248	8254
67	8261	8267	8274	8280	8287	8293	8299	8306	8312	8319
68	8325	8331	8338	8344	8351	8357	8363	8370	8376	8382
69	8388	8395	8401	8407	8414	8420	8426	8432	8439	8445
70	8451	8457	8463	8470	8476	8482	8488	8494	8500	8506
71	8513	8519	8525	8531	8537	8543	8549	8555	8561	8567
72	8573	8579	8585	8591	8597	8603	8609	8615	8621	8627
73	8633	8639	8645	8651	8657	8663	8669	8675	8681	8686
74	8692	8698	8704	8710	8716	8722	8727	8733	8739	8745
75	8751	8756	8762	8768	8774	8779	8785	8791	8797	8802
76	8808	8814	8820	8825	8831	8837	8842	8848	8854	8859
77	8865	8871	8876	8882	8887	8893	8899	8904	8910	8915
78	8921	8927	8932	8938	8943	8949	8954	8960	8965	8971
79	8976	8982	8987	8993	8998	9004	9009	9015	9020	9025
80	9031	9036	9042	9047	9053	9058	9063	9069	9074	9079
81	9085	9090	9096	9101	9106	9112	9117	9122	9128	9133
82	9138	9143	9149	9154	9159	9165	9170	9175	9180	9186
83	9191	9196	9201	9206	9212	9217	9222	9227	9232	9238
84	9243	9248	9253	9258	9263	9269	9274	9279	9284	9289
85	9294	9299	9304	9309	9315	9320	9325	9330	9335	9340
86	9345	9350	9355	9360	9365	9370	9375	9380	9385	9390
87	9395	9400	9405	9410	9415	9420	9425	9430	9435	9440
88	9445	9450	9455	9460	9465	9469	9474	9479	9484	9489
89	9494	9499	9504	9509	9513	9518	9523	9528	9533	9538
90	9542	9547	9552	9557	9562	9566	9571	9576	9581	9586
91	9590	9595	9600	9605	9609	9614	9619	9624	9628	9633
92	9638	9643	9647	9652	9657	9661	9666	9671	9675	9680
93	9685	9689	9694	9699	9703	9708	9713	9717	9722	9727
94	9731	9736	9741	9745	9750	9754	9759	9763	9768	9773
95	9777	9782	9786	9791	9795	9800	9805	9809	9814	9818
96	9823	9827	9832	9836	9841	9845	9850	9854	9859	9863
97	9868	9872	9877	9881	9886	9890	9894	9899	9903	9908
98	9912	9917	9921	9926	9930	9934	9939	9943	9948	9952
99	9956	9961	9965	9969	9974	9978	9983	9987	9991	9996

In some cases only a suggestive description of the term is given; for a precise definition, see the referenced page.

Abscissa of a point. The first coordinate of the ordered pair associated with a point. (p. 12)

Absolute maximum [minimum]. The number $f(c)$ is an **absolute maximum [minimum]** of a function f if and only if $f(c) \geq f(x)$ $[f(c) \leq f(x)]$ for all x in the domain of f. (pp. 154–155)

Absolute value. For every nonzero real number x, its **absolute value,** $|x|$, is the positive number of the pair x and $-x$. $|0| = 0$. (p. 20)

Acceleration. The rate of change of velocity with respect to time. (p. 166)

Amplitude. The maximum deviation from a central position or state, of a periodic phenomenon. For a function of the type $x \to A \sin(kx - h)$, the number $|A|$. (p. 285)

Amplitude of a simple harmonic motion. See *Simple harmonic motion.*

Angle. See *Directed angle.*

Angular speed. In circular motion, the amount of rotation per unit time. (p. 328)

Antiderivative of a function f. A function whose derivative is f. Often referred to as an *indefinite integral.* (p. 243)

Base. The number p in the exponential expression p^q. (pp. 197, 230). See also *Logarithm of x to the base a.*

Bounds for roots. If all the roots of an equation lie in an interval $\{x: a \leq x \leq b\}$, then a is a **lower bound** and b an **upper bound** for the roots of the equation. (p. 99)

Cartesian plane. A plane whose points have been put (in a particular way) into one-to-one correspondence with the set of ordered pairs of real numbers. (p. 12)

Cartesian product. The set of all ordered pairs of the elements of two sets, K and M, where the first component is from K and the second is from M, denoted by $K \times M$. (p. 12)

Commutative ring. A ring in which multiplication is commutative. (p. 32)

Complementary angles. Two angles whose sum is a right angle. (p. 289)

Composition of functions. For the functions f and g, the function $g \circ f: x \to g(f(x))$. The domain of $g \circ f$ is the set of all x in the domain of f for which $f(x)$ is in the domain of g. (p. 34)

Constant function. A function all of whose values are the same number. (p. 20)

Constant of integration. An arbitrary constant, c, which arises in integration due to the fact that if g is an antiderivative of f, so is $g + c$. (p. 245)

Continuous. A function is **continuous** at a, an element of its domain, if and only if $\lim_{x \to a} f(x) = f(a)$. A **continuous function** is one which is continuous at each number in its domain. (p. 115)

Convex downward. A segment G of the graph of a function is **convex downward** (or **concave upward**) if, given any two points P and Q on G, every point of G between P and Q lies below the chord $\overline{PQ}$. (p. 138)

Convex upward. A segment G of the graph of a function is **convex upward** (or **concave downward**) if, given any two points P and Q on G, every point of G between P and Q lies above the chord $\overline{PQ}$. (p. 139)

Cosecant function. The function $\csc\colon x \to \dfrac{1}{\sin x}$ $(\sin x \neq 0)$. (p. 313)

Cosine function. The function $\cos\colon x \to$ abscissa of P_x, where P_x is the point x units around the circle $u^2 + v^2 = 1$ from $(1, 0)$. (p. 270)

Cotangent function. The function $\text{ctn}\colon x \to \dfrac{\cos x}{\sin x}$ $(\sin x \neq 0)$. (p. 313)

Critical point. A point $(c, f(c))$ on the graph of a function f such that $f'(c) = 0$. (p. 132)

Definite integral. See *Integral.*

Degree (angle measure). If the circumference of a circle is divided into 360 equal parts, the degree measure of a central angle is the number of these parts contained in the arc intercepted by the angle if the arc is directed counterclockwise and is the negative of this number if the arc is directed clockwise. (p. 278)

Degree of a polynomial. See *Polynomial.*

Derivative. The derivative of a function f at a is $\lim_{x \to a} \dfrac{f(x) - f(a)}{x - a}$; geometrically, it is the slope of the line tangent to the graph of f at $(a, f(a))$. (p. 122)

Differentiable. A function is **differentiable** at a, an element of its domain, if its derivative at a exists. (p. 123)

Differentiable function. One which is differentiable at each element of its domain. (p. 123)

Differential equation. An equation which involves two variables and derivatives of one of these variables with respect to the other. (p. 248)

Directed angle. An ordered pair (R_1, R_2) of rays having a common endpoint, together with a rotation of R_1 into R_2. The common endpoint is the **vertex,** R_1 the **initial side,** and R_2 the **terminal side,** of the angle. (p. 277)

Directrix of a parabola. See *Parabola.*

Domain. The set of all first components of ordered pairs of a function or a relation. (p. 6)

Dummy variable. A variable which is introduced in a mathematical process but which does not appear in the final form. (p. 124)

Even function. A function f such that $f(-x) = f(x)$ for each x in its domain. (p. 273)

Exponent. The number q in the exponential expression p^q. (p. 197)

Exponential function. A function of the type $x \to a^x$ $(a > 0)$. (pp. 197, 229). See also *Natural exponential function.*

Extremum (plural: **extrema**). Either a maximum or a minimum value of a function. (p. 71)

Field. A commutative ring which has a multiplicative identity element and in which each nonzero element has a multiplicative inverse. (p. 33)

Frequency. The number of cycles completed in unit time, hence the reciprocal of the period. (p. 327)

Function. A relation in which no two different ordered pairs of numbers have the same first component. (p. 3)

Fundamental period. See *Periodic function.*

Graph of a function. The set of all points $(x, f(x))$ such that x is an element of the domain of the function. (p. 17)

"Greatest-integer" function. The function $x \to [x]$, which maps each real number x onto the greatest integer which does not exceed x. (p. 20)

Half-life. The length of time it takes half of a radioactive substance to disintegrate. (p. 253)

Harmonic motion. See *Simple harmonic motion.*

Hyperbolic cosine. The function $\cosh: x \to \dfrac{e^x + e^{-x}}{2}$. (p. 238)

Hyperbolic sine. The function $\sinh: x \to \dfrac{e^x - e^{-x}}{2}$. (p. 238)

Identity. An equation which is true for all values of the variable(s) involved for which both sides of the equation are defined. (p. 274)

Identity function. The function $x \to x$. (p. 20)

Image. See *Mapping.*

Indefinite integral. See *Antiderivative.*

Inflection point. A point P on a graph such that the graph is convex downward on an interval adjacent to P on one side and convex upward on an interval adjacent to P on the other side. (p. 139)

Initial phase. See *Phase.*

Initial side of an angle. See *Directed angle.*

Integral. Geometrically, for a positive function f defined on $a \le x \le b$, the **integral** from a to b of f is the area bounded by the graph of f, the x-axis, and the lines $x = a$ and $x = b$. (p. 204)

Intercept form. If a line has x-intercept a and y-intercept b, the **intercept form** of its equation is $\frac{x}{a} + \frac{y}{b} = 1$. (p. 62)

Inverse cosine function. The function Cos^{-1} such that $y = \text{Cos}^{-1} x$ if and only if $\cos y = x$ and $0 \leq y \leq \pi$. (p. 322)

Inverse of a function. For a one-to-one function f, the function

$$f^{-1} = \{(y, x) : (x, y) \in f\}. \quad \text{(p. 40)}$$

Inverse sine function. The function Sin^{-1} such that $y = \text{Sin}^{-1} x$ if and only if $\sin y = x$ and $-\frac{\pi}{2} \leq y \leq \frac{\pi}{2}$. (p. 321)

Inverse tangent function. The function Tan^{-1} such that $y = \text{Tan}^{-1} x$ if and only if $\tan y = x$ and $-\frac{\pi}{2} < y < \frac{\pi}{2}$. (p. 323)

Lemma. A theorem whose principal use is in proving other theorems. (p. 209)

Linear function. A function f is **linear** if there are numbers m and b such that $f(x) = mx + b$. (p. 19)

Logarithm function. See *Natural logarithm function.*

Logarithm of x to the base a. The quotient of the natural logarithm of x divided by the natural logarithm of a, denoted by $\log_a x$. (p. 232)

Lower bound for roots. See *Bounds for roots.*

Mapping. A function f **maps** a onto b if $f(a) = b$; b is the **image** of a under f and a is the **pre-image** of b under f. (p. 8)

Maximum (plural: **maxima**). See *Absolute maximum* and *Relative maximum.*

Mean position of simple harmonic motion. See *Simple harmonic motion.*

m-fold factor. If $P(x)$ and $Q(x)$ are polynomials, $P(x) = (x - a)^m Q(x)$, and $x - a$ is not a factor of $Q(x)$, then $x - a$ is called an **m-fold factor,** or a factor of **multiplicity m,** of $P(x)$. (p. 90)

Minimum (plural: **minima**). See *Absolute minimum* and *Relative minimum.*

Minute (angle measure). $\frac{1}{60}$ of a degree (in symbols, $1'$). (p. 278)

Multiplicity. See *m-fold factor.*

Natural exponential function. The inverse function of the natural logarithm function, generally denoted by $x \rightarrow e^x$. (p. 218) (The symbol E is used for this function in Chapter 5.)

Natural logarithm function. Let G be the graph of $y = \frac{1}{x}$. The **natural logarithm function** is

$$x \rightarrow \begin{cases} \text{negative of the area under } G \text{ from } x \text{ to } 1 \text{ if } 0 < x < 1 \\ \text{area under } G \text{ from } 1 \text{ to } x \text{ if } x \geq 1. \end{cases}$$

(p. 208) (Standard names for this function are log and ln; the symbol L is used in Chapter 5.)

Normal form. The equation $Ax + By + C = 0$ of a line is in **normal form** if and only if $A^2 + B^2 = 1$. (p. 62)

Odd function. Any function f such that $f(-x) = -f(x)$ for each x in its domain. (p. 273)

One-to-one function. A function f such that for any two different members x_1 and x_2 of its domain, $f(x_1) \neq f(x_2)$. (p. 38)

Ordinate. The second coordinate of the ordered pair associated with a point. (p. 12)

Parabola. The set of all points equidistant from a fixed line and a fixed point not on this line. The fixed line is called the **directrix** and the fixed point the **focus** of the parabola. (p. 75)

Period of a function. See *Periodic function.*

Period of a periodic motion. The time required for the completion of one full cycle. (p. 327)

Periodic function. A function f is **periodic** if there is a number p, $p \neq 0$, such that for every x in its domain, $x + p$ and $x - p$ are in its domain and $f(x + p) = f(x)$. The number p is a **period** of f. The least positive period of f is the **fundamental period** of f. (p. 282)

Phase. In functions of the form $x \to A \sin(kx - h)$ and $x \to A \cos(kx - h)$, the number $kx - h$ is the **phase** and $-h$ the **initial phase** of the function. (p. 295)

Point-slope form. If a line contains the point (x_1, y_1) and has slope m, the **point-slope form** of its equation is $y - y_1 = m(x - x_1)$. (p. 56)

Polynomial. An expression of the form $a_0x^n + a_1x^{n-1} + \cdots + a_{n-1}x + a_n$, where n denotes a nonnegative integer and $a_0 \neq 0$, or the indicated sum of these same terms in any other order. The numbers $a_0, a_1, \ldots, a_{n-1}, a_n$ are the **coefficients,** and n is the **degree,** of the polynomial. (p. 80)

Polynomial equation. An equation of the form $P(x) = 0$, where $P(x)$ is a polynomial. (p. 89)

Polynomial function. A function $x \to P(x)$, where $P(x)$ is a polynomial. (p. 85)

Power function. A function of the type $x \to x^a$ $(x > 0, a \in \mathcal{R})$. (p. 197)

Pre-image. See *Mapping.*

Principal values. Values of the inverse circular functions Sin^{-1}, Cos^{-1}, etc. (The ranges of these functions have been arbitrarily prescribed.) (p. 321)

Quadrant. Each of four regions into which the plane is separated by a set of coordinate axes. (p. 13)

Quadratic function. A function f is **quadratic** if there are real numbers $a \neq 0$, b, and c such that $f(x) = ax^2 + bx + c$. (p. 69)

Radian measure. For an angle θ, the **radian measure,** $m^R\theta$, is the (signed) length of the arc of a unit circle subtended by θ as a central angle. (p. 278)

Range. The set of all second components of ordered pairs of a function or a relation. (p. 6)

Reciprocal of a function. The function $x \to \dfrac{1}{g(x)}$ is the **reciprocal** of the function $x \to g(x)$. (p. 27)

Relation. Any set of ordered pairs. (p. 3)

Relative maximum [minimum]. The number $f(c)$ is a **relative maximum [minimum]** of a function f if there are numbers a and b, $a < c < b$, such that $f(c) \geq f(x)$ $[f(c) \leq f(x)]$ whenever $a < x < b$. (p. 133)

Relatively prime integers. A pair of integers having no common prime factor. (p. 93)

Ring. A set equipped with two associative operations, addition and multiplication, say, such that an additive identity and all additive inverses exist, addition is commutative, and multiplication is distributive over addition. (p. 32)

Secant function. The function sec: $x \to \dfrac{1}{\cos x}$ $(\cos x \neq 0)$. (p. 313)

Second (angle measure). $\frac{1}{60}$ of a minute (in symbols, $1''$). (p. 278)

Sector of a circle. The region bounded by two radii and an arc of a circle. (p. 279)

Signum function. The function $x \to \begin{Bmatrix} 1 & \text{if } x > 0 \\ 0 & \text{if } x = 0 \\ -1 & \text{if } x < 0 \end{Bmatrix}$, sometimes called the **sign function,** or simply sgn. (p. 21)

Simple harmonic motion. If Q is the projection on a line L of a point P describing uniform circular motion, then Q oscillates back and forth on an interval of L in **simple harmonic motion.** The midpoint of the interval is the **mean,** or **central, position of the motion,** and the distance from the mean position to an endpoint of the interval is the **amplitude.** (p. 330)

Simple root. A root of multiplicity one. (p. 95)

Sine function. The function sin: $x \to$ ordinate of P_x, where P_x is the point x units around the circle $u^2 + v^2 = 1$ from $(1, 0)$. (p. 270)

Sine wave. The graph of a function of the form

$$x \to A \sin (kx - h) \quad \text{or} \quad x \to A \cos (kx - h),$$

where A and k are positive. (p. 295)

Sinusoid. A sine wave. (p. 295)

Slope. For any two points $P_1(x_1, y_1)$ and $P_2(x_2, y_2)$, with $x_1 \neq x_2$, the **slope** of segment $\overline{P_1P_2}$ is $\dfrac{y_2 - y_1}{x_2 - x_1}$. (p. 14)

Slope-intercept form. If a line has slope m and y-intercept b, the **slope-intercept form** of its equation is $y = mx + b$. (p. 57)

Symmetric points. Two points P and Q are symmetric with respect to a line K if K is the perpendicular bisector of segment $\overline{PQ}$. (p. 42)

Tangent function. The function tan: $x \to \dfrac{\sin x}{\cos x}$ $(\cos x \neq 0)$. (p. 313)

Terminal side of an angle. See *Directed angle.*

Trigonometric cosine. The value of the **trigonometric cosine** of an angle is the value of the cosine of the radian measure of that angle. (p. 278)

Trigonometric sine. The value of the **trigonometric sine** of an angle is the value of the sine of the radian measure of that angle. (p. 278)

Two-point form. If a line contains the points $P_1(x_1, y_1)$ and $P_2(x_2, y_2)$, $x_1 \neq x_2$, the **two-point form** of its equation is $y - y_1 = \dfrac{y_2 - y_1}{x_2 - x_1}(x - x_1)$. (p. 62)

Uniform circular motion. Motion at constant speed around a given circle. (p. 327)

Upper bound for roots. See *Bounds for roots.*

Variable. A symbol which is used to represent any member of a specified set. (p. 2)

Velocity. The rate of change of position with respect to time. (p. 166)

Vertex. See *Directed angle.*

***x*-intercept** of a graph. The abscissa of a point where the graph intersects the x-axis. (p. 19)

***y*-intercept** of a graph. The ordinate of a point where the graph intersects the y-axis. (p. 19)

Zero of a function. A **zero** of a function f is a number z in the domain of f such that $f(z) = 0$. (p. 70)

ABCDEFGHIJ-D-8543210/79

ANSWERS FOR ODD-NUMBERED EXERCISES

(Written)

ANSWERS FOR ODD-NUMBERED EXERCISES (WRITTEN)

Page 5 **A** **1.** For example, (0, 1), (1, 2), (2, 3), (−1, 0); yes, a function. **3.** For example, (−1, 2), (0, 2), (1, 2), (2, 2); yes, a function. **5.** For example, (0, 1), (1, 6), (0, 2), $(1, 4\frac{1}{2})$; not a function. **7.** For example, (−1, 0), (0, −1), (1, 0), (2, 3); yes, a function. **B** **9.** For example, (−8, −2), (−1, −1), (1, 1), (8, 2); yes, a function. **11.** For example, (4, 5), (1, 2), (0, 1), (1, 2), (4, 5); yes, a function. **13.** equal **15.** unequal

Pages 10–11 **A** **1.** $\{(1, p), (2, q), (3, p), (4, q), (5, p)$; $\{(1, x), (2, y), (2, z), (3, x), (3, y), (4, z)\}$ **3.** domain: {1, 2, 3}; range: {3} **5.** domain: $\mathcal{R}$; range: $\{x: x \geq 1\}$ **7.** domain: $\mathcal{R}$; range: $\{x: x \leq 0\}$ **9.** domain: {0, 1, 4}; range: {0, 1, 2} **11.** domain: $\mathcal{R}$; range: $\mathcal{R}$ **13.** 3 **15.** $\frac{5}{4}$ **17.** $\frac{1}{2}$ **19.** −3 **21.** $\{x: x \neq -1\}$ **23.** $\{x: x \geq 1\}$ **25.** $\{x: x \geq 0 \text{ and } x \neq 1\}$ **B** **27.** $4c^2 + 2c + 1$ **29.** $\frac{1 + y^2}{y^2}$, $y \neq 0$ **31.** $\frac{1}{1 + z}$, $z \neq 0$ or −1 **33.** a, $a \neq 0$ **35.** $\frac{x + 2a}{x}$, $x \neq 0$, $a \neq 0$ **C** **37.** $h(h + 2z + 1)$ **39.** $2y - 1 + h$, $h \neq 0$

Pages 16–17

A **1. a.**

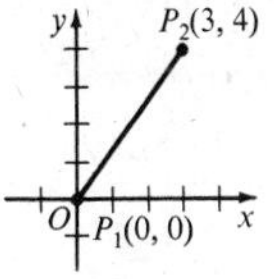

b. 5 **c.** $\frac{4}{3}$

3. a.

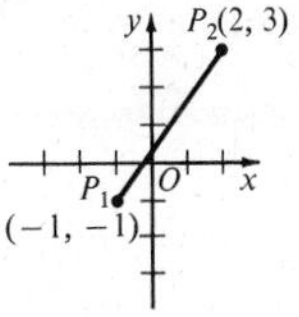

b. 5 **c.** $\frac{4}{3}$

5. a.

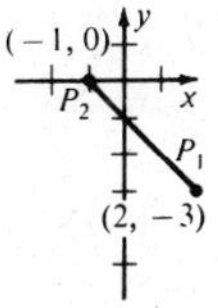

b. $3\sqrt{2}$ **c.** −1

7. a. not equilateral **b.** isosceles **c.** right **9. a.** equilateral **11. a.** not equilateral **b.** isosceles **c.** not right **13.** parallelogram **15.** not a regular quadrilateral **B** **17.** (4, 3) or (−4, −3) **19.** (7, −6) or (−5, 10) **21. a.** $\frac{1}{2}$ **b.** −2 **23. a.** $-\frac{3}{2}$ **b.** −4 **25. a.** 4 **b.** $\frac{2}{3}$

Pages 24–26

A **1.**

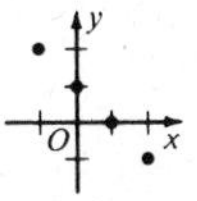

3.

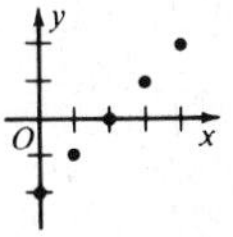

5.

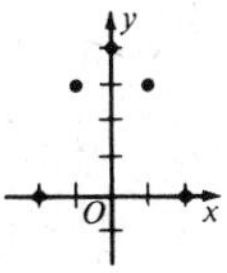

7.

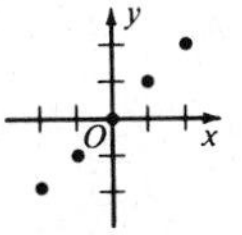

9.

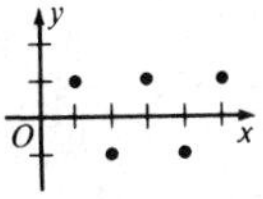

11.

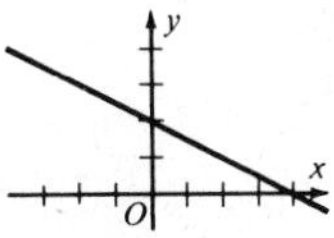

13.

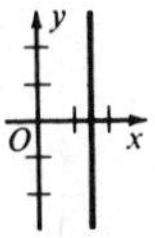

15.

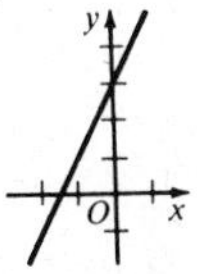

17. a.

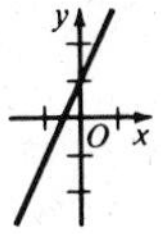

b.

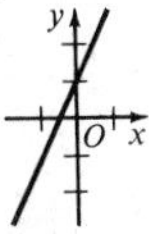

19. a.
b.

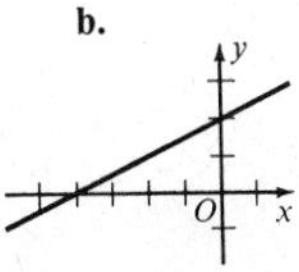

21. a.

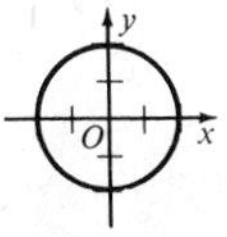

b.

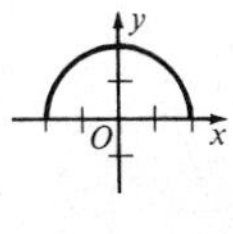

B **23.**

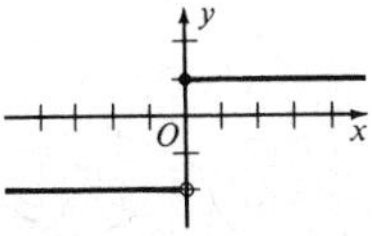

25.

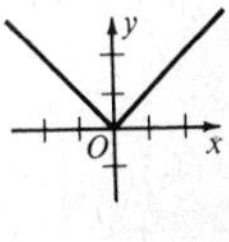

27. a.

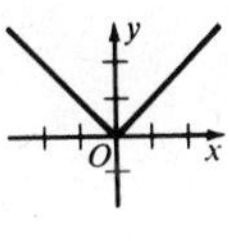

b.

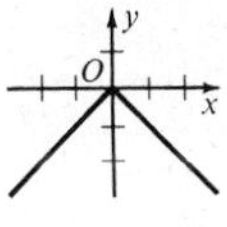

29. a.

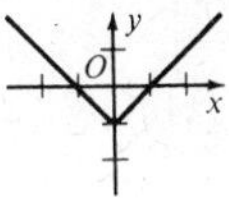

b.

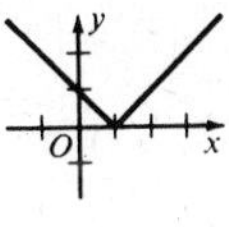

C **31.**

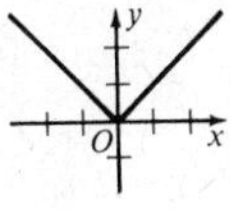

abs. value function

Pages 31–32 **A** **1.** $f + g = \{(1, 3), (2, 6), (3, 8)\}$; $f - g = \{(1, 1), (2, 2), (3, 4)\}$; $fg = \{(1, 2), (2, 8), (3, 12)\}$; $\frac{f}{g} = \{(1, 2), (2, 2), (3, 3)\}$; $g^2 = \{(1, 1), (2, 4), (3, 4)\}$. **3.** $f + g = \{(2, 6), (3, 1), (4, 9)\}$; $f - g = \{(2, 2), (3, 1), (4, 3)\}$; $fg = \{(2, 8), (3, 0), (4, 18)\}$; $\frac{f}{g} = \{(2, 2)\ (4, 2)\}$; $g^2 = \{(2, 4), (3, 0), (4, 9)\}$. **5.** $f +$

$g = \{(1, 5), (2, 6), (3, 7)\}$; $f - g = \{(1, -1), (2, 2), (3, 5)\}$; $fg = \{(1, 6), (2, 8), (3, 6)\}$; $\frac{f}{g} = \{(1, \frac{2}{3}), (2, 2), (3, 6)\}$; $g^2 = \{(1, 9), (2, 4), (3, 1)\}$. **7.** $f + g = \{(0, -1), (1, 2), (2, 5)\}$; $f - g = \{(0, 1), (1, 2), (2, 3)\}$; $fg = \{(0, 0), (1, 0), (2, 4)\}$; $\frac{f}{g} = \{(0, 0), (2, 4)\}$; $g^2 = \{(0, 1), (1, 0), (2, 1)\}$. **9.** Domain of $f + g$, fg, and $\frac{f}{g}$ is $\mathcal{R}$. $(f + g)(x) = 6x + 2$; $(fg)(x) = 12x$; $\left(\frac{f}{g}\right)(x) = 3x$. **11.** Domain of $f + g$, fg, and $\frac{f}{g}$ is $\mathcal{R}$. $(f + g)(x) = x^2 + x + 1$; $(fg)(x) = x^3 + x$; $\left(\frac{f}{g}\right)(x) = \frac{x}{x^2 + 1}$. **13.** Domain of $f + g$, fg, and $\frac{f}{g}$ is $\{x: x \neq 0\}$. $(f + g)(x) = \frac{x^3 + 1}{x}$; $(fg)(x) = x$; $\left(\frac{f}{g}\right)(x) = x^3$. **15.** Domain of $f + g$ and fg is $\mathcal{R}$; domain of $\frac{f}{g}$ is $\{x: x \neq 0\}$. $(f + g)(x) = \begin{cases} x^2 + 1 & \text{if } x > 0 \\ 0 & \text{if } x = 0 \\ x^2 - 1 & \text{if } x < 0 \end{cases}$; $(fg)(x) = \begin{cases} x^2 & \text{if } x \geq 0 \\ -x^2 & \text{if } x < 0 \end{cases}$; $\left(\frac{f}{g}\right)(x) = \begin{cases} x^2 & \text{if } x > 0 \\ -x^2 & \text{if } x < 0. \end{cases}$
17. $x^2 + x$; 0; 6 **19.** $x^3 - 2x^2 + 4$; 4; 4

B 21.

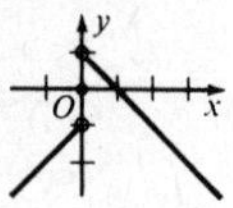

23.

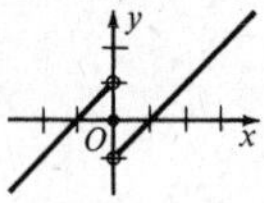

25.

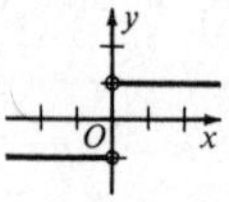

27.

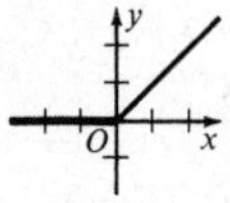

29.

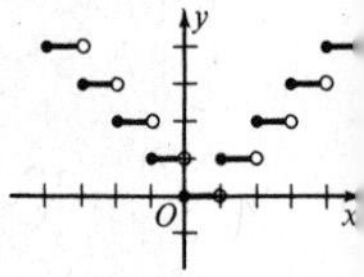

Pages 37–38 A 1. domain: $\mathcal{R}$; $(g \circ f)(x) = 4x^2 + 4$ **3.** doman: $\{x: x \geq 1\}$; $(g \circ f)(x) = \sqrt{x - 1}$ **5.** domain: $\mathcal{R}$; $(g \circ f)(x) = |x|$ **7.** domain: $\{0\}$; $(g \circ f)(x) = \sqrt{-x^2}$ **9.** $\{x: x \neq 1 \text{ or } -1\}$; $(g \circ f)(x) = \frac{1}{x^2 - 1}$ **11.** domain: $\mathcal{R}$; $(g \circ f)(x) = x^2 + 2$ **13.** domain: $\mathcal{R}$; $(g \circ f)(x) = |x + 2|$ **15.** domain: $\mathcal{R}$; $(g \circ f)(x) = |\text{sgn } x| = \begin{cases} 0 \text{ if } x = 0 \\ 1 \text{ if } x \neq 0 \end{cases}$ **17.** domain: $\{x: x \neq 0\}$; $(g \circ f)(x) = x$ **19.** domain: $\{x: x \neq 0\}$; $(g \circ f)(x) = x$ **B 21.** $f(x) = x + 1$; $g(x) = x^5$ **23.** $f(x) = x^2 + 4$; $g(x) = \sqrt{x}$ **25.** $f(x) = x^2 - 1$; $g(x) = \frac{1}{x}$

Pages 45–46 A 1. $D_{f^{-1}} = \mathcal{R}$; $f^{-1}(x) = x + 3$ **3.** $D_{f^{-1}} = \mathcal{R}$; $f^{-1}(x) = \frac{x}{2}$ **5.** $D_{f^{-1}} = \mathcal{R}$; $f^{-1}(x) = \frac{x + 1}{2}$ **7.** $D_{f^{-1}} = \{x: x \neq 0\}$; $f^{-1}(x) = \frac{1}{x}$ **9.** $D_{f^{-1}} = \{x: x \neq 0\}$; $f^{-1}(x) = \frac{1 - x}{2x}$ **11.** $D_{f^{-1}} = \{x: x \neq 1\}$; $f^{-1}(x) = \frac{x}{x - 1}$ **13.** $D_{f^{-1}} = \mathcal{R}$; $f^{-1}(x) = \sqrt[3]{x} + 2$ **15.** $D_{f^{-1}} = \mathcal{R}$; $f^{-1}(x) = x^3$ **17.** $D_{f^{-1}} = \mathcal{R}$; $f^{-1}(x) = (x + 2)^3$ **B 19.** $D_{f^{-1}} = \{x: x \neq 0\}$; $f^{-1}(x) = \frac{b}{x}$ **21.** $D_{f^{-1}} = \{x: x \neq 0\}$; $f^{-1}(x) = \frac{b - dx}{x}$ **23.** $D_{f^{-1}} = \{x: x \neq 1\}$; $f^{-1}(x) = \frac{b}{x - 1}$ **C 25.** $f^{-1}(x) = \frac{ax + b}{cx - a}$

Pages 60–62 A 1. $3x - y - 2 = 0$ **3.** $2x - y + 4 = 0$ **5.** $4x - 3y + 1 = 0$ **7.** $2x - 3y - 3 = 0$ **9.** $2x - y - 1 = 0$ **11.** $x + 3y - 6 = 0$

13.

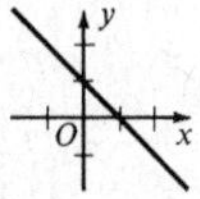

15.

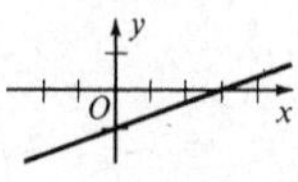

17.

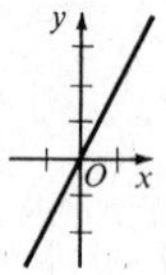

19. $f(x) = \frac{3}{2}x$ **21.** $f(x) = \frac{1}{3}x + 1$

23. $f^{-1}: x \rightarrow \frac{x}{3}$

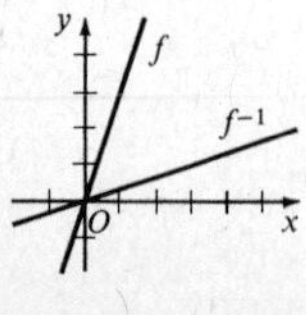

25. $f^{-1}: x \rightarrow \frac{1}{2}x - \frac{1}{2}$

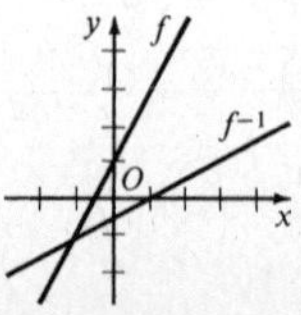

27. $f^{-1}: x \rightarrow \frac{3x - 1}{2}$

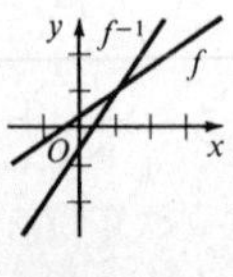

29. $g \circ f\colon x \to 2x + 3$ **31.** $g \circ f\colon x \to x$ **33.** $g \circ f\colon x \to x$ **35.** $g \circ f\colon x \to (pm)x + (pb + q)$ **37. a.** $f\colon x \to 5x + 20$ **b.** 25 in. **c.** 3 lbs. **39. a.** $v\colon t \to -32t + 1600$ **b.** up, 640 ft./sec. **c.** down, 320 ft./sec. **d.** 50 sec. after firing. **41.** $f(x) = -x - 2$ or $f(x) = -\frac{1}{3}x$ **43.** $f(x) = mx + b$ **45.** x-intercept $= a$; y-intercept $= b$

Pages 67–68 A 1. perpendicular **3.** neither **5.** perpendicular **7.** perpendicular **9. a.** $2x - y + 1 = 0$ **b.** $x + 2y - 2 = 0$ **11. a.** $x + y - 3 = 0$ **b.** $x - y - 1 = 0$ **13. a.** $x + 2y - 3 = 0$ **b.** $2x - y - 1 = 0$. **15. a.** $5x - 2y + 20 = 0$ **b.** $2x + 5y - 21 = 0$ **17. a.** $3x - 2y - 12 = 0$ **b.** $2x + 3y + 5 = 0$ **B 19. a.** $\frac{1}{2}$ **b.** -2 **21. a.** $-\frac{3}{2}$ **b.** -4 **23. a.** 4 **b.** $\frac{2}{3}$ **25. a.** $\frac{1}{2}$ **b.** -2 **27. a.** 1 **b.** -4 **29. a.** $-\frac{2}{3}$ **b.** 1

Pages 74–75 A 1. 0 **3.** $-1, 1$ **5.** $-2 + \sqrt{2}, -2 - \sqrt{2}$ **7.** 1 **9.** $-\frac{1}{2}, 1$ **11. a.** $x = 0$ **b.** $f(0) = 0$ **c.** min. **13. a.** $x = 1$ **b.** $f(1) = -1$ **c.** min. **15. a.** $x = -\frac{3}{2}$ **b.** $f(-\frac{3}{2}) = -\frac{9}{4}$ **c.** min. **17. a.** $x = \frac{1}{3}$ **b.** $f(\frac{1}{3}) = 0$ **c.** min. **19. a.** $x = 2$ **b.** $f(2) = 0$ **c.** min. **B 21.** 5 sec.; $156\frac{1}{4}$ ft. **23.** $1012\frac{1}{2}$ square feet. **C 25.** 200 ft. by 300 ft. **27.** 6 and 6; value is 72.

Pages 78–80 A 1. $y^2 = 4x$; directrix $x = -1$ **3.** $x^2 + 8y = 0$; focus $(0, -2)$ **5.** $y^2 + 10x = 0$; focus $(-\frac{5}{2}, 0)$ **7.** $2x^2 - y = 0$; focus $(0, \frac{1}{8})$; directrix $y = -\frac{1}{8}$ **9.** $3x^2 - 4y = 0$; focus $(0, \frac{1}{3})$; directrix $y = -\frac{1}{3}$

11. focus $(1, 0)$; directrix $x = -1$

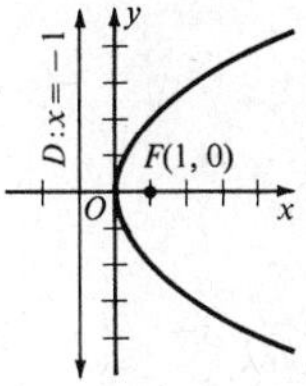

13. focus $(0, \frac{1}{4})$; directrix $y = -\frac{1}{4}$

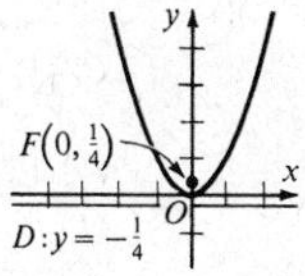

15. focus $(0, -2)$; directrix $y = 2$

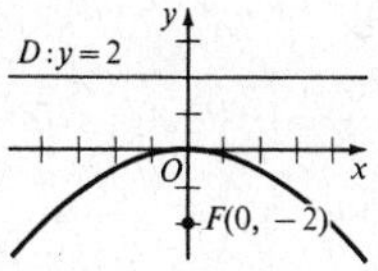

B 17. $x^2 + 6y - 9 = 0$ **19.** $y^2 + 8x - 16 = 0$ **21.** $x^2 + 4y - 8 = 0$ **23.** $x^2 + 2x + 8y - 15 = 0$ **27.** P_r and P_r' are equidistant from F and D.

Pages 84–85 A 1. $a = 0$; $b = -3$; $c = -2$; $d = -5$ **3. a.** $4x^3 - 2x^2 + 3x + 3$ **b.** $4x^3 - 4x^2 + x - 7$ **c.** $4x^5 + x^4 + 19x^3 - 15x^2 + 8x - 10$ **5. a.** $2x^3 + 2$ **b.** $-2x$ **c.** $x^6 + 2x^3 - x^2 + 1$ **7.** $Q(x) = 4x - 7$; $R(x) = -11x + 33$ **9.** $Q(x) = 1$; $R(x) = -2x$ **11.** $P(x) = (x + 2)(S(x))$ **13.** $Q(x) = 4x^2 + 5x + 11$; $R = 22$ **15.** $Q(x) = x^3 - 2x^2 + 4x - 8$; $R = 18$ **B 17.** $a = -\frac{41}{2}$ **19.** $(x - 3)^3 + 8(x - 3)^2 + 25(x - 3) + 31$

Page 88 A 1. $P(-3) = 7$ **3.** $P(1) = -1$ **5.** $S(4) = 3$ **7.** $S(-1) = -2$ **9.** $T(0) = 1$ **11.** $T(2) = 7$ **13.** $U(a) = 0$ **15.** $U(c) = 0$

17.

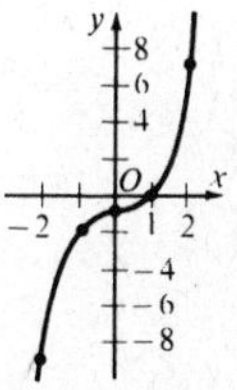

19.

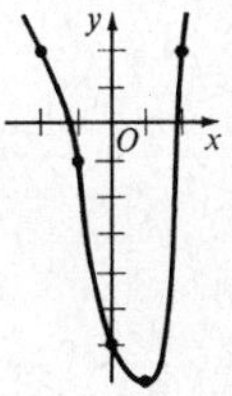

21.

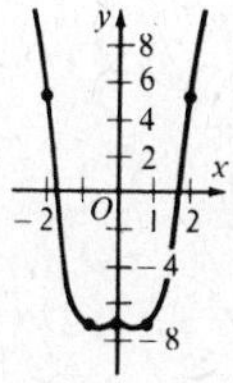

Page 92 A 1. factor **B 9.** multiplicity 2 **11.** multiplicity 2 **C 13.** $c = 0$; $d = -4$

Page 97 A 1. $-\frac{3}{2}$ **3.** None **5.** $1, -1, \frac{4}{3}$ **7.** $-\frac{1}{2}, \frac{2}{3}$ **9.** $-\frac{1}{2}, 2, -2$ **11.** $1, \frac{3}{2}$ (mult. 2), $-\frac{3}{2}$ (mult. 2) **13.** 2 and 3, 3 and 4, -2 and -3 **15.** 0 and 1, 3 and 4, 0 and -1, -3 and -4

Pages 101–102 1. 1 neg. root between -1 and -2; 2 pos. roots, one between 0 and 1 and the other between 2 and 3. **3.** 2 or 0 pos. roots; 1 neg. root **5.** 2 or 0 pos. roots; 3 or 1 neg. roots. **7.** 3 or 1 pos. roots; no neg. roots. **9.** 3 (upper); -2 (lower) **11.** 1 (upper); -2 (lower) **13.** 1 (upper); -1 (lower) **15.** Use Descartes' Rule; $P(x)$ has no pos. roots, 1 neg. root **B 17.** -2 is only root.

Page 114 A **1.** 3 **3.** 4 **5.** -2 **7.** $\frac{1}{2}$ **9.** $-\frac{1}{3}$ **11.** $\frac{1}{2}$ **13.** Answers will vary. **15.** All non-integral values of a.

Pages 119–120 A **1.** continuous **3.** continuous **5.** $x = 1$ **7.** $x = -1$ **9.** All integers except 0 **11.–13.** Answers will vary. **19.** -1 **21.** 2

Pages 125–126 A **1.** $f'(a) = 2a$ **3.** $f'(a) = -2a$ **5.** $f'(a) = 2a - 1$ **7.** $f'(a) = 6a^2$ **9.** $f'(a) = 3a^2 + 2a$ **11.** $f'(a) = -\dfrac{1}{a^2}$ **13. a.** 2 **b.** $2x - y - 1 = 0$ **15. a.** -2 **b.** $2x + y - 5 = 0$ **17. a.** 1 **b.** $x - y - 1 = 0$ **19. a.** 6 **b.** $6x - y - 4 = 0$ **21. a.** 5 **b.** $5x - y - 3 = 0$ **23. a.** -1 **b.** $x + y - 2 = 0$

B 27.

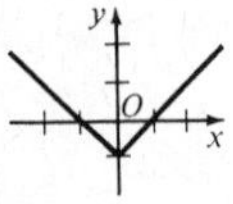

C 29.

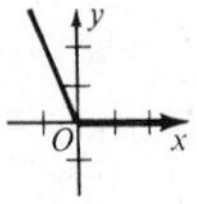

31. d.

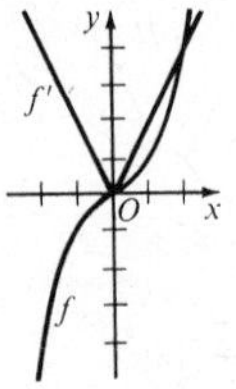

31. a. $f'(0) = 0$ **b.** $f'(x) = 2x, x > 0$ **c.** $f'(x) = -2x, x < 0$ **d.** Diagram above, far right

Pages 130–131 A **1. a.** $f'(x) = 2x + 2$ **b.** $f(-2) = 3;\ f'(-2) = -2$ **3. a.** $f'(x) = 3x^2 + 6x - 9$ **b.** $f(2) = 0;\ f'(2) = 15$ **5. a.** $f'(x) = 4x^3 + 12x^2 + 8x$ **b.** $f(1) = 2;\ f'(1) = 24$ **7.** $2x + y + 1 = 0$ **9.** $15x - y - 30 = 0$ **11.** $24x - y - 22 = 0$ **B 13.** $(-1, 2)$ **15.** $(-3, 25)$; $(1, -7)$ **17.** $(0, -7)$; $(-1, -6)$; $(-2, -7)$ **C 23.** $f'(a) \cdot x - y + f(a) - f'(a) \cdot a = 0$

Pages 136–137 A **1. a.** $(0, -1)$ **b.** falls on $\{x: x < 0\}$; rises on $\{x: x > 0\}$ **c.** See below. **d.** rel. min. -1 at $x = 0$ **3. a.** $(-1, 2)$; $(1, -2)$ **b.** rises on $\{x: x < -1\}$ and on $\{x: x > 1\}$; falls on $\{x: -1 < x < 1\}$ **c.** See below. **d.** rel. max. 2 at $x = -1$; rel. min. -2 at $x = 1$ **5. a.** no critical points **b.** f rises everywhere **c.** See below. **d.** no rel. max. or rel. min. **7. a.** $(-\frac{1}{3}, \frac{5}{27})$; $(1, -1)$ **b.** rises on $\{x: x < -\frac{1}{3}\}$ and on $\{x: x > 1\}$; falls on $\{x: -\frac{1}{3} < x < 1\}$ **c.** See below. **d.** rel. max. $\frac{5}{27}$ at $x = -\frac{1}{3}$; rel. min. -1 at $x = 1$ **9. a.** $(1, -3)$ **b.** falls on $\{x: x < 1\}$; rises on $\{x: x > 1\}$ **c.** See below. **d.** rel. min. -3 at $x = 1$ **B 11.** Answers will vary. **15.** $f: x \to x^5 + x$

1. c.

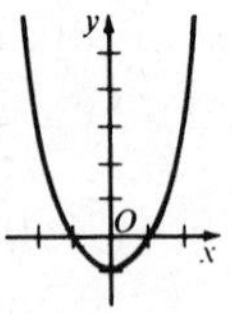

3. c.

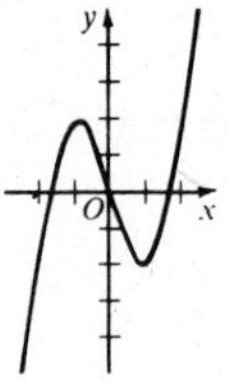

5. c.

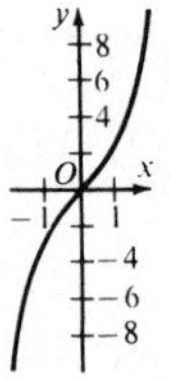

7. c.

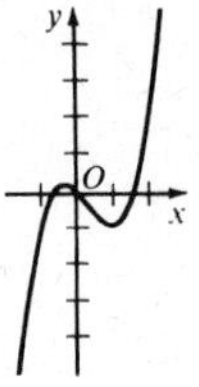

9. c.

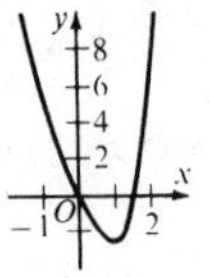

Page 142 A **1.** $g'(x) = 4x^3 - 12x^2 + 12x - 4$; $g''(x) = 12x^2 - 24x + 12$; $g'''(x) = 24x - 24$; $g^{\text{v}}(x) = 24$ **3. a.** upward on $\{x: x < 0\}$; downward on $\{x: x > 0\}$ **b.** $(0, 0)$ **c.** See below. **5. a.** upward on $\{x: x < 0\}$; downward on $\{x: x > 0\}$ **b.** $(0, 0)$ **c.** See below. **7. a.** upward on $\{x: x < \frac{1}{3}\}$; downward on $\{x: x > \frac{1}{3}\}$ **b.** $(\frac{1}{3}, -\frac{11}{27})$ **c.** See below. **9. a.** downward everywhere **b.** no inflection points. **c.** See below.

3. c.

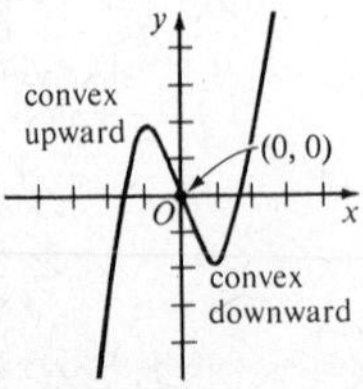

5. c.

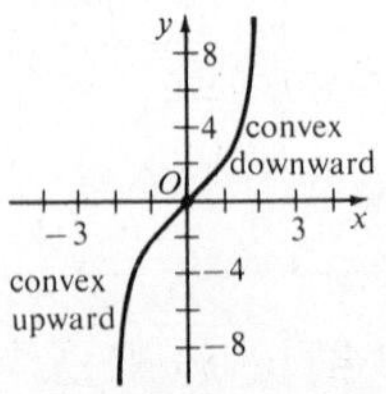

7. c.

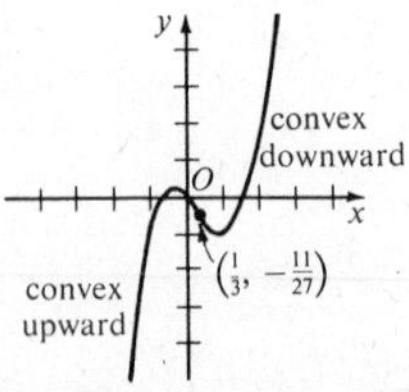

9. c.

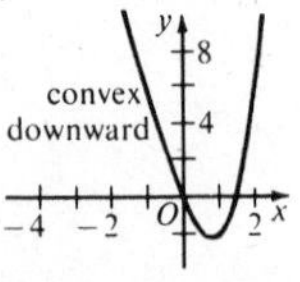

11.
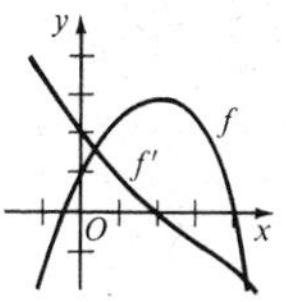

13.
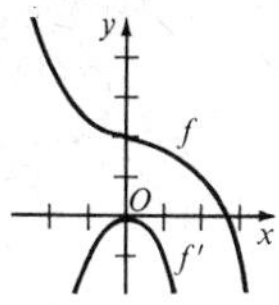

15.
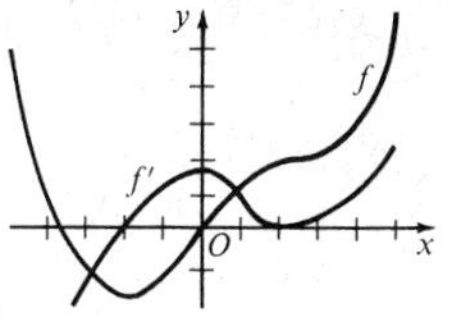

B **17.** no inflection point at (0, 0). **21.** $n - 2$

Pages 157–158 **A** **1.** $f(1) = 13$ is a rel. max.; $f(3) = 9$ is a rel. min. **3.** no extrema **5.** $f(-2) = -8$ is a rel. min.; $f(0) = 8$ is a rel. max.; $f(2) = -8$ is a rel. min. **15.** $f''(-2) = 0$, thus f''-test fails. **17.** See Ex. 5. **19.** $f(0) = 0$ is abs. min.; $f(2) = 4$ is abs. max. **21.** $f(0) = 0$ is abs. min.; $f(1) = 3$ is abs. max. **B** **23.** $f(-1)$ is a rel. max.; $f(1) = 2$ is a rel. min. **25.** $2c$

Pages 163–164 **A** **1.** 6 and 6 **3.** 4 and 8 **5.** 1800 sq. ft. **7.** 1800 sq. ft. **9.** $120\sqrt{3}$ **11.** $\frac{2a''}{3} \times \frac{2a''}{3} \times \frac{a''}{6}$; $\frac{2a^3}{27}$ cubic inches **13.** 4 p.m. that day **15.** $4' \times 4' \times 4'$ **17.** (1, 2) **19.** $(-\frac{2}{13}, 2\frac{10}{13})$ **21.** (1, 1)

Pages 168–169 **A** **1. a.** $2t - 6$ **b.** 2 **c.** -9 **d.** See below. **3. a.** $3t^2 - 12t + 9$ **b.** $6t - 12$ **c.** 4; 0 **d.** See below.

1. d.
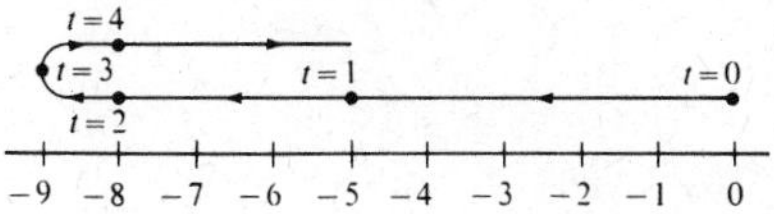

3. d.
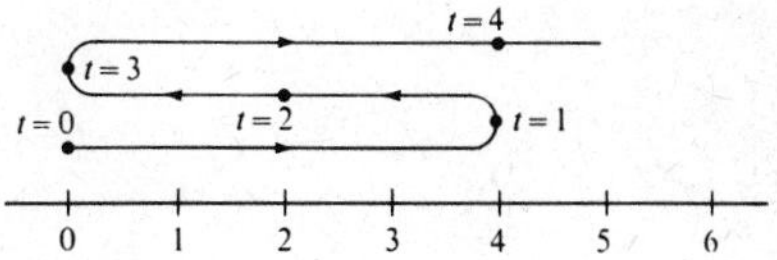

5. a. $3t^2 - 12t + 12$ **b.** $6t - 12$ **c.** 8 **d.** See at right. **7.** $A = l^2$; $\frac{dA}{dl} = 2l$ **9.** $V = \frac{4}{3}\pi r^3$; $\frac{dV}{dr} = 4\pi r^2$ **11.** $C = 2\pi r$; $\frac{dC}{dr} = 2\pi$ **13.** $V = s^3$; $\frac{dV}{ds} = 3s^2$ **15.** $P = 3s$; $\frac{dP}{ds} = 3$

5. d.
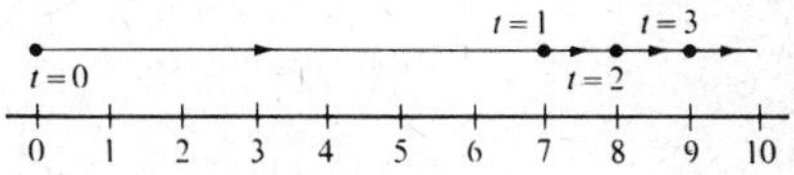

Page 173 **A** **1.** 1.414 **3.** -1.587 **5.** -1.386 **7.** 0.347 **9.** 1.180 **11.** 0.771 **13.** Use $f(x) = x^3 - a$

Pages 177–178 **A** **1.** $y' = 4x^3 + 2x$ **3.** $y' = 4x^3 + 3x^2 + 2x + 1$ **5.** $\phi'(x) = \frac{3}{2}\sqrt{x}$ **7.** $\phi'(x) = \frac{(3x + 1)\sqrt{x}}{2x}$ **9.** $\phi'(x) = \frac{1}{1 - 2x + x^2}$ **11.** $\phi'(x) = -\frac{2}{x^2 - 2x + 1}$ **13.** $\phi'(x) = \frac{\sqrt{x}\,(x - 1)}{2x^2}$ **15.** $\phi'(x) = \frac{x^2 + 2x - 1}{x^2 + 2x + 1}$ **17.** $x + y - 2 = 0$ **19.** $x + 16y - 12 = 0$

Pages 183–184 **A** **1.** $3x^2 + 6x + 3$ **3.** $4x^3 + 4x$ **5.** $4x^3 + 12x^2 + 24x + 16$ **7.** $4(x + 2)^3$ **9.** $\frac{2x}{(1 - x^2)^2}$ **11.** $20(2x + 1)^9$ **13.** $\frac{x}{\sqrt{x^2 + a^2}}$ **15.** $\frac{x + 1}{\sqrt{x^2 + 2x}}$ **B** **17.** $\frac{3\sqrt{3}}{4}a^2$ **19.** $r = \frac{2\sqrt{2}}{3}a$ and $h = \frac{4}{3}a$

Pages 188–189 **A** **1.** 4 **3.** $-\frac{8}{3}$ **5.** $-\frac{2}{11}$ **B** **7.** $\frac{1}{50}$ cm./hr. **C** **9.** 3 ft./sec. **11.** $\frac{2}{\pi}$ cu. ft./min.

Pages 201–202 **A** **1.** $\frac{y^3}{x^2}$ **3.** $-\frac{r^4s^5}{4}$ **5.** $\frac{2x}{y^2}$ **7.** $\frac{y + x}{xy}$ **9.** $-\frac{r^2 + s^2 + rs}{rs(r + s)}$ **11.** $\frac{(y^2 + x^2)^{1/2}}{xy}$ **13.** $\frac{1}{(1 - x)^{1/2}(1 + x)^{3/2}}$ **15.** $x = 1$ **17.** $x = -2$ **19.** $\frac{1}{3x^{2/3}}$ **B** **21.** $-\frac{1}{2x^{3/2}}$ **23.** $\frac{2^{4/3}}{3x^{1/3}}$ **25.** $\frac{1}{(2x + 1)^{1/2}}$ **27.** $\frac{1}{(3x + 2)^{2/3}}$ **29.** $-\frac{x}{(1 - x^2)^{1/2}}$

Pages 207–208 **A** **1.** $x = 3$ **3.** $x = 3$ **5.** $x = \frac{1}{2}$ **7.** $x = 2$ **9.** $x = \frac{q}{p}$ **B** **11. b.** 2.083 **c.** 1.283 **d.** $1.283 < A(1, 5) < 2.083$ **e.** 1.683 **13. b.** 0.760 **c.** 0.635 **d.** $0.635 < A(1, 2) < 0.760$ **e.** 0.698 **15.** Average of upper and lower estimates is the area under the dotted line for each pair of rectangles.

Page 213 **A** **1.** 3.402 **3.** −0.406 **5.** 1.673 **7.** 0.347 **9.** 1.354 **11.** −0.357 **13.** −3.913 **15.** −2.072 **17.** 3.912 **19.** 0.693 **21.** 0.406

Pages 217–218 **A** **1.** $\frac{2}{x}$ **3.** $-\frac{1}{x}$ **5.** $\frac{1}{2x}$ **7.** $-\frac{1}{3x}$ **9.** $x - y - 1 = 0$ **11.** $(e^4, 4)$ **13.** $(e^{c+1}, c + 1)$ **B** **15.** $e^2x - y - 3 = 0$ **17.** $x - e^2y + e^2 = 0$ **C** **19. a.** $f'(x) = 1 + L(x)$ **b.** $f''(x) = \frac{1}{x}$ **c.** $f\left(\frac{1}{e}\right) = -\frac{1}{e}$ is a minimum. **d.** convex downward everywhere. **e.** See at right.

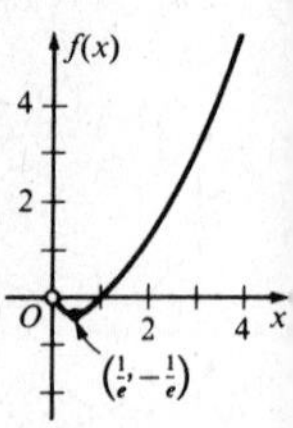

Ex. 19(e)

Page 222 **A** **1.** $x - y + 1 = 0$ **3.** $e^2x - y - e^2 = 0$ **5.** $e^ax - y + e^a(1 - a) = 0$ **7.** $f(x) = x^5$; $g'(x) = \frac{1}{5x^{4/5}}$ **9.** $f(x) = \frac{1}{x^2}$; $g'(x) = -\frac{1}{2\sqrt{x^3}}$ **B** **11.** $f'(x) = xE(x) + E(x)$; $f''(x) = xE(x) + 2E(x)$; $f'''(x) = xE(x) + 3E(x)$; $f^{\text{iv}}(x) = xE(x) + 4E(x)$; $f^{\text{v}}(x) = xE(x) + 5E(x)$ **C** **13.** $f^{(n)}(x) = xE(x) + nE(x)$

Pages 234–235 **A** **1.** 3 **3.** −1 **5.** 3 **7.** 3 **9.** $\frac{1}{5}$ **11.** 16 **13.** 15 **15.** 3 **B** **17.** $\log_a b = \frac{1}{\log_b a}$ **19.** 1.586 **21.** −1.161 **23.** 1.586 **25.** −0.861

Page 239

A **1.**

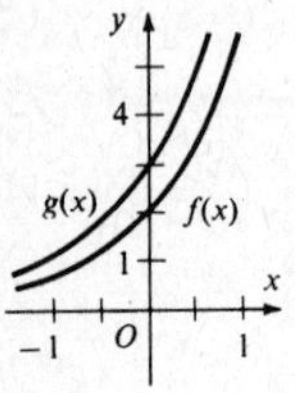

3.

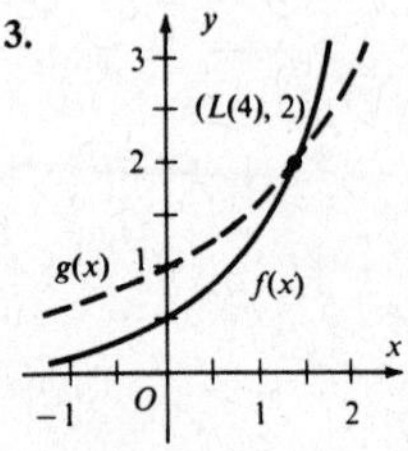

9.

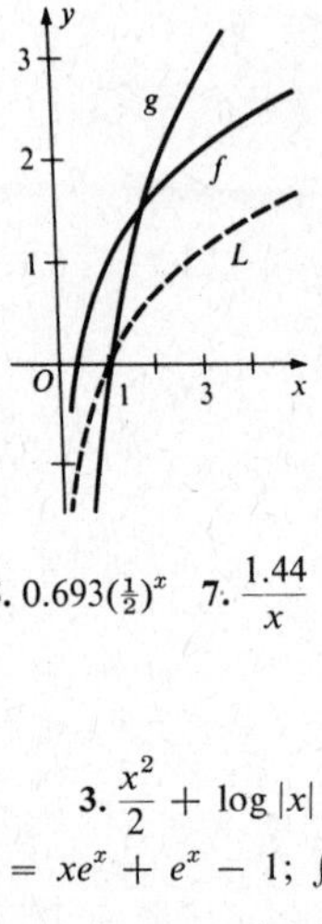

11.

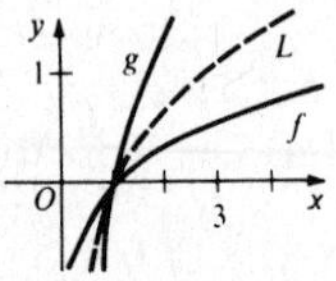

5. (L(4), 2)

Pages 242–243 **A** **1.** $0.693(2^x)$ **3.** $0.347(\sqrt{2})^x$ **5.** $0.693(\frac{1}{2})^x$ **7.** $\frac{1.44}{x}$ **9.** $\frac{2x}{3(x^2 + 1)}$ **11.** $2xe^{x^2}$ **13.** $-e^{1-x}$ **15.** $\frac{1}{x} + \frac{x}{x^2 + 1}$ **C** **23.** $g^{-1}: x \to \frac{1}{k}\log x$

Pages 246–247 **A** **1.** $\frac{x^4}{4} + \frac{x^3}{3} + \frac{x^2}{2} + x + c$ **3.** $\frac{x^2}{2} + \log|x| + c$ **5.** $x + \log|x| - \frac{1}{x} + c$ **7.** $(\log_2 e)2^x + c$ **9.** $\cosh x + c$ **B** **11.** $g'(x) = xe^x + e^x - 1$; $\int(xe^x + e^x - 1)\,dx = xe^x - x + c$ **13.** $g'(x) = \frac{1}{x^2 - 1}$; $\int\left(\frac{1}{x^2 - 1}\right)dx = \frac{1}{2}\log\frac{x - 1}{x + 1} + c$ **15.** Domain of g in Ex. 13 is $\{x: x < -1 \text{ or } x > 1\}$; domain of g in Ex. 14 is $\{x: -1 < x < 1\}$.

Pages 251–252 **A** **1.** $f(x) = x^2 - 1$ **3.** $f(x) = \frac{x^3}{3}$ **5.** $f(x) = 2e^x$ **7. a.** $s = 4t - t^2$ **b.** See below. **9. a.** $s = t^2 - 2t + 1$ **b.** See below. **11. a.** $s = \frac{t^3}{3} - 2t^2 + 3t$ **b.** See below. **13. a.** $s = e^{-2t}$ **b.** See below. **B** **15. a.** $s = -3t^2 + 12t$ **b.** See below. **17. a.** $s = t^3 - 6t^2 + 9t$ **b.** See below. **C** **19. a.** $s = \frac{1}{2}gt^2$ **b.** $v = \sqrt{2gs}$ **21. b.** $y = ce^{ax}$; $y = \sinh ax$; $y = \cosh ax$

7. b.

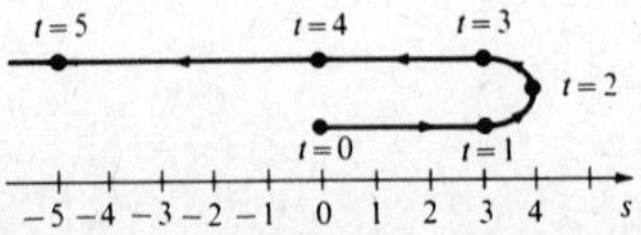

9. b.

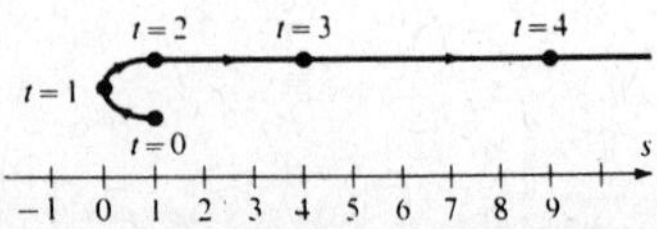

11. b.

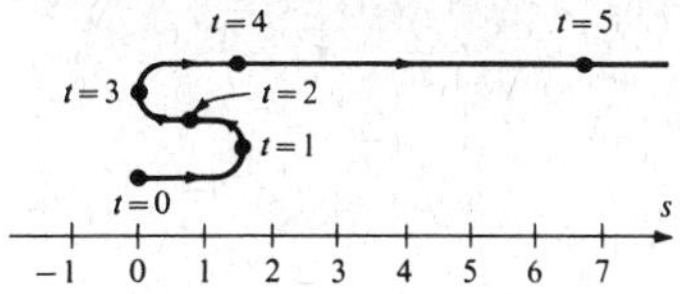

13. b.

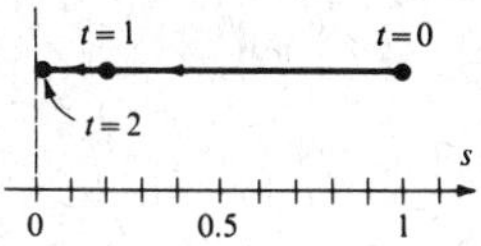

15. b.

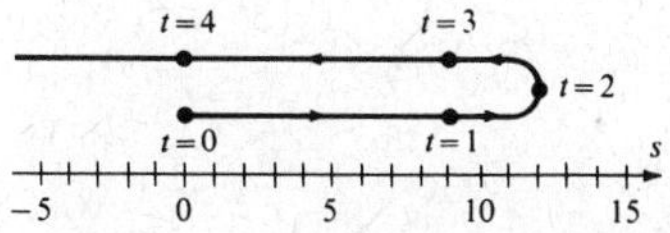

17. b.

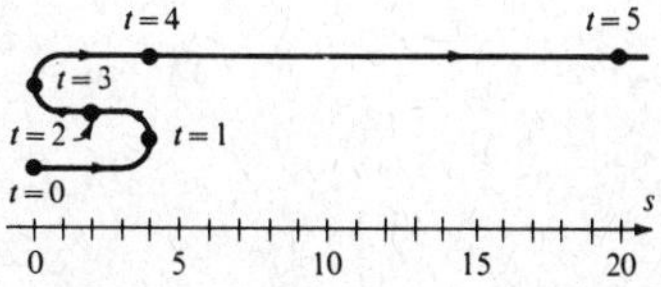

Page 257 A **1. a.** 2.61 grams **b.** 3240 years **3.** $h = -\frac{\log 2}{k}$ **5.** 63.4 minutes **B 7.** $n = n_0(2^{\frac{t}{8}})$ **9. a.** $\frac{du}{dt} = ku$, where u is the amount of sugar still undissolved. **b.** 32.7 minutes

Pages 269–270 A **1.** I **3.** III **5.** I **7.** $\frac{4}{5}$ **9.** $\frac{12}{13}$ **11.** $\frac{3}{\sqrt{10}}$ **B 13. a.** $(\frac{3}{5}, -\frac{4}{5})$ **b.** $(-\frac{3}{5}, \frac{4}{5})$ **c.** $(-\frac{3}{5}, -\frac{4}{5})$ **d.** $(\frac{4}{5}, \frac{3}{5})$ **15. a.** $(-\frac{5}{13}, -\frac{12}{13})$ **b.** $(\frac{5}{13}, \frac{12}{13})$ **c.** $(\frac{5}{13}, -\frac{12}{13})$ **d.** $(\frac{12}{13}, -\frac{5}{13})$ **17. a.** $\left(\frac{3}{\sqrt{10}}, \frac{1}{\sqrt{10}}\right)$ **b.** $\left(-\frac{3}{\sqrt{10}}, -\frac{1}{\sqrt{10}}\right)$ **c.** $\left(-\frac{3}{\sqrt{10}}, \frac{1}{\sqrt{10}}\right)$ **d.** $\left(-\frac{1}{\sqrt{10}}, \frac{3}{\sqrt{10}}\right)$ **19.** $\left(\frac{\sqrt{2}}{2}, \frac{\sqrt{2}}{2}\right)$

Pages 275–276 A **1.** $\sin\left(-\frac{\pi}{4}\right) = -\frac{\sqrt{2}}{2}$, $\cos\left(-\frac{\pi}{4}\right) = \frac{\sqrt{2}}{2}$ **3.** $\sin\frac{13\pi}{6} = \frac{1}{2}$, $\cos\frac{13\pi}{6} = \frac{\sqrt{3}}{2}$ **5.** $\sin\left(-\frac{100\pi}{3}\right) = \frac{\sqrt{3}}{2}$, $\cos\left(-\frac{100\pi}{3}\right) = -\frac{1}{2}$ **7.** $\sin\left(\frac{6n+4}{3}\pi\right) = -\frac{\sqrt{3}}{2}$, $\cos\left(\frac{6n+4}{3}\pi\right) = -\frac{1}{2}$ **9.** $x = \frac{\pi}{12}$ **11.** $x = \frac{3\pi}{4}$ **13.** $x = \frac{5\pi}{3}$ **15.** $x = \frac{\pi}{4}$ **17.** $x = \frac{\pi}{6}$ **19.** $x = \frac{\pi}{2}$ **21.** $\cos x = \frac{4}{5}$ **23.** $\cos x = -\frac{12}{13}$ **B 25.** $\cos x = \frac{2\sqrt{2}}{3}$

Pages 280–281

A 1.

$m^R\theta$	0	$\frac{\pi}{6}$	$\frac{\pi}{4}$	$\frac{\pi}{3}$	$\frac{\pi}{2}$	$\frac{2\pi}{3}$	$\frac{3\pi}{4}$	$\frac{5\pi}{6}$	π	$\frac{7\pi}{6}$	$\frac{5\pi}{4}$	$\frac{4\pi}{3}$	$\frac{3\pi}{2}$	2π
$m°\theta$	0	30	45	60	90	120	135	150	180	210	225	240	270	360
$\sin\theta$	0	$\frac{1}{2}$	$\frac{\sqrt{2}}{2}$	$\frac{\sqrt{3}}{2}$	1	$\frac{\sqrt{3}}{2}$	$\frac{\sqrt{2}}{2}$	$\frac{1}{2}$	0	$-\frac{1}{2}$	$-\frac{\sqrt{2}}{2}$	$-\frac{\sqrt{3}}{2}$	-1	0
$\cos\theta$	1	$\frac{\sqrt{3}}{2}$	$\frac{\sqrt{2}}{2}$	$\frac{1}{2}$	0	$-\frac{1}{2}$	$-\frac{\sqrt{2}}{2}$	$-\frac{\sqrt{3}}{2}$	-1	$-\frac{\sqrt{3}}{2}$	$-\frac{\sqrt{2}}{2}$	$-\frac{1}{2}$	0	1

3. 24000 radians; $\frac{4{,}320{,}000}{\pi}$ degrees **5.** $s = 3\pi$; $A = 6\pi$ **7.** $m^R\theta = \frac{\pi}{2}$; $m°\theta = 90$; $A = \frac{1}{4\pi}$ **9.** $m^R\theta = 1$; $m°\theta = \frac{180}{\pi}$; $A = \frac{1}{2}$ **11.** $r = 6$; $s = \pi$

Pages 286–287 A **1.** $f(x) \to 3\sin x$ **3.** $f(x) \to 2\sin 2x$ **5.** $f(x) \to 2\sin\frac{2\pi}{3}x$ **7.** $f(x) \to 10\sin 20\pi x$

9.

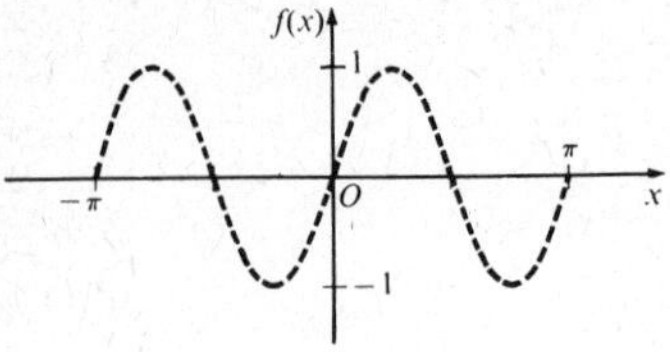

11.

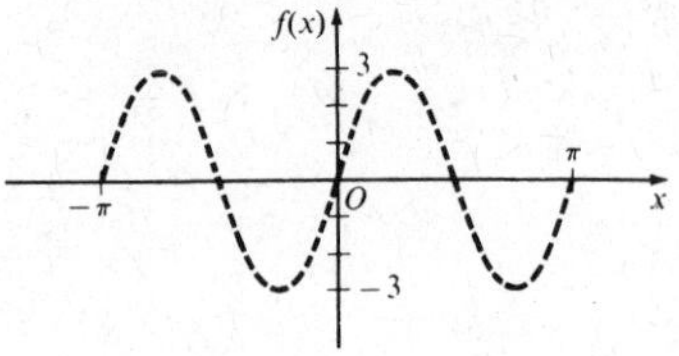

13.

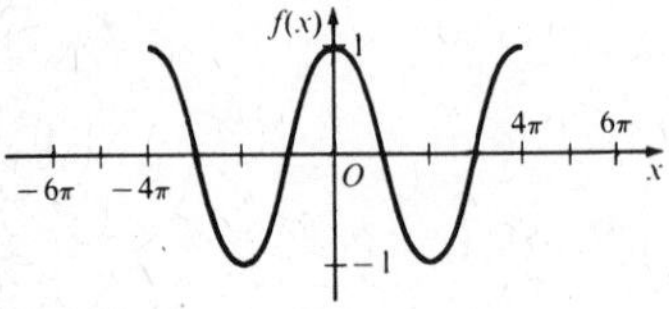

15.

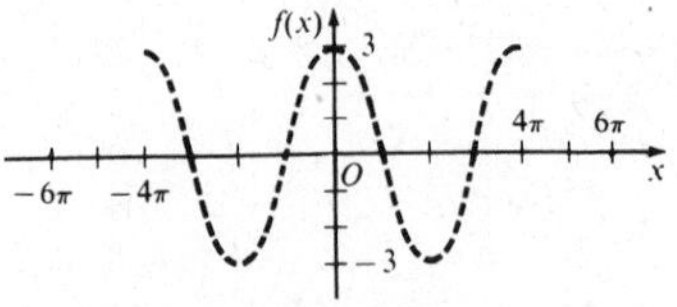

17.

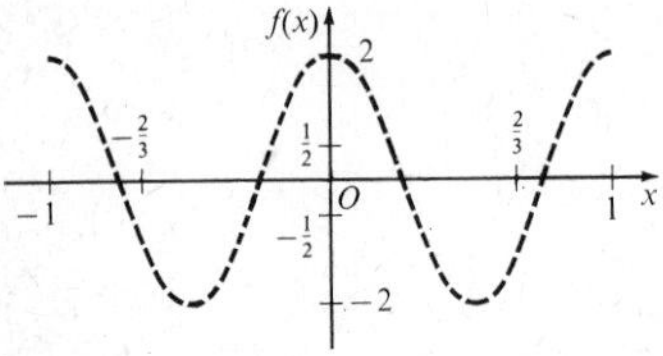

19.

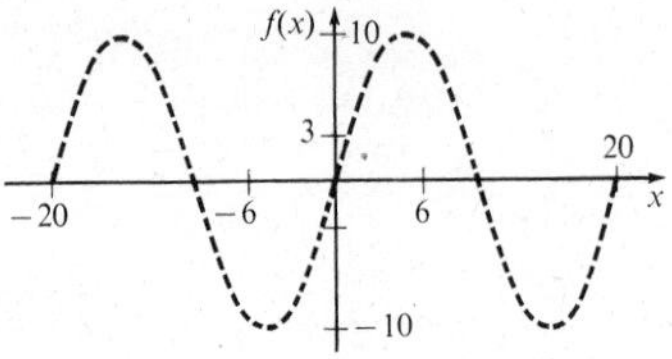

B 21.

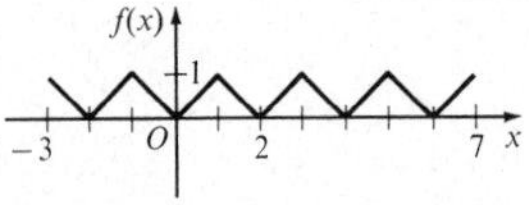

23.

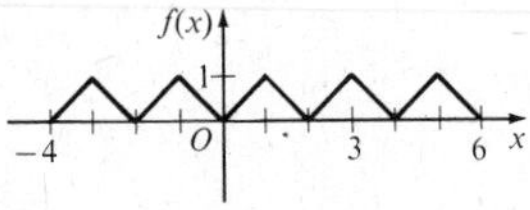

Pages 291–292 A 1. $\cos x$ **3.** $-\sin x$ **5.** $\sin x$ **7.** $-\cos x$ **9.** $-\cos x$ **11.** $\sin\frac{\pi}{12} = \frac{\sqrt{6}-\sqrt{2}}{4}$; $\sin\frac{5\pi}{12} = \frac{\sqrt{6}+\sqrt{2}}{4}$ **13.** (1) $\sin\frac{7\pi}{12} = \frac{\sqrt{6}+\sqrt{2}}{4}$; $\cos\frac{7\pi}{12} = -\frac{\sqrt{6}-\sqrt{2}}{4}$ (2) $\sin\frac{11\pi}{12} = \frac{\sqrt{6}-\sqrt{2}}{4}$; $\cos\frac{11\pi}{12} = -\frac{\sqrt{6}+\sqrt{2}}{4}$ (3) $\sin\frac{13\pi}{12} = -\frac{\sqrt{6}-\sqrt{2}}{4}$; $\cos\frac{13\pi}{12} = -\frac{\sqrt{6}+\sqrt{2}}{4}$ (4) $\sin\frac{17\pi}{12} = -\frac{\sqrt{6}+\sqrt{2}}{4}$; $\cos\frac{17\pi}{12} = -\frac{\sqrt{6}-\sqrt{2}}{4}$ (5) $\sin\frac{19\pi}{12} = -\frac{\sqrt{6}+\sqrt{2}}{4}$; $\cos\frac{19\pi}{12} = \frac{\sqrt{6}-\sqrt{2}}{4}$ (6) $\sin\frac{23\pi}{12} = -\frac{\sqrt{6}-\sqrt{2}}{4}$; $\cos\frac{23\pi}{12} = \frac{\sqrt{6}+\sqrt{2}}{4}$ **15. a.** $-\frac{24}{25}$ **b.** $\frac{7}{25}$ **c.** $\frac{3}{\sqrt{10}}$ **d.** $\frac{1}{\sqrt{10}}$ **17. a.** $\frac{4\sqrt{5}}{9}$ **b.** $\frac{1}{9}$ **c.** $-\sqrt{\frac{3+\sqrt{5}}{6}}$ **d.** $\sqrt{\frac{3-\sqrt{5}}{6}}$ **B 19.** Use $\cos z = \cos\left(2 \cdot \frac{z}{2}\right)$. **21.** $4\cos^3 x - 3\cos x$ **C 23. a.** $\cos x \cos y = \frac{1}{2}[\cos(x+y) + \cos(x-y)]$ **b.** $\sin x \cos y = \frac{1}{2}[\sin(x+y) + \sin(x-y)]$ **25. a.** $\sin a + \sin b = 2\sin\frac{a+b}{2}\cos\frac{a-b}{2}$ **b.** $\sin a - \sin b = 2\sin\frac{a-b}{2}\cos\frac{a+b}{2}$ **c.** $\cos a + \cos b = 2\cos\frac{a+b}{2}\cos\frac{a-b}{2}$

Page 298

A 1.

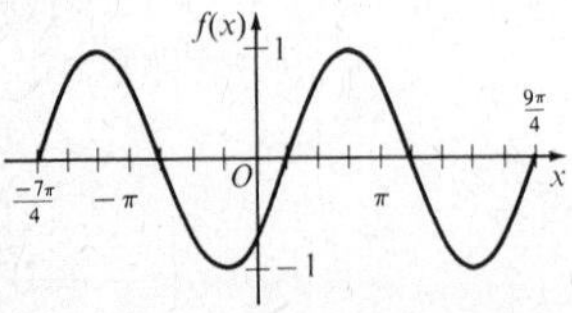

3.

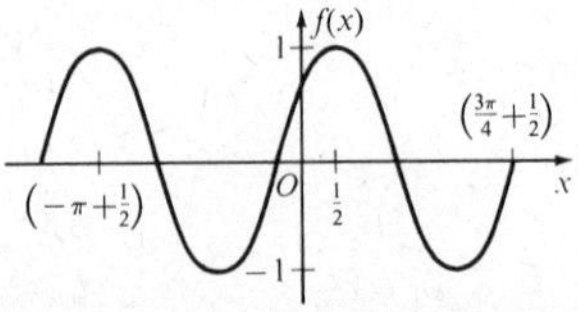

5.

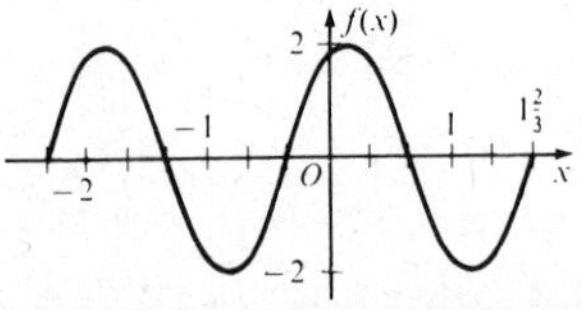

7. Solid graph below

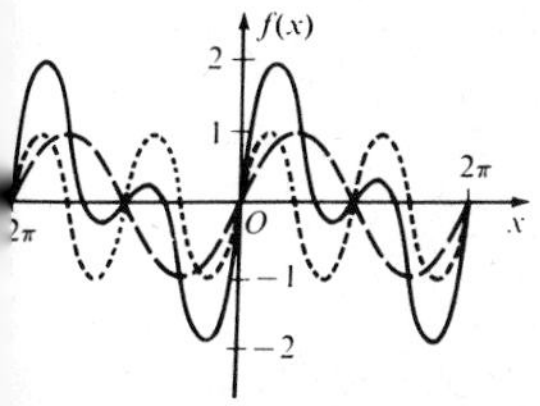

9. Solid graph below

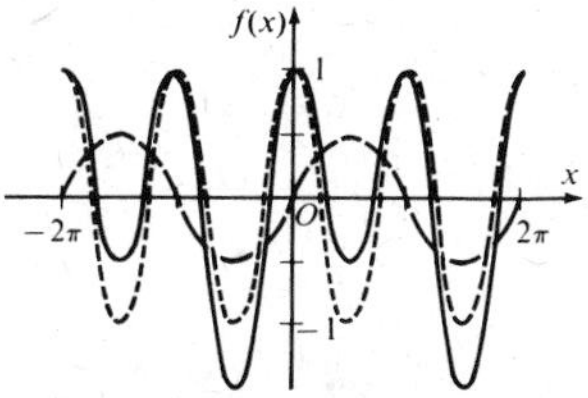

B **11.** $y = \sqrt{2} \sin\left(x + \frac{\pi}{4}\right)$

13. $y = 2 \sin\left(x - \frac{\pi}{6}\right)$

Pages 311–312 **A** **1.** $\cos^2 x - \sin^2 x$ **3.** 0 **5.** $\cos x - x \sin x$ **7.** $e^x \cos x - e^x \sin x$ **9.** $-\dfrac{\sin x}{\cos x}$ **11.** $x \cos x$; $\int x \cos x \, dx = x \sin x + \cos x + c$ **13.** $\cos^2 x$; $\int \cos^2 x \, dx = \frac{1}{2} \sin x \cos x + \frac{1}{2}x + c$ **B** **15.** $y = x$ at $x = 0$; $y = \pi - x$ at $x = \pi$; $y = x - 2\pi$ at $x = 2\pi$. **17.** $y = 1$ at $x = 0$; $y = -1$ at $x = \frac{\pi}{2}$; $y = 1$ at $x = \pi$.

19. Relative minima: $-\frac{3}{2}$ at $x = \frac{\pi}{3}$ and $-\frac{3}{2}$ at $x = \frac{5\pi}{3}$; relative maxima: -1 at $x = 0$, 3 at $x = \pi$, and -1 at $x = 2\pi$. **21.** Relative minimum: $-\dfrac{3\sqrt{3}}{2}$ at $x = \dfrac{2\pi}{3}$; relative maximum: $\dfrac{3\sqrt{3}}{2}$ at $x = \dfrac{4\pi}{3}$. **27.** See at right.

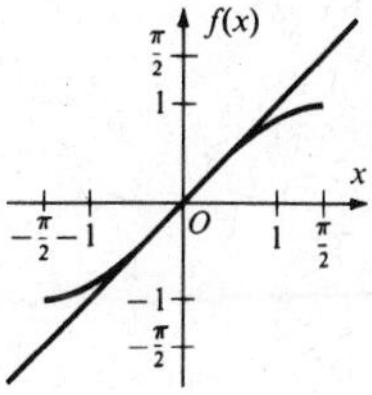

Ex. 27

C **29. a.** $f^{(n)}(x) = \begin{cases} \cos x \text{ if } \frac{n-1}{4} \text{ is a nonnegative integer} \\ -\sin x \text{ if } \frac{n-2}{4} \text{ is a nonnegative integer} \\ -\cos x \text{ if } \frac{n-3}{4} \text{ is a nonnegative integer} \\ \sin x \text{ if } \frac{n-4}{4} \text{ is a nonnegative integer} \end{cases}$

b. $f^{(n)}(x) = \begin{cases} -\sin x \text{ if } \frac{n-1}{4} \text{ is a nonnegative integer} \\ -\cos x \text{ if } \frac{n-2}{4} \text{ is a nonnegative integer} \\ \sin x \text{ if } \frac{n-3}{4} \text{ is a nonnegative integer} \\ \cos x \text{ if } \frac{n-4}{4} \text{ is a nonnegative integer} \end{cases}$

Pages 319–320 **A** **1.** valid for $\{x: \sin x \neq 0\}$ **3.** valid for $\{x: \cos x \neq 0\}$ **5.** valid for $\{x \text{ and } y: \sin(x + y) \neq 0, \sin x \neq 0, \sin y \neq 0, \cos x \neq 0, \cos y \neq 0\}$ **7.** 1, if $\sin 2x \neq 0$ **9.** $2 \cos x$, if $\sin x \neq 0$ **11.** $\sec x$, if $\sin x \neq 0$ and $\cos x \neq 0$ **13.** $\cos x = \pm\sqrt{1 - \sin^2 x}$; $\tan x = \pm \dfrac{\sin x}{\sqrt{1 - \sin^2 x}}$; $\text{ctn } x = \pm \dfrac{\sqrt{1 - \sin^2 x}}{\sin x}$; $\sec x = \pm \dfrac{1}{\sqrt{1 - \sin^2 x}}$; $\csc x = \dfrac{1}{\sin x}$ **B** **21. a.** $\tan \frac{z}{2} = \dfrac{\sin z}{1 + \cos z}$ **b.** $\text{ctn } \frac{z}{2} = \dfrac{\sin z}{1 - \cos z}$

23. $\text{ctn } 2x = \dfrac{\text{ctn}^2 x - 1}{2 \text{ ctn } x}$ **25.** $\tan^2 x$ **27.** $\sin^2 x$ **29.** $\csc x$ **31.** $\csc x$

Pages 326–327 **A** **1.** $-\frac{\pi}{6}$ **3.** $\frac{\pi}{6}$ **5.** $\frac{\pi}{4}$ **7.** 1 **9.** $\frac{4}{5}$ **11.** $\sqrt{1 - x^2}$ **B** **13.** $\frac{\pi}{2} - x$ **15.** $2x^2 - 1$ **19.** $-\dfrac{2}{\sqrt{1 - 4x^2}}$ **21.** $\dfrac{2}{4 + x^2}$ **23.** $\dfrac{1}{x^2 + 1}$ **29.** $\text{Cos}^{-1}(-x) = \pi - \text{Cos}^{-1} x$

C **31. b.** See at right.

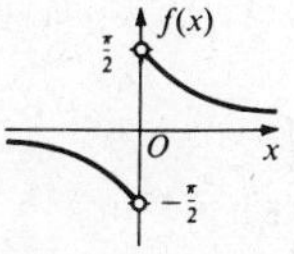

Ex. 31(b)

Pages 332–334 **A** **1. a.** $x = 3 \cos \frac{2}{3}t$, $y = 3 \sin \frac{2}{3}t$, where x and y are in feet and t is in minutes. **b.** $x = 3 \times \cos 8\pi t$, $y = 3 \sin 8\pi t$, where x and y are in feet and t is in minutes. **3. a.** $x = 12 \cos(\frac{1}{12}t + \pi)$, $y = 12 \sin(\frac{1}{12}t + \pi)$, where x and y are in inches and t is in minutes. **b.** $x = \cos\left(\frac{\pi}{18}t + \pi\right)$, $y = \sin\left(\frac{\pi}{18}t + \pi\right)$, where x and y are in feet and t is in hours. **5. a.** $x = 2 \cos(-5t)$, $y = 2 \sin(-5t)$, where x and y are in feet and t is in minutes. **b.** $x = 2 \cos(-20\pi t)$, $y = 2 \sin(-20\pi t)$, where x and y are in feet and t is in minutes. **7.** $s = 2 \sin\left(\frac{1}{4}t + \frac{\pi}{2}\right)$

B **13.** amplitude is 10 cm.; frequency is $\dfrac{3}{2\pi}$ cycles per second. **15.** $\dfrac{\sqrt{3}}{2}$